CIVIL PROCEDURE
2009

Second
Cumulative Supplement
to the
2009 Edition

Up–to–date generally to October 1, 2009

TO ACCESS THE WHITE BOOK CIVIL PROCEDURE RULES
WEBSITE AND TO REGISTER FOR THE FORMS ALERTER
SERVICE VIA HTTP://WWW.SWEETANDMAXWELL.CO.UK/
WHITEBOOK YOU NEED TO ENTER THE FOLLOWING
PASSWORD: **WB2009**

SWEET & MAXWELL      **THOMSON REUTERS**

Published in 2009 by Thomson Reuters (Legal) Limited
(Registered in England & Wales, Company No 1679046.
Registered Office and address for service:
100 Avenue Road, London, NW3 3PF) trading as Sweet & Maxwell.
Table of International and European Legislation typeset by Hobbs the Printers Ltd,
Totton, Hampshire. All other typesetting by Sweet & Maxwell electronic publishing
system.
Printed in the UK by CPI William Clowes Beccles NR34 7TL
For further information on our products and services, visit
www.sweetandmaxwell.co.uk.

*No natural forests were destroyed to make this product; only farmed timber was used
and replanted.*

British Library Cataloguing in Publication Data
A catalogue record for this book is available from the British Library

ISBN–978–1–84703–833–3

MASTER B. FONTAINE
A Master of the Senior Courts, Queen's Bench Division; Member of the Civil Procedure Rule Committee

M. GIBBON
Barrister, Maitland Chambers

JOAN GOULBOURN
Of the Public Guardianship Office

K. HOUGHTON
The Admiralty Marshal and Chief Clerk of the Admiralty and Commercial Registry

R. JAY
Solicitor

E. JEARY
Of the Court Funds Office

MASTER JERVIS KAY
Admiralty Registrar and a Master of the Senior Courts, Queen's Bench Division; One of Her Majesty's Counsel

DISTRICT JUDGE M. LANGLEY
A District Judge of the Central London County Court

C. LEWIS Q.C.
Barrister

KARON MONAGHAN Q.C.
Barrister, Matrix Chambers

HELEN MOUNTFIELD
Barrister, Matrix Chambers

MASTER J. O'HARE
A Master of the Senior Courts Costs Office

R. J. B. PARKES Q.C.
One of Her Majesty's Counsel

HER HONOUR JUDGE PATRICIA PEARL
A Circuit Judge on the South Eastern Circuit

DISTRICT JUDGE RICHARD ROBINSON
Principal Registry of the Family Division

MASTER ROSE
A Master of the Senior Courts, Queen's Bench Division

C. SANDERS
Of the Official Solicitor and Public Trustee

IAN SEWELL
Costs Clerk, Supreme Court of the United Kingdom

K. TALBOT
Barrister, Member of the New York Bar

MASTER TEVERSON
A Master of the Senior Courts, Chancery Division

MASTER VENNE
Registrar of Criminal Appeals and Master of the Crown Office

TIM WALLIS
Mediator and Solicitor with Expedite Resolution and Trust Mediation

H. WARD
Barrister

GARY WEBBER
Barrister and Mediator and a Deputy District Judge

GORDON WIGNALL
Barrister

DR VICTORIA WILLIAMS
A Deputy Master of the Senior Courts Costs Office; Barrister, Coram Chambers

SERVICE INFORMATION

Generally up–to–date to October 1, 2009

Civil Procedure 2009 published in April 2009. The Second Cumulative Supplement brings the Rules and Practice Directions up–to–date to October 1, 2009.

The Second Supplement includes:

- The new Supreme Court Rules, Practice Directions and Forms, together with expert commentary;
- Amendments to the Civil Procedure Rules and Practice Directions introduced by the Civil Procedure (Amendment) Rules 2009 (SI 2009/2092) and TSO CPR Update 5;
- The new Practice Direction 51D on Defamation Proceedings Costs Management Scheme, a costs management pilot scheme;
- New commentary on sections included in Part 35 on Experts and Assessors as part of the October Amendment Rules;
- Changes to Part 44 on General Rules about Costs;
- A completely revised Part 63 on Patents and Other Intellectual Property Claims and Practice Direction;
- A new Practice Direction relating to Companies Act Proceedings resulting from the Companies Act 2006 coming into force;
- The new eighth edition of the Admiralty and Commercial Courts Guide and related commentary. The Guide accounts for changes made by Pre Action Protocols and the Commercial Court e–working pilot;
- Updates to the Court Funds Office special and basic account interest rates;
- Updated guidance on Part 36 offers before the commencement of proceedings;
- Commentary on revised guidance on court dress from the Bar Council;
- New material on ADR concerning confidentiality in relation to mediation following the *Farm Assist* cases;
- Commentary on recent cases, including *Roult v North West Strategic Health Authority* (application to vary final order); *Imperial Cancer Research Fund v Ove Arup & Partners Limited* (application for extension of time on service of claim form); *Sharab v Prince Al–Waleed* (effect of appellant offering undertaking); and *Berezhovsky v Russian Television and Radio Broadcasting Co* (court's discretion to set aside judgment);
- Coverage of the Baden–Wurttembergische Bank case in relation to section 4 of the Civil Jurisdiction and Judgments Act 1982 (Part 74 Enforcement in Different Jurisdictions);
- Amendments made by the Constitutional Reform Act 2005, the Civil Proceedings Fees (Amendment) Order 2009 (SI 2009/1498), the Legal Services Act 2007 (Registered European Lawyers) Order 2009 (SI 2009/1497) and further amendments made by the Housing and Regeneration Act (Commencement No.5) Order 2009/1261.

We have included all material published by the Ministry of Justice up to October 1, 2009. *Civil Procedure News* will keep you abreast of developments throughout the subscription year. The 2010 edition of

Civil Procedure is due to publish in April 2010.

For further updates to the Civil Procedure Rules, Practice Directions, and to register for the Forms Alerter service and Rules Alerter service, please visit **http://www.sweetandmaxwell.co.uk/whitebook**.

Forms

The Forms Volume is no longer automatically included in the White Book Service (for new subscribers). New subscribers may order the Forms Volume separately. However, all subscribers will continue to be updated with the latest forms by way of receiving the Forms Release. We do ask that you keep your Forms Volume from one year to the next and update by way of filing the releases supplied, particularly as we cross–refer from the text of the CPR to forms in the Forms Volume and Forms CD in greater numbers this year. We avoid the duplication of forms in both the main volumes and the Forms Volume. This now includes Practice Direction forms, for which there is a new section in the Forms Volume and Forms CD.

The forms release is nominally published three times a year. In 2009, again in response to customer requests, we will not publish a paper forms release with the two supplements unless the number of new or amended forms released by the MOJ demands it (we will continue to release the Forms CD as normal). The twenty–fourth release is included with this Supplement.

Civil Procedure Forms CD and Adobe forms

Your 2009 subscription includes a CD–ROM containing all the forms provided in the Civil Procedure Forms Volume. We publish these forms as RTF/Word documents and PDFs. In addition, we have converted 100 PDFs of the most commonly used forms to allow edit and save functionality using the latest version of Adobe Reader. See the accompanying Quick Reference Card for full details of this new service.

A reminder to register for the Forms Email Alerter Service—go to **http://www.sweetandmaxwell.co.uk/whitebook** to register to receive an email notice when new court forms are published by the Court Service. You can also download the forms from our website. You will need to enter the password: **WB2009**.

If you were a subscriber to the White Book Service in 2008, please remember to retain your *White Book Forms Volume*. This will continue to be updated during the 2009 subscription year. The twenty–fourth forms release is included with this Supplement.

How to use Civil Procedure 2009

This is the Second Cumulative Supplement to Civil Procedure 2009. Updating information is referenced to the relevant paragraph in the Main Volumes. The instructions in italics explain how the added material relates to the Main Volumes.

As ever, we have endeavoured to ensure that the content of *The*

White Book is presented logically. The Civil Procedure Rules are reproduced in bold type to ensure they are easily distinguished from editorial comment and Practice Directions. Notes have been added to provide a full record of the changes to the Civil Procedure Rules. CPR Part numbers have been added to the thumb tabs at the side of each page.

Please refer to your User Guide which walks you through the navigational features and various components of *The White Book Service*, including the new cross–references to the additional content online and on CD.

Volume 1

The Civil Procedure Rules and Practice Directions (including Schs 1 and 2 containing those RSC and CCR still in force) are contained in Vol.1 with the following exceptions:

– *CPR on Specialist lists*—CPR Pts 58–63 (dealing with the Commercial Court, the Mercantile Courts, the Technology and Construction Court, Admiralty Claims and Arbitrations, and Patents and Other Intellectual Property Claims) are set out in Vol.2, Section 2.

– *CPR Pt 49—Specialist proceedings* —the proceedings dealt with under the Practice Direction to Pt 49 (Proceedings under the Companies Acts) are set out in Vol.2, Section 2.

Miscellaneous Practice Directions, Pre–Action Protocols, procedural guides and a guide to time limits are also reproduced in Vol.1.

Volume 2

The main elements of Vol.2 are the specialist areas of practice and procedure: the specialist lists dealt with by CPR Pts 58–63 and the specialist proceedings under CPR Pt 49, other specialist proceedings (e.g. Housing and Consumer) and procedural legislation. Volume 2 also includes Litigation and Procedural Topics such as Interim Remedies and Alternative Dispute Resolution.

A quick guide to finding key materials is set out below. See the separate User Guide for further information.

How to find ...
... CPR Rules and Supplementary Practice Directions (Vol.1, Section A)
The Civil Procedure Rules and Practice Directions are contained in Section A, which adopts the following paragraph system.

Part 3, r.1	para. **3.1**
Commentary to Part 3, r.1	para.3.1.1, (3.1.2 etc.)
Practice Direction supplementing Part 3	para. 3**PD**.1
Second Practice Direction supplementing Part 3	para.3B**PD**.1

The paragraph numbers appear at the top outside corner of each page.

... Rules of the Supreme Court, County Court Rules and Supplementary Practice Directions

---

Section A also contains the re–enacted Rules of the Supreme Court and County Court Rules, with all supplementary Practice Directions. The following paragraph system is used:

RSC Order 52, r.1	para.**sc**52.1
Commentary to RSC Order 52.1	para.sc52.1.**1**, (sc52.1.**2** etc.)
Practice Direction supplementing Order 52	para.sc**pd**52.1
CCR Order 1, r.6	para.**cc**1.6
Commentary to CCR Order 1, r.6	para.cc1.6.**1**

... *Miscellaneous Practice Direction (Vol.1, Section B)*
Practice Directions which are not supplementary to a rule (e.g. the Practice Direction on Insolvency Proceedings) are contained in Section B, which adopts the following paragraph system.

Practice Direction Insolvency Proceedings, etc.   para.B1–001

... *Pre–Action Protocols (Vol.1, Section C)*
The Pre–Action Protocols are contained in Section C, which adopts the following paragraph system:

Practice Direction—Protocols	para.C**0**–001
Pre–Action Protocol for Personal Injury Claims	para.C**1**–001

... *Chancery Guide*
The Chancery Guide Appears in Section 1 of Vol.2 and is numbered para.1–1 onwards.

... *Specialist Practice Directions under CPR Parts 58–63 and Specialist Court Guides, Applications under the Companies Act*
Specialist Proceedings under CPR Parts 58–63 and Specialist Court Guides, Applications under the Companies Act appear in Section 2 of Vol.2 as follows:

CPR 58	Commercial Court
CPR 59	Mercantile Courts
CPR 60	Technology and Construction Courts
CPR 61	Admiralty Claims
CPR 62	Arbitration Claims
CPR 63	Patents and other Intellectual Property Claims
Practice Direction to CPR 49	Applications Under the Companies Act

... *Forms*
The forms are located in the Civil Procedure Forms Volume and on the Forms CD.

... *Litigation and Procedural Topics...*
These are located at the end of Vol.2 in Sections 11 to 15.

Service Elements
The White Book Service allows you to choose a customised product to suit your requirements.

Civil Procedure CD and Print Service

Annual subscription includes:
CD (includes all content in Vols 1 and 2 and the Forms Volume and additional research materials)
Civil Procedure 2009 Vol.1
Civil Procedure 2009 Vol.2
Civil Procedure Forms Updates
Civil Procedure Forms Volume (on request to new subscribers)
Two paper supplements
Civil Procedure News (10 issues a year)
Internet–based primary law updating
Forms email Alerter Service
Rules email Alerter Service
Subscription price: £499 plus VAT

Civil Procedure Volumes 1 and 2

Annual subscription includes:
Civil Procedure 2009 Vol.1
Civil Procedure 2009 Vol.2
Civil Procedure Forms CD
Civil Procedure Forms Updates
Civil Procedure Forms Volume (on request to new subscribers)
Two paper supplements
Civil Procedure News (10 issues a year)
Internet–based primary law updating
Forms email Alerter Service
Rules email Alerter Service
Subscription price: £429 plus VAT

Civil Procedure Volume 1

Annual subscription includes:
Civil Procedure 2009 Vol.1
Civil Procedure Forms CD
Civil Procedure Forms Updates
Civil Procedure Forms Volume (on request to new subscribers)
Two paper supplements
Civil Procedure News (10 issues a year)
Internet–based primary law updating
Forms email Alerter Service
Rules email Alerter Service
Subscription price: £329 plus VAT

Premium Online Service

Please contact our Westlaw UK helpdesk for further information on 0800 028 2200.

Customer Services

If you have a query relating to your subscription or you wish to purchase extra copies of Civil Procedure 2009, please call our Customer Services team on:

UK direct customers: 0845 600 9355

UK trade customers: 0845 082 1032

International customers: +44 (0) 1264 388560
Or you can write to:

Customer Services
Sweet & Maxwell
Freepost
PO Box 2000
Andover
SP10 9AH
United Kingdom
Website: *http://www.sweetandmaxwell.co.uk*
Email: *sweetandmaxwell.customer.services@thomson.com*

Comments and feedback

We are always pleased to receive comments and suggestions from customers. Address correspondence to: Publishing Editor, The White Book Service, Sweet & Maxwell, 100 Avenue Road, London, NW3 3PF or email *whitebook@sweetandmaxwell.co.uk*.

The White Book Team
September 2009

CONTENTS

Section C—Pre–Action Protocols

Section D—Procedural Guides

Section E—Table of Time Limits

Volume 2

Section 1—Court Guides

Section 2—Specialist Proceedings

Section 3—Other Proceedings

TABLE OF CASES

TABLE OF STATUTES

TABLE OF INTERNATIONAL AND EUROPEAN LEGISLATION, TREATIES AND CONVENTIONS

*[**References in bold type** are to the paragraph at which that article is set out in full. All references to material in* **Volume 2** *are enclosed within square parentheses.]*

VOLUME 1

CIVIL PROCEDURE RULES

SECTION A

CIVIL PROCEDURE RULES 1998

PART 2

APPLICATION AND INTERPRETATION OF THE RULES

In the contents list the following entries have been amended:

Contents **2.0.1**

PRACTICE DIRECTION 2A—COURT OFFICES

This Practice Direction supplements CPR Part 2 **2APD.1**

Delete Practice Direction—Court Offices and substitute:

Central Office of the High Court at the Royal Courts of Justice

1 The Central Office will be divided into such departments, and the business performed in the Central Office shall be distributed among the departments in such manner, as is set out in the Queen's Bench Division Guide.

Business in the Offices of the Senior Courts

2.1(1) The offices of the Senior Courts will be open on every day **2APD.2** of the year except—

    (a) Saturdays and Sundays,

    (b) Good Friday;

    (c) Christmas Day;

    (d) a further day over the Christmas period determined in accordance with the table annexed to this Practice Direction;

    (e) Bank Holidays in England and Wales under the Banking and Financial Dealings Act 1971; and

    (f) such other days as the Lord Chancellor, with the concurrence of the Lord Chief Justice, the Master of the Rolls, the President of the Queen's Bench Division, the President of the Family Division, and the Chancellor of the High Court ("the Heads of Division") may direct.

    (2) The hours during which the offices of the Senior Courts at the Royal Courts of Justice and at the Principal Registry of the

Family Division at First Avenue House, 42–49 High Holborn, London WC1V 6NP will be open to the public are as follows—

   (a) from 10 am to 4.30 pm;

   (b) such other hours as the Lord Chancellor, with the concurrence of the Heads of Division, may from time to time direct.

(3) Every District Registry shall be open on the days and during the hours that the Lord Chancellor from time to time directs and, in the absence of any such directions, shall be open on the same days and during the same hours as the county court offices of which it forms part are open.

2.2 One of the Masters of the Queen's Bench Division (the "Practice Master") shall be present at the Central Office on every day on which the office is open for the purpose of superintending the business performed there and giving any directions which may be required on questions of practice and procedure.

County courts

2APD.3   **3.1** Every county court shall have an office or, if the Lord Chancellor so directs, two or more offices, situated at such place or places as he may direct, for the transaction of the business of the court.

3.2 Every county court office, or if a court has two or more offices at least one of those offices, will be open on every day of the year except—

   (a) Saturdays and Sundays;

   (b) Good Friday;

   (c) Christmas Day;

   (d) a further day over the Christmas period determined in accordance with the table annexed to this Practice Direction;

   (e) Bank Holidays in England and Wales under the Banking and Financial Dealings Act 1971; and

   (f) such other days as the Lord Chancellor may direct.

3.2 The hours during which any county court office is open to the public will be those published from time to time by, and available to the public on, the website of Her Majesty's Courts Service[1], or such other hours as the Lord Chancellor may from time to time direct.

Annex to Practice Direction 2A: Court Office Closures at Christmas and New Year

Christmas Day	**Bank Holiday**	**Further Day**	**New Year Bank Holiday**
2APD.4 Sunday 25 December	Monday 26 and Tuesday 27 December	Wednesday 28 December	Monday 2 January

[1] The court office opening hours are published for each court in the "Court Finder" section of the website of Her Majesty's Court Service, which can be found at: http://www.hmcourts–service.gov.uk/HMCSCourtFinder/.

Monday 25 December	Tuesday 26 December	Wednesday 27 December	Monday 1 January
Tuesday 25 December	Wednesday 26 December	Monday 24 December	Tuesday 1 January
Wednesday 25 December	Thursday 26 December	Friday 27 December	Wednesday 1 January
Thursday 25 December	Friday 26 December	Wednesday 24 December	Thursday 1 January
Friday 25 December	Monday 28 December	Thursday 24 December	Friday 1 January
Saturday 25 December	Monday 27 and Tuesday 28 December	Friday 24 December	Monday 3 January

PRACTICE DIRECTION 2B—ALLOCATION OF CASES TO LEVELS OF JUDICIARY

Delete practice direction title "Practice Direction—Allocation of Cases to Levels of Judiciary" and substitute "Practice Direction 2B—Allocation of Cases to Levels of Judiciary". **2BPD.1**

Other pre–trial Orders and Interim Remedies

In paragraph 3.1(f), for "Supreme Court Act 1981" substitute:

Senior Courts Act 1981 **2BPD.3**

Chancery Proceedings

In paragraph 5.1 for "In proceedings in the Chancery Division ... consent of the Chancellor:" substitute:

In proceedings in the Chancery Division, a Master or a district **2BPD.5** judge may not deal with the following without the consent of the Chancellor of the High Court—

Delete paragraph 5.1(k) and substitute:

    (k) making orders in proceedings in the Patents Court except—

        (i) orders by way of settlement, except settlement of procedural disputes;

       (ii) applications for extension of time;

     (iii) applications for permission to serve out of the jurisdiction;

     (iv) applications for security for costs;

      (v) other matters as directed by a judge of the court; and

     (vi) enforcement of money judgments.

County Courts

Injunctions, Anti–social Behaviour Orders and Committal

After paragraph 8.1A(2), add new paragraph (3):

    (3) section 4 or 9 of the Violent Crime Reduction Act 2006 (drink- **2BPD.8** ing banning orders).

PART 3

THE COURT'S CASE MANAGEMENT POWERS

The court's general powers of management

In rule 3.1(2) for "the court will" substitute:

3.1   **the court may**

In rule 3.1(3) for "it will" substitute:

it may

Stay of proceedings

Add new paragraph at end:

3.1.7   In *Schutz (UK) Ltd v Werit UK and Delta Containers Ltd* [2009] EWHC 131 (Pat) C sought remedies against D1 for patent infringement and, in a separate claim arising out of similar facts, sought remedies against D2 for patent infringement, trade mark infringement and passing off. C and D2 agreed to a stay of the patent infringement claim against D2 on terms that D2 agreed to be bound by the result of the action against D1. D1 and D2 contended that the remaining issues in the claim against D2 should also be stayed pending the outcome of the action against D1 whereas C contended that the two actions should be heard together so as to avoid the extra expense that separate hearings would entail, and so as to avoid the risk that different courts might make inconsistent decisions on the evidence. Kitchin J. held that the appropriate direction in this case was not a stay but an order that the actions should be heard sequentially nine months apart. As a general rule, where all the parties could afford to litigate, it made sense for two linked actions to be heard together. However, in this case D2 was considerably smaller than C, and this led to a real risk of D2 being overwhelmed by an inequality of arms. The use of sequential trials would avoid the need for both defendants to be represented throughout which would be wasteful and might unjustly prevent D2 from participating. In addition, if C won the patent infringement claims the further claims against D2 were likely to be redundant because D would be unable to continue in that line of business. If the second action did proceed, then C and D2 could reduce the risk of inconsistency by obtaining transcripts of the trial and judgment in the first action.

Stay of proceedings—pending medical examination

Add new paragraph 3.1.7.1:

3.1.7.1   In a personal injury action, the court has the power under its inherent jurisdiction and under r.3.1(2)(f) to order the stay of proceedings until such time as the claimant has agreed to an examination by the defendant's medical experts or until he has undergone medical tests. The decision whether to grant a stay involves the exercise of the court's discretion. A refusal to undergo an ordinary examination is likely to result in a stay; see *Starr v NCB* [1977] 1 W.L.R. 63; [1977] 1 All E.R. 243, CA. Where the examination involves discomfort or risk of injury the question of whether a stay should be granted is more difficult. In *Laycock v Lagoe* [1997] P.I.Q.R P518, CA; (defendant seeking MRI scan—stay refused), Kennedy L.J. set out the approach which the court should adopt on an application for such a stay. There is a two–stage test:

> "First, do the interests of justice require the test which the defendant proposes? If the answer to that is in the negative, that is the end of the matter. If the answer is 'yes', then the court should go on to consider whether the party who opposes the test has put forward a substantial reason for that test not being undertaken; a substantial reason being one that is not imaginary or illusory. In deciding the answer to that question, the court will inevitably take into account, on the one hand the interests of justice in the result of the test and the extent to which the result may progress the action as a whole; on the other hand, the weight of the objection advanced by the party who declines to go ahead with the proposed procedure, and any assertion that the litigation will only be slightly advanced if the test is undertaken. But if the [claimant], for example, has a real objection, which he articulates, to the proposed test, then the balance will come down in his favour."

4

Prospective costs cap orders

Add at start:

As from April 6, 2009, new rules 44.18 to 44.20 largely codify into the CPR the **3.1.8** practice as to costs capping which arose from the following cases.

Court's power to vary or revoke an order (r.3.1(7))

Delete the fourth and fifth paragraphs and substitute:

In Roult v North West Strategic Health Authority [2009] EWCA Civ 444; May 20, **3.1.9** 2009, unrep., the Court of Appeal gave the following guidance as to the court's power to vary or revoke an order under r.3.1(7). The grounds for invoking the power generally fall into one or other of two categories: (i) the original order was made on the basis of erroneous information (whether accidentally or deliberately given); and (ii) subsequent events, unforeseen at the time the order was made, have destroyed the basis on which it was made. In the context of case management decisions, further developments as to information or events may well justify variations in any orders previously given. However, proof of facts establishing either category may not justify any variation or revocation of a final order. This is because r.3.1(7) does not give a judge, in effect, power to hear an appeal from himself in respect of a final order relating to the whole or part of a claim. In *Roult* on the first day of the trial of a clinical negligence claim, a settlement was made which the judge approved on behalf of the claimant (C), a protected party. The settlement had been reached on the basis that C's best interests lay in him being cared for in a group home provided by the local authority and therefore a schedule setting out costs claimed in respect of independent care in his own home had been assessed at nil. The settlement also included, among certain heads of claim yet to be quantified, a claim for "costs of future care". C had subsequently entered a group home but had been removed from it by his parents after a short time. They now considered that, in fact, C's best interests lay in him being cared for in his own home. C's application to vary the approved settlement was dismissed by Christopher Clarke J. whose decision was upheld by the Court of Appeal.

After the fifteenth paragraph, add as a new paragraph:

In r.3.3(4) and (5) it is stated that, where a court makes an order of its own initiative, without hearing the parties or giving them an opportunity to make representations, a party affected by the order may apply to have it set aside, varied or stayed, and the order must contain a statement of the right to make such an application. Practice Direction (Applications) para.11.2 states that, where a court exercises its powers under r.23.8(c), and deals with an application without a hearing on the basis that it does not consider that a hearing would be appropriate, the court will treat the application as if it were proposing to make an order on its own initiative (see para.23PD11 below). It would seem that one consequence of this is that a party affected by an order made in such circumstances may apply to the court to have it set aside, varied or stayed (see further para.23.8.1 below).

Application to set aside

Add new paragraph at start:

Where a court does not consider that a hearing of an application would be ap- **3.3.2** propriate (r.23.8(c)), and considers the points made by the parties on paper, the effect of para.11.2 of Practice Direction——Applications (see para.23PD.11 below) is that the court proceeds as if it were proposing to make an order of its own initiative, with the consequence that r.3.3 applies. In such circumstances the defendant may apply to have any order made set aside, varied or discharged (r. 3.5(a)) (see e.g., *R. (Compton) v Wiltshire Primary Care Trust (Practice Note)* [2008] EWCA Civ 749; [2009] 1 W.L.R. 1436, CA, (application to set aside or vary protective costs order made without a hearing under r.23.8(c)). (See further para.23.8.1 below.)

Attempts to re–litigate decided issues

At the beginning of the last paragraph, add:

In *Walbrook Trustees (Jersey) Ltd v Fattal* [2009] EWCA Civ 297, the judge struck out **3.4.3.2** a claim brought by trustees as an abuse of process on the basis that it could have been brought in earlier proceedings. The Court of Appeal held that the judge had erred in striking out the claim, given that at the time of the earlier proceedings, the trustees did not have all the information necessary to bring their claim and had they done so the claim would have been struck out as disclosing no cause of action. It could not be an abuse of process for a party not to enforce their rights until they had the information that would prevent their case from being struck out.

Delay

At the end of the first paragraph add:

3.4.3.5 Delay, even a long delay, cannot by itself be categorised as an abuse of process without there being some additional factor which transforms the delay into an abuse (*Icebird Ltd v Winegardner* [2009] UKPC 24).

Other forms of abuse

At the end of the third paragraph add:

3.4.3.6 Similarly, in *Pickthall v Hill Dickinson LLP* [2009] EWCA Civ 543 it was held to be an abuse of process for a claimant to start proceedings in respect of a cause of action which was not vested in him in the hope that it would be assigned to him later.

At the end of the fourth paragraph add:

His decision was upheld by the Court of Appeal ([2009] EWCA Civ 542):

[50] " ... Where, as in this case, there has been a full trial, the proper course for the judge is to give judgment on the issues which have been tried. To have struck out the claims of the first and third claimants would have been to invoke a case management power not for a legitimate case management purpose (in other words, for the purpose of achieving a just and expeditious determination of the parties' rights, or avoiding an unjust determination where a party's conduct had made a safe determination impossible), but for the very different purpose of depriving those parties of their legal right to damages by way of punishment for their complicity in the second claimant's fraudulent claim, which in my judgment he had no power to do. It was open to him to impose costs sanctions on the first and third claimants, which he did, but that is a different matter."(per Toulson L.J.).

In *Zahoor v Masood* [2009] EWCA Civ 650 a similar decision was reached by a differently constituted Court of Appeal in which the words quoted above were cited with approval.

Effect of rule

After the fourth paragraph, add as new paragraphs:

3.9.1 When exercising the power under CPR r.3.9 to grant relief from sanctions for failure to comply with an unless order, the court should consider whether, at the time of the application for relief is heard, the unless order remains a proper order in the circumstances (*Tarn Insurance Services Ltd v Kirby* [2009] EWCA Civ 19, which also held that, in a case of deliberate and persistent non–compliance with orders to provide information and deliver documents made in order to safeguard proprietary claims, a proper administration of justice requires that, save in very exceptional circumstances, sanctions imposed should take effect).

In *Momson v Azeez* [2009] EWCA Civ 202, it was held (following *CIBC Mellon*, above) that the refusal to grant relief against a debarring sanction would not contravene art.6 of the European Convention on Human Rights provided that such refusal was proportionate and was for a legitimate purpose. The sanction which the court had imposed had the legitimate purpose of requiring the party to comply with an order of the court that had been made with a view to achieving a fair trial. Having decided that the party's non–compliance with the order (a disclosure order) meant that a fair trial was not possible, the judge (on the first appeal) concluded that a balancing of all the Pt 3.9 factors and a consideration also of the overriding objective required a decision that the defaulting party should not have been granted any relief against the sanction. The Court of Appeal held that that conclusion was Convention compliant and that any other conclusion would mean that litigants could with impunity avoid compliance with court orders made for the purpose of the holding of a fair trial.

PRACTICE DIRECTION—STRIKING OUT A STATEMENT OF CASE

7. Vexatious Litigants

In paragraph 7.1, for "Supreme Court Act 1981" substitute:

3PD.7 Senior Courts Act 1981

PART 5

COURT DOCUMENTS

Effect of rule

After the second paragraph, add as a new paragraph:

Paragraph 10.1 of Practice Direction (Electronic Working Pilot Scheme) (supplementing r.5.5) states that where a document filed under that scheme is one which any provision in the CPR requires should be signed by a person that provision is satisfied "by that person typing his or her name on an electronic version of the form". **5.3.1**

Permission to obtain "any other document"

Add new paragraph at end:

In *R. (Taranissi) v Human Fertilisation and Embryology Authority* [2009] EWHC 130 (Admin), January 14, 2009, unrep. (Saunders J.), an application under r.5.4C(2) by a third party, pleading justification in defending a libel claim, for permission to obtain from court records copies of a general class of documents contained in the court record of judicial review proceedings previously brought by the claimant in the libel action against a public agency, and which documents were before the judge at the judicial review permission hearing, was granted. The judge found that it seemed likely that the court record would contain documents relevant to the justification defence, and that it was in the interest of justice that the applicants should have access to them. The judge stated that the court may give permission under r.5.4C in circumstances where disclosure applications have been made in collateral proceedings. **5.4C.7**

Filing by electronic means

Add new paragraph at end:

CPR r.51.2 states that practice directions may modify or disapply any provision of the rules (a) for specified periods, and (b) in relation to proceedings in specified courts, during the period of "pilot schemes" for assessing the use of new practices and procedures in connection with proceedings. Practice Direction (Electronic Working Pilot Scheme) was made in exercise of this power. It provides for a pilot scheme under which various CPR provisions are modified for the specified period of April 1, 2009 to March 31, 2010 in relation to proceedings in the Admiralty, Commercial and London Mercantile courts of the High Court at the Royal Courts of Justice (although the operation of this pilot scheme may be extended to other courts during the period of the pilot scheme), and which applies to claims started on or after April 1, 2009. Under the scheme, in the circumstances set out in the Practice Direction, proceedings may be started and all subsequent steps may be taken electronically. As most of the provisions in the Practice Direction are examples of provisions of the type referred to in r.5.5, it is regarded as a practice direction supplementing that rule. **5.5.1**

PRACTICE DIRECTION—POSSESSION CLAIMS

Enrolment of Deeds and other Documents

In paragraph 6.1(1), for "Supreme Court" substitute:

Senior Courts **5PD.8**

PRACTICE DIRECTION—ELECTRONIC WORKING PILOT

This Practice Direction supplements CPR rule 5.5. **5CPD.0**

Add new Practice Direction—Electronic Working Pilot (paras 5CPD.0 to 5CPD.17):

This Practice Direction came into force on April 1, 2009.

General

1.1 This practice direction is made under rules 5.5 and 51.2 of the Civil Procedure Rules ("CPR"). It provides for a pilot scheme ("the Electronic Working pilot scheme") to— **5CPD.1**

(1) operate from 1st April 2009 to 31st March 2010;

(2) operate in the Admiralty, Commercial and London Mercantile

Courts of the High Court at the Royal Courts of Justice, although the operation of this pilot scheme may be extended to other courts during the period of the pilot scheme; and

(3) apply to claims started on or after 1st April 2009.

1.2(1) This practice direction provides for a pilot scheme by which, in the circumstances set out in this practice direction, proceedings may be started and all subsequent steps may be taken electronically ("Electronic Working").

(2) As an electronic system, the Electronic Working pilot scheme will operate 24 hours a day all year round, including weekends and bank holidays. This will enable claim forms to be issued and documents to be filed electronically out of normal court office opening hours. However, there will be two exceptions to this—

(a) planned "down–time": as with all electronic systems, there will be some planned periods for system maintenance and upgrades when Electronic Working will not be available; and

(b) unplanned "down–time": in the event of unplanned periods during which Electronic Working will not be available due, for example, to a system failure, power outage etc. the Electronic Working pilot scheme team will try to rectify the problem as soon as practicable.

(Paragraphs 6.8(2) and 7.2(2) contain provisions concerning the responsibility of the parties to file documents in time.)

1.3 Where proceedings are issued in the Admiralty, the Commercial or the London Mercantile Court to which CPR Part 58, Part 59 and Part 61 apply, then the Electronic Working pilot scheme will apply subject to the provisions of those Parts unless specifically excluded or revised by this practice direction.

1.4 As and when the Electronic Working pilot scheme is expanded to include the Technology and Construction Court and claims other than Part 7 claims (see paragraph 5.1), where proceedings are issued to which CPR Part 60 or Part 62 applies, then the Electronic Working pilot scheme will apply subject to the provisions of those Parts unless specifically excluded or revised by this practice direction.

1.5 This practice direction enables claimants and their legal representatives—

(1) to start electronically certain types of claim (subject to paragraph 5) in the Admiralty, Commercial and London Mercantile Courts; and

(2) where a claim has been started electronically—

(a) to file electronically all subsequent forms and documents, including but without limitation the following—

(i) requests for judgment in default;

(ii) requests for judgment on acceptance of an admission of the whole of the amount claimed;

(iii) notices that permission to serve out of the jurisdiction is not required (practice form N510);

(iv) certificates of service;

(v) statements of case and any amended statements of case;

8

   (vi) requests for further information and any replies;

   (vii) applications for an order;

   (viii) witness statements or affidavits;

   (ix) draft orders and orders for sealing; and

   (x) case summaries, lists of issues, chronologies, skeleton arguments, case management information sheets, progress monitoring information sheets and pre trial checklists; and

  (b) when and to the extent and subject as the court may specify, to inspect an electronic record of the progress of the claim and take copies as appropriate of documents on the court file.

(Paragraph 17 contains provisions about the possible expansion of the Electronic Working pilot scheme to other courts.)

1.6 This practice direction also enables defendants and other parties to the proceedings and their legal representatives—

  (a) to file electronically—

   (i) an acknowledgment of service;

   (ii) an admission or part admission;

   (iii) a defence with or without a counterclaim;

   (iv) a CPR Part 20 claim; and

   (v) those forms and documents listed at paragraph 1.5(2)(a)(iv) to (x); and

  (b) when and to the extent and subject as the court may specify, to inspect an electronic record of the progress of the claim and take copies as appropriate of documents on the court file.

1.7(1) Persons wishing to use the Electronic Working pilot scheme are required, wherever possible, to communicate with the court by means of e–mail. For the purposes of e–mail communications between the court and those persons, a person using the Electronic Working pilot scheme must—

  (a) provide the court with a single e–mail address at which that person can be contacted;

  (b) use the e–mail address provided by the court to file documents at the court; and

  (c) use the unique identification number, where provided by the court, to populate the subject line of the e–mail.

  (2) Where persons using the Electronic Working pilot scheme include their e–mail address on any court form, document or statement of case this is not confirmation or agreement that they are prepared to accept service by e–mail of documents between the parties to the proceedings or their respective legal representatives unless they expressly agree to do so. Paragraph 4.1(2)(c) of Practice Direction 6A supplementing CPR Part 6 does not apply.

1.8(1) A claim filed electronically under the Electronic Working pilot scheme will be issued by the Admiralty Court, the Commercial Court, or the London Mercantile Court as appropriate (or any other relevant court as and when the scope of the Electronic Working pilot scheme is expanded to include other courts), and the claim will proceed in that court unless it is transferred to another court.

(2) If the claim is transferred to another court which is not operating the Electronic Working pilot scheme it will come out of the scheme.

(Paragraph 15 contains further provisions about the transfer of claims.)

1.9 Unless the court orders otherwise no claim form, other document or order issued or filed with the court through the Electronic Working pilot scheme will be served by the court and service must be effected by the persons using the Electronic Working pilot scheme.

Security

5CPD.2 **2.1** Her Majesty's Courts Service will take such measures as it thinks fit to ensure the security of steps taken or information communicated or stored electronically. These may include requiring persons using Electronic Working to—

(1) enter a customer identification and password;

(2) provide personal information for identification purposes; and

(3) comply with any other security measures, as may from time to time be required before taking any of the steps mentioned in paragraph 1.5 or 1.6.

2.2 Her Majesty's Courts Service may provide—

(1) the parties or their legal representatives with the information necessary to register with the Criminal Justice Secure E–Mail facility which may be used for communication with the court; or

(2) such alternative method of encryption to promote security of e–mail communications as the court may deem appropriate.

(Paragraph 8.7 of the Practice Direction (Electronic communications and filing of documents) supplementing CPR Part 5 contains provisions concerning the transmission of documents or correspondence electronically.)

Fees

5CPD.3 **3.1** Where this practice direction provides for a fee to be paid electronically, it may be paid by—

(1) credit card;

(2) debit card; or

(3) any other method which Her Majesty's Courts Service may permit including any online facility.

3.2 In certain circumstances, a party may be entitled to a remission or part remission of fees. Her Majesty's Courts Service website contains guidance as to when this entitlement might arise. A party, who wishes to apply for remission or part remission of fees, must contact the relevant court office.

3.3 On filing electronically a form or document which requires the payment of a fee, the form will be subject to an initial automated validation to ensure all mandatory fields have been completed. Subject to such validation the form or document will be issued, sealed and returned to the person filing or requesting the issue of the form or document. Unless the fee is paid on filing the form or document, the e-mail from the court to the person filing or requesting the issue of the form or document will specify the amount of any fee required and the date by which the fee must be paid. In default of payment of any such fee, the matter will be referred to a Judge to consider whether the court should make an order of its own initiative pursuant to CPR rule 3.3.

(CPR rule 3.3(5) contains provisions about applying to the court to set aside an order made by the court on its own initiative.)

Forms

4.1 Persons using the Electronic Working pilot scheme must ensure that all forms, documents, schedules and other attachments filed at court are in PDF format. **5CPD.4**

4.2 Persons using the Electronic Working pilot scheme must, where they are available, use the PDF forms which have been created by Her Majesty's Courts Service specifically for Electronic Working.

4.3 Persons wishing to file a form or document which has not been created specifically for Electronic Working, or for some other reason a form or document is not available, must before filing the form or document—

(1) convert the document to PDF format if it is already in an electronic form; or

(2) if it is only available in hard copy scan the document into PDF format.

Types of claim which may be started using Electronic Working

5.1 The Electronic Working pilot scheme may be used initially to start CPR Part 7 claims in the Admiralty, the Commercial or the London Mercantile Court from 1st April 2009. **5CPD.5**

(Paragraph 17.2 contains provisions about the possible expansion of the Electronic Working pilot scheme to other types of claim.)

5.2 During the period of the Electronic Working pilot scheme, the scheme may be expanded to allow judgments and orders obtained in proceedings which have been started using Electronic Working to be enforced—

(1) by filing electronically requests and forms for enforcement; and

(2) by payment of the fee electronically pursuant to paragraph 3 of this practice direction.

5.3 Information concerning such expansion of the Electronic Working pilot scheme will be communicated by Her Majesty's Courts Service in such manner as is deemed appropriate including the HMCS website.

Starting a claim

6.1 A claimant may request the issue of a claim form by— **5CPD.6**

(1) obtaining the PDF form from Her Majesty's Courts Service;

(2) completing and sending the claim form and such other forms or documents as may be required to start the claim by e-mail to the address provided by the court; and

(3) paying the appropriate issue fee, in the manner provided for by paragraph 3.1 of this practice direction.

6.2 The particulars of claim may be included in the online claim form or may be filed separately in accordance with CPR rule 58.5, 59.4, or 61.3 where applicable.

6.3 As and when the Electronic Working pilot scheme is expanded to include the Technology and Construction Court, the particulars of claim may be included in the online claim form or may be filed separately in accordance with CPR rule 7.4 where applicable.

6.4 When a claim form is received electronically at the address provided by the court—

(1) subject to the automated validation referred to in paragraph 3.3, the claim form will be issued, sealed and returned to the claimant for service; but

(2) if the form fails the automated validation it will be immediately returned to the claimant together with notice of the reasons for failure.

6.5 When the court issues a claim form following filing by e–mail through Electronic Working—

(1) the court will enter on the form the date on which the claim form was received by the court through Electronic Working as the issue date;

(2) the court will accept receipt of claim forms filed through Electronic Working out of normal court office opening hours. Claim forms received by the court up to midnight will bear the date they are received as the issue date; and

(3) the court will keep a record, by electronic or other means, of when claim forms filed through Electronic Working are received.

(Paragraph 1.2(2) contains provisions about system "down–time" which may prevent immediate issue of claim forms.)

6.6(1) When the court issues a claim form through Electronic Working it will—

(a) return an electronic version in PDF format which will be sealed for service by the claimant; and

(b) return a further electronic version in PDF format which must be retained by the claimant in the event that the form needs to be amended.

(2) It is the claimant's or the claimant's legal representatives' responsibility to print and serve the claim form and any associated documents unless the court orders otherwise.

6.7 The sealed claim form will have printed on it a unique alphanumeric identification which will allow the defendant to obtain and file the acknowledgment of service through Electronic Working.

6.8(1) Any form or document which is filed electronically—

(a) must not be filed in hard copy unless the court orders or this practice direction provides otherwise;

(b) must consist of one copy only with no further copies unless requested by the court; and

(c) will receive an automated response to acknowledge receipt.

(2) Where a time limit applies, it is the responsibility of the the relevant party to ensure that the electronic form or document is filed in time.

Electronic Working response

7.1 A defendant wishing to file—

(1) an acknowledgment of service of the claim form under CPR Part 10;

(2) an admission or part admission;

(3) a defence or defence and counterclaim under CPR Part 15;

(4) a CPR Part 20 claim; or

(5) any of the documents or forms listed in paragraph 1.5(2)(a)(iv) to (x),

may instead of filing a written form, do so by obtaining the Electronic Working version of the form by using the unique identification referred to in paragraph 6.7 and filing the same electronically.

7.2(1) Where a defendant files a form or document through Electronic Working—

(a) the form or document is not filed until it is acknowledged as received by the court, whatever time it is shown to have been sent;

(b) the defendant may electronically file forms and documents through Electronic Working out of normal court office opening hours; and

(c) a form acknowledged as received electronically out of normal court office opening hours but before midnight will be treated as having been filed that day.

(2) Where a time limit applies, it remains the responsibility of the defendant to ensure that the electronic form or document is filed in time.

(3) When a document is filed electronically by the defendant an automated response will be sent to acknowledge receipt.

Counterclaim

8.1 Where a counterclaim is electronically filed using an Electronic Working form, any fee payable must be made and will be taken by the court in the manner provided for in paragraph 3 of this practice direction.

Statement of truth

9.1 CPR Part 22 and the Practice Direction supplementing that Part which requires any statement of case to be verified by a statement of truth apply to any Electronic Working forms filed electronically.

9.2 The statement of truth in an Electronic Working statement of case must be in the form—

"[I believe][The claimant believes] that the facts stated in this claim form are true."; or

"[I believe][The defendant believes] that the facts stated in this defence are true.",

as appropriate.

9.3 CPR rule 32.14, which sets out the consequences of making, or causing to be made, a false statement in a document verified by a statement of truth without an honest belief in its truth, applies to any false statement in a statement of truth in a document filed electronically.

Signature

5CPD.10 **10.1** Any provision of the CPR which requires a document to be signed by any person is satisfied by that person typing his or her name on an electronic version of the form.

Request for judgment or issue of warrant

5CPD.11 **11.1** If, in a claim started electronically using Electronic Working—

(1) the claimant wishes to apply for judgment in default in accordance with CPR Part 12; or

(2) the defendant has filed or served an admission of the whole of the claim in accordance with CPR rule 14.4,

the claimant may request judgment to be entered in default or on the admission (as the case may be) by completing and sending the electronic version of the appropriate case form to the e-mail address which will be provided to the parties.

11.2 When available under the Electronic Working pilot scheme, where judgment has been entered following a request under paragraph 11.1 and the claimant is entitled to the issue of a warrant of execution without requiring the permission of the court, the claimant may request the issue of a warrant of execution by—

(1) completing and sending an Electronic Working request form to the e-mail address which will be provided to the parties; and

(2) paying the appropriate fee in accordance with paragraph 3 of this practice direction.

11.3 A request under paragraph 11.1 or 11.2 will be treated as being filed—

(1) on the day the court acknowledges receipt of the request, if it receives it before 10 a.m. on a working day (which is any day on which the court office is open);

(2) otherwise, on the next working day after the court receives the request.

Inspecting the case record

5CPD.12 **12.1** When implemented, a facility will be provided for parties or their legal representatives to inspect an electronic record of the status of claims started using Electronic Working together with the facility to request documents in the electronic court file.

12.2 The record of each claim and its status will be automatically updated.

12.3 Information concerning the availability of this facility under the Electronic Working pilot scheme will be communicated by Her Majesty's Courts Service in such manner as is deemed appropriate including the HMCS website.

Case management of proceedings under the Electronic Working pilot scheme

5CPD.13 **13.1** Where a rule, practice direction, order of the court or court guide requires a case management bundle to be filed with the court—

    (1) the bundle must be filed in both hard copy and electronic format; and

    (2) the electronic copy must—

        (a) be filed electronically by e–mail, formatted as one PDF file not exceeding 10 megabytes, with each document in the file separately bookmarked;

        (b) in the event that it exceeds 10 megabytes, be filed on CD Rom or DVD; and

        (c) be updated as required and filed in compliance with sub–paragraphs (a) and (b) above.

13.2 The hard copy of the bundle must always correspond in all respects with the electronic copy.

Trial bundles

14.1 The trial bundle must be filed with the court in hard copy format. **5CPD.14**

14.2 An electronic copy of the trial bundle must also be filed if the court so orders, in which case it must comply with the requirements of paragraph 13.1(2) and paragraph 13.2 also applies.

14.3 The court will retain any electronic copy of the trial bundle for a period of one month after the claim has been finally determined, after which it may be deleted.

14.4 The time in paragraph 14.3 may be extended by order of the court at the request of a party or on the court's own initiative.

Transfer

15.1 If a claim is started under the Electronic Working pilot **5CPD.15** scheme, and is subsequently transferred to a court not operating under the Electronic Working pilot scheme the claimant or the claimant's legal representatives must ensure that a complete paper version of the court file is made available to the court to which the claim has been transferred.

15.2 If a claim which has not been started under the Electronic Working pilot scheme is transferred to a court operating the scheme and the claimant wishes to proceed with their claim electronically the claimant must scan or convert the documents in the court file into PDF format to ensure that the court has a complete copy of the file in PDF format.

Public kiosk service

16.1 An edited version of the electronic court file allowing access **5CPD.16** only to those documents which are available publicly will be made available through a public kiosk facility.

(CPR Part 5 contains provisions about access to court documents by non–parties.)

16.2 Persons wishing to obtain copies of publicly available documents—

    (1) may select the documents they require using the computer facilities provided by the public kiosk; and

    (2) must pay the appropriate fee.

16.3 Copies of the documents will be sent by e–mail following payment of the appropriate fee to an address supplied by the person applying for copies.

Expansion of the Electronic Working pilot scheme

5CPD.17　**17.1** The Electronic Working pilot scheme will initially operate in the Admiralty Court, the Commercial Court and the London Mercantile Court at the Royal Courts of Justice but may expand incrementally to include other courts or Divisions of the High Court at the Royal Courts of Justice, namely the Technology and Construction Court and the Chancery Division of the High Court and to include bankruptcy and insolvency proceedings.

17.2 The Electronic Working pilot scheme may be extended incrementally to widen the types of claim that may be started using Electronic Working. From a date or dates to be notified, the Electronic Working pilot scheme may be extended to—

(1) CPR Part 8 claims, arbitration claims and admiralty claims in the Admiralty, Commercial or London Mercantile Court;

(2) CPR Part 7 and Part 8 claims in the Technology and Construction Court and the Chancery Division of the High Court; and

(3) bankruptcy proceedings whether started by way of CPR Part 8 or petition.

17.3 Information concerning the expansion of the Electronic Working pilot scheme may be communicated by Her Majesty's Courts Service in such manner as is deemed appropriate including the HMCS website.

PART 6

SERVICE OF DOCUMENTS

Interpretation

6.2 *Delete title "Methods of service—general" and substitute: "Interpretation".*

"claim" "claim form"

In the second paragraph, for "The general rule is that … for the purposes of Pt 6." substitute:

6.2.3　When served together in that manner they constitute the claim form and the deemed service provisions in r.6.14 will apply to both. Where the general rule does not apply, and the particulars of claim are contained in a separate document and are not served with the claim form, that document is not "a claim form" for the purposes of Pt 6 and the deemed service provisions in r.6.26 will apply to the particulars of claim.

II. Service of the Claim Form in the Jurisdiction

Methods of service

In rule 6.3(2)(b), for "set out in the Companies Act 1985 or" substitute:

6.3　　　　　**permitted under**

In rule 6.3(3)(b), for "set out in section 725 of the Companies Act 1985." substitute:

permitted under the Companies Act 2006 as applied with modification by regulations made under the Limited Liability Partnerships Act 2000.

"electronic communication" (r.6.3(1)(d))

Delete and substitute:

Paragraph (d) of r.6.3(1) in relation to the service of claim forms is supplemented **6.3.5** by Practice Direction A (Service Within the United Kingdom) paras 4.1 to 4.3 (see para.6APD.4 below). Those provisions also supplement para.(d) of r.6.20(1) in relation to the service of documents other than the claim form and in that respect they are more fully dealt with in the commentary following r.6.20 (Methods of service of documents other than the claim form). See "Service of claim form by electronic method" at para.6.20.4 below.

The provisions paras 4.1 to 4.3 of 6APD were considered in *Andrew Brown v Innovatorone* [2009] EWHC 1376 (Comm). In that case, the claimants' solicitors issued claim forms, inter alia, against the seventh defendant ("D7"), an individual and the eighth defendant ("D8"), a partnership. The claim forms were not served but copies were sent to these defendants for information with an indication that they would be served within the four month period for service laid down by Pt 7 and that after service a stay would be sought. Subsequently, both defendants instructed solicitors each of whom later wrote to the claimants' solicitors on their firms' notepaper which stated their fax numbers, indicating that they had been instructed. However, neither stated that they had been instructed to accept service and at that stage neither had. On the last day for service within the four month period, at about two hours before midnight, the claimant's solicitors faxed claim forms (now amended to add further parties) to these defendants' respective solicitors on the said fax numbers, by way of purported service. By this stage D8 but not D7 had instructed its solicitors that they could accept service but still, neither defendant's solicitors had informed the claimants' solicitors that they were so instructed. In answer to the defendants' applications for declarations that the claim form was not validly served, the claimants maintained that this was good service, relying on r.6.3 (1)(d) and PD6A para.4.1., the combined effect of which is, they said, that when a claimant's solicitor has received correspondence from a solicitor who was acting for a defendant on notepaper containing that solicitor's fax number, a claim form can be validly served by sending it by fax to that number. The judge rejected this interpretation of the rules and PD and found that the words in PD6 para.4 (2)(a) " ... acting for the party to be served ..." refer to the situation in which the solicitor is to be served under Pt 6.7. The mere fact that a defendant's solicitor has a fax number on his note paper does not mean that the solicitor can be validly served. It is only when the claimant has been told that the solicitor can be served that service may be upon the solicitor by fax. It is r.6.7 and not r.6.3 or the Practice Direction that is concerned with when a solicitor may be served on behalf of a client. The judge supported his conclusion by reference to *Maggs v Marshall* (see *Collier v Williams* [2006] EWCA Civ 20; [2006] 1 W.L.R. 1945, CA. The claim forms had therefore not been validly served. The claimants cross applied retrospectively for an order for service by an alternative method but this was refused. See para.6.15.5 below.

Effect of rule (r.6.7)

At the end of the fourth paragraph add:

In *Thorne v Lass Salt Garvin* [2009] EWHC 100 (QB), January 28, 2009, unrep. **6.7.1** (Wyn Willams J.), it was held by the Master and on appeal that service on a solicitor defendant in a claim for professional negligence was not service on a solicitor but on the client in circumstances where the solicitors were unaware of the issue of the claim form and unaware that it was about to be served on them. In those circumstances it was not possible to regard the solicitors as being their own legal representative.

After the seventh paragraph, add as a new paragraph:

Where r.6.7 applies a solicitor may be served by fax in accordance with r.6.3 and PD6A. See *Andrew Brown v Innovatorone* [2009] EWHC 1376 (Comm) and the notes at para.6.3.5 above.

Effect of rule (r.6.11)

After the third paragraph, add as a new paragraph:

6.11.1 The claim form may, subject to para.(2) of the rule, be served on the defendant by a method or at the place specified in the contract. In this way the rule allows service of a claim form by methods and at places that may be either the same as those in r.6.3 and r.6.6 or may be different. This raises a question as to whether in the absence of a deeming provision in the contract, the deemed service provision in r.6.14 which applies to claim forms served "in accordance with this Part" applies to service by a method or at a place specified in a contract at all, or only to those methods and places within the aforementioned rules. The safer interpretation may be that the rules intend the process of service between parties under a contract to be carried out entirely within the four corners of the contract so that r.6.14 does not apply and the party serving under a contractual provision must look to fulfil the terms of the contract in order to prove valid and effective service and to serve in accordance with the contract before the expiry of the period of service allowed for the service of the claim form by the rules.

Deemed day of personal service

Add at end:

6.14.2 Thus the decisions in *Godwin v Swindon BC* [2001] EWCA Civ 641; [2002] 1 W.L.R. 997, CA and *Anderton v Clwyd CC (No.2)* [2002] EWCA Civ 933; [2002] 1 W.L.R. 3174, CA are particularly relevant to this form of service either when it is used voluntarily or when it is required to be used by another rule or Practice Direction, and the person served does not appear, so that the deeming provision must be relied on to prove that service is deemed to have taken place. It could also be a source of difficulty where the period required for service before a hearing is short. When serving proceedings issued against trespassers, r.55.5 provides that:

"(1) The court will fix a date for the hearing when it issues the claim form. (2) In a possession claim against trespassers the defendant must be served with the claim form, particulars of claim and any witness statements (a) in the case of residential property, not less than five days; and (b) in the case of other land, not less than 2 days, before the hearing date."

Where the claim is against trespassers in non–residential property who have been served personally and they do not appear at the possession hearing, the effect of the combination of this rule and r.6.14 and r.7.5(1) and the above case law would appear to be that the trespassers will not be deemed to have been served until the second business day after service was actually effected (which depending on the date of that service could be anything between the third and fifth day after) so that the hearing would have to be at least two days later than the deemed date unless the court was prepared to abridge time under r.3.1(2)(a) at the hearing or the claimant had taken the precaution, on issue of the claim form, to get an order under r.6.1(b) that the trespassers should be deemed to be served, if served personally, on completion of the relevant step required by r.6.5(3) notwithstanding r.6.14 and r.7.5(1).

"good reason to authorise"

In the first paragraph delete "An alternative service order is an exceptional order."

6.15.3 *Add new paragraph at end:*

In *Brown v Innovatorone plc.* [2009] EWHC 1376 (Comm), June 19, 2009, unrep. (Andrew Smith J.), the judge ruled that (in the circumstances) service by fax of a claim form should not be permitted to stand as good alternative service, and stated that (1) the expression "a good reason" in r.6.15(1) is a general one and is not confined to specific and limited categories of case, (2) the mere absence of prejudice to a defendant will not usually in itself be sufficient reason to make an order under r.6.15, and (3) "exceptional circumstances" are not required to justify a respective order under r.6.15(2), but the court should adopt a rigorous approach.

Retrospective operation—"steps already taken"

Add new paragraph at end:

6.15.5 In *Andrew Brown v Innovatorone* [2009] EWHC 1376 (Comm) the judge considered an application by the claimants under r.6.15(2) after he had granted the defendants a declaration that service on their solicitors by fax had not been valid since the claimants had not been told that they could serve on those solicitors and so r.6.7 did not apply.

(For a fuller note on this case, see para.6.3.5 above). While he found that (1) there was no reason to require, on such an application, that it be shown that the steps taken had actually brought the claim form to the attention of the defendant within the four month period for service and (2) the power conferred by r.6.15 was not one (unlike that in r.6.16) which could only be used in exceptional circumstances; what did have to be shown before an order was made, was "good reason" and the court should adopt a "rigorous approach" to an application for indulgence. The *Andrew Brown* case was one of solicitors leaving service of a claim form until very late and then not observing the rules for service. The application was rejected as there was no good reason for an order to be made. The judge was also of the view that there was no proper basis for confining the circumstances in which there is "good reason" to specific and limited categories of cases. The use in the rule of that expression indicates that the rule does not simply confer a discretion; it serves to emphasise that the discretion should not be exercised over–readily.

Service abroad of domestic process

Add at end:

In *Andrew Brown v Innovatorone* [2009] EWHC 1376 (Comm) the judge observed the apparent omission and stated (obiter) that: **6.15.7**

" ... in the amended rule 6.37 there is a provision that 'Where the court gives permission to serve a claim form out of the jurisdiction ...(b) it may (i) give directions about the method of service'. Although the amended CPR rule 6.37 refers to "method" of service, I do not interpret it as conferring a more restricted power that the court was generally recognised to have under the old rules and consider that so to interpret it would not respect the overriding objective and the principal of interpretation stipulated in CPR rule 1.2."

Effect of rule (r.6.16)

At the end of the first paragraph, add:

Note that r.6.1(a) states that the rules as to service apply except where "any other enactment ... makes different provision", and see the notes to r.6.28 below as to the consequences where a statute lays down the period for service.   **6.16.1**

Retrospective service dispensing orders

After the seventh paragraph, add as a new paragraph:

In *Thorne v Lass Salt Garvin* [2009] EWHC 100 (QB); January 28, 2009, unrep. (Wyn Willams J.), it was held by the Master and on appeal that service on a solicitor defendant in a claim for professional negligence was not service on a solicitor but on the client in circumstances where the solicitors were unaware of the issue of the claim form and unaware that it was about to be served on them. In those circumstances it was not possible to regard the solicitors as being their own legal representative. Service by fax without prior agreement therefore failed and the court held that although the solicitors would have no doubt acted for themselves had they had prior intimation of the claim this was only one factor and did not amount to exceptional circumstances warranting dispensing with service.   **6.16.3**

Notice and certificate of service relating to the claim form

In the table, delete the heading "Place of Service" and substitute: "Details to be certified".   **6.17**

III. Service of Documents other than the Claim Form in the United Kingdom

Methods of service

In rule 6.20(2)(b), for "set out in the Companies Act 1985 or" substitute:

permitted under   **6.20**

In rule 6.20(3)(b), for "set out in section 725 of the Companies Act 1985." substitute:

permitted under the Companies Act 2006 as applied with modification by regulations made under the Limited Liability Partnerships Act 2000.

"electronic communication" (r.6.20(1)(d))

After the second paragraph, add as a new paragraph:

6.20.3   Where persons taking advantage of the electronic working provided for by Practice Direction (Electronic Working Pilot Scheme) include their email address on any court form, document or statement of case, this is not confirmation or agreement that they are prepared to accept service by email of documents between the parties to the proceedings or their respective legal representatives unless they expressly agree to do so; Practice Direction A para.4.1(2)(c) does not apply (see para.1.7(2) of the former practice direction).

Service of claim form by electronic method (r.6.3(1)(b))

After the first paragraph, add as a new paragraph:

6.20.4   In *Brown v Innovatorone plc* [2009] EWHC 1376 (Comm), June 19, 2009, unrep. (Andrew Smith J.), where questions arose as to the efficacy of the service of a claim form by fax on a firm of solicitors who were defendants in the proceedings, it was held that para 4.1 of Practice Direction A, insofar as it applies to service by fax or other electronic means on solicitors, is restricted to those circumstances where, by operation of r.6.7 (Service of the claim form on a solicitor), the claim form must be served on the solicitors.

Effect of rule (r.6.23)

After the first paragraph, add as a new paragraph:

6.23.1   It should be noted that where a solicitor's address is not given the address must be "an address within the United Kingdom at which the party resides or carries on business". The precise wording of this rule is important because on occasions defendants attempt to give a PO Box address as an address for service. However, a person cannot "reside" at or "carry on business" at a PO Box although such a business might be carried on by using such a PO Box address. In the circumstances a PO Box would not be a valid address for service under this rule.

At the end of the fourth paragraph add:

In the case of a failure to provide an address for service the court could be asked either to order that service at an alternative place or by an alternative method be adopted or could make an order striking out the statement of case of the party in default unless an address was provided.

Address for service where service by means of electronic communication

Delete the first paragraph and substitute:

6.23.2   Express provision is made in paras (5) and (6) for the service of documents by the method of service permitted by para.(1)(d) of r.6.20, that is to say, "by fax or by other means of electronic communication". Neither of these provisions alters the requirement that the party, where a solicitor's address is not given, must give "an address within the United Kingdom at which the party resides or carries on business", that is, a physical address. To comply with the rule a party may not give just a fax number or email address for example as the actual address for service although the party may be willing to be served by those means. It is of course for the party serving to choose the method of service and that party may well prefer to serve at the actual address, for example, by post. In the case of service at the address for service where the party has indicated that it will accept service by transmission of a fax, the rule requires that the fax number given must be at the address at which the party resides or carries on business. In a case in which the party has indicated a willingness to be served by electronic means other than fax, the email address or electronic identification given by that party will be deemed to be at the address at which the party resides or carries on business.

VOLUME 1

Deemed service

After the table in r.6.25, add:

6.26 **(Paragraphs 10.1 to 10.7 of Practice Direction A supple-** **6.26**
menting this Part contain examples of how the date of deemed ser-
vice is calculated.)

Effect of rule (r.6.26)

Delete the seventh paragraph and substitute:

Note, however, that where the period for service is statutory and the statute does **6.26.1**
not provide for the CPR to apply, that limit cannot be cut down by CPR provisions as
to deemed service. See the notes to r.6.28.

Effect of rule (r.6.27)

Add at end:

and in particular the decision in *Andrew Brown v Innovatorone* [2009] EWHC 1376 **6.27.1**
(Comm) in relation to application of retrospective orders

Effect of rule (r.6.28)

Delete the third, fourth and fifth paragraphs and substitute:

Note that r.6.1(a) states that the rules as to service apply except where "any other **6.28.1**
enactment ... makes different provision", so that the above discretion may be curtailed
or overridden by statute. For example, para.22.6A(3)(d) of Practice Directions (Appeals) requires an appellant in an appeal under the Extradition Act 2003 to serve on
the CPS within a specified time a copy of the appellant's notice filed in the court (see
para.52PD.120, below). In *Mucelli v Government of Albania and Moulai v Deputy Public
Prosecutor in Creteil, France* [2009] UKHL 2; [2009] 1 W.L.R. 276, HL (conjoined appeals) the House of Lords held that para.26.6A reflects the time limits imposed by
s.26(4) and s.103(9) of the Extradition Act 2003 and that a notice of appeal must be
served as well as filed within the time limits fixed by those provisions. The power of
the court under the CPR to extend time for the taking of any step (r.3.1(2)(a)), to
make any order remedying any error of procedure (r.3.10) or to dispense with service
of documents (now under this rule in Pt 6), cannot be invoked to extend a statutory
time limit or to avoid service required by statute unless the statute so provides. In the
conjoined appeal of *Moulai v Deputy Public Prosecutor in Creteil, France* the House also
held that where a statutory provision such as s.26(4) imposes a time limit for the serving of a notice of appeal, that limit cannot be cut down by CPR provisions as to
deemed service, for example the rule deeming a fax sent after 4.30 pm to be served
on the next business day. In that case the Divisional Court ruled that by r.3.1(2)(a) or
r.3.10, the faxed notice could be deemed to have been served earlier than in accordance with the CPR (which would have deemed service of a fax sent on the last day of
the statutory period for service to have been effected on the next day) in order to hold
that the notice had been served within the statutory time limit, or that service could be
dispensed with. The House disagreed with both propositions and held that (1) the
server of the document can rely on proof of actual service by midnight on the last day
of the statutory period by whatever means and also (2) that in any event, where such a
statutory provision applies and the recipient's office is closed on the whole of the last
day of the service period, it will be validly served if it is served on the next business
day (confirming *Pritam Kaur v S Russell & Sons Ltd* [1973] Q.B. 336; [1973] 2 W.L.R.
147; [1973] 1 All E.R. 617).

In practice the power granted by the rule is useful for dispensing with the re–
service of a document; for example, where a document is attached to an application to
amend which is successful, or the recipient has already been given a copy, service of
the amended document may be dispensed with.

See the commentary on r.6.16.

General

Add new paragraph 6.33.3.1:

In cases under the Regulation, where the court takes jurisdiction on the basis of the **6.33.3.1**
claim form pursuant to r.6.33 it is important that solicitors issuing the proceedings
take particular care to ensure that they have a reasonable basis for their stated belief

and that the facts supporting it are stated in transparent fashion on the claim form: *National Navigation Co v Endesa Generacion SA* [2009] EWHC 196 (Comm), Gloster J.

At the end of the first paragraph add:

6.33.10   Central administration does not necessarily mean the same as central management and control for the purposes of art.60 of the Judgments Regulation; *Alberta Inc v Katanga Mining Ltd* [2008] EWHC 2679 (Comm); [2009] I.L.Pr. 14.

Delete the fifth paragraph and substitute:

It is incompatible with the Judgments Regulation for a court of a member state to make an order to restrain a person from commencing or continuing proceedings before the courts of another member state on the ground that such proceedings would be contrary to an arbitration agreement; *Allianz SpA v West Tankers Inc (The Front Comar) (Case C–185/07)* [2009] 1 Lloyd's Rep. 413, ECJ; [2009] 1 All E.R. (Comm) 435.

It has been held that the decision in *The Front Comar* will not prevent an English court from making a declaration to the effect that the defendant is bound by a London arbitration clause where a court in a Member State is seised of the same jurisdiction issue and further held that an English court may decline on grounds of public policy to give effect to a judgement by such a court that conflicts with the decision of the English court that such a binding clause exists; *National Navigation Co v Endesa Generacion SA* [2009] EWHC 957 (Comm), Gloster J.

The body of law to the effect that an agreement to the seat of an arbitration is akin to an exclusive jurisdiction clause remains good law and there is nothing in *The Front Comar* which impacts upon the law as developed in this jurisdiction in relation to anti–suit injunctions which prevents a party to such an agreement from seeking such relief in respect of proceedings in a country which is not a Convention or Member State; *Shashoua v Sharma* [2009] EWHC 957 (Comm).

A judgment debtor's submission to the English jurisdiction is a sufficient basis for the imposition of an anti–suit injunction restraining a challenge to the relevant judgment brought in another jurisdiction and no separate basis of jurisdiction to make the order is required under the Judgments Regulation or the CPR; *Masri v Consolidated Contractors International (UK) Ltd (No.3)* [2008] EWCA Civ 625; [2009] 2 W.L.R. 669; [2008] 2 Lloyd's Rep 301; [2008] 2 All E.R. (Comm) 1146.

Add new paragraph at end:

6.33.11   A foreign judgment against a state will be capable of enforcement in England if the foreign court would have had jurisdiction if it had applied the United Kingdom rules on sovereign immunity set out in s.2 of the State Immunity Act 1978, and if under the law of the United Kingdom the state is not immune from the process of execution; *NML Capital Ltd v Republic of Argentina* [2009] EWHC 110 (Comm); [2009] 2 W.L.R. 1332; [2009] 1 Lloyd's Rep. 378; *The Times* February 11, 2009.

After the first paragraph, add as a new paragraph:

6.33.12   Article 1(2)(d) of the Judgments Regulation does not oust the jurisdiction of the court under art.5(1) merely because the contract to which the claim relates contains an arbitration clause; *Youell v La Réunion Aérienne* [2009] EWCA Civ 175; March 11, 2009, CA, unrep.

In the fourth paragraph, for "FKI Engineering Ltd v Dewind Holdings Ltd [2008] EWCA Civ 316; [2008] I.L.Pr. 33" substitute:

FKI Engineering Ltd v Dewind Holdings Ltd [2008] EWCA Civ 316; [2009] 1 All E.R. (Comm) 118; [2008] I.L.Pr. 33

Matters relating to tort, delict or quasi–delict

In the fourth paragraph add after "giving rise to the damage.":

6.33.14   Where, pursuant to a misrepresentation, a claimant commits itself to accepting a deal and puts it beyond itself to withdraw, the place where these events occurred is that where the harmful event occurred; *Maple Leaf Macro Volatility Master Food & Rouvroy* [2009] EWHC 257 (Comm); [2009] Lloyd's Rep 475.

After the fourth paragraph, add as a new paragraph:

For a consideration of where damage occurs under art.5(3) of the Judgments Regulation when there is a failure to make a payment within the state alleged to have jurisdiction and of the distinction between direct and consequential harm see *Dolphin Maritime & Aviation Services Ltd v Sveriges Angartygs Assurans Forening* [2009] EWHC 716 (Comm).

Trusts

Delete and substitute:

Although for the purposes of the Civil Jurisdiction and Judgments Order 2001 (SI **6.33.17**
2001/3929), a choice of English law might not be conclusive, it is very difficult to see
what other circumstances would be sufficient to outweigh it, so that it would be another system of law with which the trust had its closest and most real connection. It is
more likely that a foreign choice of law in what would otherwise be an English trust
may be disregarded where it is intended to avoid some important principle of English
law; *Gomez v Gomez–Monche Vives* [2008] EWCA Civ 1065; [2009] 1 All E.R. (Comm)
127; [2009] 2 W.L.R. 950.

Article 5(6) of the Judgments Regulation does not apply to a constructive trust; *Gomez v Gomez–Monche Vives* above.

Article 5(6) of the Judgments Regulation does not apply to appointors or protectors
or to any other person with fiduciary powers who does not come within the normal
meaning of the expression "trustee"; *Gomez v Gomez–Monche Vives* above.

Priority of jurisdiction

Add new paragraph at end:

There is no relator back so as to retain jurisdiction where a claim form issued in the **6.33.19**
jurisdiction first seised is amended to add new facts adding a fresh cause of action after
another jurisdiction has also become seised of the jurisdiction; *The Underwriting Members
of Lloyd's Syndicate 980 v Sinco SA* [2008] EWHC 1842 (Comm); [2008] 2 Lloyd's Rep
500; [2009] 1 All E.R. (Comm) 272; [2008] I.L.Pr. 49.

After the third paragraph add as a new paragraph:

A jurisdiction specified in art.22 of the Judgments Regulation will only displace an- **6.33.25**
other jurisdiction where the case is principally concerned with an issue subject to the
exclusive jurisdiction provided by the article. The manner of the application of the
general test may vary according to which sub–paragraph of the article is engaged; *JP
Morgan Chase NA v Berliner Verkehrsbetriebe (BVG)* [2009] EWHC 1627 (Comm).

Delete the second paragraph and substitute:

Where the parties have entered into a complex transaction with competing jurisdic- **6.33.26**
tion clauses and the dispute is at the commercial centre of the transaction, it is those
jurisdiction clauses that are also at its centre which the parties must have intended to
apply to the dispute; *UBS AG v HSH Nordbank AG* [2009] EWCA Civ 585; see also *ACP
Capital Ltd v IFR Capital plc* [2008] EWHC 1627 (Comm); [2008] I.L.Pr. 47. It is most
unlikely that the parties to a jurisdiction clause would have intended that claims in
contract and deceit should be heard in different jurisdictions; *Maple Leaf Macro Volatility Master Food & Rouvroy* [2009] EWHC 257 (Comm); [2009] Lloyd's Rep 475.

*In the seventh paragraph, for "Deutsche Bank AG v Asia Pacific Broadband Wireless Com-
munications Inc [2008] EWHC 918 (Comm); [2008] 2 Lloyd's Rep. 177" substitute:*

Deutsche Bank AG v Asia Pacific Broadband Wireless Communications Inc [2008] EWCA
Civ 1091

Add new paragraph at end:

There is no requirement that jurisdiction clauses are not to apply if there is a
plausible allegation that the contracts, in which such clauses are contained, are vitiated
by mistake, misrepresentation, illegality, lack of authority or lack of capacity. Such a
requirement would deny the concept of separability which is as much part of European
law as of English law; *Deutsche Bank v Asia Pacific Broadband Wireless Communications Inc*
[2008] EWCA Civ 1091.

Special jurisdiction regimes

After the third paragraph, add as a new paragraph:

Proceedings between insurers are outside the scheme established by s.3 of the Judg- **6.33.27**
ments Regulation; *Youell v La Réunion Aérienne* [2009] EWCA Civ 175; March 11, 2009,
unrep., CA.

Period for responding to the claim form where permission was not required for service

Add after paragraph (1):

(Part 10 contains rules about acknowledgments of service, Part **6.35**

14 contains rules about admissions and Part 15 contains rules about defences.)

Before paragraph (2), insert the heading:

Service of the claim form on a defendant in Scotland or Northern Ireland

Before paragraph (3), insert the heading:

Service of the claim form on a defendant in a Convention territory within Europe or a Member State

Before paragraph (4), insert the heading:

Service of the claim form on a defendant in a Convention territory outside Europe

Before paragraph (5), insert the heading:

Service on a defendant elsewhere

Jurisdiction clauses

After the first paragraph add as a new paragraph:

6.37.19   Where the parties have entered into a complex transaction with competing jurisdiction clauses and the dispute is at the commercial centre of the transaction, it is those jurisdiction clauses that are also at its centre which the parties must have intended to apply to the dispute; *UBS AG v HSH Nordbank AG* [2009] EWCA Civ 585; see also *ACP Capital Ltd v IFR Capital plc* [2008] EWHC 1627 (Comm); [2008] I.L.Pr. 47.

At the end of the fifth paragraph, add:

; *Highland Crusader Offshore Partners LP v Deutsche Bank AG* [2009] EWCA 725.

In the seventh paragraph, add after "Communication Telesystems International op cit;":

; and *Highland Crusader Offshore Partners LP v Deutsche Bank AG* op cit.

Add at end:

6.37.20   *Novus Aviation Ltd v Onur Air Tasimacilik AS* [2009] EWCA Civ 122

Restraint of foreign proceedings

In the seventh paragraph for "The presence of ... [2004] 1 Lloyd's Rep. 471, CA" substitute:

6.37.23   Where a non–exclusive jurisdiction clause provides that proceedings may be brought in this jurisdiction there is no general presumption in favour of the grant of an anti–suit injunction restraining proceedings in another jurisdiction absent some unforeseeable change since the contract was made, see *Highland Crusader Offshore Partners LP v Deutsche Bank AG* [2009] EWCA Civ 725 for a detailed analysis of the jurisdiction.

At the end of the seventh paragraph add:

Proceedings in a foreign jurisdiction calculated to give an unfair advantage to creditors of a company in administration may be restrained to the extent that they are unconscionable; see *Harms Offshore AHT "Taurus" GmbH & Co v Bloom* [2009] EWCA Civ 632.

In the thirteenth paragraph, for ", Masri v Consolidated Contractors International Co [2008] EWCA Civ 625; [2008] 2 Lloyd's Rep. 301, CA", substitute:

; *Masri v Consolidated Contractors International Co (No.3)* [2008] EWCA Civ 625; [2008] 2 Lloyd's Rep. 301; [2008] 2 All E.R. (Comm) 146

In the fifteenth paragraph add after "[2003] 1 Lloyd's Rep. 267).":

The body of law to the effect that an agreement to the seat of an arbitration is akin to an exclusive jurisdiction clause remains good law and there is nothing in *The Front Comar (Case C–185/07)* [2009] 1 Lloyd's Rep. 413, ECJ; [2009] 1 All E.R. (Comm) 435 which impacts upon the law as developed in this jurisdiction in relation to anti–suit injunctions which prevents a party to such an agreement from seeking such relief where in respect of proceedings in a country which is not a Convention or Member State; *Shashoua v Sharma* [2009] EWHC 957 (Comm).

Actions against foreign states

Add at the end of point (ii):

Where permission has been given to serve a state out of the jurisdiction on the basis **6.37.24** of a mistaken legal analysis, the court has a discretion to set aside the permission but is not bound to do so where, on a correct legal analysis, the state is not in fact immune from suit; *NML Capital Ltd v Republic of Argentina* [2009] EWHC 110 (Comm); [2009] 2 W.L.R. 1332; [2009] 1 All E.R. (Comm) 69; *The Times* February 11, 2009.

Add at end as new paragraphs:

There is no general rule that, if an allegation might embarrass a foreign sovereign, it follows that it is non–justiciable; *Korea National Insurance Corporation v Allianz Global Corporate and Speciality AG* [2008] EWCA Civ 1355; *The Times* December 22, 2008.

A foreign judgment against a state will be capable of enforcement in England if the foreign court would have had jurisdiction if it had applied the United Kingdom rules on sovereign immunity set out in s.2 of the State Immunity Act 1978 and if under the law of the United Kingdom the state is not immune from the process of execution; *NML Capital Ltd v Republic of Argentina* [2009] EWHC 110 (Comm); [2009] 2 W.L.R. 1332; [2009] 1 All E.R. (Comm) 69.

In the second paragraph add after "April 5, 2001, CA":
; *Alberta Inc v Katanga Mining* [2008] EWHC 2679; [2009] I.L.Pr. 14   **6.37.29**

In the first paragraph, for "In order to ... found jurisdiction." substitute:

For the provision to apply, the contract does not necessarily have to be between the **6.37.35** parties. See *Greene Wood & McLean v Templeton Insurance Ltd* [2009] EWCA Civ 65.

Add at end:

For an analysis of the authorities in connection with permission to serve out of the **6.37.38** jurisdiction on the ground that the agreement is governed by English law. See *Novus Aviation Ltd v Onur Air Tasimacilik AS* [2009] EWCA Civ 122.

Effect of rule (r.6.38)

Add new paragraph at end:

The scope of r.6.38(1) (formerly r.6.30(2)) was comprehensively reviewed by Tom- **6.38.1** linson J. in *Vitol AS v Capro Marine Ltd* [2008] EWHC 378 (Comm); [2009] Bus L.R. 271, where the judge held that the court does not have jurisdiction to grant permission for service out of the jurisdiction of orders made under CPR Pt 71 (Orders to Obtain Information from Judgment Debtors) requiring officers of a judgment debtor company who were resident abroad to attend for questioning and to produce documents. The judge's analysis and conclusions in this case were endorsed by the House of Lords in *Masri v Consolidated Contractors International (No.4)* [2009] UKHL 43; [2009] 3 W.L.R. 385, HL (allowing an appeal from a decision of the Court of Appeal by an officer of a corporate foreign judgment debtor upon whom the judgment creditor had sought to serve a r.71.2 order out of the jurisdiction).

Methods of service—general provisions

Before paragraph (2), insert the heading:

Where service is to be effected on a party in Scotland or Northern Ireland   **6.40**

Before paragraph(3), insert the heading:

Where service is to be effected on a defendant out of the United Kingdom

Service on a defendant out of the United Kingdom (r.6.40(3) and (4))

Delete the second paragraph starting "Service by registered post".

Hague Service Convention   **6.40.5**

Delete paragraphs 6.40.9 and 6.40.10 and substitute:

Printed HMSO, Cmnd. 3986 (1969). The Convention on the service abroad of **6.40.9** judicial and extrajudicial documents in civil or commercial matters signed at the Hague on November 15, 1965 came into effect on February 10, 1969, after ratification by three States (art.27). It provides (inter alia) that each contracting state shall designate a Central Authority to receive requests for service coming from other contracting states and execute them. The Central Authority for England and Wales is the Senior Master of the Supreme Court Queen's Bench Division. Documents for service must be lodged with the Foreign Process Office, Room E10, Royal Courts of Justice, Strand, London WC2A 2LL, for onward transmission. The contracting states are at liberty to impose restrictions under certain articles of the Convention and information as to these can be obtained from the above–named Department and from the HCCH website. This multilateral Convention does not invalidate the bilateral Conventions already in force and listed in the websites referred to at the end of r.6.40. The following is a list of the States that are members of the Hague Convention Organisation and also of those States that are non–members (marked with an asterisk) who have acceded to the Convention or regard themselves as bound by earlier accession by their former colonial government. (Note that in the case of many Commonwealth countries the possibility exists of service on an agent to agent basis outside the Convention. For details consult the Foreign Process Section at the Royal Courts of Justice.)

Albania

Argentina

Antigua and Barbuda*

Bahamas*

Barbados*

Belarus

Belgium

Bosnia and Herzegovina

Botswana*

Bulgaria

Canada

China, People's Republic of

China, Hong Kong Special Administrative Region only

China, Macau Special Administrative Region only

Croatia

Cyprus

Czech Republic

Denmark

Egypt

Estonia

Finland

France (besides Metropolitan France and the Overseas Departments (French Guyana, Guadeloupe, Reunion, Martinique), the Convention applies to all of the other French overseas territories)

Germany

Greece

Hungary

Iceland (from July 1, 2009)

India

Ireland

Israel

Italy

Japan

Korea, Republic of

Kuwait*

Latvia

Lithuania

Luxembourg

Macedonia, the former Yugoslav Republic of (from September 1, 2009)

Malawi*

Mexico

Monaco

Netherlands

Norway

Pakistan*

Poland
Portugal
Romania
Russian Federation
Saint Vincent and the Grenadines*
San Marino*
Seychelles*
Slovakia
Slovenia
Spain
Sri Lanka
Sweden
Switzerland
Turkey
Ukraine
United Kingdom
U.S.A. (Includes Guam, Puerto Rico and the Virgin Islands)
Venezuela

Service abroad without permission

Rule 6.40(3) applies to a claim form which it is proposed to serve out of the juris- **6.40.10** diction without the permission of the court.

The Hague Service Convention permits the sending of "judicial documents by postal channels directly to persons abroad" provided "the state of destination does not object" to such method of service (see arts 10 and 19). Provided therefore that service by post is permitted by and effected in accordance with the law of the country in which service is effected, there is nothing in the Hague Convention or in the Brussels Convention which cuts down the scope of this permission (*Noirhomme v Walklate* [1992] 1 Lloyd's Rep. 427). However, it should be noted that many signatories to the Convention have declared their opposition to incoming service under art.10. Any party considering outgoing service to a Hague Convention Country by post should consult the HCCH website as to the relevant declarations and reservations.

Prompt execution of requests for service under the Hague Service Convention

The February 2009 quinquennial Special Commission on the practical operation of **6.40.10.1** the Hague Apostille, Service, Evidence and Access to Justice Conventions recommended the following timelines in relation to the Service Convention:

(a) If a forwarding authority has not received any acknowledgement of receipt of the request for service from the requested State within 30 calendar days following the sending of the request, it is encouraged to contact the Central Authority in the requested State to inquire about the status of the request. Such inquiry should be answered within a reasonable time.

(b) Where the request for service cannot be executed as a result of inadequate information or document(s) forwarded, the Central Authority of the requested State is encouraged to contact, as promptly as possible, the forwarding authority in order to secure the missing information or document(s).

(c) Whenever the Central Authority of the requested State is considering, under art.4, whether the request complies with the provisions of the Convention, it is encouraged to take that decision within 30 calendar days of receipt of the request.

(d) If at any time during the execution of the request for service, an obstacle arises which may significantly delay or even prevent execution of the request, the Central Authority of the requested State is encouraged to communicate with the forwarding authority as promptly as possible.

(e) A request for execution of service should be executed as promptly as possible and States are encouraged to take measures to further improve the effective operation of the Convention.

(f) If the forwarding authority has not received a certificate confirming service or non–service from the relevant authority of the requested State within a reasonable time after sending the request, it is encouraged to contact the Central Authority of the requested State to inquire about the status of the execution of the request and the inquiry should be answered within a reasonable time.

    (g) The Central Authority of the requested State is encouraged to take all reasonable and appropriate steps to execute the request until such time as the forwarding authority advises that service is no longer required.

    (h) The forwarding authority is also encouraged to specify in the request a time after which service is no longer required or inform the relevant authority of the requested State at any time that service is no longer required.

Effect of rule (r.6.41)

For "defendant files written evidence showing that such service has been duly effected." substitute:

6.41.1   claimant files written evidence showing that such service has been duly effected. When served under the Regulation procedure the certificate of service from the authority that served the documents is required.

Service Regulation

At the beginning of the third paragraph add:

6.41.2   There is no hierarchy of service methods. Further there is nothing in the Regulation that suggests that more than one method may be used at the same time though doing so might cause confusion. An application to issue duplicate claim forms for service out would be necessary in that case.

At the end of the third paragraph add:

The email address is foreignprocess.RCJhmcourts–service.gsi.gov.uk.

At the end of the fifth paragraph add:

, for incoming service. For outgoing service in Member States that have not opposed this method of service, this provision, would have to be invoked in England and Wales through the Senior Master who, in an appropriate case, would forward the papers to the Foreign and Commonwealth Office.

In the sixth paragraph, after "acknowledgement of receipt or equivalent." add:

Note, again, that this is service by the organs of a Member State and not by parties to the litigation direct.

In the seventh paragraph, for "England and Wales has indicated that it will not be effecting service under this provision." substitute:

The Ministry of Justice have notified the European Commission that "England and Wales is opposed to the possibility of direct service provided for by Article 15(1)".

In the eighth paragraph, for "The Central Body ... Queen's Bench Division" substitute:

The Central Body in England and Wales for this Regulation is the Senior Master of the Supreme Court, Queen's Bench Division (foreignprocess.RCJhmcourts–service.gsi.gov.uk)

Hague Service Convention

Delete and substitute:

6.42.2   For explanation, see para.(a) of r.6.31 (Interpretation) above. Parties to litigation in England and Wales are also able to serve in countries that are signatories to the Hague Service Convention (other than Member States covered by the EU Service Regulation) as set out in art.10 of the Convention. However, it should be noted that many signatories to the Convention have declared their opposition to incoming service under that article. Any party considering outgoing service to a Hague Service Convention State by this means should consult the HCCH website as to relevant declarations and reservations.

Method of service

6.51 *Delete title "Request for service" and substitute "Method of service".*

After service

In rule 6.52(2)(a), for "Supreme Court" substitute:

6.52   **Senior Courts**

Effect of Section V

Delete the first paragraph and substitute:

This section sets out the procedure for the incoming service of judicial documents **6.52.1**
in a non–EU Service Regulation situation, through the Senior Master in England and
Wales. Parties to foreign litigation in a country which is a signatory to the Hague
Convention on the Service of Judicial and Extrajudicial Documents, are also able to effect service in England and Wales as set out in art.10 of the Convention which states:

PRACTICE DIRECTION B—SERVICE OUT OF THE JURISDICTION

Service out of the jurisdiction where permission of the court is required

Delete title "Service out of the jurisdiction where permission of the court is not required" and **6BPD.3**
substitute: "Service out of the jurisdiction where permission of the court is required".

In paragraph 3.1(18), for "Supreme Court Act 1981" substitute:
Senior Courts Act 1981

Period for responding to an application notice

Delete "will be calculated in accordance with paragraph 6.3, 6.4 or 6.5.". **6BPD.7**

Table

In the table, the following entry has been amended:

Kazakhstan 21 **6BPD.8**

PART 7

How to Start Proceedings—The Claim Form

Interest on debts

(f) Late Payment of Commercial Debts (Interest) Act 1998

Add new section (f) at end:

This Act and commentary thereon can be found at para.9B–1324. Where it applies, **7.0.11**
interest at the higher rate provided for by this Act can be claimed (instead of interest
under the Supreme Court Act 1981 s.35A or the County Courts Act 1984 s.69) together
with the compensation payment provided for by s.5A.

Rates of interest

Delete section (f) and substitute:

    (f) *Special account rate*—The "special account" is one of two main accounts **7.0.17**
        administered by the Court Funds Office. For details of this account and histori-
        cal rates of interest see Vol.2 para.6A–171. The interest rate is fixed from time
        to time by direction of the Lord Chancellor pursuant to r.27(1) of the Court
        Funds Rules 1987. The rate was 6 per cent from February 1, 2002 but was
        reduced to 3 per cent as from February 1. 2009. It was further reduced to 1.5
        per cent as from June 1, 2009 and to only 0.5 per cent as from July 1, 2009.
        The "special account rate" is not generally used to award interest on debt or
        damages but does have a limited and well established use in personal injury
        claims pursuant to the *Jefford v Gee* [1970] 2 Q.B. 130 guidelines discussed at
        para.7.0.22. Frequently, to avoid a complicated calculation, interest is awarded
        on the special damages from the date of the accident to the date of judgment
        at one half of the special account rate.

In section (h), add new item at start of list:
Thursday, March 5, 2009—0.50

Effect of rule

Delete the third paragraph and substitute:

7.2.1   For the procedure in relation to money claims online see the note to Practice Direction—Money claim online (para.7EPD.13.1).

Service of particulars of claim

Delete and substitute:

7.4.3   Rule 7.4(1)(b) states that, where particulars of claim are not contained in or served with the claim form they "must be served" on the defendant by the claimant within 14 days after the service of the claim form; but this is subject to r.7.4(2) which states that particulars served separately "must be served" on the defendant "no later than the latest time for serving the claim form" (generally, four months after issue, see r.7.5(1)). This compounding of one mandatory requirement with another creates a trap for the unwary claimant which may be illustrated as follows. If, in a given set of proceedings, the position is that "the latest time for serving the claim form" is (say) May 30, and the claimant serves the claim form on May 20, the claimant does not have 14 days after May 20 for separate service of the particulars but only 10 days. Service of the particulars after May 30 will be service out of time, even if the service after that date happens to be effected within 14 days after the service of the claim form.

The calculation of the "latest time for serving the claim form", within r.7.4(2), requires reference to r.7.5, though in fact, unlike r.7.4(2), that rule (since October 1, 2008) says nothing about "serving" a claim form within a particular time, but about completing a "step required" by the rule within the set time. Where service is to be effected within the jurisdiction, a claim form served in accordance with Pt 6 is deemed to be served on the second business day after "completion of the relevant step under rule 7.5(1)" (see r.6.14). Presumably in such circumstances it is intended that the "latest time" within r.7.4(2) for the separate service of particulars of claim is that deemed day.

Where the particulars of claim are not served in time in accordance with r.7.4 (whether this is because the claimant misunderstood the effect of r.7.4(2) or for some other reason), an application may be made to the court for an extension of time. An application for an extension may be made either before or after the expiry of the relevant time limit. For commentary on such applications, see para.7.6.8 below.

The time limits for the separate service of particulars of claim as stated in r.7.4 do not apply to all civil proceedings to which the CPR apply. Different limits are fixed by r.58.5 (proceedings in the commercial list), r.59.4 (mercantile claims), and r.61.3 (Admiralty claims in rem).

In possession claims under Pt 55, the particulars of claim must be served with the claim form (r.55.4), so no question of time limits for the separate service of particulars arises in such proceedings.

Applications under 7.6(2)

In the first paragraph for "(see Supported by evidence, para.7.6.2 below)" substitute:

7.6.2   (see Supported by evidence, para.7.6.5 below)

Add new paragraphs at end:

F.G. Hawkes (Western) Ltd v Beli Shipping Co Ltd [2009] EWHC 1740; (Comm) [2009]

All E.R. D 207 (July) followed *Marshall v Maggs* and emphasised that the better the reason for not having served in time the more likely that an extension would be granted; incompetence or oversight by the claimant, or waiting some other development in the case might not amount to a good reason. *City and General (Holborn) Ltd v Structure Tone Ltd* [2009] EWHC 2139 TCC was an example of a claimant waiting another development, an arbitral decision, only partly relevant to the case against the applicant defendants: moreover the extension deprived those defendants of a potential limitation defence when the claimant had only issued the claim shortly before the end of the limitation period, having failed to comply with the pre–action protocol for construction and engineering disputes.

In *Duckworth v Coates* [2009] EWHC 1936 (Ch), the question was whether a series of five orders obtained without notice extending time for serving a claim form out of the jurisdiction on five defendants by a total of 12 months, were properly granted. The judge set aside the fourth and fifth orders principally on the ground that the claimant had not shown good reason for the extensions. The effect was that service of the claim form on the fifth defendant was ineffective. In addition, the judge stated that, where successive applications are made, the onus is on the applicant to ensure that on each application all relevant material is drawn to the court's attention, including whether, and if so how many, earlier extensions have been granted and the evidence upon which they were based.

By contrast, in *Imperial Cancer Research Fund v Ove Arup & Partners Ltd* [2009] EWHC 1453 (TCC), June 23, 2009, unrep. (Ramsey J.) it was held on appeal that an application by the claimant for a three month extension of time to serve the claim form had been correctly granted when the claimant needed to excavate premises to investigate a water leak and obtain expert advice to attribute liability for the defect between the defendants and other potentially liable parties, particularly when the defendants had been slow to disclose plans and documents.

Extension of time for serving particulars of claim

Delete the last paragraph and substitute:

A party who has served the claim form in accordance with r.7.5, but who has failed **7.6.8** to comply with the time limits for the separate service of particulars of claim imposed by r.7.4, may apply to the court for an extension of time for service of the particulars. A court considering whether, on such an application, it should exercise its general discretionary power, recited in r.3.1(2)(a)), to extend time for compliance with any rule (in this case r.7.4) should adopt the r.3.9 (Relief from sanctions) framework (*Price v Price* [2003] EWCA Civ 888; [2003] 3 All E.R. 911, CA).

The submissions that r.7.4(2) has the effect of abrogating the general power to extend time recited in r.3.1(2)(a), and that the strict conditions in r.7.6(3) applicable to the service of claim forms extended to service of the particulars of claim, were rejected by the Court of Appeal in *Totty v Snowden* [2001] EWCA Civ 1415; [2002] 1 W.L.R. 1384, CA, where the court explained that there are perfectly sensible reasons why there should be a strict regime in relation to extensions of time for service of claim forms and a discretionary regime in relation to extensions of time for the separate service of particulars of claim (ibid., at para.37 per Kay L.J., and para.48 per Chadwick L.J.).

In *Robert v Momentum Services Ltd* [2003] EWCA Civ 299; [2003] 1 W.L.R. 1577, CA (a case decided before *Price v Price* but not referred to in the judgment therein), the Court of Appeal held that, where a claimant, having served the claim form, has the foresight to anticipate that they will be unable to serve the particulars within time and, before time expires, applies to the court for an extension, there is no reason for the court to import the r.3.9 framework by implication into r.3.1(2)(a). This is because there is a difference in principle between, on the one hand, seeking relief from a sanction imposed for failure to comply with a rule where such failure has already occurred, and on the other hand, seeking an extension of time for doing something required by a rule before the time for doing it has arrived. The latter cannot sensibly be regarded as, or even closely analogous to, a relief from sanctions case. In such circumstance the discretion under r.3.1(2)(a) should be exercised by simply having regard to the overriding objective set out in r.1.1(2) (*ibid*).

Cases in which appeal courts have found that lower courts had erred in principle in granting or refusing applications for extensions of time for the separate service of particulars of claim, and have felt obliged to exercise the discretion afresh, are cases in which the lower court either failed to adopt the r.3.9 framework or applied it incorrectly. Usually, the errors indentified relate to the manner in which the lower court took into account the effect which the claimant's failure to comply with r.7.4 had on each party (r.3.9(1)(h)) and the effect which the granting of relief would have on each party (r.3.9(1)(i)); see *Austin v Newcastle Chronicle & Journal Ltd* [2001] EWCA Civ 834; May 18, 2001, unrep., CA; *Webster v British Gas Services Ltd* [2001] 1 All E.R. (D.) 409 (Oct) (Eady J.); *Price v Price*, op cit.

Where it would be disproportionate not to allow a claimant's application the court may, in exercise of its powers under r.3.1(3)(a), insert in the order granting an extension conditions having the effect of limiting the particulars of claim where the defendant would be disadvantaged if such conditions were not attached (*Price v Price*, op cit).

Fixed date actions

Delete the second and third paragraphs and substitute:

7.9.1 There are some types of claim which, by their nature, require a court trial but do not require an extensive, or any, pre–trial procedure. The most common examples are mortgage possession actions, rent possession actions, actions for the return of goods and some claims for the recovery of taxes and duties. These—and some other—claims have long had special forms of county court summons each specifically for the type of fixed date claim.

The Practice Directions which supplement r.7.9 relate only to claims under the Consumer Credit Act 1974; see para.7BPD.1. For the Recovery of Taxes and Duties see para.7DPD.1, for bulk claims issued at the Production Centre see para.7CPD.1, and for money claims issued online at Northampton see para.7EPD.1. Claims by mortgages and landlords seeking recovery of property are now covered by Pts 55 and 56.

Practice Directions

7.9.2 *Delete paragraph 7.9.2.*

PRACTICE DIRECTION—HOW TO START PROCEEDINGS—THE CLAIM FORM

Where to start proceedings

In paragraph 2.5, for "Supreme Court Act 1981" substitute:

7PD.2 Senior Courts Act 1981

In paragraph 2.6, for "Supreme Court Act 1981" substitute:

Senior Courts Act 1981

PRACTICE DIRECTION—PRODUCTION CENTRE

General

After paragraph 1.4(3), add new sub–paragraph (3A):

7CPD.1 (3A) The requirement in paragraph 7.3 of practice direction 16 (statements of case) for documents to be attached to the particulars of contract claims does not apply to claims to be issued by the Centre, unless the particulars of claim are served separately in accordance with paragraph 5.2 of this practice direction.

PRACTICE DIRECTION—CLAIMS FOR THE RECOVERY OF TAXES AND DUTIES

Note on Practice Direction—Claims for the Recovery of Taxes and Duties

Add new paragraph 7DPD.3.1:

7DPD.3.1 The 2005 Act (see para.3.1) provides that if an Inspector of Taxes issues a certificate of tax due in relation to an unpaid amount of a tax within a defined category of taxes and duties, in effect a defence to an issued claim cannot generally be pursued to a contested trial. Paragraph 1.1 of the Practice Direction lists the defined taxes and duties. This list was significantly extended from April 6, 2009—note that student loans repayable by an employer are included although they are neither a tax nor a duty, but certain taxes, including tax credits, are not included.

When a claim is issued for a payment of a "tax" in the list in para.1.1 and a "defence" is filed, the Practice Direction provides for the case to be issued for a short disposal hearing (in a similar way to most Pt 8 claims). The court nonetheless exceptionally (not defined) has the power at that hearing, under para.3.2 of the Practice Direction, to allocate the case to track and give directions to trial, presumably either when no certificate has been issued, or there is prima facie evidence that the certificate may be incorrect.

PRACTICE DIRECTION—MONEY CLAIM ONLINE

Starting a claim

After paragraph 5.2, add new paragraph 5.2A:

5.2A The requirement in paragraph 7.3 of practice direction 16 **7EPD.5** (statements of case) for documents to be attached to the particulars of contract claims does not apply to claims started using an online claim form, unless the particulars of claim are served separately in accordance with paragraph 5.2 of this practice direction.

Note on Practice Direction—Money Claim Online

Delete and substitute:

In 2001 a scheme was introduced for the issue of money claims electronically online **7EPD.13.1** through the Courts Service website (*http://www.hmcourts-service.gov.uk* [Accessed May 13, 2009]) (see the Practice Direction). The claim must be for less than £100,000 (excluding interest and costs), the Pt 7 procedure must be used, neither the claimant nor the defendant must be a child or a patient, the claimant must not be fees exempt or publicly funded, and the defendant must not be the Crown. Particulars of claim, if included in the claim form, must be shorter than 1,080 characters, including spaces. The claim is printed, issued and served by the Northampton Court in the usual way.

However, from April 6, 2009 a claimant may serve the particulars of claim separately from the claim form, including on the form only a brief summary of the claim, and stating that the particulars will follow (see para.5.2). The particulars must then be served within 14 days (or no later than the latest time for service of the claim form—see r.7.4(1) and (2)). The claimant must then file online within 14 days of service of the particulars, a certificate of service (para.6.1(2), but will only need to file the particulars if the claim is defended, and transferred to a county court, and then so file the particulars at that court (paras 6.3 to 6.4).

It would be simpler and preferable for the parties and the court if the Courts Service extended the number of characters allowed in the particulars section of the online claim form. This would, in many cases, avoid the need for the separate service and filing of the particulars and of a certificate of service, and would reduce the risk of possible administrative errors. Also, if longer particulars could be included on the claim form, case management judges on allocation, would less frequently need to order that "better particulars" of the claim and/or the defences in accordance with Pt 16 must be filed and served, in order to provide sufficient information to enable the judge to allocate the case to track and give directions, as is commonly the case where one or both parties are acting in person.

From October 2009 the requirement in para.3 of PD16 for documents to be attached to the particulars of contract claims does not apply to claims issued on line or through the Production Centre unless the particulars are served separately in accordance with para.5.2 of the PD. This was an oversight when the PD was amended in April 2009.

The defendant can acknowledge/admit/defend in all the usual ways and also by email to the Courts Service (see para.7.1 of the Practice Direction). Defended claims are transferred to the defendant's county court. Judgments can be entered online in undefended claims and in default and the claimant can check the position electronically without having to telephone—probably the most popular innovation. Note that Money Claim Online has been made permanent. (In October 2006 a similar online scheme was introduced for possession claims of residential property for rent arrears—see Pt 55.)

PART 8

ALTERNATIVE PROCEDURE FOR CLAIMS

Procedure where defendant objects to use Part 8 procedure

Add at end:

8.8.1   Any such order will be case specific: *Bovale v Secretary of State* [2009] 3 All E.R. 340, CA.

PRACTICE DIRECTION—ALTERNATIVE PROCEDURE FOR CLAIMS

In the table, the following entry has been amended:

8PD.9

Application under Section 42 of the Senior Courts Act 1981	Paragraph 16	Administra-tive Court	

Application under Section 42 of the Senior Courts Act 1981

8PD.16 *Delete title "Application under Section 42 of the Supreme Court Act 1981" and substitute: "Application under Section 42 of the Senior Courts Act 1981".*

In paragraph 16.1, for "section 42 of the Supreme Court Act 1981" substitute:

section 42 of the Senior Courts Act 1981

PART 11

DISPUTING THE COURT'S JURISDICTION

Effect of Part 11

In the first paragraph, for "within 10 days" substitute:

11.1.1   within 14 days

At the end of the first paragraph, add as a new paragraph:

Where a defendant enters an appearance before the English courts by acknowledgment of service, those courts possess jurisdiction under art.24 of the Judgments Regulation albeit that such a defendant does not thereby lose his entitlement to challenge the jurisdiction of the court under the CPR; *Maple Leaf Macro Volatility Master Fund v Rouvroy* [2009] EWHC 257 (Comm); [2009] Lloyd's Rep 475. Claims introduced by way of amendment also fall within art.24. A defendant, by entering an appearance accepts that the court has jurisdiction to hear any claim against him related in any way to the subject matter of the original action albeit that the defendant retains his right to challenge jurisdiction where an application to amend or join a party is made; *Maple Leaf Macro Volatility Master Fund v Rouvroy* op. cit.

In the third paragraph for ", Hoddinott v Persimmon Homes (Wessex) Ltd, The Times, December 28, 2007", substitute:

; *Hoddinott v Persimmon Homes (Wessex) Ltd* [2007] EWCA Civ 1203; [2008] 1 W.L.R. 806

In the third paragraph add after "r.11(7) and (8).":

The periods set out in r.6.35 for the service of a defence run during the time provided for a defendant to make an application under Pt 11 with the consequence that, where a challenge is not pursued, the time for service of the defence may have expired unless extended by agreement or order; see *Flame SA v Primera Maritime (Hellas) Ltd* [2009] EWHC 1973 (Comm).

After the fourth paragraph, add as a new paragraph:

Where permission has been given to serve a state out of the jurisdiction on the basis of a mistaken legal analysis, the court has a discretion to set aside the permission but is not bound to do so where, on a correct legal analysis, the state is not in fact immune from suit; *NML Capital Ltd v Republic of Argentina* [2009] EWHC 110 (Comm); [2009] 2 W.L.R. 1332; [2009] 1 All E.R. (Comm) 69.

In the fifth paragraph, for "Compliance", substitute:
Non–compliance

PART 12

DEFAULT JUDGMENT

"admission ... together with a request for time to pay"

Delete title and substitute:
    "admission ... together with a request for time to pay"Admitting a claim and request- **12.3.6**
ing time to pay is now of general application under the CPR. In the High Court and in the county court, when served with the claim form the defendant will also be served with "a form for admitting the claim" in accordance with r.7.8(1). The defendant uses that form to make an admission in accordance with Pt 14 (see rr.14.4 and 14.7). Where such an admission is filed the claimant cannot obtain a default judgment. He can instead obtain judgment on the admission: see rr.14.10, 14.11 and 14.12.

Allocation

In the second paragraph for "(£5000 – £15000)" substitute:
    (£5000–£25,000)   **12.7.6**

PART 13

SETTING ASIDE OR VARYING DEFAULT JUDGMENT

Rule 13.3(1)(b) "some other good reason"

Add new paragraph at end:
    In *Berezhovsky v Russian Television and Radio Broadcasting Co* [2009] EWHC 1733 **13.3.2**
(QB), Eady J held, in a defamation claim, that the court's discretion to set aside judgment under CPR r.13.3 was a broad one, which may be exercised if there was considered to be "some other good reason" why a defendant should be allowed to defend the claim. Where an allegation was a serious one, involving the suggestion that someone had been granted asylum on a false basis and in light of evidence obtained by threats and by drugging a relevant witness, it was plainly desirable (and indeed in the public interest) that the allegation should be given as full and fair a hearing as the circumstances permitted. Although the defendant had not acted promptly in his attempt to set aside the judgment, that may have been attributable to a genuine perception on his part that he needed to remain in hiding. It was also important to note that the primary object of most libel actions was to achieve vindication of the relevant claimant's reputation. If the claimant relied purely on a judgment obtained in default, it would be easy for those ill disposed towards him, for whatever reason, to undermine the effectiveness of that vindication. It was in the interests of both sides that a proposed plea of justification should properly be addressed.

Rule 13.3(2)—need to act promptly

Add at end:
    In *Standard Bank Plc v Agrinvest International Inc* [2009] EWHC 1692 (Comm) Field J **13.3.3**
held that although promptness may not be the controlling factor under CPR r.13.3, it is plainly a very important factor, as is evident from the fact that it is singled–out in the rule as a matter to which the court must have regard. It is a very important factor because there is a strong public interest in the finality of litigation.

PART 14

ADMISSIONS

Rule 14.1A

Add new paragraph 14.1.10:

14.1.10   Rule 14.1A(2)(a) and (b) have been amended with effect from April 6, 2009 and now refer to a "letter before claim" rather than a "letter of claim" which is the terminology used in the personal injury, disease and injury and the clinical disputes pre–action protocols.

In order to avoid any confusion from the fact that strictly r.14.3A(3) to (5) only applies to cases within these protocols in which a "letter of claim" has been sent, the Association of British Insurers (ABI), the Association of Personal Injury Lawyers (APIL), the Forum of Insurance Lawyers (FOIL) and the Motor Accident Solicitors Society (MASS) entered a memorandum of understanding on April 2, 2009 agreeing:

"that for the purpose of the personal injury, disease and illness and the clinical disputes pre–action protocols, the phrase *letter before claim* in CPR 14.1A is to be interpreted as a reference to the *letter of claim* sent in accordance with the protocols referred to in this memorandum".

PART 16

STATEMENTS OF CASE

PRACTICE DIRECTION—STATEMENTS OF CASE

Matters which must be included in the particulars of claim in certain types of claim

Personal injury claims

In paragraph 4.4(1), for "Supreme Court Act 1981" substitute:

16PD.4   Senior Courts Act 1981

PART 17

AMENDMENTS TO STATEMENTS OF CASE

Adding or substituting new cause of action (r.17.4(2))

After the eleventh paragraph, add as a new paragraph:

17.4.4   In a professional negligence claim, although an amendment raising a new allegation of breach of duty may amount to raising a new cause of action, an amendment which merely raises a new head of loss or damage can never amount to that. However, once the relevant limitation period has expired, the court should be astute not to permit claimants to raise new heads of loss or damage as a stepping stone from which to allege new breaches of duty. In Harland & Wolff PensionTrustees Ltd v *Aon Consulting Financial Services Ltd* [2009] EWHC 1557 (Ch) Warren J. permitted the claimant to raise a new head of loss or damage but only on terms that it would not subsequently seek to further amend the particulars of claim by relying on new breaches of duty in order to recover compensation under that head.

PART 22

STATEMENTS OF TRUTH

Related sources

After the last bullet point, add new bullet point:

22.0.3   • Practice Direction (Electronic Working Pilot Scheme) para.9.1 (Statement of truth)

Statement of case

Add new paragraph at end:

Practice Direction (Electronic Working Pilot Scheme) para.9.1 states that the **22.1.2** requirements in Pt 22 as to the verification by a statement of truth of any statement of case apply "to any Electronic Working forms filed electronically" in accordance with that Pilot Scheme. In these circumstances, the form of statement of truth "in an Electronic Working statement of case" is as stated in para.9.2. It should be noted that many of the forms and documents that may be filed electronically under the scheme, quite apart from statements of case, may, by virtue of provisions in CPR Pt 22 or elsewhere, have to be verified by a statement of truth. (Paragraph 9.1 is open to the interpretation that a document not normally required to be verified should be verified when filed electronically under the scheme, but presumably that is not what is intended.)

Documents in costs proceedings

At the end of the first paragraph add:

; and para.23A.4 states that where, on an application for a costs capping order **22.1.15.1** under r.44.19, the court directs that a party should file a schedule of costs that document must be supported by a statement of truth (see para.44PD.18).

PART 23

General Rules about Applications for Court Orders

Court dispensing with application notice requirement

In the last paragraph, add after "... trustees time and money).":

In *Sharab v Prince Al–Waleed* [2009] EWCA Civ 353; [2009] 2 Lloyd's Rep. 160, CA, **23.3.2** the Court of Appeal was prepared to treat an email sent to the court by the appellant's counsel after the hearing of the appeal but before judgment was delivered as an application for the court to accept an undertaking offered by the appellant.

Effect of rule

At the end of the eighth paragraph add:

Where the court deals with an application without a hearing in the circumstances **23.8.1** provided for by r.23.8(b), and the position is that the order made by the court in dealing with the application is a final order, the appropriate course to be adopted by a party dissatisfied with the order is to apply for permission to appeal (see *R. (Jones) v Nottingham City Council* [2009] EWHC 271 (Admin); January 21, 2009, unrep. (Collins J.), where the court disposed of the claimant's claim by a consent order in which the parties agreed that the matter of costs should be dealt with by the court on the parties' written submissions without a hearing and where the claimant wished to challenge the costs order made by the court).

In the last paragraph delete "(See further commentary following r.7.6.)".

PART 25

Interim Remedies and Security for Costs

Subsequent amendment of particulars of claim

Add new paragraph 25.1.25.3.1:

Where a claimant applies for and obtains from the court an order for a freezing **25.1.25.3.1** injunction on the basis that he has a particular claim (claim 1) against the defendant, but subsequently amends his particulars of claim to allege another claim (claim 2), the claimant bears the risk that if the amendment constitutes a new cause of action, and at trial he succeeds on claim 2 but fails on claim 1, the freezing order may be discharged and the cross–undertaking enforced (*Dadourian Group International Inc v Simms* [2009] EWCA Civ 169; [2009] 1 Lloyd's Rep. 601, CA). In such circumstances, when the amendment is made the claimant ought to go through the process of establishing before the court that the freezing order is properly made in support of claim 2 as well as claim 1 (*ibid*. at para.191).

Applicant's duties where application made without notice to respondent

In the fifth paragraph, add after "per Hobhouse L.J.).":

25.3.5   The law as to the discharge of freezing orders and the enforcement of undertakings where there has been material non–disclosure (whether innocent or not) was explained at first instance and on appeal in *Dadourian Group International Inc. v Simms* [2007] EWHC 1673 (Ch), July 11, 2007, unrep (Warren J.) at paras 29 to 32 and [2009] EWCA Civ 169; [2009] 1 Lloyd's Rep. 601, CA, at paras 167 to 210.

Effect of rule

Add new paragraph at end:

25.6.1   As to interim payment order applications in cases where, in the event, the question whether all or part of the award should be made payable by periodical payments under the Damages Act 1996 s.1 will arise, see commentary in para.25.7.1 below and Vol.2, para.15–110.1.

Effect of rule

At the end of the first paragraph add:

25.7.1   Rule 25.7(4) has not been amended in the light of the introduction by the Damages Act 1996 s.2 and CPR Pt 41 Section II of the court's jurisdiction to order that all or part of an award of damages in respect of personal injury is to take the form of periodical payments. So, on applications for an interim payment order, judges have been left to apply that provision to a case in which such an order might be made (*Eeles v Cobham Hire Services Ltd* [2009] EWCA Civ 204; March 13, 2009, unrep., CA, at para.7).

Condition (c): insolvent or impecunious company

In the third paragraph, add after "[2008] EWCA Civ 908":

25.13.12   ; [2009] 1 W.L.R. 751

In the fifth paragraph, add after "[2008] EWCA Civ 908":
; [2009] 1 W.L.R. 751

Particular discretionary factors where condition (c) relied on

At the end of the third paragraph add:

25.13.13   In *Spy Academy Ltd v Sakar International Inc* [2009] EWCA Civ 481 an order for security for costs was set aside on appeal: whilst the pre–condition for the making of the order was satisfied (the claimant company had no assets) there were other factors to be taken into account that pointed away from the making of such an order. Those factors were as follows: (i) the claimant had a bona fide claim; (ii) there was no realistic chance that the claimant's directors would be able to raise security; (iii) it was arguable that the claimant's impecuniosity had been brought about by the conduct of the defendant; and (iv) the application for security had been made late in the proceedings.

Proving insolvency or impecuniosity

For "An applicant for ... may not be disputed." substitute:

25.13.14   An applicant for security for costs who relies on r.25(13)(c) or upon s.726(1) of the Companies Act 1985 has to persuade the court that there is reason to believe that the company will not be able to pay costs if it is subsequently ordered to do so. It is not enough to show that the applicant has a reasonable belief to that effect: the court will take account of the evidence adduced by both sides (*Re Unisoft (No.2)* [1993] B.C.L.C. 532). However, the test to be applied is lower than a balance of probabilities test: the court is not required to reach a conclusion as to whether or not the company will later be unable to pay such costs (*Jirehouse Capital v Beller* [2008] EWCA Civ 908; [2009] 1 W.L.R. 751, CA). In practice, the insolvency or impecuniosity may not be disputed.

PRACTICE DIRECTION—INTERIM INJUNCTIONS

Urgent applications and applications without notice

Delete paragraph 4.1 and substitute:

4.1 These fall into two categories: **25PD.4**

(1) applications where a claim form has already been issued, and

(2) applications where a claim form has not yet been issued,

and, in both cases, where notice of the application has not been given to the respondent.

Search Orders

General

In paragraph 7.9(1), for "Supreme Court Act 1981" substitute:

Senior Courts Act 1981   **25PD.7**

PART 27

THE SMALL CLAIMS TRACK

Mediation in small claims cases

Delete and subsitute:

There are different "industry–led" schemes which offer potential litigants a chance **27.0.6** to mediate or go to arbitration before the start of court proceedings—for example for holiday claims. Failure to engage in alternative dispute resolution in a small claims case may attract an adverse order for costs—see para.27.14.4.

The court has the power to stay proceedings to enable the parties to engage in settlement discussions (r.26.4(1)). Rule 1.4(2)(e) considers active case management in the context of the overriding objective which includes "encouraging the parties to use alternative dispute resolution". Mediation is a variety of alternative dispute resolution—it is entirely voluntary, non–binding and private.

Attempts to encourage small claims litigants to go to private mediation through, for example, the National Mediation Helpline were not, overall, successful, because of the cost of private mediation relative to the amount in dispute.

County courts now promote a nationwide mediation scheme at no extra charge to cases allocated to the small claims track. This is a new service and is an alternative to pursuing a hearing before a judge. The allocation questionnaire (small claims track) now invites parties to agree to use the "free small claims service provided by Her Majesty's Courts Service, to help you settle your claim with the other party". If the parties agree, or at the discretion of the District Judge, they are referred to a trained mediator working in a local court. The mediator is not a judge, does not rule on disputed issues and his or her role is limited to assisting the parties to reach a settlement. The method used is usually by "shuttle diplomacy" on the telephone but the mediation can also be in person and in a few, experimental, cases, by email. The mediations last no more than an hour and if an agreement is reached the parties will usually be invited to sign a binding contract to record the terms reached; sometimes a Tomlin order is made. The scheme is, of course, not "free" as the claimant will have paid the issue fee and, depending on the amount of the claim, the allocation fee before the mediation is offered. These fees are not refunded by the Courts Service even if the mediation is successful. If mediation fails, then the case will be referred back to the court for a small claims hearing. Some cases are not suitable for mediation, for example claims arising out of road traffic accidents where neither party accepts liability or where there are outstanding issues of law. Mediation is, however, suitable for a wide range of other cases including claims for allegedly faulty goods and services. Although the mediation may take place earlier in time than a small claims hearing, the sidetracking of the case to mediation, if unsuccessful, may increase the overall length of the proceedings.

Costs where a party has behaved unreasonably (r.27.14(2)(d))

Add new paragraph at end:

27.14.4   Attention is drawn to the Practice Direction on Pre–action Conduct (49th update, April 2009) which describes the conduct the court will normally expect of the prospective parties prior to the start of proceedings. Failure to comply may result in an adverse order for costs including where a case is allocated to the small claims track (para.4.6(2) of the Practice Direction).

PART 28

THE FAST TRACK

PRACTICE DIRECTION—THE FAST TRACK

Expert Evidence

Add at end:

28PD.13   (see paragraphs 6, 7 and 9 of practice direction 35)

PART 29

THE MULTI–TRACK

PRACTICE DIRECTION—THE MULTI-TRACK

4.   Directions on Allocation

At the end of paragraph 4.8, add:

29PD.4   (see paragraphs 6, 7 and 9 of practice direction 35)

PART 31

DISCLOSURE AND INSPECTION OF DOCUMENTS

The duty to disclose

31.0.4   *Delete the tenth and eleventh paragraphs starting "Unless the court".*

Procedure for claiming a right or duty to withhold inspection

Delete and substitute:

31.3.3   See r.31.19 below.

(a) *Communications privileged although no litigation was contemplated or pending—"legal advice privilege"*

Solicitor and client

Delete the fourth paragraph and substitute:

31.3.6   This privilege extends to documents otherwise within it, although they contain statements of fact as to matters in the public domain, such as statements as to proceedings in private in the presence of the other party (*Ainsworth v Wilding* [1900] 2 Ch. 315). It extends to bills of costs relating to litigation actual or in contemplation (*Chant v Brown* (1852) 9 Ha. 790; *Turton v Barber* (1874) 17 L.R. Eq. 329) but it does not extend to a communication which took place in the presence of the opposite party, or with the opposite party (but see *Feuerheerd v LGO Co* [1918] 2 K.B. 565) or which are wholly in the public domain (*Ainsworth v Wilding*). The privilege is not affected by the fact that the action in which disclosure is sought is founded on a policy insuring the claimant against damages and costs incurred in an claim to which the disclosure relates (*Daily Express (1908) Ltd v Mountain* (1916) 32 T.L.R. 592, CA).

Legal advisers in the service of a party

For "Turco and Kingdom of Sweden ... July 4, 2008" substitute:
    Turco and Kingdom of Sweden v Council of the European Union, Joined Cases C–39/05P **31.3.9** and C–52/05P [2008] 3 C.M.L.R. 17; *The Times*, July 4, 2008

(b) *Communications privileged only when litigation was contemplated or pending—"litigation privilege"*

Solicitors and non–professional agent or third party

In the first paragraph, for "Reid v Langlois" substitute:
    Reid v Langlois 41 E.R. 1408   **31.3.12**

In the first paragraph, for "Calcraft v Guest" substitute:
    Calcraft v Guest [1898] 1 Q.B. 759

In the fourth paragraph, for "Learoyd v Halifax Joint Stock Banking Co" substitute:
    Learoyd v Halifax Joint Stock Banking Co [1893] 1 Ch. 686

(c) *Legal Professional Privilege generally*

Human Rights Act 1998

For "R v Hertfordshire ... 1 All E.R. 773, HL" substitute:
    R. v Hertfordshire CC Ex p. Green Environmental Industries [2000] 2 A.C. 412; [2000] 1 **31.3.32** All E.R. 773, HL

(d) *Other grounds of privilege*

Confidential communications

In the first paragraph, for "Alfred Crompton ... Excise (No.2) substitute:
    Alfred Crompton Amusement Machines Ltd v Commrs. of Customs and Excise (No.2) [1974] **31.3.36** A.C. 405; [1973] 3 W.L.R. 268

Without prejudice communications

Delete the first paragraph and substitute:
    The "without prejudice" rule governs the admissibility of evidence and is founded **31.3.40** upon both the public policy of encouraging litigants to settle their differences rather than litigate them to a finish, and the express or implied agreement of the parties themselves that communications in the course of their negotiations should not be admissible in evidence (*Rush & Tompkins Ltd v Greater London Council* [1989] A.C. 1280; [1988] 3 W.L.R. 939; [1988] 3 All E.R. 737, HL; *Unilever Plc v The Procter & Gamble Co* [2000] 1 W.L.R. 2436; [1999] All E.R. 691, and *Ofulue v Bossert* [2009] UKHL 16; 2 W.L.R. 749, HL). The rule applies to exclude all negotiations genuinely aimed at a settlement, whether oral or in writing, from being given in evidence. The purpose of the rule is to protect a litigant from being embarrassed by any admission or acknowledgment made purely in an attempt to achieve a settlement. There must be a dispute which is under settlement discussion and not merely the seeking of a concession as to payment of an undisputed debt sought by a debtor: *Bradford & Bingley Plc v Rashid* [2006] UKHL 37; [2006] 4 All E.R. 705, HL, a case concerning an acknowledgment within s.29(5) of the Limitation Act 1980. "Without prejudice" material will be admissible if the issue is whether or not negotiations resulted in an agreed settlement (*Walker v Wilsher* (1889) 23 Q.B.D. 335), but in relation to any other issue an admission or acknowledgment made in order to achieve a compromise should not be held against the maker of the admission or received in evidence; moreover an admission or acknowledgment made to reach a settlement with a party is not admissible in proceedings between the maker of the admission or acknowledgment and a different party,

even if such proceedings are within the same litigation (*Rush & Tompkins Ltd v Greater London Council* above). Likewise, an admission or acknowledgment regarding an unresolved issue raised in prior proceedings will not be admissible in subsequent proceedings between the same parties (*Ofulue v Bossert* [2009] UKHL 16). The right to disclosure and production of documents does not necessarily depend upon the admissibility of documents in evidence (*O'Rourke v Darbishire* [1920] A.C. 581, HL), but the general public policy that applies to protect genuine negotiations from being admissible in evidence is also extended by the Courts to protect those negotiations from being discloseable to third parties (*Rush & Tompkins Ltd v Greater London Council* (above)). Any discussions between the parties for the purpose of resolving the dispute between them are not admissible, even if the words "without prejudice" or their equivalent are not expressly used (*Chocoladefabriken Lindt & Sprungli AG v Nestle Co Ltd* [1978] R.P.C. 287). It follows that documents containing such material are themselves privileged from production. This head of privilege is not confined to admissions but applies to all bona fide without prejudice statements which touch upon the strengths or weaknesses of the parties' cases or which placed a valuation on a party's rights forming a part of the attempt to compromise the litigation; see *Unilever v Procter & Gamble*, above and *Instance v Denny Bros Printing Ltd*, *The Times*, February 28, 2000.

In the fourth paragraph, add after "(see above) at 1300":
and *Ofulue v Bossert* (above), though in this case the majority of the House of Lords held (doubting dicta of Lord Hoffmann in *Muller v Linsley & Mortimer* [1996] P.N.L.R. 74, and *Bradford & Bingley Plc v Rashid* (above)) that for reasons of legal and practical certainty it was inappropriate to create a further exception limiting the "without prejudice" rule to identifiable admissions, as opposed to acknowledgments.

Rule 31.16(3)(a), (b) and (d)

At the end of the third paragraph, add as a new paragraph:

31.16.4   In *Black v Sumitomo* (above) Rix L.J. observed at [88] that "the discretion is not confined and will depend on all the facts of the case", however he identified as

> "among the important considerations ... the nature of the injury or loss complained of; the clarity and identification of the issues raised by the complaint; the nature of the documents requested; the relevance of any protocol or pre-action inquiries; and the opportunity which the complainant has to make his case without pre-action disclosure".

See also *Gwelhayl Limited v Midas Construction Limited* [2008] EWHC 2316 (TCC); 2008 WL 4125338 and *Anglo Irish Bank Corporation Plc v West LB AG* [2009] EWHC 207 (Comm); 2009 WL 364152.

"... under any Act for disclosure by a person who is not a party to the proceedings"

At the end of the third paragraph, add as a new paragraph:

31.17.1   "The court has a clear obligation to ensure, if necessary of its own motion, that this intrusive jurisdiction is not used inappropriately even by consent. In exercising its responsibility, the court may well be assisted by submissions made on behalf of any third party the protection of whose interests requires to be considered." per Eady J. at [29] *Gary Flood v Times Newspapers Limited* [2009] EWHC 411 (QB); 2009 WL 506437.

PART 32

EVIDENCE

Effect of rule

After the third paragraph, add as a new paragraph:

32.7.1   In terms, r.32.7(1) does not give any indication as to the matters that a court should take into account in determining whether permission to cross-examine should be granted. The pre-CPR authorities indicate that the matter is not at large and that much will depend on the context in which the application to cross-examine is made. In *West London Pipeline and Storage Ltd v Total UK Ltd* [2008] EWHC 1729 (Comm), July 22, 2008, unrep. (Beatson J.) the proposition that those authorities should be discarded and that the court should concentrate on the intrinsic justice of the particular case in the light of the overriding objective was rejected and the effect of the authorities was explained (at paras 77 to 86). At an interlocutory stage a court may, in certain circumstances, order cross–examination of a person who has sworn an affidavit; for example, an affidavit sworn as a result of the order of the court that a defendant to a freezing injunction should disclose his assets (*House of Spring Gardens Ltd v Waite* [1985] F.S.R. 173, CA; *Yukong Line Ltd of Korea v Rendsburg Investments Corporation of Liberia* [1996] 2 Lloyd's Rep. 604, CA; *Motorola Credit Corporation v Uzan (No.2)* [2003] EWCA Civ 752; [2004] 1 W.L.R. 113, CA). However, the weight of authority is that cross–examination may not be ordered in the case of an affidavit of documents except in extreme cases where there is no alternative relief (*Frankenstein v Gavin's House–to–House Cycle Cleaning and Insurance Co* [1897] 2 Q.B. 62, CA; *Birmingham and Midland Motor Omnibus Co Ltd v London and North Western Railway Co* [1913] 3 K.B. 850; *Lonrho plc v Fayed (No.3), The Times* June 24, 1993, CA); see further para.31.19.1.1 above.

Effect of rule

Add new paragraphs at end:

32.14.1 The authorities show (1) that the discretion to grant permission under r.32.14(2)b) should be exercised with great caution, (2) that there must be a strong prima facie case shown against the deponent, (3) that the court (a) should be careful not to stray at this stage into the merits of the case, and (b) should consider whether the public interest requires the committal proceedings to be brought, and (4) that such proceedings should be proportionate and in accordance with the overriding objective (*Kirk v Walton* [2008] EWHC 1780 (QB); [2009] 1 All E.R. 257 (Cox J.); see also *Sony Computer Entertainment v Ball* [2004] EWHC 1192 (Ch); May 17, 2004, unrep. (Pumfrey J.)).

Where a claimant (C) was confronted with a defendant's video evidence which raised a strong prima facie case to the effect that C had committed contempt by making false statements in several documents verified by statements of truth, and the proceedings had then been settled in terms expressed in a consent order, a judge granted D's application for permission under r.32.14(2)(b) and in doing so stated that the mere fact that a claim had been settled on terms such as those agreed does not extinguish any contempt (*Kirk v Walton* op cit).

PRACTICE DIRECTION—WRITTEN EVIDENCE

Who may administer oaths and take Affidavits

In paragraph 9.1(4), for "Supreme Court" substitute:

Senior Courts

32PD.9

Penalty

In paragraph 28.1(1), for "shall" substitute:

must

32PD.28

In paragraph 28.1(2)(c), for "to him to" substitute:

that the Attorney General

In paragraph 28.1(2)(c), delete "he wishes".

Delete paragraph 28.2 and substitute:

28.2(1) A request to the Attorney General must be made in writing and sent to the Attorney General's Office at 20 Victoria Street, London, SW1H 0NF. The request must be accompanied by a copy of the order directing that the matter be referred to the Attorney General and must—

(a) identify the statement said to be false;

(b) explain—

(i) why it is false; and

(ii) why the maker knew the statement to be false at the time it was made; and

(c) explain why contempt proceedings would be appropriate in the light of the overriding objective in Part 1.

(2) The Attorney General prefers a request that comes from the court to one made direct by a party to the claim in which the alleged contempt occurred without prior consideration by the court. A request to the Attorney General is not a way of appealing against, or reviewing the decision of the judge.

Delete paragraph 28.3 and substitute:

28.3 Where a party makes an application to the court for permission to commence proceedings for contempt of court, it must be supported by written evidence of the facts and matters specified in paragraph 28.2(1) and the result of the request to the Attorney General made by the applicant.

PART 34

WITNESSES, DEPOSITIONS AND EVIDENCE FOR FOREIGN COURTS

"court ... may set it aside"

Add new paragraph at end:

34.4.3   In *Peters v Andrew* [2009] EWHC 1511 (QB), the applicants, who were non–parties to an arbitration agreement, applied to set aside witness summonses under r.34.4(2). The respondent had been granted permission by the arbitrators to apply to the High Court to issue witness summonses for the production of documents showing the itemised phone bills of both applicants. Applying, *South Tyneside BCl v Wickes Building Supplies Limited* [2004] EWHC 2428 (Comm) (see 34.3.5, above), Eady J., refused to set aside the witness summonses finding that the material sought was necessary and relevant for the purposes of the arbitration proceedings. The judge observed that, although not binding on him, the affirmative decision of the arbitrators on this issue was plainly entitled to respect. As to the intrusion into the private affairs of the applicants, the judge found that the intrusion into the private affairs of the applicants was proportionate and necessary and was limited to establishing how many communications there were between particular persons over a limited period of time. Furthermore, there was no other obvious way of obtaining the information. It had not been suggested that the contents of the calls would be disclosed.

Hague Convention countries

Add the following countries to the list:

34.13.8   Iceland
Liechtenstein
Macedonia, The Former Yugoslav Republic of

In the last paragraph after "the following countries:" insert:
Bosnia Herzegovina,

In the last paragraph after "Hungary," insert:
Iceland, India,

In the last paragraph after "Lithuania," insert:
Liechtenstein,

Dealing with deposition

In rule 34.19(2)(a), for "Supreme Court" substitute:

34.19   **Senior Courts**

PRACTICE DIRECTION—DEPOSITIONS AND COURT ATTENDANCE BY WITNESSES

Annex A

Draft Letter of Request (where the Taking of Evidence Regulation does not apply)

In the first paragraph of Annex A, for "Supreme Court of England and Wales" substitute:

Senior Courts of England and Wales

34PD.12

PART 35

EXPERTS AND ASSESSORS

In the table of contents, the following entry has been amended:

Contents

35.0.1

The Protocol on Expert Evidence

Add at end:

From October 2009 the statement of truth to be included in an expert's report, set **35.0.3** out in PD paragraph 3.37 and in the Protocol paragraph 13.5, has been amended to make it clear that experts only need to confirm to be true facts within their own knowledge.

Expert evidence in small claims

Add after "permission of the court (r.27.5).":

From October 2009 r.35.4.3 has been amended to clarify that in claims allocated to **35.0.4** the small claims track permission will only normally be given for evidence from one expert in a particular issue.

Effect of rule

At the end of the third paragraph add:

In *Clifford v Chief Constable of Hertfordshire* [2008] EWHC 2549, QB the defendant's **35.1.1** request for a computer science expert, in a claim for malicious prosecution for possessing images of child abuse in a temporary internet folder, was refused because the issue between the parties was purely factual.

Interpretation and definitions

Delete rule 35.2 and substitute:

35.2—(1) A reference to an "expert" in this Part is a reference 35.2 to a person who has been instructed to give or prepare expert evidence for the purpose of proceedings.

(2) "Single joint expert" means an expert instructed to prepare a report for the court on behalf of two or more of the parties (including the claimant) to the proceedings.

Effect of rule

Add at end:

In October 2009 r.35.2(2) was added to define a single joint expert.

35.2.1

Experts—overriding duty to the court

Delete rule 35.3(1) and substitute:

(1) It is the duty of experts to help the court on matters within 35.3 their expertise.

In rule 35.3(2), for "he has received instructions or by whom he is paid." substitute:

experts have received instructions or by whom they are paid.

Court's power to restrict expert evidence

Delete rule 35.4(2) and substitute:

35.4   **(2) When parties apply for permission they must identify—**

        (a) the field in which expert evidence is required; and

        (b) where practicable, the name of the proposed expert.

In rule 35.4(3) delete "under this rule".

After rule 35.4(3), add new paragraph (3A):

(3A) Where a claim has been allocated to the small claims track or the fast track, if permission is given for expert evidence, it will normally be given for evidence from only one expert on a particular issue.

(Paragraph 7 of practice direction 35 sets out some of the circumstances the court will consider when deciding whether expert evidence should be given by a single joint expert.)

Delete rule 35.4(4) and substitute:

(4) The court may limit the amount of a party's expert's fees and expenses that may be recovered from any other party.

Court's permission

At the end of the third paragraph add:

35.4.2   from October 2009 (r.35.4(3)).

In the fourth paragraph, for "where the court said it would ... carried out)" substitute:
where the court said it would depend upon the employees' status as experts and the nature of the work carried out and *Multiplex v Cleveland Bridge* [2008] EWHC 2220 (TCC) where, in the Wembley Stadium litigation the court dismissed a challenge by the claimant that an engineer employee of the defendant could include opinion evidence in his witness statement on the basis that it is legitimate for a construction professional to include statements of opinion that are related to the facts within his knowledge, based on his experience)

General requirement for expert evidence to be given in a written report

In rule 35.5(2), add after "If a claim is on the":

35.5   **small claims track or the**

Written questions to experts

Delete rule 35.6(1) and substitute:

35.6   **(1) A party may put written questions about an expert's report (which must be proportionate) to—**

(a) an expert instructed by another party; or

(b) a single joint expert appointed under rule 35.7.

In rule 35.6(4)(a) delete "in accordance with this rule".

Effect of rule

In the fourth paragraph, for "para.4.2" substitute:
para.5.2 — 35.6.1

Court's power to direct that evidence is to be given by a single joint expert

Delete rule 35.7 and substitute:

35.7—(1) Where two or more parties wish to submit expert evi- 35.7
dence on a particular issue, the court may direct that the evidence
on that issue is to be given by a single joint expert.

(2) Where the parties who wish to submit the evidence ("the relevant parties") cannot agree who should be the single joint expert,
the court may—

(a) select the expert from a list prepared or identified by the
relevant parties; or

(b) direct that the expert be selected in such other manner
as the court may direct.

Effect of rule

In the first paragraph add after "... under r.35.7.):
From October 2009 r.35.4.3 has been amended to the same effect. — 35.7.1

After the third paragraph, add as a new paragraph:
In October 2009 the CPRC adopted a proposal made by the CJC after consultation
that it would be helpful for Pt 35 to give more guidance to parties on when the court
might order expert evidence to be given by a single joint expert. The guidance is in a
new para.7 of the practice direction which lists the factors that the court will take into
account.

Power of court to direct evidence from lead experts

Delete and substitute:
Paragraph 6 of the practice direction was deleted from October 2009 as lead experts 35.7.2
are very rarely used and the court could make such a direction under the Part 3 case
management powers.

Instructions to a single joint expert

In rule 35.8(1), for "each instructing" substitute:

any relevant — 35.8

Delete rule 35.8(2) and substitute:

(2) When a party gives instructions to the expert that party must,
at the same time, send a copy to the other relevant parties.

In rule 35.8(4)(b), for "the instructing" substitute:

some or all of the relevant

In rule 35.8(5), for "instructing" substitute:

relevant

Power of court to direct a party to provide information

35.9 *In rule 35.9, for "available to the other party" substitute:*

available to another party

Contents of report

In rule 35.10(1), for "the relevant practice direction" substitute:

35.10   practice direction 35

Delete rule 35.10(2) and substitute:

(2) At the end of an expert's report there must be a statement that the expert understands and has complied with their duty to the court.

Discussions between experts

Delete rule 35.12(3) and substitute:

35.12   (3) The court may direct that following a discussion between the experts they must prepare a statement for the court setting out those issues on which—

(a) they agree; and

(b) they disagree, with a summary of their reasons for disagreeing.

Effect of rule

After the fourth paragraph, add as a new paragraph:

35.12.1   In October 2009 a new paragraph was added to the practice direction on the recommendation of the CJC to make it clear that experts' discussions are not mandatory unless the court orders one, and also to explain the purpose of the discussions and the need and form of joint statements.

At the end of the sixth paragraph add:

(see also para.9.3 of the practice direction—new from October 2009).

Delete the seventh paragraph and substitute:

New para.9.4 in the practice direction from October 2009 makes it clear that the norm is that parties and legal representatives will not attend experts' discussions unless the court orders otherwise, and even if they do so, the lawyers' role will normally be to answer the experts' questions or to advise them of the law.

The joint statement

Delete the first three paragraphs and substitute:

35.12.2   The experts in conjunction with the other experts of like discipline should prepare a written note signed by each of them as to matters of opinion on which they are agreed. From October 2009 new paras 9.6–9.8 give guidance on joint statements— they should be signed at the discussion or as soon as possible thereafter and the experts do not need any authority from the party of the lawyer to sign. This is to try to prevent some lawyers insisting that they must approve the draft before the expert has signed it. Whilst all experts may not agree particular points, limited agreement should be explored. Rule 34.12(5) acknowledges that, where in the course of their discussions experts reach agreement on an issue, that agreement should not bind the parties unless they expressly agree to be bound by the agreement. As a practical matter, the rule could hardly state otherwise. The parties may give their consent either prospectively or retrospectively. In practice however, it could be very difficult for a party dissatisfied with an agreement reached at a experts' discussion, to persuade the court that this agreement should, in effect, be set aside unless the party's expert had clearly stepped outside his expertise or brief, or otherwise had shown himself to be incompetent.

Add new paragraph at end:

From October 2009 a new paragraph in the practice direction requires an expert who significantly alters an opinion to include in the joint statement a note explaining this.

Expert's right to ask court for directions

Delete rule 35.14(1) and (2) and substitute:

(1) Experts may file written requests for directions for the purpose of assisting them in carrying out their functions. 35.14

(2) Experts must, unless the court orders otherwise, provide copies of the proposed requests for directions under paragraph (1)—

> **(a) to the party instructing them, at least 7 days before they file the requests; and**
>
> **(b) to all other parties, at least 4 days before they file them.**

Assessors

Delete rule 35.15 and substitute:

35.15—(1) This rule applies where the court appoints one or more persons under section 70 of the Senior Courts Act 1981 or section 63 of the County Courts Act 1984 as an assessor. 35.15

(2) An assessor will assist the court in dealing with a matter in which the assessor has skill and experience.

(3) An assessor will take such part in the proceedings as the court may direct and in particular the court may direct an assessor to—

> **(a) prepare a report for the court on any matter at issue in the proceedings; and**
>
> **(b) attend the whole or any part of the trial to advise the court on any such matter.**

(4) If an assessor prepares a report for the court before the trial has begun—

> **(a) the court will send a copy to each of the parties; and**
>
> **(b) the parties may use it at trial.**

(5) The remuneration to be paid to an assessor is to be determined by the court and will form part of the costs of the proceedings.

(6) The court may order any party to deposit in the court office a specified sum in respect of an assessor's fees and, where it does so, the assessor will not be asked to act until the sum has been deposited.

(7) Paragraphs (5) and (6) do not apply where the remuneration of the assessor is to be paid out of money provided by Parliament.

Delete Practice Direction—Experts and Assessors and substitute:

PRACTICE DIRECTION 35—EXPERTS AND ASSESSORS

Introduction
35PD.1 **1.** Part 35 is intended to limit the use of oral expert evidence to that which is reasonably required. In addition, where possible, matters requiring expert evidence should be dealt with by only one expert. Experts and those instructing them are expected to have regard to the guidance contained in the Protocol for the Instruction of Experts to give Evidence in Civil Claims annexed to this practice direction. (Further guidance on experts is contained in Annex C to the Practice Direction (Pre–Action Conduct)).

Expert Evidence – General Requirements
35PD.2 **2.1** Expert evidence should be the independent product of the expert uninfluenced by the pressures of litigation.

2.2 Experts should assist the court by providing objective, unbiased opinions on matters within their expertise, and should not assume the role of an advocate.

2.3 Experts should consider all material facts, including those which might detract from their opinions.

2.4 Experts should make it clear—

(a) when a question or issue falls outside their expertise; and

(b) when they are not able to reach a definite opinion, for example because they have insufficient information.

2.5 If, after producing a report, an expert's view changes on any material matter, such change of view should be communicated to all the parties without delay, and when appropriate to the court.

Form and Content of an Expert's Reports
35PD.3 **3.1** An expert's report should be addressed to the court and not to the party from whom the expert has received instructions.

3.2 An expert's report must:

(1) give details of the expert's qualifications;

(2) give details of any literature or other material which has been relied on in making the report;

(3) contain a statement setting out the substance of all facts and instructions which are material to the opinions expressed in the report or upon which those opinions are based;

(4) make clear which of the facts stated in the report are within the expert's own knowledge;

(5) say who carried out any examination, measurement, test or experiment which the expert has used for the report, give the qualifications of that person, and say whether or not the test or experiment has been carried out under the expert's supervision;

(6) where there is a range of opinion on the matters dealt with in the report—
  (a) summarise the range of opinions; and
  (b) give reasons for the expert's own opinion;

(7) contain a summary of the conclusions reached;

(8) if the expert is not able to give an opinion without qualification, state the qualification; and

(9) contain a statement that the expert—

(a) understands their duty to the court, and has complied with that duty; and

(b) is aware of the requirements of Part 35, this practice direction and the Protocol for Instruction of Experts to give Evidence in Civil Claims.

3.3 An expert's report must be verified by a statement of truth in the following form—

"I confirm that I have made clear which facts and matters referred to in this report are within my own knowledge and which are not. Those that are within my own knowledge I confirm to be true. The opinions I have expressed represent my true and complete professional opinions on the matters to which they refer.

(Part 22 deals with statements of truth. Rule 32.14 sets out the consequences of verifying a document containing a false statement without an honest belief in its truth.)

Information

4. Under Rule 35.9 the court may direct a party with access to information, which is not reasonably available to another party to serve on that other party a document, which records the information. The document served must include sufficient details of all the facts, tests, experiments and assumptions which underlie any part of the information to enable the party on whom it is served to make, or to obtain, a proper interpretation of the information and an assessment of its significance. **35PD.4**

Instructions

5. Cross–examination of experts on the contents of their instructions will not be allowed unless the court permits it (or unless the party who gave the instructions consents). Before it gives permission the court must be satisfied that there are reasonable grounds to consider that the statement in the report of the substance of the instructions is inaccurate or incomplete. If the court is so satisfied, it will allow the cross–examination where it appears to be in the interests of justice. **35PD.5**

Questions to Experts

6.1 Where a party sends a written question or questions under rule 35.6 direct to an expert, a copy of the questions must, at the same time, be sent to the other party or parties. **35PD.6**

6.2 The party or parties instructing the expert must pay any fees charged by that expert for answering questions put under rule 35.6. This does not affect any decision of the court as to the party who is ultimately to bear the expert's fees.

Single joint expert

7. When considering whether to give permission for the parties to rely on expert evidence and whether that evidence should be from a single joint expert the court will take into account all the circumstances in particular, whether: **35PD.7**

(a) it is proportionate to have separate experts for each party on a particular issue with reference to—

(i) the amount in dispute;

    (ii) the importance to the parties; and

    (iii) the complexity of the issue;

(b) the instruction of a single joint expert is likely to assist the parties and the court to resolve the issue more speedily and in a more cost–effective way than separately instructed experts;

(c) expert evidence is to be given on the issue of liability, causation or quantum;

(d) the expert evidence falls within a substantially established area of knowledge which is unlikely to be in dispute or there is likely to be a range of expert opinion;

(e) a party has already instructed an expert on the issue in question and whether or not that was done in compliance with any practice direction or relevant pre–action protocol;

(f) questions put in accordance with rule 35.6 are likely to remove the need for the other party to instruct an expert if one party has already instructed an expert;

(g) questions put to a single joint expert may not conclusively deal with all issues that may require testing prior to trial;

(h) a conference may be required with the legal representatives, experts and other witnesses which may make instruction of a single joint expert impractical; and

(i) a claim to privilege^{GL} makes the instruction of any expert as a single joint expert inappropriate.

Orders

35PD.8   **8.** Where an order requires an act to be done by an expert, or otherwise affects an expert, the party instructing that expert must serve a copy of the order on the expert. The claimant must serve the order on a single joint expert.

Discussions between experts

35PD.9   **9.1** Unless directed by the court discussions between experts are not mandatory. Parties must consider, with their experts, at an early stage, whether there is likely to be any useful purpose in holding an expert's discussion and if so when.

    9.2 The purpose of discussions between experts is not for experts to settle cases but to agree and narrow issues and in particular to identify:

    (i) the extent of the agreement between them;

    (ii) the points of and short reasons for any disagreement;

    (iii) action, if any, which may be taken to resolve any outstanding points of disagreement; and

    (iv) any further material issues not raised and the extent to which these issues are agreed.

    9.3 Where the experts are to meet, the parties must discuss and if possible agree whether an agenda is necessary, and if so attempt to agree one that helps the experts to focus on the issues which need to be discussed. The agenda must not be in the form of leading questions or hostile in tone.

    9.4 Unless ordered by the court, or agreed by all parties, and the experts, neither the parties nor their legal representatives may attend experts discussions.

9.5 If the legal representatives do attend—

(i) they should not normally intervene in the discussion, except to answer questions put to them by the experts or to advise on the law; and

(ii) the experts may if they so wish hold part of their discussions in the absence of the legal representatives.

9.6 A statement must be prepared by the experts dealing with paragraphs 9.2(i) – (iv) above. Individual copies of the statements must be signed by the experts at the conclusion of the discussion, or as soon thereafter as practicable, and in any event within 7 days. Copies of the statements must be provided to the parties no later than 14 days after signing.

9.7 Experts must give their own opinions to assist the court and do not require the authority of the parties to sign a joint statement.

9.8 If an expert significantly alters an opinion, the joint statement must include a note or addendum by that expert explaining the change of opinion.

Assessors

10.1. An assessor may be appointed to assist the court under rule 35.15. Not less than 21 days before making any such appointment, the court will notify each party in writing of the name of the proposed assessor, of the matter in respect of which the assistance of the assessor will be sought and of the qualifications of the assessor to give that assistance. **35PD.10**

10.2. Where any person has been proposed for appointment as an assessor, any party may object to that person either personally or in respect of that person's qualification.

10.3. Any such objection must be made in writing and filed with the court within 7 days of receipt of the notification referred to in paragraph 10.1 and will be taken into account by the court in deciding whether or not to make the appointment.

10.4. Copies of any report prepared by the assessor will be sent to each of the parties but the assessor will not give oral evidence or be open to cross–examination or questioning.

Protocol for the Instruction of Experts to give evidence in civil claims

13. Contents of Experts' Reports

Delete paragraph 13.5 and substitute:

13.5 Experts' reports must contain statements that they— **35.28**

(i) understand their duty to the court and have complied and will continue to comply with it; and

(ii) are aware of the requirements of Part 35 and practice direction 35, this protocol and the practice direction on pre–action conduct.

Experts' reports must also be verified by a statement of truth. The form of the statement of truth is as follows—

"I confirm that I have made clear which facts and matters referred to in this report are within my own knowledge and which are not. Those that are within my own knowledge I confirm to be true. The opinions I have expressed represent my true and complete professional opinions on the matters to which they refer."

This wording is mandatory and must not be modified.

PART 36

Offers to Settle

Formal or technical defects

Add new paragraph 36.1.3.1:

36.1.3.1   In spite of the wording of r.36.1(2) it has been held that if there are formal or technical defects to a Pt 36 offer, provided they cause no real uncertainty or other prejudice to the offeree, the court may order that the usual Pt 36 costs consequences will follow. See *Huntley v Simmonds* [2009] EWHC 406, QB and *AF v BG* [2009] EWCA Civ 757; [2009] All E.R. (D) 249.

Offers before the commencement of proceedings

Add new paragraph 36.3.3.1:

36.3.3.1   Rule 36.3 (2)(a) is clearly intended to make the whole Pt 36 structure available to litigants before proceedings are commenced and for offers made then to have the anticipated costs consequences later after the proceedings have been commenced. This is an innovation under the CPR because there was no provision for payments into court prior to proceedings under the RSC. One of the ambiguities left by the wording of the current Pt 36 is that it is somewhat unclear as to what the costs consequences might be of a Pt 36 offer which is made and then accepted before proceedings are commenced: rr.36.10 and 36.11 are both written in anticipation of there being extant proceedings. It is submitted that parties wanting to make Pt 36 offers in advance of proceedings should do so in terms whereby the offer expressly states that it is made on the basis that in the event of acceptance before the commencement of proceedings, the costs provisions of Pt 36 (and Pt 44 if the parties so wish) will apply, thereby binding those terms into any settlement contract.

Costs under r.36.10(4) and (5)

Add new paragraph 36.10.2:

36.10.2   In the absence of any express provision (such as in r.36.14) there is no presumption that the court would order a late accepting party to pay the other party's costs on an indemnity basis. The usual basis will be the standard one, unless, say, conduct is an issue, in which case r.44.3 will apply: *Fitzpatrick Contractors Ltd v Tyco Fire and Integrated Solutions (UK) Ltd* [2009] EWHC 274 (TCC); [2009] All E.R. (D) 70.

Enhanced interest/costs

Add at end:

36.14.3   Whether an offeror is funded under a CFA is not a relevant factor for the court to take into account when deciding to make an order under r.36.14(3). See *CEL Group Ltd v Nedlloyd Lines (UK) Ltd* [2003] EWCA Civ 1871; [2004] 1 Lloyd's Rep 338.

PART 37

Miscellaneous Provisions about Payments into Court

PRACTICE DIRECTION—MISCELLANEOUS PROVISIONS ABOUT PAYMENTS INTO COURT

Payment into court under an order, etc

In paragraph 1.1(1)(a) for "Supreme Court" substitute:

37PD.1   Senior Courts

PART 39

MISCELLANEOUS PROVISIONS RELATING TO HEARINGS

Related sources

After the last bullet point, add new bullet point:

- Practice Direction (Court Dress) (No.5) [2008] 1 W.L.R. 1700, Sup Ct. (see **39.0.3**
  Vol.2 para.B10–001)

Barristers' dress for court hearings

Add new paragraph 39.0.5:

On June 2, 2009, the Chairman of the Bar Council issued Revised Guidance indicat- **39.0.5**
ing the circumstances when barristers appearing in court should wear "court dress"
(wigs, gowns, wing collars and bands or collarettes) and when they should wear "business suits" (dark–coloured formal non–court dress as appropriate). The Guidance
draws a distinction between a hearing in the form of a trial (which is defined as including any final hearing of a CPR Pt 7 claim, a Pt 8 claim, or a Petition) and other
hearings. The Guidance states that counsel will wear court dress in the Court of
Appeal. In so far as it applies to proceedings in the High Court and the county courts,
in summary the Guidance states as follows:

High Court

- Commercial Court and Admiralty Court: business suits on all occasions
- Technology and Construction Court: business suits on all occasions
- Chancery Division: court dress for all trials and appeals and business suits on
  all other occasions
- Family Division: business suits, save for contested divorce and nullity petitions
  when court dress will be worn
- Administrative Court: court dress on all occasions
- Queen's Bench Division: court dress for trials save on the occasions mentioned
  above; business suits on all other occasions

All of the above is subject to the qualification that counsel will wear court dress
where the liberty of the subject is in issue.

County Courts

For hearings before Circuit Judges, Deputy Circuit Judges and Recorders, counsel
will wear business suits for applications (including all interim and final hearings in
children and ancillary financial relief cases). They will wear court dress for trials
(including contested divorce and nullity petitions).

In appeals in the county courts, counsel will wear business suits for appeals from
applications, and court dress for appeals from trials and appeals under sections 204
and 204A of the Housing Act 1996.

Masters, registrars and district judges

Counsel will wear business suits, save that court dress will be worn: (1) in the Chancery Division where the hearing takes place in court (and not in the judge's room),
and (2) on winding–up hearings heard by district judges in the county courts.

PRACTICE DIRECTION—MISCELLANEOUS PROVISIONS RELATING TO HEARINGS

Hearings

Delete paragraph 1.5(8) and substitute:

(8) an application for security for costs to be provided by a claim- **39PD.1**
ant who is a company or a limited liability partnership in the
circumstances set out in rule 25.13(2)(c),

PART 40

JUDGMENTS, ORDERS, SALE OF LAND ETC.

Effect of judgment before entry—altering judgment

At the end of the first paragraph add:

40.2.1   Nowadays, an order is perfected by being sealed pursuant to r.40.2(2)(b).

After the second paragraph, add as a new paragraph:

In *Paulin v Paulin* [2009] EWCA Civ 221; March 17, 2009, unrep., CA, the Court of Appeal noted that, after the decision of the court in *Stewart v Engel* (endorsing the *Barrell* jurisdiction), and with effect from May 2, 2000, the time for appeal from a decision of the High Court began to run, not from the date on which the judgment or order of the court below was sealed or otherwise perfected (as was previously stated in RSC O.59, r.4(1)), but from the date of the decision of the lower court (as is now stated in CPR r.52.4(2)(b)). The court rejected the submission that this change in effect abrogated the *Barrell* jurisdiction. In this respect the court was bound by *Hyde and South Bank Housing Association v Kain* July 27, 1989, unrep., CA, a decision turning on the pre–CPR provision regulating appeals to the court from county courts (former RSC O.59, r.19(3)), a provision which had the same effect as CPR r.52.4(2)(b).

Before the paragraph beginning "In A v B Plc" insert the following as a new paragraph:

40.2.1.A   In *Paulin v Paulin* [2009] EWCA Civ 221, March 17, 2009, unrep., CA, the trial judge reconsidered his judgment and reversed his decision, ultimately holding that a wife's application to annul a bankruptcy order against her husband should be granted. On the husband's appeal the Court of Appeal reviewed and explained the authorities on the nature of a trial court's exercise of the *Barrell* jurisdiction. The court concluded that the judge's decision to reconsider his decision upon the central question arising was flawed in that it did not even purport to be exercised in accordance with the relevant authorities; indeed the decision to reconsider was not reasoned at all. The husband did not appeal against the judge's decision to reconsider his judgment, but against the judge's ultimate (and perfected) order. Consequently the court expressed no opinion on what the court's reaction to an appeal by the husband against the judge's decision to reconsider might have been, but in this respect drew attention to the following dictum of Peter Gibson L.J. in *Robinson v Bird* op cit. (at para.11):

> "If a judge gives reasons why he is recalling his order or a draft judgment which he has sent out and those reasons are unpersuasive, that in itself does not seem to me to require the court to interfere with the perfected order unless it can be said that the judge's final judgment is thereby, or for some other reason, shown to be wrong."

In the last paragraph, add after "per Arden L.J.":

40.2.1.C   ; *Paulin v Paulin* [2009] EWCA Civ 221, March 17, 2009, CA, at para.30 per Wilson L.J.

Entry of judgment in foreign currency

Add new paragraph at end:

40.2.2   On the question as to whether in a costs order the amounts payable should be assessed in a currency other than sterling, see *Schlumberger Holdings Ltd v Electromagnetic Geoservices AS* [2009] EWHC 775 (Pat), February 23, 2009, unrep. (Mann J.)

Tomlin orders

In the fifteenth paragraph, for "Wallace v Brian Gale & Associates, The Times March 31, 1997" substitute:

40.6.2   *Wallace v Brian Gale & Associates* [1998] 1 F.L.R. 1091

Interest on costs orders in substantive proceedings

Add new paragraph at end:

40.8.11   In *Schlumberger Holdings Ltd v Electromagnetic Geoservices AS* [2009] EWHC 773 (Pat), February 24, 2009, unrep. (Mann J.) the paying party submitted that the court had power under r.40.8(1) and r.44.3(6)(g) to postpone to the date when the costs were finally quantified and certified by the costs judge the time at which interest at the judgment debt rate commenced to run. In rejecting this submission the judge held (1) it is an anomaly, but one confirmed by binding authority, that whereas the judgment debt rate applies to damages from the date of assessment, it applies to costs from the date of the costs order, (2) the judgment debt rate is fixed by statutory instrument and the court has no more power directly to adjust that rate as payable under a costs order than it does to vary the rate as payable under any other judgment, (3) under r.44.3(6)(g) the court has power to order that a paying party must pay interest on costs from or until a certain date, but neither that provision nor any other subordinate legislation gives the court power indirectly to alter the statutorily prescribed interest rate.

Other rules making different provision

In the third paragraph, add as the first item in the list:

Rule 3.3(4) and (5) (court making order of its own initiative without hearing parties). **40.9.2**

After the seventh paragraph, add as a new paragraph:

An effect of Practice Direction (Applications) para.11.2 (para.23PD11, above) is to provide that, where a court exercises its powers under r.23.8(c), and deals with an application without a hearing on the basis that it does not consider that a hearing would be appropriate, a party affected by an order made in such circumstances may apply to the court to have it set aside, varied or stayed (see further paras 3.1.9 and 23.8.1 above).

General power to vary or revoke orders

Add after "... trial on the substantive merits of an issue)).":

The rule does not give a judge, in effect, power to hear an appeal from himself in respect of a final order, and should not be used to revoke approval to a final settlement, whether of the whole or part of a claim (*Roult v North West Strategic Health Authority* [2009] EWCA Civ 444, May 20, 2009, CA, unrep. (rejecting the submission that the court's power may be exercised where a subsequent unforeseen event destroyed the assumption on which the order was made)). **40.9.3**

Jurisdiction to make declarations

After the third paragraph, add as a new paragraph:

In the several judgments delivered by the Court of Appeal in the case of *Rolls–Royce Plc v Unite the Union* [2009] EWCA Civ 387, *The Times*, May 27, 2009, CA, there are extended discussions of the power of courts to grant declaratory relief as a final remedy in the context of a claim proceeding under the CPR Pt 8 alternative procedure and raising issues under the Employment Equality (Age) Regulations 2006 likely to affect persons other than the parties before the court. **40.20.2**

Declarations without trial (judgment by consent or default and summary judgment)

After the third paragraph, add as a new paragraph:

In *Animatrix Ltd v O'Kelly* [2008] EWCA Civ 1415; December 16, 2008, unrep., CA, an intellectual property claim case in which an issue as to the assignment of rights arose and the claimants (C) sought various forms of relief, including declarations, the parties reached a compromise agreement in which C's claims for declarations were recited and by which the proceedings were stayed, principally for purpose of giving the defendant an opportunity to raise finance. On C's subsequent application to enforce the agreement, a judge rejected D's submission that the court could not properly grant declaratory relief on the summary basis sought by C without first hearing evidence on the underlying issues to which the declarations were directed (in particular the issue of the validity of the assignment: [2008] EWHC 438 (Ch)). In dismissing D's appeal the Court of Appeal stated (1) it is the established practice of the court that declarations will not be granted simply because the parties have agreed to them, (2) but it is open to the court to grant a declaration by consent where that was necessary to do justice between the parties, (3) in this case, the compromise agreement was a commercial bargain and under is terms it was not open to D to contend that C must still establish that they were the rightful owners of the relevant rights, (3) in effect, the position was the same as if D had agreed to transfer his rights (if any) and the parties **40.20.3** had agreed that in default C could seek an order for specific performance and a declaration that upon the transfer taking effect they were the owner of rights.

PRACTICE DIRECTION—JUDGMENTS AND ORDERS

Preparation of deeds or documents under an order

40BPD.2 *In paragraph 2.3(2)(c), for "Supreme Court" substitute:*

Senior Courts

Order to make an order of the Supreme Court an order of the High Court

40BPD.13 *Delete title "Order to make an order of the House of Lords an order of the High Court" and substitute: "Order to make an order of the Supreme Court an order of the High Court".*

In paragraph 13.1, for "House of Lords" substitute:

Supreme Court

In paragraph 13.2(1), for "House of Lords" substitute:

Supreme Court

In paragraph 13.2(2), for "House of Lords" substitute:

Supreme Court

In paragraph 13.2(3), for "Clerk of Parliaments" substitute:

Registrar of the Supreme Court

In paragraph 13.2(3), for "House of Lords" substitute:

Supreme Court

In paragraph 13.3, for "House of Lords" substitute:

Supreme Court

PART 41

DAMAGES

"order to take the form of periodical payments"

Add new paragraph at end:

41.4.1   As to interim payment order applications under r.25.6 in cases where, in the event, the question whether all or part of the award should be made payable by periodical payments under the Damages Act 1996 s.1 will arise, see para.25.7.1 above and Vol.2, para.15–110.1.

"the order must specify"

In the last paragraph, add after "being approved by the court.":

41.8.1   In *Long v Norwich Union Insurance Ltd* [2009] EWHC 715 (QB), April 6, 2009, unrep. (Mackay J.) it was noted that the model order is silent as to upon whom the costs of providing for the defendant at annual instalment dates evidence establishing that the claimant remained alive should fall. The judge ruled that such costs were plainly within the province of the professional deputy (whose fees had been estimated and assessed) and included such activity as the proof of life.

PART 43

SCOPE OF COST RULES AND DEFINITIONS

Definitions and application

43.2   *In rule 43.2(1)(b), for "Supreme Court" substitute:*

Senior Courts

Add after rule 43.2(1)(b):

"Costs Office" means the Senior Courts Costs Office;

In rule 43.2(1)(d)(iv), delete "Supreme Court".

In rule 43(1)(e), delete "as such".

Costs estimates

In the fifth paragraph, for "MasterCigars Direct Ltd ... [2008] 3 All E.R. 417" substitute:
MasterCigars Direct Ltd v Withers LLP [2007] EWHC 2733 (Ch); [2009] 1 W.L.R. 881   **43.2.2**

PRACTICE DIRECTION ABOUT COSTS

Section 1 Introduction

In paragraph 1.3, for "Supreme Court" substitute:

Senior Courts   **43PD.1**

In paragraph 1.3, for "Section 51 of the Supreme Court Act 1981" substitute:
Section 51 of the Senior Courts Act 1981

In paragraph 1.4, for "Supreme Court" substitute:
Senior Courts

PART 44

GENERAL RULES ABOUT COSTS

In the contents list, the following entry has been added:

Contents   **44.0.1**

Comment

After the tenth paragraph, add as a new paragraph:
    Where a partnership dispute was settled on the day of the trial, because the claim- **44.3.1** ant abandoned his claims at the door of the court and the Order which was made reflected what the defendant had sought throughout, the judge at first instance made no order as to costs. On appeal the court held that costs should have followed the event and the making of no order for costs was not a reasonable exercise of the judge's discretion: *Hannan v Maxton* [2009] EWCA Civ 8.

Judicial Review

After the ninth paragraph, add as a new paragraph:
    The Court of Appeal held that the principles to be applied under CPR r.44.3 where **44.3.7** Judicial Review proceedings had been compromised were set out in *R. (Boxall) v Waltham Forest LBC* (above). The Court of Appeal could not change the law in order to fund litigation in a way that was preferable to a party, nor could there be one rule for Judicial Review proceedings and another for civil litigation. The judge, at first instance, had made no order for costs save as to the detailed assessment on the applicant's publicly funded costs. The court stated (obiter) that judges should bear in mind the need to make reasonable and proportionate attempts to ascertain the position between

the parties and should not be tempted too readily to use the fallback position of making no order for costs: *R (Scott) v London Borough of Hackney* [2009] EWCA Civ 217.

Add new paragraphs at end:

The Court of Appeal has considered the question of costs of a respondent to an application for permission. Having referred to *Davey v Aylesbury Vale DC* (above) the court stated that when "preparation" costs are sought in addition to "acknowledgement" costs, it is for the defendant to justify those costs, which may well not be recoverable. It was undoubtedly the case that even a short form of acknowledgement did not settle itself, and study may be needed to decide what should go into it:

"In future and in accordance with principle (3) of the Sedley–Clarke principles, it will be important that the Permission Judge, who is far better placed than anyone else to decide what needed reasonably to be said, in response to a claim, should himself apply the *R (Roudham and Larling Parish Council) v Breckland Council* [2008] EWCA Civ 714.

Rule 44.3(2)

After the eleventh paragraph, add as a new paragraph:

44.3.8 In an action over music copyright the claimant failed to obtain the relief sought, but the judge made no order for costs in favour of the defendant, on the basis that although it was the successful party, it had raised and lost a number of issues thereby prolonging the hearing and in some cases without the necessary standing to do so. The defendant had also made allegations of fraud which had been rejected. The Court of Appeal held that although it was unusual to deny a successful party the recovery of the whole of its costs of trial, the judge had not misdirected himself as a matter of law, nor failed adequately to express his reasoning in his costs judgment: *Peer International Corporation v Editora Musical de Cuba* [2008] EWCA Civ 1260.

Admiralty Court

Add new paragraph at end:

44.3.8.3 In proceedings arising out of a collision of ships at sea, the fact that the successful party had been found one–third to blame for the collision was not of itself a sufficient reason to reduce the level of recoverable costs, although it did not follow that the apportionment of liability was not a relevant factor. Taking into account the offer which had been made and the parties' conduct, a fair outcome was that the successful party should recover 65 per cent of its costs: *Owners Demise Charterers and Time Charterers of "Western Neptune" v Owners and Demise Charterers of "Philadelphia Express"* [2009] EWHC 1522 (Admlty), David Steel J.

Costs of inquest

Add new paragraph 44.3.8.4:

44.3.8.4 Following the death in custody of a young man who was a drug addict, a dispute arose as to the adequacy of the care given to him by the prison authorities. At the inquest, solicitors and counsel attended with exceptional funding from the Legal Services Commission for representation. The civil claim was subsequently settled for £10,000.

90 per cent of the claimant's bill of costs related to the attendance at the inquest. On detailed assessment the Home Office argued that there should be no liability upon them to pay the costs of attending the inquest. The court held that it was common ground that the courts were entitled, at their discretion, to award costs that were of and incidental to civil proceedings pursuant to s.51 of the Supreme Court Act 1981. There was no doubt that the costs incurred prior to proceedings were capable, in principle, of being recoverable as costs in the proceedings (see *Gibson's Settlement Trusts*, 1981 Ch. 179 and the cases therein cited). Although the costs were in principle recoverable, it was not appropriate to divide the costs of an inquest by the dual role or purpose of the legal representative at the hearing, i.e. the inquest itself and the subsequent civil claim. All costs that were of and incidental to civil proceedings could be recovered: *Roach v The Home Office* [2009] EWHC 312 (QB); [2009] 3 All E.R. 510, Davis J.

Exaggeration and false claims

In the fifth paragraph, add after "February 15, 2005 CA.":

The Court of Appeal distinguished from *Painting* (above) a case in which the client **44.3.10** had exaggerated his claim but, following video evidence, reduced his claim both openly and in the course of without prejudice negotiations. The Recorder, having taken into account the circumstances, nonetheless awarded the claimant his costs. On appeal the Court of Appeal found that the Recorder was acting within his broad discretion: *Morgan v UPS* [2008] EWCA Civ 1476. In *Morgan* (above), the Court of Appeal referred to the judgment of Waller L.J. in *Straker v Tudor Rose* [2007] EWCA Civ 368:

> "The key issue is whether the judge misdirected himself. It is well known that this court will be loath to interfere with the discretion exercised by a judge in any area, but so far as costs are concerned, that principle has a special significance. The judge has the feel of a case after a trial which the Court of Appeal cannot hope to replicate and the judge must have gone seriously wrong if this court is to interfere".

Add new paragraph at end:

In an action for breach of repairing covenants in a lease the claimant claimed over £500,000 from the defendant landlord who raised preliminary issues. There was a meeting of experts, after which all that was left of the claim was an agreed figure of £1,073.50. The claimant offered to accept this sum, provided the defendant paid all his costs, which the defendant refused to do. The court formed the clear view that in the litigation the claimant was the clear loser. The court held that the claimant both before and after the institution of proceedings acted in a way which took the case out of the norm. Any proper investigation of the claim, both before the particulars of claim were served and afterwards, would have revealed that this was not a genuine claim for dilapidations. The claimant was ordered to pay the defendant's costs on the indemnity basis: *Business Environment Bow Lane Ltd v Deanwater Estates Ltd* [2008] EWHC 2003 (TCC), H.H.J. Toulmin Q.C.

Rule 44.3(6) types of order

Add new paragraphs at end:

Where proceedings were compromised, the receiving party applied, some three **44.3.14** years after the Consent Order, for an order that the costs judge dealing with assessment should be directed that the party's entitlement to costs included preparation for trial as there was no prospect that the claim would be revived. The judge, at first instance, directed that an order be drawn up whereby the costs judge was directed to carry out the assessment using the guidance set out in six specified paragraphs in the judgment. On appeal the Court of Appeal thought it highly debateable whether the judge had any jurisdiction to hear the application. Even if the judge had jurisdiction, he should not have exercised it as the matter would ordinarily go before a costs judge for detailed assessment. In addition, the judgment was extremely diffuse and it was unlikely that any costs judge would be able to follow the directions. As a matter of practice it was undesirable for judges to enter into this form of order. Any order made at the end of a judgment should stand on its own: *Richardson's Roofing Company Limited v Ballast plc; Comp Co Holdings plc; The Colman Partnership* [2009] EWCA Civ 13.

In 1998 the Judgments Act 1838 was amended so as to give the court a discretion with regard to interest (see *Powell v Herefordshire*, above and *Douglas v Hello*, above). The combined effect of the Act and the Rules is that, save where a Rule or Practice Direction otherwise provides, interest will run from the date the judgment is given, unless the court orders otherwise. There is nothing in the Statute or in the Rules which indicates that a different order is only to be made in exceptional circumstances. The Rules expressly indicate that the court may order interest to begin from a date before judgment, and the circumstances in which it is likely to do so include cases where substantial sums have been paid in costs before the judgment is given.

> "The most important criterion is that any order should reflect what justice requires. The primary purpose of an award of interest on a debt, damages or costs is to compensate the recipient for the fact that he had been precluded from obtaining a return on the money which he has had to expend on costs and has thus been out of pocket— *London Chatham and Dover Railway Company v South Eastern Railways Company* (1893) A.C. 429 at 437; *Earl of Malmsbury v Strutt and Parker* [2008] EWCA 616 (QB) paras [5] and [6]." *Fattal v Walbrook Trustees (Jersey) Limited* [2009] EWHC 1674 (Ch) Christopher Clarke J.

Rule 44.3(8) payment on account

Add new paragraph at end:

44.3.15   The court has power to order interest on an interim payment of costs. The power resides either in CPR r.52.10(2)(d) or in CPR r.44.3(6)(g) read in the context of r.44.3(8): *Multiplex Constructions (UK) Ltd v Cleveland Bridge UK Ltd* [2008] EWCA Civ 133; 118 Con. L.R., CA.

Limits on recovery under funding arrangements

In rule 44.3B(1), for "A" substitute:

44.3B Unless the court orders otherwise, a

In rule 44.3B(1)(c), delete "in the proceedings".

In rule 44.3B(1)(c), for "he" substitute:

that party

In rule 44.3B(1)(d), for "a party" substitute:

that party

After rule 44.3B(1)(d), add new sub–paragraph (e):

> **(e) any insurance premium where that party has failed to provide information about the insurance policy in question by the time required by a rule, practice direction or court order.**

(Paragraph 9.3 of the Practice Direction (Pre–Action Conduct) provides that a party must inform any other party as soon as possible about a funding arrangement entered into before the start of proceedings.)

Rule 44.4(3)—Costs on the Indemnity Basis

After the third paragraph add as a new paragraph:

44.4.3   The fact that a substantial part of a claimant's case had failed at the stage of summary judgment did not warrant an award of indemnity costs. The giving of summary judgment against the party, who had a hopeless case, was itself the norm. The requirement of proportionality was a useful brake on the escalation of costs and should not be lightly removed from any assessment of costs. The claimant was ordered to pay 90 per cent of the defendant's costs on the standard basis: *Easy Air Limited v Opal Telecom Limited* [2009] EWHC 779 (Ch), Lewison J.

Delete and substitute:

44.9.2   In a housing disrepair case the Court of Appeal had to decide the question whether that in order to make the rules and the protocol operate in the manner which must be intended, some order for pre–allocation costs is necessary and if so what. The court stated:

> "33. In our view, the answer to the question posed ... is clear. Since the promulgation of the protocol it is no longer the case that a claim is only made (for costs purposes at least) when and if litigation is begun. On the contrary, the protocol requires a claim to be advanced initially in accordance with its terms, under a warning that there is likely to be a costs penalty if it is not. The references to costs which are contained in the protocol ... clearly demonstrate that the object of the protocol is to achieve settlement of disrepair claims without recourse to litigation. Its object is very clearly that, provided the claim is justified, it ought to be settled on terms which include the payment of the tenant's reasonable costs; and costs calculated according to the track on which the claim would fall to if made by way of litigation."

The court made an order that the claimant should have her costs in the cause on the fast track up to the date when the repairs were completed. Any costs relating to the period after September 26 would remain governed by the allocation to the small claims track: *Birmingham City Council v Lee* [2008] EWCA Civ 891.

Costs–only proceedings

In rule 44.12A, add after "paragraph (4A)":
(and subject to rule 44.12B) **44.12A**

Costs only proceedings—costs in respect of insurance premium in publication cases

Add new rule 44.12B:

44.12B—(1) If in proceedings to which rule 44.12A applies it **44.12B** appears to the court that—
- (a) if proceedings had been started, they would have been publication proceedings;
- (b) one party admitted liability and made an offer of settlement on the basis of that admission;
- (c) agreement was reached after that admission of liability and offer of settlement; and
- (d) either—
  - (i) the party making the admission of liability and offer of settlement was not provided by the other party with the information about an insurance policy as required by the Practice Direction (Pre–Action Conduct); or
  - (ii) that party made the admission of liability and offer of settlement before, or within 42 days of, being provided by the other party with that information,

  no costs may be recovered by the other party in respect of the insurance premium.

(2) In this rule, "publication proceedings" means proceedings for—
- (a) defamation;
- (b) malicious falsehood; or
- (c) breach of confidence involving publication to the public at large.

Effect of rule

Add new paragraph 44.12B.1:

This rule was inserted by the Civil Procedure (Amendment) Rules 2009 (SI 2009/ **44.12B.1** 2092) and came into effect on October 1, 2009, but is subject to a transitional provision (ibid r.23) which states that r.44.12B, and the consequential amendments made to Pt 44 to accommodate it, do not apply to proceedings where the insurance policy was taken out before that date. For such proceedings the Pt 44 provisions in force immediately before that date will continue to apply as if that Part had not been amended.

The rule makes it clear that, in relation to publication cases (defamation and similar cases) insurance premiums for after the event insurance cannot be recovered by any period if the information about the insurance policy required by the rules or practice direction, was not given as required, and provides that an ATE insurance premium cannot be recovered in costs only proceedings by a party if an admission of liability leading to settlement was made by the other party within 42 days of being given the required information.

PRACTICE DIRECTION—DIRECTIONS RELATING TO PART 44—GENERAL RULES ABOUT COSTS

Section 17 Costs–Only Proceedings: Rule 44.12A

In paragraph 17.2, delete "Supreme Court". **44PD.11**

Section 19 Providing Information About Funding Arrangements: Rule 44.15

Method of giving information

In the parenthesis below paragraph 19.2, for "should" substitute:

44PD.13   must

Information which must be provided

Delete paragraph 19.4(3) and substitute:

(3) Where the funding arrangement is an insurance policy, the party must—

    (a) state the name and address of the insurer, the policy number and the date of the policy and identify the claim or claims to which it relates (including Part 20 claims if any);

    (b) state the level of cover provided by the insurance; and

    (c) state whether the insurance premiums are staged and, if so, the points at which an increased premium is payable.

Transitional Provision

After paragraph 19.5, add new paragraph 19.6:

19.6 The amendments to the parenthesis below paragraph 19.2 and to paragraph 19.4(3) do not apply where the funding arrangement was entered into before 1st October 2009 and the parenthesis below paragraph 19.2 and paragraph 19.4(3) in force immediately before that date will continue to apply to that funding arrangement as if those amendments had not been made.

Section 23 Determination Proceedings and Similar Proceedings Under the Community Legal Service (Costs) Regulations 2000

44PD.17   *In paragraph 23.2(2), delete "Supreme Court".*

In paragraph 23.2A(2)(i), delete the two instances of "Supreme Court".

Section 23A Costs Capping Orders

Estimate of costs

In paragraph 23A.3, for "rules 44.19 and 44.20(2)" substitute:

44PD.18   rule 44.19

PART 45

FIXED COSTS

Comment

In the third paragraph, for "the court refused to" substitute:
the court decided to   **45.1.1**

Amount of success fee

Add at end:
; [2009] 1 W.L.R. 853, CA.   **45.11.1**

PART 47

PROCEDURE FOR DETAILED ASSESSMENT OF COSTS AND DEFAULT PROVISIONS

Venue for detailed assessment proceedings

In rule 47.4(2), delete "Supreme Court".   **47.4**

PRACTICE DIRECTIONS RELATING TO PART 47—PROCEDURE FOR DETAILED ASSESSMENT OF COSTS AND DEFAULT PROVISIONS

Section 30 Powers of an authorised court officer: Rule 47.3

In paragraph 30.1(1) delete "Supreme Court".   **47PD.3**

Section 31 Venue for detailed assessment proceedings: Rule 47.4

In paragraph 31.1(2) delete "Supreme Court".   **47PD.4**

In paragraph 30.1A(2)(i) delete the two instances of "Supreme Court".

In paragraph 30.1A(2)(ii) delete "Supreme Court".

In paragraph 30.2(3) delete the two instances of "Supreme Court".

Section 37 Default costs certificate: Rule 47.11

In paragraph 37.7 delete "Supreme Court".   **47PD.10**

Section 42 Final costs certificate: Rule 47.16

In paragraph 42.12 delete "Supreme Court".   **47PD.15**

Section 43 Detailed assessment procedure where costs are payable out of the community legal service fund: Rule 47.17

In paragraph 43.3(g) delete "Supreme Court".   **47PD.16**

Section 49A Costs Payable by the Trustee for Civil Recovery under a Recovery Order

In paragraph 49A.4 delete "Supreme Court".   **47PD.23**

PART 48

COSTS—SPECIAL CASES

Comment

After the ninth paragraph, add as a new paragraph:

48.2.1   The court declined to make a third party costs order against a company official who had been principally involved in the management of the company's action and had often assumed a role normally played by a solicitor, because he was not the "real party" to the claim. The Board of the company had exercised control of the litigation and had independently applied their minds to the matters to be decided in the litigation. The company had risked its own assets and made arrangements for funding the litigation. That did not materially depend upon the financial contribution of the company official—the company was the real party to the litigation: *Lingfield Properties (Darlington) Limited v Padgett Lavender Associates* [2008] EWHC 2795 (QB), Tugendhat J.

After the twenty–second paragraph, add as a new paragraph:

There is no fixed rule to the effect that orders for costs can never be made against an unsuccessful opposing creditor. The test is whether it is just, in all the circumstances, to make an order against the creditor: *In the matter of Professional Computer Group Ltd* [2008] EWHC 1541 (Ch) Morgan J.

VAT Tribunal

Add new paragraph at end:

48.6.4   The principle that a successful litigant in person could not recover costs other than such sums as were recoverable at common law, namely out of pocket expenses (see *London Scottish Benefits Society v Chorley* (1883–84) LR13 Q.B.D. 872, CA) and *Buckland v Watts* (1971) Q.B. 27, CA is still applicable in the VAT Tribunal in spite of the Litigants in Person (Costs and Expenses) Act 1975. No order had been made extending the application of the Act to the VAT Tribunal: *Serpes v Revenue and Customs Commissioners* [2009] S.T.I. 449, V and D Tribunal, December 22, 2008, Angus Nicol.

General principles

Add new paragraph at end:

48.7.16   The wasted cost regime is neither a punitive nor a regulatory jurisdiction but rather a compensatory one. A person seeking orders for wasted costs has to show that the conduct complained of has caused them loss. Even where "improper, unreasonable and negligent" conduct has been shown, the court retains the discretion as to whether any order should be made. In a case where the costs of the wasted costs application amounted to several tens of thousands of pounds on each side, the court took the view that those costs were wholly disproportionate to the amount of any potentially wasted costs and on that ground alone, had no hesitation in declining to exercise its discretion to grant the relief sought: *Harrison v Harrison* [2009] EWHC 428 (QB), Mackay J.

Rule 48.8(2)

Add new paragraph at end:

48.8.2   Where, on assessment, the costs judge had applied r.48.8(2)(c) as the basis for assessment and stated that the provision was not limited to contentious cases, the paying party submitted that the case was non–contentious and should therefore be assessed on the basis of the Solicitors' (Non–Contentious Business) Remuneration Order 1994 art.3. The court found that the paying party was in fact putting forward a new case on appeal and was not entitled to put forward a new case, and in any event the judge had not found the matter to be non–contentious nor was r.48.8(2)(c) limited to contentious cases. The provisions of the Rule applied to every assessment of a solicitor's bill to his client without qualification and without any distinction between contentious and non–contentious business: *Dean & Dean Solicitors v Angel Airlines SA* [2007] EWHC 399 (QB), Mackay J.

DIRECTIONS RELATING TO PART 48—COSTS—SPECIAL CASES

Section 50 Amount of costs where costs are payable pursuant to contract: Rule 48.3

In paragraph 50.3(1), for "Supreme Court Act 1981" substitute:

Senior Courts Act 1981   **48PD.1**

GENERAL PRINCIPLES AND CASE LAW RELATING TO COSTS AND THEIR ASSESSMENT

1. Costs in specific courts and other tribunals

Competition Appeal Tribunal

Add new paragraph at end:

Although r.55(3) of the Competition Appeal Tribunal Rules 2003 indicated the **48.12.10** expected way of dealing with the costs (by assessment in the Supreme Court Costs Office) did not mean that the Tribunal did not have a discretion to assess costs itself. In the particular case which had considerable and real complexity, raising issues in respect of which the Tribunal had no particular experience, it was appropriate for the assessment of costs to be transferred to the SCCO: *Consumers Association v JJB Sports plc* [2009] CAT 2, Lord Carlisle of Berriew QC.

Guidance Notes on the Application of s.11 Access to Justice Act 1999 issued by the Senior Costs Judge

Add new paragraph at end:

A respondent, who had lost on appeal to the Court of Appeal and had the benefit of **48.14.21** CLS funding, was ordered to pay the successful appellant's costs, limited to "an amount to be determined by a costs judge". Liberty was given to the successful appellant "to apply to a High Court judge in relation to the assessment of the respondent's liability for costs and, in the event that the assessment gives rise to a shortfall under the Community Legal Services (Costs Protection) Regulations 2000". An application should have been made within three months of the order. It was in fact not made until the three years had elapsed. The court on appeal found that the costs judge had been correct to find that the application was out of time and found that the order did nothing either expressly or by implication to extend the three month period or to defer its commencement: *Liverpool Free Port Electronics Ltd v Habib Bank Limited and the Legal Services Commission* [2009] EWHC 861 (QB), Jack J.

4. Costs relating to particular types of parties and miscellaneous

Patents

At the end of the first paragraph, add as a new paragraph:

The court took an issues based approach in deciding what costs should be payable **48.15.5** by a losing party. The court examined whether there were any issues on which the paying party had won and in respect of which the receiving party should be deprived of its costs and, if so, whether it should actually pay the other party's costs of that issue. The court applied CPR r.44.3(7) by depriving the receiving party of a percentage to its overall costs. The receiving party was allowed 45 per cent of its costs, the order being pitched at a level to reflect, on a pure issue based approach, the court's decision that the receiving party should not only be deprived of its own costs but it should also meet the other party's costs: *Activis UK Ltd v Movartis AG* [2009] EWHC 502 (Ch), Warren J.

Protective Costs Orders

In the eighteenth paragraph add after "[2008] EWCA Civ 749":

; [2009] 1 W.L.R. 1436, CA   **48.15.7**

Add new paragraph at end:
There was no legal principle which would enable the court to treat a pure treaty obligation, even one adopted by the European Community, as converted into a Rule of Law directly binding on the English court. Thus the principle of the Aarhus Convention that costs should not be prohibitively expensive was, at most, a matter to which the court might have regard in exercising its discretion to make a Protective Costs Order: *Morgan v Hinton Organics (Wessex) Ltd* [2009] EWCA Civ 107.

Trustees, personal representatives

Powers of the court as to costs

After the second paragraph add new paragraphs:

48.15.9   Where proceedings were brought by Trustees to have the guidance of the court on the construction of a Trust Deed or on some question arising in the administration of a Trust, the costs of all parties were usually treated as incurred for the benefit of the Trust Fund and ordered to be paid out of it. But where a party had used the proceedings to raise issues not germane to the questions before the court, which added to the expense, the particular party was ordered to make a contribution to the costs of the Trustees on the indemnity basis. Thus, that party's conduct had been disgraceful or deserving of moral condemnation: *Grender v Dresden* [2009] EWHC 500 (Ch), Norris J.

A trustee who had wrongly applied money owned by a person to whom he owed a fiduciary duty, was ordered to pay costs on the indemnity basis and an enhanced rate of interest, where he had delayed in providing information sought prior to and during the proceedings. If the information and explanations, sought before proceedings were commenced, had been provided, the claims would not have been brought: *Curtis v Pulbrook* [2009] EWHC 1370 (Ch), Richard Sheldon QC.

PART 49

SPECIALIST PROCEEDINGS

Specialist Proceedings

Delete r.49 and substitute:

49.1   **49   These Rules apply to proceedings under—**
(a) the Companies Act 1985;
(b) the Companies Act 2006; and
(c) other legislation relating to companies and limited liability partnerships,
subject to the provision of the relevant practice direction which applies to those proceedings.

PART 51

TRANSITIONAL ARRANGEMENTS AND PILOT SCHEMES

Electronic working pilot scheme

Add new paragraph 51.1.6:

51.1.6   In April 2009, Practice Direction (Electronic Working Pilot Scheme) was made and came into effect on April 1, 2009. Publication of this practice direction in a TSO CPR Update is not expected until October 2009. This practice direction supplements r.5.5 (see para.5CPD.1 above).

PRACTICE DIRECTION—AUTOMATIC ORDERS PILOT SCHEME

Contents of this Practice Direction

Delete paragraph 1.1 and substitute:

51BPD.1   **1.1** This Practice Direction is made under rule 51.2. It provides for a pilot scheme ("the Automatic Orders Pilot Scheme") to operate in two stages.

After paragraph 1.1, add new paragraphs 1.1A and 1.1B:

1.1A The first stage will—

(1) operate from 1st October 2008 to 30th September 2009 in the county courts at Chelmsford, Newcastle, Teesside, Watford and York; and

(2) apply to claims started on or after 1st October 2008.

1.1B The second stage will—

(1) operate for a further year from 1st October 2009 to 30th September 2010 in all county courts and the High Court; and

(2) apply to all claims started on or after 1st October 2009.

PRACTICE DIRECTION—DEFAMATION PROCEEDINGS COSTS MANAGEMENT SCHEME

This Practice Direction supplements CPR Parts 29 and 44   **51DPD.1**

Add new Practice Direction (paras 51DPD.1–51DPD.6):

General

1.1 This Practice Direction is made under rule 51.2. It provides for a pilot scheme (the Defamation Proceedings Costs Management Scheme) to—

(1) operate from 1 October 2009 to 30 September 2010;

(2) operate in the Royal Courts of Justice and the District Registry at Manchester;

(3) apply to proceedings in which the claim was started on or after 1 October 2009.

(Rule 30.2(4) enables cases issued at other district registries to be transferred to London or Manchester if those court centres are more appropriate.)

1.2 The Defamation Proceedings Costs Management Scheme will apply to proceedings which include allegations of—

(1) libel;

(2) slander; and/or

(3) malicious falsehood.

1.3 The Defamation Proceedings Costs Management Scheme provides for costs management based on the submission of detailed estimates of future base costs. The objective is to manage the litigation so that the costs of each party are proportionate to the value of the claim and the reputational issues at stake and so that the parties are on an equal footing. Solicitors are already required by paragraph 2.03 of the Solicitors Code of Conduct 2007 to provide costs budgets to their clients. Accordingly, it should not be necessary for solicitors to incur substantial additional costs in providing costs budgets to the court.

Modifications of relevant practice directions

2 During the operation of the Defamation Proceedings Costs **51DPD.2** Management Scheme—

Use of costs budgets in case and costs management

(1) The practice direction supplementing Part 29 is modified by inserting after paragraph 3A—

"Case management and costs in defamation proceedings

3B In cases within the scope of the Defamation Proceedings Costs Management Scheme provided for in practice direction 51D, the court will manage the costs of the litigation as well as the case itself, making use of case management conferences and costs management conferences in accordance with that practice direction."

Estimates of costs to be detailed budgets

(2) Paragraph 6.4(1)(a) of the Costs Practice Direction does not apply to proceedings within the scope of the Defamation Proceedings Costs Management Scheme.

(3) Section 6 of the costs practice direction is modified by substituting for paragraph 6.5 the following—

"Costs budgets in defamation proceedings

6.5 In proceedings within the scope of the Defamation Proceedings Costs Management Scheme provided for in practice direction 51D the estimate of costs must be presented as a detailed budget setting out the estimated costs for the entire proceedings, in a standard template form following the precedent described as Precedent HA and annexed to that practice direction."

Preparation of the costs budget

51DPD.3   **3.1** Each party must prepare a costs budget or revised costs budget in the form of Precedent HA—

(1) in advance of any case management conference or costs management conference;

(2) for service with the pre–trial checklist;

(3) at any time as ordered to by the court.

3.2 A litigant in person shall not be required to prepare a costs budget unless the court otherwise orders.

3.3 Each party will include separately in its costs budget reasonable allowances for—

(1) intended activities, for example: disclosure, preparation of witness statements, obtaining expert reports, mediation or any other steps which are deemed necessary for the particular case;

(2) specified contingencies, for example: any application on meaning (if required); specific disclosure applications (if an opponent fails to give proper disclosure); resisting applications (if made inappropriately by opponent);

(3) disbursements, in particular, court fees, counsel's fees and any mediator or expert fees.

3.4 Each party must update its budget for each subsequent case management conference or costs management conference and for the pre–trial review. This should enable the judge to review the updated figures, in order to ascertain what departures have occurred from each side's budget and why.

Discussions between parties and exchange of budgets

4.1 During the preparation of costs budgets the parties should **51DPD.4** discuss the assumptions and the timetable upon which their respective costs budgets are based.

4.2 The parties must exchange and lodge with the court their costs budgets in the form of Precedent HA not less than 7 days before the date of the hearing for which the costs budgets are required.

4.3 A budget provided to the court will not (unless the providing party consents) be released to any other party (except a litigant in person) until that party is ready to exchange.

Effect of budget on case management and costs

5.1 The court will manage the costs of the litigation as well as the **51DPD.5** case itself in a manner which is proportionate to the value of the claim and the reputational issues at stake. For this purpose, the court may order attendance at regular hearings ("costs management conferences") by telephone wherever possible, in order to monitor expenditure.

5.2 At any case management conference, costs management conference or pre–trial review, the court will have before it the detailed costs budgets of both parties for the litigation, updated as necessary, and will take into account the costs involved in each proposed procedural step when giving case management directions.

5.3 At any case management conference, costs management conference or pre–trial review, the court will, either by agreement between the parties or after hearing argument, record approval or disapproval of each side's budget and, in the event of disapproval, will record the court's view.

5.4 Directions orders produced at the end of case management conferences and/or costs management conferences must be given to the parties on each side by their respective lawyers, together with copies of the budgets which the court has approved or disapproved.

5.5 Solicitors must liaise monthly to check that the budget is not being exceeded. In the event that the budget is exceeded, either party may apply to the court to fix a costs management conference as described in paragraph 5.1 above.

5.6 The judge conducting a detailed or summary assessment will have regard to the budget estimates of the receiving party and to any view previously expressed by the court pursuant to paragraph 5.3. Unless there has been a significant change in circumstances the judge will approve as reasonable and proportionate any costs claimed which fall within the last previously approved budget. Save in exceptional circumstances the judge will not approve as reasonable and proportionate any costs claimed which do not fall within the last previously approved budget.

Annex—Precedent HA

51DPD.6

Work done / to be done	Assumptions [to be completed as appropriate]	Disbursements	Profit Costs	Total
Pre-action costs		£0.00	£0.00	£0.00
Issue / pleadings		£0.00	£0.00	£0.00
CMC		£0.00	£0.00	£0.00
Any application on meaning		£0.00	£0.00	£0.00
Disclosure		£0.00	£0.00	£0.00
Witness statements		£0.00	£0.00	£0.00
Expert reports		£0.00	£0.00	£0.00
PTR		£0.00	£0.00	£0.00
Trial preparation		£0.00	£0.00	£0.00
Trial		£0.00	£0.00	£0.00
Settlement		£0.00	£0.00	£0.00
Contingent cost A: [explanation]		£0.00	£0.00	£0.00
Contingent cost B: [explanation]		£0.00	£0.00	£0.00
Contingent cost C: [explanation]		£0.00	£0.00	£0.00
[Insert additional contingent rows as required]				
GRAND TOTAL (including both incurred costs and estimated costs)				£0.00

comprising incurred costs of:

and estimated costs of:

Assumed into the costs of each stage should be the time costs for (a) attendance on own client (b) correspondence with the other party and (c) the general project and strategy management of completing that stage

This estimate excludes:
VAT [if applicable]
Costs of detailed assessment
Success fee [delete if no CFA]
ATE insurance premium [delete if no ATE insurance]
Other [to be completed as appropriate]

A breakdown of the above figures is found on the following pages.

Delete as applicable:		Incurred / estimated		Incurred / estimated		Incurred / estimated		Incurred / estimated		Incurred / estimated		Incurred / estimated	
	RATE (per hour)	Pre-action costs		Issue / pleadings		CMC		Any application on meaning		Disclosure		Witness statements	
		Hours	Total	Hours	Total	Hours	Total	Hours	Total	Hours	Total	Hours	Total
Solicitors' time costs [descriptions to be amended as applicable to retainer]													
Band A			£0.00		£0.00		£0.00		£0.00		£0.00		£0.00
Band B			£0.00		£0.00		£0.00		£0.00		£0.00		£0.00
Band C			£0.00		£0.00		£0.00		£0.00		£0.00		£0.00
Band D			£0.00		£0.00		£0.00		£0.00		£0.00		£0.00
Expert's costs													
Fees													
Disbursements													
Counsel's fees [indicate seniority]													
Leading counsel			£0.00				£0.00		£0.00		£0.00		£0.00
Junior counsel			£0.00				£0.00		£0.00		£0.00		£0.00
Court fees													
Disbursements													
Explanation of disbursements [details to be completed]													
Total		0	£0.00	0	£0.00	0	£0.00	0	£0.00	0	£0.00	0	£0.00

Band A - solicitors with over 8 years post qualification experience including at least 8 years litigation experience.
Band B - solicitors and legal executives with over 4 years post qualification experience including at least 4 years litigation experience.
Band C - other solicitors and legal executives and fee earners of equivalent experience.
Band D - trainee solicitors, paralegals and other fee earners.

Delete as applicable:	RATE (per hour)	Expert reports (Incurred / estimated)		PTR (Incurred / estimated)		Trial preparation (Incurred / estimated)		Trial (Incurred / estimated)		Settlement (negotiation / mediation) (Incurred / estimated)		Contingent cost A: [explanation e.g. amending pleadings] (Incurred / estimated)	
		Hours	Total	Hours	Total	Hours	Total	Hours	Total	Hours	Total	Hours	Total
Solicitors' time costs [descriptions to be amended as applicable to retainer]													
Band A			£0.00		£0.00		£0.00				£0.00		£0.00
Band B			£0.00		£0.00		£0.00				£0.00		£0.00
Band C			£0.00		£0.00		£0.00				£0.00		£0.00
Band D			£0.00		£0.00		£0.00				£0.00		£0.00
Expert's costs													
Fees													
Disbursements													
Counsel's fees [indicate seniority]													
Leading counsel			£0.00		£0.00		£0.00				£0.00		£0.00
Junior counsel			£0.00		£0.00		£0.00				£0.00		£0.00
Court fees													
Disbursements													
Explanation of disbursements [details to be completed]													
Total		0	£0.00	0	£0.00	0	£0.00		£0.00	0	£0.00	0	£0.00

Delete as applicable:	RATE (per hour)	Incurred / estimated		Incurred / estimated	
		Contingent cost B: [explanation e.g. specific disclosure application inc. hearing]		Contingent cost C: [explanation]	
		Hours	Total	Hours	Total
Solicitors' time costs					
Band A			£0.00		£0.00
Band B			£0.00		£0.00
Band C			£0.00		£0.00
Band D			£0.00		£0.00
Expert's costs					
Fees					
Disbursements					
Counsel's fees					
Leading counsel			£0.00		£0.00
Junior counsel			£0.00		£0.00
Court fees					
Disbursements					
Explanation of disbursements [details to be completed]					
Total		0	£0.00	0	£0.00

PART 52

APPEALS

Who may exercise the powers of the Court of Appeal

In the second set of parentheses under rule 52.16(7), for "House of Lords" substitute:

Supreme Court

52.16

PART 53

DEFAMATION CLAIMS

The section 3 procedure

Add at end of the fifth paragraph add:

53PD.29   ; [2009] 2 W.L.R. 314

Ruling on meaning

Add new paragraph at end:

53PD.32   Even though Pt 53 applies only to defamation claims, a ruling on meaning may also be obtained by way of preliminary issue in a malicious falsehood case: *Ajinomoto Sweeteners Europe SAS v Asda Stores Ltd* [2009] EWHC 781 (QB).

PART 54

JUDICIAL REVIEW AND STATUTORY REVIEW

Protected Costs Orders

In the first paragraph, add after "[2008] EWCA Civ 749;":

54.6.3   [2009] 1 W.L.R. 1436;

PRACTICE DIRECTION 54A—JUDICIAL REVIEW

Section I—General provisions relating to judicial review

In paragraph 1.1, for "Supreme Court Act 1981" substitute:

54APD.1   Senior Courts Act 1981

PART 55

POSSESSION CLAIMS

Possession claims relating to mortgaged residential property

Delete rule 55.10(2) and substitute:

55.10   **(2) Within 5 days of receiving notification of the date of the hearing by the court, the claimant must send a notice to—**

(a) the property, addressed to "the tenant or the occupier"; and

(b) the housing department of the local authority within which the property is located.

In rule 55.10(3) for "paragraph (2)" substitute:

paragraph (2)(a)

After rule 55.10(3), add new paragraph (3A):

(3A) The notice referred to in paragraph 2(b) must contain the information in paragraph (3) and must state the full address of the property.

In rule 55.10(4)(a) for "notice" substitute:
notices

In rule 55.10(4)(b), for "he has served it" substitute:
they have been sent

PRACTICE DIRECTION—POSSESSION CLAIMS

Residential property let on a tenancy

In paragraph 2.4, for "Supreme Court Act 1981" substitute:
Senior Courts Act 1981   **55PD.3**

55.8 — The Hearing

Add new paragraph 5.5:
5.5 The claimant must bring 2 completed copies of Form N123 to **55PD.8** the hearing.

PART 57

PROBATE AND INHERITANCE

How to start a probate claim

In paragraph 2.4, for "Supreme Court Act 1981" substitute:
Senior Courts Act 1981   **57PD.2**

Application for an order to bring in a will, etc.

In paragraph 7.1, for "Supreme Court Act" substitute:
Senior Courts Act 1981   **57PD.7**

Administration pending the determination of a probate claim

In paragraph 8.1, for "Supreme Court Act" substitute:
Senior Courts Act 1981   **57PD.8**

Starting the claim

Delete paragraph 13.1(1) and substitute:
(1) either—   **57PD.13**
    (a) a sealed or certified copy of the grant of probate or letters of administration, or
    (b) where the claim is to substitute or remove an executor and is made before a grant of probate has been issued, the original or, if the original is not available, a copy of the will; and

Production of the grant

Add new paragraph 14.3:
14.3 Where the claim is to substitute or remove an executor and **57PD.14** the claim is made before a grant of probate has been issued, paragraphs 14.1 and 14.2 do not apply. Where in such a case an order is made substituting or removing an executor a sealed copy of the order must be sent to the Principal Registry of the Family Division where it will be recorded and retained pending any application for a grant. An order sent to the Principal Registry in accordance with this paragraph must be accompanied by a note of the full name

and date of death of the deceased, if it is not apparent on the face of the order.

PART 64

ESTATES, TRUSTS AND CHARITIES

Determining certain claims without a hearing

Add new paragraph 64.2.4.1:

64.2.4.1   It should be noted that, with effect from October 1, 2009, new para.1A of Practice Direction 64A—Estates, Trusts and Charities provides that where a claim is made for an order under para.1(2)(b) of the PD (approving any sale, purchase, compromise or other transaction by a trustee, whether administrative or dispositive) (including where the remedy sought is approval of a transaction affected by conflict of interests or duties) the court may be requested to determine the claim without a hearing (see para.1A.1). The claim form may be issued without naming the defendant under r.8.2A, and no separate application for permission under that rule need be made (para.1A.2). Attention is drawn to the documentation required (by para.1A.3) to accompany the claim form. Importantly, under this new provision the court may be invited to determine the claim without a hearing, in which case it will consider whether it is one appropriate for an oral hearing or whether it can be dealt with by the judge on the papers.

Practice Direction—Pre–Action Conduct

Add new paragraph 64.3.1:

64.3.1   The PD on pre–action conduct, which came into force on April 6, 2009, will not normally apply to applications under r.64.2: see Practice Direction—Pre–action Conduct, para.2.2. It should be noted, however, that 64PDB para.7.5 provides that in an application for directions about actual or potential litigation the evidence should state inter alia whether the Practice Direction—Pre–Action Conduct has been complied with. This would include *Beddoe* applications and applications under the Administration of Justice Act 1985.

PRACTICE DIRECTION 64A—ESTATES, TRUSTS AND CHARITIES

64PD.1   *For the title "Practice Direction 64—Estates, Trusts and Charities" substitute "Practice Direction 64A—Estates, Trusts and Charities".*

I. Claims relating to the administration of estates and trusts

Examples of claims under rule 64.2(a)

In paragraph 1(2)(b), add after "by a trustee":

(whether administrative or dispositive)

Determining certain claims under rule 64.2(a) without a hearing

Add new paragraph 64PD.1A:

64PD.1A   **1A.1** Where a claim is made by a trustee for a remedy within paragraph 1(2)(b) (including a case where the remedy sought is approval of a transaction affected by conflict of interests or duties), the court may be requested to determine the claim without a hearing.

1A.2 The claim form in such a case may be issued in accordance with rule 8.2A (Issue of claim form without naming defendants), and no separate application for permission under rule 8.2A need be made.

1A.3 The claim form must be accompanied by—

(a) a witness statement setting out the material facts justifying determination without a hearing and in particular—

(i) identifying those affected by the remedy sought and

(ii) detailing any consultation of those so affected and the result of that consultation;

(b) the advice of a lawyer having a 10–year High Court qualification within the meaning of section 71 of the Courts and Legal Services Act 1990 on the merits of the claim;

(c) a draft order for the remedy sought;

(d) a statement of costs.

1A.4 If the court considers that the case does not require an oral hearing, it will proceed to consider the claim on the papers.

1A.5 If the court considers that an oral hearing is required, it will give appropriate directions.

1A.6 If the court considers it appropriate, it will make the order sought and may direct that the claimant must—

(a) serve notice of the order on the interested parties in accordance with rule 19.8A, and

(b) file a certificate of service within 7 days of doing so.

PRACTICE DIRECTION 64B—APPLICATIONS TO THE COURT FOR DIRECTIONS BY TRUSTEES IN RELATION TO THE ADMINISTRATION OF THE TRUST

For the title "Practice Direction—Applications to the Court for Directions by Trustees in Relation to the Administration of the Trust" substitute "Practice Direction 64B—Applications to the Court for Directions by Trustees in Relation to the Administration of the Trust". **64BPD.1**

PART 65

PROCEEDINGS RELATING TO ANTI–SOCIAL BEHAVIOUR AND HARASSMENT

In the table of contents, for "VI. [...]" substitute:

Contents **65.0.1**

VI. Drinking Banning Orders under the Violent Crime Reduction Act 2006

Scope of this Part

In rule 65.1(f) for "[...]" substitute:

(f) in Section VI, about applications for drinking banning orders **65.1**

and interim drinking banning orders under sections 4 and 9 of the Violent Crime Reduction Act

VI. Drinking Banning Orders under the Violent Crime Reduction Act 2006

Scope of this Section and interpretation

In rule 65.31 for "[...]" substitute:

65.31   65.31—(1) This Section applies to applications in proceedings in a county court under sub–sections (2), (3) or (5) of section 4 of the Violent Crime Reduction Act 2006 by a relevant authority, and to applications for interim orders under section 9 of that Act.

(2) In this Section—

    (a) "the 2006 Act" means the Violent Crime Reduction Act 2006;

    (b) "relevant authority" has the same meaning as in section 14(1) of the 2006 Act; and

    (c) "the principal proceedings" means any proceedings in a county court.

Application where the relevant authority is a party in principal proceedings

Add new rules 65.32 to 65.36:

65.32   65.32—(1) Subject to paragraph (2)—

    (a) where the relevant authority is the claimant in the principal proceedings, an application under section 4(2) of the 2006 Act for an order under section 4(7) of the 2006 Act must be made in the claim form; and

    (b) where the relevant authority is a defendant in the principal proceedings, an application for an order must be made by application notice which must be filed with the defence.

(2) Where the relevant authority becomes aware of the circumstances that lead it to apply for an order after its claim is issued or its defence filed, the application must be made by application notice as soon as possible thereafter.

(3) Where the application is made by application notice, it should normally be made on notice to the person against whom the order is sought.

Application where the relevant authority is not a party in principal proceedings

65.33   65.33—(1) Where the relevant authority is not a party to the principal proceedings—

    (a) an application under section 4(3) of the 2006 Act to be made a party must be made in accordance with Section I of Part 19; and

    (b) the application to be made a party and the application

for an order under section 4(7) of the 2006 Act must be made in the same application notice.

(2) The applications—

(a) must be made as soon as possible after the relevant authority becomes aware of the principal proceedings; and

(b) should normally be made on notice to the person against whom the order is sought.

Application by a relevant authority to join a person to the principal proceedings

65.34—(1) An application under section 4(5) of the 2006 Act by **65.34** a relevant authority which is a party to the principal proceedings to join a person to the principal proceedings must be made—

(a) in accordance with Section I of Part 19;

(b) in the same application notice as the application for an order under section 4(7) of the 2006 Act against the person; and

(c) as soon as possible after the relevant authority considers that the criteria in section 4(4) of the 2006 Act are met.

(2) The application notice must contain—

(a) the relevant authority's reasons for claiming that the person's conduct is material in relation to the principal proceedings; and

(b) details of the conduct alleged.

(3) The application should normally be made on notice to the person against whom the order is sought.

Evidence

65.35 An application for an order under section 4(7) of the **65.35** 2006 Act must be accompanied by written evidence, which must include evidence that section 4(7) of the Act has been complied with.

Application for an interim order

65.36—(1) An application for an interim order under section 9 **65.36** of the 2006 Act must be made in accordance with Part 25.

(2) The application should normally be made—

(a) in the claim form or application notice seeking the order; and

(b) on notice to the person against whom the order is sought.

(3) An application for an interim order may be—

(a) made without a copy of the application notice being served on the person against whom the order is sought;

(b) heard in the absence of the person against whom the order is sought,

with the permission of the court.

PART 66

CROWN PROCEEDINGS

ANNEX 2

CROWN PROCEEDINGS ACT 1947

For text of Annex 2 substitute:

66PD.4　List of Authorised Government Departments and the names and addresses for service of the person who is, or is acting for the purposes of the Act as, Solicitor for such Departments, published by the Minister for the Civil Service in pursuance of Section 17 of the Crown Proceedings Act 1947.

This list supersedes the list published on 31 August 2005

AUTHORISED GOVERNMENT DEPARTMENTS		SOLICITOR AND ADDRESSES FOR SERVICE
Advisory, Conciliation and Arbitration Service	))	The Treasury Solicitor One Kemble Street London WC2B 4TS
		(see Notes (1) and (2))
Board of Trade	)	
Cabinet Office	)	
Central Office of Information	)	
Commissioners for the Reduction of National Debt (see Note (3))	)	
Crown Prosecution Service	)	
Department for Business, Enterprise and Regulatory Reform	)	
Department for Children, Schools and Families	)	
Department for Communities and Local Government	)	
Department for Culture, Media and Sport	)	
Department of Energy and Climate Change	)	
Department for Innovation, Universities and Skills	)	
Department for International Development	))	
Department for Transport	)	
Food Standards Agency	)	
Foreign and Commonwealth Office	)	
Government Actuary's Department	)	
Government Equalities Office	)	
Health and Safety Executive	)	
Office for Standards in Education, Children's Services and Skills	)	
Her Majesty's Chief Inspector of Schools in Wales	))	
Her Majesty's Treasury	)	
Home Office	)	

Ministry of Defence)
Ministry of Justice (see Note (4)))
National Savings and Investments)
National School of Government)
Northern Ireland Office)
Ordnance Survey)
Privy Council Office)
Public Works Loan Board (see Note)
(3))
Royal Mint)
Serious Fraud Office)
Wales Office (Office of the Secretary)
of State for Wales) (see Note (5)))

Child Maintenance and Enforcement Commission Department of Health Department for Work and Pensions UK Statistics Authority	The Solicitor to the Department for Work and Pensions and the Department of Health New Court 48 Carey Street London WC2A 2LS
Crown Estate Commissioners	Legal Director The Crown Estate 16 New Burlington Place London W1S 2HX
Department for Environment, Food and Rural Affairs (see Note (5)) Forestry Commissioners	The Solicitor to the Department for Environment, Food and Rural Affairs Nobel House 17 Smith Square London SW1P 3JR
Export Credits Guarantee Department	The General Counsel Export Credits Guarantee Department P.O. Box 2200 2 Exchange Tower Harbour Exchange Square London E14 9GS
Gas and Electricity Markets Authority	Senior Legal Director Office of Gas and Electricity Markets 9 Millbank London SW1P 3GE
Her Majesty's Revenue and Customs	General Counsel and Solicitor to Her Majesty's Revenue and Customs HM Revenue and Customs South West Wing Bush House Strand London WC2B 4RD
Office of Fair Trading	General Counsel Fleetbank House 2–6 Salisbury Square London EC4Y 8JX

Postal Services Commission	The Chief Legal Adviser Postal Services Commission Hercules House 6 Hercules Road London SE1 7DB
Revenue and Customs Prosecutions Office (RCPO)	The Director Revenue and Customs Prosecutions Office New King's Beam House 22 Upper Ground London SEI 9BT
Water Services Regulation Authority (OFWAT)	Director of Legal Services and Board Secretary Water Services Regulation Authority (OFWAT) Centre City Tower 7 Hill Street Birmingham B5 4UA
Welsh Assembly Government	The Director of Legal Services to the Welsh Assembly Government Cathays Park Cardiff CF10 3NQ

NOTES

66PD.5   (1) Section 17(3) and section 18 of the Crown Proceedings Act 1947 provide as follows:

> *17(3) Civil proceedings against the Crown shall be instituted against the appropriate authorised Government department, or, if none of the authorised Government departments is appropriate or the person instituting the proceedings has any reasonable doubt whether any and if so which of those departments is appropriate, against the Attorney General.*

> *18 All documents required to be served on the Crown for the purpose of or in connection with any civil proceedings by or against the Crown shall, if those proceedings are by or against an authorised Government department, be served on the solicitor, if any, for that department, or the person, if any, acting for the purposes of this Act as solicitor for that department, or if there is no such solicitor and no person so acting, or if the proceedings are brought by or against the Attorney General, on the Solicitor for the affairs of His Majesty's Treasury.*

Proceedings brought against the Attorney General should be served on the Treasury Solicitor.

(2) The above–mentioned provisions do not apply to Scotland, where in accordance with the Crown Suits (Scotland) Act 1857, as amended by the Scotland Act 1998, civil proceedings against the Crown (other than the Scottish Administration) or any Government Department (other than the Scottish Executive) may be directed against the Advocate General for Scotland. The Advocate General's address for service is the Office of the Solicitor to the Advocate General for Scotland, Victoria Quay, Edinburgh EH6 6QQ. Civil proceedings against the Scottish Administration may be directed against the Scottish Ministers at St Andrew's House, Edinburgh EH 1 3DG, or against the Lord Advocate for and on behalf of the Scottish Executive. The Lord Advocate's address for service is 25 Chambers Street, Edinburgh, EH1 1LA.

(3) The functions of the Commissioners for the Reduction of National Debt and the Public Works Loan Board are carried out within the UK Debt Management Office.

(4) The reference to the Ministry of Justice includes a reference to the Lord Chancellor's Department.

CABINET OFFICE
WHITEHALL
LONDON SW1

(Signed) SIR GUS O'DONNELL
19th February 2009

PART 67

Proceedings Relating to Solicitors

PRACTICE DIRECTION—PROCEEDINGS RELATING TO SOLICITORS

Proceedings in the Costs Office

Delete heading to paragraph 2 and substitute "Proceedings in the Costs Office". **67PD.2**

In paragraph 2.1(1), delete "Supreme Court".

In paragraph 2.1(2), delete "Supreme Court".

In paragraph 2.2, delete "Supreme Court".

After paragraph 2.2, add new paragraph 2.3:

2.3 "Costs Office" has the same meaning as set out in rule 43.1(2)(ba).

Drawing up and Service of Orders

In paragraph 5, delete "Supreme Court". **67PD.5**

PART 68

References to the European Court

In the table of contents, the following entries have been added or amended:

Contents **68.0.1**

Interpretation

In rule 68.1, add after sub–paragraph (c):

(d) "reference" means a request to the European Court for a pre- **68.1** liminary ruling.

Making of order

Delete title "Making of order of reference" and substitute "Making of order". **68.2**

Delete rule 68.2(3) and substitute:

(3) The reference, which must contain the information required by the practice direction supplementing this Part.

Request to apply the urgent preliminary ruling procedure

After paragraph 68.2, add new rule 68.2A:

68.2A Any request by the court to the European Court that the **68.2A** preliminary ruling be dealt with under its urgent preliminary ruling procedure must be made in a document separate from the order or in a covering letter.

Transmission to the European Court

Delete rule 68.3(1) and substitute:

68.3 **(1)** **The Senior Master will send a copy of—**

    (a) **the order; and**

    (b) **where relevant, any request to apply the urgent preliminary ruling procedure**

to the Registrar of the European Court.

In rule 68.3(2), for "the proper officer" substitute:

a court officer

PRACTICE DIRECTION 68—REFERENCES TO THE EUROPEAN COURT

68PD.1 *This Practice Direction supplements CPR Part 68*

Delete paragraphs 68PD.1 to 68PD.3 and substitute:

Wording of references

1.1 Where the court intends to refer a question to the European Court it may direct the parties to produce a draft of the reference but responsibility for the terms of the reference lies with the court making the reference and not with the parties.

1.2 The reference should identify as clearly and succinctly as possible the question on which the court seeks the ruling of the European Court. In choosing the wording of the reference, it should be remembered that it will need to be translated into many other languages.

1.3 The court will incorporate the reference as a schedule to its order. The schedule must—

    (1) give the full name of the referring court;

    (2) identify the parties;

    (3) summarise the nature and history of the proceedings, including the salient facts, indicating whether these are proved or admitted or assumed;

    (4) set out the relevant rules of national law;

    (5) summarise the relevant contentions of the parties;

    (6) explain why a ruling of the European Court is sought;

    (7) identify the provisions of Community law which the European Court is being requested to interpret;

    (8) state the question on which a ruling of the European Court is sought; and

    (9) state any opinion on the answer to the question that may have been expressed by the court in the course of delivering judgment.

1.4 If some of these matters are conveniently set out in a judgment, the relevant passages should be summarised succinctly. If it is not possible to produce such a summary, only those passages that contain information of the kind referred to in paragraph 1.3 should be cited.

1.5 The reference should not exceed 20 pages in length.

Request to apply the urgent preliminary ruling procedure

1A.1 The request to the European Court to apply its urgent preliminary ruling procedure must set out— **68PD.1A**

(1) the matters of fact and law which establish the urgency;

(2) the reasons why the urgent preliminary ruling procedure applies; and

(3) in so far as possible, the court's view on the answer to the question referred to the European Court for a preliminary ruling.

Transmission to the European Court

2.1 The order containing the reference, and where relevant any request to the European Court to apply its urgent preliminary ruling procedure, must be sent to the Senior Master, Room E101, Queen's Bench Division, Royal Courts of Justice, Strand, London, WC2A 2LL, for onward transmission to the European Court. **68PD.2**

2.2 The relevant court file must also be sent to the Senior Master at the above address.

European Court Information Note

3. There are annexed to this Practice Direction— **68PD.3**

(1) an Information Note issued by the European Court; and

(2) a supplement to the Information Note following the implementation of the urgent ruling procedure applicable to references concerning the area of freedom, security and justice.

Annex 2

Information Note Supplement (2008/C 64/0)

Add new paragraph 68PD.5:

1. This note is supplementary to the existing information note on references from national courts for a preliminary ruling[1], and provides practical information on the new urgent preliminary ruling procedure applicable to references concerning the area of freedom, security and justice. The procedure is governed by Article 23a of the Protocol on the Statute of the Court of Justice and Article 104b of its Rules of Procedure[2]. **68PD.5**

2. This information is intended to assist national courts proposing to request the application of the urgent preliminary ruling procedure, and to facilitate the Court's handling of that request. In common with the existing information note, it is in no way binding.

Conditions for the application of the urgent preliminary ruling procedure

3. The urgent preliminary ruling procedure is applicable only in

---

[1] See OJ 2005 C 143, pp. 1 to 4.
[2] See OJ 2008 L 24, pp. 39 to 43.

the areas covered by Title VI (Articles 29 to 42) of the Treaty on European Union concerning police and judicial cooperation in criminal matters, and Title IV (Articles 61 to 69) of Part Three of the EC Treaty concerning visas, asylum, immigration and other policies related to free movement of persons, including judicial cooperation in civil matters.

4. Although a reference for a preliminary ruling generally calls for the national proceedings to be stayed until the Court has given its ruling, the referring court may still order protective measures to safeguard the interests of the parties pending the judgment of the Court, particularly as regards a national administrative measure based on a Community act which is the subject of a reference for a preliminary ruling on validity.

5. The Court decides whether the urgent procedure is to be applied. Such a decision is generally taken only on a reasoned request from the referring court. Exceptionally, the Court may decide of its own motion to deal with a reference under the urgent preliminary ruling procedure, where that appears to be required.

6. The urgent procedure simplifies the various stages of the proceedings before the Court, but its application entails significant constraints for the Court and for the parties and other interested persons participating in the procedure, particularly the Member States.

7. It should therefore be requested only where it is absolutely necessary for the Court to give its ruling on the reference as quickly as possible. Although it is not possible to provide an exhaustive list of such situations, particularly because of the varied and evolving nature of Community rules governing the area of freedom, security and justice, a national court or tribunal might, for example, consider submitting a request for the urgent procedure to be applied in the following situations: in the case of a person detained or deprived of his liberty, where the answer to the question raised is decisive as to the assessment of that person's legal situation or, in proceedings concerning parental authority or custody of children, where the identity of the court having jurisdiction under Community law depends on the answer to the question referred for a preliminary ruling.

The request for application of the urgent preliminary ruling procedure

8. To enable the Court to decide quickly whether the urgent preliminary ruling procedure should be applied, the request must set out the matters of fact and law which establish the urgency and, in particular, the risks involved in following the normal preliminary ruling procedure.

9. In so far as it is able to do so, the referring court should briefly state its view on the answer to be given to the question(s) referred. Such a statement makes it easier for the parties and other interested persons participating in the procedure to define their positions and facilitates the Court's decision, thereby contributing to the rapidity of the procedure.

10. The request for the urgent preliminary ruling procedure must be submitted in a form that enables the Registry of the Court to establish immediately that the file must be dealt with in a particular way. Accordingly, the request should be submitted in a document separate from the order for reference itself, or in a covering letter expressly setting out the request.

11. As regards the order for reference itself, it should be noted that relevant information is already contained in points 20 to 24 of the information note on references from national courts for a preliminary ruling. It is particularly important in an urgent situation that the order for reference should be succinct, as it helps to ensure the rapidity of the procedure.

Communication between the Court of Justice, the national court and the parties

12. As regards communication with the national court or tribunal and the parties before it, national courts or tribunals which submit a request for an urgent preliminary ruling procedure are requested to state the e–mail address or any fax number which may be used by the Court, together with the e–mail addresses or any fax numbers of the representatives of the parties to the proceedings.

13. A copy of the signed order for reference together with a request for the urgent preliminary ruling procedure can initially be sent to the Court by e–mail (ECJ–Registry@curia.europa.eu) or by fax (+352 43 37 66). Processing of the reference and of the request can then begin upon receipt of the e–mailed or faxed copy. The originals of those documents must, however, be sent to the Registry of the Court as soon as possible.

PART 69

Court's Power to Appoint a Receiver

PRACTICE DIRECTION—COURT'S POWER TO APPOINT A RECEIVER

Court's power to appoint receiver

In paragraph 1.1(1), for "Supreme Court Act 1981" substitute:
Senior Courts Act 1981

69PD.1

PART 73

Charging Orders, Stop Orders and Stop Notices

Section 15 Trusts of Land and Appointment of Trustees Act 1996

At the end of the first paragraph add:
In *Hameed v Qayyum* [2008] EWHC 2274 (Ch) the claimant succeeded in obtaining **73.10.7** an order for sale to enforce his charging order. The court rejected the wife's assertion that 100 per cent of the beneficial interest was vested in her.

PART 74

ENFORCEMENT OF JUDGMENTS IN DIFFERENT JURISDICTIONS

Registration orders

Delete rule 74.6(1)(b) and substitute:

74.6   **(b) by any of the methods of service permitted under the Companies Act 2006; or**

Appeals

After the fifth paragraph, add as a new paragraph:

74.8.1   The House of Lords referred to the European Court of Justice for a preliminary ruling on certain questions regarding the applicability of the Judgments Regulation in this case. The decision in *Meletis Apostolides v Orams* EUECJ C–420/07 (April 28, 2009) held that recognition of the judgment in England could not be refused on the grounds that the Cypriot government did not have control over the land in question, or because it would be difficult to enforce the Cypriot judgment in the Turkish–controlled area. It was held that Art.34.1 (which permits a member state to refuse to recognise another member state's judgment if it is contrary to public policy) is to be interpreted strictly, and is to be applied only in exceptional circumstances where there would otherwise be a manifest breach of public policy.

Public Policy

Add new paragraph at end:

74.10.5   In *D'Hoker v Tritan Enterprises* [2009] EWHC 949 (QB) the appellant successfully appealed against registration of an order of a Greek court on public policy grounds under art.34.1 of the Judgments Regulation. The Greek order provided for sequestration of the appellant's assets, and was similar to a freezing order in the English courts. The appellant and her husband were involved in divorce proceedings in England, and the order of the Greek court was in direct conflict with an order made in the divorce proceedings. The effect of the Greek order was to deprive the appellant of any money for the support of herself and her children or the means to instruct lawyers. It was held that the enforcement of the Greek order was contrary to public policy in England. It was said that something proximate to a denial of human rights had to be shown to involve art.34.1 of the Judgments Regulation.

Authentic instruments and approved court settlements

Add new paragraph at end:

74.10.15   In the Scottish case of *Baden–Wurttembergische Bank, AG , Petitioner* [2009] CSIH 47 before the Inner House, Court of Session, an application was made by a German bank for an order under s.4 of the Civil Jurisdiction and Judgments Act 1982 for registration of an authentic instrument pursuant to art.50 of the Brussels Convention (Article 57 of the Judgments Regulation). Article 57 of the Regulation provides that an application may be refused only if enforcement of the instrument is contrary to public policy in the State addressed. The defendant invoked the public policy exception in the statutory provision and submitted that the prayer of the petition for registration should be refused. It was accepted by reference to *Hoffman v Krieg* [1988] E.C.R.645 that the public policy exception could only apply in exceptional circumstances. It was submitted that the circumstances of the present case were exceptional in that there had been inordinate, unexplained and inexcusable delay on the Bank's part in making the application to the Scots Court. Having regard to this delay, it was submitted that to grant the order sought by the Bank would involve a violation of the appellant's rights under art.6 of the European Convention on Human Rights and that it followed that the court would be in breach of its duty in terms of s.6 of the Human Rights Act 1998 to act in a manner compatible with the Convention rights if registration of the authentic instrument were to be permitted.

The Court of Session stated that the "reasonable time guarantee" in art.6(1), is concerned, so far as relating to civil matters, with delay in the determination of civil rights and obligations by a court or tribunal which is seised with a dispute. It was said that that was made even clearer by the French version, which guarantees every person a right that his "cause" should be heard within a reasonable time by a tribunal which will decide " *contestations sur ses droits et obligations de caractère civil*". It was held that that guarantee was not engaged by a lapse of time between the execution of an authentic instrument and an application by the creditor under the deed for its registration in accordance with the Brussels Convention.

Registration of money judgments in the High Court

In rule 74.15(2), for "Supreme Court" substitute:
Senior Courts   **74.15**

Application for registration of suspension order

In rule 74.25(1), for "Supreme Court" substitute:
Senior Courts   **74.25**

Delete paragraphs 68PD.1 to 68PD.3 and substitute:

PRACTICE DIRECTION—ENFORCEMENT OF JUDGMENTS IN DIFFERENT JURISDICTIONS

Registers

In paragraph 3, for "Central Office of the Supreme Court" substitute:
Central Office of the Senior Courts   **74PD.3**

Certified copies of judgments issued under rule 74.12

In paragraph 7.1, for "Seal of the Supreme Court" substitute:
Seal of the Senior Courts   **74PD.7**

Certificates under section III of Part 74

In paragraph 8.1, for "Central Office of the Supreme Court" substitute:
Central Office of the Senior Courts   **74PD.8**

PART 76

PROCEEDINGS UNDER THE PREVENTION OF TERRORISM ACT 2005

Directions for hearing on application for permission or on a reference

Delete rule 76.10(2)(b) and substitute:

    (b) unless the court otherwise directs—   **76.10**
        (i) in the case of directions given under section 3(2)(c), that date must be no later than 7 days from the date on which the notice of the terms of the control order is delivered to the controlled person in accordance with section 7(8) of the Act; or
       (ii) in the case of directions given under section 3(6)(b) or (c), that date must be 7 days from the date on which the court's determination on the reference is made.

Applications for anonymity

Delete rule 76.19(4) and substitute:

76.19   (4)   **References in this rule—**

    (a) **to an order requiring anonymity for the controlled person are to be construed in accordance with paragraph 5(3) of the Schedule to the Act; and**

    (b) **to the controlled person, in relation to a time before the control order has been made, are to be construed in accordance with paragraph 5(4) of the Schedule to the Act.**

Functions of special advocate

At the beginning of rule 76.24(b) add:

76.24   **adducing evidence and**

Modification of the general rules of evidence and disclosure

After rule 76.26(5), add new sub-rule (5A):

76.26   **(5A) A special advocate shall be entitled to adduce evidence and to cross–examine witnesses.**

PART 79

Proceedings Under the Counter–Terrorism Act 2008

In the title to Part 79 delete "Financial Restrictions". In the contents list, add at end:

79.0.1 Contents

V. Notification orders

1. Application of this Part

Scope and interpretation

After rule 79.1(1)(b) add:

79.1   (c) **applications for a notification order under Schedule 4 to the Counter–Terrorism Act 2008.**

Procedural Guide

Add new paragraph 79.3.1:

79.3.1   See Procedural Guide 18 at para.D18–001.

4. General Provisions

Scope of this Section

In rule 79.15, for "rule 79.1(1)" substitute:
rule 79.1(1)(a) and (b)   **79.15**

Hearings

In rule 79.17(1), after "All proceedings to which" add:
Section 2 or 3 of   **79.17**

Appointment of a special advocate

In rule 79.18(1), after "in proceedings to which" add:
Section 2 or 3 of   **79.18**

In rule 79.18(3), after "any proceedings to which" add:
Section 2 or 3 of

Modification of the general rules of evidence and disclosure

In rule 79.22(1), after "any proceedings to which" add:
Section 2 or 3 of   **79.22**

In rule 79.22(2), after "Subject to the other rules in" add:
Section 2, 3 and this Section of

After rule 79.22(4), add new sub–rule (4A):
A special advocate is entitled to adduce evidence and to cross–examine witnesses.

Search for, filing of and service of material

In rule 79.23(1)(a), after "in the proceedings to which" add:
                                                                79.23

Section 2 or 3 of

In rule 79.23(3), after "the proceedings to which" add:
Section 2 or 3 of

In rule 79.23(4), after "the proceedings to which" add:
Section 2 or 3 of

Judgments

In rule 79.28(1), after "in any proceedings to which" add:
Section 2 or 3 of   **79.28**

Application by Treasury for reconsideration of order, direction or judgment

In rule 79.29(1), after "in any proceedings to which" add:
Section 2 or 3 of   **79.29**

Supply of court documents

In rule 79.30, after "to any proceedings to which" add:
Section 2 or 3 of   **79.30**

5. Notification Orders

Applications for a notification order

Add new paragraph 79.31:

79.31　**79.31—(1)　An application for a notification order under Schedule 4 to the Act must be made in accordance with Part 8.**

(2)　Where the defendant wishes to serve a notice under paragraph 2(4) of Schedule 4 to the Act, the defendant must file and serve the notice with an acknowledgment of service not more than 14 days after service of the claim form.

Schedule 1

RSC ORDER 46—WRITS OF EXECUTION: GENERAL

Effect of rule

In the first paragraph, for "O.81, r.5(2) … actions between partners)." substitute:

sc46.2.1　para.6A.4 of the Practice Direction supplementing Pt 70 (certain judgments against partners); for enforcement against a partnership, see generally para.6A of the Practice Direction (para.70PD.6A).

Issue of writ of execution

In RSC Order 46, rule 6(6)(d), for "Supreme Court" substitute:

sc46.6　Senior Courts

RSC ORDER 52—COMMITTAL

"The power … to punish for contempt of court"

In the second paragraph, add after "(Re M [1993] 3 W.L.R. 433).":

sc52.1.1　Where a local authority is in breach of a contract order it is enforceable by committal for contempt against the officer responsible for its implementation: *In re B (Minors) (Contact order: Enforcement) The Times*, March 19, 2009 (Thorpe, Wall and Moore–Bick L.JJ.).

I. Making a false statement in a document verified by a statement of truth

Add new paragraph at end:

sc52.1.16　The court should exercise great caution before giving permission to bring private proceedings for contempt of court, under CPR r.32.14, where it appears that a witness has made untrue statements under oath. Proceedings for contempt of court are public law proceedings and the court therefore had to have regard to the public interest alone. When the court gave a private person permission to pursue proceedings for contempt against a witness who was alleged to have told lies in a witness statement it allowed that person to act in a public rather than a private role, not to recover damages for his own benefit, but to pursue the public interest. The only question was whether it was in the public interest for such proceedings to be brought. Among the foremost factors to be considered were (a) the strength of the evidence tending to show not only that the statement was false but that it was known at the time to be false, (b) the circumstances in which it was made, (c) its significance having regard to the nature of the proceedings in which it was made and (d) such evidence as there might be of the maker's state of mind, including his understanding of the likely effect of the statement and the use to which it was put in the proceedings. The court would also consider whether the proceedings would be likely to justify the resources which would have to be devoted to them: *KJM Superbikes Ltd v Hinton* [2008] EWCA Civ 1280 (Mummery, Arden and Moore–Bick L.JJ.). See also *Kirk v Walton* [2008] EWHC 1780, where a similar note of caution was sounded.

Undertakings

For "Hussain v Hussain [1986] 2 W.L.R. 805; [1986] 1 All E.R. 961, CA" substitute:
  Hussain v Hussain [1986] Fam 134; [1986] 1 All E.R. 961, CA   **sc52.4.4**

RSC ORDER 54—APPLICATIONS FOR WRIT OF HABEAS CORPUS

Application for the writ

In the third paragraph, delete "(see s.14(1) of AJA 1960)".

RSC ORDER 79—ESTREAT OF RECOGNIZANCES   **sc54.1.3**

Bail

In rule 9(11), for the three instances of "House of Lords" substitute:
  the Supreme Court   **sc79.9**

RSC ORDER 109—THE ADMINISTRATION OF JUSTICE ACT 1960

Applications under Act

In rule 1(1)(a), for "House of Lords" substitute:
  Supreme Court   **sc109.1**

In rule 1(1)(b), for "House of Lords" substitute:
  Supreme Court

Release of appellant on bail

In rule 3(1), for the two instances of "House of Lords" substitute:
  Supreme Court   **sc109.3**

Release of appellant on bail by the Court of Appeal

In rule 4(1), for the two instances of "House of Lords" substitute:
  Supreme Court   **sc109.4**

In rule 1(2), for "House of Lords" substitute:
  the Supreme Court

SCHEDULE 2

CCR ORDER 1—CITATION, APPLICATION AND INTERPRETATION

Application of RSC to county court proceedings

In rule 6(d), for "Supreme Court" substitute:
  Senior Courts   **cc1.6**

CCR ORDER 29—COMMITTAL FOR BREACH OF ORDER OR UNDERTAKING

Family Proceedings

At the end of the fifth paragraph add:
  A breach of a contact order by a local authority is in principle enforceable by committal proceedings against the officer responsible for its implementation: *In re B*   **cc29.1.4**

(Minors) Contact order: Enforcement, The Times, March 19, 2009 (Thorpe, Wall and Moore–Bick L.JJ.).

CCR ORDER 39—ADMINISTRATION ORDERS

Debt relief orders

Add new paragraph cc39.0.6:

cc39.0.6   See commentary on Debt Relief Orders at Vol.2 para.3E–2859. These orders can be made if debts do not exceed £15,000 and thus will be available to some who do not come within the criteria for an administration order and may be a better solution for some who do qualify for an administration order.

SECTION C

PRE–ACTION PROTOCOLS

PRE–ACTION CONDUCT AND PROTOCOLS

Disclosure of funding arrangements

Add new paragraph C1A–13.1:

C1A–13.1   From October 2009 a party conducting litigation under a funding arrangement (a conditional fee agreement) must inform the other party within seven days of entering into the arrangement or, where the claimant has entered into an arrangement before sending a letter of claim, so inform the defendant in the letter of claim. Previously para.9.3 said "should" notify, rather than "must". If a party fails to comply and wishes to recover any after the event insurance and success fee in the litigation they must apply for relief from sanctions under CPR r.3.9.

SECTION IV—REQUIREMENTS THAT APPLY IN ALL CASES

Specific Divisions

9.3 Information about funding arrangements

In paragraph 9.3 for "should" substitute:

C1–008   must

Add after "as soon as possible"

and in any event either within 7 days of entering into the funding arrangement concerned or, where a claimant enters into a funding arrangement before sending a letter before claim, in the letter before claim

9.8 Transitional Provision

Add new paragraph 9.8:

The amendments to paragraph 9.3 do not apply to a funding arrangement entered into before the 1st October 2009 and paragraph 9.3 in force immediately before that date will continue to apply to that funding arrangement as if paragraph 9.3 had not been amended.

PRE-ACTION PROTOCOL FOR PERSONAL INJURY CLAIMS

Scope of the Protocol

In paragraph 2.3 for "£15,000 which are likely to be allocated to the fast track" substitute:

C2–003   the fast track limit and which are likely to be allocated to that track

In paragraph 2.4 for "worth more than £15,000, with a view to avoiding" substitute:

with a value of more than the fast track limit, to avoid

3.

The Protocol

Letter of Claim

In paragraph 3.9 for "£15,000" substitute:

the value of the fast track limit   **C2–012**

Annex D

The Rehabilitation Code

Delete Annex D (paragraph C2–024) and substitute:

The aim of this code is to promote the use of rehabilitation and **C2–024** early intervention in the compensation process so that the injured person makes the best and quickest possible medical, social and psychological recovery. This objective applies whatever the severity of the injuries sustained by the Claimant. The Code is designed to ensure that the Claimant's need for rehabilitation is assessed and addressed as a priority, and that the process of so doing is pursued on a collaborative basis by the claimant's lawyer and the compensator.

Therefore, in every case, where rehabilitation is likely to be of benefit, the earliest possible notification to the compensator of the claim and of the need for rehabilitation will be expected.

1. Introduction

   1.1 The purpose of the personal injury claims process is to put the individual back into the same position as he or she would have been in, had the accident not occurred, insofar as money can achieve that objective. The purpose of the rehabilitation code is to provide a framework within which the Claimant's health, quality of life and ability to work are restored as far as possible before, or simultaneously with, the process of assessing compensation.

   1.2 Although the Code is recognised by the Personal Injury Pre–Action Protocol, its provisions are not mandatory. It is recognised that the aims of the Code can be achieved without strict adherence to the terms of the Code, and therefore it is open to the parties to agree an alternative framework to achieve the early rehabilitation of the Claimant.

   1.3 However, the Code provides a useful framework within which Claimant's lawyers and the compensator can work together to ensure that the needs of injured Claimants are assessed at an early stage.

   1.4 In any case where agreement on liability is not reached it is open to the parties to agree that the Code will in any event operate, and the question of delay pending resolution of liability should be balanced with the interests of the injured party. However, unless so agreed, the Code does not apply in the absence of liability or prior to agreement on liability being reached.

1.5 In this code the expression "the compensator" shall include any loss adjuster, solicitor or other person acting on behalf of the compensator.

2. The claimant's solicitor

2.1 It should be the duty of every Claimant's solicitor to consider, from the earliest practicable stage, and in consultation with the Claimant, the Claimant's family, and where appropriate the claimant's treating physician(s), whether it is likely or possible that early intervention, rehabilitation or medical treatment would improve their present and/or long term physical and mental well being. This duty is ongoing throughout the life of the case but is of most importance in the early stages.

2.2 The Claimant's solicitors will in any event be aware of their responsibilities under section 4 of the Pre–Action Protocol for Personal Injury Claims.

2.3 It shall be the duty of a Claimant's solicitor to consider, with the Claimant and/or the Claimant's family, whether there is an immediate need for aids, adaptations, adjustments to employment to enable the claimant to keep his/her existing job, obtain suitable alternative employment with the same employer or retrain for new employment, or other matters that would seek to alleviate problems caused by disability, and then to communicate with the compensators as soon as practicable about any such rehabilitation needs, with a view to putting this Code into effect.

2.4 It shall not be the responsibility of the solicitor to decide on the need for treatment or rehabilitation or to arrange such matters without appropriate medical or professional advice.

2.5 It is the intention of this Code that the Claimant's solicitor will work with the compensator to address these rehabilitation needs and that the assessment and delivery of rehabilitation needs shall be a collaborative process.

2.6 It must be recognised that the compensator will need to receive from the Claimants' solicitors sufficient information for the compensator to make a proper decision about the need for intervention, rehabilitation or treatment. To this extent the Claimant's solicitor must comply with the requirements of the Pre–Action Protocol to provide the compensator with full and adequate details of the injuries sustained by the Claimant, the nature and extent of any or any likely continuing disability and any suggestions that may have already have been made concerning the rehabilitation and/or early intervention.

2.7 There is no requirement under the Pre–Action Protocol, or under this code, for the Claimant's solicitor to have obtained a full medical report. It is recognised that many cases will be identified for consideration under this code before medical evidence has actually been commissioned or obtained.

3. The Compensator

    3.1 It shall be the duty of the compensator, from the earliest practicable stage in any appropriate case, to consider whether it is likely that the Claimant will benefit in the immediate, medium or longer term from further medical treatment, rehabilitation or early intervention. This duty is ongoing throughout the life of the case but is most important in the early stages.

    3.2 If the compensator considers that a particular claim might be suitable for intervention, rehabilitation or treatment, the compensator will communicate this to the Claimant's solicitor as soon as practicable.

    3.3 On receipt of such communication, the Claimant's solicitor will immediately discuss these issues with the Claimant and/or the Claimant's family pursuant to his duty set out above.

    3.4 Where a request to consider rehabilitation has been communicated by the claimant's solicitor to the compensator, it will usually be expected that the compensator will respond to such request within 21 days.

    3.5 Nothing in this or any other code of practice shall in any way modify the obligations of the compensator under the Protocol to investigate claims rapidly and in any event within 3 months (except where time is extended by the claimant's solicitor) from the date of the formal claim letter. It is recognised that, although the rehabilitation assessment can be done even where liability investigations are outstanding, it is essential that such investigations proceed with the appropriate speed.

4. Assessment

    4.1 Unless the need for intervention, rehabilitation or treatment has already been identified by medical reports obtained and disclosed by either side, the need for and extent of such intervention, rehabilitation or treatment will be considered by means of an assessment by an appropriately qualified person.

    4.2 An assessment of rehabilitation needs may be carried out by any person or organisation suitably qualified, experienced and skilled to carry out the task. The claimant's solicitor and the compensator should endeavour to agree on the person or organisation to be chosen.

    4.3 No solicitor or compensator may insist on the assessment being carried out by a particular person or organisation if [on reasonable grounds] the other party objects, such objection to be raised within 21 days from the date of notification of the suggested assessor.

    4.4 The assessment may be carried out by a person or organisation which has a direct business connection with the solicitor or compensator, only if the other party agrees. The solicitor or compensator will be expected to reveal to the other party the existence of and nature of such a business connection.

5. The Assessment Process

5.1 Where possible, the agency to be instructed to provide the assessment should be agreed between the Claimant's solicitor and the compensator. The method of providing instructions to that agency will be agreed between the solicitor and the compensator.

5.2 The assessment agency will be asked to carry out the assessment in a way that is appropriate to the needs of the case and, in a simple case, may include, by prior appointment, a telephone interview but in more serious cases will probably involve a face to face discussion with the Claimant. The report will normally cover the following headings:

- The Injuries sustained by the Claimant.
- The current disability/incapacity arising from those Injuries. Where relevant to the overall picture of the Claimant's needs, any other medical conditions not arising from the accident should also be separately annotated.
- The Claimant's domestic circumstances (including mobility accommodation and employment) where relevant.
- The injuries/disability in respect of which early intervention or early rehabilitation is suggested.
- The type of intervention or treatment envisaged.
- The likely cost.
- The likely outcome of such intervention or treatment.

5.3 The report should not deal with issues relating to legal liability and should therefore not contain a detailed account of the accident circumstances.

5.4 In most cases it will be expected that the assessment will take place within 14 days from the date of the letter of referral to the assessment agency.

5.5 It must be remembered that the compensator will usually only consider such rehabilitation to deal with the effects of the injuries that have been caused in the relevant accident and will normally not be expected to fund treatment for conditions which do not directly relate to the accident unless the effect of such conditions has been exacerbated by the injuries sustained in the accident.

6. The Assessment Report

6.1 The report agency will, on completion of the report, send copies onto both the Claimant's solicitor and compensator simultaneously. Both parties will have the right to raise questions on the report, disclosing such correspondence to the other party.

6.2 It is recognised that for this assessment report to be of benefit to the parties, it should be prepared and used wholly outside the litigation process. Neither side can therefore, unless they agree in writing, rely on its contents in any subsequent litigation.

6.3 The report, any correspondence related to it and any notes created by the assessing agency to prepare it, will be covered by legal privilege and will not be disclosed in any legal proceedings unless the parties agree. Any notes or documents created in connection with the assessment process will not be disclosed in any litigation, and any person involved in the preparation of the report or involved in the assessment process, shall not be a compellable witness at Court. This principle is also set out in paragraph 4.4 of the Pre–Action Protocol.

6.4 The provision in paragraph 6.3 above as to treating the report etc as outside the litigation process is limited to the assessment report and any notes relating to it. Any notes and reports created during the subsequent case management process will be covered by the usual principle in relation to disclosure of documents and medical records relating to the Claimant.

6.5 The compensator will pay for the report within 28 days of receipt.

6.6 This code intends that the parties will continue to work together to ensure that the rehabilitation which has been recommended proceeds smoothly and that any further rehabilitation needs are also assessed.

7. Recommendations

7.1 When the assessment report is disclosed to the compensator, the compensator will be under a duty to consider the recommendations made and the extent to which funds will be made available to implement all or some of the recommendations. The compensator will not be required to pay for intervention treatment that is unreasonable in nature, content or cost or where adequate and timely provision is otherwise available. The Claimant will be under no obligation to undergo intervention, medical or investigation treatment that is unreasonable in all the circumstances of the case.

7.2 The compensator will normally be expected to respond to the Claimant's solicitor within 21 days from the date upon which the assessment report is disclosed as to the extent to which the recommendations have been accepted and rehabilitation treatment would be funded and will be expected to justify, within that same timescale, any refusal to meet the cost of recommended rehabilitation.

7.3 If funds are provided by the compensator to the Claimant to enable specific intervention, rehabilitation or treatment to occur, the compensator warrants that they will not, in any legal proceedings connected with the claim, dispute the reasonableness of that treatment, nor the agreed costs, provided of course that the Claimant has had the recommended treatment. The compensator will not, should the claim fail or be later discontinued, or any element of contributory negligence be assessed or agreed, seek to recover from the Claimant any funds that they have made available pursuant to this Code.

Annex B

Medical Negligence and Personal Injury Claims

A PROTOCOL FOR OBTAINING HOSPITAL MEDICAL RECORDS

Application on Behalf of a Patient for Hospital Medical Records for Use When Court Proceedings Are Contemplated

Use of the Forms

In the paragraph entitled "Use of the Forms" for "Supreme Court Act 1981" substitute:

C3–019 Senior Courts Act 1981

The Protocol for Possession Claims Based on Mortgage or Home Purchase Plan Arrears in Respect of Residential Property

Mortgage Arrears Protocol—editorial

Add new paragraphs at end:

C12A–001 In October 2009 an addition was made to para.6.1 to invite a lender also to consider when starting a possession claim, whether the borrower has applied to DWP for mortgage interest support (an application can, since January 2009, be made after 13 weeks of being without means to pay, whereas it was 30 weeks previously).

Also from October 2009 lenders must complete a new checklist of compliance with the protocol N123, and take two copies to the possession hearing for the claimant and the court. Failure to do this may lead to an adjournment.

Postponing the Start of a Possession Claim

Delete paragraph 6.1(1) and substitute:

C12–006 (1) submitted a claim to—

(a) the Department for Works and Pensions (DWP) for Support for Mortgage Interest (SMI); or

(b) an insurer under a mortgage payment protection policy,

and has provided all the evidence required to process a claim;

In paragraph 6.1(2) after "for payment" add:

from the DWP or

In paragraph 6.1(3) for "the insurance" substitute:

a claim to the DWP or the insurer

SECTION D

PROCEDURAL GUIDES

1. COMMENCEMENT

1.2. Part 7 or Part 8 Claim, Selection and Service

In Guide 1.2 delete text of first bullet point and substitute:

Specific occasions where Part 8 claim may be suitable   **D1–002**

> • Where court approval of a child or protected party's
> settlement (reached before issue of proceedings) is
> needed;

2. SERVICE

2.1. Service of Claims: General Rules

In Guide 2.1, delete title "Address for service (other than children and patients)" and substitute:

Address for service (other than children and protected parties)   **D2–001**

4. JUDGMENT WITHOUT TRIAL

4.6. Judgment on Admissions

In Guide 4.6, delete the entry under "Limits on right to enter judgment on admissions" and substitute:

Limits on right to enter judgment on admissions   **D4–006**

CPR r.14.1(4)   There is no right to enter judgment on admissions:
(i) in money claims where the defendant is a child or
protected party or
(ii) where the claimant is a child or protected party and
the defendant admits the whole of a money claim for a
specified sum or admits a money claim for an unspecified
sum and offers a sum in satisfaction (rr.14.5 or 14.7).

5. CASE MANAGEMENT AND SANCTIONS

5.1. Track Allocation: Rules

Under "The fast track" delete point (b) and substitute:

> (b) which has a value (for proceedings issued on or   **D5–001**
> after 6th April 2009), of not more than £25,000 or
> (for proceedings issued before 6th April 2009) of
> not more than £15,000;

5.2. Track Allocation: Procedure

Delete the text following "Track re–allocation" and substitute:

The court may change the track allocation (r.26.10).   **D5–002**
However where for example it becomes apparent that a
fast track case will probably somewhat exceed the
applicable value limit but not by a large margin the case

should not be reallocation if to do so would cause substantial disruption. However where the amount by which the value will exceed the applicable value limit is substantial, there should normally be a re–allocation even if to do so will cause delay to completion of the litigation: *Maguire v Molin* [2002] EWCA Civ 1083.

9. EXECUTION

Note

Add new paragraph D9–000:

D9–000   For guidance in selecting an appropriate form of execution procedure see Practice Direction 70.

9.14. Enforcement of decisions of bodies other than the High Court and county courts and compromises enforceable by enactment

Note

Add new paragraph D9–014:

D9–014   This Guide does not apply to any judgment to which CPR 74 applies (enforcement of overseas judgments), or to arbitration awards, or to confiscation in connection with criminal proceedings (RSC 115) or to traffic enforcement (CPR 75) (See CPR 70.5(2)).

Where an Act or SI governs the decision of a court or tribunal which is neither a County Court nor the High Court, and provides that a decision of the court or tribunal or a compromise of proceedings before that court or tribunal may enforced as if it were a court order (or as if payable under a court order)	The procedure to be adopted is that a party may enforce the decision or compromise by applying for a specific method of enforcement under CPR Pts 71 to 73 or RSC O.45 to 47 and 52 or CCR O.25 to 29 (whichever is relevant to the case).
Procedure (I)	
Other than where an Act or SI provides that a decision or compromise is enforceable or a sum of money is recoverable "if a court so orders"	Follow the relevant Court rules for execution of judgment as if the judgment or compromise were a court order but note that the party enforcing must also file at court a copy of the decision or compromise and must provide such further information is required by PD 70.
Procedure (II)	
Where an Act or SI provides that a decision or compromise is enforceable or a sum of money is recoverable "if a court so orders"	Apply for an order for payment or for enforcement in accordance with CPR 70.5(4)–(7A)
CPR 70.5(4)–(7A)	
The application for an order for enforcement	(i) if the enforcement is of a compromise which requires a person to whom a sum of money is payable under the compromise to do anything in

addition to discontinuing or not starting proceedings, the application must be made on notice and will be determined by the court (and see "Conditional compromises" below); or

CPR 70.5(4)

(ii) if the enforcement is of a compromise which does not require a person to whom a sum of money is payable to do anything in addition to discontinuing or not starting proceedings, the application may be made without notice and may be determined by a court officer without a hearing; and

CPR 70.5(4A)

(iii) in any event must be made to the court for the district where the person against whom the order is sought, resides or carries on business, unless the court otherwise orders.

"Conditional compromises"

Where the application concerns a compromise which requires a person to whom a sum of money is payable under the compromise to do anything in addition to discontinuing or not starting proceedings.
CPR 70.5(7A)

the respondent may oppose it by filing a response within 14 days of service of the application notice and if the respondent does so, the court will make such order as appears appropriate, (and in default of a response in the time provided, the court will make the order sought).

The form of application and information to be provided
CPR 70.5(5)
CPR 70.5(6)

(i) must be that specified in PD 70;
(ii) a copy of the decision or compromised must be filed with with the application;

Where order or compromise is required to be registered as an order of the High Court

Where an Act or SI provides that a decision or compromise may be enforced in the same manner as an order of the High Court if it is registered
CPR 70.5(8)

Apply for registration following the procedure in PD70 para.5.1

10. APPEALS, JUDICIAL REVIEW AND HABEAS CORPUS

10.6. Habeas Corpus (Habeas Corpus ad subjiciendum)

Add at end:

Claims for Judicial Review issued outside London

For arrangements in these cases see PD54D Judicial Review (Administrative Court (Venue))

D10–006

11. COSTS

11.4. Summary Assessment of Costs

In Guide11.4, delete the entry under "Summary assessment where children and patients are involved" and substitute:

D11–004   **Summary assessment where children and protected parties are involved**

Costs PD para.13.11   The court may not summarily assess costs where the receiving party is a child or protected party unless the solicitor acting for the child or protected party has waived the right to further costs.
The court may summarily assess costs which are payable by a child or protected party.

12. LANDLORD AND TENANT

12.4. Possession Claims: Commencement of Possession Claims On–line under PD 55B

In Guide 12.4, for "The Defendant (or any of them) must not be known to be a child or patient." substitute:

D12–004   The defendant (or any of them) must not be known to be a child or protected party.

15. INSOLVENCY

15.2. Proceedings under s.6 of the Company Directors Disqualification Act 1986 (CDDA 1986)

Under the heading "Notification of intention to apply for disqualification order", for "Secretary of State for Business, Enterprise and Regulatory Reform (formerly" substitute:

D15–002   Secretary of State for Business, Innovation and Skills, formerly the Secretary of State for Business, Enterprise and Regulatory Reform (before that known as

18. FINANCIAL RESTRICTIONS PROCEEDINGS UNDER THE COUNTER–TERRORISM ACT 2008

General Note

Add new paragraphs D18–001 to D18–004:

D18–001   By r.79.2 the Overriding Objective of the CPR is effectively modified in relation to Financial Restrictions Proceedings in that the obligation to deal with cases justly is to be read and given effect in a way which is compatible with the duty set out in r.79.2(2) namely that "The court will ensure that information is not disclosed contrary to the public interest." Rule 79.2(3) requires the court to satisfy itself that the material available to it enables it properly to determine the proceedings but that rule is expressly "without prejudice to" (r.79.2(2)).

Part IV of CPR Pt 79 applies generally to applications to the High Court to set aside Financial Restrictions Decisions and to appeals to the Court of Appeal against decisions made on applications to set aside Financial Restrictions Decisions. See Guide 17.2.

18.1 Applications to set aside Financial Restrictions Decisions

D18–002   **Where?**

CPR r.79.4   Apply to the Administrative Court

Procedure

CPR r.79.5   Use Pt 8 Claim procedure but NB that the following rules in Pt 8 are disapplied:
(a) r.8.1(3) (Court's power to disapply Part 8);
(b) r.8.2A (issue of claim form without naming defendants);

(c) r.8.4 (consequence of not filing an acknowledgment of service);
(d) r.8.5 (filing and serving written evidence);
(e) r.8.6 (evidence—general); and
(f) r.8.8 (defendant objects to use of Pt 8).

Claim form on set aside application

CPR r.79.6 The claim form must set out:
(a) the details of the financial restrictions decision;
(b) details of how the claimant is affected by the financial restrictions decision; and
(c) the grounds on which the claimant seeks to set aside the decision.

Documents to file with claim

CPR r.79.6 The claimant must file with the claim form a copy of:
(a) the written notice of the relevant financial restrictions decision made by the Treasury; or
(b) where relevant, any direction, order or licence made under Sch.7 to the Act or any freezing order made under Pt 2 of the Anti–terrorism, Crime and Security Act 2001; and
(c) any evidence, including witness statements, on which the claimant relies at that stage.

After issue of claim

CPR r.79.7 The court will fix a date for a directions hearing which will unless directed otherwise be not less than 14 days and not more than 28 days after issue of the claim form.

CPR r.79.8 The court will serve the Treasury with the claim form and the documents filed under r.79.6 and will send all parties and any special advocate notice of the directions hearing unless the date is endorsed on the claim form.

CPR r.79.10 See r.79.10 for examples of types of provisions which the court may include in directions made at the directions hearing.

Acknowledgement of service

CPR r.79.9 If a special advocate has been appointed then the Treasury must serve that advocate with a copy of its acknowledgement of service.

The Treasury's response

CPR r.79.11 If the Treasury oppose the application to set aside it must file at court its grounds for doing so and must file any evidence which it is aware of and which is relevant at that stage. The evidence must be served on the claimant unless the Treasury objects to doing so. Any evidence must be served on any special advocate.

CPR rr.79.11(3), (4) Where the Treasury objects to serving evidence r.79.25 it must make an application to withhold evidence under CPR 79.25 (see Guide 18.3).

Application for further information

CPR rr.79.11(5)–(8) The claimant or a special advocate may apply for an order for provision of further information about the Treasury's grounds for opposing the application and must specify in that application what information is sought and why. If the Treasury objects to providing the further information sought, it must apply to withhold evidence under r.79.25 (see Guide 18.3).

Filing and service of evidence (generally)

CPR 79.12

See r.79.12 for general rules as to filing and service of evidence, including any closed evidence.

Appeals against orders on applications to set aside

CPR r.79.13 and r.79.14

CPR Pt 52 applies to appeals against orders of the High Court made on applications to set aside Financial Restrictions Decisions but Part 52 is to be read subject to the modification of the Overriding Objective in r.79.2 (see note at start of Guides in this section) and the appeal is subject to the general procedural matters in Part IV of Pt 79 (as was the application to the High Court under appeal).

18.2 General procedural provisions on applications to set aside Financial Restrictions Decisions (or appeals against decisions on such applications). (Part IV of CPR 79)

D18–003   Notifications of hearings

CPR 79.16

All parties (and the special advocate if any) must be notified of the date time and place of any hearings whether or not they are entitled to attend.

Conduct of hearings

CPR r.79.17(1)
CPR 79.17(2)

All proceedings must be determined at a hearing, save in the circumstances set out in r.79.17(1). Where the court considers it necessary for a party other than the Treasury its legal representative to be excluded from a hearing in order to secure that information is not disclosed contrary to the public interest, the court will direct accordingly and will conduct that part of the hearing in private but attended by a special advocate to represent the interests of the excluded party.

Special Advocates

CPR r.79.18 and 79.19

Unless the Treasury do not oppose the claim or appeal or intend to withhold closed material from a party and his legal representatives, the Treasury must immediately give notice to the Attorney General when the Treasury is served with a Claim form, application notice or appeal notice under Pt 79 unless a special advocate has already been appointed to represent represent the interests of a party other than the Treasury and that special advocate is not prevented from communicating with that party by virtue of r.79.20.

Request for appointment of a special advocate

CPR r.79.18(3)

Any party may request the Attorney General to appoint a special advocate in proceedings under Pt 79.

Function of a special advocate

CPR r.79.19

The function of a special advocate is to represent the interests of a party other than the Treasury. Examples of matters which a special advocate may deal with appear in r.79.19.

Restrictions on communication by a special advocate

CPR r.79.20(1)
CPR r.79.20(2)

Before service of any closed material on the special advocate, the special advocate may communicate with any party or his representatives.

After the Treasury serve closed material on the special advocate, the special advocate must not communicate with any person about any matter connected with the proceedings, except in accordance with a direction of the court or for the following persons or bodies and only where necessary for administrative purposes about matters not connected with the substance of the proceedings:

(a) the court;

(b) the Treasury and any persons acting for them;

(c) the Attorney General and any persons acting for the Attorney General; and

(d) any other person, except for:

   (i) the specially represented party and that party's legal representative; and

   (ii) any other party to the proceedings (other than the Treasury) and that party's legal representative.

Communication by the specially represented party with the special advocate

CPR r.79.20(6)

The specially represented may communicate with special advocate after the Treasury have served closed material on the special advocate as but only through a legal representative in writing and the special advocate must not reply other than in accordance with directions by the court (save for a written acknowledgement of receipt to the specially represented person's legal representative).

For provisions relating to:

Objections by HM Treasury to applications by the special advocate for a direction as to communicating with the specially represented party — See r.79.21.

Modifications to usual rules as to disclosure and evidence — See rr.79.22 and 79.23.

Notice of Redacted evidence and filing of unredacted version at court — See r.79.24.

Provisions as to judgments, restrictions on release of documents from the court file, and applications by Treasury where the court proposes to serve on any other party written notice of directions made in the Treasury's absence or written judgments. — See rr.79.28, 79.29 and 79.30.

18.3 Applications by the Treasury to withhold closed material (CPR r.79.25)

D18–004 **Application**

CPR r.79.25(1)   The Treasury must apply to the court for permission to withhold closed material from another party and his legal representative. It may not rely on closed material at a hearing unless a special advocate has been appointed and attends the hearing to represent the interests of that party.

Procedure

CPR r.79.25(2)   The Treasury must file and serve on the special advocate the closed material and a statement of its reasons for withholding that material from the party.

Summary of material

CPR r.79.25(2)(c)   If the Treasury consider it possible to summarise the closed material, without disclosure contrary to the public interest, it must serve on the special advocate such a summary in a form which can be served on the specially represented party or his legal representative.

Redacted material

CPR r.79.25(3)   Where the Treasury serve on the special advocate any closed material which has been redacted on grounds other than those of legal professional privilege the Treasury must file with the court the material in an unredacted form together with an explanation of the redactions. The court will then give a direction as to what may be redacted and what must be served on the special advocate in an undredacted form.

Hearing of application to withhold

CPR r.79.26(1) and (2)   A hearing will be fixed by the court for the Treasury and the special advocate to make representations unless the special advocate does not challenge the application (and notifies such under r.79.26(2)) or the court has previously considered an application for permission to withhold substantially the same material and is satisfied that it would be just to give permission without a hearing, or the Treasury and the special advocate consent to the court deciding the issue without a hearing.

CPR r.79.26(3)   Where the court fixes a hearing of the application to withhold closed material, the special advocate may file and serve on the Treasury a reply and the Treasury may file and serve on the special advocate a response to the reply. The Treasury and the special advocate must file at least seven days before the hearing a schedule identifying the issues which cannot be agreed which must give brief reasons for their contentions on each issue in dispute and set out any proposals for the court to resolve the issues.

Absence of specially represented party

CPR r.79.26(4)
CPR r.79.20(2)   The hearing of the application to withhold closed material must take place in the absence of the specially represented party and that party's legal representative.

Grant of permission to withhold

CPR r.79.26(5)   The court will give permission to the Treasury to withhold closed material where it considers that disclosure of that material would be contrary to the public interest. The court will consider whether to direct the Treasury to serve a summary of that material on the specially represented party or that party's legal representative but ensure that such a summary does not contain material, the disclosure of which would be contrary to the public interest.

Refusal of permission to withhold

CPR r.79.26(7)   Where the court does <u>not</u> give permission to withhold closed material or directs the Treasury to serve a summary of that material on the specially represented party or that party's legal representative the Treasury is not required to do so. But if they do not do so, then at a hearing on notice the court may (if the material might be adverse to the Treasury's case or supports the case of the specially represented party) direct that the Treasury must not rely on that material or must make such concessions or take such steps as the court may specify and (in any other case) may direct that the Treasury do not rely on the material.

SECTION E

TABLE OF TIME LIMITS

TIME TABLE UNDER CPR

TABLES SHOWING THE TIMES FIXED FOR TAKING VARIOUS PROCEEDINGS

Litigation Friends Without Court Order

Delete and substitute:

A deputy appointed by the Court of Protection under the 2005 Act with power to conduct proceedings on the protected party's behalf must file an official copy of the order of the Court of Protection which confers his power to act	(a) where the deputy is to act as litigation friend for the claimant, at the time the claim is made, or (b) where the deputy is to act as a litigation friend for the a defendent at the time when they first take a step in the proceedings on behalf of the defendent (CPR r.21.5(2)).	**E1–033**
Any other person must file a certificate of suitability stating that he satisfies the conditions specified in r.21.4(3):	(a) where the person is to act as a litigation friend for a claimant, at the time when the claim is made; or (b) where the person is to act as a litigation friend for a defendant, at the time when he first takes a step in the proceedings on behalf of the defendant. (CPR r.21.5(3))	
The litigation friend must:	(a) serve the certificate of suitability on every person on whom the claim form should be served; and (b) file a certificate of service when filing the certificate of suitability. (CPR r.21.5(4))	

Litigation Friends—On Cessation of Child or Protected Party Status

Add new paragraph E1–033.1:

E1–033.1

When a party ceases to be a child at age 18	the litigation friend's appointment ceases ceases. (CPR r.21.9(1))
Where a party ceases to be a protected party	the litigation friend's appointment continues until ended by court order.(CPR r.21.9(2))
The child or protected party must then serve notice complying with CPR r.21.9(4) and if he does not do so	within 28 days after the date on which the litigation friend's appointment ceases, the court may on application, strike out any claim or defence brought by him (CPR r.21.9(5)).

VOLUME 2

CIVIL PROCEDURE RULES

SECTION 1

COURT GUIDES

1C   THE SUPREME COURT COSTS OFFICE GUIDE 2006

LIST OF COSTS JUDGES AND COSTS OFFICERS

In the table, "Miss C Bowstead" has been deleted. The following entry has been added:

Ms H Newman   2.18   **1C–2**

SECTION 2

SPECIALIST PROCEEDINGS

2A   COMMERCIAL COURT

PART 58—COMMERCIAL COURT

Related sources

After the last bullet point add new bullet point:
- Practice Direction (Electronic Working Pilot Scheme)   **2A–3**

Note

Add at end:
However *Midland Bank Ltd v Stamps* was not followed by the Court of Appeal in **2A–6**
National Westminster Bank Plc v Kitch [1996] 1 W.L.R. 1316; [1996] 4 All E.R. 495.

Electronic working

Add new paragraph 2A–9.1:
Practice Direction (Electronic Working Pilot Scheme), made by the Master of the **2A–9.1**
Rolls, came into effect on April 1, 2009. It supplements CPR r.5.5 (Filing and sending
documents) and provides for a pilot scheme, starting on April 1, 2009, and running
(initially) until March 31, 2010, by which, in the circumstances set out in the practice
direction, parties may avail themselves of arrangements for starting proceedings in the
Commercial Court at the Royal Courts of Justice (and some other courts) electronically, and also for taking all subsequent steps in the proceedings electronically (so–
called "Electronic Working"). In certain respects the practice direction modifies CPR
provisions that would otherwise apply. Paragraph 1.3 states that, where proceedings to
which CPR Pt 58 (Commercial Court) apply are issued, then the Electronic Working
pilot scheme will apply subject to the provisions of that Part unless specifically excluded
or revised by this practice direction.

The full text of this practice direction is published at para.5CPD.1 above.

Reference should be made to the Admiralty and Commercial Courts Guide, 8th edn
(2009), section B, in particular to paragraph B2.4, which provides for the request for

the issue of a Pt 7 or Pt 8 claim form being made when the Registry is closed and the circumstances when a party may request that a claim form be issued electronically; para.B3 which provides that the general directions with regard to the applicability of Protocols must be observed and that this may generally be done by a letter of claim which should be concise and not over elaborate.

Attention is also drawn to para.B13 of the Admiralty and Commercial Courts Guide which considers transfers to or from the Commercial Court and the appropriateness of commencing proceedings in the Mercantile Court before transfer into the Commercial List. See paras B13.2 and B13.5.

Note

Add new paragraph 2A–10.1:

2A–10.1   As to the claim form in a Pt 7 claim, see also the Admiralty and Commercial Courts Guide, 8th edn (2009), section B4, paras B4.1 to B4.10. Methods of service, applications for extensions of time, certificates of service and service of the claim form are considered in paras B7 to B8 of the Guide.

Further detail as to the form, content, serving and filing of the Particulars of Claim is to be found in section C of the Admiralty and Commercial Courts Guide, 8th edn (2009). As to form and content the following may be noted:

(a) statements of case should be brief and not set out evidence;

(b) they are limited to 25 pages unless permission for a longer statement of case has been obtained;

(c) they should not include lengthy portions of documents (if necessary such documents should be included in a schedule);

(d) the statement of case should be signed by the individual who drafted it and not, where the drafter is a solicitor in the name of the solicitor's firm.

As to service it is to be noted that all statements of case are to be served by the parties and not by the court (see PD58, para.9 and para.C1.8 of the Admiralty and Commercial Courts Guide, 8th edn (2009)). When filed, statements of case form part of the court record (see para C1.9 of the Admiralty and Commercial Courts Guide, 8th edn (2009)). Extensions of time for service may be agreed but the court must be notified (see PD 58 para.7.1 and para.C2.1 of the Admiralty and Commercial Courts Guide, 8th edn (2009)).

Note

Add new paragraph 2A–11.1:

2A–11.1   As to acknowledgment of service in a Pt 7 claim see also the Admiralty and Commercial Courts Guide, 8th edn (2009) section B9, paras B9.1, B9.3 and B9.4.

Note

Add new paragraph 2A–12.1:

2A–12.1   As to disputing the court's jurisdiction in a Pt 7 claim see also the Admiralty and Commercial Courts Guide, 8th edn (2009) section B10, paras B10.1 and B10.3 of the Guide.

Note

Add new paragraph 2A–13.1:

2A–13.1   As to default judgment see para.B11 of the Admiralty and Commercial Courts Guide, 8th edn (2009) which explains that the reason for the modification in r.58.8(2) is that in the Commercial Court the period for filing an acknowledgment of service is calculated from the service of the claim form.

Note

Add new paragraph 2A–15.1:

2A–15.1   With respect to the form, contents, serving and filing of a defence or reply see para.2A–10.1 above and see paras C.1.2, C3 and C4 of the Admiralty and Commercial Courts Guide, 8th edn (2009). It should be noted that a defendant (or Pt 20 defendant) who wishes to advance a positive case on mitigation (or on causation, or on quantification of damages) must provide proper details of the case, see para.C1.2(g) of the Guide. As to extensions of time for serving and filing see para.C.3.1(b) of the Guide. With respect to the necessity to file a reply, see para.C4.2 of the Guide.

Note

Add new paragraph 2A–16.1:

Guidance as to amendments to a statement of case is provided at para.C5 of the Admiralty and Commercial Courts Guide, 8th edn (2009). It is to be noted that amendments must show the original text and may be shown by using footnotes or marginal notes provided that they identify where and when an amendment has been made (see also PD58, para.8). This procedure is to be contrasted with the practice contained in PD17 para.2.2 of the CPR. **2A–16.1**

Note

Add new paragraph 2A–17.1:

The Admiralty and Commercial Courts Guide, 8th edn (2009) provides specific information with respect to Pt 8 claims in the following paragraphs: para.B5 (commencement, statement of truth and time for filing evidence in opposition to a Part 8 claim), para.B9.2 filing an acknowledgment of service, and paras 10.2 and 10.3 disputing the court's jurisdiction. **2A–17.1**

Heavy and Complex Cases

Delete and substitute:

Reference should be made to paras 10 to 12 of the Practice Direction to Pt 58 and to section D of the Admiralty and Commercial Courts Guide, 8th edn (2009) which set out the procedure to be followed in detail. The Guide particularly emphasises the key features of case management in the Commercial Court (see para D2), how and when such management conferences are to be fixed (see para.D3); how cases which are exceptional in size or complexity may be allocated to a designated judge by order of the judge in charge of the List in which case ordinarily all applications will be made to the judge so designated who will also be the trial judge (see para.D4); the use of case memoranda (see para.D5); the use of the list of issues (see para.D6); the case management bundle and its preparation (see para.D7). Detailed consideration as to the procedure to be adopted with regard to the Case Management Conference itself, including applications, attendance and the conduct of the hearing itself are set out in para.D8 of the Guide. Paragraph D10 deals with case management of Pt 20 claims, para.D12 deals with progress monitoring and paras D16, D17 and D18 are concerned with fixing trial dates, the estimates of the length of trial and pre–trial review and trial timetable. **2A–18.1**

THE ADMIRALTY AND COMMERCIAL COURTS GUIDE

Delete and substitute the Admiralty and Commercial Courts Guide (for paragraphs 2A–39.0 to 2A–205 substitute paragraphs 2A–39.0 to 2A–215):

Contents   **2A–39.0**

8th Edition: 2009

2A–39

Introduction

This edition of the Admiralty & Commercial Court Guide introduces changes designed to implement recommendations made by the Long Trials Working Party that were published in December 2007, following a pilot period in 2008 during which the Courts adopted the recommended procedures and subsequent consultations with practitioners. It also makes amendments in light of new procedures for issuing claims and applications and for communicating with the court electronically and other amendments suggested by practitioners or required by other developments. We are grateful to our colleagues for their assistance in revising the Guide, and in particular to Mr. Justice Flaux, who drew together the comments of practitioners on the proposals of the Working Party.

The Guide is intended to promote the efficient conduct of litigation in the Admiralty and Commercial Courts. It does not provide a complete blueprint for litigation and should be seen as providing guidance to be adopted flexibly and adapted to the exigencies of the particular case. It should not be understood to override in any way the Civil Procedure Rules or Practice Directions made under them, or as fettering the discretion of the judges.

We try to keep the Guide up to date, and suggestions for its improvement are always welcome.

The Hon Mr. Justice David Steel,
The Admiralty Judge

The Hon Mr. Justice Andrew Smith,
Judge in charge of the Commercial Court
30 April 2009

A.

Preliminary

A1 The procedural framework

A1.1 Proceedings in the Commercial Court are governed by the Civil Procedure **2A–40** Rules ("CPR") and Practice Directions. CPR Part 58 and its associated practice direction deal specifically with the Commercial Court. Part 61 deals with the Admiralty Court and Part 62 deals with arbitration applications. Parts 58 and 61 and their associated practice directions are set out in Appendix 1; Rule 62 and its associated practice direction is set out in Appendix 2.

A1.2 The Admiralty & Commercial Courts Guide is published with the approval of the Lord Chief Justice and the Head of Civil Justice in consultation with the Judges of the Admiralty and Commercial Courts and with the advice and support of the Admiralty Court and Commercial Court Users Committees. It is intended to provide guidance about the conduct of proceedings in the Admiralty and Commercial Courts and, within the framework of the Civil Procedure Rules and Practice Directions, to establish the practice to be followed in those courts.

A1.3 It is important to understand what the Guide is and what it is not. It provides guidance without prejudice to the provisions of the CPR and the Practice Directions. It is not itself a Practice Direction and does not constrain in any way how the judges might exercise their discretion under the Rules and Practice Directions in accordance with the overriding objective.

A1.4 Thus, the requirements of the Guide are designed to ensure effective management of proceedings in the Admiralty and Commercial Courts. On matters for which specific provision is not made by the Guide, the parties, their solicitors and counsel will be expected to act reasonably and in accordance with the spirit of the Guide.

A1.5 Pre–trial matters in the Admiralty and Commercial Courts are dealt with by the judges of those Courts: 58PD § 1.2.

A1.6 The Court expects a high level of co–operation and realism from the legal representatives of the parties. This applies to dealings (including correspondence) between legal representatives as well as to dealings with the Court.

A1.7 In order to avoid excessive repetition, the Guide has been written by reference to proceedings in the Commercial Court. Practitioners should treat the guidance as applicable to proceedings in the Admiralty Court unless the content of Part 61 or Section N of this Guide ("Admiralty") specifically requires otherwise.

A1.8 Parties may communicate with by e–mail with the Commercial and Admiralty Courts on certain matters: see Appendix 17.

A1.9 On 1 April 2009 the Commerical Court started an electronic working pilot scheme under PD Electronic Working Pilot Scheme. It is intended to develop the scheme incrementally in the Commerial and Admiralty Courts and in other courts, and up–to–date information about the scheme will be available on the Commerical Court website, www.hmcourts–service.gov.uk/infoabout/admiralcomm. See Appendix 18.

A2 The Admiralty & Commercial Registry; the Commercial Court Listing Office

2A–41 A2.1 The administrative office for the Admiralty Court and the Commercial Court is the Admiralty & Commercial Registry ("the Registry") which is located at Room EB13 in the Royal Courts of Justice, Strand, London WC2A 2LL. The Commercial Court Listing Office ("the Listing Office") is located at Room EB09 in the Royal Courts of Justice, Strand, London WC2A 2LL.

A2.2 It is important that there is close liaison between legal representatives of the parties and both the Registry and the Listing Office.

A3 The Commercial Court Users Committee

2A–42 A3.1 The success of the Court's ability to meet the special problems and continually changing needs of the commercial community depends in part upon a steady flow of information and constructive suggestions between the Court, litigants and professional advisers.

A3.2 The Commercial Court Committee has assisted in this process for many years, and it is expected to continue to do so. It is expected to play an important part in helping to ensure that the procedures of the Court enable the achievement of the "overriding objective". All concerned with the Court are encouraged to make the fullest use of this important channel of communication. Correspondence raising matters for the consideration of the Committee should be addressed to the Clerk to the Commercial Court, Royal Courts of Justice, Strand, London WC2A 2LL.

A4 Specialist associations

2A–43 A4.1 There are a number of associations of legal representatives which liaise closely with the Commercial Court. These will also play an important part in helping to ensure that the Court remains responsive to the "overriding objective".

A4.2 The associations include the Commercial Bar Association ("COMBAR"), the London Common Law and Commercial Bar Association ("LCLCBA"), the City of

London Law Society, the London Solicitors Litigation Association, the Commercial Litigators' Forum and the Admiralty Solicitors Group.

B.

COMMENCEMENT, TRANSFER AND REMOVAL

B1 Commercial cases

B1.1 Rule 58.1(2) describes a "commercial claim" as follows:

2A–44

"any claim arising out of the transaction of trade and commerce and includes any claim relating to—
   (a) a business document or contract;
   (b) the export or import of goods;
   (c) the carriage of goods by land, sea, air or pipeline;
   (d) the exploitation of oil and gas reserves or other natural resources;
   (e) insurance and re–insurance;
   (f) banking and financial services;
   (g) the operation of markets and exchanges;
   (h) the purchase and sale of commodities;
   (i) the construction of ships;
   (j) business agency; and
   (k) arbitration."

B2 Starting a case in the Commercial Court

B2.1 Except for arbitration applications which are governed by the provisions of CPR **2A–45** Part 62 and section O of the Guide, the case will be begun by a claim form under Part 7 or Part 8.

B2.2 Save where otherwise specified, references in this Guide to a claim form are to a Part 7 claim form.

B2.3 The Commercial Court may give a fixed date for trial (see section D16), but it does not give a fixed date for a hearing when it issues a claim. Rules 7.9 and 7.10 and their associated practice directions do not apply to the Commercial Court.

B2.4 A request for the issue of a Part 7 or a Part 8 claim form may be made by fax at certain times when the Registry is closed to the public: PD58 2.2. The procedure is set out in Appendix 3. Further details may be obtained from the Commercial Court website (www.hmcourts–service.gov.uk/infoabout/admiralcomm) or from the Registry. The fax number is 020 7947 6667.

B2.5 The Commercial Court may give a fixed date for trial (see section D16), but it does not give a fixed date for a hearing when it issues a claim. Rules 7.9 and 7.10 and their associated practice directions do not apply to the Commercial Court.

B3 Pre–Action Protocols

B3.1 The Practice Direction – Protocols applies to actions in the Commercial Court **2A–45.1** and usually it should be observed, although it is sometimes necessary or proper to start proceedings without following the procedures there contemplated: for example, where delays in starting proceedings might prompt forum–shopping in other jurisdictions. There is no approved protocol for actions in the Commercial Court generally, but cases in the Commercial Court are sometimes covered by an approved protocol, such as the Professional Negligence Pre–Action Protocol.

B3.2 Subject to complying with the Practice Direction and any applicable approved protocol, the parties to proceedings in the Commercial Court are not required, or generally expected, to engage in elaborate or expensive pre–action procedures, and restraint is encouraged.

B3.3 Thus, the letter of claim should be concise and it is usually sufficient to explain the proposed claim(s), identifying key dates, so as to enable the potential defendant to understand and to investigate the allegations. Only essential documents need be supplied, and the period specified for a response should not be longer than one month without good reason.

B3.4 A potential defendant should respond to a letter of claim concisely and only essential documents need by supplied. It should often be possible to respond sufficiently within the 21 days referred to in para 4.4 of the Practice Direction for acknowledgment of the letter of claim. The Practice Direction (para 4.3(c)) requires a potential defendant to give reasons if he requires longer to respond than the period specified in the letter of claim, and even if the period specified is longer than one month, a potential defendant who needs longer should explain the reasons when acknowledging the letter of claim.

B4 Part 7 claims

The form

2A–46 B4.1 A claimant starting proceedings in the Commercial Court must use practice form **N1(CC)** for Part 7 claims: PD58 § 2.4.

Marking

B3.2 In accordance with PD58 § 2.3 the claim form should be marked in the top right hand corner with the words "Queen's Bench Division, Commercial Court", and on the issue of the claim form out of the Registry the case will be entered in the Commercial List. Marking the claim form in this way complies sufficiently with PD7 § 3.6(3).

Statement of value

B4.3 Rule 16.3, which provides for a statement of value to be included in the claim form, does not apply in the Commercial Court: rule 58.5(2).

Particulars of claim and the claim form

B4.4 Although particulars of claim may be served with the claim form, this is not a requirement in the Commercial Court. However, if the particulars of claim are not contained in or served with the claim form, the claim form must contain a statement that if an acknowledgment of service is filed indicating an intention to defend the claim, particulars of claim will follow: rule 58.5(1)(a).

B4.5 If particulars of claim do not accompany the claim form they must be served within 28 days after the defendant has filed an acknowledgment of service indicating an intention to defend the claim: rule 58.5(1)(c).

B4.6 The three forms specified in rule 7.8(1) must be served with the claim form. One of these is a form for acknowledging service: rule 58.5(1)(b).

Statement of truth

B4.7

(a) A claim form must be verified by a statement of truth: rule 22.1. Unless the court otherwise orders, any amendment to a claim form must also be verified: rule 22.1(2).
(b) The required form of statement of truth is set out at PD7 § 7.2.
(c) A claim form will remain effective even where not verified by a statement of truth, unless it is struck out: PD22 § 4.1
(d) In certain cases the statement of truth may be signed by a person other than the party on whose behalf it is served or its legal representative: section C1.8–1.9.

Trial without service of particulars of claim or a defence

B4.8 The attention of the parties and their legal representatives is drawn to rule 58.11 which allows the court to order (before or after the issue of a claim form) that the case shall proceed without the filing or service of particulars of claim or defence or of any other statement of case. This facility is to be used with caution. It is unlikely to be appropriate unless all the issues have already been clearly defined in previous exchanges between the parties either in the course of a pre–claim form application or in previous correspondence and then only when the issues are of law or construction.

Interest

B4.9 The claim form (and not only the particulars of claim) must comply with the requirements of rules 16.4(1)(b) and 16.4(2) concerning interest: rule 58.5(3).

B4.10 References to particulars of claim in rule 12.6(1)(a) (referring to claims for interest where there is a default judgment) and rule 14.14(1)(a) (referring to claims for interest where there is a judgment on admissions) may be treated as references to the claim form: rules 58.8(2) and 58.9(3).

B5 Part 8 claims

Form

B5.1 A claimant who wishes to commence a claim under CPR Part 8 must use **2A–47** practice form **N208(CC)**: PD58 § 2.4.

B5.2 Attention is drawn to the requirement in rule 8.2(a) that where a claimant uses the Part 8 procedure his claim form must state that Part 8 applies. Similarly, PD7 § 3.3 requires that the claim form state (if it be the case) that the claimant wishes his claim to proceed under Part 8 or that the claim is required to proceed under Part 8.

Marking and statement of truth

B5.3 Sections B3.2 (marking) and B3.7 (statement of truth) also apply to a claim form issued under Part 8.

Time for filing evidence in opposition to a Part 8 claim

B5.4 A defendant to a Part 8 claim who wishes to rely on written evidence must file and serve it within 28 days after filing an acknowledgment of service: rule 58.12.

B6 Part 20 claims

Form

B6.1 Adapted versions of the Part 20 claim form and acknowledgment of service **2A–48** (Practice Forms no. **N211** and **N213**) and of the related Notes to Part 20 claimant and Part 20 defendant have been approved for use in the Commercial Court.

B7 Service of the claim form

Service by the parties

B7.1 Claim forms issued in the Commercial List are to be served by the parties, not **2A–49** by the Registry: PD58 § 9.

Methods of service

B7.2 Methods of service are set out in CPR Part 6, which is supplemented by a Practice Direction.

B7.3 PD6 § § 2.1 and 3.1 concern service by document exchange and other means, including fax and other electronic means. There are specific provisions about when a solicitor acting for a party may be served.

Applications for extension of time

B7.4 Applications for an extension of time in which to serve a claim form are governed by rule 7.6. Rule 7.6(3)(a), which refers to service of the claim form by the court, does not apply in the Commercial Court.

B7.5 The evidence required on an application for an extension of time is set out in PD7 § 8.2. In an appropriate case it may be presented by an application notice verified by a statement of truth and without a separate witness statement: rule 32.6(2).

Certificate of service

B7.6 When the claimant has served the claim form he must file a certificate of service: rule 6.14(2). Satisfaction of this requirement is relevant, in particular, to the claimant's ability to obtain judgment in default (see Part 12) and to the right of a non–party to search for, inspect and take a copy of the claim form under rule 5.4(2)(a).

B8 Service of the claim form out of the jurisdiction

2A–50 B8.1 Service of claim forms outside the jurisdiction without permission is governed by rules 6.32– 6.35, and where rule 6.35(5) applies by PD6B.

B8.2 Applications for permission to serve a claim form out of the jurisdiction are governed by rules 6.36 and 6.37 and PD6B. A guide to the appropriate practice is set out in Appendix 15.

B8.3 Service of process in some foreign countries may take a long time to complete; it is therefore important that solicitors take prompt steps to effect service.

B9 Acknowledgment of service

2A–51 *Part 7 claims*

B9.1

(a) A defendant must file an acknowledgment of service in every case: rule 58.6(1). An adapted version of practice form **N9** (which includes the acknowledgment of service) has been approved for use in the Commercial Court.
(b) The period for filing an acknowledgment of service is calculated from the service of the claim form, whether or not particulars of claim are contained in or accompany the claim form or are to follow service of the claim form. Rule 9.1(2), which provides that in certain circumstances the defendant need not respond to the claim until particulars of claim have been served on him, does not apply: rule 58.6(1).

Part 8 claims

B9.2

(a) A defendant must file an acknowledgment of service in every case: rule 58.6(1). An adapted version of practice form **N210** (acknowledgment of service of a Part 8 claim form) has been approved for use in the Commercial Court. A copy of this practice form (Form **N210(CC)**) is included at the end of the Guide, together with adapted versions of the notes for claimants and defendants on completing and replying to a Part 8 claim form.
(b) The time for filing an acknowledgment of service is calculated from the service of the claim form.

Acknowledgment of service in a claim against a firm

B9.3

(a) PD10 § 4.4 allows an acknowledgment of service to be signed on behalf of a partnership by any of the partners or a person having the control or management of the partnership business, whether he be a partner or not.
(b) However, attention is drawn to Schedule 1 to the CPR which includes, with modifications, provisions previously contained in RSC Order 81 concerning acknowledgment of service by a person served as a partner who denies his liability as such. (see also the note at the end of CPR Part 10).

Time for filing acknowledgment of service

B9.4

(a) Except in the circumstances described in section B8.4(b) and B8.4(c), or is otherwise ordered by the court, the period for filing an acknowledgment of service is

14 days after service of the claim form.

(b) If the claim form has been served out of the jurisdiction without the permission of the court under rules 6.32 and 33, the time for filing an acknowledgment of service is governed by rule 6.35, save that in all cases time runs from the service of the claim form: rule 58.6(3).

(c) If the claim form has been served out of the jurisdiction with the permission of the court under rule 6.36 the time for filing an acknowledgment of service is governed by rule 6.37.5, see Practice Direction B supplementing rule 6 and the table to which it refers, save that in all cases time runs from the service of the claim form: rule 58.6(3).

B10 Disputing the court's jurisdiction

Part 7 claims   **2A–52**

B10.1

(a) If the defendant intends to dispute the court's jurisdiction or contend that the court should not exercise its jurisdiction he must:

   (i) file an acknowledgment of service— rule 11(2); and

   (ii) issue an application notice seeking the appropriate relief.

(b) An application to dispute the court's jurisdiction must be made within 28 days after filing an acknowledgment of service: rule 58.7(2).

(c) If the defendant wishes to rely on written evidence in support of that application, he must file and serve that evidence when he issues the application. In an appropriate case it may be presented by an application notice verified by a statement of truth and without a separate witness statement: CPR 32.6(2).

(d) The parties to that application should consider at the time of the application or as soon as possible thereafter whether the application is a 'heavy application' within Section F6.1 likely to last more than half a day but for which the automatic timetable provisions in PD 58 para 13.2 and F6.3–F6.5 will not for any reason be appropriate. If any party considers that special timetabling is required otherwise than in accordance with those automatic provisions it should at once so inform all other parties and the Listing Office. Unless a timetable covering those matters covered by Section F6.3 to F6.5 can be agreed forthwith, the applicant must without delay inform the Listing Office that a directions hearing will be required. For the purposes of such a hearing all parties must by 1pm on the day before that hearing lodge with the Listing Office a brief summary of the issues of fact and law likely to arise on the application, a list of witnesses of fact whose witness statements or affidavits are likely to be adduced by that party, a list of expert witnesses on whose report that party intends to reply, an estimate of how long the hearing will take and how much pre–hearing reading will be required by the judge and a proposed pre–hearing timetable.

(e) If the defendant makes an application under rule 11(1), the claimant is not bound to serve particulars of claim until that application has been disposed of: rule 58.7(3).

Part 8 claims

B10.2

(a) The provisions of section B10.1(a)–(c) also apply in the case of Part 8 claims.

(b) If the defendant makes an application under rule 11(1), he is not bound to serve any written evidence on which he wishes to rely in opposition to the substantive claim until that application has been disposed of: rule 11.9.

Effect of an application challenging the jurisdiction

B10.3 An acknowledgment of service of a Part 7 or Part 8 claim form which is followed by an application challenging the jurisdiction under Part 11 does not constitute a submission by the defendant to the jurisdiction: rules 11(3) and 11(7).

B10.4 If an application under Part 11 is unsuccessful, and the court then considers giving directions for filing and serving statements of case (in the case of a Part 7 claim) or evidence (in the case of a Part 8 claim), a defendant does not submit to the jurisdiction merely by asking for time to serve and file his statement of case or evidence, as the case may be.

B11 Default judgment

2A–53 B11 Default judgment is governed by Part 12 and PD12. However, because in the Commercial Court the period for filing the acknowledgment of service is calculated from service of the claim form, the reference to "particulars of claim" in PD12 § 4.1(1) should be read as referring to the claim form: PD58 § 6(1).

2A–54 B12 Admissions

B12

(a) Admissions are governed by CPR Part 14, and PD14, except that the references to "particulars of claim" in PD14 § § 2.1, 3.1 and 3.2 should be read as referring to the claim form: PD58 § 6(2).

(b) Adapted versions of the practice forms of admission (practice forms no. **N9A** and no. **N9C**) have been approved for use in the Commercial Court.

B13 Transfer of cases into and out of the Commercial List

2A–55 B13.1 The procedure for transfer and removal is set out in PD58 § 4. All such applications must be made to the Commercial Court: rule 30.5(3).

B13.2 Although an order to transfer a case to the Commercial List may be made at any stage, any application for such an order should normally be made at an early stage in the proceedings. It might be appropriate for some cases to be brought in a Mercantile Court and managed in its early stages in a Mercantile Court before being transferred to the Commercial List.

B13.3 Transfer to the Commercial List may be ordered for limited purposes only, but a transferred case will normally remain in the Commercial List until its conclusion.

B13.4 An order transferring a case out of the Commercial List may be made at any stage, but will not usually be made after a pre–trial timetable has been fixed at the case management conference (see section D8).

B13.5 Some commercial cases may more suitably, or as suitably, be dealt with in one of the Mercantile Courts or the London Mercantile Court. Parties should consider whether it would be more appropriate to begin proceedings in one of those courts and the Commercial Judge may on his own initiative order the case to be transferred there. Guidance on practical steps for transferring cases to the London Mercantile Court and to the Mercantile Courts is contained in a Guidance Note at Appendix 19.

C.

PARTICULARS OF CLAIM, DEFENCE AND REPLY

2A–56 C1 Form, content, serving and filing

C1.1

(a) Particulars of claim, the defence and any reply must be set out in separate consecutively numbered paragraphs and be as brief and concise as possible. They should not set out evidence.

(b) Statements of case should be limited to 25 pages in length. The court will give permission for a longer statement of case to be served where a party shows good reasons for doing so, and if it does the court might require that a summary of the statement of case is also served. Any application to serve a statement of case longer than 25 pages should be made on paper to the court briefly stating the reasons for exceeding the 25 page limit.

(c) It is seldom necessary for the proper understanding of the statement of case to include substantial parts of a lengthy document, but if this is necessary the passages in question should be set out in a schedule rather than in the body of the case.

(d) The document must be signed by the individual person or persons who drafted it, not, in the case of a solicitor, in the name of the firm alone.

(e) Documents should be in the form stipulated in the Practice Direction to CPR part 5, including that there should be numbered paragraphs and numbered pages.

C1.2

(a) Particulars of claim, the defence and also any reply must comply with the provisions of rules 16.4 and 16.5, save that rules 16.5(6) and 16.5(8) do not apply.

(b) The requirements of PD16 § 7.4–8.1 (which relate to claims based upon oral agreements, agreements by conduct and Consumer Credit Agreements and to reliance upon evidence of certain matters under the Civil Evidence Act 1968) should be treated as applying to the defence and reply as well as to the particulars of claim.

    (i) full and specific details should be given of any allegation of fraud, dishonesty, malice or illegality; and

    (ii) where an inference of fraud or dishonesty is alleged, the facts on the basis of which the inference is alleged must be fully set out.

(d) Any legislative provision upon which an allegation is based must be clearly identified and the basis of its application explained.

(e) Any provision of The Human Rights Act 1998 (including the Convention) on which a party relies in support of its case must be clearly identified and the basis of its application explained.

(f) Any principle of foreign law or foreign legislative provision upon which a party's case is based must be clearly identified and the basis of its application explained.

(g) It is important that if a defendant or Part 20 defendant wishes to advance by way of defence or defence to counterclaim a positive case on causation, mitigation or quantification of damages, proper details of that case should be included in the defence or Part 20 defence at the outset or, if not then available, as early as possible thereafter.

C1.3

(a) PD16 § 7.3 relating to a claim based upon a written agreement should be treated as also applying to the defence, unless the claim and the defence are based on the same agreement.

(b) In most cases attaching documents to or serving documents with a statement of case does not promote the efficient conduct of the proceedings and should be avoided.

(c) If documents are to be served at the same time as a statement of case they should normally be served separately from rather than attached to the statement of case.

(d) Only those documents which are obviously of critical importance and necessary for a proper understanding of the statement of case should be attached to or served with it. The statement of case must itself refer to the fact that documents are attached to or served with it.

(e) An expert's report should not be attached to the statement of case and should not be filed with the statement of case at the Registry. A party must obtain permission from the court in order to adduce expert evidence at trial and therefore any party which serves an expert's report without obtaining such permission does so at his own risk as to costs.

(f) Notwithstanding PD16 § 7.3(1), a true copy of the complete written agreement may be made available at any hearing unless the court orders otherwise.

Adapted versions of the practice forms of defence and counterclaim have been approved for use in the Commercial Court.

Statement of truth

C1.4 Particulars of claim, a defence and any reply must be verified by a statement of truth: rule 22.1. So too must any amendment, unless the court otherwise orders: rule 22.1(2); see also section C5.4.

C1.5 The required form of statement of truth is as follows:

    (i) for particulars of claim, as set out in PD7 § 7.2 or PD16 § 3.4;

    (ii) for a defence, as set out in PD15 § 2.2 or PD16 § 12.2;

    (iii) for a reply the statement of truth should follow the form for the particulars of claim, but substituting the word "reply" for the words "particulars of claim" (see PD22 § 2.1).

C1.6 Rule 22.1(5), (6) and (8) and PD22 § 3 state who may sign a statement of truth.

For example, if insurers are conducting proceedings on behalf of many claimants or defendants a statement of truth may be signed by a senior person responsible for the case at a lead insurer, but

(i) the person signing must specify the capacity in which he signs;

(ii) the statement of truth must be a statement that the lead insurer believes that the facts stated in the document are true; and

(iii) the court may order that a statement of truth also be signed by one or more of the parties.

See PD22 § 3.6B.

C1.7 A statement of case remains effective (although it may not be relied on as evidence) even where it is not verified by a statement of truth, unless it is struck out: PD22 § § 4.1–4.3.

Service

C1.8 All statements of case are served by the parties, not by the court: PD58 § 9.

Filing

C1.9 The statements of case filed with the court form part of the permanent record of the court.

C2 Serving and filing particulars of claim

2A–57 C2.1 Subject to any contrary order of the court and unless particulars of claim are contained in or accompany the claim form:

(i) the period for serving particulars of claim is 28 days after filing an acknowledgment of service: rule 58.5(1)(c);

(ii) the parties may agree extensions of the period for serving the particulars of claim. However, any such agreement and brief reasons must be evidenced in writing and notified to the court, addressed to the Listing Office: PD58 § 7.1;

C2.2 The court may make an order overriding any agreement by the parties varying a time limit: PD58 § 7.2.

C2.3 The claimant must serve the particulars of claim on all other parties. A copy of the claim form will be filed at the Registry on issue. If the claimant serves particulars of claim separately from the claim form he must file a copy within 7 days of service together with a certificate of service: rule 7.4(3).

C3 Serving and filing a defence

2A–58 C3.1 The defendant must serve the defence on all other parties and must at the same time file a copy with the court.

C3.2

(a) If the defendant files an acknowledgment of service which indicates an intention to defend the period for serving and filing a defence is 28 days after service of the particulars of claim, subject to the provisions of rule 15.4(2). (See also Appendix 15 for cases where the claim form has been served out of the jurisdiction).

(b) The defendant and the claimant may agree that the period for serving and filing a defence shall be extended by up to 28 days: rule 15.5(1). However, any such agreement and brief reasons must be evidenced in writing and notified to the court, addressed to the Case Management Unit: PD58 § 7.1.

(c) An application to the court is required for any further extension. If the parties are able to agree that a further extension should be granted, a draft consent order should be provided together with a brief explanation of the reasons for the extension.

C3.3 The general power to agree variations to time limits contained in rule 2.11 and PD58 § 7.1 enables parties to agree extensions of the period for serving and filing a defence that exceed 28 days. The length of extension must in all cases be specified, and any such agreement must be evidenced in writing and comply with the requirements of section C2.1.

C3.4 The claimant must notify the Listing Office by letter when all defendants who intend to serve a defence have done so. This information is material to the fixing of the case management conference (see section D3.1).

C4 Serving and filing a reply

C4.1 Subject to section C4.3, the period for serving and filing a reply is 21 days after service of the defence: rule 58.10(1). **2A–59**

C4.2 A claimant who does not file a reply does not admit what is pleaded in the defence and a claimant who files a reply that does not deal with something pleaded in the defence is not taken to admit it. A reply should be served only when necessary and then only plead what is necessary: it should not repeat what is pleaded in the particulars of claim.

C4.3

(a) A reply must be filed at the same time as it is served: rule 15.8(b); rule 15.8(a) does not apply in proceedings in the Commercial List.
(b) The reply should be served before case management information sheets are provided to the court (see section D8.5). In the normal case, this will allow the parties to consider any reply before completing the case management information sheet, and allow time for the preparation of the case memorandum and the list of issues each of which is required for the case management conference (see sections D5–D7).

C4.3 In some cases, more than 21 days may be needed for the preparation, service and filing of a reply. In such cases an application should be made on paper for an extension of time and for a postponement of the case management conference. The procedure to be followed when making an application on paper is set out in section F4.

C4.4 Any reply must be served by the claimant on all other parties: rule 58.10(1).

C5 Amendment
2A–60

C5.1

(a) Amendments to a statement of case must show the original text, unless the court orders otherwise: PD58 § 8.
(b) Amendments may be shown by using footnotes or marginal notes, provided they identify precisely where and when an amendment has been made.
(c) Unless the court so orders, there is no need to show amendments by colour–coding.
(d) If there have been extensive amendments it may be desirable to prepare a fresh copy of the statement of case. However, a copy of the statement of case showing where and when amendments have been made must also be made available.

C5.2 All amendments to any statement of case must be verified by a statement of truth unless the court orders otherwise: rule 22.1(2).

C5.3 Questions of amendment, and consequential amendment, should wherever possible be dealt with by consent. A party should consent to a proposed amendment unless he has substantial grounds for objecting to it.

C5.4 Late amendments should be avoided and may be disallowed.

D.

CASE MANAGEMENT IN THE COMMERCIAL COURT

D1 Generally

D1.1 All proceedings in the Commercial List will be subject to management by the court. **2A–61**

D1.2 All proceedings in the Commercial List are automatically allocated to the multi–track and consequently Part 26 and the rules relating to allocation do not apply: rule 58.13(1).

D1.3 Except for rule 29.3(2) (legal representatives to attend case management conferences and pre–trial reviews) and rule 29.5 (variation of case management timetable), Part 29 does not apply to proceedings in the Commercial List: rule 58.13(2).

D1.4 If a party has a legal representative, all case management conferences must be attended by such a representative who is familiar with the case and has sufficient authority to deal with any issues that are likely to arise: rule 29.3(2).

Editorial note

2A–61.1   See Heavy and Complex Cases at para.2A–18.1, above.

D2 Key features of case management in the Commercial Court

2A–62 D2 Case management is governed by rule 58.13 and PD58 § 10. In a normal commercial case commenced by a Part 7 claim form, case management will include the following 12 key features:

(1) statements of case will be exchanged within fixed or monitored time periods;

(2) a case memorandum, a list of issues and a case management bundle will be produced at an early point in the case;

(3) the case memorandum, list of issues and case management bundle will be amended and updated or revised on a running basis throughout the life of the case and will be used by the court at every stage of the case;. In particular the list of issues will be used as a tool to define what factual and expert evidence is necessary and the scope of disclosure;

(4) the court itself will approve or settle the list of issues and may require the further assistance of the parties and their legal representatives in order to do so;

(5) a mandatory case management conference will be held shortly after statements of case have been served, if not before (and preceded by the parties lodging case management information sheets identifying their views on the requirements of the case);

(6) at the case management conference the court will (as necessary) discuss the issues in the case and the requirements of the case with the advocates retained in the case. The court will set a pre–trial timetable and give any other directions as may be appropriate;

(7) after statements of case have been served, the parties will serve a disclosure schedule or schedules. At the first case management conference, the court will discuss with the advocates retained in the case by reference to the list of issues the strategy for disclosure set out in the disclosure schedules with a view to ensuring that disclosure and searches for documents are proportionate to the importance of the issues in the case to which the disclosure relates and avoiding subsequent applications for specific disclosure;

(8) before the progress monitoring date the parties will report to the court, using a progress monitoring information sheet, the extent of their compliance with the pre–trial timetable;

(9) on or shortly after the progress monitoring date a judge will (without a hearing) consider progress and give such further directions as he thinks appropriate;

(10) if at the progress monitoring date all parties have indicated that they will be ready for trial, all parties will complete a pre–trial checklist;

(11) in many cases there will be a pre–trial review; in such cases the parties will be required to prepare a trial timetable for consideration by the court;

(12) throughout the case there will be regular reviews of the estimated length of trial, including how much pre–trial reading should be undertaken by the judge.

D3 Fixing a case management conference

2A–63 D3.1 A mandatory case management conference will normally take place on the first available date 6 weeks after all defendants who intend to serve a defence have done so. This will normally allow time for the preparation and service of any reply (see section C4).

D3.2

(a) If proceedings have been started by service of a Part 7 claim form, the claimant must take steps to fix the date for the case management conference with the Listing Office in co–operation with the other parties within 14 days of the date when all defendants who intend to file and serve a defence have done so: PD58 § 10.2(a). The parties should bear in mind the need to allow time for the preparation and service of any reply.

(b) If proceedings have been begun by service of a Part 8 claim form, the claimant must take steps to fix a date for the case management conference with the Listing Office in co–operation with the other parties within 14 days of the date when all defendants who wish to serve evidence have done so: PD58 § 10.2(b).

D3.3

(a) In accordance with section C3 the Registry will expect a defence to be served and filed by the latest of:

    (i) 28 days after service of particulars of claim (as certified by the certificate of service); or

    (ii) any extended date for serving and filing a defence as notified to the court in writing following agreement between the parties; or

    (iii) any extended date for serving and filing a defence as ordered by the court on an application.

(b) If within 28 days after the latest of these dates has passed for each defendant, the parties have not taken steps to fix the date for the case management conference, the Listing Office will inform the Judge in Charge of the List, and at his direction will take steps to fix a date for the case management conference without further reference to the parties.

D3.4 If the proceedings have been transferred to the Commercial List, the claimant must apply for a case management conference within 14 days of the date of the order transferring them, unless the judge held, or gave directions for, a case management conference when he made the order transferring the proceedings: PD58 § 10.3.

D3.5 If the claimant fails to make an application as required by the rules, any other party may apply for a case management conference: PD58 § 10.5.

D3.6

(a) In some cases it may be appropriate for a case management conference to take place at an earlier date.

(b) Any party may apply to the court in writing at an earlier time for a case management conference: PD58 § 10.4. A request by any party for an early case management conference should be made in writing to the Judge in Charge of the List, on notice to all other parties, at the earliest possible opportunity.

D3.7 If before the date on which the case management conference would be held in accordance with section D3 there is a hearing in the case at which the parties are represented, the business of the case management conference will normally be transacted at that hearing and there will be no separate case management conference.

D3.8 The court may fix a case management conference at any time on its own initiative. If it does so, the court will normally give at least 7 days notice to the parties: PD58 § 10.6.

D3.9 A case management conference may not be postponed or adjourned without an order of the court.

D4 Designated judge

D4.1 Cases which are exceptional in size or complexity or in having a propensity to **2A–64** give rise to numerous pre–trial applications may be allocated to a designated judge.

D4.2 An application for the appointment of a designated judge should be made in writing to the Judge in Charge of the List at the time of fixing the case management conference.

D4.3 If an order is made for allocation to a designated judge, the designated judge will preside at all subsequent pre–trial case management conferences and other hearings. Normally all applications in the case, other than applications for an interim payment, will be determined by the designated judge and he will be the trial judge.

D5 Case memorandum

2A–65 D5.1 In order that the judge conducting the case management conference may be informed of the general nature of the case and the issues which are expected to arise, after service of the defence and any reply the solicitors and counsel for each party shall draft an agreed case memorandum.

D5.2 The case memorandum should contain:

(i) a short and uncontroversial description of what the case is about; and

(ii) a very short and uncontroversial summary of the material procedural history of the case.

D5.3 Unless otherwise ordered, the solicitors for the claimant are to be responsible for producing and filing the case memorandum, and where appropriate for revising it.

D5.4 The case memorandum should not refer to any application for an interim payment, to any order for an interim payment, to any voluntary interim payment, or to any payment or offer under CPR Part 36 or Part 37.

D5.5

(a) It should be clearly understood that the only purpose of the case memorandum is to help the judge understand broadly what the case is about. The case memorandum does not play any part in the trial. It is unnecessary, therefore, for parties to be unduly concerned about the precise terms in which it is drafted, provided it contains a reasonably fair and balanced description of the case. Above all the parties must do their best to spend as little time as practicable in drafting and negotiating the wording of the memorandum and keep clearly in mind the need to limit costs.

(b) Accordingly, in all but the most exceptional cases it should be possible for the parties to draft an agreed case memorandum. However, if it proves impossible to do so, the claimant must draft the case memorandum and send a copy to the defendant. The defendant may provide its comments to the court (with a copy to the claimant) separately.

(c) The failure of the parties to agree a case memorandum is a matter which the court may wish to take into account when dealing with the costs of the case management conference.

D6 List of issues

2A–66 D6.1 After service of the defence (and any reply), the solicitors and counsel for each party shall produce an agreed list of the important issues in the case. The list should include both issues of fact and issue of law. A separate section of the document should list what is common ground between the parties (or any of them, specifying which).

D6.2

(a) The list of issues is intended to be a neutral document for use as a case management tool at all stages of the case by the parties and the court. Neither party should attempt to draft the list in terms which advance one party's case over that of another.

(b) It is unnecessary, therefore, for parties to be unduly concerned about the precise terms in which the list of issues is drafted, provided it presents the structure of the case in a reasonably fair and balanced way. Above all the parties must do their best to spend as little time as practicable in drafting and negotiating the wording of the list of issues and keep clearly in mind the need to limit costs.

(c) Accordingly, in most cases it should be possible for the parties to draft an agreed list of issues. However, if it proves impossible to do so, the claimant must draft the list and send a copy to the defendant. The defendant may provide its comments or alternative suggested list to the court (with a copy to the claimant) separately.

D6.3

(a) A draft (or drafts) of the list of issues is to be available to the court prior to the first case management conference. It is intended that at that stage the draft list should be in a general form, identifying the key issues and the structure of the parties' contentions, rather than setting out all detailed sub–issues.

(b) At the first case management conference and any subsequent case management conferences which take place, the court will review and settle the draft list of issues with a view to refining it and identifying important sub–issues as appropriate and as required in order to manage the case. Accordingly the list of issues may be developed, by expansion or reduction as the case progresses.

D6.4 The list of issues will be used by the court and the parties as a case management tool as the case progresses to determine such matters as the scope of disclosure and of factual and expert evidence and to consider whether issues should be determined summarily or preliminary issues should be determined.

D6.5 The list of issues is a tool for case management purposes and is not intended to supersede the pleadings which remain the primary source for each party's case. If at any stage of the proceedings, any question arises as to the accuracy of the list of issues, it will be necessary to consult the pleadings, in order to determine what issues arise.

D7 Case management bundle

Preparation

D7.1 Before the case management conference (see sections D3 and D8), a case **2A–67** management bundle should be prepared by the solicitors for the claimant: PD58 § 10.8.

Contents

D7.2 The case management bundle should contain the documents listed below (where the documents have been created by the relevant time):

(i) the claim form;

(ii) all statements of case (excluding schedules), except that, if a summary has been prepared, the bundle should contain the summary, not the full statement of case;

(iii) the case memorandum (see section D5);

(iv) the list of issues (see section D6);

(v) the case management information sheets and the pre–trial timetable if one has already been established (see sections D8.5 and D8.9);

(vi) the principal orders in the case;

(vii) any agreement in writing made by the parties to disclose documents without making a list or any agreement in writing that disclosure (or inspection or both) shall take place in stages.

See generally PD58 § 10.8.

D7.3 It is also useful for the case management bundle to include all disclosure schedules stating what search each party intends to make pursuant to Rule 31.7 when giving standard disclosure of electronic and other documents and what search he expects of the other party (or parties).

D7.4 The case management bundle should not include a copy of any order for an interim payment.

Lodging the case management bundle

D7.5 The case management bundle should be lodged with the Listing Office at least 7 days before the (first) case management conference (or earlier hearing at which the parties are represented and at which the business of the case management conference may be transacted: see section D3.7).

Preparation and upkeep

D7.6 The claimant (or other party responsible for the preparation and upkeep of the case management bundle), in consultation with the other parties, must revise and update the case management bundle as the case proceeds: PD58 § 10.9. The claimant should attend at the Listing Office for this purpose at the following stages:

(i) within 10 days of the case management conference, in order to add the pre–trial timetable (or any other order made at the case management conference) and an updated case memorandum;

(ii) within 10 days of an order being made on an application, if in the light of the order or the application it is necessary to add a copy of the order made (as a principal order in the case) or an updated case memorandum;

(iii) within 14 days of the service of any amended statement of case (or summary), in order to substitute a copy of the amended statement of case (or summary) for that which it replaces and to incorporate an updated case memorandum and (if appropriate) a revised list of issues;

(iv) within 10 days of any other revision to the case memorandum or list of issues, in order to incorporate the revised document.

D8 Case Management Conference

2A–68 *Application to postpone the case management conference*

D8.1

(a) An application to postpone the case management conference must be made within 21 days after all defendants who intend to serve a defence have done so.

(b) The application will be dealt with on paper unless the court considers it appropriate to direct an oral hearing.

Attendance at the case management conference

D8.2 Clients need not attend a case management conference unless the court otherwise orders. A representative who has conduct of the case must attend from each firm of solicitors instructed in the case. At least one of the advocates retained in the case on behalf of each party should also attend.

D8.3

(a) The case management conference is a very significant stage in the case. Although parties are encouraged to agree proposals for directions for the consideration of the court, directions will not normally be made by consent without the need for attendance.

(b) The general rule in the Commercial Court, as the Commercial and Admiralty Courts Guide makes clear, is that there must be an oral Case Management Conference (CMC) at court.

(c) However, there are cases which are out of the ordinary where it may be possible to dispense with an oral hearing if the issues are straightforward and the costs of an oral hearing cannot be justified.

(d) In such a case, if the parties wish to ask the Court to consider holding the CMC on paper, they must lodge all the appropriate documents (see D8.3(e)) by no later than 12 noon on the Tuesday of the week in which the CMC is fixed for the Friday. That timing will be strictly enforced. If all the papers are not provided by that time, the CMC must be expected to go forward to an oral hearing. If the failure to lodge the papers is due to the fault of one party and it is for that reason an oral CMC takes place, that party will be at risk as to costs.

(e) With the papers (which will include the Case Management bundle with the information sheets fully completed by each party), the parties must lodge a draft Order and draft list of issues (both agreed by the parties) for consideration by the Judge and a statement signed by each advocate:

(i) confirming that the parties have considered and discussed all the relevant issues and brought to the Court's attention anything that was unusual; and

(ii) setting out information about any steps that had been taken to resolve the dispute by ADR, any future plans for ADR or an explanation as to why ADR would not be appropriate.

(iii) giving a time estimate for the trial, specifically stating how much pre–trial reading by the judge will be required.

(f) In the ordinary course of things it would be unlikely that any case involving expert evidence or preliminary issues would be suitable for a CMC on paper. In cases involving expert evidence, the Court is anxious to give particular scrutiny to that evidence, given the cost such evidence usually involves and the need to focus that evidence. In cases where preliminary issues are sought, the Court will need to examine the formulation of those issues and discuss whether they are really appropriate.

Applications

D8.4

(a) If by the time of the case management conference a party wishes to apply for an order in respect of a matter not covered by Questions (1)–(16) in the case management information sheet, the application should be made at the case management conference.

(b) In some cases notice of such an application may be given in the case management information sheet itself: see section D8.5(c).

(c) In all other cases the applicant should ensure that an application notice and any supporting evidence is filed and served in time to enable the application to be heard at the case management conference.

Materials: case management information sheet and case management bundle

D8.5

(a) All parties attending a case management conference must complete a case management information sheet: PD58 § 10.7. A standard form of case management information sheet is set out in Appendix 6. The information sheet is intended to include reference to all applications which the parties would wish to make at a case management conference.

(b) A completed case management information sheet must be provided by each party to the court (and copied to all other parties) at least 7 days before the case management conference.

(c) Applications not covered by the standard questions raised in the case management information sheet should be entered under Question (17). No other application notice is necessary if written evidence will not be involved and the 7 day notice given by entering the application on the information sheet will in all the circumstances be sufficient to enable all other parties to deal with the application.

D8.6 The case management bundle must be provided to the court at least 7 days before the case management conference: PD58 § 10.8.

The hearing

D8.7 The court's power to give directions at the case management conference is to be found in rules 3.1 and 58.13(4). At the case management conference the judge will:

    (i) discuss the issues in the case by reference to the draft list of issues, and settle a list of issues;

    (ii) discuss the requirements of the case (including issues of disclosure by reference to the disclosure schedule or schedules), with the advocates retained in the case;

    (iii) fix the entire pre–trial timetable, or, if that is not practicable, fix as much of the pre–trial timetable as possible; and

    (iv) in appropriate cases make an ADR order.

D8.8 At the Case Management Conference, and again at the Pre–Trial Review, active consideration will be given, by reference to the list of issues, to the possibility of the trial or summary determination of a preliminary issue or issues the resolution of which is likely to shorten the proceedings. An example is a relatively short question of law which can be tried without significant delay (though the implications of a possible appeal for the remainder of the case cannot be lost sight of). The court may suggest the trial of a preliminary issue, but it will rarely make an order without the concurrence of at least one of the parties. Active consideration will also be given to whether any issues are suitable for summary determination pursuant to CPR Part 24.

D8.9

(a) Rules 3.1(2) and 58.13(4) enable the court at the case management conference to stay the proceedings while the parties try to settle the case by alternative means. The case management information sheet requires the parties to indicate whether a stay for such purposes is sought.

(b) In an appropriate case an ADR order may be made without a stay of proceedings. The parties should consider carefully whether it may be possible to provide for ADR in the pre–trial timetable without affecting the date of trial.

(c) Where a stay has been granted for a fixed period for the purposes of ADR the court has power to extend it. If an extension of the stay is desired by all parties, a judge will normally be prepared to deal with an application for such an extension if it is made before the expiry of the stay by letter from the legal representatives of one of the parties. The letter should confirm that all parties consent to the application.

(d) An extension will not normally be granted for more than four weeks unless clear reasons are given to justify a longer period, but more than one extension may be granted.

The pre–trial timetable

D8.10 The pre–trial timetable will normally include:

(i) a progress monitoring date (see section D12 below); and

(ii) a direction that the parties attend upon the Clerk to the Commercial Court to obtain a fixed date for trial.

Variations to the pre–trial timetable

D8.11

(a) The parties may agree minor variations to the time periods set out in the pre–trial timetable without the case needing to be brought back to the court provided that the variation

(i) will not jeopardise the date fixed for trial;

(ii) does not relate to the progress monitoring date; and

(iii) does not provide for the completion after the progress monitoring date of any step which was previously scheduled to have been completed by that date.

(b) The court should be informed in writing of any such agreement.

D8.12 If in any case it becomes apparent that variations to the pre–trial timetable are required which do not fall within section D8.11 above, the parties should apply to have the case management conference reconvened immediately. The parties should not wait until the progress monitoring date.

D9 Case management conference: Part 8 claims

2A–69 D9 In a case commenced by the issue of a Part 8 claim form, a case management conference will normally take place on the first available date 6 weeks after service and filing of the defendant's evidence. At that case management conference the Court will make such pre–trial directions as are necessary, adapting (where useful in the context of the particular claim) those of the case management procedures used for a claim commenced by the issue of a Part 7 claim form.

D10 Case management conference: Part 20 claims

2A–70 D10.1 Wherever possible, any party who intends to make a Part 20 claim should do so before the hearing of the case management conference dealing with the main claim.

D10.2 Where permission to make a Part 20 claim is required it should be sought at the case management conference in the main claim.

D10.3 If the Part 20 claim is confined to a counterclaim by a defendant against a claimant alone, the court will give directions in the Part 20 claim at the case management conference in the main claim.

D10.4 If the Part 20 claim is not confined to a counterclaim by a defendant against a claimant alone, the case management conference in the main claim will be reconvened on the first available date 6 weeks after service by the defendant of the new party of parties to the proceedings.

D10.5 All parties to the proceedings (i.e. the parties to the main claim and the parties to the Part 20 claim) must attend the reconvened case management conference. There will not be a separate case management conference for the Part 20 claim alone.

D10.6 In any case involving a Part 20 claim the court will give case management directions at the same case management conferences as it gives directions for the main claim: PD58 § 12. The court will therefore normally only give case management directions at hearings attended by all parties to the proceedings.

D10.7 The provisions of D10.4, D10.5 and D10.6 apply equally to Part 20 claims brought by parties who are not also parties to the main claim.

D11 Management throughout the case

D11 The court will continue to take an active role in the management of the case **2A–71** throughout its progress to trial. Parties should be ready at all times to provide the court with such information and assistance as it may require for that purpose.

D12 Progress monitoring

Fixing the progress monitoring date

D12.1 The progress monitoring date will be fixed at the case management conference **2A–72** and will normally be after the date in the pre–trial timetable for exchange of witness statements and expert reports.

Progress monitoring information sheet

D12.2 At least 3 days (i.e. three clear days) before the progress monitoring date the parties must each send to the Case Management Unit (with a copy to all other parties) a progress monitoring information sheet to inform the court:

(i) whether they have complied with the pre–trial timetable, and if they have not, the respects in which they have not; and

(ii) whether they will be ready for a trial commencing on the fixed date specified in the pre–trial timetable, and if they will not be ready, why they will not be ready.

D12.3 A standard form of progress monitoring information sheet is set out in Appendix 12.

D12.4 The progress monitoring information sheets are referred to the judge in charge of the list.

D12.5 Upon considering progress monitoring information sheet, the court may, particularly if there has been significant non–compliance with the pre–trial timetable, direct a date by which further information sheet are to be sent to the court.

D13 Reconvening the case management conference

D13.1 If in the view of the court the information given in the progress monitoring **2A–73** sheets justifies this course, the court may direct that the case management conference be reconvened.

D13.2 At a reconvened hearing of the case management conference the court may make such orders and give such directions as it considers appropriate. If the court is of the view that due to the failure of the parties or any of them to comply with the case management timetable the trial cannot be fairly and efficiently conducted on the date fixed, it may vacate the trial date and make such order for costs as is appropriate.

D14 Pre–trial checklist

D14 Not later than three weeks before the date fixed for trial each party must send to **2A–74** the Listing Office (with a copy to all other parties) a completed checklist confirming final details for trial (a "pre–trial checklist") in the form set out in Appendix 13.

2A-75 **D15 Further information**

D15.1

(a) If a party declines to provide further information requested under Part 18, the solicitors or counsel who are to appear at the application for the parties concerned must communicate directly with each other in an attempt to reach agreement before any application is made to the court.

(b) No application for an order that a party provide further information will normally be listed for hearing without prior written confirmation from the applicant that the requirements of this section D15.1(a) have been complied with.

(c) The court will only order further information to be provided if satisfied that the information requested is strictly necessary to understand another party's case.

D15.2 Because it falls within the definition of a statement of case (see rule 2.3(1)) a response providing further information under CPR Part 18 must be verified by a statement of truth.

D16 Fixed trial dates

2A-76 D16.1 Most cases will be given fixed trial dates immediately after the pre–trial timetable has been set at the case management conference.

D16.2 A fixed date for trial is given on the understanding that if previous fixtures have been substantially underestimated or other urgent matters need to be heard, the trial may be delayed. Where such delay might cause particular inconvenience to witnesses or others involved in the trial, the Clerk to the Commercial Court should be informed well in advance of the fixed date.

D17 Estimates of length of trial

2A-77 D17.1 At the case management conference an estimate will be made of the minimum and maximum lengths of the trial. The estimate should include time for pre–trial reading by the judge and specify what time has been allowed for that purpose. The estimate will appear in the pre–trial timetable and will be the basis on which a date for trial will be fixed.

D17.2 The court examines with particular care longer estimates, and will wish to consider with the assistance of advocates whether in the case of particularly long trials all the issues in the trial should be heard at the same hearing: see section J2.

D17.3 If a party subsequently instructs new advocate(s) to appear on its behalf at the trial, the Listing Office should be notified of that fact within 14 days. Advocates newly instructed should review the estimate of the minimum and maximum lengths of the trial, and submit to the Listing Office a signed note revising or confirming the estimate as appropriate.

D17.4 A confirmed estimate of the minimum and maximum lengths of the trial, signed by the advocates who are to appear at the trial, should be attached to the pre–trial checklist.

D17.5 It is the duty of all advocates who are to appear at the trial to seek agreement, if possible, on the estimated minimum and maximum lengths of trial.

D17.6 The provisional estimate and (after it is given) the confirmed estimate must be kept under review by the advocates who are to appear at the trial. If at any stage an estimate needs to be revised, a signed revised estimate (whether agreed or not) should be submitted by the advocates to the Clerk to the Commercial Court.

D17.7 Accurate estimation of trial length is of great importance to the efficient functioning of the court. The court will be guided by, but will not necessarily accept, the estimates given by the parties.

D18 Pre–Trial Review and trial timetable

2A-78 D18.1 The court will order a pre–trial review in any case in which it considers it appropriate to do so.

D18.2 A pre–trial review will normally take place between 8 and 4 weeks before the date fixed for trial, but might be earlier in particularly long or complex cases.

D18.3 Whenever possible the pre–trial review will be conducted by the trial judge. It should be attended by the advocates who are to appear at the trial: PD58 § 11.2.

D18.4 Before the pre–trial review or, if there is not to be one, not later than 7 days before the trial is due to commence, the parties must attempt to agree a timetable for the trial providing for oral submissions, examinations in chief (if any) and cross–examination of witnesses of fact and expert witnesses: PD58 § 11.3. The claimant must file a copy of the draft timetable at least two days before the date fixed for the pre–trial review; any differences of view should be clearly identified and briefly explained: PD58 § 11.4. At the pre–trial review the judge may set a timetable for the trial and give such other directions for the conduct of the trial as he considers appropriate.

D19 Orders   2A–79

D19.1

(a) Except for orders made by the court on its own initiative under rule 3.3, and unless the court otherwise orders, every judgment or order will be drawn up by the parties and rule 40.3 is modified accordingly: rule 58.15(1).

(b) Consent orders are to be drawn up in accordance with the procedure described in section F9.

(c) All other orders are to be drawn up in draft by the parties and dated in the draft with the date of the judge's decision. The claimant is to have responsibility for drafting the order, unless it was made on the application of another party in which case that other party is to have the responsibility.

(d) Two copies of the draft, signed by the parties themselves, or by their solicitors or counsel, must be lodged with the Registry **within five days** of the decision of the court reflected in the draft.

D19.2 If the court orders that an act be done by a certain date without specifying a time for compliance, the latest time for compliance is 4.30 p.m. on the day in question.

D19.3 Orders that are required to be served must be served by the parties, unless the court otherwise directs.

E.

DISCLOSURE

E1 Generally

E1.1 The court will seek to ensure that disclosure is no wider than appropriate. **2A–80** Anything wider than standard disclosure will need to be justified.

E1.2 The obligations imposed by an order for disclosure continue until the proceedings come to an end. If, after a list of documents has been prepared and served, the existence (present or past) of further documents to which the order applies comes to the attention of the disclosing party, that party must prepare and serve a supplemental list.

E1.3 When making standard disclosure, a party is required to make a reasonable search for documents and state in his disclosure statement any limits that he has placed upon his search on the grounds that it would be unreasonable: rule 31.7.

E2 Procedure in advance of disclosure

E2.1 At the first case management conference the court will normally wish to consider **2A–81** one or more of the following:

   (i) ordering standard disclosure: rule 31.5(1);

   (ii) dispensing with or limiting standard disclosure: rule 31.5(2);

   (iii) ordering sample disclosure;

(iv) ordering disclosure in stages;

(v) ordering disclosure otherwise than by service of a list of documents, for example, by service of copy documents; and

(vi) ordering specific disclosure: rule 31.12.

E2.2 Among other things the court will normally wish to consider, by reference to the list of issues, the scope of standard disclosure. This is standard disclosure as defined by rule 31.6. Where standard disclosure is ordered a party is required to disclose only:

(i) the documents on which he relies; and

(ii) documents which—

— adversely affect his own case;

— adversely affect another party's case; or

— support another party's case; and

(iii) documents which he is required to disclose by any relevant practice direction.

E2.3 When considering disclosure at the first case management conference the court will normally be assisted by a disclosure schedule produced by each party, indicating (by reference to categories of documents, the location of documents and the period of time covered by the documentation and otherwise) what documentation the party recognises should be covered by standard disclosure, and whether he intends to place any, and if so what, limits upon his search on the basis that it would be unreasonable. The court will normally invite the observations of other parties upon the proposals in a disclosure schedule with a view to determining the proper extent of disclosure and any proper limits upon the search for documents before the parties make disclosure.

E2.4 A party who contends that to search for a category or class of document would be unreasonable (see rule 31.7) should also indicate this in his case management information sheet (see Appendix 6).

E2.5 All parties should have regard to issues which may specifically arise concerning electronic data and documents in accordance with 31PD.2A:

(a) Rule 31.4 contains a broad definition of a document. This extends to electronic documents, including e–mail and other electronic communications, word processed documents and databases. In addition to documents that are readily accessible from computer systems and other electronic devices and media, the definition covers those documents that are stored on servers and back–up systems and electronic documents that have been "deleted". It also extends to additional information stored and associated with electronic documents known as metadata. In most cases metadata is unlikely to be relevant.

(b) The parties should, prior to the first Case Management Conference, discuss any issues that may arise regarding searches for and the preservation of electronic documents. This may involve the parties providing information about the categories of electronic documents within their control, the computer systems, electronic devices and media on which any relevant documents may be held, the storage systems maintained by the parties and their document retention policies. In the case of difficulty or disagreement, the matter should be referred to a judge for directions at the earliest practical date, if possible at the first Case Management Conference. For this purpose the parties should before any such hearing co–operate to provide the court with an explicit account of the issues as to retrieval and disclosure of electronic documents which have arisen and where proportionality is in issue each party should provide the court with an informed estimate of the volume of documents involved and the cost of their retrieval and disclosure.

(c) The parties should co–operate at an early stage as to the format in which electronic copy documents are to be provided on inspection. In the case of difficulty or disagreement, the matter should be referred to a Judge for directions at the earliest practical date, if possible at the first Case Management Conference.

(d) The existence of electronic documents impacts upon the extent of the reasonable search required by Rule 31.7 for the purposes of standard disclosure. The factors that may be relevant in deciding the reasonableness of a search for electronic documents include (but are not limited to) the following:

(i) The number of documents involved.

(ii) The nature and complexity of the proceedings.

(iii) The ease and expense of retrieval of any particular document. This includes:

    (1) The accessibility of electronic documents or data including e–mail communications on computer systems, servers, back–up systems and other electronic devices or media that may contain such documents taking into account alterations or developments in hardware or software systems used by the disclosing party and/or available to enable access to such documents.

    (2) The location of relevant electronic documents, data, computer systems, servers, back–up systems and other electronic devices or media that may contain such documents.

    (3) The likelihood of locating relevant data.

    (4) The cost of recovering any electronic documents.

    (5) The cost of disclosing and providing inspection of any relevant electronic documents.

    (6) The likelihood that electronic documents will be materially altered in the course of recovery, disclosure or inspection.

(iv) The significance of any document which is likely to be located during the search.

(e) It may be reasonable to search some or all of the parties' electronic storage systems. In some circumstances, it may be reasonable to search for electronic documents by means of keyword searches (agreed as far as possible between the parties) even where a full review of each and every document would be unreasonable. There may be other forms of electronic search that may be appropriate in particular circumstances.

(f) Whether or not the parties draw to the court's attention particular areas of difference or disagreement, the court will normally at the first case management conference wish to consider whether the burden of dislcosure, in terms of time, cost and business disruption, can properly be reduced (for example by use of electronic search tools and deduplication software).

E3 Disclosure procedure

E3.1 In order to comply with rule 31.10(3) (which requires the list to identify the **2A–82** documents in a convenient order and manner and as concisely as possible) it will normally be necessary to list the documents in date order, to number them consecutively and to give each a concise description. In some cases, it will be useful to give each document a "Bates number" identifying the party disclosing it (such as C101 or D(1) 202). However, where there is a large number of documents all falling within a particular category the disclosing party may (unless otherwise ordered) list those documents as a category rather than individually.

E3.2 Each party to the proceedings must serve a separate list of documents. This applies even if two or more parties are represented by the same firm of solicitors.

E3.3 If the physical structure of a file may be of evidential value (e.g. a placing or chartering file) solicitors should make one complete copy of the file in the form in which they received it before any documents are removed for the purpose of giving disclosure or inspection.

E3.4 Unless the Court directs otherwise, the disclosure statement must comply with the requirements of rules 31.7(3) and 31.10(6). In particular, it should

(i) expressly state that the disclosing party believes the extent of the search to have been reasonable in all the circumstances; and

(ii) draw attention to any particular limitations on the extent of the search adopted for reasons of proportionality and give the reasons why they were adopted.

E3.5 The disclosure statement for standard disclosure should begin with the following words:

"[I/we], [name(s)] state that [I/we] have carried out a reasonable and proportionate search to locate all the documents which [I am/here name the party is] required to disclose under [the order made by the Court or the agreement in writing made between the parties] on the [] day of [] 20[]."

E3.6 The disclosure statement for standard disclosure should end with the following certificate:

"[I/we] certify that [I/we] understand the duty of disclosure and to the best of [my/our] knowledge [I have/here name the party has] carried out that duty. [I/we] certify that the list above is a complete list of all documents which are or have been in [my/here name the party's] control and which [I am/here name the party is] obliged under [the said order or the said agreement in writing] to disclose."

E3.7 An adapted version of practice form N265 (list of documents: standard disclosure) has been approved for use in the Commercial Court. The court may at any stage order that a disclosure statement be verified by affidavit.

E3.8

(a) For the purposes of PD31 § 4.3 the court will normally regard as an appropriate person any person who is in a position responsibly and authoritatively to search for the documents required to be disclosed by that party and to make the statements contained in the disclosure statement concerning the documents which must be disclosed by that party.

(b) A legal representative may in certain cases be an appropriate person.

(c) An explanation why the person is considered an appropriate person must still be given in the disclosure statement.

(d) A person holding an office or position in the disclosing party but who is not in a position responsibly and authoritatively to make the statements contained in the disclosure statement will not be regarded as an appropriate person to make the disclosure statement of the party.

(e) The court may of its own initiative or on application require that a disclosure statement also be signed by another appropriate person.

E4 Specific disclosure

2A–83 E4.1 Specific disclosure is defined by rule 31.12(2).

E4.2 An order for specific disclosure under rule 31.12 may in an appropriate case direct a party to carry out a thorough search for any documents which it is reasonable to suppose may adversely affect his own case or support the case of the party applying for disclosure or which may lead to a train of enquiry which has either of these consequences and to disclose any documents located as a result of that search: PD31 § 5.5.

E4.3 Where an application is made for specific disclosure the party from whom disclosure is sought should provide to the applicant and to the Court information as to the factors listed in E2.5(d) above and its documents retention policy, to the extent such information is relevant to the application. At the hearing of the application, the Court may take into account the factors listed in E2.5(d) as well as the width of the request and the conduct of the parties.

E4.4 The court may at any stage order that specific disclosure be verified by affidavit or witness statement.

E4.5 Applications for ship's papers are provided for in rule 58.14.

2A–84 ### E5 Authenticity

E5.1

(a) Where the authenticity of any document disclosed to a party is not admitted, that party must serve notice that the document must be proved at trial in accordance with CPR 32.19. Such notice must be served by the latest date for serving witness statements or within 7 days of disclosure of the document, whichever is later.

(b) Where, apart from the authenticity of the document itself, the date upon which a document or an entry in it is stated to have been made or the person by whom the document states that it or any entry in it was made or any other feature of the document is to be challenged at the trial on grounds which may require a witness to be called at the trial to support the contents of the document, such challenge

(i) must be raised in good time in advance of the trial to enable such witness or witnesses to be called;

(ii) the grounds of challenge must be explicitly identified in the skeleton argument or outline submissions in advance of the trial.

(c) Where, due to the late disclosure of a document it or its contents or character cannot practicably be challenged within the time limits prescribed in (a) or (b), the challenge may only be raised with the permission of the court and having regard to the Overriding Objective (CPR 1.1).

F.

APPLICATIONS

F1 Generally

F1.1

(a) Applications are governed by CPR Part 23 and PD23 as modified by rule 58 and PD58. As a result

(i) PD23 § § 1 and 2.3–2.6 do not apply;

(ii) PD23 § § 2.8 and 2.10 apply only if the proposed (additional) application will not increase the time estimate (including the estimate for the judge's pre-hearing reading time) already given for the hearing for which a date has been fixed; and

(iii) PD23 § 3 is subject in all cases to the judge's agreeing that the application may proceed without an application notice being served.

(b) An adapted version of practice form **N244** (application notice) has been approved for use in the Commercial Court.

F1.2 An application for a consent order must include a draft of the proposed order signed on behalf of all parties to whom it relates: PD58 § 14.1.

F1.3 The requirement in PD23 § 12.1 that a draft order be supplied on disk does not apply in the Commercial Court since orders are generally drawn up by the parties: PD58 § 14.2.

Service

F1.4 Application notices are served by the parties, not by the court: PD58 § 9.

Evidence

F1.5

(a) Particular attention is drawn to PD23 § 9.1 which points out that even where no specific requirement for evidence is set out in the Rules or Practice Directions the court will in practice often need to be satisfied by evidence of the facts that are relied on in support of, or in opposition to, the application.

(b) Where convenient the written evidence relied on in support of an application may be included in the application notice, which may be lengthened for this purpose: see rule 32.6(2).

Time for service of evidence

F1.6 The time allowed for the service of evidence in relation to applications is governed by PD58 § 13.

Hearings

F1.7

(a) Applications (other than arbitration applications) will be heard in public in accordance with rule 39.2, save where otherwise ordered.

(b) With certain exceptions, arbitration applications will normally be heard in private: rule 62.10(3). See section O.

(c) An application without notice for a freezing injunction or a search order will often need to be heard in private in the interests of justice and therefore be heard in private: see rule 39.2(3).

F1.8 Parties should pay particular attention to PD23 § 2.9 which warns of the need to anticipate the court's wish to review the conduct of the case and give further management directions. The parties should be ready to give the court their assistance and should be able to answer any questions that the court may ask for this purpose.

F1.9 PD23 § § 6.1–6.5 and § 7 deal with the hearing of applications by telephone (other than an urgent applications out of court hours) and the hearing of applications using video–conferencing facilities. These methods may be considered when an application needs to be made before a particular Commercial Judge who is currently on circuit. In most other cases applications are more conveniently dealt with in person.

F2 Applications without notice

2A–86 F2.1 All applications should be made on notice, even if that notice has to be short, unless

(i) any rule or Practice Direction provides that the application may be made without notice; or

(ii) there are good reasons for making the application without notice, for example, because notice would or might defeat the object of the application.

F2.2 Where an application without notice does not involve the giving of undertakings to the court, it will normally be made and dealt with on paper, as, for example, applications for permission to serve a claim form out of the jurisdiction, and applications for an extension of time in which to serve a claim form.

F2.3 Any application for an interim injunction or similar remedy will require an oral hearing.

F2.4

(a) A party wishing to make an application without notice which requires an oral hearing before a judge should contact the Clerk to the Commercial Court at the earliest opportunity.
(b) If a party wishes to make an application without notice at a time when no commercial judge is available he should apply to the Queen's Bench Judge in Chambers (see section P1.1).

F2.5 On all applications without notice it is the duty of the applicant and those representing him to make full and frank disclosure of all matters relevant to the application.

F2.6 The papers lodged for the application should include two copies of a draft of the order sought. Save in exceptional circumstances where time does not permit, all the evidence relied upon in support of the application and any other relevant documents must be lodged in advance with the Clerk to the Commercial Court. If the application is urgent, the Clerk to the Commercial Court should be informed of the fact and of the reasons for the urgency. Counsel's estimate of reading time likely to be required by the court should also be provided.

F3 Expedited applications

2A–87 F3.1 The Court will expedite the hearing of an application on notice in cases of sufficient urgency and importance.

F3.2 Where a party wishes to make an expedited application a request should be made to the Clerk to the Commercial Court on notice to all other parties.

2A–88 F4 Paper applications

F4.1

(a) Although contested applications are usually best determined at an oral hearing, some applications may be suitable for determination on paper.

(b) Attention is drawn to the provisions of rule 23.8 and PD23 § 11. If the applicant considers that the application is suitable for determination on paper, he should ensure before lodging the papers with the court

    (i) that the application notice together with any supporting evidence has been served on the respondent;

    (ii) that the respondent has been allowed the appropriate period of time in which to serve evidence in opposition;

    (iii) that any evidence in reply has been served on the respondent; and

    (iv) that there is included in the papers

        (A) the written consent of the respondent to the disposal of the application without a hearing; or

        (B) a statement by the applicant of the grounds on which he seeks to have the application disposed of without a hearing, together with confirmation that the application and a copy of the grounds for disposing of without a hearing have been served on the respondent and a statement of when they were served.

        (c) Where a previous application in the case has been determined by a judge of the Commercial Court whether at a hearing or on paper, it is helpful for the application to indicate clearly when lodging the papers, the identity of the judge who last considered the matter, so that so far as reasonably practicable, the papers can be placed before that judge.

(d) Only in exceptional cases will the court dispose of an application without a hearing in the absence of the respondent's consent.

F4.2

(a) Certain applications relating to the management of proceedings may conveniently be made in correspondence without issuing an application notice.

(b) It must be clearly understood that such applications are not applications without notice and the applicant must therefore ensure that a copy of the letter making the application is sent to all other parties to the proceedings.

(c) Accordingly, the following procedure should be followed when making an application of this kind:

    (i) the applicant should first ascertain whether the application is opposed by the other parties;

    (ii) if it is, the applicant should apply to the court by letter stating the nature of the order which it seeks and the grounds on which the application is made;

    (iii) a copy the letter should be sent (by email or fax, where possible) to all other parties at the same time as it is sent to the court;

    (iv) any other party wishing to make representations should do so by letter within two days (i.e. two clear days) of the date of the applicant's letter of application. The representations should be sent (by email or fax, where possible) to the applicant and all other parties at the same time as they are sent to the court;

    (v) the court will advise its decision by letter to the applicant. The applicant must forthwith copy the court's letter to all other parties, by email or fax where possible.

F5 Ordinary applications

F5.1 Applications likely to require an oral hearing lasting half a day or less are **2A–89** regarded as "ordinary" applications.

F5.2 Ordinary applications will generally be heard on Fridays, but may be heard on other days. Where possible, the Listing Office will have regard to the availability of advocates when fixing hearing dates.

F5.3

(a) The timetable for ordinary applications is set out in PD58 § 13.1 and is as follows:

    (i) evidence in support must be filed and served with the application;

    (ii) evidence in answer must be filed and served within 14 days thereafter;

    (iii) evidence in reply (if any) must be filed and served within 7 days thereafter.

(b) This timetable may be abridged or extended by agreement between the parties provided that any date fixed for the hearing of the application is not affected: PD58 § 13.4. In appropriate cases, this timetable may be abridged by the Court.

F5.4 An application bundle (see section F11) must be lodged with the Listing Office by 1 p.m. one clear day before the date fixed for the hearing. The case management bundle will also be required on the hearing; this file will be passed by the Listing Office to the judge.

F5.5 Save in very short and simple cases, skeleton arguments must be provided by all parties. These must be lodged with the Listing Office and served on the advocates for all other parties to the application by 1 p.m. on the day before the date fixed for the hearing (i.e. the immediately preceding day) together with an estimate of the reading time likely to be required by the court. Guidelines on the preparation of skeleton arguments are set out in Part 1 of Appendix 9.

[EDITORIAL NOTE: The next paragraph is F5.7]

F5.7 Thus, for an application estimated for a half day or less and due to be heard on a Friday:

    (i) the application bundle must be lodged by 1 p.m. on Wednesday; and

    (ii) skeleton arguments must be lodged by 1 p.m. on Thursday.

If, for reasons outside the reasonable control of the advocate a skeleton argument cannot be delivered to the Listing Office by 1pm, the clerk of the judge hearing the application should be informed before 1pm and the skeleton argument should be delivered direct to the clerk of the judge listed to hear the application and in any event not later than 4pm the day before the hearing.

F5.8 The applicant should, as a matter of course, provide all other parties to the application with a copy of the application bundle at the cost of the receiving party. Further copies should be supplied on request, again at the cost of the receiving party.

F5.9 Problems with the lodging of bundles or skeleton arguments should be notified to the Clerk to the Commercial Court as far in advance as possible. **If the application bundle or skeleton argument is not lodged by the time specified, the application may be stood out of the list without further warning.**

F6 Heavy applications

2A–90 F6.1 Applications likely to require an oral hearing lasting more than half a day are regarded as "heavy" applications.

F6.2 Heavy applications normally involve a greater volume of evidence and other documents and more extensive issues. They accordingly require a longer lead–time for preparation and exchange of evidence. Where possible the Listing Office will have regard to the availability of advocates when fixing hearing dates.

F6.3 The timetable for heavy applications is set out in PD58 § 13.2 and is as follows:

    (i) evidence in support must be filed and served with the application;

    (ii) evidence in answer must be filed and served within 28 days thereafter;

    (iii) evidence in reply (if any) must be filed and served as soon as possible, and in any event within 14 days of service of the evidence in answer.

F6.4 An application bundle (see section F11) must be lodged with the Listing Office by 4 p.m. two days (i.e. two clear days) before the date fixed for the hearing together with a reading list and an estimate for the reading time likely to be required by the court as agreed between the counsel or other advocates to appear on the application. The case management bundle will also be required on the hearing; this file will be passed by the Listing Office to the judge.

F6.5 Skeleton arguments must be lodged with the Listing Office and served on the advocates for all other parties to the application as follows:

    (i) applicant's skeleton argument (with chronology unless one is unnecessary, and with a dramatis personae if one is warranted), by 4 p.m. two days (i.e. two clear days) before the hearing;

(ii) respondent's skeleton argument, by 4 p.m. one day (i.e. one clear day) before the hearing.

Guidelines on the preparation of skeleton arguments are set out in Part 1 of Appendix 9.

F6.6 Thus, for an application estimated for more than half a day and due to be heard on a Thursday:
(i) the application bundle and the applicant's skeleton argument must be lodged by 4 p.m. on Monday;
(ii) the respondent's skeleton argument must be lodged by 4 p.m. on Tuesday.

F6.7 The applicant must, as a matter of course, provide all other parties to the application with a copy of the application bundle at the cost of the receiving party. Further copies must be supplied on request, again at the cost of the receiving party.

F6.8 Problems with the lodging of bundles or skeleton arguments should be notified to the Clerk to the Commercial Court as far in advance as possible. **If the application bundle or skeleton argument is not lodged by the time specified, the application may be stood out of the list without further warning**.

F7 Evidence

F7.1 Although evidence may be given by affidavit, it should generally be given by witness statement, except where it can conveniently be given in the application notice (see rule 32.6(2) and except where PD32 requires evidence to be given on affidavit (as, for example, in the case of an application for a freezing injunction or a search order: PD32 § 1.4). In other cases the Court may order that evidence be given by affidavit: PD32 § 1.4(1) and 1.6. **2A–91**

F7.2 Witness statements and affidavits must comply with the requirements of PD32, save that photocopy documents should be used unless the court orders otherwise.

F7.3

(a) Witness statements must be verified by a statement of truth signed by the maker of the statement: rule 22.1.
(b) At hearings other than trial an applicant may rely on the application notice itself, and a party may rely on his statement of case, if the application notice or statement of case (as the case may be) is verified by a statement of truth: rule 32.6(2).
(c) A statement of truth in an application notice may also be signed as indicated in sections C1.8 and C1.9 above.

F7.4 Proceedings for contempt of court may be brought against a person who makes, or causes to be made, a false statement in a witness statement (or any other document verified by a statement of truth) without an honest belief in its truth: rule 32.14(1).

F8 Reading time

2A–92

F8

(a) It is essential for the efficient conduct of the court's business that the parties inform the court of the reading required in order to enable the judge to dispose of the application within the time allowed for the hearing and of the time likely to be required for that purpose. Accordingly
(i) in the case of all heavy applications and in the case of other applications if any advocate considers that the time required for reading is likely to exceed one hour, each party must lodge with the Listing Office not later than 1pm two clear days before the hearing of the application a reading list with an estimate of the time likely to be required by the court for reading;
(ii) in the case of all other applications each party must lodge with the Listing Office by 1pm on the day before the date fixed for the hearing of an application (ie the immediately preceding day) a reading list with an estimate of the time required to complete the reading;
(iii) each reading list should identify the material on both sides which the court needs to read.

(iv) if possible, the parties should provide the reading list in an agreed document, but if necessary each party should provide its own list.

(b) Failure to comply with these requirements may result in the adjournment of the hearing.

2A–93 F9 Applications disposed of by consent

F9.1

(a) Consent orders may be submitted to the court in draft for approval and initialling without the need for attendance.

(b) Two copies of the draft, one of which (or a counterpart) must be signed on behalf of all parties to whom it relates, should be lodged at the Registry. The copies should be undated. The order will be dated with the date on which the judge initials it, but that does not prevent the parties acting on their agreement immediately if they wish.

(c) The parties should act promptly in lodging the copies at the Registry. If it is important that the orders are made by a particular date, that fact (and the reasons for it) should be notified in writing to the Registry.

F9.2 For the avoidance of doubt, this procedure is not normally available in relation to a case management conference or a pre–trial review. Whether or not the parties are agreed as between themselves on the directions that the court should be asked to consider giving at a case management conference or a pre–trial review, attendance will normally be required. See section D8.3.

F9.3 Where an order provides a time by which something is to be done the order should wherever possible state the particular date by which the thing is to be done rather than specify a period of time from a particular date or event: rule 2.9.

F10 Hearing dates, time estimates and time limits

2A–94 F10.1 Dates for the hearing of applications to be attended by advocates are normally fixed after discussion with the counsel's clerks or with the solicitor concerned.

F10.2 The efficient working of the court depends on accurate estimates of the time needed for the oral hearing of an application including a considered estimate of the judge's pre–hearing reading. Over–estimating can be as wasteful as under–estimating.

F10.3 Subject to section F10.4, the Clerk to the Commercial Court will not accept or act on time estimates for the oral hearing of applications where those estimates exceed the following maxima:

Application to set aside service:	4 hours
Application for summary judgment:	4 hours
Application to set aside or vary interim remedy:	4 hours
Application to set aside or vary default judgment:	2 hours
Application to amend statement of case:	1 hour
Application for specific disclosure:	1 hour
Application for security for costs:	1 hour

F10.4 A longer listing time will only be granted upon application in writing specifying the additional time required and giving reasons why it is required. A copy of the written application should be sent to the advocates for all other parties in the case at the same time as it is sent to the Listing Office.

F10.5

(a) Not later than five days before the date fixed for the hearing the applicant must provide the Listing Office with his current estimate of the time required to dispose of the application.

(b) If at any time either party considers that there is a material risk that the hearing of the application will exceed the time currently allowed it must inform the Listing Office immediately.

F10.6

(a) All time estimates should be given on the assumption that the judge will have read in advance the skeleton arguments and the documents identified in the reading list. In this connection attention is drawn to section F8.

(b) A time estimate for an ordinary application should allow time for judgment and consequential matters; a time estimate for a heavy application should not.

F10.7 Save in the situation referred to at section F10.8, a separate estimate must be given for each application, including any application issued after, but to be heard at the same time as, another application.

F10.8 A separate estimate need not be given for any application issued after, but to be heard at the same time as, another application where the advocate in the case certifies in writing that

(i) the determination of the application first issued will necessarily determine the application issued subsequently; or

(ii) the matters raised in the application issued subsequently are not contested.

F10.9 If it is found at the hearing that the time required for the hearing has been significantly underestimated, the judge hearing the application may adjourn the matter and may make any special costs orders (including orders for the immediate payment of costs and wasted costs orders) as may be appropriate.

F10.10 Failure to comply with the requirements for lodging bundles for the application will normally result in the application not being heard on the date fixed at the expense of the party in default (see further sections F5.9 and F6.8 above). An order for immediate payment of costs may be made.

F11 Application bundles   2A–95

F11.1

(a) Attention is drawn to appendix 10, which deals with the preparation of bundles.

(b) Bundles for use on applications may be compiled in any convenient manner but must contain the following documents (preferably in separate sections in the following order)

(i) a copy of the application notice;

(ii) a draft of the order which the applicant seeks;

(iii) a copy of the statements of case;

(iv) copies of any previous orders which are relevant to the application;

(v) copies of the witness statements and affidavits filed in support of, or in opposition to, the application, together with any exhibits.

(c) Copies of the statements of case and of previous orders in the action should be provided in a separate section of the bundle. They should not be exhibited to witness statements.

(d) Witness statements and affidavits previously filed in the same proceedings should be included in the bundle at a convenient location. They should not be exhibited to witness statements.

(e) Where for the purpose of the application it is likely to be necessary for the court to read in chronological order correspondence or other documents located as exhibits to different affidavits or witness statements, copies of such documents should be filed and paged in chronological order in a separate composite bundle or bundles which should be agreed between the parties. If time does not permit agreement on the contents of the composite bundle, it is the responsibility of the applicant to prepare the composite bundle and to lodge it with the Listing Office by 4pm two clear days before the hearing in the case of heavy applications and one clear day before the hearing in the case of all other applications.

F12 Chronologies, indices and dramatis personae

F12.1 For most applications it is of assistance for the applicant to provide a **2A–96** chronology which should be cross–referenced to the documents. Dramatis personae are often useful as well.

F12.2 Guidelines on the preparation of chronologies and indices are set out in Part 2 of Appendix 9.

F13 Authorities

2A–97 F13.1 On some applications there will be key authorities that it would be useful for the judge to read before the oral hearing of the application. Copies of these authorities should be provided with the skeleton arguments.

F13.2 It is also desirable for bundles of the authorities on which the parties wish to rely to be provided to the judge hearing the application as soon as possible after skeleton arguments have been exchanged.

F13.3 Authorities should only be cited when they contain some principle of law relevant to an issue arising on the application and where their substance is not to be found in the decision of a court of higher authority.

F14 Costs

2A–98 F14.1 Costs are dealt with generally at section J13.

F14.2 Reference should be also be made to the rules governng the summary assessment of costs for shorter hearings contained in Parts 43 and 44. Active consideration will generally be given by the court to adopting the summary assessment procedure in all cases where the schedule of costs of the successful party is no more than £100,000, but the parties should always be prepared for the court to assess costs summarily even where the costs exceed this amount.

F14.3 In carrying out a summary assessment of costs, the court may have regard amongst other matters to
    (i) advice from a Commercial Costs Judge or from the Chief Costs Judge on costs of specialist solicitors and counsel;
    (ii) any survey published by the London Solicitors Litigation Association showing the average hourly expense rate for solicitors in London;
    (iii) any information provided to the court at its request by one or more of the specialist associations (referred to at section A4.2) on average charges by specialist solicitors and counsel.

F14.4 Reference should also be made to CPR 44.3(8). Active consideration will generally be given by the court to making an order for a payment on account of costs if they are not assessed summarily.

F15 Interim injunctions

2A–99 *Generally*

F15.1

(a) Applications for interim injunctions are governed by CPR Part 25.
(b) Applications must be made on notice in accordance with the procedure set out in CPR Part 23 unless there are good reasons for proceeding without notice.

F15.2 A party who wishes to make an application for an interim injunction must give the Clerk to the Commercial Court as much notice as possible.

F15.3

(a) Except when the application is so urgent that there has not been any opportunity to do so, the applicant must issue his claim form and obtain the evidence on which he wishes to rely in support of the application before making the application.
(b) On applications of any weight, and unless the urgency means that this is not possible, the applicant should provide the court at the earliest opportunity with a skeleton argument.
(c) An affidavit, and not a witness statement, is required on an application for a freezing order or a search order: PD25 § 3.1.

Fortification of undertakings

F15.4

(a) Where the applicant for an interim remedy is not able to show sufficient assets within the jurisdiction of the Court to provide substance to the undertakings given, particularly the undertaking in damages, he may be required to reinforce his undertakings by providing security.
(b) Security will be ordered in such form as the judge decides is appropriate but may, for example, take the form of a payment into court, a bond issued by an insurance company or a first demand guarantee or standby credit issued by a first–class bank.
(c) In an appropriate case the judge may order a payment to be made to the applicant's solicitors to be held by them as officers of the court pending further order. Sometimes the undertaking of a parent company may be acceptable.

Form of order

F15.5 Standard forms of wording for freezing injunctions and search orders are set out in Appendix 5. The forms have been adapted for use in the Commercial Court and should be followed unless the judge hearing a particular application orders otherwise.

F15.6 A phrase indicating that an interim remedy is to remain in force until judgment or further order means that it remains in force until the delivery of a final judgment. If an interim remedy continuing after judgment is required, say until judgment has been satisfied, an application to that effect must be made (see further section K1).

F15.7 It is good practice to draft an order for an interim remedy so that it includes a proviso which permits acts which would otherwise be a breach of the order to be done with the written consent of the solicitor of the other party or parties. This enables the parties to agree in effect to variations (or the discharge) of the order without the necessity of coming back to the court.

Freezing injunctions

F15.8

(a) Freezing injunctions made on an application without notice will provide for a return date, unless the judge otherwise orders: PD25 § 5.1(3). In the usual course, the return date given will be a Friday (unless a date for a case management conference has already been fixed, in which event the return date given will in the usual course be that date).
(b) If, after service or notification of the injunction, one or more of the parties considers that more than 15 minutes will be required to deal with the matter on the return date the Listing Office should be informed forthwith and in any event no later than 4 p.m. on the Wednesday before the Friday fixed as the return date.
(c) If the parties agree, the return date may be postponed to a later date on which all parties will be ready to deal with any substantive issues. In this event, an agreed form of order continuing the injunction to the postponed return date should be submitted for consideration by a judge and if the order is made in the terms submitted there will be no need for the parties to attend on the day originally fixed as the return date.
(d) In such a case the defendant and any other interested party will continue to have liberty to apply to vary or set aside the order.

F15.9 A provision for the defendant to give notice of any application to discharge or vary the order is usually included as a matter of convenience but it is not proper to attempt to fetter the right of the defendant to apply without notice or on short notice if need be.

F15.10 As regards freezing orders in respect of assets outside the jurisdiction, the standard wording in relation to effects on third parties should normally incorporate wording to enable overseas branches of banks or similar institutions which have offices within the jurisdiction to comply with what they reasonably believe to be their obligations under the laws of the country where the assets are located or under the proper law of the relevant banking or other contract relating to such assets.

F15.11 Any bank or third party served with, notified of or affected by a freezing injunction may apply to the court without notice to any party for directions, or notify the court in writing without notice to any party, in the event that the order affects or may affect the position of the bank or third party under legislation, regulations or procedures aimed to prevent money laundering.

Search orders

F15.12 Attention is drawn to the detailed requirements in respect of search orders set out in PD25 § § 7.1–8.3. The applicant for the search order will normally be required to undertake not to inform any third party of the search order or of the case until after a specified date.

Applications to discharge or vary freezing injunctions and search orders

F15.13 Applications to discharge or vary freezing injunctions and search orders are treated as matters of urgency for listing purposes. Those representing applicants for discharge or variation should ascertain before a date is fixed for the hearing whether, having regard to the evidence which they wish to adduce, the claimant would wish to adduce further evidence in opposition. If so, all reasonable steps must be taken by all parties to agree upon the earliest practicable date at which they can be ready for the hearing, so as to avoid the last minute need to vacate a fixed date. In cases of difficulty the matter should be referred to a judge who may be able to suggest temporary solutions pending the hearing.

F15.14 If a freezing injunction or a search order is discharged on an application to discharge or vary, or on the return date, the judge will consider whether it is appropriate that he should assess damages at once and direct immediate payment by the applicant. Where the judge considers that the hearing for the assessment of damages should be postponed to a future date he will give such case management directions as may be appropriate for the assessment hearing, including, if necessary, disclosure of documents and exchange of witness statements and experts' reports.

Applications under section 25 of the Civil Jurisdiction and Judgments Act 1982

F15.15 A Part 8 claim form (rather than an application notice: cf. rule 25.4(2)) must be used for an application under section 25 of the Civil Jurisdiction and Judgments Act 1982 ("Interim relief in England and Wales and Northern Ireland in the absence of substantive proceedings"). The modified Part 8 procedure used in the Commercial Court is referred to at section B4 above.

F16 Security for costs

2A–100 F16.1 Applications for security for costs are governed by rules 25.12–14.

F16.2 The applicable practice is set out in Appendix 16.

G.

ALTERNATIVE DISPUTE RESOLUTION ("ADR")

G1 Generally

2A–101 G1.1 While emphasising its primary role as a forum for deciding commercial cases, the Commercial Court encourages parties to consider the use of ADR (such as, but not confined to, mediation and conciliation) as an alternative means of resolving disputes or particular issues.

G1.2 Whilst the Commercial Court remains an entirely appropriate forum for resolving most of the disputes which are entered in the Commercial List, the view of the Commercial Court is that the settlement of disputes by means of ADR

(i) significantly helps parties to save costs;

(ii) saves parties the delay of litigation in reaching finality in their disputes;

(iii) enables parties to achieve settlement of their disputes while preserving their existing commercial relationships and market reputation;

(iv) provides parties with a wider range of solutions than those offered by litigation; and

(v) is likely to make a substantial contribution to the more efficient use of judicial resources.

G1.3 The Commercial Judges will in appropriate cases invite the parties to consider whether their dispute, or particular issues in it, could be resolved through ADR.

G1.4 Legal representatives in all cases should consider with their clients and the other parties concerned the possibility of attempting to resolve the dispute or particular issues by ADR and should ensure that their clients are fully informed as to the most cost effective means of resolving their dispute.

G1.5 Parties who consider that ADR might be an appropriate means of resolving the dispute or particular issues in the dispute may apply for directions at any stage, including before service of the defence and before the case management conference.

G1.6 At the case management conference if it should appear to the judge that the case before him or any of the issues arising in it are particularly appropriate for an attempt at settlement by means of ADR but that the parties have not previously attempted settlement by such means, he may invite the parties to use ADR.

G1.7 The judge may, if he considers it appropriate, adjourn the case for a specified period of time to encourage and enable the parties to use ADR. He may for this purpose extend the time for compliance by the parties or any of them with any requirement under the rules, the Guide or any order of the Court. The judge in making an order providing for ADR will normally take into account, when considering at what point in the pre–trial timetable there should be compliance with such an order, such matters as the costs likely to be incurred at each stage in the pre–trial timetable if the claim is not settled, the costs of a mediation or other means of dispute resolution, how far the prospects of a successful mediation or other means of dispute resolution are likely to be enhanced by completion of pleadings, disclosure of documents, provision of further information under CPR 18, exchange of factual witness statements or exchange of experts' reports.

G1.8 The Judge may further consider in an appropriate case making an ADR Order in the terms set out in Appendix 7.

G1.9

(a) The Clerk to the Commercial Court keeps some published information on individuals and bodies that offer ADR and arbitration services. If the parties are unable to agree upon a neutral individual or panel of individuals to act as a mediator or give an early neutral evaluation, the normal form of ADR order set out in Appendix 7 contains at paragraph 3 a mandatory requirement that the case management conference should be restored to enable the court to facilitate agreement on a neutral or panel of neutrals. In order to avoid the cost of a restored case management hearing, the parties may agree to send to the court their respective list of available neutrals, so as to enable the judge to suggest a name from those lists. In any other case the parties may by consent refer to the judge for assistance in reaching such agreement.
(b) The court will not recommend any individual or body to act as a mediator or arbitrator.

G1.10 At the case management conference or at any other hearing in the course of which the judge makes an order providing for ADR he may make such order as to the costs that the parties may incur by reason of their using or attempting to use ADR as may in all the circumstances seem appropriate. The orders for costs are normally costs in the case, meaning that if the claim is not settled, the costs of the ADR procedures, will follow the ultimate event, or that each side shall bear its own costs of those procedures if the case is not settled.

G1.11 In some cases it may be appropriate that an ADR order should be made following judgment if application is made for permission to appeal. In such cases the court may adjourn the application for permission to appeal while making an ADR order providing for ADR procedures to be completed within a specified time and, failing settlement with that period, for the application for permission to appeal to be restored.

G1.12 At the case management conference the court may consider that an order directed to encouraging bilateral negotiations between the parties' respective legal representatives is likely to be a more cost–effective and productive route to settlement then can be offered by a formal ADR or ENE Order. In such a case the court will set a date by which there is to be a meeting between respective solicitors and their respective clients' officials responsible for decision–taking in relation to the case in question.

G2 Early neutral evaluation

2A–102 G2.1 In appropriate cases and with the agreement of all parties the court will provide a without–prejudice, non–binding, early neutral evaluation ("ENE") of a dispute or of particular issues.

G2.2 The approval of the Judge in Charge of the List must be obtained before any ENE is undertaken.

G2.3 If, after discussion with the advocates representing the parties, it appears to a judge that an ENE is likely to assist in the resolution of the dispute or of particular issues, he will, with the agreement of the parties, refer the matter to the Judge in Charge of the List.

G2.4

(a) The Judge in Charge of the List will nominate a judge to conduct the ENE.
(b) The judge who is to conduct the ENE will give such directions for its preparation and conduct as he considers appropriate.

G2.5 The judge who conducts the ENE will take no further part in the case, either for the purpose of the hearing of applications or as the judge at trial, unless the parties agree otherwise.

H.

Evidence for Trial

H1 Witnesses of fact

Preparation and form of witness statements

2A–103 H1.1 Witness statements must comply with the requirements of PD32. The following points are also emphasised

(i) the function of a witness statement is to set out in writing the evidence in chief of the witness; as far as possible, therefore, the statement should be in the witness's own words;

(ii) it should be as concise as the circumstances of the case allow without omitting any significant matters;

(iii) it should not contain lengthy quotations from documents;

(iv) it is seldom necessary to exhibit documents to a witness statement;

(v) it should not engage in (legal or other) argument;

(vi) it must indicate which of the statements made in it are made from the witness's own knowledge and which are made on information or belief, giving the source for any statement made on information or belief;

(vii) it must contain a statement by the witness that he believes the matters stated in it are true; proceedings for contempt of court may be brought against a person if he makes, or causes to be made, a false statement in a witness statement without an honest belief in its truth: rule 32.14(1).

(viii) it must comply with any direction of the court about its length.

H1.2 It is usually convenient for a witness statement to follow the chronological sequence of events or matters dealt with (32PD19.2) . It is helpful for it to indicate to which issue in the list of issues the particular passage in the witness statement relates, either by a heading in the statement or in a marginal notation or by some other convenient method.

H1.3 It is improper to put pressure of any kind on a witness to give anything other than his own account of the matters with which his statement deals. It is also improper to serve a witness statement which is known to be false or which it is known the maker does not in all respects actually believe to be true.

Fluency of witnesses

H1.4 If a witness is not sufficiently fluent in English to give his evidence in English, the witness statement should be in the witness's own language and a translation provided.

H1.5 If a witness is not fluent in English but can make himself understood in broken English and can understand written English, the statement need not be in his own words provided that these matters are indicated in the statement itself. It must however be written so as to express as accurately as possible the substance of his evidence.

Witness statement as evidence in chief

H1.6

(a) Where a witness is called to give oral evidence, his witness statement is to stand as his evidence in chief unless the Court orders otherwise: rule 32.5(2).
(b) In an appropriate case the trial judge may direct that the whole or any part of a witness's evidence in chief is to be given orally. Notice of any such application for such an order should be given as early as is reasonably convenient. It is usually reasonable for any such application to be made at a pre–trial review if one is held.

Additional evidence from a witness

H1.7

(a) A witness giving oral evidence at trial may with the permission of the court amplify his witness statement and give evidence in relation to new matters which have arisen since the witness statement was served: rule 32.5(3). Permission will be given only if the Court considers that there is good reason not to confine the evidence of the witness to the contents of his witness statement: rule 32.5(4).
(b) A supplemental witness statement should normally be served where the witness proposes materially to add to, alter, correct or retract from what is in his original statement. Permission will be required for the service of a supplemental statement. Such application should be made at the pre–trial review or, if there is no pre–trial review, as early as possible before the start of the trial. If application is made at any later stage, the applicant must provide compelling evidence explaining its delay in adducing such evidence.
(c) It is the duty of all parties to ensure that the statements of all factual witnesses intended to be called or whose statements are to be tendered as hearsay statements should be exchanged simultaneously unless the court has otherwise ordered. Witnesses additional to those whose statements have been initially exchanged may only be called with the permission of the court which will not normally be given unless prompt application is made supported by compelling evidence explaining the late introduction of that witness's evidence.

Notice of decision not to call a witness

H1.8

(a) If a party decides not to call to give oral evidence at trial a witness whose statement has been served but wishes to rely upon the evidence, he must put in the statement as hearsay evidence unless the court otherwise orders: rule 32.5. If he proposes to put the evidence in as hearsay evidence, reference should be made to rule 33.2.
(b) If the party who has served the statement does not put it in as hearsay evidence, any other party may do so: rule 32.5(5).

Witness summonses

H1.9

(a) Rules 34.2–34.8 deal with witness summonses, including a summons for a witness to attend court or to produce documents in advance of the date fixed for trial.

(b) Witness summonses are served by the parties, not the court.

H2 Expert witnesses

Application for permission to call an expert witness

2A–104 H2.1 Any application for permission to call an expert witness or serve an expert's report should normally be made at the case management conference. The party applying for such permission will normally be expected to identify to which issue or issues in the list of issues the proposed expert evidence relates, and to propose any amendments to the list of issues that might be required for this purpose. The court may limit the length of an expert report.

H2.2 Parties should bear in mind that expert evidence can lead to unnecessary expense and they should be prepared to consider the use of single joint experts in appropriate cases. In many cases the use of single joint experts is not appropriate and each party will generally be given permission to call one expert in each field requiring expert evidence. These are referred to in the Guide as "separate experts".

H2.3 When the use of a single joint expert is contemplated, the court will expect the parties to co–operate in developing, and agreeing to the greatest possible extent, terms of reference for that expert. In most cases the terms of reference will (in particular) identify in detail what the expert is asked to do, identify any documentary materials he is asked to consider and specify any assumptions he is asked to make.

Provisions of general application in relation to expert evidence

H2.4 The provisions set out in Appendix 11 to the Guide apply to all aspects of expert evidence (including expert reports, meetings of experts and expert evidence given orally) unless the court orders otherwise. Parties should ensure that they are drawn to the attention of any experts they instruct at the earliest opportunity.

Form and content of expert's reports

H2.5 Expert's reports must comply with the requirements of PD35 § § 1 and 2.

H2.6

(a) In stating the substance of all material instructions on the basis of which his report is written as required by rule 35.10(3) and PD35 § 1.2(8) an expert witness should state the facts or assumptions upon which his opinion is based.

(b) The expert must make it clear which, if any, of the facts stated are within his own direct knowledge.

(c) If a stated assumption is, in the opinion of the expert witness, unreasonable or unlikely he should state that clearly.

(d) The expert's report must be limited to matters relevant to the issue or issues in the list of issues to which the relevant expert evidence relates and for which permission to call such expert evidence has been given.

H2.7 It is useful if a report contains a glossary of significant technical terms.

H2.8 Where the evidence of an expert, such as a surveyor, assessor, adjuster, or other investigator is to be relied upon for the purpose of establishing primary facts, such as the condition of a ship or other property as found by him at a particular time, as well as for the purpose of deploying his expertise to express an opinion on any matter related to or in connection with the primary facts, that part of his evidence which is to be relied upon to establish the primary facts, is to be treated as factual evidence to be incorporated into a factual witness statement to be exchanged in accordance with the order for the exchange of factual witness statements. The purpose of this practice is to avoid postponing disclosure of a party's factual evidence until service of expert reports.

Statement of truth

H2.9

(a) The report must be signed by the expert and must contain a statement of truth in accordance with Part 35.

(b) Proceedings for contempt of court may be brought against a person if he makes, or causes to be made, without an honest belief in its truth, a false statement in an expert's report verified in the manner set out in this section.

Request by an expert to the court for directions

H2.10 An expert may file with the court a written request for directions to assist him in carrying out his function as expert, but

(i) at least 7 days before he does so (or such shorter period as the court may direct) he should provide a copy of his proposed request to the party instructing him; and

(ii) at least 4 days before he does so (or such shorter period as the court may direct) he should provide a copy of his proposed request to all other parties.

Exchange of reports

H2.11 In appropriate cases the court will direct that the reports of expert witnesses be exchanged sequentially rather than simultaneously. The sequential exchange of expert reports may in many cases save time and costs by helping to focus the contents of responsive reports upon true rather than assumed issues of expert evidence and by avoiding repetition of detailed factual material as to which there is no real issue. Sequential exchange is likely to be particularly effective where experts are giving evidence of foreign law or are forensic accountants. This is an issue that the court will normally wish to consider at the case management conference.

Meetings of expert witnesses

H2.12 The court will normally direct a meeting or meetings of expert witnesses before trial. Sometimes it may be useful for there to be further meetings during the trial itself.

H2.13 The purposes of a meeting of experts are to give the experts the opportunity

(i) to discuss the expert issues;

(ii) to decide, with the benefit of that discussion, on which expert issues they share or can come to share the same expert opinion and on which expert issues there remains a difference of expert opinion between them (and what that difference is).

H2.14 Subject to section H2.16 below, the content of the discussion between the experts at or in connection with a meeting is without prejudice and shall not be referred to at the trial unless the parties so agree: rule 35.12(4).

H2.15 Subject to any directions of the court, the procedure to be adopted at a meeting of experts is a matter for the experts themselves, not the parties or their legal representatives.

H2.16 Neither the parties nor their legal representatives should seek to restrict the freedom of experts to identify and acknowledge the expert issues on which they agree at, or following further consideration after, meetings of experts.

H2.17 Unless the court orders otherwise, at or following any meeting the experts should prepare a joint memorandum for the court recording

(i) the fact that they have met and discussed the expert issues;

(ii) the issues on which they agree;

(iii) the issues on which they disagree; and

(iv) a brief summary of the reasons for their disagreement.

H2.18 If experts reach agreement on an issue that agreement shall not bind the parties unless they expressly agree to be bound by it.

Written questions to experts

H2.19

(a) Under rule 35.6 a party may, without the permission of the court, put written questions to an expert instructed by another party (or to a single joint expert) about his report. Unless the court gives permission or the other party agrees, such questions must be for the purpose only of clarifying the report.

(b) The court will pay close attention to the use of this procedure (especially where separate experts are instructed) to ensure that it remains an instrument for the helpful exchange of information. The court will not allow it to interfere with the procedure for an exchange of professional opinion at a meeting of experts, or to inhibit that exchange of professional opinion. In cases where (for example) questions that are oppressive in number or content are put, or questions are put for any purpose other than clarification of the report, the court will not hesitate to disallow the questions and to make an appropriate order for costs against the party putting them.

Documents referred to in experts' reports

H2.20 Unless they have already been provided on inspection of documents at the stage of disclosure, copies of any photographs, plans, analyses, measurements, survey reports or other similar documents relied on by an expert witness as well as copies of any unpublished sources must be provided to all parties at the same time as his report.

H2.21

(a) Rule 31.14(e) provides that (subject to rule 35.10(4)) a party may inspect a document mentioned in an expert's report. In a commercial case an expert's report will frequently, and helpfully, list all or many of the relevant previous papers (published or unpublished) or books written by the expert or to which the expert has contributed. Requiring inspection of this material may often be unrealistic, and the collating and copying burden could be huge.

(b) Accordingly, a party wishing to inspect a document in an expert report should (failing agreement) make an application to the court. The court will not permit inspection unless it is satisfied that it is necessary for the just disposal of the case and that the document is not reasonably available to the party making the application from an alternative source.

Trial

H2.22 At trial the evidence of expert witnesses is usually taken as a block, after the evidence of witnesses of fact has been given. The introduction of additional expert evidence after the commencement of the trial can have a severely disruptive effect. Not only is it likely to make necessary additional expert evidence in response, but it may also lead to applications for further disclosure of documents and also to applications to call further factual evidence from witnesses whose statements have not previously been exchanged. Accordingly, experts' supplementary reports must be completed and exchanged not later than the progress monitoring date and the introduction of additional expert evidence after that date will only be permitted upon application to the trial judge and if there are very strong grounds for admitting it.

H3 Evidence by video link

2A–105 H3.1 In an appropriate case permission may be given for the evidence of a witness to be given by video link. If permission is given the court will give directions for the conduct of this part of the trial.

H3.2 The party seeking permission to call evidence by video link should prepare and serve on all parties and lodge with the Court a memorandum dealing with the matters outlined in the Video Conferencing Guidance contained in Annex 3 to PD32 (see Appendix 14) and setting out precisely what arrangements are proposed. Where the proposal involves transmission from a location with no existing video–link facility, experience shows that questions of feasibility, timing and cost will require particularly close investigation.

H3.3 An application for permission to call evidence by video link should be made, if possible, at the case management conference or, at the latest, at any pre–trial review. However, an application may be made at an even later stage if necessary. Particular attention should be given to the taking of evidence by video link whenever a proposed witness will have to travel from a substantial distance abroad and his evidence is likely to last no more than half a day.

H3.4 In considering whether to give permission for evidence to be given in this way the court will be concerned in particular to balance any potential savings of costs against the inability to observe the witness at first hand when giving evidence.

H4 Taking evidence abroad

H4.1 In an appropriate case permission may be given for the evidence of a witness to be taken abroad. CPR Part 34 contains provisions for the taking of evidence by deposition, and the issue of letters of request. **2A–106**

H4.2 In a very exceptional case, and subject in particular to all necessary approvals being obtained and diplomatic requirements being satisfied, the court may be willing to conduct part of the proceedings abroad. However, if there is any reasonable opportunity for the witness to give evidence by video link, the court is unlikely to take that course.

J.

TRIAL

J1 Expedited trial

J1.1 The Commercial Court is able to provide an expedited trial in cases of sufficient urgency and importance. **2A–107**

J1.2 A party seeking an expedited trial should apply to the Judge in Charge of the Commercial List on notice to all parties at the earliest possible opportunity. The application should normally be made after issue and service of the claim form but before service of particulars of claim.

J2 Trials of issues

J2.1 The court may direct a separate trial of any issue under rule 3.1(2)(i). It will sometimes be advantageous to have a separate trial of particular issues with other issues being heard either by the same judge or by another judge of the Commercial Court or in another court or tribunal. For example, where liability is tried first in the Commercial Court, the assessment of damages can be referred to a judge of the Technology and Construction Court or to a Master, or the parties may choose to ask an arbitrator to decide them. The same approach can be applied to other factual questions. **2A–108**

J2.2 Under rule 3.1(2)(j), (k) and (l) the court may decide the order in which issues are to be tried, may exclude an issue from consideration and may dismiss or give judgment on a claim after a decision on a preliminary issue. The court is likely to consider this by reference to the list of issues. Particularly in long trials, it will sometimes be advantageous to exercise these powers, and accordingly hear the evidence relevant to some issues before moving on to the evidence relevant to others; and the judge will sometimes decide some issues before moving on to hear the evidence relevant to other issues.

J3 Documents for trial

J3.1 Bundles of documents for the trial must be prepared in accordance with Appendix 10. **2A–109**

J3.2 The number, content and organisation of the trial bundles must be approved by the advocates with the conduct of the trial.

J3.3 Apart from certain specified documents, trial bundles should include only necessary documents: 39PD3.2(11). Consideration must always be given to what documents are and are not relevant and necessary. Where the court is of the opinion that costs have been wasted by the copying of unnecessary documents it will have no hesitation in making a special order for costs against the person responsible.

J3.4 The number content and organisation of the trial bundles should be agreed in accordance with the following procedure

(i) the claimant must submit proposals to all other parties at least 6 weeks before the date fixed for trial; and

(ii) the other parties must submit details of additions they require and any suggestions for revision of the claimant's proposals to the claimant at least 4 weeks before the date fixed for trial.

This information must be supplied in a form that will be most convenient for the recipient to understand and respond to. The form to be used should be discussed between the parties before the details are supplied.

J3.5

(a) It is the responsibility of the claimant's legal representative to prepare and lodge the agreed trial bundles: see 39PD34.
(b) If another party wishes to put before the court a bundle that the claimant regards as unnecessary he must prepare and lodge it himself.

J3.6

(a) Preparation of the trial bundles must be completed not later than 2 weeks before the date fixed for trial unless the court orders otherwise.
(b) Any party preparing a trial bundle should, as a matter of course, provide all other parties who are to take part in the trial with a copy, at the cost of the receiving party: 39PD3.10. Further copies should be supplied on request, again at the cost of the receiving party.

J3.7 Unless the court orders otherwise, a full set of the trial bundles must be lodged with the Listing Office at least 7 days before the date fixed for trial.

J3.8 If bundles are lodged late, this may result in the trial not commencing on the date fixed, at the expense of the party in default. An order for immediate payment of costs may be made.

J3.9 If oral evidence is to be given at trial, the claimant should provide a clean unmarked set of all relevant trial bundles for use in the witness box: 39PD3.10. The claimant is responsible for ensuring that these bundles are kept up to date throughout the trial.

J4 Information technology at trial

2A–110 J4.1 The use of information technology at trial is encouraged where it is likely substantially to save time and cost or to increase accuracy.

J4.2 If any party considers that it might be advantageous to make use of information technology in preparation for, or at, trial, the matter should be raised at the first case management conference. This is particularly important if it is considered that document handling systems would assist disclosure and inspection of documents or the use of documents at trial. In any event, at the first case management conference, even if neither party itself raises the use of information technology, the parties must expect the court to consider its use, including its use in relation to trial bundles.

J4.3 Where information technology is to be used for the purposes of presenting the case at trial the same system must be used by all parties and must be made available to the court. In deciding whether and to what extent information technology should be used at the trial the court will have regard to the financial resources of the parties and will consider whether it is appropriate that, having regard to the parties' unequal financial resources, it is appropriate that the party applying for the use of such information technology should initially bear the cost subject to the court's ultimate order as to the overall costs following judgment.

J5 Reading lists, authorities and trial timetable

2A–111 J5.1 Unless the court orders otherwise, a single reading list approved by all advocates must be lodged with the Listing Office not later than 1 p.m. two days (i.e. two clear days) before the date fixed for trial together with an estimate of the time required for reading.

J5.2

(a) If any party objects to the judge reading any document in advance of the trial, the objection and its grounds should be clearly stated in a letter accompanying the trial bundles and in the skeleton argument of that party.
(b) Parties should consider in particular whether they have any objection to the judge's reading the witness statements before the trial.
(c) In the absence of objection, the judge will be free to read the witness statements and documents in advance.

J5.3

(a) A composite bundle of the authorities referred to in the skeleton arguments should be lodged with the Listing Office as soon as possible after skeleton arguments have been exchanged.
(b) Unless otherwise agreed, the preparation of the bundle of authorities is the responsibility of the claimant, who should provide copies to all other parties. Advocates should liaise in relation to the production of bundles of authorities to ensure that the same authority does not appear in more than one bundle.

J5.4 Cases which are unreported and which are also not included in the index of Judgments of the Commercial Court and Admiralty Court of England and Wales should normally only be cited where the advocate is ready to give an assurance that the transcript contains a statement of some relevant principle of law of which the substance, as distinct from some mere choice of phraseology, is not to be found in any judgment that has appeared in one of the general or specialised series of law reports. The index of Judgments of the Commercial Court and Admiralty Court of England and Wales can be found www.hmcourt–service.gov.uk/infoabout/admiralcomm/index.htm via the link to "Searchable index of court cases" (at bottom of the box on right hand side of Commercial Court and Admiralty Court).

J5.5

(a) When lodging the reading list the claimant should also lodge a trial timetable.
(b) A trial timetable may have been fixed by the judge at the pre–trial review (section D18.4 above). If it has not, a trial timetable should be prepared by the advocate(s) for the claimant after consultation with the advocate(s) for all other parties.
(c) If there are differences of view between the advocate(s) for the claimant and the advocate(s) for other parties, these should be shown.
(d) The trial timetable will provide for oral submissions, witness evidence and expert evidence over the course of the trial. On the first day of the trial the judge may fix the trial timetable, subject to any further order.
(e) The court may restrict evidence or submissions to ensure compliance with the trial timetable.

J6 Skeleton arguments etc. at trial

J6.1 Written skeleton arguments should be prepared by each party. Guidelines on **2A–112** the preparation of skeleton arguments are set out in Part 1 of Appendix 9.

J6.2 Unless otherwise ordered, the skeleton arguments should be served on all other parties and lodged with the court as follows

(i) by the claimant, not later than 1 p.m. two days (i.e. two clear days) before the start of the trial;

(ii) by each of the defendants, not later than 1 p.m. one day (i.e. one clear day) before the start of the trial.

J6.3 In heavier cases it will often be appropriate for skeleton arguments to be served and lodged at earlier times than indicated at section J6.2. The timetable should be discussed between the advocates and may be the subject of a direction in the pre–trial timetable or at any pre–trial review.

J6.4 The claimant should provide a chronology with his skeleton argument. Indices (i.e. documents that collate key references on particular points, or a substantive list of the contents of a particular bundle or bundles) and dramatis personae should also be provided where these are likely to be useful. Guidelines on the preparation of chronologies and indices are set out in Part 2 of Appendix 9.

J6.5 So far as possible skeleton arguments should be limited in length to 50 pages. Where the advocate or advocates for trial consider that it is not possible to comply with that limit, the matter should be discussed with the trial judge at the pre–trial review or in correspondence.

J7 Trial sitting days and hearing trials in public

2A–113 J7.1 Trial sitting days will not normally include Fridays.

J7.2 Where it is necessary in order to accommodate hearing evidence from certain witnesses or types of witness, the court may agree to sit outside normal hours.

J7.3 The general rule is that a hearing is to be in public: rule 39.2(1).

J8 Oral opening statements at trial

2A–114 J8.1 Oral opening statements should as far as possible be uncontroversial and in any event no longer than the circumstances require. Even in a very heavy case, oral opening statements may be very short. There remains some confusion amongst advocates as to what is necessary to adduce a document other than a witness statement or expert report in evidence. Whereas there can be no doubt that any disclosed document can be relied on as evidence of the facts contained in it or as evidence of its existence or the use to which it was put, see Civil Evidence Act 1995 S.2(4) and CPR 32.19 the mere inclusion of a document in the agreed trial bundles does not in itself mean that it is being adduced in evidence by either party: see Appendix 10. For this to happen either the parties must agree that the document in question is to be treated as put in evidence by one or other of them and the judge so informed or they must actively adduce the document in evidence by some other means. This might be done by counsel inviting the judge to read the document relied upon before the calling of oral evidence. The appropriate procedure will be a matter for the judgment of the advocates in each case. However, whichever course is adopted, it will not normally be appropriate for reliance to be placed in final speeches on any document, not already specifically adduced in evidence by one of the means described.

J8.2 At the conclusion of the opening statement for the claimant the advocates for each of the other parties will usually each be invited to make a short opening statement.

J9 Applications in the course of trial

2A–115 J9.1 It will not normally be necessary for an application notice to be issued for an application which is to be made during the course of the trial, but all other parties should be given adequate notice of the intention to apply.

J9.2 Unless the judge directs otherwise the parties should prepare skeleton arguments for the hearing of the application.

J10 Oral closing submissions at trial

2A–116 J10.1 All parties will be expected to make oral closing submissions, whether or not closing submissions have been made in writing. It is a matter for the advocate to consider how in all the circumstances these oral submissions should be presented.

J10.2 Unless the trial judge directs otherwise, the claimant will make his oral closing submissions first, followed by the defendant(s) in the order in which they appear on the claim form with the claimant having a right of reply.

2A–117 ### J11 Written closing submissions at trial

J11.1

(a) In a more substantial trial, the court will normally also require closing submissions in writing before oral closing submissions.

(b) In such a case the court will normally allow an appropriate period of time after the conclusion of the evidence to allow the preparation of these submissions.

(c) Even in a less substantial trial the court will normally require a skeleton argument on matters of law.

J12 Judgment

J12.1

(a) When judgment is reserved the judge may deliver judgment orally or by handing down a written judgment.

(b) If the judge intends to hand down a written judgment a copy of the draft text marked

"*Draft Judgment*"

and bearing the rubric:

" *This is a judgment to which the Practice Direction supplementing CPR Part 40 applies. It will be handed down on at in Court No . This Judgment is confidential to the parties and their legal representatives and accordingly neither the draft itself nor its substance may be disclosed to any other person or used in the public domain. The parties must take all reasonable steps to ensure that its confidentiality is preserved. No action is to be taken (other than internally) in response to the draft, before judgment has been formally pronounced. A breach of any of these obligations may be treated as a contempt of court. The official version of the judgment will be available from the Mechanical Recording Department of the Royal Courts of Justice once it has been approved by the judge.*

The court is likely to wish to hand down its judgment in an approved final form. Counsel should therefore submit any list of typing corrections and other obvious errors in writing (Nil returns are required) to the clerk to , by fax to 020 7947 or via email at , by on , so that changes can be incorporated, if the judge accepts them, in the handed down judgment."

will normally be supplied to the advocates one clear day before the judgment is to be delivered.

(c) Advocates should inform the judge's clerk not later than noon on the day before judgment is to be handed down of any typographical or other errors of a similar nature which the judge might wish to correct. This facility is confined to the correction of textual mistakes and is not to be used as the occasion for attempting to persuade the judge to change the decision on matters of substance.

(d) The requirement to treat the text as confidential must be strictly observed. Failure to do so amounts to a contempt of court.

J12.2

(a) Judgment is not delivered until it is formally pronounced in open court.

(b) Copies of the approved judgment will be made available to the parties, to law reporters and to any other person wanting a copy.

(c) The judge may direct that the written judgment stand as the definitive record and that no transcript need be made. Any editorial corrections made at the time of handing down will be incorporated in an approved official text as soon as possible, and the approved official text, so marked, will be available from the Mechanical Recording Department.

J12.3 If at the time of pronouncement of the judgment any party wishes to apply for permission to appeal to the Court of Appeal, that application should be supported by written draft grounds of appeal.

J13 Costs

J13.1 The rules governing the award and assessment of costs are contained in CPR **2A–119** Parts 43 to 48.

J13.2 The summary assessment procedure provided for in Parts 43 and 44 also applies to trials lasting one day or less.

K.

AFTER TRIAL

2A–120 **K1 Continuation, variation and discharge of interim remedies and undertakings**

K1.1

(a) Applications to continue, vary or discharge interim remedies or undertakings should be made to a Commercial Judge, even after trial.
(b) If a party wishes to continue a freezing injunction after trial or judgment, care should be taken to ensure that the application is made before the existing freezing injunction has expired.

K2 Accounts and enquiries

2A–121 K2.1 The court may order that accounts and inquiries be referred to a judge of the Technology and Construction Court or to a Master. Alternatively, the parties may choose to refer the matter to arbitration.

K3 Enforcement

2A–122 K3.1 Unless the court orders otherwise, all proceedings for the enforcement of any judgment or order for the payment of money given or made in the Commercial Court will be referred automatically to a master of the Queen's Bench Division or a district judge: PD58 § 1.2(2).

K3.2 Applications in connection with the enforcement of a judgment or order for the payment of money should accordingly be directed to the Registry which will allocate them to the Admiralty Registrar or to one of the Queen's Bench masters as appropriate.

K4 Assessment of damages or interest after a default judgment

2A–123 K4.1 Unless the court orders otherwise, the assessment of damages or interest following the entry of a default judgment for damages or interest to be assessed will be carried out by the Admiralty Registrar or one of the Queen's Bench masters to whom the case is allocated by the Registry.

L.

MULTI–PARTY DISPUTES

L1 Early consideration

2A–124 L1.1 Cases which involve, or are expected to involve, a large number of claimants or defendants require close case management from the earliest point. The same is true where there are, or are likely to be, a large number of separate cases involving the same or similar issues. Both classes of case are referred to as "multi–party" disputes.

L1.2

(a) The Judge in Charge of the List should be informed as soon as it becomes apparent that a multi–party dispute exists or is likely to exist and an early application for directions should be made.
(b) In an appropriate case an application for directions may be made before issue of a claim form. In some cases it may be appropriate for an application to be made without notice in the first instance.

L2 Available procedures

2A–125 L2.1 In some cases it may be appropriate for the court to make a Group Litigation Order under Part 19 of the Rules. In other cases it may be more convenient for the court to exercise its general powers of management. These include powers

　　(i) to dispense with statements of case;

　　(ii) to direct parties to serve outline statements of case;

　　(iii) to direct that cases be consolidated or managed and tried together;

　　(iv) to direct that certain cases or issues be determined before others and to stay other proceedings in the meantime;

　　(v) to advance or put back the usual time for pre–trial steps to be taken (for example the disclosure of documents by one or more parties or a payment into court).

L2.2 Attention is drawn to the provisions of Section III of Part 19, rules 19.10–19.15 and the practice direction supplementing Section III of Part 19. Practitioners should note that the provisions of Section III of Part 19 give the court additional powers to manage disputes involving multiple claimants or defendants. They should also note that a Group Litigation Order may not be made without the consent of the Lord Chief Justice: PD19B § 3.3(1).

L2.3 An application for a Group Litigation Order should be made in the first instance to the Judge in Charge of the List: PD19B § 3.5.

M.

LITIGANTS IN PERSON

M1 The litigant in person

M1.1 Litigants in person appear less often in the Commercial Court than in some **2A–126** other courts. Their position requires special consideration.

M2 Represented parties

M2.1 Where a litigant in person is involved in a case the court will expect solicitors **2A–127** and counsel for other parties to do what they reasonably can to ensure that he has a fair opportunity to prepare and put his case.

M2.2 The duty of an advocate to ensure that the court is informed of all relevant decisions and legislative provisions of which he is aware (whether favourable to his case or not) and to bring any procedural irregularity to the attention of the court during the hearing is of particular importance in a case where a litigant in person is involved.

M2.3 Further, the court will expect solicitors and counsel appearing for other parties to ensure that the case memorandum, the list of issues and all necessary bundles are prepared and provided to the court in accordance with the Guide, even where the litigant in person is unwilling or unable to participate.

M2.4 If the claimant is a litigant in person the judge at the case management conference will normally direct which of the parties is to have responsibility for the preparation and upkeep of the case management bundle.

M2.5 At the case management conference the court may give directions relating to the costs of providing application bundles, trial bundles and, if applicable, transcripts of hearings to the litigant in person.

M3 Companies without representation

M3.1 Although rule 39.6 allows a company or other corporation with the permission **2A–128** of the court to be represented at trial by an employee, the complexity of most cases in the Commercial Court makes that unsuitable. Accordingly, permission is likely to be given only in unusual circumstances.

N.

ADMIRALTY

N1 General

N1.1 Proceedings in the Admiralty Court are dealt with in Part 61 and its associated **2A–129** practice direction.

N1.2 The Admiralty & Commercial Courts Guide has been prepared in consultation with the Admiralty Judge. It has been adopted to provide guidance about the conduct of proceedings in the Admiralty Court. The Guide must be followed in the Admiralty Court unless the content of Part 61, its associated practice direction or the terms of this section N require otherwise.

N1.3 One significant area of difference between practice in the Commercial Court and practice in the Admiralty Court is that many interlocutory applications are heard by the Admiralty Registrar who has all the powers of the Admiralty judge save as provided otherwise: rule 61.1(4).

N2 The Admiralty Court Committee

2A–130 N2.1 The Admiralty Court Committee provides a specific forum for contact and consultation between the Admiralty Court and its users. Its meetings are usually held in conjunction with the Commercial Court Users Committee. Any correspondence should be addressed to the Deputy Admiralty Marshal, Royal Courts of Justice, Strand, WC2A 2LL.

N3 Commencement of proceedings, service of Statements of Case and associated matters

2A–131 N3.1 Sections B and C of this guide apply to all Admiralty claims except:
　　(i) a claim in rem;
　　(ii) a collision claim; and
　　(iii) a limitation claim.

N4 Commencement and early stages of a claim in rem

2A–132 N4.1 The early stages of an in rem claim differ from those of other claims.

The procedure is governed generally by rule 61.3 and PD61 § § 3.1–3.11.

N4.2 In addition, the following sections of the Guide apply to claims in rem: B4.3, B4.7–B4.11, B7.4–B7.6, C1.1–C1.6, C1.8 and C2.1(ii)–C5.4.

N4.3 Subject to PD61 § 3.7, section C1.7 of the Guide also applies to claims in rem.

N4.4 After an acknowledgement of service has been filed a claim in rem follows the procedure applicable to a claim proceeding in the Commercial List, save that the Claimant is allowed 75 days in which to serve his particulars of claim: PD61 § 3.10.

N5 The early stages of a Collision Claim

2A–133 N5.1 Where a collision claim is commenced in rem, the general procedure applicable to claims in rem applies subject to rule 61.4 and PD61 § § 4.1–4.5.

N5.2 Where a collision claim is not commenced in rem the general procedure applicable to claims proceeding in the Commercial List applies subject to rule 61.4 and PD61 § § 4.1–4.5.

N5.3 Service of a claim form out of the jurisdiction in a collision claim (other than a claim in rem) is permitted in the circumstances identified in rule 61.4(7) only and the procedure set out in Appendix 15 of the Guide should be adapted accordingly.

N5.4 One particular feature of a collision action is that the parties must prepare and file a Collision Statement of Case. Prior to the coming into force of Part 61, a Collision Statement of Case was known as a Preliminary Act and the law relating to Preliminary Acts continues to apply to Collision Statements of Case: PD61 § 4.5.

N5.5 The provisions of Appendix 4 apply to part 2 of a Collision Statement of Case (but not to part 1).

N5.6 Every party is required, so far as it is able, to provide full and complete answers to the questions contained in part 1 of the Collision Statement of Case. The answers should descend to a reasonable level of particularity.

N5.7 The answers to the questions contained in part 1 are treated as admissions made by the party answering the questions and leave to amend such answers will be granted only in exceptional circumstances. As to the principles applicable to the amendment of particulars of claim in a collision claim reference should be made to the judgment of Gross J. in *The Topaz* [2003] 2 Lloyd's Rep 19.

N6 The early stages of a Limitation Claim

N6.1 The procedure governing the early stages of a limitation claim differs **2A–134** significantly from the procedure relating to other claims and is contained in rule 61.11 and PD61 § 10.1.

N6.2 Service of a limitation claim form out of the jurisdiction is permitted in the circumstances identified in rule 61.11 (5) only and the procedure set out in Appendix 15 of the Guide should be adapted accordingly.

N7 Issue of documents when the Registry is closed

N7.1 When the Registry is closed (and only when it is closed) an Admiralty claim **2A–135** form may be issued on the following designated fax machine: 020 7947 6245 and only on that machine.

N7.2 The procedure to be followed is set out in Appendix 3 of the Guide.

N7.3 The issue of an Admiralty claim form in accordance with the procedure set out in Appendix 3 shall have the same effect for all purposes as a claim form issued in accordance with the relevant provisions of rule 61 and PD61.

N7.4 When the Registry is closed (and only when it is closed) a notice requesting a caution against release may be filed on the following designated fax machine: 020 7947 6245 and only on that machine. This machine is manned 24 hours a day by court security staff (telephone 020 7947 6260).

N7.5 The notice requesting the caution should be transmitted with a note in the following form for ease of identification by security staff:
"CAUTION AGAINST RELEASE
Please find notice requesting caution against release of the ... (*name ship/identify cargo*) ... for filing in the Admiralty & Commercial Registry."

N7.6 The notice must be in Admiralty Form No. **ADM11** and signed by a solicitor acting on behalf of the applicant.

N7.7 Subject to the provisions of sections N7.9 and N7.10 below, the filing of the notice takes place when the fax is recorded as having been received.

N7.8 When the Registry is next open to the public, the filing solicitor or his agent shall attend and deliver to the Registry the document which was transmitted by fax together with the transmission report. Upon satisfying himself that the document delivered fully accords with the document received by the Registry, the court officer shall stamp the document delivered with the time and date on which the notice was received, enter the same in the caution register and retain the same with the faxed copy.

N7.9 Unless otherwise ordered by the court, the stamped notice shall be conclusive proof that the notice was filed at the time and on the date stated.

N7.10 If the filing solicitor does not comply with the foregoing procedure, or if the notice is not stamped, the notice shall be deemed never to have been filed.

N8 Case Management

N8.1 The case management provisions of the Guide apply to Admiralty claims save **2A–136** that
(i) In Admiralty claims the case management provisions of the Guide are supplemented by PD61 § § 2.1–2.3 which make provision for the early classification and streaming of cases;
(ii) In a collision case the claimant should apply for a case management conference within 7 days after the last Collision Statement of Case is filed;
(iii) In a limitation claim where the right to limit is not admitted and the claimant seeks a general limitation decree, the claimant must, within 7 days after the date of the filing of the defence of the defendant last served or the expiry of the time for doing so, apply to the Admiralty Registrar for a case management conference: PD61 § 10.7;
(iv) In a collision claim or a limitation claim a mandatory case management conference will normally take place on the first available date 5 weeks after the date when

the claimant is required to take steps to fix a date for the case management conference;

(v) In a limitation claim, case management directions are initially given by the Registrar: PD61 § 10.8;

(vi) In the Admiralty Court, the Case Management Information Sheet should be in the form in Appendix 6 of this Guide but should also include the following questions

1. Do any of the issues contained in the List of Issues involve questions of navigation or other particular matters of an essentially Admiralty nature which require the trial to be before the Admiralty Judge?

2. Is the case suitable to be tried before a Deputy Judge nominated by the Admiralty Judge?

3. Do you consider that the court should sit with nautical or other assessors? If you intend to ask that the court sit with one or more assessors who is not a Trinity Master, please state the reasons for such an application.

N9 Evidence

2A–137 N9.1 In collision claims, section H1.5 and Appendix 8 are subject to the proviso that experience has shown that it is usually desirable for the main elements of a witness' evidence in chief to be adduced orally.

Authenticity

N9.2

(a) Where the authenticity of any document disclosed to a party is not admitted, that party must serve notice that the document must be proved at trial in accordance with CPR 32.19. Such notice must be served by the latest date for serving witness statements or within 7 days of disclosure of the document, whichever is later.

(b) Where, apart from the authenticity of the document itself, the date upon which a document or an entry in it is stated to have been made or the person by whom the document states that it or any entry in it was made or any other feature of the document is to be challenged at the trial on grounds which may require a witness to be called at the trial to support the contents of the document, such challenge

(i) must be raised in good time in advance of the trial to enable such witness or witnesses to be called;

(ii) the grounds of challenge must be explicitly identified in the skeleton argument or outline submissions in advance of the trial.

(c) Where, due to the late disclosure of a document it or its contents or character cannot practicably be challenged within the time limits prescribed in (a) or (b), the challenge may only be raised with the permission of the court and having regard to the Overriding Objective (CPR 1.1).

Skeleton arguments in Collision Claims

N9.3 In collision claims the skeleton argument of each party must be accompanied by a plot or plots of that party's case or alternative cases as to the navigation of vessels during and leading to the collision. All plots must contain a sufficient indication of the assumptions used in the preparation of the plot.

N10 Split trials, accounts, enquiries and enforcement

2A–138 N10.1 In collision claims it is usual for liability to be tried first and for the assessment of damages and interest to be referred to the Admiralty Registrar.

N10.2 Where the Admiralty Court refers an account, enquiry or enforcement, it will usually refer the matter to the Admiralty Registrar.

N11 Release of vessels out of hours

2A–139 N11.1 This section makes provision for release from arrest when the Registry is closed.

N11.2 An application for release under rule 61.8(4)(c) or (d) may, when the Registry is closed, be made in, and only in, the following manner

(i) The solicitor for the arrestor or the other party applying must telephone the security staff at the Royal Courts of Justice (020 7947 6260) and ask to be contacted by the Admiralty Marshal, who will then respond as soon as practicably possible;

(ii) Upon being contacted by the Admiralty Marshal the solicitor must give oral instructions for the release and an oral undertaking to pay the fees and expenses of the Admiralty Marshal as required in Form No. **ADM12**;

(iii) The arrestor or other party applying must then send a written request and undertaking on Form No. **ADM12** by fax to a number given by the Admiralty Marshal;

(iv) The solicitor must provide written consent to the release from all persons who have entered cautions against release (and from the arrestor if the arrestor is not the party applying) by sending such consents by fax to the number supplied by the Admiralty Marshal;

(v) Upon the Admiralty Marshal being satisfied that no cautions against release are in force, or that all persons who have entered cautions against release, and if necessary the arrestor, have given their written consent to the release, the Admiralty Marshal shall effect the release as soon as practicable.

N11.3 Practitioners should note that the Admiralty Marshal is not formally on call and therefore at times may not be available to assist. Similarly the practicalities of releasing a ship in some localities may involve the services of others who may not be available outside court hours.

N11.4 This service is offered to practitioners for use during reasonable hours and on the basis that if the Admiralty Marshal is available and can be contacted he will use his best endeavours to effect instructions to release but without guarantee as to their success.

N12 Use of postal facilities in the Registry

N12.1 Applications together with the requisite documents may be posted to: **2A–140**

The Admiralty and Commercial Registry,

Room EB15,

Royal Courts of Justice,

Strand,

London WC2A 2LL.

N12.2 In addition to the classes of business for which the use of postal facilities is permitted by the CPR or the Commercial Court Guide, the filing of the following classes of documents is also permitted in Admiralty matters

(i) Requests for cautions;

(ii) Collision Statements of Case.

N12.3

(a) Documents sent by post for filing must be accompanied by two copies of a list of the documents sent and an envelope properly addressed to the sender.

(b) On receipt of the documents in the Registry, the court officer will, if the circumstances are such that had the documents been presented personally they would have been filed, cause them to be filed and will, by post, notify the sender that this has been done. If the documents would not have been accepted if presented personally the court officer will not file them but will retain them in the Registry for collection by the sender and will, by post, so inform the sender.

(c) When documents received through the post are filed by the court officer they will be sealed and entered as filed on the date on which they were received in the Registry.

N13 Insurance of arrested property

N13.1 The Marshal will not insure any arrested property for the benefit of parties at **2A–141** any time during the period of arrest (whether before or after the lodging of an application for sale, if any).

N13.2 The Marshal will use his best endeavours (but without any legal liability for failure to do so) to advise all parties known to him as being on the record in actions in rem against the arrested property, including those who have filed cautions against release of that property, before any such property moves or is moved beyond the area covered by the usual port risks policy.

N13.3 In these circumstances, practitioners' attention is drawn to the necessity of considering the questions of insuring against port risks for the amount of their clients' interest in any property arrested in an Admiralty action and the inclusion in any policy of a "Held Covered" clause in case the ship moves or is moved outside the area covered by the usual port risks policy. The usual port risks policy provides, among other things, for a ship to be moved or towed from one berth to another up to a distance of five miles within the port where she is lying.

N14 Assessors

2A–142 14.1 In collision claims and other cases involving issues of navigation and seamanship, the Admiralty Court usually sits with assessors. The parties are not permitted to call expert evidence on such matters without the leave of the court: rule 61.13.

14.2 Parties are reminded of the practice with regard to the disclosure of any answers to the court's questions and the opportunity for comment on them as set out in the Judgment of Gross J. in *The Global Mariner* [2005] 1 Lloyd's Rep 699 at p702.

14.3 Provision is made in rule 35.15 for assessors' remuneration. Provisions for assessors' remuneration are set out in QB *Practice Direction* [2007] 1 WLR 2508. The usual practice is for the court to seek an undertaking from the claimant to pay the remuneration on demand after the case has concluded.

O.

ARBITRATION

2A–143 ### O1 Arbitration claims

O1.1

(a) Applications to the court under the Arbitration Acts 1950– 1996 and other applications relating to arbitrations are known as "arbitration claims".
(b) The procedure applicable to arbitration claims is to be found in Part 62 and its associated practice direction. Separate provision is made

> (i) by Section I for claims relating to arbitrations to which the Arbitration Act 1996 applies;
> (ii) by Section II for claims relating to arbitrations to which the Arbitration Acts 1950– 1979 ("the old law") apply; and
> (iii) by Section III for enforcement proceedings.

(c) For a full definition of the expression "arbitration claim" see rule 62.2(1) (claims under the 1996 Act) and rule 62.11(2) (claims under the old law).
(d) Part 58 applies to arbitration claims in the Commercial Court insofar as no specific provision is made by Part 62: rule 62.1(3).

Claims under the Arbitration Act 1996

O2 Starting an arbitration claim

2A–144 O2.1 Subject to section O2.3 an arbitration claim must be started by the issue of an arbitration claim form in accordance with the Part 8 procedure: rule 62.3(1).

O2.2 The claim form must be substantially in the form set out in Appendix A to practice direction 62: PD62 § 2.2.

O2.3 An application to stay proceedings under section 9 of the Arbitration Act 1996 must be made by application notice in the proceedings: rule 62.3(2).

O2.4 Where a question arises as to whether an arbitration agreement is null and void, inoperative or incapable of being performed the court may deal with it in the same way as provided by rule 62.8(3) which applies where a question arises as to whether an arbitration agreement has been concluded or the dispute which is the subject matter of the proceedings falls within the terms of such an agreement.

O3 The arbitration claim form

O3.1 The arbitration claim form must contain, among other things, a concise statement of the remedy claimed and, if an award is challenged, the grounds for that challenge: rule 62.4(1).

O3.2 Reference in the arbitration claim form to a witness statement or affidavit filed in support of the claim is not sufficient to comply with the requirements of rule 62.4(1).

O4 Service of the arbitration claim form

O4.1 An arbitration claim form issued in the Admiralty & Commercial Registry must be served by the claimant.

O4.2

(a) The rules governing service of the claim form are set out in Part 6 of the Civil Procedure Rules.
(b) Unless the court orders otherwise an arbitration claim form must be served on the defendant within 1 month from the date of issue: rule 62.4(2).

O4.3

(a) An arbitration claim form may be served out of the jurisdiction with the permission of the court: rule 62.5(1).
(b) Rules 6.40– 6.46 apply to the service of an arbitration claim form out of the jurisdiction: rule 62.5(3).

O4.4 The court may exercise its powers under rules 6.15 and/or 6.37(5)(b) to permit service of an arbitration claim form on a party at the address of the solicitor or other representative acting for him in the arbitration: PD62 § 3.1.

O4.5 The claimant must file a certificate of service within 7 days of serving the arbitration claim form: PD62 § 3.2.

O5 Acknowledgment of service

O5.1

(a) A defendant must file an acknowledgment of service of the arbitration claim form in every case: rule 58.6(1).
(b) An adapted version of practice form **N210** (acknowledgment of service of a Part 8 claim form) has been approved for use in the Commercial Court.

O5.2 The time for filing an acknowledgment of service is calculated from the service of the arbitration claim form.

O6 Standard directions

O6.1 The directions set out in PD62 § 6.2–6.7 apply unless the court orders otherwise.

O6.2 The claimant should apply for a hearing date as soon as possible after issuing an arbitration claim form or (in the case of an appeal) obtaining permission to appeal.

O6.3 A defendant who wishes to rely on evidence in opposition to the claim must file and serve his evidence within 21 days after the date by which he was required to acknowledge service: PD62 § 6.2.

O6.4 A claimant who wishes to rely on evidence in response to evidence served by the defendant must file and serve his evidence within 7 days after the service of the defendant's evidence: PD62 § 6.3.

O6.5 An application for directions in a pending arbitration claim should be made by application notice under Part 23. Where an arbitration application involves recognition and/or enforcement of an agreement to arbitrate and that application is challenged on the grounds that the parties to the application were not bound by an agreement to arbitrate, it will usually be necessary for the court to resolve that issue in order to determine the application. For this purpose it may be necessary for there to be disclosure of documents and/or factual and/or expert evidence. In that event, it is the responsibility of those advising the applicant to liaise with the other party and to arrange with the Listing Office for a case management conference to be listed as early as possible to enable the court to give directions as to the steps to be taken before the hearing of the application.

O7 Interim remedies

O7.1 An application for an interim remedy under section 44 of the Arbitration Act 1996 must be made in an arbitration claim form: PD62 § 8.1.

O8 Challenging the award

Challenge by way of appeal

2A–145 O8.1 A party wishing to appeal against the award of an arbitrator or umpire must set out in the arbitration claim form

  (i) the question of law on which the appeal is based; and

  (ii) a succinct statement of the grounds of appeal,

identifying the relevant part(s) of the award and reasons.

O8.2 If the appeal is brought with the agreement of the other parties to the proceedings, a copy of their agreement in writing must be filed with the arbitration claim form.

O8.3 A party seeking permission to appeal must

  (i) state in his arbitration claim form the grounds on which he contends that permission to appeal should be given PD62 § 12.1; and

  (ii) file and serve with the arbitration claim form any written evidence on which he wishes to rely for the purposes of satisfying the court of the matters referred to in section 69(3) of the 1996 Act: PD62 § 12.2.

O8.4

(a) If the defendant wishes to oppose the claimant's application for permission to appeal he must file a witness statement setting out

  (i) the grounds on which he opposes the grant of permission; and

  (ii) any evidence on which he relies in relation to the matters mentioned in section 69(3) of the 1996 Act: PD62 § § 12.3(1) and (2).
  (b) If the defendant wishes to contend that the award should be upheld for reasons other than those expressed in the award, he must set out those reasons in his witness statement: PD62 § 12.3(3).

O8.5 The court will normally determine applications for permission to appeal without an oral hearing. If the court considers that an oral hearing is required, it will give further directions as appropriate.

Challenging an award for serious irregularity

O8.6

(a) An arbitration claim challenging an award on the ground of serious irregularity under section 68 of the 1996 Act is appropriate only in cases where there are grounds for thinking

    (i) that an irregularity has occurred which

    (ii) has caused or will cause substantial injustice to the party making the challenge.

(b) An application challenging an award on the ground of serious irregularity should therefore not be regarded as an alternative to, or a means of supporting, an application for permission to appeal.

O8.7 The challenge to the award must be supported by evidence of the circumstances on which the claimant relies as giving rise to the irregularity complained of and the nature of the injustice which has been or will be caused to him.

O8.8 If the nature of the challenge itself or the evidence filed in support of it leads the court to consider that the claim has no real prospect of success, the court may exercise its powers under rule 3.3(4) to dismiss the application summarily. In such cases the applicant will have the right to apply to the court to set aside the order and to seek directions for the hearing of the application.

Multiple claims

O8.9 If the arbitration claim form includes both a challenge to an award by way of appeal and a challenge on the ground of serious irregularity, the applications should be set out in separate sections of the arbitration claim form and the grounds on which they are made separately identified.

O8.10 In such cases the papers will be placed before a judge to consider how the applications may most appropriately be disposed of. It is usually more appropriate to dispose of the application to set aside or remit the award before considering the application for permission to appeal.

O9 Time limits

O9.1 An application to challenge an award under sections 67 or 68 of the 1996 Act or **2A–146** to appeal under section 69 of the Act must be brought within 28 days of the date of the award: **see** section 70(3).

O9.2 The court has power to vary the period of 28 days fixed by section 70(3) of the 1996 Act: rule 62.9(1). However, it is important that any challenge to an award be pursued without delay and the court will require cogent reasons for extending time.

O9.3 An application to extend time made **before** the expiry of the period of 28 days must be made in a Part 23 application notice, but the application notice need not be served on any other party: rule 62.9(2) and PD62 § 11.1(1).

O9.4 An application to extend time made **after** the expiry of the period of 28 days must be made in the arbitration claim form in which the applicant is seeking substantive relief: rule 62.9(3)(a).

O9.5 An application to vary the period of 28 days will normally be determined without a hearing and prior to the consideration of the substantive application: PD62 § 10.2.

Claims under the Arbitration Acts 1950–1979

O10 Starting an arbitration claim

O10.1 Subject to section O10.2 an arbitration claim must be started by the issue of an **2A–147** arbitration claim form in accordance with the Part 8 procedure: rule 62.13(1).

O10.2 The claim form must be substantially in the form set out in Appendix A to PD62 § 2.2.

O10.3 An application to stay proceedings on the grounds of an arbitration agreement must be made by application notice in the proceedings: rule 62.13(2).

O11 The arbitration claim form

O11.1 An arbitration claim form must state the grounds of the claim or appeal: rule 62.15(5)(a).

O11.2 Reference in the arbitration claim form to the witness statement or affidavit filed in support of the claim is not sufficient to comply with the requirements of rule 62.15(5)(a).

O12 Service of the arbitration claim form

O12.1 An arbitration claim form issued in the Admiralty & Commercial Registry must be served by the claimant.

O12.2 The rules governing service of the claim form are set out in Part 6 of the Civil Procedure Rules.

O12.3

(a) An arbitration claim form may be served out of the jurisdiction with the permission of the court: rule 62.16(1).
(b) Rules 6.40– 6.46 apply to the service of an arbitration claim form out of the jurisdiction: rule 62.16(4).

O12.4 Although not expressly covered by PD62, the court may in an appropriate case exercise its powers under rule 6.15 and/or 6.37(5) to permit service of an arbitration claim form on a party at the address of the solicitor or other representative acting for him in the arbitration.

O12.5 The claimant must file a certificate of service within 7 days of serving the claim form.

2A–148 Acknowledgment of service

O13.1

(a) A defendant must file an acknowledgment of service in every case: rule 58.6(1).
(b) An adapted version of practice form **N210** (acknowledgment of service of a Part 8 claim form) has been approved for use in the Commercial Court.

O13.2 The time for filing an acknowledgment of service is calculated from the service of the arbitration claim form.

O14 Standard directions

O14.1 Where the claim or appeal is based on written evidence, a copy of that evidence must be served with the arbitration claim form: rule 62.15(5)(b).

O14.2 Where the claim or appeal is made with the consent of the arbitrator or umpire or other parties, a copy of every written consent must be served with the arbitration claim form: rule 62.15(5)(c).

O14.3 An application for directions in a pending arbitration claim should be made by application notice under Part 23.

O15 Interim remedies

O15.1 An application for an interim remedy under section 12(6) of the 1950 Act must be made in accordance with Part 25.

O15.2 The application must be made by arbitration claim form.

O15.3 A claim under section 12(4) of the 1950 Act for an order for the issue of a witness summons to compel the attendance of a witness before an arbitrator or umpire where the attendance of the witness is required within the district of a District Registry may be started in that Registry: rule 62.14.

O16 Challenging the award

Challenge by way of appeal

O16.1 A party wishing to appeal against the award of an arbitrator or umpire must **2A–149** file and serve with the arbitration claim form a statement of the grounds for the appeal, specifying the relevant part(s) of the award and reasons: rule 62.15(6).

O16.2 A party seeking permission to appeal must also file and serve with the arbitration claim form any written evidence in support of the contention that the question of law concerns a term of the contract or an event which is not "one off": rule 62.15(6).

O16.3 Any written evidence in reply must be filed and served not less than 2 days before the hearing of the application for permission to appeal: rule 62.15(7).

O16.4 A party who wishes to contend that the award should be upheld for reasons other than those set out in the award and reasons must file and serve on the claimant a notice specifying the grounds of his contention not less than 2 days before the hearing of the application for permission to appeal: rule 62.15(8).

O16.5 Applications for permission to appeal will be heard orally, but will not normally be listed for longer than half an hour. Skeleton arguments should be lodged.

Claims to set aside or remit the award

O16.6 A claim to set aside or remit an award on the grounds of misconduct should not be regarded as an alternative to, or a means of supporting, an application for permission to appeal.

O16.7 The directions set out in PD62 § § 6.2–6.7 should be followed unless the court orders otherwise.

Multiple claims

O16.8 If the arbitration claim form includes both an appeal and an application to set aside or remit the award, the applications should be set out in separate sections of the arbitration claim form and the grounds on which they are made separately identified.

O16.9 The court may direct that one application be heard before the other or may direct that they be heard together, as may be appropriate. It is usually more appropriate to dispose of the application to set aside or remit the award before considering the application for permission to appeal.

O17 Time limits   **2A–150**

O17.1

(a) Time limits governing claims under the 1950 and 1979 Acts are set out in rule 62.15.
(b) Different time limits apply to different claims. It is important to consult rule 62.15 to ensure that applications are made within the time prescribed.
(c) The court has power under rule 3.1(2) to vary the time limits prescribed by rule 62.15, but will require cogent reasons for doing so.

Provisions applicable to all arbitrations

Enforcement of awards

O18.1 All applications for permission to enforce awards are governed by Section III **2A–151** of Part 62, rule 62.17.

O18.2 An application for permission to enforce an award in the same manner as a judgment may be made without notice, but the court may direct that the arbitration claim form be served, in which case the application will continue as an arbitration claim in accordance with the procedure set out in Section I: rule 62.18(1)–(3).

O18.3 An application for permission to enforce an award in the same manner as a judgment must be supported written evidence in accordance with rule 62.18(6).

O18.4

(a) Two copies of the draft order must accompany the application.
(b) If the claimant wishes to enter judgment, the form of the judgment must correspond to the terms of the award.
(c) The defendant has the right to apply to the court to set aside an order made without notice giving permission to enforce the award and the order itself must state in terms

    (i) that the defendant may apply to set it aside within 14 days after service of the order or, if the order is to be served out of the jurisdiction, within such other period as the court may set; and

    (ii) that it may not be enforced until after the end of that period or any application by the defendant to set it aside has been finally disposed of: rule 62.18(9) and (10).

Matters of general application

O19 Transfer of arbitration claims

2A–152 O19.1 An arbitration claim which raises no significant point of arbitration law or practice will normally be transferred

    (i) if a rent–review arbitration, to the Chancery Division;

    (ii) if a construction or engineering arbitration, to the Technology and Construction Court;

    (iii) if an employment arbitration, to the Central London County Court Mercantile List.

O19.2 Salvage arbitrations will normally be transferred to the Admiralty Court.

O20 Appointment of a Commercial Judge as sole arbitrator or umpire

O20.1 Section 93 of the Arbitration Act 1996 provides for the appointment of a Commercial Judge as sole arbitrator or umpire. The Act limits the circumstances in which a Judge may accept such an appointment.

O20.2 Enquiries should be directed to the Judge in charge of the Commercial List or the Clerk to the Commercial Court.

P.

MISCELLANEOUS

2A–153 **P1 Out of hours emergency arrangements**

P1.1

(a) When the Listing Office is closed, solicitors or counsel's clerks should in an emergency contact the Clerk to the Queen's Bench Judge in Chambers by telephone through the security desk at the Royal Courts of Justice: PD58 § 2.2.
(b) The telephone number of the security desk is included in the list of addresses and contact details at the end of the Guide.

P1.2 When the Listing Office is closed an urgent hearing will initially be dealt with by the Queen's Bench Judge in Chambers who may dispose of the application himself or make orders allowing the matter to come before a Commercial Judge at the first available opportunity.

P2 Index of decisions of the Commercial and Admiralty Courts

P2.1 An Index has been prepared on a subject–matter basis of unreported **2A–154** Commercial Court and Admiralty Court judgments from 1995 onwards. The Index is updated regularly.

P2.2 The Index is provided as a service to litigants and to the legal profession, and to assist the Commercial Court and the Admiralty Court to maintain reasonable consistency of approach in those areas of law and procedure most frequently before them.

P2.3 The index of Judgments of Commercial Court and Admiralty Court of England and Wales is available to all Internet users and can be found at: www.hmcourts–service.gov.uk/infoabout/admiralcomm/index.htm via the link to "Searchable index of court cases" (at bottom of the box on right hand side of Commercial Court and Admiralty Court).

P2.4 The judgments referred to in the Index are kept in the Registry. They may be consulted there.

P2.5 Copies of the judgments referred to in the Index may be obtained from the Registry (or where there is difficulty, from the clerk to the judge) unless the judgment is in the form of a transcript, in which case copies should be obtained from the shorthand writers or other transcript agency.

APPENDIX 1

Editorial note
Part 58 (Commercial Court)—reproduced at paras 2A–1 *et seq.*   **2A–155**
Part 61 (Admiralty Court)—reproduced at paras 2D–1 *et seq.*
Practice Direction to Part 58—reproduced at paras 2A–22 *et seq.*
Practice Direction to Part 61—reproduced at paras 2D–85 *et seq.*

APPENDIX 2

Editorial note
Part 62 (Arbitration)—reproduced at paras 2E–1 *et seq.*   **2A–156**
Practice Direction to Part 62—reproduced at paras 2E–46 *et seq.*

APPENDIX 3

PROCEDURE FOR ISSUE OF CLAIM FORM WHEN REGISTRY CLOSED
(See section B2.4 of the Guide.)   **2A–157**

Procedure
The procedure is as follows:

1. The claim form must be signed by a solicitor acting on behalf of the claimant, and must not require the permission of the Court for its issue (unless such permission has already been given).

2. The solicitor causing the claim form to be issued ("the issuing solicitor") must

(i) endorse on the claim form the endorsement shown below and sign that endorsement;

(ii) send a copy of the claim form so endorsed to the Registry by fax for issue under this section; and

(iii) when he has received a transmission report stating that the transmission of the claim form to the Registry was completed in full and the time and the date of the transmission, complete and sign the certificate shown below.

3. When the Registry is next open to the public after the issue of a claim form in accordance with this procedure the issuing solicitor or his agent shall attend and

deliver to the Registry the document which was transmitted by fax (including the endorsement and the certificate), or if that document has been served, a true and certified copy of it, together with as many copies as the Registry shall require and the transmission report.

4. When the proper officer at the Registry has checked and is satisfied that the document delivered under paragraph 3 fully accords with the document received under paragraph 2, and that all proper fees for issue have been paid, he shall allocate a number to the case, and seal, mark as "original" and date the claim form with the date on which it was issued (being, as indicated below, the date when the fax is recorded at the Registry as having been received).

5. As soon as practicable thereafter the issuing solicitor shall inform any person served with the unsealed claim form of the case number, and (on request) shall serve any such person with a copy of the claim form sealed and dated under paragraph 4 above (at such address in England and Wales as the person may request) and the person may, without paying a fee, inspect and take copies of the documents lodged at the Registry under paragraphs 2 and 3 above.

Effect of issue following request by fax

2A–158   The issue of a claim form in accordance with this procedure takes place when the fax is recorded at the Registry as having been received, and the claim form bearing the endorsement shall have the same effect for all purposes as a claim form issued under CPR Part 7 [or 8, as the case may be]. Unless otherwise ordered the sealed version of the claim form retained by the Registry shall be conclusive proof that the claim form was issued at the time and on the date stated. If the procedure set out in this Appendix is not complied with, the court may declare (on its own initiative or on application) that the claim form shall be treated as not having been issued.

Endorsement

2A–159   A claim form issued pursuant to a request by fax must be endorsed as follows:

1. This claim form is issued under paragraph 2.2 of the Commercial Court practice direction and may be served notwithstanding that it does not bear the seal of the Court.

2. A true copy of this claim form and endorsement has been transmitted to the Admiralty and Commercial Registry, Royal Courts of Justice, Strand, London WC2A 2LL, at the time and date certified below by the solicitor whose name appears below ("the issuing solicitor").

3. It is the duty of the issuing solicitor or his agent to attend at the Registry when it is next open to the public for the claim form to be sealed.

4. Any person upon whom this unsealed claim form is served

(a) will be notified by the issuing solicitor of the number of the case;

(b) may require the issuing solicitor to serve a copy of the sealed claim form at an address in England and Wales; and

(c) may inspect without charge the documents which have been lodged at the Registry by the undersigned solicitor.

5. I, the issuing solicitor, undertake to the Court, to the defendants named in this claim form, and to any other person upon whom this claim form may be served:

(a) that the statement in paragraph 2 above is correct;

(b) that the time and date given in the certificate with this endorsement are correct;

(c) that this claim form is a claim form which may be issued under section 2.2 and Appendix A of the Commercial Court practice direction;

(d) that I will comply in all respects with the requirements of Appendix A of the Commercial Court practice direction;

(e) that I will indemnify any person served with the claim form before it is sealed against any loss suffered as a result of the claim form being or becoming invalid in accordance with Appendix A of the Commercial Court practice direction.

(Signed)

Solicitor for the claimant"

[**Note**: the endorsement may be signed in the name of the firm of solicitors rather than an individual solicitor, or by solicitors' agents in their capacity as agents acting on behalf of their professional clients.]

Certificate

An issuing solicitor must sign a certificate in the following form: **2A–160**

"I certify that I have received a transmission report confirming that the transmission of a copy of this claim form to the Registry by fax was fully completed and that the time and date of transmission to the Registry were *[enter the time and date shown on the transmission report]*.

Dated

(Signed)

Solicitor for the claimant."

[**Note**: the certificate may be signed in the name of the firm of solicitors rather than an individual solicitor, or by solicitors' agents in their capacity as agents acting on behalf of their professional clients.]

APPENDIX 4

STATEMENTS OF CASE

The following principles apply to all statements of case and should, as far as **2A–161** possible, also be observed when drafting a Part 8 claim form, which will not contain, or be followed by, particulars of claim:

1. The document must be as brief and concise as possible.

2. The document must be set out in separate consecutively numbered paragraphs and sub–paragraphs.

3. So far as possible each paragraph or sub–paragraph should contain no more than one allegation.

4. The document must deal with the case on a point by point basis to allow a point by point response.

5. Where particulars are given of any allegation or reasons given for a denial, the allegation or denial should be stated first and the particulars or reasons for it listed one by one in separate numbered sub–paragraphs.

6. A party wishing to advance a positive case should set that case out in the document; a simple denial is not sufficient.

7. Any matter which, if not stated, might take another party by surprise should be stated.

8. Where they will assist:

(i) headings should be used; and

(ii) abbreviations and definitions should be established and used, and a glossary annexed.

9. Contentious headings, abbreviations and definitions should not be used. Every effort should be made to ensure that headings, abbreviations and definitions are in a form that will enable them to be adopted without issue by the other parties.

10. Particulars of primary allegations should be stated as particulars and not as primary allegations.

11. If it is necessary to rely upon a substantial amount of detailed factual information or lengthy particulars in support of an allegation, these should be set out in schedules or appendices.

12. Particular care should be taken to set out only those factual allegations which are necessary to support the case. Evidence should not be included.

13. A response to particulars set out in a schedule should be set out in a corresponding schedule.

14. If it is necessary for the proper understanding of the statement of case to include substantial parts of a lengthy document the passages in question should be set out in a schedule rather than in the body of the case.

15. Contentious paraphrasing should be avoided.

16. The document must be signed by the individual person or persons who drafted it, not, in the case of a solicitor, in the name of the firm alone.

17. The document must not be longer than 25 pages unless the court has given permission for a longer document.

Appendix 5

Forms of Freezing Injunction and Search Order

2A–162

adapted for use in the Commercial Court

** FREEZING INJUNCTION **

IN THE HIGH COURT OF JUSTICE
QUEEN'S BENCH DIVISION
COMMERCIAL COURT

Before The Honourable Mr Justice [   ]

Claim No.

BETWEEN

Claimant(s)/Applicant(s)

– and –

Defendant(s)/Respondent(s)

PENAL NOTICE

If you [   ][1] disobey this order you may be held to be in contempt of court and may be imprisoned, fined or have your assets seized.

Any other person who knows of this order and does anything which helps or permits the Respondent to breach the terms of this order may also be held to be in contempt of court and may be imprisoned, fined or have their assets seized.

THIS ORDER

1. This is a Freezing Injunction made against [   ] ("the Respondent") on [   ] by Mr Justice [   ] on the application of [   ] ("the Applicant").

2. This order was made at a hearing without notice to the Respondent. The Respondent has a right to apply to the court to vary or discharge the order—see paragraph 13 below.

3. There will be a further hearing in respect of this order on [   ] ("the return date"[2]).

[4. If there is more than one Respondent

    (a) unless otherwise stated, references in this order to "the Respondent" mean both or all of them; and

    (b) this order is effective against any Respondent on whom it is served or who is given notice of it.]

---

[1] Insert name of Respondent(s).

[2] In the Commercial Court, usually 14 days after the injunction was granted, particularly where parties are outside the jurisdiction.

FREEZING INJUNCTION

[For injunction limited to assets in England and Wales]

5. Until after the return date or further order of the court, the Respondent must not remove from England and Wales or in any way dispose of, deal with or diminish the value of any of his assets which are in England and Wales up to the value of £

[For worldwide injunction]

5. Until the return date or further order of the court, the Respondent must not—

    (1) remove from England and Wales any of his assets which are in England and Wales up to the value of £   ; or

    (2) in any way dispose of, deal with or diminish the value of any of his assets whether they are in or outside England and Wales up to the same value.

[For either form of injunction]

6. Paragraph 5 applies to all the Respondent's assets whether or not they are in his own name, whether they are solely or jointly owned and whether the Respondent is interested in them legally, beneficially or otherwise. For the purpose of this order the Respondent's assets include any asset which he has the power, directly or indirectly, to dispose of or deal with as if it were his own. The Respondent is to be regarded as having such power if a third party holds or controls the asset in accordance with his direct or indirect instructions.

7. This prohibition includes the following assets in particular—

    (a) the property known as [*title/address*] or the net sale money after payment of any mortgages if it has been sold;

    (b) the property and assets of the Respondent's business [known as [*name*]] [carried on at [*address*]] or the sale money if any of them have been sold; and

    (c) any money in the account numbered [*account number*] at [*title/address*].

    (d) any interest under any trust or similar entity including any interest which can arise by virtue of the exercise of any power of appointment, discretion or otherwise howsoever.

[For injunction limited to assets in England and Wales]

8. If the total value free of charges or other securities ("unencumbered value") of the Respondent's assets in England and Wales exceeds £   , the Respondent may remove any of those assets from England and Wales or may dispose of or deal with them so long as the total unencumbered value of his assets still in England and Wales remains above £   .

[For worldwide injunction]

8. (1) If the total value free of charges or other securities ("unencumbered value") of the Respondent's assets in England and Wales exceeds £   , the Respondent may remove any of those assets from England and Wales or may dispose of or deal with them so long as the total unencumbered value of the Respondent's assets still in England and Wales remains above £   .

    (2) If the total unencumbered value of the Respondent's assets in England and Wales does not exceed £   , the Respondent must not remove any of those assets from England and Wales and must not dispose of or deal with any of them. If the Respondent has other assets outside England and Wales, he may dispose of or deal with those assets outside England and Wales so long as the total unencumbered value of all his assets whether in or outside England and Wales remains above £   .

PROVISION OF INFORMATION

9. (1) Unless paragraph (2) applies, the Respondent must [within   hours of service of this order] and to the best of his ability inform the Applicant's solicitors of all his assets [in England and Wales] [worldwide] [exceeding £   in value[1]] whether in his own name or not and whether solely or jointly owned, giving the value, location and details of all such assets.

---

[1] In most cases, careful consideration will need to be given to inserting a lower limit of say £10,000 or equivalent below which value assets need not be disclosed.

(2) If the provision of any of this information is likely to incriminate the Respondent, he may be entitled to refuse to provide it, but is recommended to take legal advice before refusing to provide the information. Wrongful refusal to provide the information is contempt of court and may render the Respondent liable to be imprisoned, fined or have his assets seized.

10. Within [] working days after being served with this order, the Respondent must swear and serve on the Applicant's solicitors an affidavit setting out the above information[1].]

PROVISION OF INFORMATION

11. (1) This order does not prohibit the Respondent from spending £   a week towards his ordinary living expenses and also £   [*or* a reasonable sum] on legal advice and representation. [But before spending any money the Respondent must tell the Applicant's legal representatives where the money is to come from.]

[(2) This order does not prohibit the Respondent from dealing with or disposing of any of his assets in the ordinary and proper course of business, but before doing so the Respondent must tell the Applicant's legal representatives.]

(3) The Respondent may agree with the Applicant's legal representatives that the above spending limits should be increased or that this order should be varied in any other respect, but any agreement must be in writing.

(4) The order will cease to have effect if the Respondent—

(a) provides security by paying the sum of £   into court, to be held to the order of the court; or

(b) makes provision for security in that sum by another method agreed with the Applicant's legal representatives.

COSTS

12. The costs of this application are reserved to the judge hearing the application on the return date.

VARIATION OR DISCHARGE OF THIS ORDER

13. Anyone served with or notified of this order may apply to the court at any time to vary or discharge this order (or so much of it as affects that person), but they must first inform the Applicant's solicitors. If any evidence is to be relied upon in support of the application, the substance of it must be communicated in writing to the Applicant's solicitors in advance.

INTERPRETATION OF THIS ORDER

14. A Respondent who is an individual who is ordered not to do something must not do it himself or in any other way. He must not do it through others acting on his behalf or on his instructions or with his encouragement.

15. A Respondent which is not an individual which is ordered not to do something must not do it itself or by its directors, officers, partners, employees or agents or in any other way.

PARTIES OTHER THAN THE APPLICANT AND RESPONDENT

16. **Effect of this order**

It is a contempt of court for any person notified of this order knowingly to assist in or permit a breach of this order. Any person doing so may be imprisoned, fined or have their assets seized.

17. **Set off by banks**

This injunction does not prevent any bank from exercising any right of set

---

[1] Consideration should also be given to amalgamating paragraphs 9 and 10 of the draft Order, so as to require only one disclosure exercise, verified by Affidavit.

off it may have in respect of any facility which it gave to the respondent before it was notified of this order.

18. **Withdrawals by the Respondent**

No bank need enquire as to the application or proposed application of any money withdrawn by the Respondent if the withdrawal appears to be permitted by this order.

[For worldwide injunction]

19. **Persons outside England and Wales**

(1) Except as provided in paragraph (2) below, the terms of this order do not affect or concern anyone outside the jurisdiction of this court.

(2) The terms of this order will affect the following persons in a country or state outside the jurisdiction of this court–

    a. the Respondent or his officer or agent appointed by power of attorney;

    b. any person who–

        i. is subject to the jurisdiction of this court;

        ii. has been given written notice of this order at his residence or place of business within the jurisdiction of this court; and

        iii. is able to prevent acts or omissions outside the jurisdiction of this court which constitute or assist in a breach of the terms of this order; and

    c. any other person, only to the extent that this order is declared enforceable by or is enforced by a court in that country or state.

[For worldwide injunction]

20. **Assets located outside England and Wales**

Nothing in this order shall, in respect of assets located outside England and Wales, prevent any third party from complying with—

(1) what it reasonably believes to be its obligations, contractual or otherwise, under the laws and obligations of the country or state in which those assets are situated or under the proper law of any contract between itself and the Respondent; and

(2) any orders of the courts of that country or state, provided that reasonable notice of any application for such an order is given to the Applicant's solicitors.

COMMUNICATIONS WITH THE COURT

All communications to the court about this order should be sent to Room EB09, Royal Courts of Justice, Strand, London WC2A 2LL quoting the case number. The telephone number is 020 7947 6826.

The offices are open between 10 a.m. and 4.30 p.m. Monday to Friday.

SCHEDULE A—AFFIDAVITS

The Applicant relied on the following affidavits—

    [name]   [number of affidavit]   [date sworn]   [filed on behalf of]

(1)

(2)

SCHEDULE B—UNDERTAKINGS GIVEN TO THE COURT BY THE APPLICANT

(1) If the court later finds that this order has caused loss to the Respondent, and decides that the Respondent should be compensated for that loss, the Applicant will comply with any order the court may make. (3)1 (4)1 (5)1(i)1 copies of the affidavits and exhibits containing the evidence relied upon by the Applicant, and any other documents provided to the court on the making of the application; (ii)1 the claim form; and (iii)1 an application notice for continuation of the order.

[(2) The Applicant will—

    (a) on or before [*date*] cause a written guarantee in the sum of £   to be issued from a bank with a place of business within England or Wales, in respect of any order the court may make pursuant to paragraph (1) above; and

    (b) immediately upon issue of the guarantee, cause a copy of it to be served on the Respondent.]

(3) As soon as practicable the Applicant will issue and serve a claim form [in the form of the draft produced to the court] [claiming the appropriate relief].

(4) The Applicant will [swear and file an affidavit] [cause an affidavit to be sworn and filed] [substantially in the terms of the draft affidavit produced to the court] [confirming the substance of what was said to the court by the Applicant's counsel/solicitors].

(5) The Applicant will serve upon the Respondent [together with this order] [as soon as practicable]—

    (i) copies of the affidavits and exhibits containing the evidence relied upon by the Applicant, and any other documents provided to the court on the making of the application;

    (ii) the claim form; and

    (ii) an application notice for continuation of the order.

[(6) Anyone notified of this order will be given a copy of it by the Applicant's legal representatives.]

(7) The Applicant will pay the reasonable costs of anyone other than the Respondent which have been incurred as a result of this order including the costs of finding out whether that person holds any of the Respondent's assets and if the court later finds that this order has caused such person loss, and decides that such person should be compensated for that loss, the Applicant will comply with any order the court may make.

(8) If this order ceases to have effect (for example, if the Respondent provides security or the Applicant does not provide a bank guarantee as provided for above) the Applicant will immediately take all reasonable steps to inform in writing anyone to whom he has given notice of this order, or who he has reasonable grounds for supposing may act upon this order, that it has ceased to have effect.

[(9) The Applicant will not without the permission of the court use any information obtained as a result of this order for the purpose of any civil or criminal proceedings, either in England and Wales or in any other jurisdiction, other than this claim.]

[(10) The Applicant will not without the permission of the court seek to enforce this order in any country outside England and Wales [or seek an order of a similar nature including orders conferring a charge or other security against the Respondent or the Respondent's assets].]

NAME AND ADDRESS OF APPLICANT'S LEGAL REPRESENTATIVES

The Applicant's legal representatives are—

[Name, address, reference, fax and telephone numbers both in and out of office hours and e–mail]

2A–162.1   ****SEARCH ORDER****

IN THE HIGH COURT OF JUSTICE
QUEEN'S BENCH DIVISION
COMMERCIAL COURT

Before The Honourable Mr Justice [**]**

                                            Claim No.

BETWEEN

– and –

PENAL NOTICE

If you [   ]¹ disobey this order you may be held to be in contempt of court and may be imprisoned, fined or have your assets seized.

Any other person who knows of this order and does anything which helps or permits the Respondent to breach the terms of this order may also be held to be in contempt of court and may be imprisoned, fined or have their assets seized.

THIS ORDER

1. This is a Search Order made against [   ] ("the Respondent") on [   ] by Mr Justice [   ] on the application of [   ] ("the Applicant"). The Judge read the Affidavits listed in Schedule F and accepted the undertakings set out in Schedules C, D and E at the end of this order.

2. This order was made at a hearing without notice to the Respondent. The Respondent has a right to apply to the court to vary or discharge the order—see paragraph 27 below.

3. There will be a further hearing in respect of this order on [   ] ("the return date").

4. If there is more than one Respondent—

   (a) unless otherwise stated, references in this order to "the Respondent" mean both or all of them; and

   (b) this order is effective against any Respondent on whom it is served or who is given notice of it.

5. This order must be complied with by—

   (a) the Respondent;

   (b) any director, officer, partner or responsible employee of the Respondent; and

   (c) if the Respondent is an individual, any other person having responsible control of the premises to be searched.

THE SEARCH

6. The Respondent must permit the following persons²—

   (a) [   ] ("the Supervising Solicitor);

   (b) [   ], a solicitor in the firm of [   ], the Applicant's solicitors; and

   (c) up to [   ] other persons³ being [their identity or capacity] accompanying them,

   (together "the search party"), to enter the premises mentioned in Schedule A to this order and any other premises of the Respondent disclosed under paragraph 18 below and any vehicles under the Respondent's control on or around the premises ("the premises") so that they can search for, inspect, photograph or photocopy, and deliver into the safekeeping of the Applicant's solicitors all the documents and articles which are listed in Schedule B to this order ("the listed items").

7. Having permitted the search party to enter the premises, the Respondent must allow the search party to remain on the premises until the search is complete. In the event that it becomes necessary for any of those persons to

---

¹ Insert name of Respondent(s).

² Where the premises are likely to be occupied by an unaccompanied woman and the Supervising Solicitor is a man, at least one of the persons accompanying him should be a woman.

³ None of these persons should be people who could gain personally or commercially from anything they might read or see on the premises, unless their presence is essential.

leave the premises before the search is complete, the Respondent must allow them to re–enter the premises immediately upon their seeking re–entry on the same or the following day in order to complete the search.

RESTRICTIONS ON SEARCH

8. This order may not be carried out at the same time as a police search warrant.

9. Before the Respondent allows anybody onto the premises to carry out this order, he is entitled to have the Supervising Solicitor explain to him what it means in everyday language.

10. The Respondent is entitled to seek legal advice and to ask the court to vary or discharge this order. Whilst doing so, he may ask the Supervising Solicitor to delay starting the search for up to 2 hours or such other longer period as the Supervising Solicitor may permit. However, the Respondent must—

    (a) comply with the terms of paragraph 27 below;

    (b) not disturb or remove any listed items; and

    (c) permit the Supervising Solicitor to enter, but not start to search.

PROVISION OF INFORMATION

11. Before permitting entry to the premises by any person other than the Supervising Solicitor, the Respondent may, for a short time (not to exceed two hours, unless the Supervising Solicitor agrees to a longer period), gather together any documents he believes may be [incriminating or][1] privileged and hand them to the Supervising Solicitor for him to assess whether they are [incriminating or] privileged as claimed. If the Supervising Solicitor decides that any of the documents may be [incriminating or] privileged or is in any doubt as to their status, he will exclude them from the search and retain them in his possession pending further order of the court.

12. If the Respondent wishes to take legal advice and gather documents as permitted, he must first inform the Supervising Solicitor and keep him informed of the steps being taken.

PROVISION OF INFORMATION

13. No item may be removed from the premises until a list of the items to be removed has been prepared, and a copy of the list has been supplied to the Respondent, and he has been given a reasonable opportunity to check the list.

14. The premises must not be searched, and items must not be removed from them, except in the presence of the Respondent.

15. If the Supervising Solicitor is satisfied that full compliance with paragraphs 13 or 14 is not practicable, he may permit the search to proceed and items to be removed without fully complying with them.

DELIVERY UP OF ARTICLES/DOCUMENTS

16. The Respondent must immediately hand over to the Applicant's solicitors any of the listed items, which are in his possession or under his control, save for any computer or hard disk integral to any computer. Any items the subject of a dispute as to whether they are listed items must immediately be handed over to the Supervising Solicitor for safe keeping pending resolution of the dispute or further order of the court.

17. The Respondent must immediately give the search party effective access to the computers on the premises, with all necessary passwords, to enable the computers to be searched. If they contain any listed items the Respondent must cause the listed items to be displayed so that they can be read and copied.[2] The Respondent must provide the Applicant's Solicitors with copies of all listed items contained in the computers. All reasonable steps shall be taken by the Applicant and the Applicant's solicitors to ensure that no damage is done to any computer or data. The Applicant and his representatives may not themselves search the Respondent's computers unless they have sufficient expertise to do so without damaging the Respondent's system.

---

[1] References to incriminating documents should be omitted from orders made in intellectual property proceedings, where the privilege against self–incrimination does not apply – see paragraph 8.4 of the practice direction.

[2] If it is envisaged that the Respondent's computers are to be imaged (i.e. the hard drives are to be copied wholesale, thereby reproducing listed items and other items indiscriminately), special provision needs to be made and independent computer specialists need to be appointed, who should be required to give undertakings to the court.

PROVISION OF INFORMATION

18. The Respondent must immediately inform the Applicant's Solicitors (in the presence of the Supervising Solicitor) so far as he is aware—

    (a) where all the listed items are;

    (b) the name and address of everyone who has supplied him, or offered to supply him, with listed items;

    (c) the name and address of everyone to whom he has supplied, or offered to supply, listed items; and

    (d) full details of the dates and quantities of every such supply and offer.

19. Within [ ] working days after being served with this order the Respondent must swear and serve an affidavit setting out the above information.[1]

PROHIBITED ACTS

20. Except for the purpose of obtaining legal advice, the Respondent must not directly or indirectly inform anyone of these proceedings or of the contents of this order, or warn anyone that proceedings have been or may be brought against him by the Applicant until 4.30 p.m. on the return date or further order of the court.

21. Until 4.30 p.m. on the return date the Respondent must not destroy, tamper with, cancel or part with possession, power, custody or control of the listed items otherwise than in accordance with the terms of this order.

22. [Insert any negative injunctions.]

23. [Insert any further order]

COSTS

24. The costs of this application are reserved to the judge hearing the application on the return date.

RESTRICTIONS ON SERVICE

25. This order may only be served between [ ] a.m./p.m. and [ ] a.m./p.m. [and on a weekday].[2]

26. This order must be served by the Supervising Solicitor, and paragraph 6 of the order must be carried out in his presence and under his supervision.

VARIATION AND DISCHARGE OF THIS ORDER

27. Anyone served with or notified of this order may apply to the court at any time to vary or discharge this order (or so much of it as affects that person), but they must first inform the Applicant's solicitors. If any evidence is to be relied upon in support of the application, the substance of it must be communicated in writing to the Applicant's solicitors in advance.

INTERPRETATION OF THIS ORDER

28. Any requirement that something shall be done to or in the presence of the Respondent means—

    (a) if there is more than one Respondent, to or in the presence of any one of them; and

    (b) if a Respondent is not an individual, to or in the presence of a director, officer, partner or responsible employee.

29. A Respondent who is an individual who is ordered not to do something must not do it himself or in any other way. He must not do it through others acting on his behalf or on his instructions or with his encouragement.

30. A Respondent which is not an individual which is ordered not to do something must not do it itself or by its directors, officers, partners, employees or agents or in any other way.

COMMUNICATIONS WITH THE COURT

All communications to the court about this order should be sent to Room EB09, Royal Courts of Justice, Strand, London WC2A 2LL quoting the case number. The telephone number is 020 7947 6826.

---

[1] The period should ordinarily be longer than the period in paragraph (2) of Schedule D, if any of the information is likely to be included in listed items taken away of which the Respondent does not have copies.

[2] Normally, the order should be served in the morning (not before 9.30 a.m.) and on a weekday to enable the Respondent more readily to obtain legal advice.

The offices are open between 10 a.m. and 4.30 p.m. Monday to Friday.

SCHEDULE A
THE PREMISES

SCHEDULE B
THE LISTED ITEMS

SCHEDULE C
UNDERTAKINGS GIVE TO THE COURT BY THE APPLICANT

(1) If the court later finds that this order or carrying it out has caused loss to the Respondent, and decides that the Respondent should be compensated for that loss, the Applicant will comply with any order the court may make. Further if the carrying out of this order has been in breach of the terms of this order or otherwise in a manner inconsistent with the Applicant's solicitors' duties as officers of the court, the Applicant will comply with any order for damages the court may make.

[(2) As soon as practicable the Applicant will issue a claim form [in the form of the draft produced to the court] [claiming the appropriate relief].]

(3) The Applicant will [swear and file an affidavit] [cause an affidavit to be sworn and filed] [substantially in the terms of the draft affidavit produced to the court] [confirming the substance of what was said to the court by the Applicant's counsel/solicitors].

(4) The Applicant will not, without the permission of the court use any information or documents obtained as a result of carrying out this order nor inform anyone else of these proceedings except for the purposes of these proceedings (including adding further Respondents) or commencing civil proceedings in relation to the same or related subject matter to these proceedings until after the return date.

(5) The Applicant will maintain pending further order the sum of £ [[0]11] in an account controlled by the Applicant's solicitors.]

[(6) The Applicant will insure the items removed from the premises.]

SCHEDULE D
UNDERTAKINGS GIVEN BY THE APPLICANT'S SOLICITORS

(1) The Applicant's solicitors will provide to the Supervising Solicitor for service on the Respondent—

    (i) a service copy of this order;

    (ii) the claim form (with defendant's response pack) or, if not issued, the draft produced to the court;

    (iii) an application for hearing on the return date;

    (iv) copies of the affidavits [or draft affidavits] and exhibits capable of being copied containing the evidence relied upon by the applicant;

    (v) a note of any allegation of fact made orally to the court where such allegation is not contained in the affidavits or draft affidavits read by the judge; and

    (vi) a copy of the skeleton argument produced to the court by the Applicant's [counsel/solicitors].

(2) The Applicants' solicitors will answer at once to the best of their ability any question whether a particular item is a listed item.

(3) Subject as provided below the Applicant's solicitors will retain in their own safe keeping all items obtained as a result of this order until the court directs otherwise.

(4) The Applicant's solicitors will return the originals of all documents obtained as a result of this order (except original documents which belong to the Applicant) as soon as possible and in any event within [two] working days of their removal.

SCHEDULE E
UNDERTAKINGS GIVEN BY THE SUPERVISING SOLICITOR

(1) The Supervising Solicitor will use his best endeavours to serve this order upon the Respondent and at the same time to serve upon the Respondent the other documents required to be served and referred to in paragraph (1) of Schedule D.

(2) The Supervising Solicitor will offer to explain to the person served with the order its meaning and effect fairly and in everyday language, and to inform him of his right to take legal advice (such advice to include an explanation that the Respondent may be entitled to avail himself of [the privilege against self–incrimination or] [legal professional privilege]) and to apply to vary or discharge this order as mentioned in paragraph 27 above.

(3) The Supervising Solicitor will retain in the safe keeping of his firm all items retained by him as a result of this order until the court directs otherwise.

(4) Within [48] hours of completion of the search the Supervising Solicitor will make and provide to the Applicant's solicitors, the Respondent or his solicitors and to the judge who made this order (for the purposes of the court file) a written report on the carrying out of the order.

SCHEDULE F
AFFIDAVITS

The Applicant relied on the following affidavits—

[name]   [number of affidavit]   [date sworn]   [filed on behalf of]

(1)

(2)

NAME AND ADDRESS OF APPLICANT'S SOLICITORS

The Applicant's solicitors are—

[Name, address, reference, fax and telephone numbers both in and out of office hours.]

APPENDIX 6

CASE MANAGEMENT INFORMATION SHEET

The information supplied should be printed in bold characters   **2A–163**

Case Management Information Sheet

Party lodging information sheet:

Name of solicitors:

Name(s) of advocates for trial:

[Note: This Sheet should normally be completed with the involvement of the advocate(s) instructed for trial. If the claimant is a litigant in person this fact should be noted at the foot of the sheet and proposals made as to which party is to have responsibility for the preparation and upkeep of the case management bundle.]

(1) By what date can you give standard disclosure?

(2) In relation to standard disclosure, do you contend in relation to any category or class of document under rule 31.6(b) that to search for that category or class would be unreasonable? If so, what is the category or class and on what grounds do you so contend?

(3) Is specific disclosure required on any issue? If so, please specify.

(4) By what dates can you (a) give specific disclosure or (b) comply with a special disclosure order?

(5) May the time periods for inspection at rule 31.15 require adjustment, and if so by how much?

(6) Are amendments to or is information about any statement of case required? If yes, please give brief details of what is required.

(7) Can you make any additional admissions? If yes, please give brief details of the additional admissions.

(8) Are any of the issues in the case suitable for trial as preliminary issues?

(9) (a) On the evidence of how many witnesses of fact do you intend to rely at trial (subject to the directions of the Court)? Please give their names, or explain why this is not being done.

(b) By what date can you serve signed witness statements?

(c) How many of these witnesses of fact do you intend to call to give oral evidence at trial (subject to the directions of the Court)? Please give their names, or explain why this is not being done.

(d) Will interpreters be required for any witness?

(e) Do you wish any witness to give oral evidence by video link? Please give his or her name, or explain why this is not being done. Please state the country and city from which the witness will be asked to give evidence by video link.

(10) (a) On what issues may expert evidence be required?

(b) Is this a case in which the use of a single joint expert might be suitable (see rule 35.7)?

(c) On the evidence of how many expert witnesses do you intend to rely at trial (subject to the directions of the Court)? Please give their names, or explain why this is not being done. Please identify each expert's field of expertise.

(d) By what date can you serve signed expert reports?

(e) When will the experts be available for a meeting or meetings of experts?

(f) How many of these expert witnesses do you intend to call to give oral evidence at trial (subject to the directions of the Court)? Please give their names, or explain why this is not being done.

(g) Will interpreters be required for any expert witness?

(h) Do you wish any expert witness to give oral evidence by video link? Please give his or her name, or explain why this is not being done. Please state the country and city from which the witness will be asked to give evidence by video link.

(11) What are the advocates' present provisional estimates of the minimum and maximum lengths of the trial?

(12) What is the earliest date by which you believe you can be ready for trial?

(13) Is this a case in which a pre–trial review is likely to be useful?

(14) Is there any way in which the Court can assist the parties to resolve their dispute or particular issues in it without the need for a trial or a full trial?

(15) (a) Might some form of Alternative Dispute Resolution procedure assist to resolve or narrow the dispute or particular issues in it?

(b) Has the question at (a) been considered between the client and legal representatives (including the advocate(s) retained)?

(c) Has the question at (a) been explored with the other parties in the case?

(d) Do you request that the case is adjourned while the parties try to settle the case by Alternative Dispute Resolution or other means?

(e) Would an ADR order in the form of Appendix 7 to the Commercial Court Guide be appropriate?

(f) Are any other special directions needed to allow for Alternative Dispute Resolution?

(16) What other applications will you wish to make at the Case Management Conference?

(17) Does provision need to be made in the pre–trial timetable for any application or procedural step not otherwise dealt with above? If yes, please specify the application or procedural step.

(18) Are there, or are there likely in due course to be, any related proceedings (e.g. a Part 20 claim)? Please give brief details.

[Signature of solicitors]

Note: This information sheet must be lodged with the Clerk to the Commercial Court at least 7 days before the Case Management Conference (with a copy to all other parties): see section D8.5 of the Commercial Court Guide.

APPENDIX 7

DRAFT ADR ORDER

1. On or before [*] the parties shall exchange lists of 3 neutral individuals who are **2A–164** available to conduct ADR procedures in this case prior to [*]. Each party may [in addition] [in the alternative] provide a list identifying the constitution of one or more panels of neutral individuals who are available to conduct ADR procedures in this case prior to [*].

2. On or before [*] the parties shall in good faith endeavour to agree a neutral individual or panel from the lists so exchanged and provided.

3. Failing such agreement by [*] the Case Management Conference will be restored to enable the Court to facilitate agreement on a neutral individual or panel.

4. The parties shall take such serious steps as they may be advised to resolve their disputes by ADR procedures before the neutral individual or panel so chosen by no later than [*].

5. If the case is not finally settled, the parties shall inform the Court by letter prior to [disclosure of documents/exchange of witness statements/exchange of experts' reports] what steps towards ADR have been taken and (without prejudice to matters of privilege) why such steps have failed. If the parties have failed to initiate ADR procedures the Case Management Conference is to be restored for further consideration of the case.

6. [Costs].

Note: The term "ADR procedures" is deliberately used in the draft ADR order. This is in order to emphasise that (save where otherwise provided) the parties are free to use the ADR procedure that they regard as most suitable, be it mediation, early neutral evaluation, non–binding arbitration etc.

APPENDIX 8

STANDARD PRE–TRIAL TIMETABLE

1. [Standard disclosure is to be made by [*], with inspection [*] days after notice.] **2A–165**

2. Signed statements of witnesses of fact, and hearsay notices where required by rule 33.2, are to be exchanged not later than [*].

3. Unless otherwise ordered, witness statements are to stand as the evidence in chief of the witness at trial.

4. Signed reports of experts
   (i) are to be confined to one expert for each party from each of the following fields of expertise: [*];

(ii) are to be confined to the following issues: [*];

(iii) are to be exchanged [sequentially/simultaneously];

(iv) are to be exchanged not later than [date or dates for each report in each field of expertise].

5. Meeting of experts

(i) The meeting of experts is to be by [*];

(ii) The joint memorandum of the experts is to be completed by [*];

(iii) Any short supplemental expert reports are to be exchanged [sequentially/simultaneously] by not later than [date or dates for each supplemental report].

6. [If the experts' reports cannot be agreed, the parties are to be at liberty to call expert witnesses at the trial, limited to those experts whose reports have been exchanged pursuant to 4. above.]

[Or: The parties are to be at liberty to apply to call as expert witnesses at the trial those experts whose reports they have exchanged pursuant to 4. above, such application to be made not earlier than [*] and not later than [*].]

7. Preparation of trial bundles to be completed in accordance with Appendix 10 to the Commercial Court Guide by not later than [*].

8. The provisional estimated length of the trial is [*]. This includes [*] pre–trial reading time.

9. Within [*] days the parties are to attend on the Clerk to the Commercial Court to fix the date for trial which shall be not before [*].

10. The progress monitoring date is [*]. Each party is to lodge a completed progress monitoring information sheet with the Clerk to the Commercial Court at least 3 days before the progress monitoring date (with a copy to all other parties).

11. Each party is to lodge a completed pre–trial checklist not later than 3 weeks before the date fixed for trial.

12. [There is to be a pre–trial review not earlier than [*] and not later than [*]].

13. Save as varied by this order or further order, the practice and procedures set out in the Admiralty & Commercial Courts Guide are to be followed.

14. Costs in the case.

15. Liberty to restore the Case Management Conference.

Appendix 9

Skeleton Arguments, Chronologies and Indices

Part 1 Skeleton arguments

2A–166 1. A skeleton argument is intended to identify both for the parties and the court those points which are, and are not, in issue and the nature of the argument in relation to those points that are in issue. It is not a substitute for oral argument.

2. Skeleton arguments must therefore

(a) identify concisely:

(i) the nature of the case generally and the background facts insofar as they are relevant to the matter before the court;

(ii) the propositions of law relied on with references to the relevant authorities;

(iii) the submissions of fact to be made with references to the evidence;

(b) be in numbered paragraphs and state the name of the advocate(s) who prepared them; and

(c) should avoid arguing the case at length.

Part 2 Chronologies and indices

3. As far as possible chronologies and indices should not be prepared in a **2A–167** tendentious form. The ideal is that the court and the parties should have a single point of reference that all find useful and are happy to work with.

4. Where there is disagreement about a particular event or description, it is useful if that fact is indicated in neutral terms and the competing versions shortly stated.

5. If time and circumstances allow its preparation, a chronology or index to which all parties have contributed and agreed can be invaluable.

6. Chronologies and indices once prepared can be easily updated and are of continuing usefulness throughout the life of the case.

Appendix 10

Preparation of Bundles

1. The preparation of bundles requires a high level of co–operation between legal **2A–168** representatives for all parties. It is the duty of all legal representatives to co–operate to this high level.

2. Bundles should be prepared as follows:

(i) No more than one copy of any one document should be included, unless there is good reason for doing otherwise;

(ii) Contemporaneous documents, and correspondence, should be included in chronological order;

(iii) Where a contract or similar document is central to the case it may be included in a separate place provided that a page is inserted in the chronological run of documents to indicate

(A) the place the contract or similar document would have appeared had it appeared chronologically and

(B) where it may be found instead;

(iv) Documents in manuscript, or not fully legible, should be transcribed; the transcription should be marked and placed adjacent to the document transcribed;

(v) Documents in a foreign language should be translated; the translation should be marked and placed adjacent to the document transcribed; the translation should be agreed, or, if it cannot be agreed, each party's proposed translation should be included;

(vi) If a document has to be read across rather than down the page, it should be so placed in the bundle as to ensure that the top of the text is nearest the spine;

(vii) No bundle should contain more than 300 pages;

(viii) Bundles should not be overfilled, and should allow sufficient room for later insertions. Subject to this, the size of file used should not be a size that is larger than necessary for the present and anticipated contents;

(ix) Bundles should be paginated, in the bottom right hand corner and in a form that can clearly be distinguished from any existing pagination on the document;

(x) Bundles should be indexed, save that a chronological bundle of contemporaneous documents need not be indexed if an index is unlikely to be useful;

(xi) Bundles should be numbered and named on the outside and on the inside front cover, the label to include the short title of the case, and a description of the bundle (including its number, where relevant).

3. Documents within bundles should be marked as follows:

(i) When copy documents from exhibits have been included in the bundle(s), then unless clearly unnecessary, the copy of the affidavit or witness statement to which the documents were exhibited should be marked in the right hand margin (in manuscript if need be) to show where the document referred to may be found in the bundle(s).

(ii) Unless clearly unnecessary, where copy documents in a bundle are taken from the disclosure of more than one party the documents should be marked in the top right hand corner (in manuscript if need be) to show from which party's disclosure the copy document has been taken;

(iii) Where there is a reference in a statement of case or witness statement to a document which is contained in the trial bundles a note should be made in the margin (if necessary in manuscript) identifying the place where that document is to be found.

Unless otherwise agreed this is the responsibility of the party tendering the statement of case or witness statement.

4. For the trial a handy–sized core bundle should normally be provided containing the really important documents in the case. The documents in this bundle should be paginated, but each page should also bear its bundle and page number reference in the main bundles. It is particularly important to allow sufficient room for later insertions (see paragraph 2(viii) above).

5. Large documents, such as plans, should be placed in an easily accessible file.

6.

(a) When agreeing bundles for trial, legal representatives should bear in mind the effect of the Civil Evidence Act 1995 and of rules 33.2(3) (notice requiring proof of authenticity) and 32.19 (hearsay notices).

(b) Pursuant to those provisions, documents which have not been the subject of a notice served in accordance with rule 32.19(2) (requiring proof of authenticity) will be admissible as evidence of the truth of their contents even if there has been non–compliance with the notice requirements of s. 2(1) of the 1995 Act and rule 33.2 (see s. 2(4) of the Act). Accordingly, save for documents in respect of which there has been a timely notice to prove authenticity, all documents in the trial bundle will be admissible in evidence without more.

(c) The fact that documents in the trial bundle are admissible in evidence does not mean that all such documents form part of the evidence in the trial. It is the trial advocate's responsibility to indicate clearly to the court before closing his or her case the written evidence which forms part of that case. This should be done in the written opening statement or in the oral opening statement if the document is then available. Documents which have not previously been put in evidence before the closure of the parties' cases should not normally be referred to as evidence in the course of final speeches.

Appendix 11

Expert Evidence—Requirements of General Application

2A–169 1. It is the duty of an expert to help the court on the matters within his expertise: rule 35.3(1). This duty is paramount and overrides any obligation to the person from whom the expert has received instructions or by whom he is paid: rule 35.3(2).

2. Expert evidence presented to the court should be, and should be seen to be, the independent product of the expert uninfluenced by the pressures of litigation.

3. An expert witness should provide independent assistance to the court by way of objective unbiased opinion in relation to matters within his expertise. An expert witness should never assume the role of an advocate.

4. An expert witness should not omit to consider material facts which could detract from his concluded opinion.

5. An expert witness should make it clear when a particular question or issue falls outside his expertise.

6. If an expert's opinion is not properly researched because he considers that insufficient data is available, this must be stated in his report with an indication that the opinion is no more than a provisional one.

7. In a case where an expert witness who has prepared a report is unable to confirm that the report contains the truth, the whole truth and nothing but the truth without some qualification, that qualification must be stated in the report.

8. If, after exchange of reports, an expert witness changes his view on a material matter having read another expert's report or for any other reason, such change of view should be communicated in writing (through the party's legal representatives) to the other side without delay, and when appropriate to the court.

APPENDIX 12

PROGRESS MONITORING INFORMATION SHEET
The information supplied should be printed in bold characters

2A–170

[SHORT TITLE OF CASE and FOLIO NUMBER]

Fixed trial date/provisional range of dates for trial specified in the pre–trial timetable:

Party lodging information sheet:

Name of solicitors:

Name(s) of advocates for trial:

[Note: this information sheet should normally be completed with the involvement of the advocate(s) instructed for trial]

(1) Have you complied with the pre–trial timetable in all respects?

(2) If you have not complied, in what respects have you not complied?

(3) Will you be ready for a trial commencing on the fixed date (or, where applicable, within the provisional range of dates) specified in the pre–trial timetable?

(4) If you will not be ready, why will you not be ready?

[*Signature of solicitors*]

Note: This information sheet must be lodged with the Listing Office at least 3 days before the progress monitoring date (with a copy to all other parties): see section D12.2 of the Guide.

APPENDIX 13

PRE–TRIAL CHECKLIST
The information supplied should be printed in bold characters

2A–171

[SHORT TITLE OF CASE and FOLIO NUMBER]

a. Trial date:

b. Party lodging checklist:

c. Name of solicitors:

d. Name(s) of advocates for trial:

[**Note**: this checklist should normally be completed with the involvement of the advocate(s) instructed for trial.]

1. Have you completed preparation of trial bundles in accordance with Appendix 10 to the Commercial Court Guide?

2. If not, when will the preparation of the trial bundles be completed?

3. Which witnesses of fact do you intend to call?

4. Which expert witness(es) do you intend to call (if directions for expert evidence have been given)?

5. Will an interpreter be required for any witness and if so, have any necessary directions already been given?

6. Have directions been given for any witness to give evidence by video link? If so, have all necessary arrangements been made?

7. What are the advocates' confirmed estimates of the minimum and maximum lengths of the trial? (A confirmed estimate of length signed by the advocates should be attached).

8. What is your estimate of costs already incurred and to be incurred at trial for the purposes of section 46 of the Practice Direction supplementing CPR Part 43? (If the trial is not expected to last more than **one day** the estimate should be substantially in the form of a statement of costs as illustrated in Form H of the Schedule of Costs Forms annexed to the Practice Direction).

[Signature of solicitors]

VIDEO CONFERENCING GUIDANCE (ANNEX 3 TO PD32)

Editorial note

The Video Conferencing Guidance contained in this Appendix reproduces the Guidance in Annex 3 of Practice Direction—Evidence; see Vol.1 para.32PD.33.

2A–172

[THE NEXT PARAGRAPH IS 2A–175.]

Appendix 15

Service Out of the Jurisdiction: Related Practice

2A–175   Service out of the jurisdiction without permission

1. (a) Before issuing a claim form or seeking permission to serve out of the jurisdiction, it is necessary to consider whether the jurisdiction of the English courts is affected by the Civil Jurisdiction and Judgments Act 1982. Where each claim in the claim form is a claim which the Court has by virtue of the Civil Jurisdiction and Judgments Act 1982 power to hear and determine, service of the claim form out of the jurisdiction may be effected without permission provided that, in the case of service in Scotland or Northern Ireland, the relevant requirements of rules 6.32 and 6.34 are satisfied; and, in the case of service out of the United Kingdom, the relevant requirements of rules 6.33 and 6.34 are satisfied.

These requirements include the requirement to file with the claim form a notice containing a statement of the grounds on which the claimant is entitled to serve the claim form out of the jurisdiction and to serve a copy of that notice with the claim form. In the case of service out of the jurisdiction of the United Kingdom, paragraph 2.1 of PD6B requires the notice to be in the form of practice form N510 in order to comply with rule 6.34. Rule 6.34(2) provides that, if the claimant fails to file such a notice, the consequence is that the claim form may only be served once the claimant has filed the requisite notice or if the court gives permission.

(b) Because of the significance of (amongst other things) the concept of "first seisure" in the context of Council Regulation (EC) No 44/2001 of 22 December 2001 on jurisdiction and the recognition and enforcement of judgments in civil and commercial matters ("the Judgment Regulation"), it is very important that the statement as to the grounds upon which the claimant is entitled to serve the claim form out of the jurisdiction is accurate and made with care. If entitlement to serve out of the jurisdiction without leave is wrongly asserted, a claimant may be ordered to pay the costs of a defendant's application to strike out the claim or set aside serve of the claim form on an indemnity basis.

(c) Rule 6.35 sets out the time periods during which a defendant must respond to a claim form where permission was not required for service, depending on whether the defendant is:

   (i) in Scotland or Northern Ireland;
   (ii) in a Member State or a Convention Territory; or
   (iii) elsewhere.

Paragraph 6 of PDB sets out the periods for responding in the case of defendants served elsewhere.

These provisions are subject to the modifications set out in rule 58 in relation to Commercial Court Cases, including, but not limited to

   (i) that a defendant must file an acknowledgement of service in every case; and
   (ii) that the time periods provided by rule 6.35 apply after service of the claim form.

2A–176   Application for permission: statement in support

2. (a) The grounds upon which a claimant may apply for the court's permission to serve a claim form out of the jurisdiction pursuant to rule 6.36 (in circumstances where neither rule 6.32 nor rule 6.33 applies) are set out in paragraph 3.1 of PDB.

(b) An application for permission under rule 6.36 must set out:

   (i) the ground in PD6B relied on as giving the court jurisdiction to order service out, together with a summary of the facts relied on as bringing the case within each such paragraph;
   (ii) where the application is made in respect of a claim referred to in paragraph 3.1(3) of PD6B, the grounds on which the claimant believes that there is between the claimant and the defendant a real issue which it is reasonable for the court to try;

(iii) the belief of the claimant that the claim has a reasonable prospect of success; and

(iv) the defendant's address or, if not known, in what place or country the defendant is or is likely to be found.

(c) The claimant should also present evidence of the considerations relied upon as showing that the case is a proper one in which to subject a party outside the jurisdiction to proceedings within it (stating the grounds of belief and sources of information); exhibit copies of the documents referred to and any other significant documents; and draw attention to any features which might reasonably be thought to weigh against the making of the order sought. Where convenient the written evidence should be included in the form of application notice, rather than in a separate witness statement. The form of application notice may be extended for this purpose.

Application for permission: copies of draft order
2A–177

3. (a) specify the periods within which the defendant must:
   (i) file an acknowledgement of service;
   (ii) serve or file an admission;
   (iii) file a defence; and

   (b) set out any other directions sought by the claimant as to:
   (i) the method of service;
   (ii) the terms of any order sought giving permission to serve other documents out of the jurisdiction;

The relevant periods referred to in sub–paragraphs (a)(i)–(iii) above are specified in paragraphs 6.1–6.6 of PDB, and in the Table at the end of that Practice Direction.

Application for permission: copy or draft of claim form

4. A copy or draft of the claim form which the applicant intends to issue and serve **2A–178** must be provided to the judge who will usually initial it. If the endorsement to the claim form includes causes of action or claims not covered by the grounds on which permission to serve out of the jurisdiction can properly be granted, permission will be refused unless the draft is amended to restrict it to proper claims. Where the application is for the issue of a concurrent claim form, the documents submitted must also include a copy of the original claim form.

Arbitration matters

5. Service out of the jurisdiction in arbitration matters is governed by Part 62. As to **2A–179** the 1968 Convention on Jurisdiction in the context of arbitration, see Article 1(4), which applies rules 6.40– 6.46. The Judgment Regulation does not apply to "arbitration" (see Article 1.(2)(d)), but what proceedings fall within the category of arbitration and what do not, may be a difficult question: see The Front Comor, 10 February 2009, Case C–185/07.

Practice under rules 6.32 and 6.33
2A–180

6. (a) Although a Part 7 claim form may contain or be accompanied by particulars of claim, there is no need for it to do so and in many cases particulars of claim will be served after the claim form: rule 58.5.

(b) A defendant should acknowledge service in every case: rule 58.6(1).

(c) The period for filing an acknowledgment of service will be calculated from the service of the claim form, whether or not particulars of claim are to follow: rule 58.6.

(d) The periods for filing an acknowledgement of service and a defence are set out respectively in rule 6.35(2) (in relation to claim forms served in Scotland and Northern Ireland); in rule 6.35(3) (in relation to claim forms served pursuant to rule 6.33 on a defendant in a Convention Territory within Europe or a Member State); in rule 6.35(4) (in relation to claim forms served pursuant to rule 6.33 on a defendant in a Convention Territory outside Europe); and in paragraphs 6.1, 6.3, 6.4 and the Table in PDB in relation to claim forms served pursuant to rule 6.33 on a defendant in a country elsewhere: rule 6.35(5).

2A–180.1 Practice under rule 6.36

7. (a) Although a Part 7 claim form may contain or be accompanied by particulars of claim, there is no need for it to do so and in many cases particulars of claim will be served after the claim form: rule 58.5. If the claim form states that particulars of claim are to follow, there is no need to obtain further permission to serve out of the jurisdiction: rule 6.38(2).

However, permission must be obtained to serve any other document out of the jurisdiction: rule 6.38(2); other than in cases where the defendant has given an address for service in Scotland and Northern Ireland: rule 6.38(3).

(b) A defendant should acknowledge service in every case: rule 58.6(1).

(c) The periods for filing an acknowledgment of service will be calculated from the service of the claim form, whether or not particulars of claim are to follow: rule 58.6.

(d) The period for serving, and filing, particulars of claim (where they were not contained in the claim form and did not accompany the claim form) will be calculated from acknowledgment of service: rule 58.5(1)(c).

(e) The period for serving and filing the defence will be calculated from service of the particulars of claim: rule 58.10(2).

8. Time for serving and filing a defence is calculated:

(a) by reference to the number of days listed in the Table in PDB after service of the particulars of claim; or

(b) where the defendant has filed an acknowledgement of service, the number of days listed in the Table plus an additional 14 days after service of the particulars of claim: paragraph 6.4 of PDB.

9. There is some uncertainty whether the court's powers under rule 6.37 and rule 6.40 to give directions about the "method" of service include a specific power to make an order for service of documents to which Section IV of Part 6 applies by an alternative method (e.g. service on solicitors within the jurisdiction or service on a party by email); see the Notes in the 2009 Edition of Civil Procedure Rules Part 6 at paras 6.15.1 and 6.15.7. To date, the Commercial and Admiralty Court judges have taken the view that they do have such power and, in appropriate cases, have made orders providing for alternative methods of service, in cases where the criteria for serving the claim form out of the jurisdiction are satisfied. However, in circumstances where such alternative service is not permitted by the law of the country in which the defendant is to be served, rule 6.40(3) and (4) would appear to prevent such orders being made.

Practice under rule 6.41—service in accordance with the Service Regulation

2A–180.2 10. If a party wishes to effect service of the claim form or other document in accordance with the Service Regulation, then the procedure to be adopted differs depending upon whether service is being made pursuant to rule 6.33 (service of the claim form, and other documents, out of the jurisdiction where the permission of the court is not required), or whether it is being made pursuant to rules 6.36 and 6.37 (service of the claim form, and other documents, out of the jurisdiction where the permission of the court is required).

11. In the former case (service without permission), the claimant must file the relevant documents referred to in rule 6.41(2) with the Registry. If the documents are in order, the relevant court officer will seal the claim form and forward the documents to the Senior Master of the Queen's Bench Division in accordance with rule 6.41(3).

12. In the latter case (service with permission), the claimant must first obtain permission from a judge to serve the relevant documents out of the jurisdiction, together with a direction pursuant to rule 6.37 that one, or the, method of service is to be in accordance with the Service Regulation. Once such an order has been made,

the relevant court officer will seal the claim form and forward the documents to the Senior Master in accordance with rule 6.41(3).

13. In either case, once the documents have been forwarded by the Registry to the Senior Master, any queries thereafter about the progress of such service should be directed to the Senior Master.

Appendix 16

Security for Costs: Related Practice

First applications

1. First applications for security for costs should not be made later than at the Case **2A–181** Management Conference and in any event any application should not be left until close to the trial date. Delay to the prejudice of the other party or the administration of justice might well cause the application to fail, as will any use of the application to harass the other party. Where it is intended to make an application for security at the Case Management Conference the procedure, and timetable for evidence, for an ordinary application must be followed (see section F5 of the Guide).

Successive applications

2. Successive applications for security can be granted where the circumstances **2A–182** warrant. If a claimant wishes to seek to preclude any further application it is incumbent on him to make that clear.

Evidence

3. An affidavit or witness statement in support of an application for security for costs **2A–183** should deal not only with the residence of the claimant (or other respondent to the application) and the location of his assets but also with the practical difficulties (if any) of enforcing an order for costs against him.

Investigation of the merits of the case

4. Investigation of the merits of the case on an application for security is strongly **2A–184** discouraged. It is usually only in those cases where it can be shown without detailed investigation of evidence or law that the claim is certain or almost certain to succeed or fail will the merits be taken into consideration.

Undertaking by the applicant

5. In appropriate cases an order for security for costs may only be made on terms **2A–185** that the applicant gives an undertaking to comply with any order that the court may make if the court later finds that the order for security for costs has caused loss to the claimant and that the claimant should be compensated for such loss. Such undertakings are intended to compensate claimants in cases where no order for costs is ultimately made in favour of the applicant.

Stay of proceedings

6. It is not usually convenient or appropriate to order an automatic stay of the **2A–186** proceedings pending the provision of the security. It leads to delay and may disrupt the preparation of the case for trial, or other hearing. Experience has shown that it is usually better to give the claimant (or other relevant party) a reasonable time within which to provide the security and the other party liberty to apply to the court in the event of default. This enables the court to put the claimant to his election and then, if appropriate, to dismiss the case.

Amount of security

7. Where the dispute on an application for security for costs relates to the correct **2A–187** evaluation of the amount of costs likely to be allowed to a successful defendant on an assessment of costs, parties should consider whether it would be advantageous for the judge hearing the application to sit with a Costs Judge as an informal assessor. The judge himself may take such an initiative.

APPENDIX 17

COMMERCIAL COURT USER E-MAIL GUIDANCE

Introduction

2A-188 1. This guidance sets out how parties may communicate by e-mail with the Commercial and Admiralty Courts on certain matters.

Restrictions

2A-189 2. A party should not use e-mail to take any step in a claim which requires a fee to be paid for that step. If a party sends by e-mail a document for which a fee is payable upon filing, the document will be treated as not having been filed.

3. Where a party sends or lodges a document by e-mail he should still comply with any rule or practice direction requiring the document to be served on any other person.

4. Nothing in this guidance requires any person to accept service of a document by e-mail.

The subject line

2A-190 5. The subject line of the e-mail should contain only the following information which should be in the following order:

    a. First, the proper title of the claim (abbreviated as necessary) with the claimant named first and the defendant named second; unless the action is an Admiralty action, the name of the ship should not be used:

    b. Second, the claim number.

Form and content of the e-mail

2A-191 6. Correspondence and documents may be sent either as text or attachments, except that documents required to be in a practice form should be sent in that form as attachments using one of the formats specified in paragraph 17.

7. Parties must not use e-mail to send any document which exceeds 40 pages in the aggregate of normal typescript in length or 2 MB whichever is the smaller. Documents may not be subdivided to comply with this requirement.

8. Where a party files a document by e-mail, he should not send a hard copy in addition, unless there are good reasons for so doing or the Court requires.

9. Parties are advised to bear in mind when sending correspondence or documents of a confidential or sensitive nature that the security of e-mails cannot be guaranteed.

10. Where a time limit applies, it remains the responsibility of the party to ensure that the document is filed in time. Parties are advised to allow for delays or downtime on their server or the servers used by the Court.

Attachments

2A-192 11. Attachments should be in one of the following formats:

    a. Microsoft Word viewer/reader (.doc) in Word 1997 or later format

    b. Rich Text Format as (.rtf) files

    c. Plain/Formatted Text as (.txt) files

    d. Hypertext documents as (.htm) files

    e. Adobe Acrobat as (.pdf) files minimum viewer version 4

Receipt of e-mail by the Court

2A-193 12. A document is not filed until the e-mail is received by the court at the addressee's computer terminal, whatever time it is shown to have been sent.

13. The time of receipt of an e-mail at the addressee's computer terminal will be recorded.

14. If an e–mail is received after 4 p.m. it will be treated as having been received on the next day the court office is open.

15. If a response to the subject matter of the e–mail is not received within a reasonable period, the sender should assume that the court has not received it and should send the e–mail again, or file the document by another means.

16. Parties should not telephone to enquire as to the receipt of an e–mail. They should observe the procedure set out in paragraph 15.

Replies to e–mails sent to the court

17. The court will normally send any reply by e–mail to documents or **2A–194** correspondence sent by e–mail.
  a. All replies will be sent to the e–mail address from which the e–mail has been sent. If the sender wishes the reply to be copied to other parties or to another e–mail address used by the sender of the message, such e–mail addresses must be specified in the copy line.
  b. The Court will not send copies to clients or others not on the record; the copy line must therefore not contain the addresses of such persons.
  c. The e–mail should also contain in the body of the e–mail the name and telephone number of the sender.

Note: It is important that each firm or set of chambers considers putting in place a system to deal with the absence of the individual who has sent the e–mail and to whom the Court will ordinarily reply. Two possible solutions are:
  a. A central mail box within each firm, either from which the e–mail is sent to the Court (and which will therefore receive the reply) or to which it is copied by the individual sender who sends it direct to the Court (and who will receive a copy of the reply);
  b. a second individual e–mail address within the firm to which the reply will be copied so that any reply can be monitored.

It must be for each firm and set of chambers to devise its own system.

Communication with the Clerk to a Commercial Judge

18. No documents or correspondence should be sent by e–mail to the Clerk to a **2A–195** Commercial Judge dealing with a case, unless:
  a. an arrangement is made with the Clerk in each specific instance in which e–mail is to be used;
  b. if such an arrangement is made, the e–mail must be copied to the appropriate Listing Office Address, The Registry Address, or the Admiralty Marshal Address, as the case may be.

Appendix 18

Commercial Court Electronic Working Pilot Scheme

Introduction   2A–196

1. On 1 April 2009 the Commercial Court began a electronic working pilot scheme. It allows claims to be brought by issuing a claim form electronically, other documents to be filed electronically in those cases and an electronic court file to be used and inspected.

2. The intention is for the pilot scheme to be developed incrementally. Initially it covers only Part 7 claims in the Commercial Court and shortly such claims in the Admiralty Court issued by registered users. It is intended that it should soon be developed to include Part 8 claims and arbitration claims. Up–to–date information about the scheme can be found on the Commercial Court website (www.hmcourts–service.gov.uk/infoabout/admiralcomm).

3. The pilot scheme is taking place under Practice Direction (Electronic Working Pilot

Scheme): see CPR Part 51. The practice direction is set out at the end of this appendix.

Operation of the scheme

4. The electronic scheme operated 24 hours every day and so claim forms can be issued and documents can be filed in cases to which the scheme applies outside normal court office opening hours. However, the scheme is not operated (i) during planned "down–time" and (ii) during "unplanned down–time". See PD (EWPS) 1.2(2). If the scheme is not operating, claim forms can be issued outside normal court hours by fax: see PD 58 2.2, and para B2.4 and Appendix 3 of the Guide.

Fees

5. Under the scheme fees may be paid by credit or debit card. If fees are not paid in accordance with the court's specifications, the court may make an order under CPR 3.3, including, in an appropriate case, an order striking out a claim or an application. See PD (EWPS) 3.1, 3.3, 8.1.

Forms

6. All forms filed at court under the scheme must be in PDF formal, and where they are available, the PDF forms created for the scheme must be used. If necessary forms must be converted into PDF format before they are filed. See PD (EWPS) para 4.1, 4.2, 4.3.

Starting claims

7. The procedure for starting a claim under the scheme is set out in PD (EWPS) para 6. The court will enter on the claim form as the issue date the date when the claim form was received by the court electronically: PD (EWPS) para 6.5. A claim form is issued on the date entered on the form by the court: CPR 7.2(2).

Defendants

8. Where a claim is started electronically, a defendant may file documents electronically. Any fees (for example, payable by a defendant making a counterclaim or an application) must be paid when and in the manner stipulated by the court. See para 5 above, and PD (EWPS) paras 7 and 8.

Statements of truth and signatures

9. Attention is drawn to paras 9 and 10 of the PD (EWPS), which deal with statements of truth and signatures.

Hard copies of documents

10. All trial bundles must be filed in hard copy format; PD (EWPS) para 14.

11. The court may require any other bundle to be provided in hard copy: PD (EWPS) para 13.

Note: During the course of this pilot scheme the court and Judges, with the assistance of court users, will be learning from experience what bundles (other than trial bundles) need be filed in hard copy. Please consult the Commercial Court website or telephone the court for up–to–date guidance.

PRACTICE DIRECTION—ELECTRONIC WORKING PILOT

2A–197   *Note*—For text of practice direction, see para.5CPD.0 above.

APPENDIX 19

GUIDANCE ON PRACTICAL STEPS FOR TRANSFERRING CASES TO THE MERCANTILE COURTS

1. If a case is suitable for transfer to a Mercantile Court, either party can apply to the **2A–214** Commercial Judge prior to the CMC for transfer or, if no such application is made, the Commercial Judge will normally consider this with the parties at the CMC. He will expect the parties to have considered this issue prior to the CMC. Among the factors that the parties should consider are the size and complexity of the claim, the location of the parties and their legal advisers and the convenience of the witnesses. If transfer is contemplated, the parties should also contact the appropriate listing officer (at the telephone numbers set out at paragraph 9) to ascertain likely trial dates.

2. If the case is one that is suitable for transfer and a decision is made to transfer prior to the CMC, the Commercial Judge will order that the case be transferred to a Mercantile Court and the CMC will take place at the Mercantile Court.

3. If the case is one that is suitable for transfer and a decision is made to transfer at the CMC, the Commercial Judge will, in order to save the costs of a further hearing in the Mercantile Court, usually make all the directions with the appropriate timetable down to trial in the same way as if the case were to remain in the Commercial Court, including a direction to fix the trial date through the appropriate listing officer (see paragraph 9 below) within a specified period of time. If, as is usually the case, it is thought desirable to give the parties time to try and settle the case through direct negotiation or ADR, this will be built into the timetable.

4. The Commercial Judge will consider the time at which transfer is to take place and this must be specified in the Order. The Commercial Judge will decide whether he considers a PTR or further CMC appears necessary at that stage.

5. The Order must be drawn up in the usual way and lodged with the Commercial Registry Room EB13 in the RCJ.
   - If the draft Order was not initialled in court by the Judge, the Order will then be sent to the Judge who made the Order to be approved. That normally takes 3–4 days.
   - If the draft Order was initialled in court by the Judge at the hearing, the Order can be brought straight up to the Registry to be sealed.

6. Once the Order comes back, the Registry will put the Order in the various out trays for the solicitors clerks to collect. If the Order was sent in via the post, then the Registry will return it via the post or, if the firm of solicitors are not one of the regular users, the Registry will inform them of the procedure as to how to collect the Order.

7. Once the Order is sealed, the transfer from the Commercial Court is during normal circumstances effected by the Registry within one week; the transfer is effected by the Registry sending the court file and the Order to the Mercantile Court as the case may be. The Registry will also inform all parties on record once the case has been transferred.

8. The Mercantile Court will then receive all the papers which were on the Commercial Court file and they will give the case one of their own numbers and inform the parties.

9. The case will then continue in exactly the same way as if at the Commercial Court save that the hearing date must be fixed with the listing office at the Mercantile Court within the time limit specified in the Order. The parties must contact the specialist listing officer at the Court to which the case has been transferred. The telephone and fax numbers of the listing officers for the specialist list are:

London Mercantile Court

020 7947 6826

Fax 020 7947 7670

E–mail: comct.listing@hmcourts–service.gsi.gov.uk

Birmingham:

0121 681 3035

Fax 0121 250 6730

E–mail: birmingham.mercantile@hmcourts–service.gsi.gov.uk

Bristol:

0117 910 6706

Fax 0117 910 6727

E–mail: bristolmercantilelisting@hmcourts–service.gsi.gov.uk

Leeds:

0113 306 2461

Fax 0113 306 2392

E–mail: e–filing@leeds.countycourt.gsi.gov.uk

Newcastle:

0191 201 2047

Fax 0191 201 2000

E–mail: hearings@newcastle.countycourt.gsi.gov.uk

Liverpool/Manchester:

0161 240 5307

Fax 0161 240 5398

E–mail: highcourtspecialisthearings@manchester.countycourt.gsi.gov.uk

Wales and Chester:

02920 376483

Fax 02920 376475

E–mail: hearings@cardiff.countycourt.gsi.gov.uk

Parties are asked to speak to the specialist listing officers who will tell them of the facilities available at other Courts.

11. The Commercial Court monitors compliance with its Orders through the provision of progress monitoring information sheets which have to be provided by the Progress Monitoring Date specified in the Order. The standard directions for the Mercantile Courts provide for a Progress Monitoring Date; such a date should therefore be provided for in any Order. The Mercantile Courts monitor progress in

accordance with paragraph 8 of the Mercantile Courts Practice Direction supplemental to Part 59. A PTR (either in court or by telephone conference) may be held in the Mercantile Courts if the parties make a request or the Mercantile Judge so directs.

12. The parties are expected to keep the listing officer of the Court to which the case is transferred apprised of any settlement of the case. Where the Commercial Judge has not made all the directions or the parties need to make an application either orally or in writing, then the appropriate directions will be considered and made by the Mercantile Judge.

ADDRESSES AND CONTACT DETAILS

The Admiralty Marshal: **2A–215**

    Room EB12

    Royal Courts of Justice

    Strand

    London WC2A 2LL

    Tel: 020 7947 6111

    Fax: 020 7947 7671

The Admiralty & Commercial Registry:

    Room EB13

    Royal Courts of Justice

    Strand,

    London WC2A 2LL

    Tel: 020 7947 6112

    Fax: 020 7947 6245

    DX 44450 STRAND

The Admiralty & Commercial Court Listing Office:

    Room EB09

    Royal Courts of Justice

    Strand,

    London WC2A 2LL

    Tel: 020 7947 6826

    Fax: 020 7947 7670

    DX 44450 STRAND

The Secretary to the Commercial Court Committee:

    Mrs Angela Hodgson

    Room EB09

    Royal Courts of Justice

    Strand

    London WC2A 2LL

    Tel: 020 7947 6826

    Fax: 020 7947 7670

    DX 44450 STRAND

Out of hours emergency number: (Security Office at Royal Courts of Justice): 020 7947 6260.

Fax number for the procedure under sections B3.11 and B4.4 of the Guide for the issue of claim forms when the Registry is closed: 020 7947 6667.

2B   MERCANTILE COURTS

Part 59—Mercantile Courts

Related sources

After the last bullet point add new bullet point:

2B–2.1   • Practice Direction (Electronic Working Pilot Scheme)

Electronic working

Add new paragraph 2B–4.1:

2B–4.1   Practice Direction (Electronic Working Pilot Scheme), made by the Master of the Rolls, came into effect on April 1, 2009. It supplements CPR r.5.5 (Filing and sending documents) and provides for a pilot scheme, starting on April 1, 2009, and running (initially) until March 31, 2010, by which, in the circumstances set out in the practice direction, parties may avail themselves of arrangements for starting proceedings in London Mercantile Courts at the Royal Courts of Justice (and some other courts) electronically, and also for taking all subsequent steps in the proceedings electronically (so–called "Electronic Working"). In certain respects the practice direction modifies CPR provisions that would otherwise apply. Paragraph 1.3 states that, where proceedings to which CPR Pt 59 (Mercantile Courts) apply are issued, then the Electronic Working pilot scheme will apply subject to the provisions of that Part unless specifically excluded or revised by this practice direction.

The full text of this practice direction is published at para.5CPD.1 above.

2C   PROCEEDINGS IN THE TECHNOLOGY AND CONSTRUCTION COURT

Part 60—Technology and Construction Court Claims

General

In rule 60.1(4) for "Supreme Court Act 1981" substitute:

2C–4   **Senior Courts Act 1981**[1]

2D   ADMIRALTY JURISDICTION AND PROCEEDINGS

Part 61—Admiralty Claims

Related sources

After the last bullet point add new bullet point:

2D–3   • Practice Direction (Electronic Working Pilot Scheme)

Electronic working

Add new paragraph 2D–5.1:

2D–5.1   Practice Direction (Electronic Working Pilot Scheme), made by the Master of the Rolls, came into effect on April 1, 2009. It supplements CPR r.5.5 (Filing and sending documents) and provides for a pilot scheme, starting on April 1, 2009, and running

---

[1] 1981 c.54. Renamed by the Constitutional Reform Act 2005 s.59 and Sch.11, para.1 with effect from October 1, 2009 (SI 2009/1604).

(initially) until March 31, 2010, by which, in the circumstances set out in the practice direction, parties may avail themselves of arrangements for starting proceedings in the Admiralty Court at the Royal Courts of Justice (and some other courts) electronically, and also for taking all subsequent steps in the proceedings electronically (so–called "Electronic Working"). In certain respects the practice direction modifies CPR provisions that would otherwise apply. Paragraph 1.3 states that, where proceedings to which CPR Pt 61 (Admiralty Claims) apply are issued, then the Electronic Working pilot scheme will apply subject to the provisions of that Part unless specifically excluded or revised by this practice direction.

Scope and interpretation

In rule 61.1(2)(a) for "section 20 of the Senior Courts Act 1981" substitute:

section 20 of the Senior Courts Act 1981[1]   2D–6

In rule 61.1(2)(d) for "Supreme Court Act 1981" substitute:

Senior Courts Act 1981

Admiralty jurisdiction

Add at end:

Applied by *Christopher Clarke Jin Cherney v Deripsaka* [2008] EWHC 1530 (Comm); **2D–7** [2009] 1 All E.R. (Comm) 333.

Claims against two or more "sister" ships

Add at end:

The Banco was distinguished by the Singapore Court of Appeal in *Permina Samudra* **2D–10** [1978] 1 Lloyds Rep. 315 but subsequently applied in *The Berny* [1979] Q.B. 80; [1978 1 All E.R. 1065; [1977] 2 Lloyds Rep 533 and followed in Scotland by the Court of Sessions: *The Afala* [1995] 2 Lloyd's Rep 286.

Admiralty claims

In rule 61.2(1)(a)(v), for "Supreme Court Act 1981" substitute:

Senior Courts Act 1981[2]   2D–16

Renewal of claim form

Add at end:

See also *The Helen Roth* [1980] Q.B. 273; [1980] 2 W.L.R. 549; [1980] 1 All E.R. **2D–26** 1078; [1980] 1 Lloyd's Rep. 477 as to the effect of a sale before the claim form was renewed.

Special provisions relating to collision claims

In rule 61.4(7), for "section 22(2)(a), (b) or (c) of the Supreme Court Act 1981" substitute:

section 22(2)(a), (b) or (c) of the Senior Courts Act 1981[3] 2D–29

---

[1] 1981 c.54; s.20 was amended by the Merchant Shipping (Salvage and Pollution) Act 1994 (c.28) s.1(6) and Sch. 2, para.6; the Merchant Shipping Act 1995 (c.21) s.314(2) and Sch.13, para.59 and by the Merchant Shipping and Maritime Security Act 1997 (c.28) s.29(1) and Sch. 6, para.2. Renamed by the Constitutional Reform Act 2005 s.59 and Sch.11, para.1 with effect from October 1, 2009 (SI 2009/1604).

[2] 1981 c.54. Renamed by the Constitutional Reform Act 2005 s.59 and Sch.11, para.1 with effect from October 1, 2009 (SI 2009/1604)

Damages

Add at end:

2D–33.1   The following cases, cited in *The Front Ace*, are also of importance in assessing damages: *The Oropesa* [1943] P. 32; [1943] 1 All E.R. 211; (1942) 74 Ll. L. Rep. 86; (CA) which provides that a claimant is entitled to damages unless there has been a break in the chain of causation; *Owners of the Steamship Gracie v Owners of the Steamship Argentino (The Argentino)* (1889) L.R. 14 App. Cas. 519; (HL) on the methodology to be adopted in cases where a claimant has lost a fixture as a result of the collision and *Allied Maples Group Ltd v Simmons & Simmons* [1995] 1 W.L.R. 1602; [1995] 4 All E.R. 907; [1996] C.L.C. 153 on the question of whether a deduction should be made for the chance of obtaining a replacement contract.

Release pursuant to Merchant Shipping Act 1995

Add at end:

2D–54   See also *The Wladyslaw Lokotiek* [1978] 2 Lloyd's Rep. 520.

Limitation claims

In rule 61.11(5)(a), for "section 22(2)(a), (b) or (c) of the Supreme Court Act 1981" substitute:

2D–73   **section 22(2)(a), (b) or (c) of the Senior Courts Act 1981[1];**

Practice Direction—Admiralty Claims

Arrest

Delete paragraph 5.3(2) and substitute:

2D–96   (2) in a claim against a ship by virtue of section 21(4) of the Senior Courts Act 1981—

(a) the name of the person who would be liable on the claim if it were not commenced in rem;

(b) that the person referred to in sub–paragraph (a) was, when the right to bring the claim arose

(i) the owner or charterer of; or

(ii) in possession or in control of,

the ship in connection with which the claim arose; and

(c) that at the time the claim form was issued the person referred to in sub–paragraph (a) was either—

(i) the beneficial owner of all the shares in the ship in respect of which the warrant is required; or

(ii) the charterer of it under a charter by demise;

(3) in the cases set out in rules 61.5(5) and (6) that the relevant notice has been sent or served, as appropriate; and

(4) in the case of a claim in respect of liability incurred under section 153 of the Merchant Shipping Act 1995, the facts relied on as establishing that the court is not prevented from considering the claim by reason of section 166(2) of that Act.

---

[3] 1981 c.54. Renamed by the Constitutional Reform Act 2005 s.59 and Sch.11, para.1 with effect from October 1, 2009 (SI 2009/1604).

[1] 1981 c.54. Renamed by the Constitutional Reform Act 2005 s.59 and Sch.11, para.1 with effect from October 1, 2009 (SI 2009/1604).

Note

Add new paragraph 2D–96.1:
Amended by the Constitutional Reform Act 2005 s.59 and Sch.11, para.1 with effect **2D–96.1** from October 1, 2009 (SI 2009/1604).

Claim in reference. See para.13.2 above

For "Vol.3, Form 181 (2003 Issue)":
Vol.3, Form 185 (2008 Issue) **2D–128**

Senior Courts Act 1981

Delete title "Supreme Court Act 1981" and substitute "Senior Courts Act 1981". **2D–145**

2E ARBITRATION PROCEEDINGS

For "Supreme Court Act 1981" substitute:
Senior Courts Act 1981 **2E–380**

Note

In the first paragraph, for "and the Civil Procedure (Modification of Enactments) Order 2002." substitute:
, the Civil Procedure (Modification of Enactments) Order 2002 and the Constitutional **2E–381** Reform Act 2005 s.59 and Sch.11, para.1 with effect from October 1, 2009 (SI 2009/ 1604).

2F INTELLECTUAL PROPERTY PROCEEDINGS

PART 63—INTELLECTUAL PROPERTY CLAIMS

Delete Part 63 and substitute:

Contents **2F–1**

Scope of this Part and interpretation

2F–2   63.1—(1)   This Part applies to all intellectual property claims
including—
>   (a) registered intellectual property rights such as—
>>   (i) patents;
>>   (ii) registered designs; and
>>   (iii) registered trade marks; and
>   (b) unregistered intellectual property rights such as—
>>   (i) copyright;
>>   (ii) design right;
>>   (iii) the right to prevent passing off; and
>>   (iv) the other rights set out in the practice direction.
>   (2) In this Part—
>>   (a) "the 1977 Act" means the Patents Act 1977[1];
>>   (b) "the 1988 Act" means the Copyright, Designs and Patents
>>   Act 1988[2];
>>   (c) "the 1994 Act" means the the Trade Marks Act 1994[3];
>>   (d) "the Comptroller" means the Comptroller General of
>>   Patents, Designs and Trade Marks;
>>   (e) "patent" means a patent under the 1977 Actor a supple-
>>   mentary protection certificate granted by the Patent Of-
>>   fice under Article 10(1) of Council Regulation (EEC) No.
>>   1768/92[4] or of Regulation (EC) No. 1610/96 of the
>>   European Parliament and the Council[5] and includes any
>>   application for a patent or supplementary protection cer-
>>   tificate;
>>   (f) "Patents Court"

means the Patents Court of the High Court constituted as part of
the Chancery Division by section 6(1) of the Senior Courts Act
1981[6];

---

[1] 1977 c.37.
[2] 1988 c.48.
[3] 1994 c.26.
[4] OJ No L182, 2.7.1992, p.1.
[5] OJ No L198, 8.8.1996, p.30.
[6] 1981 c.54. Renamed by the Constitutional Reform Act 2005, s.59, Sch.11, para.1 with effect
from October 1, 2009 (SI 2009/1604).

(g) "patents county court" means a county court designated as a patents county court under section 287(1) of the 1988 Act;

(h) "patents judge" means a person nominated under section 291(1) of the 1988 Act as the patents judge of a patents county court[1];

(i) "the practice direction" means the Practice Direction supplementing this Part;

(j) "the register" means whichever of the following registers is appropriate—

(i) patents maintained by the Comptroller under section 32 of the 1977 Act;

(ii) designs maintained by the registrar under section 17 of the Registered Designs Act 1949[2];

(iii) trade marks maintained by the registrar under section 63 of the 1994 Act;

(iv) Community trade marks maintained by the Office for Harmonisation in the Internal Market under Article 83 of Council Regulation (EC) 40/94[3];

(v) Community designs maintained by the Office for Harmonisation in the Internal Market under Article 72 of Council Regulation (EC) 6/2002[4]; and

(vi) plant varieties maintained by the Controller under regulation 12 of the Plant Breeders' Rights Regulations 1998[5]; and

(k) "the registrar" means—

(i) the registrar of trade marks; or

(ii) the registrar of registered designs,

whichever is appropriate.

(3) Claims to which this Part applies are allocated to the multi–track.

I. Patents and Registered Designs

Scope of Section I and allocation

63.2—(1) This Section applies to—   2F–3

(a) any claim under—

(i) the 1977 Act;

(ii) the Registered Designs Act 1949;

(iii) the Defence Contracts Act 1958; and

(b) any claim relating to—

(i) Community registered designs;

(ii) semiconductor topography rights; or

(iii) plant varieties.

(2) Claims to which this Section applies must be started in—

(a) the Patents Court; or

(b) a patents county court.

Specialist list

63.3 Claims in the Patents Court and a patents county court 2F–4
form specialist lists for the purpose of rule 30.5.

---

[1] SI 2005/2292.
[2] 1949 c.88.
[3] OJ No.L11, 14.1.1994, p.1.
[4] OJ No.L3, 5.1.2002, p.1.
[5] S.I. 1998/1027.

Patents Judge

2F–5   63.4—(1) Subject to paragraph (2), proceedings in a patents county court will be dealt with by the patents judge of that court.

(2) When a matter needs to be dealt with urgently and it is not practicable or appropriate for the patents judge to deal with such a matter, the matter may be dealt with by another judge with appropriate specialist experience nominated by the Chancellor of the High Court.

Starting the claim

2F–6   63.5 Claims to which this Section applies must be started—
   (a) by a Part 7 claim form; or
   (b) in existing proceedings under Part 20.

Claim for infringement or challenge to validity of a patent or registered design

2F–7   63.6 A statement of case in a claim for infringement or a claim in which the validity of a patent or registered design is challenged must contain particulars as set out in the practice direction.

Defence and reply

2F–8   63.7 Part 15 applies with the modification—
   (a) to rule 15.4(1)(b) that in a claim for infringement under rule 63.6, the period for filing a defence where the defendant files an acknowledgment of service under Part 10 is 42 days after service of the particulars of claim;
   (b) that where rule 15.4(2) provides for a longer period to file a defence than in rule 63.7(a), then the period of time in rule 15.4(2) will apply; and
   (c) to rule 15.8 that the claimant must—
      (i) file any reply to a defence; and
      (i) serve it on all other parties,
   within 21 days of service of the defence.

Case management

2F–9   63.8—(1) Parties do not need to file an allocation questionnaire.
   (2) The following provisions only of Part 29 apply—
      (a) rule 29.3(2) (legal representatives to attend case management conferences);
      (b) rule 29.4 (the court's approval of agreed proposals for the management of proceedings); and
      (c) rule 29.5 (variation of case management timetable) with the exception of paragraph (1)(b) and (c).

(3) As soon as practicable the court will hold a case management conference which must be fixed in accordance with the practice direction.

Disclosure and inspection

2F–10   63.9 Part 31 is modified to the extent set out in the practice direction.

Application to amend a patent specification in existing proceedings

63.10—(1) An application under section 75 of the 1977 Act for 2F–11
permission to amend the specification of a patent by the proprietor
of the patent must be made by application notice.

(2) The application notice must—
- (a) give particulars of—
  - (i) the proposed amendment sought; and
  - (ii) the grounds upon which the amendment is sought;
- (b) state whether the applicant will contend that the claims
prior to the amendment are valid; and
- (c) be served by the applicant on all parties and the Comptroller within 7 days of it being filed.

(3) The application notice must, if it is reasonably possible, be
served on the Comptroller electronically.

(4) Unless the court otherwise orders, the Comptroller will, as
soon as practicable, advertise the application to amend in the
journal.

(5) The advertisement will state that any person may apply to the
Comptroller for a copy of the application notice.

(6) Within 14 days of the first appearance of the advertisement
any person who wishes to oppose the application must file and
serve on all parties and the Comptroller a notice opposing the application which must include the grounds relied on.

(7) Within 28 days of the first appearance of the advertisement
the applicant must apply to the court for directions.

(8) Unless the court otherwise orders, the applicant must within
7 days serve on the Comptroller any order of the court on the
application.

(9) In this rule "the journal" means the journal published pursuant to rules under section 123(6) of the 1977 Act.

Court's determination of question or application

63.11—(1) This rule applies where the Comptroller—   2F–12
- (a) declines to deal with a question under section 8(7), 12(2),
37(8) or 61(5) of the 1977 Act;
- (b) declines to deal with an application under section 40(5)
of the 1977 Act; or
- (c) certifies under section 72(7)(b) of the 1977 Act that the
court should determine the question whether a patent
should be revoked.

(2) Any person seeking the court's determination of that question
or application must start a claim for that purpose within 14 days of
receiving notification of the Comptroller's decision.

(3) A person who fails to start a claim within the time prescribed
by rule 63.11(2) will be deemed to have abandoned the reference or
application.

(4) A party may apply to the Comptroller or the court to extend
the period for starting a claim prescribed by rule 63.11(2) even
where the application is made after expiration of that period.

Application by employee for compensation

63.12—(1) An application by an employee for compensation 2F–13
under section 40(1) or (2) of the 1977 Act must be made—

(a) in a claim form; and

(b) within the period prescribed by paragraphs (2), (3) and (4).

(2) The prescribed period begins on the date of the grant of the patent and ends 1 year after the patent has ceased to have effect.

(3) Where the patent has ceased to have effect as a result of failure to pay renewal fees, the prescribed period continues as if the patent has remained continuously in effect provided that—

(a) the renewal fee and any additional fee are paid in accordance with section 25(4) of the 1977 Act; or

(b) restoration is ordered by the Comptroller following an application under section 28 of the 1977 Act.

(4) Where restoration is refused by the Comptroller following an application under section 28 of the 1977 Act, the prescribed period will end 1 year after the patent has ceased to have effect or 6 months after the date of refusal, whichever is the later.

II. Registered Trade Marks and Other Intellectual Property Rights

Allocation

2F–14   63.13—(1) Claims relating to matters arising out of the 1994 Act and other intellectual property rights set out in the practice direction must be started in—

(a) the Chancery Division;

(b) a patents county court; or

(c) save as set out in the practice direction, a county court where there is also a Chancery District Registry.

III. Service of Documents and Participation by the Comptroller

Service of documents

2F–15   63.14—(1) Subject to paragraph (2), Part 6 applies to service of a claim form and any document in any proceedings under this Part.

(2) A claim form relating to a registered right may be served—

(a) on a party who has registered the right at the address for service given for that right in the United Kingdom Patent Office register, provided the address is within the United Kingdom; or

(b) in accordance with rule 6.32(1), 6.33(1) or 6.33(2) on a party who has registered the right at the address for service given for that right in the appropriate register at—

(i) the United Kingdom Patent Office; or

(ii) the Office for Harmonisation in the Internal Market.

(3) Where a party seeks any remedy (whether by claim form, counterclaim or application notice), which would if granted affect an entry in any United Kingdom Patent Office register, that party must serve on the Comptroller or registrar—

(a) the claim form, counterclaim or application notice;

(b) any other statement of case where relevant (including any amended statement of case); and

(c) any accompanying documents.

Participation by the Comptroller

63.15 Where the documents set out in rule 63.14(3) are served, **2F–16** the Comptroller or registrar—

    (a) may take part in proceedings; and

    (b) need not serve a defence or other statement of case unless the court orders otherwise.

IV. Appeals

Appeals from the Comptroller

63.16—(1) Part 52 applies to appeals from decisions of the **2F–17** Comptroller and the registrar.

(2) Appeals about patents must be made to the Patents Court, and other appeals to the Chancery Division.

(3) Where Part 52 requires a document to be served, it must also be served on the Comptroller or registrar, as appropriate.

PRACTICE DIRECTION 63—INTELLECTUAL PROPERTY CLAIMS
This Practice Direction supplements CPR Part 63

Delete "Practice Direction—Patents and Other Intellectual Property Claims" and substitute:

Contents of this Practice Direction

1.1 This practice direction is divided into four sections— **2F–18**

- Section I – Provisions about patents and those other rights within the scope of Section I of Part 63
- Section II – Provisions about registered trade marks and other intellectual property rights
- Section III—Provisions about appeals.
- Section IV—Provisions about final orders

I. Provisions about Patents and those other Rights within the Scope of Section I of Part 63

Scope of Section I

2.1 This Section applies to claims within the scope of Section 1 of **2F–19** Part 63.

Starting the claim (rule 63.5)

3.1 A claim form to which this Section applies must— **2F–20**

    (a) be marked "Chancery Division Patents Court" or "Patents County Court" as the case may be, in the top right hand corner below the title of the court, and

    (b) state the number of any patent or registered design to which the claim relates.

Claim for infringement or challenge to validity (rule 63.6)

4.1 In a claim for infringement of a patent— **2F–21**

    (1) the statement of case must—

        (a) show which of the claims in the specification of the patent are alleged to be infringed; and

(b) give at least one example of each type of infringement alleged; and

(2) a copy of each document referred to in the statement of case, and where necessary a translation of the document, must be served with the statement of case.

4.2 Where the validity of a patent or registered design is challenged—

(1) the statement of case must contain particulars of—

    (a) the remedy sought; and

    (b) the issues except those relating to validity of the patent or registered design;

(2) the statement of case must have a separate document attached to and forming part of it headed "Grounds of Invalidity" which must—

    (a) specify the grounds on which validity of the patent or registered design is challenged; and

    (b) include particulars that will clearly define every issue (including any challenge to any claimed priority date) which it is intended to raise; and

(3) a copy of each document referred to in the Grounds of Invalidity, and where necessary a translation of the document, must be served with the Grounds of Invalidity.

4.3 Where in an application in which the validity of a patent or a registered design is challenged, the Grounds of Invalidity include an allegation—

(1) that the invention is not a patentable invention because it is not new or does not include an inventive step, the particulars must specify details of the matter in the state of the art relied on, as set out in paragraph 4.4;

(2) that the specification of the patent does not disclose the invention clearly enough and completely enough for it to be performed by a person skilled in the art, the particulars must state, if appropriate, which examples of the invention cannot be made to work and in which respects they do not work or do not work as described in the specification; or

(3) that the registered design is not new or lacks individual character, the particulars must specify details of any prior design relied on, as set out in paragraph 4.4.

4.4 The details required under paragraphs 4.3(1) and 4.3(3) are—

(1) in the case of matter or a design made available to the public by written description, the date on which and the means by which it was so made available, unless this is clear from the fact of the matter; and

(2) in the case of matter or a design made available to the public by use—

    (a) the date or dates of such use;

    (b) the name of all persons making such use;

    (c) the place of such use;

    (d) any written material which identifies such use;

    (e) the existence and location of any apparatus employed in such use; and

(f) all facts and matters relied on to establish that such matter was made available to the public.

4.5 In any proceedings in which the validity of a patent is challenged, where a party alleges that machinery or apparatus was used before the priority date of the claim the court may order inspection of that machinery or apparatus.

4.6 If the validity of a patent is challenged on the ground that the invention did not involve an inventive step, a party who wishes to rely on the commercial success of the patent must state in the statement of case the grounds on which that party so relies.

Case management (rule 63.8)

5.1 The following paragraphs only of the practice direction **2F–22** supplementing Part 29 apply—

(1) paragraph 5 (case management conferences)—
  (a) excluding paragraph 5.9; and
  (b) modified so far as is made necessary by other specific provisions of this practice direction; and
(2) paragraph 7 (failure to comply with case management directions).

5.2 Case management will be dealt with by—

(1) a judge of the Patents Court, a patents judge or a Master, but
(2) a Master may only deal with the following matters—
  (a) orders by way of settlement, except settlement of procedural disputes;
  (b) applications for extension of time;
  (c) applications for permission to serve out of the jurisdiction;
  (d) applications for security for costs;
  (e) other matters as directed by a judge of the court; and
  (f) enforcement of money judgments.

5.3 The claimant must apply for a case management conference within 14 days of the date when all defendants who intend to file and serve a defence have done so.

5.4 Where the claim has been transferred, the claimant must apply for a case management conference within 14 days of the date of the order transferring the claim, unless the court held or gave directions for a case management conference when it made the order transferring the claim.

5.5 Any party may, at a time earlier than that provided in paragraphs 5.3 and 5.4, apply in writing to the court to fix a case management conference.

5.6 If the claimant does not make an application in accordance with paragraphs 5.3 and 5.4, any other party may apply for a case management conference.

5.7 The court may fix a case management conference at any time on its own initiative.

5.8 Not less than 4 days before a case management conference, each party must file and serve an application notice for any order which that party intends to seek at the case management conference.

5.9 Unless the court orders otherwise, the claimant, or the party who makes an application under paragraph 5.6, in consultation with the other parties, must prepare a case management bundle containing—

(1) the claim form;

(2) all other statements of case (excluding schedules), except that, if a summary of a statement of case has been filed, the bundle must contain the summary, and not the full statement of case;

(3) a pre–trial timetable, if one has been agreed or ordered;

(4) the principal orders of the court; and

(5) any agreement in writing made by the parties as to disclosure,

and provide copies of the case management bundle for the court and the other parties at least 4 days before the first case management conference or any earlier hearing at which the court may give case management directions.

5.10 At the case management conference the court may direct that—

(1) a scientific adviser under section 70(3) of the Senior Courts Act 1981 or under section 63(1) of the County Courts Act 1984 be appointed; and

(2) a document setting out basic undisputed technology should be prepared.

(Rule 35.15 applies to scientific advisers.)

5.11 Where a trial date has not been fixed by the court, a party may apply for a trial date by filing a certificate which must—

(1) state the estimated length of the trial, agreed if possible by all parties;

(2) detail the time required for the judge to consider the documents;

(3) identify the area of technology; and

(4) assess the complexity of the technical issues involved by indicating the complexity on a scale of 1 to 5 (with 1 being the least and 5 the most complex).

5.12 The claimant, in consultation with the other parties, must revise and update the documents, referred to in paragraph 5.9 appropriately as the case proceeds. This must include making all necessary revisions and additions at least 7 days before any subsequent hearing at which the court may give case management directions.

Disclosure and inspection (rule 63.9)

2F–23   **6.1** Standard disclosure does not require the disclosure of documents that relate to—

(1) the infringement of a patent by a product or process where—

    (a) not less than 21 days before the date for service of a list of documents the defendant notifies the claimant and any other party of the defendant's intention to serve—

        (i) full particulars of the product or process alleged to infringe; and

        (ii) any necessary drawings or other illustrations; and

    (b) on or before the date for service the defendant serves on the claimant and any other party the documents referred to in paragraph 6.1(1)(a);

(2) any ground on which the validity of a patent is put in issue, except documents which came into existence within the period—

    (a) beginning two years before the earliest claimed priority date; and

    (b) ending two years after that date; and

(3) the issue of commercial success.

6.2 The particulars served under paragraph 6.1(1)(b) must be accompanied by a signed written statement which must state that the person making the statement—

(1) is personally acquainted with the facts to which the particulars relate;

(2) verifies that the particulars are a true and complete description of the product or process alleged to infringe; and

(3) understands that he or she may be required to attend court in order to be cross–examined on the contents of the particulars.

6.3 Where the issue of commercial success arises, the patentee must, within such time limit as the court may direct, serve a schedule containing—

(1) where the commercial success relates to an article or product—

    (a) an identification of the article or product (for example by product code number) which the patentee asserts has been made in accordance with the claims of the patent;

    (b) a summary by convenient periods of sales of any such article or product;

    (c) a summary for the equivalent periods of sales, if any, of any equivalent prior article or product marketed before the article or product in sub–paragraph (a); and

    (d) a summary by convenient periods of any expenditure on advertising and promotion which supported the marketing of the articles or products in sub–paragraphs (a) and (c); or

(2) where the commercial success relates to the use of a process—

    (a) an identification of the process which the patentee asserts has been used in accordance with the claims of the patent;

    (b) a summary by convenient periods of the revenue received from the use of such process;

    (c) a summary for the equivalent periods of the revenues, if any, received from the use of any equivalent prior art process; and

    (d) a summary by convenient periods of any expenditure which supported the use of the process in sub–paragraphs (a) and (c).

Experiments

7.1 A party seeking to establish any fact by experimental proof **2F–24** conducted for the purpose of litigation must, at least 21 days before service of the application notice for directions under paragraph 7.3, or within such other time as the court may direct, serve on all parties a notice—

(1) stating the facts which the party seeks to establish; and

(2) giving full particulars of the experiments proposed to establish them.

7.2 A party served with a notice under paragraph 7.1—

(1) must within 21 days after such service, serve on the other party a notice stating whether or not each fact is admitted; and

(2) may request the opportunity to inspect a repetition of all or a number of the experiments identified in the notice served under paragraph 7.1.

7.3 Where any fact which a party seeks to establish by experimental proof is not admitted, that party must apply to the court for permission and directions by application notice.

Use of models or apparatus

2F–25   **8.1** A party that intends to rely on any model or apparatus must apply to the court for directions at the first case management conference.

Time estimates for trial, trial bundle, reading guide and detailed trial timetable

2F–26   **9.1** Not less than one week before the beginning of the trial, each party must inform the court in writing of the estimated length of its—

(1) oral submissions;

(2) examination in chief, if any, of its own witnesses; and

(3) cross–examination of witnesses of any other party.

9.2 At least four days before the date fixed for the trial, the claimant must file—

(1) the trial bundle;

(2) a reading guide for the judge; and

(3) a detailed trial timetable which should be agreed, if possible.

9.3 The reading guide filed under paragraph 9.2 must—

(1) be short and, if possible, agreed;

(2) set out the issues, the parts of the documents that need to be read on each issue and the most convenient order in which they should be read;

(3) identify the relevant passages in text books and cases, if appropriate; and

(4) not contain argument.

Application to amend a patent specification in existing proceedings (rule 63.10)

2F–27   **10.1** Where the application notice is served on the Comptroller electronically under rule 63.10(3), the applicant must comply with any requirements for the sending of electronic communications to the Comptroller.

10.2 Not later than two days before the first hearing date the applicant, the Comptroller if wishing to be heard, the parties to the proceedings and any other opponent, must file and serve a document stating the directions sought.

Request to limit a European patent (UK) under the European Patent Convention

11.1 Paragraphs 11.2 to 11.4 apply where there are proceedings **2F–28** before the court in which the validity of a European patent (UK) may be put in issue.

11.2 Where the proprietor of the European patent (UK) intends to file a request under Article 105a of the European Patent Convention to limit the European patent (UK) by amendment of the claims, the proprietor must serve on all the parties to the proceedings a copy of the intended request (including a copy of the intended complete version of the amended claims and, as the case may be, of the amended description and drawings) at least 28 days prior to filing the request with the European Patent Office.

11.3 Where a copy of an intended request is served on the party in accordance with paragraph 11.2, any party may apply to the court for such directions or other order as may be appropriate.

11.4 Reference to "European Patent Convention" means the Convention on the Grant of European Patents of 5th October 1973 as amended from time to time.

Application by employee for compensation (rule 63.12)

12.1 Where an employee applies for compensation under section **2F–29** 40(1) or (2) of the 1977 Act, the court will at the case management conference give directions as to—

(1) the manner in which the evidence, including any accounts of expenditure and receipts relating to the claim, is to be given at the hearing of the claim and if written evidence is to be given, specify the period within which witness statements must be filed; and

(2) the provision to the claimant by the defendant or a person deputed by the defendant, of reasonable facilities for inspecting and taking extracts from the accounts by which the defendant proposes to verify the accounts in sub–paragraph (1) or from which those accounts have been derived.

Communication of information to the European Patent Office

13.1 The court may authorise the communication of any such in- **2F–30** formation in the court files as the court thinks fit to—

(1) the European Patent Office; or

(2) the competent authority of any country which is a party to the European Patent Convention.

13.2 Before authorising the communication of information under paragraph 13.1, the court will permit any party who may be affected by the disclosure to make representations, in writing or otherwise, on the question of whether the information should be disclosed.

Order affecting entry in the register of patents or designs

14.1 Where any order of the court affects the validity of an entry **2F–31** in the register, the party in whose favour the order is made, must serve a copy of such order on the Comptroller within 14 days.

14.2 Where the order is in favour of more than one party, a copy of the order must be served by such party as the court directs.

European Community designs

2F–32   **15.1** The Patents Court and the patents county court at the Central London County Court are the designated Community design courts under Article 80(5) of Council Regulation (EC) 6/2002.

15.2 Where a counterclaim is filed at the Community design court, for a declaration of invalidity of a registered Community design, the Community design court will inform the Office for Harmonisation in the Internal Market of the date on which the counterclaim was filed, in accordance with Article 86(2) of Council Regulation (EC) 6/2002.

15.3 On filing a counterclaim under paragraph 15.2, the party filing it must inform the Community design court in writing that it is a counterclaim to which paragraph 15.2 applies and that the Office for Harmonisation in the Internal Market needs to be informed of the date on which the counterclaim was filed.

15.4 Where a Community design court has given a judgment which has become final on a counterclaim for a declaration of invalidity of a registered Community design, the Community design court will send a copy of the judgment to the Office for Harmonisation in the Internal Market, in accordance with Article 86(4) of Council Regulation (EC) 6/2002.

15.5 The party in whose favour judgment is given under paragraph 15.4 must inform the Community design court at the time of judgment that paragraph 15.4 applies and that the Office for Harmonisation in the Internal Market needs to be sent a copy of the judgment.

II. Provisions about Registered Trade Marks and Other Intellectual Property Rights

Allocation (rule 63.13)

2F–33   **16.1** The other intellectual property rights referred to in rule 63.13 are—

(1) copyright;

(2) rights in performances;

(3) rights conferred under Part VII of the 1988 Act;

(4) design right;

(5) Community design right;

(6) association rights;

(7) moral rights;

(8) database rights;

(9) unauthorised decryption rights;

(10) hallmarks;

(11) technical trade secrets litigation;

(12) passing off;

(13) protected designations of origin, protected geographical indications and traditional speciality guarantees;

(14) registered trade marks; and

(15) Community trade marks.

16.2 There are Chancery district registries at Birmingham, Bristol, Caernarfon, Cardiff, Leeds, Liverpool, Manchester, Mold, Newcastle upon Tyne and Preston.

16.3 The county courts at Caernarfon, Mold and Preston do not have jurisdiction in relation to registered trade marks and Community trade marks.

Starting the claim

17.1 A claim form to which Section II of Part 63 applies must be **2F–34** marked in the top right hand corner "Intellectual Property" below the title of the court in which it is issued.

17.2 In the case of claims concerning registered trade marks and Community trade marks, the claim form must state the registration number of any trade mark to which the claim relates.

Reference to the court by the registrar or the Comptroller

18.1 This paragraph applies where—   **2F–35**

(1) an application is made to the registrar under the 1994 Act and the registrar refers the application to the court; or

(2) a reference is made to the Comptroller under section 246 of the 1988 Act and the Comptroller refers the whole proceedings or a particular question or issue to the court under section 251(1) of that Act.

18.2 Where paragraph 18.1 applies, the applicant under the 1994 Act or the person making the reference under section 246 of the 1988 Act, as the case may be, must start a claim seeking the court's determination of the reference within 14 days of receiving notification of the decision to refer.

18.3 If the person referred to in paragraph 18.2 does not start a claim within the period prescribed by that paragraph, that person will be deemed to have abandoned the reference.

18.4 The period prescribed under paragraph 18.2 may be extended by—

(1) the registrar or the Comptroller as the case may be; or

(2) the court

where a party so applies, even if the application is not made until after the expiration of that period.

Application to the court under section 19 of the 1994 Act

19.1 Where an application is made under section 19 of the 1994 **2F–36** Act, the applicant must serve the claim form or application notice on all identifiable persons having an interest in the goods, materials or articles within the meaning of section 19 of the 1994 Act.

Order affecting entry in the register of trade marks

20.1 Where any order of the court affects the validity of an entry **2F–37** in the register, the provisions of paragraphs 14.1 and 14.2 apply.

European Community trade marks

21.1 The Chancery Division, the patents county court at the **2F–38** Central London County Court and the county courts where there is also a Chancery district registry, except Caernarfon, Mold and Preston, are designated Community trade mark courts for the purposes of Article 91(1) of Council Regulation (EC) 40/94.

21.2 Where a counterclaim is filed at the Community trade mark court, for revocation or for a declaration of invalidity of a Community trade mark, the Community trade mark court will inform the Office of Harmonisation in the Internal Market of the date on which the counterclaim was filed, in accordance with Article 96(4) of Council Regulation (EC) 40/94.

21.3 On filing a counterclaim under paragraph 21.2, the party filing it must inform the Community trade mark court in writing that it is a counterclaim to which paragraph 21.2 applies and that the Office for Harmonisation in the Internal Market needs to be informed of the date on which the counterclaim was filed.

21.4 Where the Community trade mark court has given a judgment which has become final on a counterclaim for revocation or for a declaration of invalidity of a Community trade mark, the Community trade mark court will send a copy of the judgment to the Office for Harmonisation in the Internal Market, in accordance with Article 96(6) of Council Regulation (EC) 40/94.

21.5 The party in whose favour judgment is given under paragraph 21.4 must inform the Community trade mark court at the time of judgment that paragraph 21.4 applies and that the Office for Harmonisation in the Internal Market needs to be sent a copy of the judgment.

Claim for additional damages under section 97(2), section 191J(2) or section 229(3) of the 1988 Act

2F–39   **22.1** Where a claimant seeks to recover additional damages under section 97(2), section 191J(2) or section 229(3) of the 1988 Act, the particulars of claim must include—

    (1) a statement to that effect; and

    (2) the grounds for claiming them.

Application for delivery up or forfeiture under the 1988 Act

2F–40   **23.1** An applicant who applies under section 99, 114, 195, 204, 230 or 231 of the 1988 Act for delivery up or forfeiture must serve—

    (1) the claim form; or

    (2) application notice, where appropriate,

on all identifiable persons who have an interest in the goods, material or articles within the meaning of section 114, 204 or 231 of the 1988 Act.

Association rights

2F–41   **24.1** Where an application is made under regulations made under section 7 of the Olympic Symbol etc (Protection) Act 1995, the applicant must serve the claim form or application notice on all identifiable persons having an interest in the goods, materials or articles within the meaning of the regulations.

III. Provisions about Appeals

Reference to the court by an appointed person

2F–42   **25.1** This paragraph applies where a person appointed by the Lord Chancellor to hear and decide appeals under section 77 of the 1994 Act, refers an appeal to the Chancery Division under section 76(3) of the 1994 Act.

25.2 The appellant must file a claim form seeking the court's determination of the appeal within 14 days of receiving notification of the decision to refer.

25.3 The appeal will be deemed to have been abandoned if the appellant does not file a claim form within the period prescribed by paragraph 25.2.

25.4 The period prescribed under paragraph 25.2 may be extended by—

(1) the person appointed by the Lord Chancellor; or

(2) the court

where the appellant so applies, even if such application is not made until after the expiration of that period.

IV. Provisions about Final Orders

Costs

26.1 Where the court makes an order for delivery up or destruc- 2F–43 tion of infringing goods, or articles designed or adapted to make such goods, the person against whom the order is made must pay the costs of complying with that order unless the court orders otherwise.

26.2 Where the court finds that an intellectual property right has been infringed, the court may, at the request of the applicant, order appropriate measures for the dissemination and publication of the judgment to be taken at the expense of the infringer.

2G COMPANIES ACT PROCEEDINGS

PRACTICE DIRECTION 49A—APPLICATIONS UNDER THE COMPANIES ACTS AND RELATED LEGISLATION

This Practice Direction supplements CPR Part 49   2G–7

Delete Practice Direction—Applications under the Companies Acts and Related Legislation and substitute:

Section I.

General

Definitions

1. In this practice direction—

   "the 1985 Act" means the Companies Act 1985;

   "the 2006 Act" means the Companies Act 2006;

   "the CJPA" means the Criminal Justice and Police Act 2001;

   "the EC Regulation" means Council Regulation (EC) No. 2157/ 2001 of 8 October 2001 on the Statute for a European Company (SE);

   "Part VII FSMA" means Part VII of the Financial Services and Markets Act 2000;

   "the Cross–Border Mergers Regulations" means the Companies (Cross–Border Mergers) Regulations 2007.

Application of this practice direction

2G–8 2. This practice direction applies to proceedings under—

    (a) the 1985 Act;

    (b) the 2006 Act (except proceedings under Chapter 1 of Part 11 or Part 30 of that Act);

    (c) section 59 of the CJPA;

    (d) Articles 22, 25 and 26 of the EC Regulation;

    (e) Part VII FSMA; and

    (f) the Cross–Border Mergers Regulations.

(Part 19 and the practice direction supplementing Part 19 contain provisions about proceedings under Chapter 1 of Part 11 of the 2006 Act (derivative claims)).

Application of this practice direction to certain proceedings in relation to limited liability partnerships

2G–9 3. This practice direction applies to proceedings under the 1985 Act and 2006 Act as applied to limited liability partnerships by regulations made under the Limited Liability Partnerships Act 2000.

Title of documents

2G–10 4.(1) The claim form in proceedings under the 1985 Act, the 2006 Act, Part VII FSMA, the EC Regulation or the Cross–Border Mergers Regulations, and any application, affidavit, witness statement, notice or other document in such proceedings, must be entitled "In the matter of [the name of the company in question] and in the matter of [the relevant law]", where "[the relevant law]" means "the Companies Act 1985", "the Companies Act 2006", " Part VII of the Financial Services and Markets Act 2000", "Council Regulation (EC) No 2157/2001 of 8 October 2001 on the Statute for a European Company (SE)" or "the Companies (Cross–Border Merger) Regulations 2007", as the case may be.

    (2) Where a company changes its name in the course of proceedings, the title must be altered by—

    (a) substituting the new name for the old; and

    (b) inserting the old name in brackets at the end of the title.

Starting proceedings and notification of application made

2G–11 5.(1) Proceedings to which this practice direction applies must be started by a Part 8 claim form—

    (a) unless a provision of this or another practice direction provides otherwise, but

    (b) subject to any modification of that procedure by this or any other practice direction.

    (2) The claim form—

    (a) will, where issued in the High Court, be issued out of the Companies Court or a Chancery district registry; or

    (b) will, where issued in a county court, be issued out of a county court office.

    (3) Where this practice direction requires a party to proceedings to notify another person of an application, such notification must, unless the court orders otherwise, be given by sending

to that other person a copy of the claim form as soon as reasonably practicable after the claim form has been issued.

Section II.

Particular applications under the 2006 Act

References to provisions of the 2006 Act in this Section

6. In this Section, a reference to a section by number, not otherwise identified, is to the section so numbered in the 2006 Act.

2G–12

Company generally to be made a party to a claim under the 2006 Act

7.(1) Where in a claim under the 2006 Act the company concerned is not the claimant, the company is to be made a defendant to the claim unless—

2G–13

   (a) any other enactment, the CPR or this or another practice direction makes a different provision; or

   (b) the court orders otherwise.

(2) Where an application is made in the course of proceedings to which the company is or is required to be a defendant, the company must be made a respondent to the application unless—

   (a) any other enactment, the CPR or this or another practice direction makes a different provision; or

   (b) the court orders otherwise.

Applications under section 169 (Director's right to protest against removal)

8.(1) This paragraph applies to an application for an order under section 169(5).

2G–14

(2) The claimant must notify the director concerned of the application.

Applications under section 244 (Disclosure under court order of protected information)

9.(1) This paragraph applies to an application for an order under section 244.

2G–15

(2) The claimant must notify the director concerned of the application.

Applications under section 295 (Application not to circulate members' statement) or section 317 (Application not to circulate members' statement)

10.(1) This paragraph applies to an application for an order under section 295 or 317.

2G–16

(2) The claimant must notify each member who requested the circulation of the relevant statement of the application.

Proceedings under section 370 (Unauthorised donations – enforcement of directors' liabilities by shareholder action)

11. Proceedings to enforce a director's liability under section 370 must be started by a Part 7 claim form.

2G–17

Proceedings under section 456 (Application in respect of defective accounts or directors' report)

2G–18   **12.**(1) This paragraph applies to an application for a declaration under section 456(1).

(2) The claimant must notify any former director who was a director at the time of the approval of the annual accounts or directors' report of the application.

Proceedings under section 511, 514, 515 or 518 (Representations or statements made by the auditor)

2G–19   **13.**(1) This paragraph applies to an application for an order under section 511(6), 514(7), 515(7) or 518(9).

(2) The claimant must notify the auditor of the application.

Proceedings under section 527 (Members' powers to require website publication of audit concerns)

2G–20   **14.**(1) This paragraph applies to an application for an order under section 527(5).

(2) The claimant must, unless the court orders otherwise, notify each member who requested a statement to be placed on the website of the application.

Proceedings under Parts 26 and 27 of the 2006 Act (Applications to sanction a compromise or arrangement)

2G–21   **15.**(1) This paragraph applies to an application for an order under Parts 26 and 27 of the 2006 Act to sanction a compromise or arrangement.

(2) Where the application is made by the company concerned, or by a liquidator or administrator of the company, there need be no defendant to the claim unless the court so orders.

(3) The claim form must be supported by written evidence, including—

(a) statutory information about the company; and

(b) the terms of the proposed compromise or arrangement.

(4) The claim form must seek—

(a) directions for convening a meeting of creditors or members or both, as the case requires;

(b) the sanction of the court to the compromise or arrangement, if it is approved at the meeting or meetings, and a direction for a further hearing for that purpose; and

(c) a direction that the claimant files a copy of a report to the court by the chairman of the meeting or of each meeting.

Proceedings under section 955 (Takeovers – enforcement by the court)

2G–22   **16.** Proceedings for an order under section 955 must be started by a Part 7 claim form.

Proceedings under section 968 (Takeovers – effect on contractual restrictions)

2G–23   **17.** Proceedings to recover compensation under section 968(6) must be started by a Part 7 claim form.

Applications under section 1132 (Production and inspection of documents where offence suspected)

18.(1) This paragraph applies to an application for an order under section 1132. **2G–24**

(2) No notice need be given to any person against whom the order is sought.

Section III.

Other applications

Applications under the EC Regulation—Article 25

19.(1) In this paragraph and paragraphs 20 and 21— **2G–25**

(a) a reference to an Article by number is a reference to the Article so numbered in the EC Regulation; and

(b) 'SE' means a European public limited–liability company (Societas Europaea) within the meaning of the EC Regulation.

(1A) Any document that is filed with the court must, if not in English, be accompanied by a translation of that document into English—

(a) certified by a notary public or other qualified person; or

(b) accompanied by written evidence confirming that the translation is accurate.

(2) An application for a certificate under Article 25(2)—

(a) must set out the pre–merger acts and formalities applicable to the applicant company;

(b) must be accompanied by evidence that those acts and formalities have been completed; and

(c) must be accompanied by copies of—

(i) the draft terms of merger, as provided for in Article 20;

(ii) the entry in the London Gazette containing the particulars specified in Article 21;

(iii) a directors' report;

(iv) an expert's report; and

(v) the resolution of the applicant company approving the draft terms of merger in accordance with Article 23.

(3) In paragraph (2)(c)—

'directors' report' in relation to a company means a report by the directors of the company containing the information required by section 908 of the 2006 Act;

'expert's report' in relation to a company means a report to the members of the company drawn up in accordance with—

(a) section 909 of the 2006 Act; or

(b) Article 22.

(4) There need be no defendant to the application.

Applications under the EC Regulation—Article 22 (Appointment of an independent expert)

20.(1) An application under Article 22 for the appointment of an independent expert must be made— **2G–26**

(a) where the application is made at the same time as or after the application under Article 25(2) for the approval of the pre–merger acts and formalities has been filed with the court, by application notice pursuant to Part 23; or

(b) where no application under Article 25(2) has been made, by a Part 8 claim form.

(2) The application (whether by a claim form or application notice, as the case may be) must be accompanied by evidence in support of the application.

Applications under the EC Regulation—Article 26

2G–27 **21.**(1) Where under Article 26(2) a merging company is required to submit a certificate to the High Court, that company must, if no other merging company has begun proceedings under Article 26, start such proceedings by way of a Part 8 claim form.

(2) There need be no defendant to the claim.

(3) The claim form—

(a) must name the SE and all of the merging companies;

(b) must be accompanied by the documents referred to in sub–paragraph (5); and

(c) must be served on each of the other merging companies.

(4) Where under Article 26(2) a merging company is required to submit a certificate to the High Court, and proceedings under Article 26 have already been begun, the company—

(a) must, not more than 14 days after service on it of the claim form, file an acknowledgment of service and serve it on each of the other merging companies; and

(b) must file the documents, in relation to each merging company, referred to in sub–paragraph (5) within the time limit specified in Article 26(2), and serve copies of them on each of the other merging companies.

(5) The documents in relation to each merging company are—

(a) the certificate issued under Article 25(2) in respect of the company;

(b) a copy of the draft terms of merger approved by the company;

(c) evidence that arrangements for employee involvement have been determined by the company pursuant to Council Directive 2001/86/EC of 8 October 2001 supplementing the Statute for a European company with regard to the involvement of employees; and

(d) evidence that the SE has been formed in accordance with Article 26(4).

Applications under the Cross–Border Mergers Regulations

2G–28 **22.**(1) In this paragraph and paragraphs 23 to 25 a reference to a regulation by number is a reference to the regulation so numbered in the Cross–Border Mergers Regulations.

(2) Any document that is filed with the court must, if not in English, be accompanied by a translation of that document into English—

(a) certified by a notary public or other qualified person; or
(b) accompanied by written evidence confirming that the translation is accurate.

Application for approval of pre–merger requirements

23.(1) This paragraph applies to an application under regulation 6.   **2G–29**

(2) There need be no defendant to the application.

(3) The application must—.
(a) set out the pre–merger acts and formalities required by regulations 7 to 10 and 12 to 15 applicable to the applicant company; and
(b) be accompanied by evidence that those acts and formalities have been completed properly.

(4) Where an application under regulation 11 to summon a meeting of creditors has been made, the court will not determine the application under regulation 6 to approve the pre–merger requirements until the result of the meeting is known.

(5) Where the court makes an order certifying that all pre–merger acts and formalities have been completed properly, the applicant must draw up the order and file it no later than 7 days after the date on which the order was made so that it can be sealed^{GL} by the court. The court will seal^{GL} and return the order to the applicant within 15 days of receipt.

Application for appointment of independent expert or to summon a meeting of members or creditors

24.(1) This paragraph applies to—   **2G–30**
(a) an application for the appointment of an independent expert under regulation 9;
(b) an application under regulation 11 for an order to summon a meeting of members or creditors or both.

(2) The application must be made—
(a) where the application is made at the same time as or after the application for approval of the pre–merger acts and formalities under regulation 6 has been filed with the court, by application notice pursuant to Part 23; or
(b) where no application under regulation 6 has been made, by a Part 8 claim form.

(3) The application (whether by claim form or application notice, as the case may be) must be accompanied by evidence in support of the application.

Application for the approval of the completion of the merger

25.(1) This paragraph applies to an application under regulation 16.   **2G–31**

(2) The application must be made by a Part 8 claim form.

(3) There need be no defendant to the application.

(4) The claim form must be accompanied by—
(a) the documents referred to in regulation 16(1)(b), (c) and (e);
(b) where appropriate, evidence that regulation 16(1)(f) has been complied with; and

(c) such other evidence as may be required to enable the court to decide the application.

(5) Where the court makes an order under regulation 16 approving the merger, it will fix a date on which the consequences of the merger are to take effect.

Applications under section 59 of the CJPA

2G–32   **26.**(1) In sub–paragraphs (2) to (8)—

(a) a reference to a section by number, not otherwise identified, is a reference to the section so numbered in the CJPA; and

(b) references to a relevant interest in property have the same meaning as in section 59 of the CJPA.

(2) This paragraph applies to applications under section 59 in respect of property seized in exercise of the power conferred by section 448(3) of the 1985 Act (including any additional powers of seizure conferred by section 50 that are exercisable by reference to that power).

(3) The application must be supported by evidence—

(a) that the claimant has a relevant interest in the property to which the application relates; and

(b) in the case of an application under section 59(2), that one or more of the grounds set out in section 59(3) is satisfied in relation to the property.

(4) Where the claimant has a relevant interest in the property, the defendants to the claim are to be—

(a) the person in possession of the property; and

(b) any other person who appears to have a relevant interest in the property.

(5) Where the claimant is in possession of the property, the defendants are to be—

(a) the person from whom the property was seized; and

(b) any other person who appears to have a relevant interest in the property.

(6) In the case of an application for the return of seized property, the claimant must serve a copy of the claim form and the claimant's evidence in support of it on the person specified, by the notice given under section 52 when the property was seized, as the person to whom notice of such an application should be given.

(7) If the claimant knows the identity of the person who seized the property, the claimant must also notify that person of the application.

(8) When the court issues the claim form it will fix a date for the hearing.

Section IV.

Conduct of proceedings

Reduction of capital—evidence

2G–33   **27.**(1) In the case of an application to confirm a reduction in capital, if any shares were issued otherwise than for cash—

(a) for any shares so issued on or after 1st January 1901, it is sufficient to set out in the application the extent to which the shares are, or are treated as being, paid up; and

(b) for any shares so issued between 1st September 1867 and 31st December 1900, the application must also show that the requirement as to the filing of the relevant contract with the Registrar of Joint Stock Companies in section 25 of the Companies Act 1867 was complied with.

Section V.

Miscellaneous

Service of documents

28. The parties are responsible for service of documents in proceedings to which this practice direction applies. **2G–34**

Transitional provisions

29. A claim started, or an application made, before 1st October 2007 may be continued in accordance with the practice direction in force on 30th September 2007 as if it had not been revoked. **2G–35**

SECTION 3

OTHER PROCEEDINGS

3A HOUSING

Editorial introduction

In the first paragraph, for "Birmingham CC v Shafi [2008] EWCA Civ 1186; October 30, 2008" substitute:

Birmingham CC v Shafi [2008] EWCA Civ 1186; [2009] 3 All E.R. 127; October 30, 2008 **3A–57.4**

RENT ACT 1977

Reasonable

After the third paragraph, add as a new paragraph:

In *Lee v Whitehouse* [2009] EWCA Civ 375, May 14, 2009, Rimer L.J. said that: **3A–190**
"the question is not whether it is reasonable for the landlord to claim possession, but whether it is reasonable to make the order" (para.29) ... It required [the trial judge] to look at the question from all the angles, in particular by considering the effect on the parties not just if an order was made, but also if it was not (para.30)".

ECHR Art 8 and reasonableness

In the first paragraph for "Birmingham City Council v Doherty [2008] UKHL 57, July 30, 2008, [2008] 3 W.L.R. 636" substitute:

Birmingham City Council v Doherty [2008] UKHL 57, [2009] 1 A.C. 367, [2008] 3 W.L.R. 636 **3A–192**

Add at end:

See too *Liverpool City Council v Doran* [2009] EWCA Civ 146, March 3, 2009, where Toulson L.J. said that *Doherty v Birmingham City Council* [2008] UKHL 57; [2009] 1 A.C.

367, [2008] 3 W.L.R. 636 had "created a new battleground area" (para.46). He described the effect of *Doherty* as being two–fold:

> "49. First, there is no formulaic or formalistic restriction of the factors which may be relied upon by the licensee in support of an argument that the council's decision to serve a notice to quit, and seek a possession order, was one which no reasonable council would have taken. Such factors are not automatically irrelevant simply because they may include the licensee's personal circumstances, such as length of time of occupation. . . .
>
> 50. Secondly, the question whether the council's decision was one which no reasonable person would have made is to be decided by applying public law principles as they have been developed at common law, and not through the lens of the convention."

Whether or not a "council's decision was unreasonable has to be decided by applying public law principles as they have been developed at common law [and] it is to be remembered that those principles are not frozen" (para.52). He continued "it is likely to be a rare case indeed where a council decides to issue a notice to quit and seek a possession order without any ground on which a reasonable council might have done so" (para.55).

Restriction on discretion of court in making orders for possession of land

For "(Admiral Taverns ... November 25, 2008." substitute:

3A–293   *(Admiral Taverns (Cygnet) Limited v Daniel and Daly* [2008] EWCA Civ 1501, November 25, 2008; *The Times,* January 12, 2009).

Senior Courts Act 1981

3A–293.1   (1981 c.54)

Delete title "Supreme Court Act 1981" and substitute "Senior Courts Act 1981".

Housing Act 1985

Note

For "Birmingham City Council v Doherty [2008] UKHL 57, July 30, 2008, [2008] 3 W.L.R. 636" substitute:

3A–320   *Birmingham City Council v Doherty* [2008] UKHL 57, [2009] 1 A.C. 367, [2008] 3 W.L.R. 636

Security of tenure

In section 82(1), for "except by obtaining an order" substitute:

3A–343   except as

Delete sections 82(1A) and (2) and substitute:

(1A) The tenancy may be brought to an end by the landlord—
    (a) obtaining—
        (i) an order of the court for the possession of the dwelling–house, and
        (ii) the execution of the order,
    (b) obtaining an order under subsection (3), or
    (c) obtaining a demotion order under section 82A.

(2) In the case mentioned in subsection (1A)(a), the tenancy ends when the order is executed.

Note

For "This section has also been amended by ... see below." substitute:

3A–344   This section has also been amended by the Housing and Regeneration Act 2008

Sch.11, Pt I, para.2 (for transitional provisions see para.14) with effect from May 20, 2009 (SI 2009/1261) (c.66).

Security of tenure

In the third paragraph for ", This amendment is not yet in force." substitute:

This amendment was brought into force on May 20, 2009 by the Housing and **3A–348** Regeneration Act 2008 (Commencement No.5) Order 2009 SI 2009/1261 (c.66).

"reasonable"—nuisance and annoyance

In the fourth paragraph, add after "(2001) 33 H.L.R. 810, CA":

and *Wandsworth LBC v Webb* [2008] EWCA Civ 1421 November 12, 2008; *The Times,* **3A–375** January 5, 2009, where Sedley L.J. observed that it was not permissible to use a possession order as a means to bring pressure to bear on a tenant to modify the behaviour of an individual over whom they had no control

appeals on questions of reasonableness

Add new paragraph at end:

In *Bracknell Forest BC v Green* [2009] EWCA Civ 238, March 20, 2009 Mummery **3A–376** L.J. said that it is for judges in the county court to "carry out the balancing exercise and assess the relative weight of all the circumstances relevant to the decision". By its very nature a decision on reasonableness is difficult to appeal. "The role of the Court of Appeal under Pt 52 CPR is, in general, limited to a review of the decision of the lower court. The appeal is not a re–hearing or re–trial of the case" [22, 23]. He referred to Lord Hoffmann's "valuable analysis of the appellate function" in cases such as *Biogen v Medeva Plc* [1997] R.P.C. 1, and his overall conclusion that appellate courts should be "very cautious in differing from the judge's evaluation" of the facts in cases where a reference to, or an application of, an imprecise legal standard to the facts of the case is a matter of degree rather than of principle." In Mummery L.J.'s words:

> "the appeal process is not there merely for having another go at the kind of fact–based issue that the lower court is often better placed to assess than a law oriented appellate court is. ... [The Court of Appeal] should be slow to upset [a county court judge's] evaluation of reasonableness on the possession order issue, unless it is clear that he acted under an error of principle or unless his decision was obviously wrong" [29, 30].

ECHR Article 8 and reasonableness

For "Birmingham City Council v Doherty [2008] UKHL 57, July 30, 2008, [2008] 3 W.L.R. 636" substitute:

Birmingham City Council v Doherty [2008] UKHL 57, [2009] 1 A.C. 367, [2008] 3 **3A–377** W.L.R. 636

Extended discretion of court in certain proceedings for possession

3A–380

In section 85(3)(a) delete "or payments in respect of occupation after the termination of the tenancy (mesne profits)".

Delete sections 85(5) and (5A).

Note

Delete and substitute:

Amended by the Family Law Act 1996 Sch.8, para.53, the Civil Partnership Act 2004 **3A–381** s.82 and Sch.9, para.18 and the Housing and Regeneration Act 2008 Sch.11, Pt I, para.3(2), (4) (for transitional provisions see para.14) with effect from May 20, 2009 (SI 2009/1261) (c.66). The amendment made by Sch.11, Pt I, para.3(3) is not yet in force and is printed as part of the Housing and Regeneration Act 2008—see below.

Extended discretion of court in certain proceedings for possession

3A–384

In the eighth paragraph, for "Porter v Shepherds Bush ... December 10, 2008" substitute:
Porter v Shepherds Bush Housing Association [2008] UKHL 70; [2009] 2 W.L.R. 78

"Brent LBC v Knightley (1997) 29 H.L.R. 857, CA and Marshall v Bradford MBC [2001] EWCA Civ 594; [2002] H.L.R. 22" substitute:
Brent LBC v Knightley (1997) 29 H.L.R. 857, CA; *Marshall v Bradford MBC* [2001] EWCA Civ 594; [2002] H.L.R. 22) and *Austin v Southwark LBC* [2009] EWCA Civ 66, February 16, 2009

Effect of breach of a suspended or postponed possession order

3A–385

In the first paragraph for "(not yet in force, but printed below)" substitute:
(on May 19, 2009—the Schedule is printed below)

In the first paragraph for "depends" substitute:
depended

In the last paragraph, add after"[2008] EWCA Civ 660":
[2009] 1 W.L.R. 1269;

Revival of secure tenancies

3A–386

In the second paragraph, for "Islington LBC ... December 10, 2008" substitute:
Islington LBC v Honeygan–Green [2008] UKHL 70; [2009] 2 W.L.R. 78

Warrants and the ECHR

3A–389

In the first paragraph, for "[2001] 1 W.L.R. 1537" substitute:
[2002] 1 W.L.R. 1537

In the first paragraph for "Birmingham City Council v Doherty [2008] UKHL 57, July 30, 2008, [2008] 3 W.L.R. 636" substitute:
Birmingham City Council v Doherty [2008] UKHL 57, [2009] 1 A.C. 367, [2008] 3 W.L.R. 636

Persons qualified to succeed tenant

3A–402

At the end of the fifth paragraph add:
However, mere physical presence is not enough to amount to "residing with" for the purposes of s.87. There must, to a significant degree, be an intention which can be characterised as making a home with the tenant. Just staying in the property is not enough (*Islington LBC v Freeman* [2009] EWCA Civ 536; June 11, 2009 and *Swanbrae Ltd v Elliott* (1987) 19 H.L.R. 86, CA).

In the ninth paragraph, for "It comes to an end if the terms ... not yet in force." substitute:
The law used to be that such tenancies came to an end if the terms of a suspended possession order were breached (s.85(5) and *Brent LBC v Knightley* (1997) 29 H.L.R. 857, CA)—but now the Housing and Regeneration Act 2008 Sch.11 below provides that secure tenancies continue until any warrant for possession is executed.

"member of the tenant's family"

For "Birmingham City Council v Doherty [2008] UKHL 57, July 30, 2008, [2008] 3 W.L.R. 636" substitute:

3A–412
Birmingham City Council v Doherty [2008] UKHL 57, [2009] 1 A.C. 367, [2008] 3 W.L.R. 636

Family intervention tenancies

Add new paragraph 3A–487.1:

3A–487.1
4ZA.—(1) A tenancy is not a secure tenancy if it is a family intervention tenancy.

(2) But a tenancy mentioned in sub–paragraph (1) becomes a secure tenancy if the landlord notifies the tenant that it is to be regarded as a secure tenancy.

(3) In this paragraph "a family intervention tenancy" means, subject to sub–paragraph (4), a tenancy granted by a local housing authority in respect of a dwelling–house—

   (a) to a person ("the new tenant") against whom a possession order under section 84 in respect of another dwelling–house—
- (i) has been made, in relation to a secure tenancy, on ground 2 or 2A of Part 1 of Schedule 2;
- (ii) could, in the opinion of the authority, have been so made in relation to such a tenancy; or
- (iii) could, in the opinion of the authority, have been so made if the person had had such a tenancy; and

   (b) for the purposes of the provision of behaviour support services.

(4) A tenancy is not a family intervention tenancy for the purposes of this paragraph if the local housing authority has failed to serve a notice under sub–paragraph (5) on the new tenant before the new tenant entered into the tenancy.

(5) A notice under this sub–paragraph is a notice stating—
- (a) the reasons for offering the tenancy to the new tenant;
- (b) the dwelling–house in respect of which the tenancy is to be granted;
- (c) the other main terms of the tenancy (including any requirements on the new tenant in respect of behaviour support services);
- (d) the security of tenure available under the tenancy and any loss of security of tenure which is likely to result from the new tenant agreeing to enter into the tenancy;
- (e) that the new tenant is not obliged to enter into the tenancy or (unless otherwise required to do so) to surrender any existing tenancy or possession of a dwelling–house;
- (f) any likely action by the local housing authority if the new tenant does not enter into the tenancy or surrender any existing tenancy or possession of a dwelling–house.

(6) The appropriate national authority may by regulations made by statutory instrument amend sub–paragraph (5).

(7) A notice under sub–paragraph (5) must contain advice to the new tenant as to how the new tenant may be able to obtain assistance in relation to the notice.

(8) The appropriate national authority may by regulations made by statutory instrument make provision about the type of advice to be provided in such notices.

(9) Regulations under this paragraph may contain such transitional, transitory or saving provision as the appropriate national authority considers appropriate.

(10) A statutory instrument containing (whether alone or with other provision) regulations under this paragraph which amend or repeal any of paragraphs (a) to (f) of sub–paragraph (5) may not be made—
- (a) by the Secretary of State unless a draft of the instrument has been laid before, and approved by a resolution of, each House of Parliament; and
- (b) by the Welsh Ministers unless a draft of the instrument has been laid before, and approved by a resolution of, the National Assembly for Wales.

(11) Subject to this, a statutory instrument containing regulations made under this paragraph—
- (a) by the Secretary of State is subject to annulment in pursuance of a resolution of either House of Parliament; and
- (b) by the Welsh Ministers is subject to annulment in pursuance of a resolution of the National Assembly for Wales.

(12) In this paragraph—

"appropriate national authority"—
- (a) in relation to England, means the Secretary of State; and
- (b) in relation to Wales, means the Welsh Ministers;

   "behaviour support agreement" means an agreement in writing about behaviour and the provision of support services made between the new tenant and the local housing authority concerned (or between persons who include those persons);

   "behaviour support services" means relevant support services to be provided by any person to—
- (a) the new tenant; or
- (b) any person who is to reside with the new tenant; for the purpose of addressing the kind of behaviour which led to the new tenant falling within sub–paragraph (3)(a);

   "family intervention tenancy" has the meaning given by sub–paragraph (3);

   "family intervention tenancy" has the meaning given by sub–paragraph (3);

"the new tenant" has the meaning given by sub–paragraph (3)(a);
"relevant support services" means support services of a kind identified in
a behaviour support agreement and designed to meet such needs of the
recipient as are identified in the agreement.

Note

In the first paragraph, for "and the Housing and Regeneration Act 2008 (Consequential Provisions) Order 2008 ... see below." substitute:

3A–497 , the Housing and Regeneration Act 2008 (Consequential Provisions) Order 2008 (SI 2008/3002) para.28, and the Housing and Regeneration Act 2008 s.297 with effect from January 1, 2009 (CO 2008/3068).

Sch.1, para.4—accommodation for homeless persons

In the second paragraph for "Birmingham City Council v Doherty [2008] UKHL 57, July 30, 2008, [2008] 3 W.L.R. 636" substitute:

3A–502 Birmingham City Council v Doherty [2008] UKHL 57, [2009] 1 A.C. 367, [2008] 3 W.L.R. 636

SECURITY OF TENURE

Security of tenure

Delete section 5(1) and substitute:

3A–748 **5.**—(1) An assured tenancy cannot be brought to an end by the landlord except by—

   (a) obtaining—

      (i) an order of the court for possession of the dwelling–house under section 7 or 21, and

      (ii) the execution of the order,

   (b) obtaining an order of the court under section 6A (demotion order), or

   (c) in the case of a fixed term tenancy which contains power for the landlord to determine the tenancy in certain circumstances, by the exercise of that power, and, accordingly, the service by the landlord of a notice to quit is of no effect in relation to a periodic assured tenancy.

(1A) Where an order of the court for possession of the dwelling–house is obtained, the tenancy ends when the order is executed.

In section 5(2)(a), add after "an order of the court":

of the kind mentioned in subsection (1)(a) or (b) or any other order of the court

Note

For "This section has also been amended ... see below." substitute:

3A–749 This section has also been amended by the Housing and Regeneration Act 2008 Sch.11, Pt I, para.6 (for transitional provisions see para.14) with effect from May 20, 2009 (SI 2009/1261) (c.66).

Orders for possession

In section 7(7), for "on the day on which the order takes effect" substitute:

3A–769 in accordance with section 5(1A)

Note

For "This section has also been amended ... see below." substitute:

This section has also been amended by the Housing and Regeneration Act 2008 **3A–770**
Sch.11, Pt I, para.7 (for transitional provisions see para.14) with effect from May 20,
2009 (SI 2009/1261) (c.66).

ECHR art 8 and reasonableness

*For "Birmingham City Council v Doherty [2008] UKHL 57, July 30, 2008, [2008] 3 W.L.R.
636" substitute:*

Birmingham City Council v Doherty [2008] UKHL 57, [2009] 1 A.C. 367, [2008] 3 **3A–781**
W.L.R. 636

Breach of suspended possession orders

For "Knowsley Housing Trust ... December 10, 2008" substitute:

Knowsley Housing Trust v White [2008] UKHL 70; [2009] 2 W.L.R. 78 **3A–783**

Extended discretion of court in possession claims

In section 9(3), delete "or payments in respect of occupation after the termination of the tenancy **3A–802**
(mesne profits)".

Delete section 9(5) and (5A).

Note

For "This section has also been amended by ... see below." substitute:

This section has also been amended by the Housing and Regeneration Act 2008 **3A–803**
Sch.11, Pt I, para.8(2), (4) (for transitional provisions see para.14) with effect from
May 20, 2009 (SI 2009/1261) (c.66). The amendment made by Sch.11, Pt I, para.8(3)
is not yet in force and is printed as part of the Housing and Regeneration Act 2008—
see below.

Recovery of possession on expiry or termination of assured shorthold tenancy

In section 21(3), for "on the day on which the order takes effect" substitute:

in accordance with section 5(1A) **3A–889**

After section 21(4), add new subsection (4A).

(4A) Where a court makes an order for possession of a dwelling–
house by virtue of subsection (4) above, the assured shorthold tenancy
shall end in accordance with section 5(1A).

Note

For "This section has also been amended ... see below." substitute:

This section has also been amended by the Housing and Regeneration Act 2008 **3A–890**
Sch.11, Pt I, para.9 (for transitional provisions see para.14) with effect from May 20,
2009 (SI 2009/1261) (c.66).

Family intervention tenancies

Add new paragraph 3A–953.1:

12ZA.—(1) A family intervention tenancy. **3A–953.1**
(2) But a family intervention tenancy becomes an assured tenancy if the landlord
notifies the tenant that it is to be regarded as an assured tenancy.
(3) In this paragraph "a family intervention tenancy" means, subject to sub–
paragraph (4), a tenancy granted by a registered provider of social housing or a
registered social landlord ("the landlord") in respect of a dwelling–house—
        (a) to a person ("the new tenant") against whom a possession order under
           section 7 in respect of another dwelling–house—

      (i) has been made, in relation to an assured tenancy, on ground 14 or 14A of Part 2 of Schedule 2;

      (ii) could, in the opinion of the landlord, have been so made in relation to such a tenancy; or

      (iii) could, in the opinion of the landlord, have been so made if the person had had such a tenancy; and

  (b) for the purposes of the provision of behaviour support services.

(4) A tenancy is not a family intervention tenancy for the purposes of this paragraph if the landlord has failed to serve a notice under sub–paragraph (5) on the new tenant before the new tenant entered into the tenancy.

(5) A notice under this sub–paragraph is a notice stating—

  (a) the reasons for offering the tenancy to the new tenant;

  (b) the dwelling–house in respect of which the tenancy is to be granted;

  (c) the other main terms of the tenancy (including any requirements on the new tenant in respect of behaviour support services);

  (d) the security of tenure available under the tenancy and any loss of security of tenure which is likely to result from the new tenant agreeing to enter into the tenancy;

  (e) that the new tenant is not obliged to enter into the tenancy or (unless otherwise required to do so) to surrender any existing tenancy or possession of a dwelling–house;

  (f) any likely action by the landlord if the new tenant does not enter into the tenancy or surrender any existing tenancy or possession of a dwelling–house.

(6) The appropriate national authority may by regulations made by statutory instrument amend sub–paragraph (5).

(7) A notice under sub–paragraph (5) must contain advice to the new tenant as to how the new tenant may be able to obtain assistance in relation to the notice.

(8) The appropriate national authority may by regulations made by statutory instrument make provision about the type of advice to be provided in such notices.

(9) Regulations under this paragraph may contain such transitional, transitory or saving provision as the appropriate national authority considers appropriate.

(10) A statutory instrument containing (whether alone or with other provision) regulations under this paragraph which amend or repeal any of paragraphs (a) to (f) of sub–paragraph (5) may not be made—

  (a) by the Secretary of State unless a draft of the instrument has been laid before, and approved by a resolution of, each House of Parliament; and

  (b) by the Welsh Ministers unless a draft of the instrument has been laid before, and approved by a resolution of, the National Assembly for Wales.

(11) Subject to this, a statutory instrument containing regulations made under this paragraph—

  (a) by the Secretary of State is subject to annulment in pursuance of a resolution of either House of Parliament; and

  (b) by the Welsh Ministers is subject to annulment in pursuance of a resolution of the National Assembly for Wales.

(12) In this paragraph—

"appropriate national authority"—

  (a) in relation to England, means the Secretary of State; and

  (b) in relation to Wales, means the Welsh Ministers;

    "behaviour support agreement" means an agreement in writing about behaviour and the provision of support services made between the new tenant, the landlord and the local housing authority for the district in which the dwelling–house which is to be subject to the new tenancy is situated (or between persons who include those persons);

    "behaviour support services" means relevant support services to be provided by any person to—

  (a) the new tenant; or

  (b) any person who is to reside with the new tenant; for the purpose of addressing the kind of behaviour which led to the new tenant falling within sub–paragraph (3)(a);

    "family intervention tenancy" has the meaning given by sub–paragraph (3);

    "family intervention tenancy" has the meaning given by sub–paragraph (3);

    "landlord" has the meaning given by sub–paragraph (3);

"local housing authority" (and the reference to its district) has the same meaning as in the Housing Act 1985 (see sections 1 and 2(1) of that Act);
In this paragraph—
"the new tenant" has the meaning given by sub–paragraph (3)(a);
"registered social landlord" has the same meaning as in Part 1 of the Housing Act 1996;
"relevant support services" means support services of a kind identified in a behaviour support agreement and designed to meet such needs of the recipient as are identified in the agreement.

Note

For "the Housing and Regeneration Act 2008 ... see below." substitute:
, the Housing and Regeneration Act 2008 (Consequential Provisions) Order 2008 **3A–958** (SI 2008/3002) para.40, and the Housing and Regeneration Act 2008 s.297 with effect from January 1, 2009 (CO 2008/3068).

Paragraph 8

Add after "(SI 1998/1967)":
, as amended,   **3A–967**

Introductory tenancies

In the thirteenth paragraph for "Birmingham City Council v Doherty [2008] UKHL 57, July 30, 2008, [2008] 3 W.L.R. 636" substitute:
Birmingham City Council v Doherty [2008] UKHL 57, [2009] 1 A.C. 367, [2008] 3 **3A–1070** W.L.R. 636

Introductory tenants and the Human Rights Act 1998

In the second paragraph for "Birmingham City Council v Doherty [2008] UKHL 57, July 30, 2008, [2008] 3 W.L.R. 636" substitute:
Birmingham City Council v Doherty [2008] UKHL 57, [2009] 1 A.C. 367, [2008] 3 **3A–1071** W.L.R. 636

PROCEEDINGS FOR POSSESSION

Proceedings for possession

Delete section 127(1) and substitute:

127.—(1) The landlord may only bring an introductory tenancy to **3A–1095** an end by obtaining—
   (a) an order of the court for the possession of the dwelling–house, and
   (b) the execution of the order.
(1A) In such a case, the tenancy ends when the order is executed.

In section 127(2), for "such an order" substitute:
   an order of the kind mentioned in subsection (1)(a)

Delete section 127(3).

Amendment

Delete and substitute:
   Amended by the Housing and Regeneration Act 2008 Sch.11, Pt I, para.11 (for **3A–1095.1** transitional provisions see para.14) with effect from May 20, 2009 (SI 2009/1261) (c.66).

Effect of beginning proceedings for possession

In section 130(2)(a) for "in pursuance of ... of the court), or" substitute: **3A–1107**
   in accordance with section 127(1A), or

In section 130(3)(b), for "section 127(2) and (3)" substitute:

section 127(1A) and (2)

Amendment

Delete and substitute:

3A–1107.1   Amended by the Housing and Regeneration Act Sch.11, Pt I, para.12 (for transitional provisions see para.14) with effect from May 20, 2009 (SI 2009/1261) (c.66).

PROCEEDINGS FOR POSSESSION

Proceedings for possession

Delete section 143D(1) and substitute:

3A–1137   **143D.**—(1) The landlord may only bring a demoted tenancy to an end by obtaining —

> (a) an order of the court for the possession of the dwelling–house, and
>
> (b) the execution of the order.

(1A) In such a case, the tenancy ends when the order is executed.

Delete section 134D(3).

Amendment

Delete and substitute:

3A–1137.1   Amended by the Housing and Regeneration Act Sch.11, Pt I, para.13 (for transitional provisions see para.14) with effect from May 20, 2009 (SI 2009/1261) (c.66).

Domestic violence

Delete the last paragraph and substitute:

3A–1255   A woman who flees domestic violence and is taken in by a women's refuge normally remains "homeless" while at the refuge because it is not accommodation that it would be reasonable for her to continue to occupy indefinitely (for the purposes of s.175(3)) (*Moran v Manchester City Council* [2009] UKHL 36, July 1, 2009; *The Times*, July 7, 2009. See too *R. v Ealing LBC ex p Sidhu* (1982) 2 H.L.R. 41, CA).

Inquiry into cases of homelessness or threatened homelessness

Add new section 184(3A):

3A–1281   (3A) If the authority decide that a duty is owed to the applicant under section 193(2) or 195(2) but would not have done so without having had regard to a restricted person, the notice under subsection (3) must also—

> (a) inform the applicant that their decision was reached on that basis,
>
> (b) include the name of the restricted person,
>
> (c) explain why the person is a restricted person, and
>
> (d) explain the effect of section 193(7AD) or (as the case may be) section 195(4A).

Add new subsection (7):

(7) In this Part "a restricted person" means a person—

    (a) who is not eligible for assistance under this Part,

    (b) who is subject to immigration control within the meaning of the Asylum and Immigration Act 1996, and

    (c) either—

        (i) who does not have leave to enter or remain in the United Kingdom, or

        (ii) whose leave to enter or remain in the United Kingdom is subject to a condition to maintain and accommodate himself, and any dependants, without recourse to public funds.

Amendment

Delete and substitute:

Amended for certain purposes by the Housing and Regeneration Act 2008 Sch.15, Pt I, para.3, with effect from March 2, 2009 (SI 2009/415; for purposes see art.2).   **3A–1281.1**

ELIGIBILITY FOR ASSISTANCE

Persons from abroad not eligible for housing assistance

In section 184(4) for "another person" substitute:

a person falling within subsection (5)   **3A–1289**

Add new section 185(5):

(5) A person falls within this subsection if the person—

    (a) falls within a class prescribed by regulations made under subsection (2); but

    (b) is not a national of an EEA State or Switzerland.

Note

For "Section 185 has been ... see below." substitute:

Amended for certain purposes by the Housing and Regeneration Act 2008 Sch.15, Pt I, para.4, with effect from March 2, 2009 (SI 2009/415; for purposes see art.2).   **3A–1290**

Persons from abroad not eligible for housing assistance

After the third paragraph ending "(persons from abroad).", add as a new paragraph:

The Allocation of Housing and Homelessness (Eligibility) (England) (Amendment) Regulations 2009 (SI 2009/358) provide that certain British citizens who were living in Zimbabwe but who came or come to the UK between February 28, 2009 and March 18, 2011, pursuant to an offer from the government to assist their settlement in the UK, are to be treated as eligible, notwithstanding that they are not habitually resident in the United Kingdom.   **3A–1296**

Dependent children

In the fourth paragraph, add after "June 1998, Legal Action 14, QBD)":

—but see now *Holmes–Moorehouse v Richmond–upon–Thames RLBC* [2009] 1 W.L.R. 413; [2009] 3 All E.R. 277. If parents have separated, in considering whether a child might reasonably be expected to live with an applicant, a local authority is entitled to take account of the fact that the child may already have a home with the other parent and that the consequence of awarding priority need might be the provision of accommodation to the applicant which would be under–occupied for much of the time. As a result: **3A–1323**

> "it will be only in exceptional circumstances that it would be reasonable to expect a child who has a home with one parent to be provided under Part VII with another so that he can reside with the other parent as well" (para.21).

Such "exceptional circumstances" might arise where there is a disabled child and care of both parents is imperative.

"act or omission in good faith"

In the first paragraph, add after "(1991) 23 H.L.R. 260, QBD).":

3A-1342   The use of the phrase "good faith" carries a connotation of some kind of impropriety, or some element of misuse or abuse of the legislation (*Ugiagbe v Southwark LBC* [2009] EWCA Civ 31, February 10, 2009; *The Times*, February 18, 2009, where the claimant had been in ignorance of a relevant fact and had acted in "good faith"—not intentionally homeless).

Duty to persons with priority need who are not homeless intentionally

In section 193(3A), add after "subject to the duty under this section":

3A-1361   in a case which is not a restricted case

Add new section 193(3B):

(3B) In this section "a restricted case" means a case where the local housing authority would not be satisfied as mentioned in subsection (1) without having had regard to a restricted person.

Add new sections 193(7AA) to (7AD):

(7AA) In a restricted case the authority shall also cease to be subject to the duty under this section if the applicant, having been informed of the matters mentioned in subsection (7AB)—

    (a) accepts a private accommodation offer, or

    (b) refuses such an offer.

(7AB) The matters are—

    (a) the possible consequence of refusal of the offer, and

    (b) that the applicant has the right to request a review of the suitability of the accommodation.

(7AC) For the purposes of this section an offer is a private accommodation offer if—

    (a) it is an offer of an assured shorthold tenancy made by a private landlord to the applicant in relation to any accommodation which is, or may become, available for the applicant's occupation,

    (b) it is made, with the approval of the authority, in pursuance of arrangements made by the authority with the landlord with a view to bringing the authority's duty under this section to an end, and

    (c) the tenancy being offered is a fixed term tenancy (within the meaning of Part 1 of the Housing Act 1988) for a period of at least 12 months.

(7AD) In a restricted case the authority shall, so far as reasonably practicable, bring their duty under this section to an end as mentioned in subsection (7AA).

In subsection (7B), for "The authority" substitute:

In a case which is not a restricted case, the authority

In subsection (7C), for "The applicant" substitute:

In a case which is not a restricted case, the applicant

Add new subsection (7F)(ab):

    (ab) approve a private accommodation offer; or

Note

Add after "Sch.1, para.13":

Amended for certain purposes by the Housing and Regeneration Act 2008 Sch.15, **3A–1362**
Pt I, para.5, with effect from March 2, 2009 (SI 2009/415; for purposes see art.2).

Duty to persons with priority need who are not homeless intentionally

In point (b), delete: "In Birmingham City Council v Aweys ... are owed the same duty."　　　**3A–1374**

"secure that accommodation is available for occupation"

Delete the second paragraph and substitute:

In *Birmingham City Council v Ali and Aweys* [2009] UKHL 36; July 1, 2009; *The Times*, **3A–1375**
July 7, 2009, it was held that an authority can perform its main housing duty under
the Housing Act 1996 Pt 7 by arranging for an applicant to stay in existing unsatisfactory accommodation for a short period, but is not performing its duty if it simply accepts the homelessness application and adds the applicant to its allocation scheme for
long term housing;

Add new paragraph at end:

An offer of accommodation which is not suitable for occupation at the date it falls to
be accepted can operate as a performance of the housing duty if accompanied with
certain binding and enforceable assurances about what work will be carried out to it
after acceptance (*Boreh v Ealing LBC* [2008] EWCA Civ 1176, October 29, 2008).

Duties in case of threatened homelessness

In section 195(3A), add after "the duty under this section":

in a case which is not a restricted threatened homelessness case　　　**3A–1380**

In section 195(4), add after "Where":

in a case which is not a restricted threatened homelessness case,

In subsection (4), add after "duty under section 193":

in a case which is not a restricted case (within the meaning of that
section)

Add new sections 195(4A) and (4B):

(4A) Where, in a restricted threatened homelessness case, in pursuance of the duty under subsection (2) the authority secure that accommodation other than that occupied by the applicant when he
made his application is available for occupation by him, the provisions of section 193(3) to (9) (period for which duty owed) apply,
with any necessary modifications, in relation to the duty under this
section as they apply in relation to the duty under section 193 in a
restricted case (within the meaning of that section).

(4B) In subsections (3A) to (4A) "a restricted threatened homelessness case" means a case where the local housing authority would not
be satisfied as mentioned in subsection (1) without having had regard
to a restricted person.

Note

For "Section 195 ... see below." substitute:

Amended for certain purposes by the Housing and Regeneration Act 2008 Sch.15, **3A–1381**
Pt I, para.6, with effect from March 2, 2009 (SI 2009/415; for purposes see art.2).

Note

For "The amendment was brought into force ... Order 2008 SI 3068" substitute:

3A–1406   The amendment was brought into force in England on December 1, 2008 by the Housing and Regeneration Act 2008 (Commencement No.2 and Transitional, Saving and Transitory Provisions) Order 2008 (SI 2008/3068) and in Wales on March 30, 2009 by the Housing and Regeneration Act 2008 (Commencement No.1) (Wales) Order 2009 (SI 2009/773) (w.65) (c.48).

Right to request review of decision

Add new section 202(1)(g):

3A–1417   (g) any decision of a local housing authority as to the suitability of accommodation offered to him by way of a private accommodation offer (within the meaning of section 193).

In subsection(1A), for "as mentioned in ... under subsection (1)(f)" substitute:

as mentioned in section 193(5), (7) or (7AA) may under subsection (1)(f) or (as the case may be) (g)

Note

For ". Section 202 has also ... see below." substitute:

3A–1418   and the Housing and Regeneration Act 2008 Sch.16 with effect from December 1, 2008 (SI 2008/3068), and Sch.15, Pt I, para.7 and Sch.16, for certain purposes with effect from March 2, 2009 (SI 2009/415; for purposes see art.2).

Reviews

In the fourth paragraph for "Johnston v Lambeth LBC [2008] EWCA Civ 690 ... June 30, 2008" substitute:

3A–1425   ● *Johnston v Lambeth LBC* [2008] EWCA Civ 690; [2009] H.L.R. 10; *The Times* June 30, 2008

In the bulleted list in the third paragraph, add at the start of the third paragraph of the third bullet (beginning "cf. Gilby v Westminster ..."):

Even if, on a literal construction of the words of Allocation of Housing and Homelessness (Review Procedures) Regulations (SI 1999/71) reg.8(2), there has been no "deficiency or irregularity" in the original decision, a broad reading of the regulation requires a reviewing officer to give an applicant an opportunity to address him or her (orally or in writing) before making an adverse decision on wholly different grounds (*Banks v Kingston–upon–Thames RLBC* [2008] EWCA Civ 1443, December 17, 2008);

Section 202 reviews, s.204 appeals and the ECHR

Add at end:

3A–1432   See too *Ali v Birmingham City Council* [2008] EWCA Civ 1228, November 7, 2008; [2009] 2 All E.R. 501.

Index of defined expressions: Part VII

In the table, below "relevant authority" add:

3A–1486   restricted person   section 184(7)

Note

For ". Section 218 has been ... see below." substitute:

and the Housing and Regeneration Act 2008 Sch.15, para.8, for certain purposes **3A–1487** with effect from March 2, 2009 (SI 2009/415; for purposes see art.2).

Housing and Regeneration Act 2008

Commencement

Add new paragraph 3A–1674.1:

Brought into force on December 1, 2008 for certain purposes, by the Housing and **3A–1674.1** Regeneration Act 2008 (Commencement No.2 and Transitional, Saving and Transitory Provisions) Order 2008 (SI 2008/3068) art.4(4).

Implementation   **3A–1679**

Delete paragraph 3A–1679.

Commencement

Delete and substitute:

Brought into force with effect from December 1, 2008 for certain purposes, by the **3A–1683** Housing and Regeneration Act 2008 (Commencement No.2 and Transitional, Saving and Transitory Provisions) Order 2008 (SI 2008/3068) art.4(4).

Commencement

Delete and substitute:

Brought into force for certain purposes with effect from March 2, 2009 by the **3A–1686** Housing and Regeneration Act 2008 (Commencement No.1 and Saving Provisions) Order 2009 (SI 2009/415).

Commencement

Add new paragraph 3A–1715.1:

Part 2 brought into force for the purpose of enabling the appropriate national **3A–1715.1** authority to make orders under that Part, with effect from December 1, 2008 by the Housing and Regeneration Act 2008 (Commencement No.2 and Transitional, Saving and Transitory Provisions) Order 2008 (SI 2008/3068) art.4(4).

Commencement

Add new paragraph 3A–1725.1

Paragraphs 1–10 brought into force for the purpose of enabling the Secretary of **3A–1725.1** State to make regulations under the Landlord and Tenant Act 1987 s.42A, with effect from December 1, 2008 by the Housing and Regeneration Act 2008 (Commencement No.2 and Transitional, Saving and Transitory Provisions) Order 2008 (SI 2008/3068) art.4(4).

Commencement

Add new paragraph 3A–1733:

Brought into force for certain purposes with effect from March 2, 2009 by the **3A–1733** Housing and Regeneration Act 2008 (Commencement No.1 and Saving Provisions) Order 2009 (SI 2009/415).

3B   BUSINESS TENANCIES

tenancy

Add at end:

Note that that it is not possible for a tenant to serve a request for a new tenancy **3B–134** under s.26 unless the lease is for a "for a term of years certain exceeding one year" (e.g. see *Manton Securities Ltd v Nazam* [2008] EWCA Civ 805).

s.30(1)(c) other substantial breaches of obligations, or any other reason connected with the tenant's use or management of the holding

Add new paragraph at end:

3B–179   In *Fowles v Heathrow Airport Ltd* [2008] EWCA Civ 1270 the trial judge found that the tenant had been in flagrant and persistent breaches of planning control some of which at least amounted to the commission of criminal offences and refused to order the grant of a new lease. On appeal the tenant submitted that it was "only if the renewal of the tenancy necessarily involves a criminal offence in the use of the land that such a prospect becomes a relevant consideration". The submission was rejected as "virtually unarguable". It was contrary to common sense and the broad language of para.(c). The judge was entitled to exercise the discretion in the way that he did. Indeed "it would have been perverse for the court to have ordered the respondent to grant the new tenancy to the appellant" (per Lawrence Collins L.J.).

3C CONTEMPT OF COURT ACT 1981

Enforcement of fines imposed by certain superior courts

In section 16(4), for "House of Lords" substitute:

3C–46   Supreme Court

Note

Delete and substitute:

3C–47   Amended by the Senior Courts Act 1981 s.152(4) and Sch.7; the Industrial Tribunals Act 1996 s.45 and Sch.3, the Powers of Criminal Courts (Sentencing) Act 2000 Sch.9, para.85 and the Constitutional Reform Act 2005 s.40 and Sch.9, para.35(2), with effect from October 1, 2009 (SI 2009/1604).

SUPPLEMENTAL

Interpretation

In section 19, for "House of Lords [Supreme Court]" substitute:

3C–50   Supreme Court

Note

Delete and substitute:

3C–51   Amended by the Senior Courts Act 1981 s.152(4) and Sch.7; the Industrial Tribunals Act 1996 s.45 and Sch.3, the Powers of Criminal Courts (Sentencing) Act 2000, Sch.9, para.85 and the Constitutional Reform Act 2005 s.40 and Sch.9, para.35(2), with effect from October 1, 2009 (SI 2009/1604).

3D PROCEEDINGS UNDER THE HUMAN RIGHTS ACT 1998

Section 2(1)

Add at end:

3D–9   ; [2008] 3 W.L.R. 636; [2009] 1 All E.R. 653

In the second paragraph, add after "[2007] UKHL 46": [2008] 1 A.C. 440;

3D–16   [2007] UKHL 46; [2008] 1 A.C. 440; [2007] 3 W.L.R. 681

Add at end:

   For the boundary between interpretation and amendment see too *AS (Somalia) v Secretary of State for the Home Department* [2009] UKHL 32; [2009] 1 W.L.R. 1385

Declaration of incompatibility

In section 4(5)(a) for "the House of Lords;" substitute:

the Supreme Court;   **3D–17**

Note

Add at end:

Further amended by the Constitutional Reform Act 2005 s.40 Sch.9 para.66.   **3D–18**

At the start of the fifth paragraph add:

Whether to make a declaration of incompatibility is a matter for the court's discre- **3D–19**
tion: see *Secretary of State for the Home Department v Nasseri* [2009] UKHL 23; [2009] 2
W.L.R. 1190.

Public Authorities

Acts of public authorities

Delete section 6(4) and substitute:

[Omitted]   **3D–23**

Section 6(1)

Add at end:

; [2008] 3 W.L.R. 681   **3D–24**

Section 6(1) and 6(3)

*Delete "YL v Birmingham City Council [2007] UKHL 27;[2007] 3 W.L.R. 112; [2007] 3 All
E.R. 957; The Times, June 21, 2007" and substitute:*

YL v Birmingham City Council [2007] UKHL 27; [2008] 1 A.C. 95; [2007] 3 W.L.R. **3D–25**
112; [2007] 3 All E.R. 957; *The Times,* June 21, 2007

Add at end:

and *London & Quadrant Housing Trust v Weaver* [2009] EWCA Civ 587; [2009] 25 E.G.
137 (CS). For the meaning of "public authority" under the provisions of the Freedom
of Information Act 2000 see *Sugar v British Broadcasting Corporation* [2009] UKHL 9;
[2009] 1 W.L.R. 430

Section 9(4)

Add new paragraph 3D–27.1:

Subsection (4) provided that "Parliament" in subs.(3) did not include the House of **3D–27.1**
Lords in its judicial capacity. Upon the establishment of the Supreme Court of the
United Kingdom this subsection was omitted by the Constitutional Reform Act 2005
s.40 Sch.9 para.66.

Section 7(5)

Add at end:

The defence under s.7(5) is a limitation defence in the ordinary sense and does not **3D–34.1**
limit the jurisdiction of the court: see *M(A Child) v Ministry of Justice* [2009] EWCA Civ
419.

At the end of the first paragraph add:

Damages under s.8 should only be awarded if, taking into account other awards **3D–41**
which could be made under different heads, it is necessary to do so in order to afford
just satisfaction: see *Dobson v Thames Water Utilities Ltd* [2009] EWCA Civ 28; [2009] 3
All ER 319; [2009] UKHRR 617.

Add new paragraph 3D–48.1:

For the procedure to be followed in seeking to exclude the media from family law **3D–48.1**
proceedings, see *Re (X) (A Child)* [2009] EWCA 1728, Fam.

Appointment to European Court of Human Rights

In section 18(4)(a), for "Supreme Court Act 1981" substitute:

3D–60   Senior Courts Act 1981

Note

Delete and substitute:

3D–61   Amended by the Constitutional Reform Act 2005 ss.15(1) and 59, Sch.4, para.278 and Sch.11, para.1.

3E   INSOLVENCY PROCEEDINGS

15. Bankruptcy petition

In paragraph 15.8, for "Supreme Court Accounts Office", substitute:

3E–15   Senior Courts Accounts Office

Debt Relief Orders

Add new paragraphs 3E–2859 to 3E–2861:

3E–2859   Section 251A in Pt 7A of the Insolvency Act 1986 (inserted by the Tribunals, Courts and Enforcement Act 2007) provides for "Debt Relief Orders" ("DRO"). Such orders are very limited in scope but where one is available is an alternative to a Bankruptcy Order, or possibly even a county court administration order.

The Insolvency (Amendment) Rules 2009 (SI 2009/642) brought these orders into force as from April 1, 2009. They are a new form of personal insolvency procedure that entails the making administratively by the Official Receiver (not the court) of a DRO on the application of the individual debtor. The effect of the order is to stay enforcement by creditors and to discharge the debts after a period of one year. While the DRO is in force the debtor is subject to similar restrictions to bankruptcy.

The court plays no part in the making of a DRO. Application is direct to the Official Receiver through an approved intermediary (see *http://www.insolvency.gov.uk* [Accessed May 14, 2009] for more details and a list of approved intermediaries). The Official Receiver makes the order if satisfied that the criteria are met.

Criteria for a Debt Relief Order

3E–2860   To apply for a DRO debtors must:

(a) be unable to pay their debts;

(b) owe less than £15,000;

(c) not own their own home;

(d) have assets with a total value not exceeding £300 (additionally, a car not exceeding a value of £1,000 is permitted);

(e) after tax, national insurance and normal household expenses, have disposable income of no more than £50 a month;

(f) be domiciled in England and Wales;

(g) not have been subject of a DRO within the last six years;

(h) not be involved in another formal insolvency procedure.

Limited role of the court

3E–2861   The DRO is made by the Official Receiver not the court. However, any debtor or creditor dissatisfied with the decision of the Official Receiver may apply to the court. Further, the Official Receiver can apply to the court for directions and either a debtor or creditor can apply for an extension of the moratorium period. Additionally, the court could refuse to make a bankruptcy order or an administration order if satisfied that a DRO would be more appropriate.

3F PERSONAL INJURY

Model orders

Delete and substitute:

In *Thompstone v Tameside Hospital NHS Foundation Trust* [2008] EWHC 2948 (QB), **3F–48.1**
December 2, 2008, unrep. the High Court extensively discussed the form of order
under s.2 where the court makes provision as to the mechanics of indexation of
periodical payments, and the judgment provides model forms of order. The model
forms of order are available at para.3F–48.60.2+.

Award of provisional damages

In article 4, for "Supreme Court Act 1981" substitute:

Senior Courts Act 1981   **3F–61**

Note

Add at end:

Article 4 amended by the Constitutional Reform Act 2005 s.59 and Sch.11, para.1 **3F–62**
with effect from October 1, 2009 (SI 2009/1604).

Premature claims for funeral expenses

Add new paragraph 3F–78.1:

Note that claims for funeral expenses in personal injury cases can arise firstly, **3F–78.1**
where expenses are incurred by the dependents of the deceased and the Fatal Accidents Act 1976 s.3(5) applies (supra.), and also where they are incurred by the
deceased's estate and the Law Reform (Miscellaneous Provisions) Act 1934 s.1(2)(c)
applies. A living claimant cannot claim for anticipated funeral expenses based on a
reduced life expectancy. See *Watson v Cakebread Robey Ltd* [2009] EWHC 1695 (QB).

3H CONSUMER CREDIT AND CONSUMER LAW

Meaning of credit

Subsection (1)

After the third paragraph, add as a new paragraph:

Under a funding agreement the claimants were to provide funds of 50 millions of **3H–26**
euros, to use the funds to purchase share warrants, to transfer these warrants to the
borrower, a special purchase vehicle (an SPV) (to be set up by the defendants) and
then to have the funds repaid one year later by the borrower (the SPV) together with
an uplift of 25%. Until the SPV (a corporate body) was set up, the defendants were to
be jointly and severally liable for the borrower's liability under the agreement. This
funding agreement was held not to amount to the provision of "credit" to the
defendants: *Maple Leaf Macro Volatility Master Fund v Rouvroy and Trylinski* [2009]
EWHC 257 (Comm); [2009] C.C.L.R. 9

Subsection(4)

*For "and London North Securities Ltd v Meadows [2005] EWCA Civ 956; [2005] C.C.L.R. 7"
substitute:*

, *London North Securities Ltd v Meadows* [2005] EWCA Civ 956; [2005] C.C.L.R. 7 and **3H–29**
Blackhorse Ltd v Hanson [2009] EWCA Civ 73; [2009] C.C.L.R. 6

Multiple agreements

In the second paragraph, add after "on the facts found it unnecessary to rule upon it.":

In *Heath v Southern Pacific Mortgage Limited* [2009] EWHC 103 (Ch); [2009] C.C.L.R. **3H–58**
7, H.H. Judge Purle QC, considered both *Ocwen v Coxall and Coxall* and *London North
Securities Ltd v Williams and Williams* to have been wrongly decided, holding that section
18 does not treat every agreement which falls into two or more different categories as
necessarily being an agreement in parts.

Reopening of extortionate agreements

Restrictions on court's ability to re–open agreement

Add new paragraph at end:

3H–323   In *Nolan v Wright* [2009] EWHC 305; [2009] C.C.L.R. 8 Judge Hodge Q.C., held that a claim to re–open a credit bargain as being extortionate was statute barred after 12 years from the date of the agreement unless the claim extended to a claim for repayment of money previously paid in which case the relevant period was six years, the period in the latter case possibly not beginning until the date the money had been paid to the creditor. Considering himself bound to do so by the decision in *Rahman*, he rejected the suggestion (at the start of this paragraph) that "the Limitation Act has no application all where the debtor makes the application to re–open the credit agreement (e.g. to be relieved of the obligation to pay a sum) as part of his *defence*".

Power to declare rights of parties

Add after "s.113(3)(d) and (4).":

3H–350   A court has no power to grant a section 142 declaration where an agreement is closed, that is where the regulated agreement has been fully performed and it is therefore impossible for the creditor to apply for an enforcement order: *Watson v Progressive Financial Services Ltd, T/A Welcome Finance* [2009] C.C.L.R.10 (Liverpool Cty Ct).

3J   DIRECTORS DISQUALIFICATION PROCEEDINGS

Editorial note

Restrictions imposed by Disqualification Orders and Disqualification Undertakings

In the second paragraph for "Secretary of State for Business, Enterprise and Regulatory Reform (formerly" substitute:

3J–8   Secretary of State for Business, Innovation and Skills (formerly the Secretary of State for Business, Enterprise and Regulatory Reform (before that known as

Date of commencement of proceedings

For "Secretary of State v Vohora [2007] EWHC 2656 (Ch); The Times, December 10, 2007" substitute:

3J–9   *Secretary of State v Vohora* [2007] EWHC 2656 (Ch); [2009] B.C.C. 369

Part II

Disqualification applications

3J–13   *Delete footnote three.*

Affidavits

In the second paragraph, add after "[1998] Ch. 71":

3J–26   ; [2009] B.C.C. 375

3K   CIVIL RECOVERY PROCEEDINGS

Registers

In paragraph 7C, for "Central Office of the Supreme Court" substitute:

3K–18   Central Office of the Senior Courts

SECTION 4

SUPREME COURT OF THE UNITED KINGDOM APPEALS

Editorial Introduction

Delete Section 4 House of Lords Appeals and substitute Section 4 Supreme Court of the United Kingdom Appeals:

The Constitutional Reform Act 2005 (c.4) received the Royal Assent in March 2005. **4–0.1** (For text of this statute, see para.9A–962 below.) Provisions in Pt 3 of the Act (ss.23 to 53) dealing with the establishment of the Supreme Court of the United Kingdom came into effect on October 1, 2009.

Supreme Court Rules

Section 45 of the 2005 Act gives the President of the Supreme Court power to make **4–0.2** rules (to be known as Supreme Court Rules) governing the practice and procedure to be followed in the Court. Before making rules the President must consult the Lord Chancellor and the professional bodies referred to in s.45(4)). For the purpose of enabling rules to be enacted before the commencement date, this section was modified by the Constitutional Reform Act 2005 (Temporary Modifications) Order 2006 (SI 2006/227) to give the senior Law Lord power to make rules in the first instance. The procedure for the enactment in statutory instrument of rules made by the President is set out in s.45. The procedure for bringing Supreme Court Rules into effect differs from that which applies to the bringing into effect of Civil Procedure Rules (see Sect.12 para.12–3 below). The Lord Chancellor has no power to disallow or alter rules submitted to him by the President. The Supreme Court Rules 2009 (SI 2009/1603) were made by the senior Law Lord in June 2009 and the Lord Chancellor directed that they should come into effect on October 1, 2009. For transitional arrangements, see r.55. See further, commentary following r.2 below.

Practice Directions and Forms

Practice directions are issued by the President of the Court (initially by the senior **4–0.3** Law Lord) to supplement the Rules (see commentary following r.3 below) and to prescribe Forms (see r.4).

The practice directions issued are as follows (see para.4A–56 et seq. below):

Practice Direction 1 (General Note and Jurisdiction)
Practice Direction 2 (The Registry of the Supreme Court)
Practice Direction 3 (Applications for Permission to Appeal)
Practice Direction 4 (Notice of Appeal)
Practice Direction 5 (Papers for the Appeal Hearing)
Practice Direction 6 (The Appeal Hearing)
Practice Direction 7 (Applications, Documents, Forms and Orders)
Practice Direction 8 (Miscellaneous Matters)
Practice Direction 9 (The Human Rights Act 1998)
Practice Direction 10 (Devolution Jurisdiction)
Practice Direction 11 (The European Court of Justice)
Practice Direction 12 (Criminal Proceedings)
Practice Direction 13 (Costs)
Practice Direction 14 (Filing Documents in the Registry of the Supreme Court by electronic means)

Practice Directions 2 to 11 and 13 and 14 govern civil proceedings. Practice Direction 12 is dedicated to criminal proceedings; Practice Directions 2 to 11 apply to criminal proceedings, subject to any modifications or additional provisions made by Practice Direction 12.

The Practice Directions are, in large part, based on the Directions and Standing Orders that formerly regulated judicial proceedings in the House of Lords. (Sometimes this provenance is revealed by the fact that terminology used follows those sources and not modern terminology used in the Rules). Generally the Practice Directions read rather more like a Court Guide than traditional practice directions. The great proportion of the material in them consists of re–statements of, or paraphrases of, provisions found in the Rules or in primary legislation governing the jurisdiction of the Court (but not infrequently the exact provision repeated is not acknowledged).

The prescribed Forms are published in Annex 1 to Practice Direction 7 (Applications, Documents, Forms and Orders) and are as follows:

Form 1 (Application for permission/notice of appeal);

Form 2 (Application form);

Form 3 (Notice of objection/acknowledgment by respondent).

For convenience these Forms are set out at paras 4–197 to 4–199 below.

Jurisdiction of the Court

4–0.4   In para.1.1.1 of Practice Direction 1 it is explained that the jurisdiction of the Court corresponds to that formerly exercised by the House of Lords in its judicial capacity under the Appellate Jurisdiction Acts 1876 and 1888 (which are repealed) together with devolution matters under the Scotland Act 1998, the Northern Ireland Act 1998 and the Government of Wales Act 2006, which are transferred to the Supreme Court from the Judicial Committee of the Privy Council. The jurisdiction of the Supreme Court is defined by s.40 of, and Sch.9 to, the 2005 Act. By s.40(5) of the 2005 Act the Court has power to determine any question necessary to be determined for the purposes of doing justice in an appeal to it under any enactment (in effect, re–enacting s.4 of the 1876 Act as interpreted). The Court's jurisdiction is fully explained in Section 2 of Practice Direction 1.

Supreme Court Rules 2009

4–0   (S.I. 2009 No. 1903)

Arrangement of Rules

Part 1

Interpretation and scope

PART 1

INTERPRETATION AND SCOPE

Citation and commencement

1. These Rules may be cited as the Supreme Court Rules 2009 4–1 and shall come into force on 1st October 2009.

Effect of rule

4–1.1   These Rules came into effect on a date directed by the Lord Chancellor as provided by s.45 of the 2005 Act. The legislation establishing the Supreme Court came into effect on the same date. See further, Editorial Introduction para. 4–0.2 above.

The Rules apply, with any necessary modifications, to appeals which were proceeding, and petitions for leave which were lodged, in the House of Lords before the commencement date; see r.55 (Transitional arrangements).

Scope and objective

4–2   **2.—(1)   These Rules apply to civil and criminal appeals to the Court and to appeals and references under the Court's devolution jurisdiction.**

(2) The overriding objective of these Rules is to secure that the Court is accessible, fair and efficient.

(3) The Court must interpret and apply these Rules with a view to securing that the Court is accessible, fair and efficient and that unnecessary disputes over procedural matters are discouraged.

Effect of rule

4–2.1   This rule reflects provisions in the 2005 Act.

Scope—The Rules govern the practice and procedure to be followed by the Court when exercising its jurisdiction (s.45(1) of the 2005 Act). The jurisdiction of the Court corresponds to that of the House of Lords in its judicial capacity, together with devolution matters. The Court's jurisdiction is summarised in Section 2 of Practice Direction 1. "Devolution jurisdiction" is defined in r.3(2). If any procedural question arises which is not dealt with by these Rules, the Court or the Registrar may adopt any procedure that is consistent with the overriding objective, the 2005 Act and these Rules (r.9(7)).

Objective—In the 2005 Act, subs.(3) of s.45 (Making of rules) states that the President of the Supreme Court must exercise the power to make Supreme Court Rules with a view to securing that (a) the Court is accessible, fair and efficient, and (b) the rules are both simple and simply expressed. This provision is reflected in para.(2) ("overriding objective") and in para.(3) of r.1. Apart from r.9(7) there is no express reference to the overriding objective in the Rules and none of operational significance in any of the Practice Directions.

Interpretation

4–3   **3.—(1)   In these Rules—**

"the Act" means the Constitutional Reform Act 2005;

"the Court" means the Supreme Court of the United Kingdom;

"Justice" means a judge of the Court and includes its President and Deputy President;

"the Registrar" means the Registrar of the Court;

"the Registry" means the Registry of the Court.

(2) In these Rules except where the context otherwise requires—

"appellant" means a person who files an application for permission to appeal or who files a notice of appeal;

"business day" means any day other than a Saturday, Sunday, Christmas Day, Good Friday or a bank holiday under the Banking and Financial Dealings Act 1971[1], in England and Wales;

"certificate of service" means a certificate given under rule 6;

"counsel" includes any person with the right to be heard as an advocate at a full hearing before the Court;

---

[1] 1971 c.80.

"court below" means the court from which an appeal (or application for permission to appeal) is made to the Court;

"court officer" means the Registrar or a member of the court staff;

"devolution jurisdiction" means the jurisdiction transferred to the Court by section 40 of, and Schedule 9 to, the Act;

"electronic means" means CD ROMs, memory sticks, email, fax or other means of electronic communication of the contents of documents;

"filing" means filing in the Registry in accordance with rule 7 and related expressions have corresponding meanings;

"form" and the "appropriate form" have the meanings given by rule 4;

"panel of Justices" means a panel of at least three Justices;

"party" means an appellant, a respondent and a person who has been given permission to intervene under rule 26;

"the relevant officer" means—

(a) in relation to proceedings in England and Wales, the Attorney General and, in relation to proceedings that particularly affect Wales, the Counsel General to the Welsh Assembly Government,

(b) in relation to proceedings in Scotland, the Advocate General for Scotland and the Lord Advocate; and

(c) in relation to proceedings in Northern Ireland, the Advocate General for Northern Ireland and (when section 22 of the Justice (Northern Ireland) Act 2002 comes into force[1]) the Attorney General for Northern Ireland;

"requisite number of copies" means the number of copies which are to be provided under the relevant practice direction or as directed by the Court;

"respondent" includes a respondent to an application for permission to appeal and means—

(a) a person other than the appellant who was a party to the proceedings in the court below and who is affected by the appeal; and

(b) a person who is permitted by the Court to be a party to the appeal;

"service" and related expressions have the meanings given by rule 6;

"solicitor" includes any person authorised to provide legal services other than as counsel in connection with proceedings before the Court.

(3) References in these Rules to a practice direction means a practice direction issued by the President of the Court.

(4) References in these Rules or in any form to a party's signing, filing or serving any document or taking any other procedural step include the signature, filing or service of that document or the taking of such other procedural step by the party's solicitor.

---

[1] 2002 c. 26.

(5) Where any of these Rules or any practice direction requires a document to be signed, that requirement shall be satisfied if the signature is printed by computer or other mechanical means.

(6) Where these Rules require or permit the Court to perform an act of a formal or administrative character, that act may be performed by a court officer.

Effect of rule

4–3.1   The expressions referred to in r.3(1) are not subject to qualification. None of the expressions defined in the 2005 Act is of particular use in interpreting the Rules. Insofar as they do assist, Interpretation Act 1978 s.11 applies. The Rules must be interpreted by the Court with a view to securing the objective stated in r.2(3).

"the Court"—For obvious reasons, throughout the Rules there are many references to "the Court", but in some rules there are references to "the Supreme Court" (r.29). Throughout the practice directions the expression "Supreme Court" is more commonly used than "Court".

"Justice"— Section 40(6) of the 2005 Act states that the judges other than the President and Deputy President are to be styled "Justices of the Supreme Court". Within the Rules, "Justice" includes the President and the Deputy President (r.3(2)).

"Registrar" and "Registry"—The Registrar is an officer appointed by the President of the Court (s.49). For opening times of the Registry and postal and email addresses and telephone numbers, see Practice Direction 2 (The Registry of the Supreme Court). In the Rules, "court officer" means the Registrar or a member of the court staff (r.3(2)).

Interpretation Act 1978—Generally this Act applies to subordinate legislation and would therefore apply to the Rules.

Interpretation of particular terms (r.3(2))

4–3.2   The terms and expressions listed in r.3(2) apply except where the context otherwise requires. The ones likely to be of most use in day–to–day practice are those relevant to the service and filing of Forms and documents. Expressions related to "filing" (which means filing in the Registry) would include "lodge" (r.54), and probably "submit" (r.48(1) and "provide" (r.7 and r.22). (For methods of filing, see r.7.) Methods of service are listed in r.6 and it is provided that "service and related expressions have the meanings given by rule 6". Related expressions would include submitting (r.22.2) and giving notice (rr.38(1), 40(1) and 49(4)). It may be noted that the expression "business day", which is referred to in r.6 (Service) and r.7 (Filing), is defined in accordance with legislation applicable in England and Wales (cf. CPR r.6.2). Throughout the practice directions there are numerous references to the filing and service of Forms and documents (most of them appearing where particular rules are restated or paraphrased, rather than where points of practice not expressly dealt with in the Rules are stipulated or explained).

Practice Directions (r.3(3))

4–3.3   Practice directions are issued by the President of the Court (initially by the senior Law Lord) to supplement the Rules (1) to provide general guidance and assistance to parties and their legal representatives, and (2) to provide for the Forms (see r.4) to be used (Practice Direction 1 para.1.1.3).

Procedural step by the party's solicitor (r.3(4))

4–3.4   "Solicitor" includes any person authorised to provide legal services other than as counsel in connection with proceedings before the Court. (r.3(2)). In certain circumstances, the signature of a party's counsel may be required; see Practice Direction 4 (Notice of Appeal) para.4.2.2.

Signature of document by mechanical means (r.3(5))

4–3.5   This rule accords with CPR r.5.3 (see Vol.1, para.5.3). Rule 5.3 is helpfully supplemented by Practice Direction (Court Documents) para.1 (see Vol.1 para.5PD.1), but no comparable provision appears in the practice directions supplementing the SCR.

Act of a formal or administrative character (r.3(6))

This rule accords with CPR r.2.5(1) (see Vol.1, para.2.5.3). In terms it does not **4–3.6**
include acts required to be performed by practice directions.

Forms

**4.—(1) In these Rules, a form means a form set out in a practice 4–4
direction and a reference to the "appropriate form" means the
form provided by the relevant practice direction for any particular
case.**

**(2) The forms shall be used in the cases to which they apply, and
in the circumstances for which they are provided by the relevant
practice direction, but a form may be varied by the Court or a party
if the variation is required by the circumstances of a particular
case.**

Effect of rule

The Forms to be used in conjunction with the Rules are not prescribed by the Rules **4–4.5**
but are prescribed by practice direction. The Rules and the practice directions refer to
a wide variety of documents other than the prescribed Forms. All documents placed
before the Court must comply with the strictures stated in Practice Direction 5 (Papers
for the Appeal Hearing) para.5.1.2. (Paragraphs 5.1.1 and 5.1.2 are repeated in
Practice Direction 6 (The Appeal Hearing) paras 6.1.1 and 6.1.2.) Paragraph 7.2.1 of
Practice Direction 7 (Applications, Documents, Forms and Orders) states that all
formal documents for the Court must be produced on A4 paper, securely bound on
the left, using both sides of the paper and warns that documents which are not legible
or which are not produced in the authorised form or which are unsatisfactory for
some other similar reason will not be accepted by the Registry. (Provisions to similar
effect are found elsewhere in the practice directions; notably in Practice Direction 3
(Applications for Permission to Appeal) para.3.1.3, and Practice Direction (Notices of
Appeal) para.4.2.1.) The Registrar may refuse to accept a document unless the relevant fee has been paid (r.45).

Forms—In para.1.1.5 of Practice Direction 1, r.4 is summarised and it is explained
that three forms are set out in Annex 1 to Practice Direction 7 (Applications, Documents, Forms and Orders). They are: Form 1 (Application for permission/ notice of
appeal), Form 2 (Application form), Form 3 (Notice of objection/acknowledgement by
respondent) (see paras 4–197 to 4–199 below). As their titles suggest, Forms 1 and 3
may be used for more than one purpose. Form 2 is to be used in a variety of
circumstances.

It is expressly provided that parties may consult the Registry at any stage of preparation of an application for permission to appeal or of a notice of appeal, and may
submit applications and notices in draft for approval (Practice Direction 3 (Applications for Permission to Appeal) para.3.1.2, Practice Direction 4 (Notices of Appeal)
para.4.2.1). Insofar as r.4(2) permits the variation of any Form by the Court or a party
if the variation is required by the particular circumstances of the case it follows CPR
r.4(2).

Documents—Throughout the Rules and practice directions there are references to
various documents that may have to be produced during the appeal process and for
which none of the prescribed Forms is appropriate. The principal documents falling
into this category are: the statement of facts and issues, the appendix, the appellant's
and respondent's cases, the core volumes and authorities volumes. to the Court for appeal hearings. Parties may if they wish follow the former practice in House of Lords
appeals but are not required to do so. Where parties are in any doubt as to how documents should be presented they should consult the Registrar and discuss the practice
which should be adopted. However, it should be noted that, despite the apparent
generosity of what is said in paras 5.1.1 and 6.1.1, the practice directions contain some
provisions applicable to the manner in which documents are presented to the Court
which are quite prescriptive.

Time limits

**5.—(1) The Court may extend or shorten any time limit set by 4–5
these Rules or any relevant practice direction (unless to do so would
be contrary to any enactment).**

(2) **The Court may exercise these powers either on an application by one or more parties or without an application being made.**

(3) **The Registrar must notify the parties when a time limit is varied under this rule.**

(4) **An application for an extension of time may be granted after the time limit has expired.**

(5) **Where a party to a proposed appeal has applied for public funding and the Registrar is informed of the application, the time limits in rules 11 and 19 shall be extended until 28 days after the final determination of the application for public funding.**

(6) **When the period specified—**

(a) **by these Rules or a practice direction, or**

(b) **by any judgment or court order,**

for doing any act at the Registry ends on a day on which the Registry is closed, that act shall be in time if done on the next day on which the Registry is open.

Effect of rule

4–5.1   The effects of this rule and provisions referred to in it are explained in Practice Direction 2 (The Registry of the Supreme Court) at para.2.1.12 et seq. The Registry may accept an application for permission to appeal or a notice of appeal which is out of time if the application sets out the reason(s) why it was not filed within the time limit and it is in order in all other respects (*ibid.* para.2.1.13). The Registrar may reject an application for permission to appeal solely on the ground that it is out of time (*ibid.* para.2.1.15).

In order to achieve indicative timetables for the expedited hearing of proceedings, the Court will set aside or vary the time limits and practice directions that normally apply to applications and appeals (see further Practice Direction 3 (Applications for Permission to Appeal) para.3.4.4 et seq.).

A decision made by the Court in exercise of powers conferred by r.5 is a procedural decision within r.9 and, generally, may be made by a single justice or the Registrar without an oral hearing.

Determination of public funding application (r.5(5))

4–5.2   The Rule time limits automatically extended in the circumstances referred to in r.5(5) are for the filing of an application for permission to appeal (r.11) and for filing of a notice of appeal where permission is not required (r.19). The giving of notification to the Registrar of the public funding application is a pre–condition. Notification must be given far enough before the expiry of the original time limits to ensure that the appeal is not dismissed as being out of time; a copy of the order appealed from must be submitted by the applicant with the notification (Practice Direction 8 (Miscellaneous Matters) para.8.12.4). Note also *ibid.* para.8.12.5 (Effect of application by respondent for public funding/legal aid), and para.8.12.6 (Issue of public funding/legal aid certificate). Where r.5(5) takes effect, time is extended until 28 days after the determination of the application for public funding, including any appeals against a refusal of funding (*ibid.* para.8.12.3).

An appellant, a respondent and a person who has been given permission to intervene under r.26 may be "a party to a proposed appeal", unless the context otherwise requires (r.3(2)).

Period for doing any act at the Registry (r.5(6))

4–5.3   For opening times of the Registry, see Practice Direction 2 (The Registry of the Supreme Court) para.2.1.3.

Time limit set by Rules

4–5.4   These are set, not by weeks or months, but by number of days (except in r.48(1)). Principal time limits set by Rules for the taking of procedural steps after particular events in civil proceedings include: r.9(5) (14 days for filing application for review of Registrar's decision); r.11(1) (28 days for filing of application for permission to appeal); r.13(1) (14 days for respondent's objection to application for permission to appeal); r.14(2) (7 days for filing of further documents in support of application for permission to appeal); r.18(1)(c) (14 days for filing notice of intention to proceed with appeal); r.19(2) (42 days for filing notice of appeal where permission not required); r.21(1) (14 days for filing respondent's notice); r.22(1) (112 days for filing documents for appeal hearing); r.23 (filing of core volumes 14 days before date fixed for hearing); r.25(4) (42 days for filing notice of cross–appeal); r.30(4) (7 days for filing notice of objection to procedural application); r.39(2) (21 days for disposal of documents application). Time limits are imposed for various purposes in Rule provisions dealing with the making of orders for costs; see, r.48(1) (submission of claim for costs "within three months", r.48(4) and (5) (claim for costs), r.49(7) (assessment of costs), r.53(1) (appeal from assessment of costs). Other provisions impose time limits on actions to be taken by the Court or the Registrar, e.g. r.16(2) (invitation to parties to file written submissions as to grant of permission to appeal on terms), r.40(1) (notice to Crown where incompatibility issue arising), or particular parties, e.g. r.43(3) (notice of intention to appeal by Comptroller).

Prominent examples of time limits for the making of applications for permission to appeal being fixed, not by Rules, but by other enactments, include cases involving civil contempt of court (Administration of Justice Act 1960 s.2), and "leapfrog" appeals from the High Court (Administration of Justice Act 1969 s.13). See further, r.11 (Filing an application).

Provisions within the Rules and in other enactments affecting time limits for applying for permission to appeal and applications to extend such limits in criminal proceedings are explained in Practice Direction 12 (Criminal Proceedings) para.12.3. No extension may be granted in respect of an application for permission to appeal made under the Extradition Act 2003 ss.32 and 114.

Time limit set by relevant practice direction

Throughout the practice directions, the many provisions in the Rules fixing time **4–5.5** limits are restated (sometimes more than once). (In some instances, the Rule provenance of the time limit restated is not acknowledged.) Time limits fixed by practice direction provisions, and not by Rules (or any other enactment), are rare.

Service

6.—(1)   A document may be served by any of the following **4–6** methods—

(a) personal service;

(b) first class post (or an alternative service which provides for delivery on the next working day);

(c) (with the consent of the party to be served) through a document exchange;

(d) (with the consent of the party to be served or at the direction of the Registrar) by electronic means in accordance with the relevant practice direction.

(2) Where the address of the person on whom a document is to be served is unknown, the Registrar may direct that service is effected by an alternative method of service.

(3) A document served by first–class post or through a document exchange will be taken to have been served on the second day after it was posted or left at the document exchange, as the case may be (not including days which are not business days).

(4) A certificate of service must give details of the persons served, the method of service used and must state the date on which the document was served personally, posted, delivered to the document exchange or sent electronically, as the case may be.

Effect of rule

4–6.1   A number of provisions in the Rules stipulate that particular documents should be served by one party on another. Those relating to formal documents include: r.12 (application for permission to appeal), r.13(2) (respondent's notice of objection), r.15(2) (intervener's submissions), r.18(2) (re–sealed application for permission to appeal), r.20(1) (notice of appeal), r.21(2) (respondent's notice), r.25(4)(a) (notice of cross–appeal), r.30(3) (procedural application), r.30(4) (notice of objection to procedural application), r.48(3) (service of claim for costs on paying party), r.48(4) (service of points of dispute on receiving party), and r.48(5) (service of receiving party's response to points of dispute on paying party).

Rule 6 is not concerned with the questions as to which documents should be served upon whom and when, but with the "method" of service permitted. The methods stated are not exhaustive. (The methods of service listed in r.6(1) accord with the methods of filing listed in r.7(1).)

References in the Rules to a party's serving any document include service of that document by the party's solicitor (r.3(4)).

In r.3(2) it is provided that "service and related expressions have the meanings given by rule 6". Related expressions would include submitting (r.22.2) and giving notice (rr.38(1), 40(1) and 49(4)). Cf., r.15(4)(b) ("appellant must notify"); r.48(2) (receiving party "must supply").

In r.6(1)(b) "alternative service" has same meaning as "other service" in CPR r.6.3(1)(b). For explanation, see Vol.1, para.6.3.3. Rule 6(1)(b) refers to next working day (not next "business day").

Consent of party to be served (r.6(1))

4–6.2   Paragraph 2.1.23 of Practice Direction 2 (The Registry of the Supreme Court) states that a party or his solicitor will be taken to have consented to a particular method of service if, for example, their writing paper includes a fax number or a numbered box at a document exchange unless they have indicated in writing that they are not willing to accept service by that particular method. (Apart from that paragraph there is no practice direction provision dealing with service by electronic means inter partes.) The Registrar may direct that a document be served by electronic means. For meaning of "electronic means" see r.3(2) and commentary following r.7.

Time limits (r.6(3))

4–6.3   Some time limits imposed by provisions in the Rules for the taking of certain procedural steps are calculated from the date on which a formal document was served (e.g. rr.13(1), 21(1), 30(4)). For this reason (and others) it is important that the date of service should not be a matter for doubt. In cases where the method of service adopted is by first–class post or by a document exchange, r.6(3) fixes the date of service (which may not accord with the actual date upon which the document was received). It is important to note that, in the Rules, "business day", is defined in accordance with legislation applicable in England and Wales, and not with that applicable in other constituent parts of the United Kingdom (r.3(2)).

Certificate of service (r.6(4))

4–6.4   Provisions in the Rules stipulating that particular documents should be served by one party on another add the requirement that, when the document is filed, a certificate of service (complying with r.6(4)) must be filed with it. The certificate must be included either in the original document and signed or a separate certificate of service must be provided (Practice Direction 2 (The Registry of the Supreme Court) para.2.1.24).

Service before filing

4–6.5   Documents such as applications for permission to appeal (r.12), notices of appeal (r.20), and interveners' applications (r.15) must be served on the persons referred to in the rules applicable, in accordance with r.6 or with any relevant statutory provisions (e.g. provisions in the Companies Acts 1985 and Companies Act 2006), before they are filed (see Practice Direction 2 (The Registry of the Supreme Court) para.2.1.23). Procedural applications (and objections thereto) must be served on the persons referred to in r.30 before filing. The Registry will not issue an application for permission to appeal or other document unless (amongst other things) it has been properly served on the respondents (*ibid.* para.2.1.11).

Filing

7.—(1) A document may be filed by any of the following 4–7
methods—

(a) personal delivery;

(b) first class post (or an alternative service which provides for
delivery on the next working day);

(c) through a document exchange;

(d) (with the consent of the Registrar) by electronic means in accordance with the relevant practice direction.

(2) A document filed by first–class post or through a document
exchange will be taken to have been filed on the second day after it
was posted or left at the document exchange, as the case may be
(not including days which are not business days).

(3) Except with the consent of the Registrar, the contents of documents—

(a) filed in hard copy must also be provided to the Registry by
electronic means, and

(b) filed by electronic means must also be provided to the Registry in hard copy,

in accordance with the relevant practice direction.

(4) A court officer must seal the following documents when they
are filed—

(a) an application for permission to appeal,

(b) a notice of objection or acknowledgement by the respondent,

(c) a notice of appeal,

(d) an application form,

and may place the seal on the document by hand or by printing a
facsimile of the seal on the document whether electronically or
otherwise.

(5) A document purporting to bear the Court's seal shall be
admissible in evidence without further proof.

Effect of rule

A number of provisions in the Rules stipulate that particular documents should be **4–7.1**
filed. Except where the context otherwise requires, "filing" means filing in the Registry
in accordance with r.7, and "related expressions" have corresponding meanings
(r.3(2)).

Rule 7 is not concerned with questions as to which documents should be filed and
when, or the form they should be in, but with the "method" of filing permitted.
Paragraph (1) of r.7 is similar to para.(1) of r.6. Reference should be made to the commentary following r.6 accordingly.

In para.2.1.7 et seq. of Practice Direction 2 (The Registry of the Supreme Court)
the effects of r.7 are re–stated and attention is drawn to the Registrar's power to refuse
to accept a document under r.8(3) which does not comply with any provision in the
Rules or any relevant practice direction.

In a number of instances, a fee is payable upon the filing of a document; see Annex
2 of Practice Direction 7 (Applications, Documents, Forms and Orders). The Registrar
may refuse to accept a document (or refuse to allow a party to take any step) unless
the relevant fee is paid (r.45).

Time limits (r.7(2))

Provisions in the Rules (and in practice directions) requiring formal documents and **4–7.2**
other documents to be filed usually further require that they be filed within a particular time; e.g. r.11(1) (application for permission to appeal), r.16(2) (invited written
submissions), r.18(1) (intention to proceed), r.14(2) (further documents in support of
application), r.23 (core volumes).

Some time limits imposed by provisions in the Rules for the taking of certain procedural steps are calculated from the date on which a document was filed; e.g. r.22(1) (Documents for appeal hearing), r.25(4)(a) (Cross–appeal), r.26(1) (Intervention). Rule 7(2) is a deeming provision (similar to r.6(3)) having the effect of fixing the filing date in the circumstances to which it applied. See further commentary on r.6(3) above. Where a document is filed by electronic means the time and date of its receipt is fixed in accordance with para.14.4 of Practice Direction 14 (Filing Documents in the Registry of the Supreme or by electronic means).

Filing by electronic means (r.7.5(3))

4–7.3   Except where the context otherwise requires, in the Rules "electronic means" means CD–ROMs, memory sticks, email, fax or other means of electronic communication of the contents of documents. The relevant practice direction referred to in r.7(1)(d) and r.7(2) is Practice Direction 14 (Filing Documents in the Registry of the Supreme Court by electronic means).

Sealing of filed documents (r.7(4))

4–7.4   In terms, para.(4) of r.7 is similar to CPR r.2.6. For commentary on r.2.6, see Vol.1, para.2.6.1 et seq.

Sealed documents as evidence (r.7(5))

4–7.5   Section 55(2) of the 2005 Act states that every document purporting to be sealed with the official seal of the Supreme Court is to be received in evidence in all parts of the United Kingdom without further proof. See further, "Sealed documents as evidence" Vol.1, para.2.6.3.

Non–compliance with these Rules

4–8   **8.—(1) Any failure by a party to comply with these Rules or any relevant practice direction shall not have the effect of making the proceedings invalid.**

(2) Where any provision in these Rules or any relevant practice direction is not complied with, the Court may give whatever directions appear appropriate, having regard to the seriousness of the non–compliance and generally to the circumstances of the case.

(3) In particular, the Registrar may refuse to accept any document which does not comply with any provision in these Rules or any relevant practice direction and may give whatever directions appear appropriate.

(4) Directions given under this rule may include the summary dismissal of an appeal or debarring a respondent from resisting an appeal.

Effect of rule

4–8.1   Paragraph (1) of r.8 demonstrates an abundance of caution. It has a similar effect to CPR r.3.10, the descendant of a rule introduced many years ago for the purpose of redressing the effects of an unfortunate line of authority that never applied to proceedings in the House of Lords (see Vol.1, para.3.10.1).

Paragraph (2) of r.8 is consistent with the statutory requirement that the Court's Rules should be "fair and efficient" (s.45(3) of the 2005 Act) and with the objective that unnecessary disputes over procedural matters (particularly those stimulated by excessive formalism) should be discouraged (r.1(3)).

Non–compliance with Rules and practice directions provisions is not to be encouraged. The Court's procedures have to be protected from abuse. The powers referred to in para.(3) of r.8 may have severe effects. Where an appellant is guilty of non–compliance, presumably the Court has power to stay the appeal.

Some rules have the effect of preventing a party from taking a procedural step to progress an appeal or from participating in a particular part of the appeal process without first having complied with certain conditions (e.g. r.13(3) and r.21(3)). In effect, such provisions contain their own sanctions.

In addition to the powers referred to in para.(3) of r.8, the Registrar has power under r.45 to refuse to accept a document for filing (or to refuse to allow a party to take any step) unless the relevant fee payable for filing a document is paid. The powers of the Registrar (including powers referred to in para.(3)) exercisable where an appellant has failed to comply with r.14(2) (filing of further documents in support of application for permission to appeal) are explained in para.3.2.3 of Practice Direction 3 (Applications for Permission to Appeal). Note also r.11(2)(c).

A decision made in exercise of the powers conferred by r.8 is a procedural decision within r.9 and, subject to r.9(2), may be made by a single justice or the Registrar without an oral hearing. Rule 9(2) states that any contested application for a direction under r.8(4) shall be referred to a panel of Justices who may hold an oral hearing.

Procedural decisions

9.—(1) Subject to paragraph (2), the powers of the Court under 4–9 **the following rules may be exercised by a single Justice or the Registrar without an oral hearing—**

- **(a) rule 5 (time limits),**
- **(b) rule 8 (non–compliance with Rules),**
- **(c) rule 33 (change of interest),**
- **(d) rule 34 (withdrawal of appeal),**
- **(e) rule 35 (advocate to the Court and assessors),**
- **(f) rule 36 (security for costs),**
- **(g) rule 37 (stay of execution) and**
- **(h) rule 41 (devolution jurisdiction).**

(2) Any contested application—

- **(a) alleging contempt of the Court; or**
- **(b) for a direction under rule 8 dismissing an appeal or debarring a respondent from resisting an appeal; or**
- **(c) for security for costs,**

shall be referred to a panel of Justices who shall, in a case of alleged contempt, and may, in any other case, hold an oral hearing.

(3) Where under these Rules any matter falls to be decided by a single Justice, that Justice may, where it appears appropriate, direct an oral hearing or may refer the matter to a panel of Justices to be decided with or without an oral hearing.

(4) Where under these Rules any matter falls to be decided by the Registrar, the Registrar may—

- **(a) direct an oral hearing;**
- **(b) refer the matter to a single Justice (and paragraphs (1) and (3) shall then apply);**
- **(c) refer the matter to a panel of Justices to be decided with or without an oral hearing.**

(5) A party may apply for a decision of the Registrar to be reviewed by a single Justice (in which case paragraphs (1) and (3) shall apply) and any application under this rule must be made in the appropriate form and be filed within 14 days of the Registrar's decision.

(6) Subject to rule 27, oral hearings on procedural matters must be heard in open court or in a place to which the public are admitted.

(7) If any procedural question arises which is not dealt with by these Rules, the Court or the Registrar may adopt any procedure that is consistent with the overriding objective, the Act and these Rules.

Effect of rule

4–9.1   The principal effect of this rule is to allocate certain proceedings in which procedural decisions fall to be made and contested contempt proceedings for determination by the Registrar, a single Justice or a panel of Justices, and to indicate whether or not an oral hearing is required. Generally, procedural decisions are made in proceedings commenced by a procedural application as provided by r.30.

Paragraph (7) of r.9 stands alone and does not qualify other parts of the rule. It is an important provision, in effect enacting the inherent power of the Court to regulate its own processes. Though "procedural question" is not a term of art, its meaning is clear enough.

The terms of r.9 (excluding para.(7)) are re–stated in Section 3 of Practice Direction 1. The Registrar, when exercising powers under r.9(1), will normally make a decision without an oral hearing (*ibid.* para.1.3.5).

The appropriate form (r.9(5)) is Form 2. A fee is payable upon filing (Practice Direction 7 (Applications, Documents, Forms and Orders) Annex 2).

A panel of Justices (r.5(3) and r.5(4)) means a panel of at least three Justices (r.3(2)). The Registrar's jurisdiction does not extend to the contested applications referred to in r.9(2).

Rule 27 is concerned with oral hearings of appeals and not with oral hearings on procedural matters. The purpose of the reference to r.27 in r.9(6) would appear to be to make it clear that the Court, when holding an oral hearing under r.9, has the limiting powers referred to in r.27.

PART 2

APPLICATION FOR PERMISSION TO APPEAL

Form of application

4–10   **10.—(1) Every application to the Court for permission to appeal shall be made in the appropriate form.**

(2) An application for permission to appeal must be made first to the court below, and an application may be made to the Supreme Court only after the court below has refused to grant permission to appeal.

Effect of rule

4–10.1   The provisions in Pt 2 (rr.10 to 17) apply to an application for permission to cross–appeal (r.25(3)).

Generally the Court's permission to appeal is required. Appeals in which the Court's permission is not required do not go through the Pt 2 process but are commenced by notice of appeal filed under r.19 (Form and filing of notice where permission is not required) and then proceed in accordance with the provisions of Pt 3 (Commencement and preparation of appeal).

Applications for permission to appeal are considered by a panel of (at least three) Justices, initially on paper and without a hearing (see r.16(1)). Throughout Practice Direction 3 (Applications for Permission to Appeal) and Practice Direction 13 (Costs), though not in the Rules in Pt 2, such a panel is referred to as an "Appeal Panel".

The rules in Pt 2 (rr.10 to 17) are supplemented by Practice Direction 3 (Applications for Permission Appeal).

Where permission to appeal is required, application must first be made to the court below (r.10(2)).

Rule 10 deals with the form of an application for permission to appeal. For form of a notice of appeal, see r.18 and r.19.

The appropriate form for an application for permission to appeal is Form 1 (see Practice Direction 7 (Applications, Documents, Forms and Orders) Annex 2). Detailed provisions as to the form and content of such applications are found in paras 3.1.1 to 3.1.5 of Practice Direction 3 (Applications for Permission to Appeal). The application should set out briefly the facts and points of law and include a summary why permission should be granted (*ibid.* para.3.1.2).

Where an appellant (or a respondent) seeks a declaration of incompatibility or seeks to challenge an act of a public authority under the Human Rights Act 1998, the practice in para.4.2.12 of Practice Direction 4 (Notices of Appeal) applies. See further r.40 and commentary following that rule.

If an appellant seeks a reference to the Court of Justice of the European Court of Justice, the practice in para.4.2.13 of Practice Direction 4 (Notices of Appeal) applies. See further r.42 and commentary following that rule.

For detailed information about the titles of cases in applications for permission to appeal, see Practice Direction 2 (The Registry of the Supreme Court) para.2.1.18 et seq.

Filing of application

11.—(1) Subject to any enactment which makes special provision 4–11 **with regard to any particular category of appeal, an application for permission to appeal must be filed within 28 days from the date of the order or decision of the court below.**

(2) The Registrar may refuse to accept any application on the ground that—

(a) the Court does not have jurisdiction under section 40 of the Act to issue it;

(b) it contains no reasonable grounds; or

(c) it is an abuse of process,

and may give whatever directions appear appropriate.

(Section 2 of the Administration of Justice Act 1960 provides that an application for permission to appeal to the Supreme Court in a case involving civil contempt of court must be filed within 14 days, beginning with the date on which the application for permission is refused by the court below.)

(Section 13 of the Administration of Justice Act 1969 provides that an application for permission to appeal to the Supreme Court in a "leapfrog appeal" from the High Court must be filed within one month from the date on which the High Court judge grants a certificate under section 12.)

Effect of rule

Rule 11(1) fixes (subject to any enactment) a time limit for the making of applica- **4–11.1** tions for permission to appeal. The application must be filed in the Court's Registry (see r.7 and commentary thereon). Before filing the application must be served as provided by r.12.

Time runs from the date of the order or decision of the court below. In proceedings to which the CPR apply, every judgment or order must bear the date on which it was given or made (CPR r.40(2)).

For fee payable on filing application for permission to appeal, see Practice Direction 7 (Practice Direction 7 (Applications, Documents, Forms and Orders) Annex 2.

When an application for permission to appeal is filed it will be sealed by a member of staff in the Registry (r.7(4)).

For provisions as to the documents to be filed in support of an application for permission to appeal, see r.14.

An application for permission to appeal, or any other document filed under these Rules, may be amended as provided by r.30(5); see commentary following r.30.

Refusal of application for permission to appeal (r.11(2))

The powers given to the Registrar by r.11(2) are strikingly wide. Decisions made by **4–11.2** the Registrar under r.11(2) are not procedural decisions within r.9. Presumably, when refusing an application (or if minded to do so) the Registrar might under r.9(4) (which arguably applies to any matter and is not confined to procedural matters) direct that the matter be referred to a single Justice or to a panel of Justices. Presumably, also, the Registrar's decision to refuse an application under r.11(2) would be a decision reviewable at the instigation of a party by a single Justice under r.9(5).

In a given case, the Court's lack of jurisdiction under s.40 of the 2005 Act is likely to be clear enough, but lack of reasonable grounds or abuse of process will not always be obvious.

Presumably, the fact that the point of law raised in the application for permission to appeal was "hypothetical" or "academic", or the fact that an event had occurred depriving an appeal of practical significance to the parties (within r.33(d)), would provide grounds for refusal; see further commentary following r.33.

The most important restriction on the Court's jurisdiction under s.40, insofar as it extends to appeals to the Court from any order or judgment of the Court of Appeal in England and Wales in civil proceedings, is that imposed by s.54(4) of the Access to Justice Act 1999. That provision prevents the Court from entertaining an application for permission to appeal from a refusal by the Court of Appeal to grant leave to appeal to the Court of Appeal from a judgment or order of a lower court. (For other statutory restrictions, see Practice Direction 1 para.1.2.7.)

Public funding of applicant

4–11.3   Where a party to a proposed appeal has applied for public funding and the Registrar is informed of the application, the time limit in r.11(1) (and in r.19(2)) is extended until 28 days after the final determination of the application for public funding (r.5(5)). See further commentary following r.5.

A party to an appeal, including an applicant for permission to appeal, to whom a public funding or legal aid certificate has been issued must as soon as possible thereafter file a copy at the Registry; any emergency certificate and subsequent amendments and the authority for leading counsel must also be filed (Practice Direction 8 (Miscellaneous Matters) para.8.12.2).

Extension of time for filing application for permission

4–11.4   The Court may extend any time limit set by these Rules, including that set by r.11(1) (and as extended by r.5(5)), unless to do so would be contrary to any enactment (r.5(1)). The time limits set by s.2 of the 1960 Act and s.13 of the 1969 Act (referred to in the signpost at the end of r.11) may be extended by the Court (see further commentary following r.5).

Jurisdiction under s.40 (r.11(2))

4–11.5   The Court's jurisdiction under s.40 of the 2005 Act is summarised in Section 2 of Practice Direction 1. The Court's jurisdiction under the Administration of Justice Act 1960 s.2 (civil contempt appeals) is explained in para.1.2.8 and the jurisdiction under the Administration of Justice Act 1969 s.13 ("leapfrog" appeals) in para.1.2.17 et seq. of that practice direction (see further para. 4–59 below). The limited circumstances in which an appeal may be made to the Court against the refusal of the court below to grant permission to appeal to apply for judicial review are explained in paras 1.2.20 and 1.2.21.

Where the Court does not have jurisdiction, the Registrar will inform the appellant in writing accordingly (Practice Direction 1, para.1.2.6). An applicant may use that letter for the purpose satisfying the requirement, laid down by the European Convention on Human Rights art.35, that all domestic remedies must be exhausted before an appeal can be made to the European Court of Human Rights (*ibid.*).

"Leapfrog" appeals

4–11.6   Under s.13 of the 1969 Act, before an application for permission to appeal is made to the Court a certificate of the High Court in England and Wales or Northern Ireland must first be obtained. For an explanation of the procedure and practice relating to the granting of the requisite judge's certificate by the court below, and for applying to the Court for permission to appeal direct to the Court, see Practice Direction 3 (Applications for Permission to Appeal) paras 3.6.2 to 3.6.16.

For issues arising where permission for a "leapfrog" appeal is granted on terms, see commentary following r.16.

Rule 43 and directions in Practice Direction 8 (Miscellaneous Matters) para.8.11 apply to leapfrog appeals from an order for the revocation of a patent made under s.32 or s.61 of the Patents Act 1949 or under s.72 of the Patents Act 1977. See further commentary following r.43.

Appeals in habeas corpus proceedings

For the handling of applications for permission to appeal in habeas corpus proceed- **4–11.8** ings, see Practice Direction 3 (Applications for Permission to Appeal) paras 3.6.7 and 3.6.8.

Withdrawal of application for permission to appeal

An application for permission to appeal may be withdrawn with the written consent **4–11.8** of all parties or with the permission of the Court; see r.34 and commentary following.

Service of application

12. Before the application is filed, a copy must be served— 4–12

   (a) on every respondent, and

   (b) on any person who was an intervener in the court below,

and, when the application is filed, the appellant must file a certificate of service.

Effect of rule

For practice direction provisions relevant to service of an application for permission **4–12.1** to appeal, see Practice Direction 2 (The Registry of the Supreme Court) para.2.1.23, and Practice Direction 3 (Applications for Permission to Appeal) para.3.1.6.

See further commentary following r.6 (Service), including commentary on certificates of service.

Notice of objection by respondent

13.—(1) Each respondent who wishes to object to the application 4–13 must, within 14 days after service, file notice of objection in the appropriate form together with a certificate of service.

(2) Before the notice is filed, a copy must be served on—

   (a) the appellant,

   (b) any other respondent, and

   (c) any person who was an intervener in the court below.

(3) A respondent who does not file notice under this rule will not be permitted to participate in the application and will not be given notice of its progress.

Effect of rule

The terms of this rule are re–stated in Practice Direction 3 (Applications for Permis- **4–13.1** sion to Appeal) paras 3.1.8 to 3.1.10. When they file a notice of objection in accordance with r.13, respondents may submit written objections giving their reasons why permission to appeal should be refused; for details of practice to be followed, see *ibid.* para.3.3.6 et seq.

The appropriate form for a notice of objection is Form 3 (see Practice Direction 7 (Applications, Documents, Forms and Orders) Annex 1.

For fee payable on filing of notice of objection, see Practice Direction 7 (Applications, Documents, Forms and Orders) Annex 2.

For commentary on service of documents including notices of objection, see commentary following r.6 (Service), including commentary on certificates of service.

Where an oral hearing of an application for permission to appeal is directed under r.16(2), every respondent who has given notice under r.13 will be informed of the date of the oral hearing (r.17(1)). Where a respondent does not give such notice, r.13(3) applies (see also r.21(3)).

Subject to exceptions, a respondent who wishes to argue that the order appealed from should be varied must obtain permission to cross–appeal from the Court (r.25(2); see further Practice Direction 8 (Miscellaneous Matters) para.8.3.1.

Filing of notice of objection

The original notice in Form 3 together with three copies must be filed at the Regis- **4–13.2** try together with the prescribed fee. For the relevant fee, see Annex 2 to Practice

Direction 7 (Applications, Documents, Forms and Orders). A certificate of service complying with r.6(4) must be included in Form 3 and signed or a separate certificate of service must be provided (Practice Direction 3 (Applications for Permission to Appeal) para.3.1.9).

When a notice of objection is filed, it will be sealed by a member of staff in the Registry (r.7(4)) (Practice Direction (Applications for Permission to Appeal) para.3.1.8).

Costs

4–13.3   For costs of respondents' objections, see Practice Direction 3 (Applications for Permission to Appeal) para.3.5.1 et seq. An order for costs will not be made in favour of a respondent who has not given notice (Practice Direction 3 (Applications for Permission to Appeal) para.3.1.10).

Documents in support of application

4–14   **14.—(1) The requisite number of copies of the application must be filed together with—**

(a) a copy of the order appealed from, and

(b) (if separate) a copy of any order refusing permission to appeal

and, if the order appealed from is not immediately available, the application should be filed without delay and the order filed as soon as it is available.

(2) The appellant must file the further documents required for the use of the Court within 7 days after filing the application.

Effect of rule

4–14.1   For detailed provisions relating to compliance with r.14(1) and 14(2), including provisions as to the form of presentation of documents, the number of copies to be filed, and applications for extension of time for complying with r.14, see Practice Direction 3 (Applications for Permission to Appeal) paras 3.1.7 and 3.2.1. Where the required papers are not filed within eight weeks after the filing of the application and no good reason is given for the delay, the Registrar may (a) refer the application to an Appeal Panel without the required accompanying papers, (b) dismiss the application, or (c) give such other directions as appear appropriate under r.8 (*ibid.* para.3.2.3).

Time limits for the filing of applications for permission to appeal are fixed by r.11(1). The purpose of the requirement in r.17 to the effect that applications "should be filed without delay" would seem to be that of making it clear that the non–availability of copies of the order appealed from should not delay filing of the documents required by r.14.

Documents filed under r.14 may be amended as provided by r.30(5); see commentary following r.30.

Interventions in applications

4–15   **15.—(1) Any person and in particular—**

(a) any official body or non–governmental organization seeking to make submissions in the public interest or

(b) any person with an interest in proceedings by way of judicial review,

may make written submissions to the Court in support of an application for permission to appeal and request that the Court takes them into account.

(2) Before the submissions are filed, a copy must be served on—

(a) the appellant,

(b) every respondent, and

(c) any person who was an intervener in the court below

and the requisite number of copies of the submissions must be filed together with a certificate of service.

(3) Any submissions which are made shall be referred to the panel of Justices which considers the application for permission to appeal.

(4) If permission to appeal is granted—

(a) a person whose submissions were taken into account by the panel will be notified but, if that person wishes to intervene in the appeal, an application must be made under rule 26;

(b) the appellant must notify any person who was an intervener in the court below whether or not that person made submissions under this rule.

Effect of rule

This rule is re–stated in, and supplemented by, Practice Direction 3 (Applications **4–15.1** for Permission to Appeal) para.3.3.17 et seq. Four copies of the submissions must be filed, together with a certificate of service (*ibid*. para.3.3.17).

For service of documents, including service of written submissions under r.15(2), see commentary following r.6, including commentary on certificates of service.

Where a person makes written submissions under r.15 and those submissions are taken into account under r.16, and permission to appeal is granted, the re–sealed application for permission standing as the notice of appeal should be served on that person by the appellant (r.18(2)). Further, in those circumstances that person may apply to the Court under r.26(1) for permission to intervene in the appeal.

Consideration on paper

16.—(1) Every admissible application for permission to appeal **4–16** (together with any submissions made under rule 15 and any respondent's notice of objection) shall be considered on paper without a hearing by a panel of Justices.

(2) The panel may—

(a) grant or refuse permission to advance all or any of the grounds of appeal;

(b) invite the parties to file written submissions within 14 days as to the grant of permission on terms (whether as to costs or otherwise); or

(c) direct an oral hearing.

(3) Where the panel has invited the parties' submissions as to terms, it shall reconsider the application on paper without a hearing and may refuse permission or grant permission (either unconditionally or on terms) to advance all or any of the grounds of appeal.

(4) Where the panel grants permission to advance limited grounds of appeal it shall (unless it directs otherwise) be taken to have refused permission to advance the other grounds.

(5) An order of the Court shall be prepared and sealed by the Registrar to record any decision made under this rule.

Effect of rule

The Court's practice in the several outcomes referred to in r.16(2) is amplified in **4–16.1** Practice Direction 3 (Applications for Permission to Appeal) para.3.3.2 et seq.

Once the required papers under r.14 are filed at the Registry, the r.16 procedure is normally completed within eight sitting weeks (excluding any oral hearing). Requests for an expedited disposal of the application for permission to appeal and for an expedited hearing of the appeal in proceedings involving liberty of the subject, urgent medical intervention or the well–being of children, or under the Hague Convention etc, may be made in writing to the Registrar (r.31) (see further Practice Direction 3 (Applications for Permission to Appeal) paras 3.4.3 to 3.4.7, and note Practice Direction 4 (Notice of Appeal) para.4.8.1, and Practice Direction 6 (The Appeal Hearing) para.6.2.4).

The appellant, any recognised intervener and all respondents who have filed notice of objection under r.13, are sent a copy of the order sealed by the Registrar recording the decision of the panel of Justices (Practice Direction 3 (Applications for Permission to Appeal) para.3.3.19). (A person whose submissions were taken into account under r.15, or who was an intervener in the court below, may apply to the Court for permission to intervene in the appeal, should it proceed (see r.26).)

Where the panel of Justices grants permission for a "leapfrog" appeal on terms, and the prospective appellant declines to proceed on the basis of those terms, that party may instead pursue an appeal to the Court of Appeal in the usual way (*R. (Jones) v Ceredigion County Council v Jones (No.2)* [2007] UKHL 24; [2009] 1 W.L.R. 1400, HL) (see also Practice Direction 3 (Applications for Permission to Appeal) paras 3.3.11 and 3.6.16).

Oral hearing of application

4–17 **17.—(1) Where the panel has directed an oral hearing, the appellant and every respondent who has given notice under rule 13 will be informed of the date of the oral hearing.**

(2) An order of the Court shall be prepared and sealed by the Registrar to record any decision made under this rule.

Effect of rule

4–17.1 For Court's practice where the panel of Justices directs an oral hearing under r.16(2) and r.17 applies, see Practice Direction 3 (Applications for Permission to Appeal) para.3.3.12 et seq. Oral permission hearings usually last for 30 minutes.

PART 3

COMMENCEMENT AND PREPARATION OF APPEAL

Form and filing of notice where permission granted by the Court

4–18 **18.—(1) Where the Court grants permission to appeal, rules 19 and 20 shall not apply and**

> **(a) the application for permission to appeal shall stand as the notice of appeal;**
>
> **(b) the grounds of appeal shall be limited to those on which permission has been granted;**
>
> **(c) the appellant must, within 14 days of the grant by the Court of permission to appeal, file notice under this rule of an intention to proceed with the appeal.**

(2) When notice is filed under rule 18(1)(c), the application for permission to appeal will be re–sealed and the appellant must then—

> **(a) serve a copy on each respondent and on any person who was an intervener in the court below or whose submissions were taken into account under rule 15; and**
>
> **(b) file the requisite number of copies and a certificate of service.**

(3) In any other case an appellant must file a notice of appeal under rule 19.

Effect of rule

See commentary following r.20.

4–18.1

Form and filing of notice where permission not required

19.—**(1) Every notice of appeal shall be made in the appropriate** **4–19**
form.

(2) The notice of appeal together with the requisite number of
copies must be filed within 42 days of the date of the order or deci-
sion of the court below.

(3) The appellant must also file—

(a) a copy of the order appealed from and

(b) (if separate) a copy of the order granting permission to appeal
and, if the order appealed from is not immediately available, the
notice of appeal must be filed without delay and the order filed as
soon as it is available.

Effect of rule

See commentary following r.20.

4–19.1

Service of notice

20.—**(1) Before the notice of appeal is filed, a copy must be** **4–20**
served on each respondent and on any person who was an
intervener in the court below.

(2) When the notice of appeal is filed, the appellant must file a
certificate of service.

Effect of rules 18 to 20

Rules 19 and 20 apply where the applicant does not require permission to appeal **4–20.1**
from the Court. Rule 18 applies (and rr.19 and 20 do not) where the applicant did
require permission to appeal and was granted such permission by the Court under the
Pt 2 process.

Notice of intention to proceed (r.18(1))

Where r.18 applies, the successful applicant, now the appellant, is not required to **4–20.2**
file a notice of appeal; the application for permission stands as the notice of appeal.
But the applicant/appellant is required to file a notice of intention to proceed with the
appeal; whereupon the application for permission to appeal is re–sealed. The appellant must then serve a copy of the re–sealed document (now in effect a notice of appeal) and otherwise comply with r.18(2). The rules as to service of documents as stated
in r.6 apply to the service of the re–sealed document referred to in r.18(2).

For fee payable on filing of notice of intention to proceed with an appeal, see
Practice Direction 7 (Applications, Documents, Forms and Orders) Annex 2.

In r.34 (Withdrawal etc of application for permission to appeal or of appeal, sub–
r.(3) states that, in that rule "a notice of appeal" includes an application for permission
to appeal which (under r.18) stands as a notice of appeal.

Complying with r.18(2)

In para.3.4.1 of Practice Direction 3 (Applications for Permission to Appeal) the **4–20.3**
terms of r.18 are re–stated and it is explained that the original and three copies of the
re–sealed document together with a certificate of service (complying with r.6(4)) must
be filed. In para.3.4.2 it is further provided that, where an appellant is unable to file
notice of an intention to proceed under r.18 within the time limit of 14 days, a formal
application for an extension of time must be made in Form 2. The respondent's views
on the extension of time should be sought and, if possible, those views should be communicated to the Registry. The application will be referred to the Registrar and, if it is
granted, the appellant must then comply with r.18(2) and para.3.4.1. See also Practice
Direction 4 (Notice of Appeal) para.4.3.3.

Within 112 days after the filing of the notice under r.18(1)(c) the appellant must file the documents referred to in r.22(1).

Each respondent who intends to participate in the appeal must, within 14 days after service under r.18(2)(a) file notice in the appropriate form with a certificate of service (see r.21(1)).

Complying with r.19

4–20.4 The terms of r.19 are re–stated and amplified in paras 4.3.1 and 4.3.2 of Practice Direction 4 (Notice of Appeal). The number of documents to be filed is explained in para.4.3.1 (see also Practice Direction 7 (Applications, Documents, Forms and Orders) para.7.2.3).

The appropriate form for a notice of appeal is Form 1 (see Practice Direction 7 (Applications, Documents, Forms and Orders) Annex 1).

For fee payable on filing of notice of appeal, see Practice Direction 7 (Applications, Documents, Forms and Orders) Annex 2.

When a notice of appeal is filed it will be sealed by a member of staff in the Registry (r.7(4)).

A notice of appeal may be amended as provided by r.30(5); see commentary following r.30 and note Practice Direction 4 (Notice of Appeal) para.4.2.1.

Rule 19(2) states that time the 42 day time limit runs from the date of the order or decision of the court below. In proceedings to which the CPR apply, every judgment or order must bear the date on which it was given or made (CPR r.40(2)). Where a party to a proposed appeal has applied for public funding and the Registrar is informed of the application, the time limit in r.19(2) shall be extended until 28 days after the final determination of the application for public funding (r.5(5)).

The time limit in r.19(2) may be varied by the Court (r.5(1)). Paragraph 4.4.1 of Practice Direction 4 (Notice of Appeal) contains directions relating to applications for extension of this time limit.

Provisions in Pt 2 are designed to ensure that applicants for permission to appeal provide the Court and potential respondents with certain information. An appellant to whom r.19 applies, in effect, by–passes the Pt 2 process and commences proceedings by filing a notice of appeal. Provisions as to the form and content of notices of appeal are found in Practice Direction 4 (Notice of Appeal) paras 4.2.1 to 4.2.4. For obvious reasons the requirements of those provisions are similar to those applicable to applications for permission to appeal (see Practice Direction 3 (Applications for Permission to Appeal) paras 3.1.1 to 3.1.5).

Where an appellant seeks a declaration of incompatibility or seeks to challenge an act of a public authority under the Human Rights Act 1998, the notice of appeal should accord with the directions in para.4.2.12 of Practice Direction 4 (Notices of Appeal). See further r.40 and commentary following that rule.

Where an appellant seeks a reference to the Court of Justice of the European Court of Justice, the notice of appeal should accord with the directions in para.4.2.13 of Practice Direction 4 (Notices of Appeal) applies. See further r.42 and commentary following that rule.

Service of notice of appeal (r.20)

4–20.5 Rule 20 is to be read together with r.19. Paragraph 4.2.15 of Practice Direction 4 (Notice of Appeal) re–states r.20 and, in relation to certificates of service, draws attention to r.6(4) and explains that such certificates must be included in Form 1 and signed or a separate certificate of service must be provided. See also Practice Direction 2 (The Registry of the Supreme Court) para.2.1.24.

The rules as to service of documents as stated in r.6 apply to the service of the copy of the notice of appeal as required by r.20(1).

Each respondent who intends to participate in the appeal must, within 14 days after service under r.20 file notice in the appropriate form with a certificate of service (r.21(1)).

Cross–appeals

4–20.6 Where there is a cross–appeal the provisions of Pt 3, including rr.18 to r.20, apply with appropriate modifications. Rule 25(4)(a) (which is drafted with the circumstances envisaged by both r.18 and r.19 in mind) states that either the application for permission to cross–appeal to the Court shall stand as a notice of cross–appeal, or such a notice (in the appropriate form) shall be filed and served within 42 days of the grant by the Court of permission to appeal or of the filing of the notice of appeal. See further Practice Direction 8 (Miscellaneous Matters) para.8.3.

Case titles

For detailed information about the titles of cases in applications for permission to **4–20.7** appeal and in notices of appeal, see Practice Direction 2 (The Registry of the Supreme Court) para.2.1.18 et seq, and Practice Direction 4 (Notice of Appeal) para.4.2.5 et seq.

Requests for an expedited hearing of an appeal

In proceedings involving liberty of the subject, urgent medical intervention or the **4–20.8** well–being of children, or under the Hague Convention, etc., such requests may be made in writing to the Registrar; see further Practice Direction 4 (Notice of Appeal) para.4.8.1, Practice Direction 6 (The Appeal Hearing) para.6.2.4, and commentary on r.31.

Requests for anonymity and reporting restrictions For directions concerning requests for orders under the Children and Young Persons Act 1933 s.39 and the Contempt of Court Act 1981, see Practice Direction 4 (Notice of Appeal) paras 4.2.10 and 4.2.11. Such request should be made as soon as possible after the appeal is commenced under Pt 3.

Request for appointment of an advocate to the Court

See r.35 and commentary thereon.   **4–20.9**

Request for attendance of assessor at hearing

See r.35 and commentary thereon.   **4–20.10**

Request to record, film or broadcast proceedings

See Practice Direction 8 (Miscellaneous Matters) para.8.17.1.   **4–20.11**

Acknowledgement by respondent

21.—(1) Each respondent who intends to participate in the ap- **4–21** **peal must, within 14 days after service under rule 18(2)(a) or 20, file notice in the appropriate form together with a certificate of service.**

(2) Before the notice is filed, a copy must be served on—

(a) the appellant,

(b) any other respondent, and

(c) any person who was an intervener in the court below or whose submissions were taken into account under rule 15.

(3) A respondent who does not file notice under this rule will not be permitted to participate in the appeal and will not be given notice of its progress.

Effect of rule

The appropriate form is Form 3; see Practice Direction 3 (Applications for Permis- **4–21.1** sion to Appeal) Annex 1). For fee payable on filing notice of acknowledgement by respondent, see *ibid.* Annex 2.

Paragraphs 4.6.1, 4.6.2 and 4.6.4 of Practice Direction 4 (Notice of Appeal) re–state r.21 and, in relation to certificates of service, para.4.6.2 draws attention to r.6(4) and explains that such certificates must be included in Form 3 and signed or a separate certificate of service must be provided. See also Practice Direction 2 (The Registry of the Supreme Court) para.2.1.24.

The original respondent's acknowledgement notice together with three copies must be filed at the Registry (Practice Direction 4 (Notice of Appeal) para.4.6.3).

The rules as to service of documents as stated in r.6 apply to the service of the copy of the respondent's notice of acknowledgement as required by r.21(2).

A respondent may apply under r.5 for an extension of the time limit fixed by r.21(1).

An order for costs will not be made in favour of a respondent who has not given notice of acknowledgement under r.21 (Practice Direction 4 (Notice of Appeal) para.4.6.4.

Documents for appeal hearing

4–22   **22.—(1) Within 112 days after the filing of the notice under rule 18(1)(c) or the filing of the notice of appeal, the appellant must file—**

(a) a statement of the relevant facts and issues; and

(b) an appendix (prepared in accordance with the relevant practice direction) of the essential documents which were in evidence before, or which record the proceedings in, the courts below.

(2) Both the statement and the appendix must be submitted to, and agreed with, every respondent before being filed.

(3) Within 7 days after the filing of the statement and the appendix, every party must—

(a) notify the Registrar that the appeal is ready for listing, and

(b) specify the number of hours that their respective counsel estimate to be necessary for their oral submissions

and the Registrar will subsequently inform the parties of the date fixed for the hearing.

(4) The appellant and every respondent (and any intervener and advocate to the Court) must then sequentially exchange their respective written cases and file them, and every respondent (and any intervener and advocate to the Court) must for the purposes of rule 23 provide copies of their respective written cases, in compliance with the relevant practice direction.

Effect of rule

4–22.1   Rules 22 to 24 go together. They are supplemented by Practice Direction 5 (Papers for the Appeal Hearing), and by Practice Direction 6 (The Appeal Hearing).

For fees for filing a statement of facts and issues and the appendix (referred to in r.22(1)), see Practice Direction 7 (Applications, Documents, Forms and Orders) Annex 2.

Documents filed under rr.22 to 24 may be amended as provided by r.30(5); see commentary following r.30.

With the consent of the Registrar, documents (including those referred to in rr.22 to 24) may be filed by electronic means in accordance with Practice Direction 14 (Filing Documents in the Registry of the Supreme Court by electronic means) (r.7(1)(d)).

If the appellant is unable to comply with a time limit imposed by r.22(1), an application for an extension of time must be made (r.5), and in that event paras 5.2.3 to 5.2.5 of Practice Direction 5 (Papers for the Appeal Hearing) apply.

All documents placed before the Court must comply with para.5.1.2 of Practice Direction 5 (Papers for the Appeal Hearing). Paragraphs (1) and (2) of r.22 refer to papers for the appeal hearing in the form of (a) a statement of the relevant facts and issues, and (b) an appendix of the essential documents. These documents must comply with paras 5.1.3 to 5.1.5. The number of copies of each of these papers to be filed is stated in para.5.2.6. For prescribed fees payable upon filing, see Practice Direction 7 (Applications, Documents, Forms and Orders) Annex 2.

A table summarising provisions found elsewhere dealing with the number of documents (including the several documents referred to in r.22) usually to be provided by the appellants, respondents and interveners for the Registry and "for other side" for the hearing of an appeal is found in Practice Direction 7 (Applications, Documents, Forms and Orders) para.7.2.3.

Rule 22(3) imposes certain duties on "every party". Rule 25(4)(c) states that, where there is a cross–appeal the appellant shall remain "primarily responsible" for the preparation of all of the papers for the appeal and for giving the Registrar notice of the matters referred to in r.22(3).

It would seem that, insofar as rr.22 to 24 and the practice directions supplementing them require parties to exchange documents or to provide documents one to another, the parties may consent to this being done by electronic means. This is because expressions such as "exchanging" or "providing" are expressions related to "service" (see r.3(2)) and therefore may be effected by the electronic means of service of documents permitted by r.6(1)(d). However, although r.6.1(d) anticipates it, there is no relevant practice direction dedicated to the service of documents by one party to an appeal upon another by "electronic means" (as defined in r.3(2)). However, para.2.1.23 of Practice Direction 2 (The Registry of the Supreme Court) does provide that a party or his solicitor will be taken to have consented to a particular method of service if, for example, their writing paper includes a fax number or a numbered box at a document exchange unless they have indicated in writing that they are not willing to accept service by that particular method.

In the period during which the procedural steps stated in rr.22 to 24 are taken it may become apparent to the Court or to the parties that a directions hearing should be held. In that event, the provisions of para.6.2.5 of Practice Direction 6 (The Appeal Hearing) apply.

Written cases

The written case is the statement of a party's argument in the appeal. The Court **4–22.2** does not prescribe any maximum length but the Court favours brevity and a case should be a concise summary of the submissions to be developed. Detailed directions concerning written cases (including information concerning form, exchange, filing and the number of copies to be filed) are given in Practice Direction 6 (The Appeal Hearing) para.6.3.1 et seq. These directions stipulate time limits for the filing and exchange of written cases. Rule 22(4) anticipates the duty imposed on the appellant by r.23 and para.6.3.11 of the practice direction states that, to enable the appellant to discharge that duty, the respondent and any other party who has filed a case must provide the appellant with a further 10 copies of their written case.

Exhibits

Parties who require exhibits to be available for inspection at the hearing must apply **4–22.3** to the Registrar for permission for the exhibits to be brought to the Court before the hearing (see Practice Direction 8 (Miscellaneous Matters) para.8.6.1, and Practice Direction 12 (Criminal Proceedings) para.12.14.1).

Fresh evidence

See Practice Direction 6 (The Appeal Hearing) para.6.3.3. **4–22.4**

Cross–appeals

Where there is a cross–appeal, rr.22 to 24 (and the other rules in Pt 3) apply with **4–22.5** appropriate modifications (r.25(4)). In particular, para.(b) of r.25(4) states that, where there is a cross–appeal, there shall be a single statement of facts and issues, a single appendix of essential documents (divided if necessary into parts) and a single case for each party in respect of the appeal and the cross–appeal (and each case should state clearly that it is in respect of both the appeal and the cross–appeal). Paragraph 8.3 of Practice Direction 8 (Miscellaneous Matters) includes directions as to the filing of documents (and numbers of copies) and relevant time limits where there is a cross–appeal.

Fixing the hearing date

For directions supplementing r.22(3), including requests for expedited hearings **4–22.6** (r.31), see Practice Direction 6 (The Appeal Hearing) paras 6.2.1 to 6.2.4 and paras 6.6.1 to 6.6.3. The Registrar will on request inform the parties of the intended constitution of the Court for the appeal hearing (para.6.6.7).

If a party wishes to have a stenographer present at the hearing or to obtain a full transcript of the hearing, he must notify the Registrar not less than 7 days before the hearing (para.6.6.6). (Any costs of the stenographer or of transcription must be borne by the party making such a request; *ibid.*).

The core volumes

23. As soon as the parties' cases have been exchanged and in 4–23 **any event not later than 14 days before the date fixed for the hear-**

necessarily being an agreement in parts. ing the appellant must file the requisite number of core volumes and, if necessary, additional volumes containing further parts of the appendix, in compliance with the relevant practice direction.

Effect of rule

4–23.1   This rule imposes duties on the appellant (to be discharged the assistance of other parties as required by r.22(4)). Detailed directions concerning core volumes (including information concerning form, party cooperation in preparation, filing and the number of copies to be filed) are given in Practice Direction 6 (The Appeal Hearing) para.6.4.1 et seq. (note also para.6.3.11). As to number of core volumes to be filed and exchanged, see also table following para.7.2.3 of Practice Direction 7 (Applications, Documents, Forms and Orders).

For filing of core volumes in electronic form, see Practice Direction 14 (Filing Documents in the Registry of the Supreme Court by electronic means).

See further, commentary following r.22 as relevant to r.23.

Authorities

4–24   **24.   The volumes of authorities that may be referred to during the hearing must be prepared in accordance with the relevant practice direction and the requisite number of copies of the volumes of authorities must be filed by the appellant at the same time as the core volumes.**

Effect of rule

4–24.1   This rule imposes duties on the appellant. Detailed directions concerning volumes of authorities (including information concerning form, party cooperation in preparation, filing and the number of copies to be filed) are given in Practice Direction 6 (The Appeal Hearing) paras 6.5.1 to 6.5.8. Supplemental or additional volumes of authorities should be avoided. In order to produce the volumes of authorities, parties may download text from electronic sources; but the volumes of authorities must be filed in paper form (para.6.5.6).

As to number of volumes of authorities to be filed and exchanged, see also table following para.7.2.3 of Practice Direction 7 (Applications, Documents, Forms and Orders).

For filing of volumes of authorities in electronic form, see Practice Direction 14 (Filing Documents in the Registry of the Supreme Court by electronic means).

The cost of preparing the volumes of authorities falls to the appellants, but is ultimately subject to the decision of the Court as to the costs of the appeal (Practice Direction 6 (The Appeal Hearing) para.6.5.8).

See further, commentary following r.22 as relevant to r.24.

Cross–appeals

4–25   **25.—(1) A respondent who wishes to argue that the order appealed from should be upheld on grounds different from those relied on by the court below, must state that clearly in the respondent's written case (but need not cross–appeal).**

(2) Except where—

(a) leave is required from the Court of Session for an appeal from that court, or

(b) an appeal lies to the Court as of right,

a respondent who wishes to argue that the order appealed from should be varied must obtain permission to cross–appeal from the Court.

(3) Part 2 of these Rules shall apply (with appropriate modifications) to an application to the Court for permission to cross–appeal and (if practicable) applications for permission to appeal and to cross–appeal shall be considered together by the same panel of Justices.

(4) Where there is a cross–appeal, this Part of these Rules shall apply with appropriate modifications and in particular—

    (a) either the application for permission to cross–appeal to the Court shall stand as a notice of cross–appeal, or such a notice (in the appropriate form) shall be filed and served within 42 days of the grant by the Court of permission to appeal or of the filing of the notice of appeal;

    (b) there shall be a single statement of facts and issues, a single appendix of essential documents (divided if necessary into parts) and a single case for each party in respect of the appeal and the cross–appeal (and each case should state clearly that it is in respect of both the appeal and the cross–appeal); and

    (c) the appellant shall remain primarily responsible for the preparation of all the papers for the appeal and for notifying the Registrar under rule 22(3).

Effect of rule

The substance of r.25 is restated in para.8.3.1 of Practice Direction 8 (Miscellaneous **4–25.1** Matters) and important and detailed directions as to practice follow thereafter, including directions as to the filing of documents (and numbers of copies) and relevant time limits. (See further commentary following r.22 (Documents for appeal hearing).) Where permission to cross–appeal is required, an application for permission may only be filed after permission to appeal has been granted to the original applicant for permission to appeal (*ibid.* para.8.3.2).

The provisions in Pt 2 (Application for permission to appeal) (rr.10 to 17) apply to an application for permission to cross–appeal (r.25(3)).

Where there is a cross–appeal, the provisions of Pt 3 (Commencement and preparation of appeal) (rr.18 to 26) apply with appropriate modifications (r.25(4)). See further commentary following r.20 and r.22.

For the purposes of r.34 (Withdrawal etc of application for permission to appeal or of appeal, "a notice of appeal" includes an application for permission to cross–appeal which (under r.25(4)(a)) stands as a notice of cross–appeal (r.34(3)).

No security for costs is required in cross–appeals (Practice Direction 4 (Notice of Appeal) para.4.7.4).

Intervention

26.—(1) After permission to appeal has been granted by the 4–26 Court or a notice of appeal has been filed, any person and in particular—

    (a) any official body or non–governmental organization seeking to make submissions in the public interest,

    (b) any person with an interest in proceedings by way of judicial review,

    (c) any person who was an intervener in the court below or whose submissions were taken into account under rule 15,

may apply to the Court for permission to intervene in the appeal.

(2) An application under this rule must be made in the appropriate form and shall be considered on paper by a panel of Justices who may refuse permission to intervene or may permit intervention—

    (a) by written submissions only; or

    (b) by written submissions and oral submissions

and any oral submissions may be limited to a specified duration.

(3) **No permission is required—**

(a) **for an intervention by the Crown under section 5 of the Human Rights Act 1998, or**

(b) **for an intervention by the relevant officer in a case where the Court is exercising its devolution jurisdiction.**

(For rules relating to Human Rights Act issues and the Court's devolution jurisdiction see rules 40 and 41.)

Effect of rule

4–26.1   A person who is not a party to an application for permission to appeal may apply for permission to intervene in accordance with r.15. (See further commentary following r.15.) A person who is not a party to an appeal may apply in accordance with r.26 for permission to intervene in the appeal. An intervener under r.15 who wishes to intervene in the appeal must make a formal application under r.26. The application should be made in Form 2. Rule 26 is supplemented by Practice Direction 6 (The Appeal Hearing) para.6.9. These directions include time limits for the making of applications to intervene.

Paragraph 8.8.2 of Practice Direction 8 (Miscellaneous Matters) draws attention to paras 2 and 3 of Lord Hoffmann's opinion in *E v Chief Constable of the Royal Ulster Constabulary* [2008] UKHL 66; [2008] 3 W.L.R. 1208, HL, where his Lordship (i) said that it is not the role of an intervener to be an additional counsel for one of the parties, (ii) stressed that an intervention is of no assistance if it merely repeats points which the appellant or respondent has already made, and (iii) expressed the hope that interveners "will avoid unnecessarily taking up the time of the House in this way".

Orders for costs will not normally be made in favour of or against interveners (see r.46(3), and note Practice Direction 6 (The Appeal Hearing) para.6.9.5).

In these Rules, except where the context otherwise requires, "party" includes a person who has been given permission to intervene under r.26 (r.3(2)). If an application for permission to appeal is granted, a person who has intervened in the application and whose submissions were taken into account will be notified, but if that person wishes to intervene in the appeal, an application must be made under r.26 (r.15(4)).

PART 4

HEARING AND DECISION OF APPEAL

Hearing in open court

4–27   27.—(1) **Every contested appeal shall be heard in open court except where it is necessary in the interests of justice or in the public interest to sit in private for part of an appeal hearing.**

(2) **Where the Court considers it necessary for a party and that party's representative to be excluded from a hearing or part of a hearing in order to secure that information is not disclosed contrary to the public interest, the Court must conduct the hearing, or that part of it from which the party and the representative are excluded, in private but the Court may exclude a party and any representative only if a person who has been appointed as a special advocate to represent the interests of that party is present when the party and the representative are excluded.**

(3) **Where the Court decides it is necessary for the Court to sit in private, it shall announce its reasons for so doing publicly before the hearing begins.**

(4) **Hearings shall be conducted in accordance with—**

(a) **the relevant practice direction, and**

(b) **any directions given by the Court**

and directions given by the Court may limit oral submissions to a specified duration.

Effect of rule

Part 4 is concerned with appeal hearings, and not with hearings of procedural applications or of applications for permission to appeal. More specifically, para.(1) of r.27 is concerned with the hearing of contested appeals. Paragraph (2) of r.27 is concerned with special contingencies. Special advocates are likely to be appointed in proceedings under the Prevention of Terrorism Act 2005 or in financial restriction proceedings under the Counter–Terrorism Act 2008. (For provisions in the CPR comparable to r.27(2) and applying, respectively, to proceedings under the 2005 Act and 2008 Act, see CPR r.76.22 and 79.17(2); not also CPR r.39.2.) **4–27.1**

Paragraph 6.6.4 of Practice Direction 6 (The Appeal Hearing) states that only in wholly exceptional circumstances will the Court consider sitting in private. Any request for the Court to sit in private should be addressed to the Registrar and should be copied to the other parties. The request should set out fully the reasons why it is made and the request together with any objections filed by the other parties will normally be referred to the presiding Justice.

The rule that oral hearings on procedural matters must be heard in open court or in a place to which the public are admitted (r.9(6)) is expressed as subject to r.27.

Detailed assessments of costs are conducted in public (Practice Direction 13 (Costs) para.1.3).

For requests for anonymity and reporting restrictions at contested appeal hearings or other oral hearings, see commentary following r.20.

Appeal hearings to be conducted in accordance with directions

Paragraph (4) of r.27 is not concerned with the circumstances in which the Court may sit in private but with the conduct of the appeal hearing generally. Relevant practice direction provisions are found in para.6.6 of Practice Direction 6 (The Appeal Hearing). An example of a direction given by the Court would be a direction under r.32 as to the grouping of appeals for hearing together or consecutively. **4–27.2**

New submissions after argument

If, after the conclusion of the argument on an appeal, a party wishes to bring to the notice of the Court new circumstances which have arisen and which might affect the decision or order of the Court, the directions in para.8.9.1 of Practice Direction 8 (Miscellaneous Matters) apply. **4–27.3**

Judgment

28. A judgment may be— **4–28**

(a) delivered in open court; or

(b) if the Court so directs, promulgated by the Registrar.

Effect of rule

Practice Direction 6 (The Appeal Hearing) para.6.8 supplements this rule and deals with the place and time of judgment, the attendance of counsel at handing down, and the conditions under which judgments are released in advance. It is expressly provided that where judgment is to be promulgated by the Registrar, copies will be made available for collection by counsel or a solicitor at the Registry on a day notified in advance (para.6.8.2). **4–28.1**

Orders

29.—(1) In relation to an appeal or a reference, the Supreme Court has all the powers of the court below and may— **4–29**

(a) affirm, set aside or vary any order or judgment made or given by that court;

(b) remit any issue for determination by that court;

(c) order a new trial or hearing;

(d) make orders for the payment of interest;

(e) make a costs order.

(2) An order of the Supreme Court may be enforced in the same manner as an order of the court below or of the appropriate superior court.

(3) For the purposes of paragraph (2) "the appropriate superior court" means—

(a) in the case of an appeal or reference from a court in England and Wales, the High Court;

(b) in the case of an appeal or reference from a court in Scotland—

(i) where the appeal or reference is in civil proceedings, the Court of Session; and

(ii) where the appeal or reference is in criminal proceedings, the High Court of Justiciary;

(c) in the case of an appeal or reference from a court in Northern Ireland, the High Court in Northern Ireland.

(4) In the case of references other than those mentioned in paragraph (3) "the appropriate superior court" in paragraph (2) means—

(a) where the reference is under the Scotland Act 1998, the Court of Session;

(b) where the reference is under the Northern Ireland Act 1998, the High Court in Northern Ireland; and

(c) where the reference is under the Government of Wales Act 2006, the High Court.

(5) Every order of the Court shall be prepared and sealed by the Registrar who may invite written submissions as to the form of the order.

Effect of rule

4–29.1   Paragraph (1) of r.29 is to the same effect as CPR r.52.10(2) (Appeal court's powers). For the Court's powers as to costs and their exercise; see Pt 7 (Fees and Costs).

Enforcement of court's order (r.29(2))

4–29.2   For basic information as to the enforcement of the Court's orders in England and Wales, see Practice Direction 8 (Miscellaneous Matters) paras 8.18.1 to 8.18.3. For enforcement in Scotland or Northern Ireland, see *ibid.* para.8.18.4.

Order of the court (r.29(5))

4–29.3   Paragraph (5) of r.29 is supplemented by para.7.4 of Practice Direction 7 (Applications, Documents, Forms and Orders). In an order made under r.29 the amount of any assessed costs will be inserted, but if that order is drawn up before the assessment has been completed, the amount assessed will be certified by the Registrar (r.52).

PART 5

FURTHER GENERAL PROVISIONS

Procedural applications

4–30   30.—(1) Every procedural application to the Court must be made in the appropriate form for general procedural applications unless a particular form is provided for a specific case.

(2) An application must be made in the appropriate form and must—

(a) set out the reasons for making the application, and

(b) where necessary, be supported by written evidence.

(3) A copy of the application must be served on every other party before it is filed and, when the application is filed, the applicant must file a certificate of service.

(4) A party who wishes to oppose an application must, within 7 days after service, file notice of objection in the appropriate form and must (before filing) serve a copy on the applicant and any other parties.

(5) An application for permission to appeal, a notice of appeal or any other document filed under these Rules may be amended on application under this rule or with the permission of the Registrar on such terms as appear appropriate, and the Registrar may invite the parties' written submissions on any application to amend.

Effect of rule

Provisions in Practice Direction 7 (Applications, Documents, Forms and Orders) **4–30.1** supplement paras (1) to (4) of this rule. An application should be made as soon as it becomes apparent that it is necessary or expedient (para.7.1.1). An application must be made in Form 2 (*ibid.* para.7.1.2) and should be served on all the other parties before it is filed (r.30(1)(3)). The original notice must bear a certificate of service on the other parties (para.7.1.7). The appropriate form for a notice of objection (r.30(4)) is Form 3 (para.7.1.4). For number of copies of application and any notice of objection to be filed, see para.7.1.7.

For fees for filing procedural applications, including an application for a decision of the Registrar to be reviewed and for permission to intervene in an appeal, and a notice of objection to a procedural application, see Practice Direction 7 (Applications, Documents, Forms and Orders) Annex 2.

Generally, procedural applications (including opposed applications) are dealt with without a hearing (para.7.1.6). In the event of an oral hearing of an opposed application by a Panel of Justices authorities are not normally cited (para.7.1.8).

Certificate of service

A certificate of service is a certificate given under r.6 (r.3.1(2)). A certificate of ser- **4–30.2** vice which complies with r.6(4) must be included either in the original procedural application and signed or a separate certificate of service must be provided (Practice Direction 2 (The Registry of the Supreme Court) para.2.1.24).

Evidence in support of application

For directions as to the filing and serving of any evidence in support of an applica- **4–30.3** tion, see Practice Direction 7 (Applications, Documents, Forms and Orders) para.7.1.3, and (where an oral hearing ordered) para.7.1.8. Parties to an application for a consent order must ensure that they provide any material needed to satisfy the Court that it is appropriate to make the order (para.7.1.5).

For guidance on documents which may need to be filed in support of an application, see Practice Direction 7 (Applications, Documents, Forms and Orders) para.7.1.3.

Amendment of filed document (r.30(5))

Paragraph (5) of r.30 is important. It is relevant to the amendment of a procedural **4–30.4** application made in Form 2, but is not confined to such a document. For the exercise of the Registrar's power under r.30(5) to amend a document in the form of a notice of appeal, see Practice Direction 4 (Notice of Appeal) para.4.2.1.

Requests for expedition

31.—(1) Any request for urgent consideration of an application 4–31 for permission to appeal or for an expedited hearing must be made to the Registrar.

(2) Wherever possible the views of all parties should be obtained before such a request is made.

Effect of rule

4–31.1   For circumstances in which requests for expedition might be made and relevant practice, see Practice Direction 3 (Applications for Permission to Appeal) paras 3.4.3 to 3.4.7, Practice Direction 4 (Notice of Appeal) para.4.8.1, Practice Direction (The Appeal Hearing) para.6.2.4.

See, further, commentary following r.16 and r.20.

Grouping appeals

4–32   **32.   The Registrar may direct that appeals raising the same or similar issues shall be heard either together or consecutively by the Court constituted by the same Justices and may give any consequential directions that appear appropriate.**

Effect of rule

4–32.1   This rule is supplemented by Practice Direction 8 (Miscellaneous Matters) para.8.2.

Change of interest

4–33   **33.   The Court must be informed promptly of—**

(a) the death or bankruptcy of any individual party;

(b) the winding up or dissolution of any corporate party;

(c) any compromise of the subject matter of an appeal;

(d) any event which does or may deprive an appeal of practical significance to the parties,

and the Court may give any consequential directions that appear appropriate.

Effect of rule

4–33.1   A decision made in exercise of the Court's powers under r.33 is a procedural decision within r.9.

Death of party (r.33(a))

4–33.2   For practice where a party to an appeal dies before the hearing (including that relating to an application to substitute a new party in this circumstances), see Practice Direction 8 (Miscellaneous Matters) para.8.4.

Bankruptcy or winding up (r.33(a))

4–33.3   For practice where a party to an appeal is adjudicated bankrupt or a corporate party is ordered to be wound up before the hearing (including that relating to an application to pursue the appeal nonetheless), see Practice Direction 8 (Miscellaneous Matters) para.8.1.

Compromise (r.33(c))

4–33.4   Paragraph 8.5.1 of Practice Direction 8 (Miscellaneous Matters) states that it is the duty of counsel and solicitors in any pending appeal, if an event occurs which arguably disposes of the dispute between the parties, either to ensure that the appeal is withdrawn by consent or, if there is no agreement on that course, to bring the facts promptly to the attention of the Registrar and to seek directions. See further r.34 and commentary thereon.

Event depriving appeal of practical significance (r.33(d))

4–33.5   The Court must be informed of any event which does or may deprive an appeal of practical significance to the parties (r.33(c)). (There is no reason why "parties" in this context should not have the meaning given in r.3(2) and should therefore include an intervener.) An obvious such event would be where the parties consent to the appeal being withdrawn, see r.34. Another might be where an event had occurred that rendered "academic" or "hypothetical" the point of law raised by the appeal. For authorities on question whether appeal courts should decline jurisdiction in such circumstances (including House of Lords authority), see Vol.1 para.9A–77. The fact that an appeal has been deprived of its significance to the parties does not mean that it may not retain a wider significance.

Withdrawal etc of application for permission to appeal or of appeal

34.—**(1) An application for permission to appeal or a notice of 4–34 appeal may be withdrawn with the written consent of all parties or with the permission of the Court on such terms as appear appropriate.**

(2) The Court may set aside or vary the order appealed from by consent and without an oral hearing if satisfied that it is appropriate so to do.

(3) In this rule "a notice of appeal" includes an application for permission to appeal or cross–appeal which (under rule 18 or rule 25) stands as a notice of appeal or cross–appeal.

Effect of rule

A decision made in exercise of the Court's powers under r.34 is a procedural deci- **4–34.1** sion within r.9.

For practice where application is made to withdraw an application for permission to appeal, see Practice Direction 8 (Miscellaneous Matters) para.8.16.2.

For practice where application is made to withdraw an appeal that has not been listed, see *ibid.* para.8.16.3.

An appeal that has been listed for hearing may be withdrawn by order of the Court on application; for practice, see *ibid.* para.8.16.4.

Advocate to the Court and assessors

35.—**(1) The Court may request the relevant officer to appoint, 4–35 or may itself appoint, an advocate to the Court to assist the Court with legal submissions.**

(2) In accordance with section 44 of the Act the Court may, at the request of the parties or of its own initiative, appoint one or more independent specially qualified advisers to assist the Court as assessors on any technical matter.

(3) The fees and expenses of any advocate to the Court or assessor shall be costs in the appeal.

Effect of rule

A decision made in exercise of the Court's powers under r.35 is a procedural deci- **4–35.1** sion within r.9.

Assessors

Section 44(1) of the 2005 Act states that, if the Court thinks it expedient in any **4–35.2** proceedings, it may hear and dispose of the proceedings wholly or partly with the assistance of one or more specially qualified advisers appointed by it. Rule 35(2) qualifies s.44(1) by adding that such advisers should be appointed "to assist the Court as assessors on any technical matter". Section 44(2) states that any remuneration payable to an adviser is to be determined by the Court unless agreed between the adviser and the parties to the proceedings, and s.44(3) states that any remuneration shall form part of the costs of the proceedings; r.35(3) states that an assessor's fees and expenses shall be costs in the appeal.

Specialist advisers provide assistance to the Court and are strictly independent of the parties to the appeal (Practice Direction 8 (Miscellaneous Matters) para.8.13.1).

Any party to an appeal may apply in writing to the Registrar for specialist advisers appointed by the Court to attend the hearing (*ibid.*).

Advocate to the Court

4–35.3   The "relevant officer" is, as provided by r.3(2), in relation to proceedings in England and Wales coming before the Court, the Attorney General.

A request for an advocate to the Court to be appointed in an appeal should be made in writing to the Registrar. Any request should indicate whether the other parties to the appeal support the request (Practice Direction 8 (Miscellaneous Matters) para.8.13.2).

For memorandum from the Lord Chief Justice and the Attorney General on requests for the appointment of an advocate to court in relation to proceedings in England and Wales, see Vol.1, para.39.8.1.

Security for costs

4–36   **36.—(1) The Court may on the application of a respondent order an appellant to give security for the costs of the appeal and any order for security shall determine—**

(a) the amount of that security, and

(b) the manner in which, and the time within which, security must be given.

(2) An order made under this rule may require payment of the judgment debt (and costs) in the court below instead of, or in addition to, the amount ordered by way of security for costs.

Effect of rule

4–36.1   A decision made in exercise of the Court's powers under r.36 is a procedural decision within r.9.

This rule is supplemented by Practice Direction 4 (Notice of Appeal) para.4.7.1 et seq. An application for security should be made in Form 2 (see Practice Direction 7 (Applications, Documents, Forms and Orders) para.7.1 and Annex 2).

As an application for security is a procedural application it should be made in accordance with r.30. The application should be made as soon as it becomes apparent that an application is necessary or expedient (Practice Direction 7 (Applications, Documents, Forms and Orders) para.7.1.1).

No security for costs is required in cross–appeals (*ibid.* para.4.7.2). No security for costs is required in criminal appeals (Practice Direction 12 (Criminal Proceedings) para.12.8.1). For payment of security, see Practice Direction 8 (Miscellaneous Matters) para.8.7.1.

Failure to provide security as required will result in the appeal being struck out by the Registrar although the appellant may apply to reinstate the appeal (Practice Direction 4 (Notice of Appeal) para.4.7.5.

For directions as to the deposit with the Court of security money (in cash or by cheque), see Practice Direction 8 (Miscellaneous Matters) para.8.7.1.

For payment out of any security for costs lodged with the Court, see r.54.

Stay of execution

4–37   **37. Any appellant who wishes to obtain a stay of execution of the order appealed from must seek it from the court below and only in wholly exceptional circumstances will the Court grant a stay.**

Effect of rule

4–37.1   A decision made in exercise of the Court's powers under r.37 is a procedural decision within r.9. The rule assumes that the Court has power to order a stay. The Court has all the powers of the court below (r.29(1)) including, presumably, the power to order a stay pending an appeal.

Filing a notice of appeal or an application for permission to appeal does not in itself place a stay of execution on any order appealed from. A party seeking such a stay must apply to the court appealed from, not to the Court; the Court cannot stay an interlocutor of the Court of Session (Court of Session Act 1988 s.41(2)) (see Practice Direction 8 (Miscellaneous Matters) para.8.14.1).

Change of solicitor and London agents

38.—(1) If a party for whom a solicitor is acting wishes to change 4–38
solicitors, that party or the new solicitor must give the Registrar
and the former solicitor written notice of the change.

(2) Until such notices are given the former solicitor shall
continue to be treated as the party's solicitor.

(3) Solicitors practising outside London may appoint London
agents and additional costs incurred by not appointing London
agents may be disallowed.

Effect of rule

In this context, "solicitor" includes any person authorised to provide legal services 4–38.1
other than as counsel in connection with proceedings before the Court (see r.3(2)).

Paragraph (3) of r.38 is restated in Practice Direction 4 (Notice of Appeal)
para.4.2.14.

Disposal of documents

39.—(1) All documents filed become the property of the Court 4–39
and original documents must be retained in the records of the
Registry.

(2) Other documents shall be destroyed unless the Registrar (on
a written application made within 21 days of the end of the proceed-
ings) directs otherwise.

(3) All documents held by the Court may be inspected by the
press or members of the public on application to the Registrar but
the Registrar may refuse an application for reasons of commercial
confidentiality, national security or in the public interest.

(4) Before allowing an application for inspection under this rule,
the Registrar may impose terms or conditions such as the redaction
of certain material where such a condition is necessary in the
interests of justice or in the public interest.

Effect of rule

The heading to this rule is misleading. The rule deals with two quite distinct mat- 4–39.1
ters; disposal of documents by destruction, and inspection of documents by non–
parties.

Document disposal

Paragraph (2) of r.39 is supplemented by Practice Direction 7 (Applications, Docu- 4–39.2
ments, Forms and Orders) para.7.2.5. No documents submitted in connection with an
application for permission to appeal can be returned (*ibid.*). Rule 29(2) states that an
application to the Registrar should be made within 21 days of the end of proceedings;
in para.7.2.5 it is stated that the application should be made within 14 days of judgment in the appeal.

Inspection of documents held by the Court

Paragraph (3) of r.39 is amplified in Practice Direction 7 (Applications, Documents, 4–39.3
Forms and Orders) para.7.2.6, where it is stated that non–parties inspecting documents must comply with any anonymity orders made in the proceedings, any data

protection requirements, as well as with any conditions imposed by the Registrar under the rule. (Rule 39(3) may be contrasted with CPR r.5.4C (supply of documents to non–party from court records).)

For fees payable on requests for copies of documents, see Practice Direction 7 (Applications, Documents, Forms and Orders) Annex 2.

PART 6

PARTICULAR APPEALS AND REFERENCES

Human Rights Act issues

4–40   **40.—(1) Where an appeal raises a question of incompatibility under section 4 of the Human Rights Act 1998[1] and the Crown is not already a party to the appeal, the Registrar shall give 21 days' notice of the question to the Crown.**

(2) If notice is given that the Crown wishes to be joined, the appropriate Minister or other person shall be joined accordingly.

(3) If such a question arises for the first time during the course of an appeal hearing the Court will if necessary adjourn the proceedings to enable the Registrar to give notice under paragraph (1).

Effect of rule

4–40.1   It is explained in para.1.2.23 of Practice Direction 1 that the Human Rights Act 1998 applies to the Court and issues under that statute will often arise on appeals to the Court; but the Act does not confer any general right of appeal.

Rule 40 is supplemented by Practice Direction 9 (The Human Rights Act 1998), where detailed provisions as to practice and procedure are laid down, first for appeals involving declarations of incompatibility, and secondly, for other appeals under the 1998 Act.

Devolution jurisdiction

4–41   **41.—(1) Appeals or references under the Court's devolution jurisdiction shall in general be dealt with in accordance with these Rules but the Court shall give special directions as and when necessary, and in particular as to—**

(a) **any question referred under section 33 of the Scotland Act 1998[2], section 11 of the Northern Ireland Act 1998[3] or section 96, 99 or 112 of the Government of Wales Act 2006[4],**

(b) **any reference of a devolution issue[5],**

(c) **any direct references under paragraph 33 or 34 of Schedule 6 to the Scotland Act 1998, paragraph 33 or 34 of Schedule 10 to the Northern Ireland Act 1998 or paragraph 29 or 30 of Schedule 9 to the Government of Wales Act 2006.**

---

[1] 1998 c. 42.

[2] 1998 c. 46; section 33 provides for the scrutiny of proposed Acts of the Scottish Parliament by the Supreme Court.

[3] 1998 c. 47; section 11 provides for the scrutiny of proposed Acts of the Northern Ireland Assembly by the Supreme Court.

[4] 2006 c. 32; sections 96, 99 and 112 provide for the scrutiny of proposed Orders in Council, proposed Assembly Measures and proposed Acts of the National Assembly for Wales by the Supreme Court.

[5] A devolution issue is defined in Schedule 6 to the Scotland Act 1998, Schedule 10 to the Northern Ireland Act 1998 and Schedule 9 to the Government of Wales Act 2006.

(2) A reference made by the relevant officer is made by filing the reference and by serving a copy on any other relevant officer who is not already a party and who has a potential interest in the proceedings.

(3) A reference must state the question or issue to be decided by the Court.

(4) The Registrar shall give notice of the question or issue to the appropriate relevant officer where that officer is not already a party to any proceedings.

Effect of rule

The jurisdiction of the Court in devolution matters is explained in Practice Direc- **4–41.2** tion 1 para.1.2.24, and (in greater detail) in Practice Direction 10 (Devolution Jurisdiction) para.10.1. Rule 41(1) states that appeals or references under the Court's devolution jurisdiction shall in general be dealt with in accordance with the Rules. Practice Direction 10 restates r.41 and amplifies its provisions in certain respects. In addition it explains that devolution matters can reach the Court in four ways and contains directions as to each, some of which impose time limits for the taking of certain procedural steps (see paras 10.2 to 10.5 inclusive). In relation to the second way (appeals from UK superior courts) the practice direction briefly explains the normal effects of provisions in Pt 2 and Pt 3.

For meaning of "relevant officer", see r.3(2).

A decision made in exercise of the Court's powers under r.41 is a procedural decision within r.9.

For fees payable on references under the devolution jurisdiction, see Practice Direction 7 (Applications, Documents, Forms and Orders) Annex 2.

Court of Justice of the European Communities

42.—(1) Where it is contended on an application for permission **4–42**
to appeal that it raises a question of Community law which should
be the subject of a reference under Article 234 of the Treaty
establishing the European Community and permission to appeal is
refused, the panel of Justices will give brief reasons for its decision.

(2) Where on an application for permission to appeal a panel of
Justices decides to make a reference under Article 234 before
determining the application, it will give consequential directions as
to the form of the reference and the staying of the application (but
it may if it thinks fit dispose of other parts of the application at
once).

(3) Where at the hearing of an appeal the Court decides to make
a reference under Article 234 it will give consequential directions
as to the form of the reference and the staying of the appeal (but it
may if it thinks fit dispose of other parts of the appeal at once).

(4) An order of the Court shall be prepared and sealed by the
Registrar to record any decision made under this rule.

Effect of rule

Community law requires that the Supreme Court (as the domestic court of last **4–42.1** resort) should refer to the Court of Justice of the European Communities any doubtful questions of Community law necessary to its decision.

If an appellant seeks a reference to the Court of Justice, this should be stated clearly in the notice of appeal, and the appellant must notify the Registrar in writing (Practice Direction 4 (Notice of Appeal) para.4.2.13). In Section 7 of Form 1, which is to be used for applications for permission to appeal (as well as for notices of appeal), the applicant is required to state whether the Court is to be asked to make a reference to the Court of Justice.

Practice Direction 11 (The European Court of Justice) supplements r.42. This

Practice Direction, in addition to amplifying r.42, contains provisions stating the practice and procedure to be followed if, after the Court of Justice has given judgment, a further hearing by the Court is required.

Costs of reference

4–42.2   The Court of Justice does not make orders for costs. The costs of the reference are included in the order of the Supreme Court disposing of the appeal; and, if necessary, are assessed by the Costs Officers of the Court (Practice Direction 11 (The European Court of Justice) para.11.1.10).

Revocation of patents

4–43   43.—(1) **On any appeal under sections 12 and 13 of the Administration of Justice Act 1969[1] from an order for revocation of a patent the appellant must serve notice of the appeal on the Comptroller–General of Patents ("the Comptroller") as well as on every respondent.**

(2) A respondent who decides not to oppose the appeal must serve notice of that decision on the Comptroller together with the relevant statements of case.

(3) The Comptroller shall within 14 days serve on the appellant and file a notice stating whether or not the Comptroller intends to appear on the appeal.

(4) Where notice is given under paragraph (3), the Comptroller may appear on the appeal.

Effect of rule

4–43.1   This rule applies from where there is a direct ("leapfrog") appeal from the High Court from an order made by the High Court for the revocation of a patent made under the Patents Act 1949 s.32 or s.61, or the Patents Act 1977 s.72. The rule is re-stated, and directions are given, in Practice Direction 8 (Miscellaneous Matters) para.8.11. The 14 day time limit referred to in r.43(3) runs from the date on which the Comptroller receives notice of the respondent's decision (para.8.11.4). The Court may make such orders for the postponement or adjournment of the hearing of the appeal as may appear necessary for the purpose of giving effect to these provisions (para.8.11.6).

Criminal appeals

4–44   44. **The Court must apply in accordance with the relevant practice direction the code of practice for victims issued under section 32 of the Domestic Violence, Crime and Victims Act 2004.[2]**

Effect of rule

4–44.1   The jurisdiction of the Court in criminal proceedings is explained in Practice Direction 1 para.1.2. Appeals to the Court in criminal proceedings in England and Wales or Northern Ireland are subject to special restrictions limiting such appeals to cases of general public importance (para.1.2.10). There is no appeal in criminal proceedings from the High Court of Justiciary or any other court in Scotland, but issues relating to criminal proceedings in Scotland may come before the Supreme Court as devolution issues under the Scotland Act 1998 (*ibid.*).

Practice Direction 12 (Criminal Proceedings) contains detailed provisions for the handling of criminal appeals by the Court and affects a wide range of matters of pro-

---

[1] 1969 c. 58; section 12 has been amended by the Courts Act 1971 (c.23), Schedule 11 Part IV, Judicature (Northern Ireland) Act 1978 (c.23) section 122(1)(2), Schedule 6 paragraph 13, Schedule 7, Part I and the Supreme Court Act 1981 (c.54), section 152(4), Schedule 7.
[2] 2004 c. 28.

cedure and practice. The Practice Directions governing civil proceedings (they are Practice Directions 1 to 11, 13 and 14) apply to criminal proceedings in the Court subject to any modifications or additional provisions made by Practice Direction 12 (*ibid.* para.12.1.2).

Although, in large part, Practice Direction 12 simply re–states the effects of particular Rules and provisions in other practice directions as they apply to criminal appeals, it also makes some modifications and additions. Consequently, care must be taken in reading its provisions alongside the Rules and other practice directions.

For practice relating to the giving effect, in criminal appeals to the Court, to the victims code of practice issued under the Domestic Violence, Crime and Victims Act 2004 s.42, see Practice Direction 12 (Criminal Proceedings) para.12.15.

PART 7

FEES AND COSTS

Fees

45. Where a fee is prescribed by any order made under section 52 of the Act, the Registrar may refuse to accept a document or refuse to allow a party to take any step unless the relevant fee is paid. 4–45

Effect of rule

The fees which are payable in the Court are prescribed by the Supreme Court Fees Order 2009 (SI 2009/2131) made under s.52 of the 2005 Act. For fees payable, see Annex 2 to Practice Direction 7 (Applications, Documents, Forms and Orders) (replicating Sch.1 to the 2009 Order). The Registry will not issue an application for permission to appeal or other document unless (amongst other things) the prescribed fee is paid or a request for fee remission from court fees is made (Practice Direction 2 (The Registry of the Supreme Court) para.2.1.11). 4–45.1

Any fees paid are not refunded, even if it is decided that an application for permission to appeal is inadmissible or if an application or other proceeding is withdrawn (ibid para.2.1.31).

Payments of fees may be made in cash or by banker's draft or cheque made payable to "The Supreme Court of the United Kingdom" (Practice Direction 8 (Miscellaneous Matters) para 8.7.1).

Fee waiver and remission

In circumstances where a party would suffer financial hardship by the payment of fees, the requirement to pay fees may be waived. Schedule 2 of the 2009 Order applies for the purpose of ascertaining whether a party is entitled to a remission or part remission of a prescribed fee. This Schedule is similar to Sch.2 of the Civil Proceedings Fees Order 2008 (see para.10–1 below), adjusted to take into account legislation applicable in Northern Ireland and Scotland, and with the Chief Executive of the Supreme Court authorised to remit fees in those particular circumstances in which the Lord Chancellor is so authorised under the 2008 Order (a variation that demonstrates the independence of the Court from the Executive branch of Government). 4–45.2

Any request for fee remission should be made to the Registrar (who is "the court officer" for the purposes of art.7 of Sch.2), supported by evidence of the party's means (Practice Direction 2 (The Registry of the Supreme Court) para.2.1.29). The Registrar may then grant full or part remission of the relevant fee. Remission of fees is usually granted where a remission of fees has been granted in the court below.

Orders for costs

46.—(1) The Court may make such orders as it considers just in respect of the costs of any appeal, application for permission to appeal, or other application to or proceeding before the Court. 4–46

(2) The Court's powers to make orders for costs may be exercised

either at the final determination of an appeal or application for permission to appeal or in the course of the proceedings.

(3) Orders for costs will not normally be made either in favour of or against interveners but such orders may be made if the Court considers it just to do so (in particular if an intervener has in substance acted as the sole or principal appellant or respondent).

Effect of rules 46 to 53

4–46.1   In relation to an appeal or a reference, the Supreme Court has all the powers of the court below and may make a costs order (r.29(1)(e)).

Rules 46 to 53 are supplemented by Practice Direction 13 (Costs). This practice direction contains a comprehensive code dealing with the entitlement to costs of parties to cases dealt with by the Court, with the assessment of costs, and with the procedure for the detailed assessment of costs by Costs Officers appointed by the President of the Court under r.49. Subject to some minor variations, Practice Direction 13 follows in structure and in detail the Practice Directions Applicable to Judicial Taxations in the House of Lords (March 2007). Detailed provisions for the assessment of costs are contained in Section 1. Forms of bill of costs are set out in Section 2. Whereas the Judicial Taxation Directions contained two forms of the summary to be included in a completed bill of costs, one for general use and the other (requiring certain additional information) where costs are payable under a certificate of public funding or representation order, Section 3 of Practice Direction 13 contains a form for the summary adaptable to both circumstances, followed by the Allocatur form. Section 5 contains guideline figures for the provisional assessment of costs.

For the fees payable on the assessment of a bill of costs, see Annex 2 to Practice Direction 7 (Applications, Documents, Forms and Orders).

For provisions relevant to the award of costs where an application for permission to appeal in civil proceedings is determined by the Court, see Practice Direction 3 (Applications for Permission to Appeal) para.3.5.

For provisions relevant to the award of costs where an application for permission to appeal in criminal proceedings is determined by the Court, see Practice Direction 12 (Criminal Appeals) para.12.5.

Related provisions

4–46.2   Some provisions found elsewhere in the Rules and in other supplementing practice directions deal with issues relating to costs. The principal ones (some of which are restated in Practice Direction 13) are outlined immediately below.

Conditional fee agreements may properly be made by parties to appeals before the Court (see Practice Direction 6 (The Appeal Hearing) para.6.7.2, and Practice Direction 13 (Costs) para.28.1).

An order for costs will not be made in favour of a respondent who has not given notice of acknowledgement under r.21 (Practice Direction 4 (Notice of Appeal) para.4.6.4).

Generally, only junior counsel's fees will be allowed for any stage of an application for permission to appeal (Practice Direction 3 (Applications for Permission to Appeal) para.3.4.8).

The fees of two counsel only for any party at an appeal hearing are allowed on assessment unless the Court orders otherwise on application at the hearing (Practice Direction 6 (The Appeal Hearing) para.6.3.7, and Practice Direction 13 (Costs) para.16.5).

Solicitors outside London who decide to appoint London agents may be disallowed on any assessment of costs any additional costs incurred as a result of that decision (r.38(3)).

The cost of preparing the volumes of authorities (r.24) falls to the appellants, but is ultimately subject to the decision of the Court as to the costs of the appeal (Practice Direction 6 (The Appeal Hearing) para.6.5.8).

A party requesting the services of a stenographer at an appeal hearing for the purpose of providing a transcript of the proceedings bears the costs involved (Practice Direction 6 (The Appeal Hearing) para.6.6.6).

Submissions as to costs

47.—(1) If a party wishes to defer making submissions as to **4–47** costs until after judgment, the Court must be informed of this not later than at the close of the oral argument.

(2) If the Court accedes to the request it will give such directions as appear appropriate and it may, in particular, give directions—

(a) for the hearing of oral submissions as to costs immediately after judgment;

(b) for the simultaneous or sequential filing of written submissions as to costs within a specified period after judgment;

(c) for the hearing of oral submissions after the filing of written submissions.

Effect of rule

Where a party makes written submissions as to costs under r.47, the original and **4–47.1** seven copies of the submissions must be filed at the Registry and copies should be sent to other parties to the appeal (Practice Direction 6 (The Appeal Hearing) para.6.7.1). Written costs submissions are considered on paper.

Claim for costs

48.—(1) Where the Court has made an order for costs, the claim **4–48** for costs must be submitted to the Registrar within three months beginning with the date on which the costs order was made.

(2) The form and contents of a claim for costs must comply with the relevant practice direction and the receiving party must supply such further particulars, information and documents as the Registrar may direct.

(3) The receiving party must serve a copy of a claim for costs on the paying party.

(4) Within 21 days beginning with the day on which a claim for costs is served, the paying party may (or, in the circumstances specified in the relevant practice direction, must) file points of dispute and, if so, must serve a copy on the receiving party.

(5) Within 14 days beginning with the day on which points of dispute are served, the receiving party may file a response and, if so, must serve a copy on the paying party.

Effect of rule

For form and content of claim for cost, see Practice Direction 13 (Costs) Section 1 **4–48.1** para.7.

Assessment of costs

49.—(1) Every detailed assessment of costs shall be carried out **4–49** by two costs officers appointed by the President and—

(a) one costs officer must be a Costs Judge (a Taxing Master of the Senior Courts), and

(b) the second may be the Registrar.

(2) A disputed assessment shall be dealt with at an oral hearing.

(3) An assessment may provide for the costs of the assessment procedure.

(4) The Registrar will give the receiving party and the paying party written notice of the date of the assessment.

(5) Where one of the parties so requests or in the circumstances specified in the relevant practice direction, the Registrar may make a provisional assessment of costs without the attendance of the parties.

(6) The Registrar must inform the parties in writing of the outcome of a provisional assessment and, if a party is dissatisfied with the outcome, or if points of disagreement cannot be resolved in correspondence, the Registrar shall appoint a date for an oral hearing.

(7) Any request for an oral hearing following a provisional assessment of costs must be made within 14 days of the receipt of the Registrar's decision on the assessment.

Effect of rule

4–49.1   For directions as to provisional assessment, see Practice Direction 13 (Costs) Section 1 para.14.

Before s.59 of the 2005 Act came into force, the office of Taxing Master of the Senior Courts was the office of Taxing Master of the Supreme Court becomes Taxing Master of the Senior Courts (see Pt II of Sch.2 to the 1981 Act).

Basis of assessment

4–50   **50.—(1)** Where the Court is to assess the amount of costs it will assess those costs—

(a) on the standard basis, or

(b) on the indemnity basis,

in the manner specified by rule 51 or (where appropriate) on the relevant bases that apply in Scotland or Northern Ireland.

(2) Where—

(a) the Court makes an order about costs without indicating the basis on which the costs are to be assessed, or

(b) the Court makes an order for costs to be assessed on a basis other than one specified in paragraph (1),

the costs will be assessed on the standard basis.

(3) This rule applies subject to any order or direction to the contrary.

Effect of rule

4–50.1   See commentary following r.51.

The standard basis and the indemnity basis

4–51   **51.—(1)** Costs assessed on the standard basis are allowed only if they are proportionate to the matters in issue and are reasonably incurred and reasonable in amount.

(2) Any doubt as to whether costs assessed on the standard basis are reasonably incurred and are reasonable and proportionate in amount will be resolved in favour of the paying party.

(3) Costs assessed on the indemnity basis are allowed only if they are reasonably incurred and reasonable in amount.

(4) Any doubt as to whether costs assessed on the indemnity basis are reasonably incurred and are reasonable in amount will be resolved in favour of the receiving party.

Effect of rule

4–51.1   For directions as to basis of assessment, see Practice Direction 13 (Costs) Section 1 para.10.

Amount of assessed costs to be specified

52. The amount of any assessed costs will be inserted in the or- 4–52 der made under rule 29 but, if that order is drawn up before the assessment has been completed, the amount assessed will be certified by the Registrar.

Effect of rule

The Court has all the powers of the court below and r.29(1)(e) expressly states that **4–52.1** the Court may make a costs order.

For directions as to certificates, see Practice Direction 13 (Costs) Section 1 para.24.

Appeal from assessment

53.—(1) A party who is dissatisfied with the assessment of costs 4–53 made at an oral hearing may apply for that decision to be reviewed by a single Justice and any application under this rule must be made in the appropriate form and be filed within 14 days of the decision.

(2) The single Justice may (without an oral hearing) affirm the decision made on the assessment or may, where it appears appropriate, refer the matter to a panel of Justices to be decided with or without an oral hearing.

(3) An application may be made under this rule only on a question of principle and not in respect of the amount allowed on any item in the claim for costs.

Effect of rule

An application for an appeal by way of review of an assessment decision is made in **4–53.1** Form 2 under r.30. For relevant directions as to practice and procedure supplementing the provisions of r.53, see Practice Direction 13 (Costs) Section 1 para.18.

Payment out of security for costs

54. Any security for costs lodged by an appellant will be dealt 4–54 with by the Registrar in accordance with the directions of the Court.

Effect of rule

For deposit of security for costs, see r.36 and commentary following.   **4–54.1**

PART 8

TRANSITIONAL ARRANGEMENTS

Transitional arrangements

55.—(1) Unless the Court or the Registrar directs otherwise, 4–55 these Rules shall apply, with any necessary modifications, to appeals which were proceeding, and petitions for leave which were lodged, in the House of Lords before 1st October 2009.

(2) The Court or the Registrar may give special directions, as and when necessary, in relation to appeals which were proceeding, and petitions for leave which were lodged, in the House of Lords before 1st October 2009 notwithstanding anything that was done in accordance with the Practice Directions and Standing Orders of the House of Lords.

Effect of rule

4–55.1   The power to give directions exercisable by "the Court or the Registrar" under this rule do not fall under r.9 (Procedural decisions). Presumably, they are exercisable by a single Justice.

PRACTICE DIRECTIONS

PRACTICE DIRECTION 1

Section 1 The Supreme Court—General Note

4–56   **1.1.1** The Supreme Court of the United Kingdom was established by Part 3 of the Constitutional Reform Act 2005 ("the Act"), coming into force on 1st October 2009. Its jurisdiction corresponds to that of the House of Lords in its judicial capacity under the Appellate Jurisdiction Acts 1876 and 1888 (which are repealed) together with devolution matters under the Scotland Act 1998, the Northern Ireland Act 1998 and the Government of Wales Act 2006, which are transferred to the Supreme Court from the Judicial Committee of the Privy Council. The jurisdiction of the Supreme Court is defined by section 40 of, and Schedule 9 to, the Act.

1.1.2 Under section 45 of the Act, the senior Lord of Appeal in Ordinary has, after consulting the Lord Chancellor, the General Council of the Bar of England and Wales, the Law Society of England and Wales, the Faculty of Advocates of Scotland, the Law Society of Scotland, the General Council of the Bar of Northern Ireland, the Law Society of Northern Ireland and other bodies likely to be affected by the Rules, made the Supreme Court Rules, which are published as S.I. 2009/1603. The Rules, which come into force on 1st October 2009, apply to civil and criminal appeals to the Court and to appeals and references under the Court's devolution jurisdiction.

1.1.3 The overriding objective of the Supreme Court Rules is to secure that the Court is accessible, fair and efficient and the senior Lord of Appeal in Ordinary, the President of the Supreme Court, has issued these Practice Directions to supplement the Supreme Court Rules, to provide for the forms to be used in the Supreme Court and to provide general guidance and assistance to parties and their legal representatives.

Transitional arrangements

1.1.4 Rule 55 of the Supreme Court Rules makes transitional arrangements for appeals and applications which were filed before 1st October 2009. Unless the Court or the Registrar directs otherwise, the Rules apply, with any necessary modifications, to any appeals and applications which were lodged in the House of Lords before 1st October 2009 and the Court or the Registrar may give special directions in these circumstances.

Forms

1.1.5 The Practice Directions provide for a number of forms and a reference in the Supreme Court Rules or in these Practice Directions to a form by number means the form so numbered in the relevant practice direction. The forms are to be used in the cases to which they apply or in the particular circumstances for which they are provided but a form may be varied by the Court or a party if the variation is required by the circumstances of a particular case. The forms are set out in Annex 1 to Practice Direction 7.

Jurisdiction

1.1.6 The jurisdiction of the Supreme Court corresponds to that of the House of Lords in its judicial capacity together with devolution matters and its jurisdiction is summarised in Section 2 of this Practice Direction.

Section 2 The Jurisdiction of the Supreme Court

Civil Appeals

1.2.1 The key provisions in relation to civil appeals are subsections **4–57** (2) and (3) of section 40 of the Act:

(2) An appeal lies to the Court from any order or judgment of the Court of Appeal in England and Wales in civil proceedings.

(3) An appeal lies to the Court from any order or judgment of a court in Scotland if an appeal lay from that court to the House of Lords at or immediately before the commencement of this section.

1.2.2 The principal provisions relating to civil appeals from Scotland are in section 40 of the Court of Session Act 1988 as amended by the Act. (But see also sections 24, 27 (5), 32(5), 41, 42, 43 and 52(3) as amended for further matters of detail.)

1.2.3 The principal provisions relating to civil appeals from Northern Ireland are in section 42 of the Judicature (Northern Ireland) Act 1978 as amended by the Act. See also sections 43 (preserving leapfrog appeals), 44 (contempt) and 45 (habeas corpus), as amended.

1.2.4 Schedule 9 of the Act also amends a large number of statutes which gave rights of appeal (often limited to issues of law) to the House of Lords; these are replaced by corresponding rights of appeal to the Supreme Court.

1.2.5 Section 40(6) of the Act provides:

An appeal under subsection (2) lies only with the permission of the Court of Appeal or the Supreme Court; but this is subject to provision under any other enactment restricting such an appeal.

The most important general restriction on rights of appeal is section 54(4) of the Access to Justice Act 1999.[1] The effect of this provision is that the Supreme Court may not entertain any appeal against an order of the Court of Appeal refusing permission for an appeal to the Court of Appeal from a lower court.

1.2.6 Where the Supreme Court does not have jurisdiction, the Registrar will inform the appellant in writing that the Supreme Court does not have jurisdiction. The European Court of Human Rights accepts this letter as setting out the jurisdiction of the Supreme Court

---

[1] Section 54 of the Access to Justice Act 1999 does not extend to Northern Ireland and the Civil Procedure Rules do not apply there, but the rule in *Lane v Esdaile* (see *Lane v Esdaile* [1891] AC 10) applies to Northern Ireland.

in the litigation, for the purpose of determining whether the appellant has satisfied the requirement, laid down by Article 35 of the European Convention on Human Rights, that all domestic remedies must be exhausted before an appeal can be made to the Strasbourg Court.

Other statutory restrictions

1.2.7 There are other statutory restrictions on the Court's jurisdiction. The following are excluded from the Court's jurisdiction and are inadmissible–

(a) appeals from incidental decisions of the Court of Appeal which may be called into question by rules of court: see Supreme Court Act 1981, section 58 (as amended by Access to Justice Act 1999, section 60);

(b) applications brought by a person in respect of whom the High Court has made an order under section 42 of the Supreme Court Act 1981 (restriction of vexatious legal proceedings);[1]

(c) applications for permission to appeal from a decision of the Court of Appeal on any appeal from a county court in any probate proceedings;[2]

(d) applications for permission to appeal from a decision of the Court of Appeal on an appeal from a decision of the High Court on a question of law under Part III of the Representation of the People Act 1983 (legal proceedings);[3]

(e) applications for permission to appeal against the refusal by the Court of Appeal to reopen[4] a previously concluded appeal or application for permission to appeal.[5]

Civil contempt of court cases

1.2.8 In cases involving civil contempt of court, an appeal may be brought under section 13 of the Administration of Justice Act 1960.[6] Permission to appeal is required and an application for permission must first be made to the court below. If that application is refused, an application for permission to appeal may then be made to the Supreme Court. Where the decision of the court below is a decision on appeal under the same section of the same Act, permission to appeal to the Supreme Court is only granted if the court below certifies that a point of law of general public importance is involved in that decision and if it appears to that court or to the Supreme Court, as the case may be, that the point is one that ought to be considered by the Supreme Court. Where the court below refuses to grant the certificate required, an application for permission to appeal is not accepted for filing in the Supreme Court.

---

[1] It is open to such a person to seek to appeal the section 42 order itself if that order was the subject of an appeal to the Court of Appeal.

[2] County Courts Act 1984 s 82.

[3] Representation of the People Act 1983 s 157(1).

[4] Under the rule in *Taylor v Lawrence* [2002] EWCA Civ 90 the Court of Appeal can in exceptional circumstances re–open an appeal or application for permission to appeal after it has given a final judgment.

[5] Civil Procedure Rules, r 52.17.

[6] Or, in Northern Ireland, under Judicature (Northern Ireland) Act 1978 s 44.

Time limit for applying for permission to appeal (civil appeals)

1.2.9 The time limit for applying for permission to appeal in civil cases (other than civil contempt of court or habeas corpus) is 28 days from the date of the order appealed from. The Supreme Court may extend this time limit.

Criminal Appeals

1.2.10 Appeals to the Supreme Court in criminal proceedings in **4–58** England and Wales or Northern Ireland are subject to special restrictions limiting such appeals to cases of general public importance. As before, there is no appeal in criminal proceedings from the High Court of Justiciary or any other court in Scotland, but issues relating to criminal proceedings in Scotland may come before the Supreme Court as devolution issues under the Scotland Act 1998.

England and Wales (except courts–martial)

1.2.11 Appeals to the Supreme Court in criminal proceedings in England and Wales are regulated by sections 33 and 34 of the Criminal Appeal Act 1968 and sections 1 and 2 of the Administration of Justice Act 1960 as amended (in each case) by section 88 of the Courts Act 2003 and section 40 of, and Schedule 9 to, the Act. All such appeals may be made at the instance of the accused or the prosecutor. Section 13 of the Administration of Justice Act 1960 (as amended) extends the scope of sections 1 and 2, with some qualifications, to appeals relating to contempt of court (civil or criminal). Sections 36 to 38 of the Criminal Appeal Act 1968 (as amended) contain ancillary provisions about bail, detention and attendance at appeal hearings.

1.2.12 Any appeal under these provisions requires the permission of the court below or the Supreme Court, which may be granted (except for a first appeal in a contempt of court matter) only if (i) the court below certifies that a point of general public importance is involved and (ii) it appears to the court below or to the Supreme Court that the point is one which ought to be considered by the Supreme Court.

1.2.13 Section 36 of the Criminal Justice Act 1972 (as amended) permits the Court of Appeal to refer a point of law to the Supreme Court where (after an acquittal) the Attorney–General has referred the point of law to the Court of Appeal.

Northern Ireland

1.2.14 Similar provisions apply to appeals in criminal proceedings in Northern Ireland: see sections 31 and 32 of the Criminal Appeal (Northern Ireland) Act 1980 and section 41 of, and Schedule 1 to, the Judicature (Northern Ireland) Act 1978 as amended (in each case) by section 105 of the Courts Act 2003 and section 40 of, and Schedule 9 to, the Act.

Courts–Martial

1.2.15 Similar provisions apply to appeals from the Courts–Martial Appeal Court: see sections 39 and 40 of the Courts–Martial (Appeals) Act 1968 as amended by section 91 of the Courts Act 2003 and section 40 of, and Schedule 9 to, the Act.

Time limit for applying for permission to appeal (criminal appeals)

1.2.16 As a result of amendments made by the Courts Act 2003 the time limit for applying for permission to appeal is 28 days from the date of the decision to be appealed from, or (if later) the date when reasons for the decision are given. The Supreme Court may extend time except in appeals under the Extradition Act 2003 (see sections 32 and 33 of that Act).

Leapfrog appeals

4–59　**1.2.17** Under sections 12 to 16 of the Administration of Justice Act 1969 as amended, appeals in civil matters may exceptionally be permitted to be made direct to the Supreme Court from (i) the High Court in England and Wales (ii) a Divisional Court in England and Wales and (iii) the High Court of Northern Ireland. These appeals are generally called leapfrog appeals.

1.2.18 Such appeals are permitted only if (i) the judge certifies (immediately after judgment or on an application within 14 days) that the "relevant conditions" are satisfied, that a sufficient case has been made out to justify an application for permission to appeal to the Supreme Court, and that all parties consent; (ii) the Supreme Court (on an application made within one month, a time limit which may be extended by the Supreme Court) gives permission for the appeal and (iii) it is not a case of contempt of court or one in which an appeal to the Court of Appeal (or the Court of Appeal of Northern Ireland) (a) would not have lain even with permission or (b) would not have had leave granted for it.

1.2.19 The "relevant conditions" (set out in section 12(3) of the Administration of Justice Act 1969) are that a point of general public importance is involved and that it either:

> "(a) relates wholly or mainly to the construction of an enactment or of a statutory instrument, and has been fully argued in the proceedings and fully considered in the judgment of the judge in the proceedings, or
>
> (b) is one in respect of which the judge is bound by a decision of the Court of Appeal or of the Supreme Court in previous proceedings, and was fully considered in the judgments given by the Court of Appeal or the Supreme Court (as the case may be) in those previous proceedings."

(In the case of leapfrog appeals from Northern Ireland the above references to the Court of Appeal must be read as references to the Court of Appeal of Northern Ireland.)

Judicial review in England and Wales: civil matters

4–60　**1.2.20** An application for permission to apply for judicial review is made to the Administrative Court (which is part of the Queen's Bench Division of the High Court). If the judge in the Administrative Court refuses the application without a hearing, an application can be made for the decision to be reconsidered at a hearing. Where permission to apply for judicial review has been refused by the Administrative Court after reconsideration at an oral hearing, the applicant may appeal against the refusal of permission. Such an appeal must be filed in the Court of Appeal within 7 days. For such an appeal to be successful, the applicant needs to be granted both i) permission to appeal against the Administrative Court's determination; and ii) permission to apply for judicial review.

1.2.21 If the Court of Appeal refuses permission to appeal to it against the Administrative Court's refusal of permission to apply for judicial review, there is no appeal to the Supreme Court. The Supreme Court has no jurisdiction to entertain such an appeal: *R v Secretary of State for Trade and Industry, ex parte Eastaway* [2000] 1 WLR 2222 applying the principle in *Lane v Esdaile* [1891] AC 10. However, if the Court of Appeal (a) grants permission to appeal to it against the Administrative Court's refusal of permission to apply for judicial review, but then (b) itself refuses permission to apply for judicial review, the Supreme Court does have jurisdiction to hear an appeal against that refusal: *R v Hammersmith and Fulham LBC, ex parte Burkett* [2002] 1WLR 1593.

1.2.22 Similar provisions apply in Scotland and Northern Ireland.

Human Rights

1.2.23 The Human Rights Act 1998 applies to the Supreme Court **4–61** and issues under that statute will often arise on appeals to the Supreme Court. But the Human Rights Act 1998 does not confer any general right of appeal beyond those mentioned in this Practice Direction. As to declarations of incompatibility, see rule 40 and Practice Direction 9 (Human Rights Act issues).

Devolution Matters

1.2.24 Devolution matters raise issues of constitutional importance **4–62** as to the purported or proposed exercise of a function by a member of the Scottish Executive, a Minister in Northern Ireland or a Northern Ireland department or the Welsh Ministers or as to the legislative competence of the Scottish Parliament under the Scotland Act 1998, the Northern Ireland Assembly under the Northern Ireland Act 1998, and the Welsh Assembly under the Government of Wales Act 2006. Under these Acts, as amended by Part 2 of Schedule 9 to the Act, the Supreme Court has an appellate jurisdiction in proceedings for the determination of a devolution issue and special statutory powers to consider referred questions, including questions referred by the relevant law officer or Ministers. The principal provisions are in sections 33 and 98 of, and paras 10, 11, 12, 13, 22, 23, 30, 31, 33 and 34 of Schedule 6 to, the Scotland Act 1998 (as amended by Part 2 of Schedule 9 to the Act); sections 11 and 79 of, and paras 9, 10, 19, 20, 28, 29, 30, 31, 33 and 34 of Schedule 10 to, the Northern Ireland Act 1998 (as amended by Part 2 of Schedule 9 to the Act), and section 96 of, and paras 10, 11, 18, 19, 20, 21, 27, 28, 29 and 30 of Schedule 9 to, the Government of Wales Act 2006.

See rule 41 and Practice Direction 10 (Devolution Issues).

References under Art. 234

1.2.25 Community law requires that the Supreme Court (as the **4–63** domestic court of last resort) should refer to the Court of Justice of the European Communities any doubtful questions of Community law necessary to its decision. See rule 42 and Practice Direction 11 (Court of Justice of the European Communities).

Section 3 The exercise of the Supreme Court's jurisdiction

4–64   **1.3.1** Some of the powers of the Court may be exercised by a single Justice and by the Registrar. Rule 9 makes specific provision for procedural decisions. If any procedural question arises which is not dealt with by the Rules, the Court or the Registrar may adopt any procedure that is consistent with the overriding objective, the Act and the Rules: rule 9(7).

1.3.2 *Procedural Decisions* Except where rule 9(2) (see paragraph 1.3.4) applies, the powers of the Court under the following rules may be exercised by a single Justice or the Registrar without an oral hearing—

> rule 5 (time limits),
> rule 8 (non–compliance with Rules),
> rule 11 (rejection of applications),
> rule 33 (change of interest),
> rule 34 (withdrawal of appeal),
> rule 35 (advocate to the Court and assessors),
> rule 36 (security for costs),
> rule 37 (stay of execution) and
> rule 41 (devolution jurisdiction).

1.3.3 The single Justice may direct an oral hearing or may refer the matter to a panel of (at least three) Justices to be decided with or without an oral hearing: rule 9(3).

1.3.4 A contested application

(a) alleging contempt of the Court; or
(b) for a direction under rule 8 dismissing an appeal or debarring a respondent from resisting an appeal; or
(c) for security for costs,

has to be referred to a panel of three Justices: rule 9(2). In a case of an alleged contempt, an oral hearing must be held; in any other case the Justices may hold an oral hearing.

1.3.5 The Registrar will normally make a decision without an oral hearing but may direct an oral hearing. The Registrar may also refer the matter to a single Justice (and paragraphs 1.3.2 and 1.3.3 then apply) or to a panel of three Justices for decision.

1.3.6 A party who is dissatisfied with a decision of the Registrar may apply for that decision to be reviewed by a single Justice. Any application must be made in Form 2 and must be filed within 14 days of the Registrar's decision: rule 9(5). A fee is payable and the procedure in paragraphs 1.3.2 and 1.3.3 applies. See paragraph 7.1 of Practice Direction 7 for applications and for the relevant fee see Annex 2 to Practice Direction 7.

1.3.7 Oral hearings on procedural matters are normally heard in open court or in a place to which the public are admitted.

PRACTICE DIRECTION 2—THE REGISTRY OF THE SUPREME COURT

4–65   **2.1.1** The Registry of the Supreme Court is situated on the ground floor of the building in Parliament Square which houses the Supreme

Court, the former Middlesex Guildhall. The staff of the Registry act under the guidance and supervision of the Registrar. The Registry of the Judicial Committee of the Privy Council is situated in the same room and the staff of that Registry act under the guidance and supervision of the Registrar of the Privy Council. Where a member of staff of one Registry is not available, a member of staff of the other Registry will try to assist.

2.1.2 The postal address of the Supreme Court is

The Supreme Court of the United Kingdom, Parliament Square, London SW1P 3BD DX 157230 Parliament Square 4

The telephone numbers are 020 7960 1991, 1992

The email address for the Registry is registry@supremecourt.gsi.gov.uk

The Registry is open from 10.00 a.m. to 4.30 p.m. on Mondays to Thursdays during the law terms[1] and from 10 a.m. to 4.00 p.m. on Fridays and outside the law terms. During August the Registry is open from 10.00 a.m. to 2.00 p.m.

2.1.3 The Registry is open on every day of the year except

(a) Saturdays and Sundays,

(b) the Thursday before Good Friday, Good Friday and the day after Easter Monday,

(c) during the Christmas vacation,

(d) Bank Holidays in England and Wales under the Banking and Financial Dealings Act 1971, and

(e) such other days as the Registrar, with the agreement of the President and the Chief Executive, may direct.

The "Christmas vacation" is the two week period over Christmas Day and New Year's Eve and in 2009, for example, starts on 21 December 2009 and ends on 2 January 2010. At a time when the Registry is closed, the Registrar can for urgent business be contacted via the Supreme Court switchboard on 020 7960–1900.

2.1.4 Enquiries about fees and the filing of documents, papers and volumes should be addressed to Registry. The management of the Supreme Court's list is dealt with by the listing officer under the direction of the Registrar and enquiries about the listing of appeals should be addressed to the listing officer in the first instance. Enquiries about the assessment of costs should be addressed to the Registrar or the costs clerk.

2.1.5 Cheques and drafts for fees should be made payable to "The Supreme Court of the United Kingdom".

2.1.6 Cheques and drafts for security money should be made payable to "UK Supreme Court Security Fund Account".

Filing Documents in the Registry of the Supreme Court

2.1.7 A document may be filed in the Registry "by any of the fol- **4–66** lowing methods—

(a) personal delivery;

(b) first class post (or an alternative service which provides for delivery on the next working day);

---

[1] The law terms are the four terms of the year during which the Supreme Court holds its sittings see Practice Direction 6 paragraph 6.2.1.

(c) through a document exchange;

(d) (with the consent of the Registrar) by electronic means in accordance with [...] practice direction" 14: rule 7(1).

When an application for permission to appeal, a notice of appeal, a notice of objection, an acknowledgement by a respondent or an application is filed, it will be sealed by a member of staff in the Registry: rule 7(4).

2.1.8 A document filed by first–class post or through a document exchange will be taken to have been filed on the second day after it was posted or left at the document exchange, as the case may be (not including days which are not business days): rule 7(2). Business days are defined by rule 3(2) and mean any day other than a Saturday, Sunday, Christmas Day, Good Friday or a bank holiday under the Banking and Financial Dealings Act 1971, in England and Wales. Where a document is received on a business day at a time when the Registry is closed, the document will be taken to have been filed in time and the Registrar may give whatever consequential directions appear appropriate.

2.1.9 Except with the consent of the Registrar, "the contents of documents (a) filed in hard copy must also be provided to the Registry by electronic means, and (b) filed by electronic means must also be provided to the Registry in hard copy," in accordance with the relevant practice direction: rule 7(3). See Practice Direction 14 for filing by electronic means.

2.1.10 The Registrar may refuse to accept any document which is illegible or does not comply with any provision in the Rules or any relevant practice direction. On refusing to accept a document, the Registrar will give whatever directions appear appropriate. (See rule 8.)

2.1.11 The Registry will not issue an application for permission to appeal or other document unless:

(a) it has been properly served on the respondents (see rule 6);

(b) all the required documents are supplied; and

(c) the prescribed fee is paid or a request for fee remission from court fees is made

(see paragraphs 2.1.28–2.1.30).

Time limits

4–67   **2.1.12** Rule 10(2) provides that an application for permission to appeal must be made first to the court below and an application may be made to the Supreme Court only after the court below has refused to grant permission to appeal. Where an application is made to the Supreme Court, the Rules provide for the following time limits to apply.

(a) Except in cases of contempt of court and in leapfrog appeals, an application for permission to appeal must be filed "within 28 days from the date of the order or decision of the court below": rule 11. This period runs from the date of the substantive order appealed from, not from the date on which the order is sealed or the date of any subsequent procedural order (e.g. an order refusing permission to appeal).

(b) A notice of appeal must be filed within 42 days of the date of the order or decision of the court below: rule 19(2). This period runs from the date of the substantive order appealed from, not from the date on which the order is sealed or the date of any subsequent procedural order (e.g. an order granting permission to appeal).

(c) If an appellant has applied for public funding, the Registrar must be informed in writing within the original 28 or 42 day period that public funding has been applied for. The above periods are then extended to 28 days after the final determination of the application for funding, including any appeals. (See rules 5(2) and 11.)

2.1.13 The Registry may accept an application for permission to appeal or a notice of appeal which is out of time if the application sets out the reason(s) why it was not filed within the time limit and it is in order in all other respects.

2.1.14 The Justices or the Registrar may extend or shorten any time limit set by the Rules unless to do so would be contrary to any statutory provision. They may do so either on an application by one or both parties or without an application being made. An application for an extension of time may be granted after the time limit has expired. The Registrar will notify the parties when a time limit is varied. (See rule 5.)

2.1.15 The Registrar may reject an application for permission to appeal solely on the ground that it is out of time.

(See paragraphs 1.2.9 and 1.2.16 of Practice Direction 1 for general time limits for permission applications. For special cases see paragraph 2.1.16 and for notices of appeal see paragraph 4.3.1 of Practice Direction 4.)

Special cases: contempt of court and leapfrog appeals

2.1.16 An application for permission to appeal in   **4–68**

(a) a case involving civil contempt of court must be filed within 14 days, beginning with the date of the refusal of permission by the court below; and

(b) a "leapfrog appeal" from the High Court must be filed within one month from the date on which the High Court judge grants a certificate under section 12 of the Administration of Justice Act 1969.

Form of application for permission to appeal and notice of appeal

2.1.17 The form of an application for permission to appeal is dealt **4–69** with in paragraphs 3.1.1–3.1.5 of Practice Direction 3. The form of a notice of appeal is dealt with in paragraphs 4.2.1–4.2.4 of Practice Direction 4.

Case title

2.1.18 Applications for permission to appeal and appeals carry the same title as in the court below, except that the parties are described as appellant(s) and respondent(s). For reference purposes, the names of parties to the original proceedings who are not parties to the appeal should nevertheless be included in the title: their names should be enclosed in square brackets. The names of all parties should be given in the same sequence as in the title used in the court below.

2.1.19 Applications for permission to appeal and appeals in which trustees, executors etc. are parties are titled in the short form, for example *Trustees of John Black's Charity (Respondents) v. White (Appellant)*.

2.1.20 In any application or appeal concerning children or where in the court below the title used has been such as to conceal the identity of one or more parties to the proceedings, this fact should be clearly drawn to the attention of the Registry at the time of filing, so that the title adopted in the Supreme Court can take account of the need for anonymity. Applications involving children are normally given a title in the form B (Children).

2.1.21 In case titles involving the Crown, the abbreviation "R" meaning "Regina" is used. "R" is always given first. So case titles using this abbreviation take the form R v Jones (Appellant) or R v Jones (Respondent) (as the case may be) or R (on the application of Jones) (Appellant) v Secretary of State for the Home Department (Respondent).

2.1.22 Apart from the above, Latin is not used in case titles.

Service

4–70   **2.1.23** Documents such as applications for permission to appeal and notices of appeal must be served by the party or their solicitors on the respondents or their solicitors, in accordance with rule 6 or with any relevant statutory provisions,[1] before they are filed. A party or his solicitor will be taken to have consented to a particular method of service if, for example, their writing paper includes a fax number or a numbered box at a document exchange unless they have indicated in writing that they are not willing to accept service by that particular method.

2.1.24 A certificate of service which complies with rule 6(4) by giving details of the persons served, the method of service used and the date on which the document was served personally, posted, delivered to the document exchange or sent electronically, must be included either in the original document and signed or a separate certificate of service must be provided.

Supporting documents

4–71   **2.1.25** See paragraph 3.1.7 of Practice Direction 3 for the documents which must be filed with an application for permission to appeal.

2.1.26 See paragraph 4.3.2 of Practice Direction 4 for the documents which must be filed with a notice of appeal.

2.1.27 See paragraph 7.1.3 of Practice Direction 7 for guidance on documents which may need to be filed in support of an application.

Fees

4–72   **2.1.28** The fees which are payable in the Supreme Court are prescribed by an order made under section 52 of the Act and rule 45 allows the Registrar to refuse to accept a document or to allow a party to take any step unless the relevant fee is paid.

---

[1] The Companies Act 1985 and the Companies Act 2006 provide for the method of service on companies and limited liability partnerships.

2.1.29 In circumstances where a party would suffer financial hardship by the payment of fees, the requirement to pay fees may be waived (see the Supreme Court Fees Order 2009, S.I. 2009/2131). Any request for fee remission should be made to the Registrar, supported by evidence of the party's means. The Registrar may then grant full or part remission of the relevant fee. Remission of fees is usually granted where a remission of fees has been granted in the court below.

2.1.30 For the fees payable in the Supreme Court see Annex 2 to Practice Direction 7.

2.1.31 Any fees paid are not refunded, even if it is decided that an application for permission to appeal is inadmissible or if an application or other proceeding is withdrawn.

PRACTICE DIRECTION 3—APPLICATIONS FOR PERMISSION TO APPEAL

Form of application for permission to appeal

3.1.1 Applications for permission to appeal are considered by an **4–73** Appeal Panel, consisting of at least three Justices. Applications are generally decided on paper, without a hearing, and it is essential that the application is in the correct form.

3.1.2 An application for permission to appeal must be produced in Form 1 on A4 paper, securely bound on the left, using both sides of the paper. (See Annex 1 to Practice Direction 7 for Form 1.) The application should set out briefly the facts and points of law and include a summary of the reasons why permission should be granted. Applications which are not legible or which are not produced in the required form will not be accepted. Parties may consult the Registry at any stage of preparation of the application, and may submit applications in draft for approval. Amendments to applications are allowed where the Registrar is satisfied that this will assist the Appeal Panel and will not unfairly prejudice the respondents or cause undue delay. Any amendments must be served on the respondents (see paragraph 3.1.6).

3.1.3 If an application for permission to appeal

(a) asks the Supreme Court to depart from one of its own decisions or from one made by the House of Lords;

(b) seeks a declaration of incompatibility under the Human Rights Act 1998; or

(c) seeks a reference to the Court of Justice of the European Communities,

this should be stated clearly in the application and full details must be given.

3.1.4 An application for permission to appeal must be signed by the appellant or his agent.

3.1.5 The application for permission to appeal should include the neutral citation of the judgment appealed against, the references of any law report in the courts below, and subject matter catchwords for indexing (whether or not the case has been reported). This can conveniently be done in Section 9 of Form 1.

Service

3.1.6 A copy of the application (and any amendment to it) must be served on the respondents or their solicitors, and on any person who was an intervener in the court below in accordance with rule 6, before it is filed. A certificate of service (giving the full name and address of the respondents or their solicitors) must be included in the original application and signed or a separate certificate of service must be provided. See rule 6(4) and paragraph 2.1.24 of Practice Direction 2. Additional supporting documents other than those set out in paragraphs 3.1.7 and 3.2.1 (additional papers) are not normally accepted.

Supporting documents

3.1.7 In order to comply with rule 14(1), the original application together with 3 copies must be filed at the Registry together with the prescribed fee, a copy of the order appealed against and, if separate, a copy of the order of the court below refusing permission to appeal. For the relevant fee see Annex 2 to Practice Direction 7. If the substantive order appealed against is not immediately available, the application should be filed within the required time limit, and the order filed as soon it is available. For the relevant time limits for filing an application for permission to appeal see paragraphs 2.1.12–2.1.16 of Practice Direction 2. Where an appellant is unable to file his permission application within the relevant time limit, an application for an extension of time must be made in Section 7 of Form 1. The respondent's views on the extension of time should be sought and, if possible, those views should be communicated to the Registry. The application for an extension of time will be referred to the Registrar and, if it is granted, the appellant must then comply with rule 14 and paragraph 3.2.1. When an application for permission to appeal is filed, it will be sealed by a member of staff in the Registry: rule 7(4).

Objections by respondents

4–74   **3.1.8** Each "respondent who wishes to object to the application must, within 14 days after service, file notice of objection" in Form 3 together with a certificate of service: rule 13(1). (See Annex 1 to Practice Direction 7 for Form 3.) The original notice together with 3 copies must be filed at the Registry together with the prescribed fee. For the relevant fee see Annex 2 to Practice Direction 7. When a notice of objection is filed, it will be sealed by a member of staff in the Registry: rule 7(4).

3.1.9 Before filing, a respondent must serve a copy of the notice on the appellant, any other respondent and any person who was an intervener in the court below: rule 13(2). A certificate of service (giving the full name and address of the persons served) must be included in Form 3 and signed or a separate certificate of service must be provided. See rule 6(4) and paragraph 2.1.24 of Practice Direction 2.

3.1.10 A respondent who files notice will be permitted to participate in the application and will be given notice of its progress: rule 13(3). An order for costs will not be made in favour of a respondent who has not given notice.

Additional papers

3.2.1 To comply with rule 14(2), the following additional papers **4–75** must be filed by the appellant for use by the Appeal Panel within 7 days after the filing of the application:

(a) **four** copies of the application;

(b) **four** copies of the order appealed against;

(c) if separate from the order at (b) above, **four** copies of the order of the court below refusing permission to appeal to the Supreme Court;

(d) **four** copies of the official transcript of the judgment of the court below;[1]

(e) **four** copies of the final order(s) of all other courts below;

(f) **four** copies of the official transcript of the final judgment(s) of all other courts below;

(g) **four** copies of any unreported judgment(s) cited in the application or judgment of a court below;

(h) **four** copies of a document which sets out the history of the proceedings. (See rule 14.)

No other papers are required, and documents other than those listed above will not be accepted unless requested by the Appeal Panel. Documents which are not clearly legible or which are not in the required style or form (see paragraph 3.1.2) will not be accepted.

3.2.2 The additional papers must be presented in the form required by paragraph 5.1.2 of Practice Direction 5.

3.2.3 Where the required papers are not filed within 8 weeks after the filing of the application and no good reason is given for the delay, the Registrar may

(a) refer the application to an Appeal Panel without the required accompanying papers;

(b) dismiss the application, or

(c) give such other directions as appear appropriate under rule 8.

Consideration on paper

3.3.1 The Appeal Panel decides first whether an application for **4–76** permission to appeal is admissible (that is, whether the Court has jurisdiction to entertain an appeal). The Court's jurisdiction is summarised in section 2 of Practice Direction 1. If the Appeal Panel determines that an application is inadmissible, it will refuse permission on that ground alone and not consider the content of the application. The Appeal Panel gives a reason for deciding that the application is inadmissible.

3.3.2 If the Appeal Panel decides that an application is admissible, rule 16 provides that the Panel may then:

(a) refuse permission (see paragraph 3.3.4);

(b) give permission (see paragraph 3.3.5);

(c) invite the parties to file written submissions as to the grant of

---

[1] If the judgment has been published in a report which is ordinarily received in court, copies of the report may be filed instead of transcripts. Transcripts of judgments marked "in draft" are not accepted without certification by the relevant court that the copy is the final version of the judgment.

permission on terms whether as to costs or otherwise (see paragraphs 3.3.6 – 3.3.11);

(d) direct an oral hearing (see paragraphs 3.3.12–3.3.16).

3.3.3 Permission to appeal is granted for applications that, in the opinion of the Appeal Panel, raise an arguable point of law of general public importance which ought to be considered by the Supreme Court at that time, bearing in mind that the matter will already have been the subject of judicial decision and may have already been reviewed on appeal. An application which in the opinion of the Appeal Panel does not raise such a point of law is refused on that ground. The Appeal Panel gives brief reasons for refusing permission to appeal.

Permission refused

3.3.4 If the Appeal Panel decides that permission should be refused, the parties are notified that the application is refused and they are sent a copy of the order sealed by the Registrar which records the Panel's decision.

Permission given outright

3.3.5 If the Appeal Panel decides that an appeal should be entertained without further proceedings, it grants permission outright and the parties are sent a copy of the order sealed by the Registrar which records the Panel's decision.

Respondents' objections

3.3.6 Respondents may submit written objections giving their reasons why permission to appeal should be refused when they file notice of objection in accordance with rule 13. Exceptionally a respondent could seek to file more fully reasoned objections or might be asked to do so by the Appeal Panel. In such circumstances further objections should be filed

(a) within 14 days of any invitation by the Appeal Panel to do so; or

(b) within 14 days of an application for permission to appeal being referred for an oral hearing.

3.3.7 Respondents' objections should set out briefly the reasons why the application should be refused or make submissions as to the terms upon which permission should be granted (for example, on costs). One original and 4 copies of the respondents' written objections must be filed in the Registry. The objections must be produced on A4 paper, securely fastened, using both sides of the paper.

3.3.8 A copy of the respondents' objections should be sent to the solicitors for the other parties. In certain circumstances the Appeal Panel may invite further submissions from the appellant in the light of the respondents' objections, but appellants do not have a right to comment on respondents' objections. Where the Appeal Panel does not require further submissions to make its decision, the parties are sent a copy of the order sealed by the Registrar which records the Panel's decision. Where the Appeal Panel proposes terms for granting permission, paragraph 3.3.11 applies.

3.3.9 For the costs of respondents' objections, see paragraph 3.5.

3.3.10 Respondents who are unable to meet the deadlines set out in paragraph 3.3.6 must write to the Registrar requesting an extension of time for filing their written objections.

Permission given on terms

3.3.11 If the Appeal Panel is considering granting permission to appeal on terms:

(a) the Panel proposes the terms and the parties have the right to make submissions on the proposed terms within 14 days of the date of the Panel's proposal;

(b) the Panel will then decide whether to grant permission (unconditionally or on terms);

(c) prospective appellants who are granted permission to appeal subject to terms that they are unwilling to accept may decline to pursue the appeal;

(d) in an application for permission to appeal under the "leapfrog" procedure (see paragraph 3.6.1), prospective appellants who decline to proceed on the basis of the terms proposed by the Appeal Panel may instead pursue an appeal to the Court of Appeal in the usual way[1]

Application referred for oral hearing

3.3.12 In all cases where further argument is required, an application for permission to appeal is referred for an oral hearing.

3.3.13 Respondents may seek to file more fully reasoned objections within 14 days of being informed that the application has been referred for a hearing (see paragraph 3.3.6(b)).

3.3.14 When an application is referred for an oral hearing, the appellant and all respondents who have filed notice of objection under rule 13 are notified of the date of the hearing before the Appeal Panel. Parties may be heard before the Appeal Panel by counsel, by solicitor, or in person. If counsel are briefed, solicitors should ensure that the Registry is notified of their names. Only a junior counsel's fee is allowed on assessment (see paragraph 3.4.8).

3.3.15 Oral permission hearings usually last for 30 minutes. The panel will normally give its decision orally at the end of the hearing.

3.3.16 All the parties are sent a copy of the order sealed by the Registrar which records the Panel's decision.

Interventions in applications for permission to appeal

3.3.17 Any person (and in particular (i) any official body or non– **4–77** governmental organization who seeks to make submissions in the public interest or (ii) any person with an interest in proceedings by way of judicial review) may make written submissions to the Court in support of an application for permission to appeal. See rule 15. Before the submissions are filed, a copy must be served on

(a) the appellant,

(b) every respondent and

---

[1] *Ceredigion County Council v Jones and others* [2007] UKHL 24.

(c) any person who was an intervener in the court below.

Four copies of the submissions must be filed together with a certificate of service.

3.3.18 Any submissions which are made are referred to the panel of Justices which considers the application for permission to appeal. Where the panel decides to take the submissions into account and grants permission to appeal, the person making them will be notified. If permission to appeal is granted, a formal application must be made under rule 26 if the intervener wishes to intervene in the appeal. See Practice Direction 7 – Applications.

Sealed Orders

3.3.19 The appellant, any recognised intervener and all respondents who have filed notice of objection under rule 13 are sent a copy of the order sealed by the Registrar which records the Panel's decision.

Filing notice to proceed

4–78　**3.4.1** Where permission to appeal is granted by the Supreme Court, the application for permission to appeal will stand as the notice of appeal and the grounds of appeal are limited to those on which permission has been granted. The appellant must, within 14 days of the grant by the Court of permission to appeal, file notice under rule 18 that he wishes to proceed with his appeal. When the notice is filed, the application for permission to appeal will re–sealed and, in order to comply with rule 18(2), the appellant must then serve a copy on each respondent, on any recognised intervener (that is, an intervener whose submissions have been taken into account under rule 15) and on any person who was an intervener in the court below and file the original and 3 copies together with a certificate of service. See rule 6(4) and paragraph 2.1.24 of Practice Direction 2.

3.4.2 Where an appellant is unable to file notice under rule 18 within the time limit of 14 days, a formal application for an extension of time must be made in Form 2: see paragraph 7.1 of Practice Direction 7 for applications. The respondent's views on the extension of time should be sought and, if possible, those views should be communicated to the Registry. The application will be referred to the Registrar and, if it is granted, the appellant must then comply with rule 18(2) and paragraph 3.4.1.

Expedition

3.4.3 Once the required papers are filed at the Registry (under paragraph 3.2.1), the procedure described above is normally completed within eight sitting weeks (excluding any oral hearing). In cases involving liberty of the subject, urgent medical intervention or the well–being of children (see paragraph 3.4.4), a request for expedition may be made in writing to the Registrar. See rule 31.

Expedited hearing of proceedings under the Hague Convention etc

4–79　**3.4.4** The *Convention on the Civil Aspects of International Child Abduction* (the Hague Convention) deals with the wrongful removal and retention of children from their habitual country of residence. The Revised Brussels II Regulation also deals with these matters.[1] In the Supreme Court an expedited timetable applies. The parties must therefore inform the Registrar that the proceedings fall under the Convention or Regulation. The Court normally gives judgment within six weeks of the commencement of proceedings but this can only be achieved with the fullest co-operation of the parties.

3.4.5 The following timetable may be taken as a general guideline:

(a) an application for permission to appeal is decided by an Appeal Panel within 7 days of being filed;

(b) an appeal is heard within 21 days of a decision to grant permission to appeal;

(c) the result of the appeal is given immediately after the end of the hearing with reasons given later or, if judgment is reserved, the result of the appeal and the reasons are given within 2 weeks of the end of the hearing.

3.4.6 In order to achieve the above timetable the Court will set aside or vary the time limits and practice directions that normally apply to applications and appeals.

3.4.7 Abridged procedures and special rules for the production of documents are applied to meet the circumstances of each application and appeal. The following timetable for the production of documents is therefore indicative only:

(a) the statement of facts and issues is filed within 7 days of the decision to grant permission to appeal;

(b) the appellant's case is filed within 10 days of the decision to grant permission to appeal (or, if the relevant day falls on a Saturday or Sunday, the following Monday);

(c) the respondent's case is filed within 14 days of the decision to grant permission to appeal;

(d) the core volumes (if required) and the volumes of authorities are filed within 17 days of the decision to grant permission to appeal (or, if the relevant day falls on a Saturday or Sunday, the following Monday).

Counsel

3.4.8 Appellants and respondents to an application for permission **4–80** to appeal may instruct leading or junior counsel, but on any assessment of costs only junior counsel's fees will be allowed for any stage of an application for permission to appeal, even if a public funding or legal aid certificate provides for leading counsel. The only exception to this practice is where leading counsel who conducted the case in the court below are instructed by the Legal Services Commission or legal aid authorities to advise on the merits of an appeal.

Costs

3.5.1 Where an unsuccessful application for permission to appeal is **4–81** determined without an oral hearing, costs may be awarded as follows:

[1] Council Regulation (EC) No 2201/2003.

(a) to a publicly funded or legally aided appellant, reasonable costs incurred in preparing papers for the Appeal Panel;

(b) to a publicly funded or legally aided respondent, only those costs necessarily incurred in attending the client, attending the appellant's agents, considering the application for permission to appeal, filing notice of objection under rule 13 and, where applicable, preparing respondent's objections to the application;

(c) to an unassisted respondent where the appellant is publicly funded or legally aided, payment out of the Community Legal Service Fund (pursuant to section 11 of the Access to Justice Act 1999[1]) of costs as specified at (b) above;

(d) to a respondent where neither party is publicly funded or legally aided, costs as specified at (b) above.

3.5.2 Where costs are sought under (c) or (d) above, the application may be made by letter addressed to the Registrar or may be included in a bill of costs filed in the Registry conditional upon the application being granted.

3.5.3 Where an application for permission to appeal is referred for an oral hearing and is dismissed, application for costs must be made by the respondent at the end of the hearing. No order for costs will be made unless a request is made at that time.

3.5.4 Where permission to appeal is granted, costs of the application for permission become costs in the appeal.

3.5.5 The reasonable costs of objecting to an unsuccessful application for permission to appeal will normally be awarded to the respondent, subject to any order for costs made by the Appeal Panel. If permission to appeal is granted, the costs of respondent's objections become costs in the appeal.

3.5.6 Bills of costs must be filed within three months from the date of the decision of the Appeal Panel or from the date on which an application for permission to appeal is withdrawn in accordance with rule 34. For the withdrawal of an application see paragraph 8.16.2 of Practice Direction 8. If an extension of the three month period is desired, application must be made in writing to the Registrar and copies of all such correspondence sent to all interested parties. In deciding whether to grant an application for an extension of time made after the expiry of the three month period, the Registrar takes into account the circumstances set out in paragraph 6 of Practice Direction 13.

3.5.7 For the fees payable on the assessment of a bill of costs, see Annex 2 to Practice Direction 7. For the assessment of costs, see rules 48–53 and Practice Direction 13. For security for costs see paragraph 4.7.1 of Practice Direction 4.

Withdrawal of application for permission to appeal

3.5.8 This is dealt with in paragraph 8.16.2 of Practice Direction 8.

---

[1] Also pursuant to r 5(2) Community Legal Service (Cost Protection) Regulations 2000 and in accordance with the procedural requirements of rr 9, 10 Community Legal Service (Costs) Regulations 2000 (as amended); or Legal Aid Act 1988 s 18; or in Scotland pursuant to Legal Aid (Scotland) Act 1986 s 19; or in Northern Ireland pursuant to Legal Aid Advice and Assistance (N.I.) Order 1981 Article 16.

Leapfrog appeals

3.6.1 In certain cases an appeal lies direct from the High Court in **4–82** England and Wales or in Northern Ireland to the Supreme Court see paragraph 1.2.17 of Practice Direction 1. A certificate of the High Court must first be obtained and the permission of the Supreme Court then given before the appeal may proceed.[1] Such appeals are known as "leapfrog" appeals.

Judge's certificate

3.6.2 An application for a certificate may be made by any of the parties to any civil proceedings in the High Court before a single judge or before a Divisional Court. The application should be made immediately after the trial judge gives judgment in the proceedings or, if no such application is made, within 14 days from the date on which judgment was given.

3.6.3 The judge may grant a certificate under section 12 of the Administration of Justice Act 1969 if he is satisfied (a) that the relevant conditions are fulfilled; (b) that a sufficient case has been made to justify taking to the Supreme Court an application for permission; and (c) that all the parties to the proceedings consent to the grant of a certificate.

3.6.4 The relevant conditions are that a point of law of general public importance is involved in the judge's decision, and that that point of law either (a) relates wholly or mainly to the construction of an enactment or of a statutory instrument and has been fully argued in the proceedings and fully considered in the judgment of the judge in the proceedings[2], or (b) is one in respect of which the judge is bound by a decision of the Court of Appeal, the House of Lords or the Supreme Court in previous proceedings and was fully considered in the judgments of the Court of Appeal, the House of Lords or Supreme Court in those previous proceedings.[3]

3.6.5 The judge may not grant a certificate in cases where no appeal would lie (with or without permission) from the judge's decision to the Court of Appeal, apart from the provisions of the Administration of Justice Act 1969. Similarly, a certificate may not be granted where no appeal would lie (with or without permission) from the Court of Appeal on an appeal from the judge's decision. Where no appeal would lie from the judge's decision to the Court of Appeal except with the permission of the judge or the Court of Appeal, no certificate may be granted unless it appears to the judge that it would be a proper case for granting such permission.

3.6.6 No certificate may be given where the judge's decision concerns punishment for contempt of court.

3.6.7 No appeal lies against the grant or refusal of a certificate, but if a certificate is refused the applicant may appeal to the Court of Appeal from the High Court's decision in the normal way, once the time for applying for a certificate has expired.

Application for permission to appeal direct from High Court

3.6.8 At any time within one month from the date on which the

---

[1] Administration of Justice Act 1969 ss 12–15.
[2] Administration of Justice Act 1969 s 12(3)(a).
[3] Administration of Justice Act 1969 s 12(3)(b).

judge grants the certificate, or such extended time as the Supreme Court may allow, any of the parties may apply to the Supreme Court for permission to appeal.[1] Application is made in accordance with paragraph 3.1 of this Practice Direction. If any party to the proceedings in the High Court is not a party to the application, the application must be endorsed with a certificate of service on that party.

3.6.9 One copy of the judge's certificate must be filed with the application. The application should indicate whether the judge's certificate was granted under section 12(3)(a) or section 12(3)(b) of the Administration of Justice Act 1969.

3.6.10 The following additional papers for use by the Appeal Panel must be filed within seven days of the filing of the application:

  (a) **four** additional copies of the application;
  (b) **four** copies of the order of the High Court;
  (c) **four** additional copies of the High Court's certificate, if not contained in the order; and
  (d) **four** copies of the transcript of the judgment of the High Court.[2]

These additional papers must be presented in the form required by paragraph 5.1.2 of Practice Direction 5. No other papers are required, and documents other than those listed above will not be normally accepted.

3.6.11 Applications for permission to appeal are normally determined by an Appeal Panel without a hearing.

3.6.12 In applications where the certificate has been granted by the judge under section 12(3)(a) of the 1969 Act, the Appeal Panel only grants permission to appeal where:

  (a) there is an urgent need to obtain an authoritative interpretation by the Supreme Court;
  (b) the case is one in which permission to appeal to the Supreme Court would have been granted if it had not been brought direct to the Supreme Court and the judgment had been that of the Court of Appeal; and
  (c) it does not appear likely that any additional assistance could be derived from a judgment of the Court of Appeal.

Similarly, where the certificate has been granted under section 12(3)(b) of the 1969 Act, the Appeal Panel only grants permission where:

  (i) the case is not distinguishable from the case that was the subject of the previous decision;
  (ii) the previous case was fully considered in a previous judgment after argument that appears to have been adequate; and
  (iii) the case is one in which permission to appeal to the Supreme Court would have been granted if it had not been brought direct to the Supreme Court and the judgment had been that of the Court of Appeal.

---

[1] Administration of Justice Act 1969 s 13(1).
[2] If the judgment has been published in a report which is ordinarily received in court, copies of the report may be filed in lieu of transcripts. Transcripts of judgments marked as in draft are not acceptable without certification by the relevant court that the copy is the final version of the judgment.

3.6.13 The appellant and all respondents who have filed notice of objection under rule 13 are sent a copy of the order sealed by the Registrar which records the Panel's decision.

Extensions of time

3.6.14 Where an appellant is unable to file his application within the time limit, an application for an extension of time must be made in Section 7 of Form 1. The respondent's views on the extension of time should be sought and, if possible, those views should be communicated to the Registry. The application for an extension of time will be referred to the Registrar or an Appeal Panel and, if it is granted, the appellant must then comply with rule 14 and paragraph 3.2.1.

Proceedings after permission to appeal is granted or refused

3.6.15 If the Appeal Panel grants permission to appeal without terms, no appeal from the decision of the judge lies to the Court of Appeal but only to the Supreme Court. The appeal is brought in accordance with Practice Direction 4 and the usual requirements apply. However, an appeal does lie to the Court of Appeal from the judge's decision (i) where no application is made to the Supreme Court within the one month period after the judge has granted the certificate; or (ii) where permission to appeal direct to the Supreme Court has been refused by the Appeal Panel.

3.6.16 Prospective appellants who decline to proceed on the basis of the terms proposed by the Appeal Panel may instead pursue an appeal to the Court of Appeal in the usual way.[1]

Habeas corpus

3.6.17 Proceedings for a writ of habeas corpus in England and **4–83** Wales are subject to the procedures governing criminal appeals to the Supreme Court. These are set out in Practice Direction 12. In proceedings for a writ of habeas corpus, an appeal lies from the Queen's Bench Divisional Court to the Supreme Court at the instance of the defendant or prosecutor with the permission either of the Divisional Court or the Supreme Court. No certificate stating a point of law of general public importance is required.[2]

3.6.18 Such an application is normally determined by an Appeal Panel without an oral hearing. The appellant and all respondents who have filed notice of objection under rule 13 are sent a copy of the order sealed by the Registrar which records the Panel's decision.

PRACTICE DIRECTION 4—NOTICE OF APPEAL

General note

4.1.1 The practice is that where permission to appeal is granted by **4–84** the Supreme Court, the application for permission to appeal will stand as the notice of appeal and the grounds of appeal are limited

---

[1] *Ceredigion County Council v Jones and others* [2007] UKHL 24.
[2] Administration of Justice Act 1969 ss 1, 15(3); Judicature (Northern Ireland) Act 1978, s 45(3).

to those on which permission has been granted: rule 18(1). The appellant must, within 14 days of the grant by the Court of permission to appeal, file notice under rule 18(1)(c) that he wishes to proceed with his appeal. When the notice is filed, the application for permission to appeal will be re–sealed and the appellant must then serve a copy on each respondent, on any recognized intervener (that is, an intervener whose submissions have been taken into account under rule 15) and on any intervener in the court below; and file the original and 3 copies: rule 18(2). In any other case an appellant must file a notice of appeal in Form 1. (See Annex 1 to Practice Direction 7 for Form 1.

Form of notice of appeal

4–85   **4.2.1** A notice of appeal must be produced in Form 1 on A4 paper, securely bound on the left, using both sides of the paper. (See Annex 1 to Practice Direction 7 for Form 1.) Notices which are not legible or which are not produced in the required form will not be accepted. Parties may consult the Registry at any stage of preparation of the notice, and may submit notices in draft for approval. Amendments to notices are allowed where the Registrar is satisfied that this will assist the Court and will not unfairly prejudice the respondents or cause undue delay. Any amendments must be served on the respondents (see paragraph 4.2.15).

4.2.2 Where permission to appeal has been obtained, the notice of appeal must be signed by the appellants or their agents. In appeals where permission to appeal is not required (for example, in most Scottish appeals) the notice of appeal must be certified as reasonable by two counsel from the relevant jurisdiction and signed by them.[1] In Scottish appeals a certificate of difference of opinion must also be included where appropriate.

4.2.3 The notice of appeal should include the neutral citation of the judgment appealed against, the references of any law report in the courts below, and subject matter catchwords for indexing (whether or not the case has been reported). This can conveniently be done in Section 9 of Form 1.

4.2.4 If an appellant

(a) asks the Supreme Court to depart from one of its own decisions or from one made by the House of Lords;

(b) seeks a declaration of incompatibility under the Human Rights Act 1998; or

(c) seeks a reference to the Court of Justice of the European Communities,

this should be stated clearly in the notice of appeal and full details must be given.

Case title

4.2.5 Notices of appeal to the Supreme Court carry the same title

---

[1] In such cases, counsel's signatures are required even if the appellants propose to conduct the appeal in person. The term "counsel" is defined by rule 2 and, for the purposes of this provision, "counsel" includes an enrolled solicitor with a right of audience in the Supreme Court: see the Solicitors (Scotland) Act 1980, s.25A as amended by the Constitutional Reform Act 2005, Sch 9 para 32).

as in the court below, except that the parties are described as appellant(s) and respondent(s). For reference purposes, the names of parties to the original proceedings who are not parties to the appeal should nevertheless be included in the title: their names should be enclosed in square brackets. The names of all parties should be given in the same sequence as in the title used in the court below.

4.2.6 Notices of appeal in which trustees, executors, etc. are parties are titled in the short form, for example *Trustees of John Black's Charity (Respondents) v. White (Appellant)*.

4.2.7 In any notice of appeal concerning children or where in the court below the title used has been such as to conceal the identity of one or more parties to the proceedings, this fact should be clearly drawn to the attention of the Registry at the time the notice of appeal is filed, so that the title adopted in the Supreme Court can take account of the need for anonymity. Notices of appeal involving children are normally given a title in the form *B (Children)* (see also paragraph 4.2.10).

4.2.8 In case titles involving the Crown, the abbreviation "R" meaning "Regina" is used. "R" is always given first. Case titles using this abbreviation take the form *R v Jones (Appellant)* or *R v Jones (Respondent)* (as the case may be) or *R (on the application of Jones) (Appellant) v Secretary of State for the Home Department (Respondent)*.

4.2.9 Apart from the above, Latin is not used in case titles.

Anonymity and reporting restrictions

4.2.10 In any appeal concerning children, the parties, in addition to considering the case title to be used, should also consider whether it would be appropriate for the Court to make an order under section 39 of the Children and Young Persons Act 1933[1] (reporting restrictions). The parties should always inform the Registry if such an order has been made by a court below. A request for such an order to be made by the Court should be made in writing, preferably on behalf of all parties to the appeal, as soon as possible after the commencement of the appeal and not later than 14 days before the start of the hearing.

4.2.11 Paragraph 4.2.10 also applies to a request for an order under section 4 of the Contempt of Court Act 1981 (contemporary reports of proceedings).

Human Rights Act 1998

4.2.12 Where an appellant or a respondent seeks a declaration of incompatibility or seeks to challenge an act of a public authority under the Human Rights Act 1998, the appropriate section of Form 1 or Form 3 must be completed. Parties should set out briefly in their cases the arguments involved and state whether the point was taken below. The Crown has a right to be joined as a party to the appeal where a question of incompatibility is raised (see rule 40 and Practice Direction 9).

References to the European Court

4.2.13 If an appellant seeks a reference to the Court of Justice of

---

[1] Extended to Scotland by the Children and Young Persons (Scotland) Act 1963, s 57(3).

the European Communities, this should be stated clearly in the notice of appeal and special provisions apply: see rule 42 and Practice Direction 11. The appellant must also notify the Registrar in writing.

London agents
4.2.14 Solicitors outside London may appoint London agents. Those who decide not to do so should note that any additional costs incurred as a result of that decision may be disallowed on any assessment of costs.

Service
4.2.15 A copy of the notice of appeal must be served on the respondents or their solicitors, on any recognized intervener (under rule 15) and on any person who was an intervener in the court below, in accordance with rule 6, before it is filed. A certificate of service (giving the full name and address of the respondents or their agents) must be included in Form 1 and signed or a separate certificate of service must be provided. See rule 6(4) and paragraph 2.1.24 of Practice Direction 2.

Filing a notice of appeal
4–86 **4.3.1** A notice of appeal must be filed in the Registry within 42 days of the date of the order or decision of the court below (see rule 19). However, this time limit may be varied by the Court under rule 5. For other relevant time limits see paragraphs 2.1.12–2.1.16 of Practice Direction 2. When a notice of appeal is filed, it will be sealed by a member of staff in the Registry: rule 7(4).

4.3.2 In order to comply with rule 19(2), the original notice of appeal together with 3 copies must be filed at the Registry with the prescribed fee. For the relevant fee see Annex 2 to Practice Direction 7. If permission to appeal was granted by the court below, a copy of the order appealed from must also be filed and, if separate, a copy of the order granting permission to appeal to the Supreme Court: rule 19(3). If the order appealed from is not immediately available, *"the notice of appeal should be filed without delay and the order filed as soon as it is available"*: rule 19(3).

Filing notice to proceed under rule 18
4–87 **4.3.3** Where under rule 18(1)(a) an application for permission to appeal stands as a notice of appeal, the appellant must, within 14 days of the grant by the Court of permission to appeal, file notice that he wishes to proceed with his appeal. See paragraph 3.4.1 of Practice Direction 3 for filing notice to proceed and paragraph 3.4.2 where an appellant is unable to file notice within the prescribed time limit.

Out of time appeals
4–88 **4.4.1** Where an appellant is unable to file a notice of appeal within the relevant time limit, an application for an extension of time must be made in Section 7 of Form 1. The respondent's views on the extension of time should be sought and, if possible, those views should be communicated to the Registry. The application for an

extension of time will be referred to the Registrar and, if it is granted, the appellant must comply with rule 19 and paragraph 4.3.2.

Fees

4.5.1 For the fees payable on filing a notice of appeal and on filing **4–89** notice to proceed under rule 18 see Annex 2 to Practice Direction 7.

Acknowledgement by respondent

4.6.1 Each *"respondent who intends to participate in the appeal must,* **4–90** *within 14 days after service under rule 18(2)(a) or rule 20, file notice"* in Form 3: rule 21(1). (See Annex 1 to Practice Direction 7 for Form 3.) (Where under rule 18(1)(a) an application for permission to appeal stands as a notice of appeal, the time limit for a respondent to give notice under rule 21 runs from the date on which he is served with a resealed copy of the application.) Form 3 must be produced on A4 paper, securely fastened, using both sides of the paper.

4.6.2 Before filing, a respondent must serve a copy of Form 3 on the appellant, any other respondent and any person who was an intervener in the court below or whose submissions were taken into account under rule 15: see rule 21(2). A certificate of service (giving the full name and address of the persons served) must be included in Form 3 and signed or a separate certificate of service must be provided. See rule 6(4) and paragraph 2.1.24 of Practice Direction 2.

4.6.3 The original notice together with 3 copies must be filed at the Registry with the prescribed fee. For the relevant fee see Annex 2 to Practice Direction 7. When Form 3 is filed, it will be sealed by a member of staff in the Registry: rule 7(4).

4.6.4 A respondent who does not give notice under rule 21 will not be permitted to participate in the appeal and will not be given notice of its progress: rule 21(3). An order for costs will not be made in favour of a respondent who has not given notice.

Security for costs

4.7.1 Orders for security for costs under rule 36 will be sparingly **4–91** made but the Court may, on the application of a respondent, order an appellant to give security for the costs of the appeal and any order for security will determine

  (a) the amount of that security, and

  (b) the manner in which, and the time within which, security must be given.

An application for security should be made in the general form of application, Form 2 (see paragraph 7.1 of, and Annex 1 to, Practice Direction 7). An order made under rule 36 may require payment of the judgment debt (and costs) in the court below instead of, or in addition to, the amount ordered by way of security for costs.

4.7.2 For payment of security see paragraph 8.7.1 of Practice Direction 8.

4.7.3 The following are generally not required to give security for costs:

  (a) an appellant who has been granted a certificate of public funding/legal aid;

  (b) an appellant in an appeal under the Child Abduction and Custody Act 1985;

(c) a Minister or Government department.

4.7.4 No security for costs is required in cross–appeals.

4.7.5 Failure to provide security as required will result in the appeal being struck out by the Registrar although the appellant may apply to reinstate the appeal. See paragraph 7.1 of Practice Direction 7.

Expedition

4–92   **4.8.1** In cases involving liberty of the subject, urgent medical intervention or the well–being of children (see paragraph 3.4.4 of Practice Direction 3), a request for expedition may be made in writing to the Registrar. See rule 31. Wherever possible the views of all parties should be obtained before a request for an expedited hearing is made.

PRACTICE DIRECTION 5—PAPERS FOR THE APPEAL HEARING

General note

4–93   **5.1.1** The Supreme Court does not wish to impose very detailed requirements as to the manner in which documents are presented to the Court for appeal hearings. Parties may if they wish follow the former practice in House of Lords appeals but are not required to do so. Where parties are in any doubt as to how documents should be presented they should consult the Registrar and discuss the practice which should be adopted. The provisions of paragraphs 5.1.2 to 5.1.5 must, however, be strictly complied with.

5.1.2 All documents placed before the Court must be

(a) printed or reproduced (both as to font size and otherwise) so as to be easily legible;

(b) reproduced on paper of A4 size, printed on both sides; and

(c) (unless this causes great difficulty) presented in bound form, properly labelled and indexed.

Documents must be presented in a form which is robust, manageable and not excessively heavy. **Duplication of material must be avoided particularly where two or more appeals are heard together.** See Practice Direction 6 for core volumes, cases and authorities volumes.

5.1.3 The statement of facts and issues must be a single document, drafted initially by the appellant but "submitted to, and agreed with, every respondent before being filing": rule 22(2). The statement must set out the relevant facts and, if the parties cannot agree as to any matter, the statement should make clear what items are disputed. The statement should contain references to every law report of the proceedings below, and should state the duration of the proceedings below. It should be signed by counsel for all parties.

5.1.4 The appendix should contain only such material as is necessary for understanding the legal issues and the argument to be presented to the Supreme Court (see rule 22(2)). It should not contain documents which were not in evidence below, nor should it contain transcripts of the proceedings or evidence below unless they are essential to the legal argument. If necessary, the appendix should be prepared in several parts, only the most essential documents being included in Part 1; only Part 1 will be included in the core volumes. The appendix must be submitted to, and agreed with, every respondent before being filing: rule 22(2).

5.1.5 Documents must be included in the appendix in the following order—

(a) the order appealed against;

(b) if separate from the order at (a) above, the order refusing permission to appeal to the Supreme Court;

(c) the official transcript of the judgment of the court below;[1]

(d) the final order(s) of all other courts below;

(e) the official transcript of the final judgment(s) of all other courts below;

(f) (where they are necessary for understanding the legal issues and the argument) the relevant documents filed in the courts below;

(g) (where they are necessary for understanding the legal issues and the argument) the relevant documents and correspondence relating to the appeal.

All documents must be numbered, and each part of the Appendix must include a list of its contents.

Time limits

5.2.1 The statement of facts and issues and the appendix must be **4–94** filed by the appellant within 112 days after the filing of the notice under rule 18(1)(c) or the filing of the notice of appeal: rule 22(1).

5.2.2 If the appellant is unable to comply with the relevant time limit, an application for an extension of time must be made. (See rule 5 and paragraph 5.2.3.)

Extensions of time for filing the statement of facts and issues and the appendix

5.2.3 Appellants who are unable to complete preparation of the statement and appendix within the time limit may apply to the Registrar for an extension of that time under rule 5. Any application must be made in the general form of application, Form 2, (see Annex 1 to Practice Direction 7) and should explain the reason(s) why an extension is needed.

5.2.4 The Registrar may grant an application for an extension of time, provided that it does not prejudice the preparation for the hearing or its proposed date. The time limits provided by the Rules are, however, generous and applicants for an extension of time must set out in some detail why they are unable to comply with any relevant time limit.

Respondents' consent

5.2.5 Respondents are expected not to withhold unreasonably

---

[1] If the judgment has been published in a report which is ordinarily received in court, copies of the report may be filed instead of transcripts. Transcripts of judgments marked "in draft" are not accepted without certification by the relevant court that the copy is the final version of the judgment.

their consent to an application for an extension of time. Appellants are advised to communicate the views of respondents to the Registry since, if they raise no objection, the application may be dealt with on paper.

Filing the Statement and Appendix

4–95 **5.2.6** When the statement and appendix are ready,

(a) **the original and 7 copies** of the statement,

(b) **eight copies** of Part 1 of the appendix and

(c) **10 copies** of Parts 2 etc. (if any)

must be filed at the Registry with the prescribed fee. (For the fee payable, see Annex 2 to Practice Direction 7.)

5.2.7 Within 7 days after filing the statement and the appendix, the parties must comply with rule 22(3) by notifying the Registrar that the appeal is ready to list and providing a time estimate (see paragraph 6.2.1 of Practice Direction 6).

PRACTICE DIRECTION 6—THE APPEAL HEARING

General note

4–96 **6.1.1** The Supreme Court does not wish to impose very detailed requirements as to the manner in which documents are presented to the Court for appeal hearings. Parties may if they wish follow the former practice in House of Lords appeals but are not required to do so. Where parties are in any doubt as to how documents should be presented they should consult the Registrar and discuss the practice which should be adopted. The provisions of paragraph 6.1.2 must, however, be strictly complied with.

6.1.2 All documents placed before the Court must be

(a) reproduced or printed (both as to font size and otherwise) so as to be easily legible;

(b) reproduced on paper of A4 size, printed on both sides; and

(c) (unless this causes great difficulty) presented in bound form, properly labelled and indexed.

Documents must be presented in a form which is robust, manageable and not excessively heavy. Duplication of material must be avoided particularly where two or more appeals are heard together. See Practice Direction 5 for the statement of facts and issues and the appendix.

Fixing the hearing date

4–97 **6.2.1** Within 7 days after the filing of the statement of facts and issues and the appendix (see paragraphs 5.1.3 and 5.2.1 of Practice Direction 5), the parties must notify the Registrar that the appeal is ready to list and...specify the number of hours that their respective counsel estimate to be necessary for their oral submissions: rule 22(3). Time estimates must be as accurate as possible since, subject to the Court's discretion, they are used as the basis for arranging the Court's list. The sittings of the Court (or the 'law terms') are four in each year, that is to say:

(a) the Michaelmas sittings which begin on 1 October and end on 21 December;

(b) the Hilary sittings which begin on 11 January and end on the Wednesday before Easter Sunday;

(c) the Easter sittings which begin on the second Tuesday after Easter Sunday and end on the Friday before the spring holiday; and

(d) the Trinity sittings which begin on the second Tuesday after the spring holiday and end on 31 July.

The 'spring holiday' means the bank holiday falling on the last Monday in May or any day appointed instead of that day under section 1(2) of the Banking and Financial Dealings Act 1971.

6.2.2 Subject to any directions by the Court before or at the hearing, counsel are expected to confine their submissions to the time indicated in their estimates. The Registrar **must** be informed at once of any alteration to the original estimate. Not more than two days are normally allowed for the hearing of an appeal and appeals are listed for hearing on this basis. Estimates of more than two days must be fully explained in writing to the Registrar and may be referred to the presiding Justice.

6.2.3 The Registrar will subsequently inform the parties of the date fixed for the hearing. The appellant and every respondent (and any intervener or advocate to the Court) "must then sequentially exchange their respective written cases and file them", and every respondent (and any intervener or advocate to the Court) must provide copies of their respective written cases to the appellant for the preparation of the core volumes: rule 22(4). (See paragraph 6.3 for cases).

Requests for expedition

6.2.4 Any request for an expedited hearing should be made to the Registrar. Wherever possible the views of all parties should be obtained before a request is made. **4–98**

Directions hearings

6.2.5 Where it considers it to be appropriate, the Court may decide that a directions hearing should be held. A directions hearing will normally be held before 3 Justices. Any request for a directions hearing should be made to the Registrar. Wherever possible the views of all parties should be obtained before a request is made. **4–99**

Appellants' and Respondents' cases

6.3.1 The case is the statement of a party's argument in the appeal. The Court does not prescribe any maximum length but the Court favours brevity and a case should be a concise summary of the submissions to be developed. **4–100**

6.3.2 The case should be confined to the heads of argument that counsel propose to submit at the hearing and omit material contained in the statement of facts and issues (see paragraph 5.1.3 of Practice Direction 5).

6.3.3 If either party is abandoning any point taken in the courts below, this should be made plain in their case. If they intend to apply in the course of the hearing for permission to introduce a new point not taken below, this should also be indicated in their case and the Registrar informed. If such a point involves the introduction of fresh evidence, application for permission must be made either in the case or by filing an application for permission to adduce the fresh evidence (see paragraph 7.1 of Practice Direction 7 for applications).

6.3.4 If a party intends to invite the Court to depart from one of its own decisions or from a decision of the House of Lords, this intention must be clearly stated in a separate paragraph of their case, to which special attention must be drawn. A respondent who wishes to contend that a decision of the court below should be affirmed on grounds other than those relied on by that court must set out the grounds for that contention in their case.

6.3.5 Transcripts of unreported judgments should only be cited when they contain an authoritative statement of a relevant principle of law not to be found in a reported case or when they are necessary for the understanding of some other authority.

6.3.6 All cases must conclude with a numbered summary of the reasons upon which the argument is founded, and must bear the signature of at least one counsel for each party to the appeal who has appeared in the court below or who will be briefed for the hearing before the Court.

6.3.7 The filing of a case carries the right to be heard by two counsel. The fees of two counsel only for any party are allowed on assessment unless the Court orders otherwise on application at the hearing. The Costs Officers have no discretion to allow fees for more than two counsel unless the Court has, on application at the hearing, made such an order: see paragraph 16.5 of Practice Direction 13.

Separate cases

6.3.8 Parties whose interests in the appeal are passive (for example, stakeholders, trustees, executors, etc.) are not required to file a separate case but should ensure that their position is explained in one of the cases filed.

Filing and exchange of cases

6.3.9 No later than five weeks before the proposed date of the hearing, the appellants must file at the Registry the original and 7 **copies** of their case and serve it on the respondents.

6.3.10 No later than 3 weeks before the proposed date of the hearing, the respondents must serve on the appellants a copy of their case in response and file at the Registry the original and 7 **copies** of their case, as must any other party filing a case (for example, an intervener or advocate to the court).

6.3.11 The number of copies of cases exchanged should be enough to meet the requirements of counsel and solicitors and should not usually exceed eight. To enable the appellants to file the core volumes, the respondents and any other party who has filed a case must also provide the appellants with **10** further copies of their case.

6.3.12 Following the exchange of cases, further arguments by either side may not without permission be submitted in advance of the hearing.

Form of cases

6.3.13 Cases must be produced on A4 paper, securely bound on the left, using both sides of the paper with:

(a) numbered paragraphs; and

(b) signatures of counsel at the end, above their printed names.

The core volumes and authorities volumes

6.4.1 As soon as the parties' cases have been exchanged and in any **4–101** event not later than 14 days before the date fixed for the hearing the appellant must file core volumes in accordance with paragraph 6.4.3 and (if necessary) additional volumes containing further parts of the appendix.

6.4.2 Copies of all authorities that may be referred to during the hearing must be filed by the appellant at the same time as the core volumes. See paragraph 6.5.1–6.5.8.

6.4.3 In addition to the documents already filed, the appellant must file 10 bound core volumes. Each core volume must contain in the following order:

(a) Form 1—a copy of the notice of appeal or the re–sealed application for permission to appeal;

(b) notice of cross–appeal (if any);

(c) statement of facts and issues;

(d) appellants' and respondents' cases, with cross–references to the Appendix and authorities volume(s);

(e) case of the advocate to the court or intervener, if any;

(f) Part 1 of the appendix; and

(g) index to the authorities volume(s).

Form of core volumes

6.4.4 The core volumes:

(a) should be bound, preferably with plastic comb binding and with blue (or, for criminal appeals, red) card covers;

(b) should include tabs for each of the documents set out in paragraph 6.4.3, preferably with the name of the document on the tab;

(c) should show on the front cover a list of the contents and the names and addresses of the solicitors for all parties;

(d) must indicate (by e.g. a label (printed in landscape) attached to the plastic spine) the volume number (in roman numerals) and the short title of the appeal.

For volumes in electronic form see Practice Direction 14.

Provision of documents

6.4.5 To enable the appellants to produce the core volumes, the respondents must provide the appellants' solicitors with a further 10 copies of the respondents' case in addition to the cases already exchanged.

6.4.6 Respondents should arrange with the appellants' solicitors for the delivery to them of such core volumes as the respondents' counsel and agents require.

Authorities

6.5.1 A joint set of authorities, jointly produced, should be **4–102** complied for the appeal. Ten copies of the joint set of authorities must be filed at the same time as the core volumes. The appellants have the initial responsibility for producing the authorities volumes and for filing them at the Registry but, to enable the appellants to file the volumes, the respondents must provide the appellants with 10 copies of any authorities which the respondents require but which the appellants do not, or arrange with the appellants for their photocopying. Respondents should arrange with the appellants for the delivery to them of such authorities volumes as the respondents' counsel and agents require. **Supplemental or additional volumes of authorities should be avoided.**

Form and content of authorities volumes

6.5.2 The authorities should be collected together into one or more volumes or folders. The volumes of authorities should have a separate index and authorities should appear in alphabetical order. Authorities should (where appropriate) be further divided into the categories: domestic, Strasbourg, foreign and academic material. The volumes of authorities should

(a) be A4 size reproduced as one page per view (with any authorities smaller than A4 being enlarged);

(b) separate each authority by numbered dividers;

(c) contain an index to that volume; the first volume must also contain an index to all the volumes;

(d) be numbered consecutively on the cover and spine with numerals at least point 72 in size for swift identification of different volumes during the hearing;

(e) have printed clearly on the front cover the title of the appeal and the names of the solicitors for all parties;

(f) have affixed to the spine a sticker indicating clearly the volume number and short title of the appeal.

6.5.3 In an appeal where there is a large number of volumes of authorities, it is helpful to produce an index of indexes, separate from the index contained in the first authorities volume.

6.5.4 The volumes of authorities should be filed in the Registry preferably in separate containers from the core volumes.

6.5.5 Where a case is not reported in the Law Reports or Session Cases, references to other recognised reports may be given. In Revenue appeals, Tax Cases or Simon's Tax Cases may be cited but, wherever possible, references to the case in the Law Reports or Session Cases should also be given.

6.5.6 In order to produce the volumes of authorities, parties may download text from electronic sources; but the volumes of authorities must be filed in paper form. See Practice Direction 14 for provisions in relation to electronic volumes.

6.5.7 In certain circumstances (for example, when during the hearing it becomes apparent that a particular authority is needed but is not in the volumes of authorities), the Supreme Court Library can arrange for copies of authorities to be made available at the hearing. Parties must themselves provide ten copies of any other authority or of unreported cases. They must similarly provide copies of any authority of which notice has not been given.

6.5.8 The cost of preparing the volumes of authorities falls to the appellants, but is ultimately subject to the decision of the Court as to the costs of the appeal.

The hearing

6.6.1 The Registrar lists appeals taking into account the conve- **4–103** nience of all the parties. Provisional dates are agreed with the parties well in advance of the hearing and every effort is made to keep to these dates. Counsel, solicitors and parties are, however, advised to hold themselves in readiness during the week before and the week following the provisional date given. Solicitors receive formal notification shortly before the hearing.

6.6.2 Parties should inform the Registry as early as possible of the names of counsel they have briefed.

6.6.3 The Court usually hears appeals on Mondays from 11.00am to 1pm and from 2pm to 4pm and on Tuesdays to Thursdays from 10.30am to 1pm and from 2 to 4pm.

6.6.4 Only in wholly exceptional circumstances will the Court consider sitting in private. Any request for the Court to sit in private should be addressed to the Registrar and should be copied to the other parties. The request should set out fully the reasons why it is made and the request together with any objections filed by the other parties will normally be referred to the presiding Justice.

6.6.5 No more than two counsel will be heard on behalf of a party (or a single counsel on behalf of an intervener permitted to make oral submissions).

6.6.6 If a party wishes to have a stenographer present at the hearing or to obtain a full transcript of the hearing, he must notify the Registrar not less than 7 days before the hearing. Any costs of the stenographer or of transcription must be borne by the party making such a request.

6.6.7 The Registrar will on request inform the parties of the intended constitution of the Court for the hearing of a forthcoming appeal; this will be subject to possible alteration. Counsel should assume that the Court will have read the printed cases and the judgment under appeal but not all the papers which have been filed.

6.6.8 The Justices should be addressed as 'My Lord' or 'My Lady' as the case may be.

6.6.9 Some hearings will be filmed and broadcast on television. See paragraph 8.17.1 of Practice Direction 8.

Costs

6.7.1 Rule 46 deals with orders for costs. If counsel seek an order **4–104** other than that costs should be awarded to the successful party, they may make written submissions in accordance with rule 47 if the Court so directs. If a party wishes to defer making submissions as to costs until after judgment, the Court must be informed of this not later than at the close of the oral argument. If the Court

> "accedes to the request it will give such directions as appear appropriate and it may, in particular, give directions—
>
> (a) for the hearing of oral submissions as to costs immediately after judgment;

(b) *for the simultaneous or sequential filing of written submissions as to costs within a specified period after judgment;*

(c) *for the hearing of oral submissions after the filing of written submissions":* rule 47(2).

The original and 7 copies of any written submissions must be filed at the Registry. Copies should also be sent to the other parties to the appeal. Costs submissions are considered on paper.

Conditional fee agreements

4–105   **6.7.2** Conditional fee agreements may properly be made by parties to appeals before the Supreme Court.[1] It is open to the officer assessing costs to reduce the percentage uplift recoverable under a conditional fee agreement if he considers it to be excessive. The costs officer decides questions of percentage uplift in accordance with the principles set out in *Designers Guild Limited v. Russell Williams (Textiles) Limited (trading as Washington DC)* [2003] 2 Costs LR 204. If a party appearing before the Court seeks a ruling that the percentage uplift provided for in a conditional fee agreement should be wholly disallowed on legal grounds, such a ruling should (unless otherwise ordered) be expressly sought from the Court before the end of the hearing. *This paragraph does not apply to appeals from Scotland or Northern Ireland.*

Judgment

Place and time of judgment

4–106   **6.8.1** Judgments are given on a day notified in advance. One week's notice is normally given. If judgment is to be handed down on a Wednesday, copies will be released on the previous Thursday. All corrections are to be submitted by midday on the following Monday.

Attendance of counsel

6.8.2 One junior counsel for each party or group of parties who have filed a case may attend when judgment is delivered in open court, but the attendance of counsel is not required. If counsel do attend, they should be familiar with the subject matter of the appeal and with the options for its disposal. Where judgment is to be promulgated by the Registrar, copies will be made available for collection by counsel or a solicitor at the Registry on a day notified in advance.

Conditions under which judgments are released in advance

6.8.3 The judgment of the Court is made available to certain persons before judgment is given. When, for example, judgment is given on a Wednesday morning, it is made available to counsel from 10.30 am on the previous Thursday morning. In releasing the judgment, the Court gives permission for the contents to be disclosed to counsel, solicitors (including solicitors outside London who have appointed London agents) and in–house legal advisers in a client

---

[1] Conditional fee agreements are sanctioned by the Courts and Legal Services Act 1990, as amended by the Access to Justice Act 1999.

Government department. The contents of the judgment and the result of the appeal may be disclosed to the client parties themselves 24 hours before the judgment is to be given unless the Court or the Registrar directs otherwise. A direction will be given where there is reason to suppose that disclosure to the parties would not be in the public interest.

6.8.4 It is the duty of counsel to check the judgment for typographical errors and minor inaccuracies. In the case of apparent error or ambiguity in the judgment, counsel are requested to inform the Head of Judicial Support as soon as possible. This should be done by e-mail to judicialsupport@supremecourt.gsi.gov.uk, no later than two working days before the date judgment is to be given. The purpose of disclosing the judgment is not to allow counsel to re-argue the case and attention is drawn to the opinions of Lord Hoffmann and Lord Hope in *R (Edwards) v Environment Agency* [2008] UKHL 22, [2008] 1WLR 1587.

6.8.5 Accredited members of the media may also be given a copy of the judgment in advance. The contents of this document are subject to a strict embargo, and are not for publication, broadcast or use on club tapes before judgment has been delivered. The documents are issued in advance on the strict understanding that no approach is made to any person or organisation about their contents before judgment is given.

Intervention

6.9.1 A person who is not a party to an appeal may apply in accordance with rule 26 for permission to intervene in the appeal. An intervener under rule 15 who wishes to intervene in the appeal must make a formal application under rule 26.　**4–107**

6.9.2 An application should be made in the general form of application, Form 2, (see paragraph 7.1 of Practice Direction 7 for applications) and should state whether permission is sought for both oral and written interventions or for written intervention only. The application should be filed with the prescribed fee and confirmation of the consent of the appellants and respondents in the appeal. If their consent is refused, the application must be endorsed with a certificate of service on them, with a brief explanation of the reasons for the refusal.

6.9.3 Applications for permission to intervene should be filed at least 6 weeks before the date of hearing of the appeal. If permission is given, written submissions must be filed and also given to the appellants and respondents for incorporation into the core volumes at least 3 weeks before the hearing. Failure to meet these deadlines increases the burden on the parties in preparing their cases and the core volumes, and may delay the hearing of the appeal.

6.9.4 All counsel instructed on behalf of an intervener with permission to address the Court should attend the hearing unless specifically excused.

6.9.5 Subject to the discretion of the Court, interveners bear their own costs and any additional costs to the appellants and respondents resulting from an intervention are costs in the appeal. Orders for costs "will not normally be made either in favour of or against interveners but such orders may be made if the Court considers it just to do so (in particular if an intervener has in substance acted as the sole or principal appellant or respondent)": rule 46(3).

Specialist advisers and advocates to the Court

4–108   **6.10.1** For a request for a specialist adviser or an advocate to the Court to be appointed in an appeal see paragraphs 8.13.1 and 8.13.2 of Practice Direction 8.

PRACTICE DIRECTION 7—APPLICATIONS, DOCUMENTS, FORMS AND ORDERS

Applications

4–109   **7.1.1** Applications are governed by rule 30. An application should be made as soon as it becomes apparent that an application is necessary or expedient.

7.1.2 An application must be made in Form 2 and should be served on all the other parties before it is filed: rule 30(1)(3).

7.1.3 An application must state what order the applicant is seeking and, briefly, why the applicant is seeking the order: see rule 30(2). Certain applications (e.g. for security) should be supported by written evidence. Although there may be no requirement to provide evidence in support, it should be borne in mind that, as a practical matter, the Court will often need to be satisfied by evidence of the facts that are relied on in support of or for opposing the application. Evidence must be filed as well as served on the respondents.

7.1.4 A party *"who wishes to oppose an application must, within 7 days after service, file notice of objection"* in Form 3 and *"must (before filing) serve a copy on the applicant and any other parties"*: rule 30(4).

7.1.5 The parties to an application for a consent order must ensure that they provide any material needed to satisfy the Court that it is appropriate to make the order.

7.1.6 Applications will be dealt with without a hearing wherever possible. Unless the Registrar directs otherwise, opposed procedural applications are referred to a Panel of Justices and may be decided with or without an oral hearing.

7.1.7 **The original and 3 copies** of the application must be filed, with the prescribed fee. The original application must bear a certificate of service on the other parties and must clearly indicate whether the other parties consent or refuse to consent to the application. **The original and 3 copies** of the notice of objection must be filed, with the prescribed fee. The original notice must bear a certificate of service on the other parties.

7.1.8 If the Panel of Justices orders an oral hearing, the parties may seek permission to adduce affidavits, witness statements and such other documents as they may wish. **Eight copies** are required. Copies of such documents must be served on the other parties before the oral hearing. Authorities are not normally cited before the Panel.

Documents

Preparation

4–110   **7.2.1** All formal documents for the Supreme Court must be produced on A4 paper, securely bound on the left, using both sides of the paper. Documents which are not legible or which are not produced in the authorised form or which are unsatisfactory for some other similar reason are not accepted.

7.2.2 See paragraph 7.2.4 for a list of the provisions governing the form of documents which are to be filed.

Number of documents required

7.2.3 The following table shows the numbers of documents usually required for the hearing of an appeal. The numbers shown are the minimum prescribed by the Rules. Actual requirements must be subject to agreement and depend on the number of parties, counsel and solicitors concerned, and on the special circumstances of each appeal. Copies for the use of the party originating the documents are not included in the numbers indicated.

The appellants must provide:

Document	For Registry	For other side
Notice of appeal	Original and 3 copies on filing	One on service
Statement of facts and issues	Original and 7 copies	As arranged
Appendix Part 1	8	One in advance otherwise as arranged
Appendix Part 2 and any subsequent Parts	10	One in advance otherwise as arranged
Case	Original and 7 copies no later than five weeks before the hearing	As arranged on exchange
Core volumes	10 no later than two weeks before the hearing	As arranged
Authorities volumes	10 no later than two weeks before the hearing	As arranged

The respondents (and any interveners) must provide:

Document	For Registry	For other side
Case	Original and 7 copies no later than three weeks before the hearing	As arranged on exchange; 10 for core volumes
Respondents' additional documents (if any)	10	As arranged

Form of documents

7.2.4 Reference should be made to the following Practice Directions for the form of documents—

> For Statement of facts and issues: see Practice Direction 5 paragraph 5.1.3
>
> For Appendix: see Practice Direction 5 paragraph 5.1.4
>
> For Cases: see Practice Direction 6 paragraph 6.3
>
> For Core volumes: see Practice Direction 6 paragraph 6.4
>
> For Volumes of authorities: see Practice Direction 6 paragraph 6.5.

Disposal of documents

7.2.5 All forms and supporting documents which are filed become the property of the Court. No documents submitted in connection with an application for permission to appeal can be returned. Certain documents submitted in connection with an appeal may be returned, on application to the Registrar within 14 days of judgment in the appeal. Original documents are retained.

7.2.6 Documents filed for the use of the Court may be inspected by persons who are not a party to the appeal on application under rule 39. Such persons must comply with any anonymity orders, data protection requirements and/or conditions imposed by the Registrar under rule 39.

Forms

4–111   **7.3.1** Rule 4 provides for the forms which are to be used in the Supreme Court.

7.3.2 The following forms are set out in Annex 1 to this Practice Direction.

> Form 1 Application for permission/notice of appeal
>
> Form 2 Application form
>
> Form 3 Notice of objection/acknowledgement by respondent

Orders

Draft order

4–112   **7.4.1** After the Court has given judgment, the Registrar will send a draft order to all parties who filed a case. The drafts must be returned to the Registrar within 7 days of the date of receipt (unless otherwise directed), either approved or with suggested amendments. If amendments are proposed, they must be submitted to the solicitors for the other parties, who should indicate their approval or disagreement both to the solicitors submitting the proposals and to the Registrar.

Final order

7.4.2 A copy of the sealed final order is sent to the solicitors for all parties.

Annex 1

4–113   Form 1 Application for permission/notice of appeal

Form 2 Application form

Form 3 Notice of objection/acknowledgement by respondent

Editorial note
The Forms mentioned in the previous paragraph can be found at paras 4–197 to **4–113.1**
4–199 below.

Annex 2

Fees payable in the Supreme Court
The fees set out in column (2) of the table below are payable in the **4–114**
Supreme Court in respect of the items described in column (1) of the
table.

No fee in column (2) is payable in respect of criminal proceedings,
other than the fee payable on submitting a claim for costs.

In relation to its devolution jurisdiction the fees set out in column
(3) of the table are payable in respect of the items described in column (1) of the table.

(1) Number and description of fee	*(2)* Amount of fee	*(3)* Amount of fee
1 Application for permission to appeal		
1.1 On filing an application for permission to appeal.	£800	£400
1.2 On filing notice of objection to an application for permission to appeal.	£160	£160
2 Appeals, etc		
2.1 On filing notice under rule 18(1)(c) of the 2009 Rules of an intention to proceed with an appeal.	£800	£400
2.2 On filing a notice of appeal.	£1600	£400
2.3 On filing a reference under the Supreme Court's devolution jurisdiction. No fee is payable where the reference is made by a court.	n/a	£200
2.4 On filing notice under rule 21(1) of the 2009 Rules (acknowledgement by respondent).	£320	£160
2.5 On filing a statement of relevant facts and issues and an appendix of essential documents.	£4820	£800
3 Procedural applications		
3.1 On filing an application for a decision of the Registrar to be reviewed.	£1500	£200
3.2 On filing an application for permission to intervene in an appeal.	£800	£200
3.3 On filing any other procedural application.	£350	£200
3.4 On filing notice of objection to a procedural application.	£150	£150

(1) Number and description of fee	(2) Amount of fee	(3) Amount of fee
4 Costs		
4.1 On submitting a claim for costs.	2.5% of the sum claimed	2.5% of the sum claimed
4.2 On certification by the Registrar under rule 52 of the 2009 Rules of the amount of assessed costs, or on receipt of an order showing the amount.	2.5% of the sum claimed	2.5% of the sum claimed
5 Copying		
5.1 On a request for a copy of a document (other than where fee 5.2 or 5.3 applies)—		
(a) for ten pages or less;	£5	£5
(b) for each subsequent page.	50p	50p
5.2 On a request for a copy of a document to be provided on a computer disk or in other electronic form, for each such copy.	£5	£5
5.3 On a request for a certified copy of a document.	£20	£20

PRACTICE DIRECTION 8—MISCELLANEOUS MATTERS

Bankruptcy or winding up

4–115   **8.1.1** If a party to an appeal is adjudicated bankrupt or a corporate body is ordered to be wound up, their solicitor must give immediate notice in writing to the other parties and to the Registrar, who must also be provided with a certified copy of the bankruptcy or winding up order. The bankrupt party (or his trustee in bankruptcy) or the liquidator must file an application to pursue the appeal and the appeal cannot proceed until the application has been approved.

8.1.2 An application to pursue the appeal must be filed within 42 days of the date of the notice.

8.1.3 The form of application and the procedure for any supplemental case follows that for death of a party (see paragraph 8.4 below).

Grouping or linking of appeals

4–116   **8.2.1** The Registrar may direct that appeals raising the same or similar issues are heard either together or consecutively by the court constituted by the same Justices and may give any consequential directions that appear appropriate.

8.2.2 The Registrar should be consulted on whether grouping or linking is likely to be appropriate. A principal consideration will be to avoid wherever possible separate representation by counsel and any duplication in the submissions made or in the documents produced for the hearing.

Cross–appeals

8.3.1 A respondent who wishes to argue that the order appealed **4–117** from should be upheld on grounds different from those relied on by the court below, must state that clearly in his written case but need not cross–appeal: rule 25(1). A respondent who wishes to argue that the order appealed from should be varied must obtain permission to cross–appeal except in cases where *"leave is required from the Court of Session for an appeal from that court or...an appeal lies...as of right"*: rule 25(2). Except in those cases, applications for permission to cross–appeal should be made by the respondents directly to the Supreme Court.

8.3.2 Where permission to cross–appeal is required, an application for permission may only be filed after permission to appeal has been granted to the original applicant for permission to appeal. **The original and 3 copies** of the application for permission to cross–appeal must be filed. Where permission to cross–appeal is granted by the Supreme Court, the application for permission to cross–appeal will stand as the notice of appeal and the appellant must then comply with rule 18 and paragraph 3.4.1 of Practice Direction 3.

8.3.3 If permission to cross–appeal is not required, the notice of cross–appeal must be filed with the prescribed fee within 42 days of the filing of the original appeal. **The original and 3 copies** of the notice of cross–appeal must be filed. In a notice of cross–appeal, the original appellant is designated as original–appellant/cross–respondent and the original respondent is designated as original–respondent/cross–appellant.

8.3.4 A cross–appeal may be presented out of time in accordance with paragraph 4.4.1 of Practice Direction 4. For the fees payable for cross–appeals see Annex 2 to Practice Direction 7.

8.3.5 Argument in respect of a cross–appeal must be included by each party in their case in the original appeal. Such an inclusive case must clearly state that it is filed in respect of both the original and cross–appeals.

8.3.6 In a cross–appeal, the cases on the original appeal must be filed 5 weeks before the hearing. The cross–appellants' case for the cross–appeal must be filed 3 weeks before the hearing as part of their reply to the original appellants' case. The original appellants/cross–respondents may reply to the case for the cross–appeal in their case filed in the core volumes.

8.3.7 There is only one Appendix for the original appeal and cross–appeal, and documents in respect of the appeal and cross–appeal must be included in the same Appendix. The original–appellants/cross–respondents are responsible for filing the Statement and Appendix and for notifying the Registrar that the appeal and cross–appeal are ready for listing (including payment of the fee).

8.3.8 The provisions of the above paragraphs apply to appeals from Scotland with the appropriate modifications.

Death of a party

8.4.1 If a party to an appeal dies before the hearing, immediate **4–118** notice of the death must be given in writing to the Registrar and to the other parties. The appeal cannot proceed until a new party has been appointed to represent the deceased person's interest.

8.4.2 The application to substitute the new party must be filed with the prescribed fee within 42 days of the date of notice of death. It should explain the circumstances in which it is being filed. It must be endorsed with a certificate of service on all other parties.

8.4.3 If the death takes place after the case for the deceased person has been filed but before the appeal has been heard, the appellants must file a supplemental case setting out the information about the newly–added parties.

Dispute between parties settled

4–119   **8.5.1** It is the duty of counsel and solicitors in any pending appeal, if an event occurs which arguably disposes of the dispute between the parties, either to ensure that the appeal is withdrawn by consent or, if there is no agreement on that course, to bring the facts promptly to the attention of the Registrar and to seek directions. See further paragraph 8.16 below.

Exhibits

4–120   **8.6.1** Parties who require exhibits to be available for inspection at the hearing must apply to the Registrar for permission for the exhibits to be brought to the Court before the hearing.

Fees and security for costs

4–121   **8.7.1** Payments of fees and deposits of security money may be made in cash or by banker's draft or cheque. If an appellant wishes to pay in cash, the Registry may only accept cash up to £10,000, in order to comply with money laundering regulations. Drafts and cheques for fees must be made payable to 'The Supreme Court of the United Kingdom'. Drafts and cheques for security money must be made payable to 'UK Supreme Court Security Fund Account'.

Interveners

4–122   **8.8.1** A person who is not a party to an application for permission to appeal may apply for permission to intervene in accordance with rule 15. See paragraph 3.3.17 of Practice Direction 3. A person who is not a party to an appeal may apply for permission to intervene in accordance with rule 26. See paragraph 6.9 of Practice Direction 6.

8.8.2 Attention is drawn to paragraphs 2 and 3 of Lord Hoffmann's opinion in In *re E (a child) (Northern Ireland)* [2008] UKHL 66, (2008) Times, November 19, where he said this.

> "2. It may however be of some assistance in future cases if I comment on the intervention by the Northern Ireland Human Rights Commission. In recent years the House has frequently been assisted by the submissions of statutory bodies and non–governmental organisations on questions of general public importance. Leave is given to such bodies to intervene and make submissions, usually in writing but sometimes orally from the bar, in the expectation that their fund of knowledge or particular point of view will enable them to provide the House with a more rounded picture than it would otherwise obtain. The House is grateful to such bodies for their help.

3. An intervention is however of no assistance if it merely repeats points which the appellant or respondent has already made. An intervener will have had sight of their printed cases and, if it has nothing to add, should not add anything. It is not the role of an intervener to be an additional counsel for one of the parties. This is particularly important in the case of an oral intervention. I am bound to say that in this appeal the oral submissions on behalf of the NIHRC only repeated in rather more emphatic terms the points which had already been quite adequately argued by counsel for the appellant. In future, I hope that interveners will avoid unnecessarily taking up the time of the House in this way."

New submissions

8.9.1 If, after the conclusion of the argument on an appeal, a party **4–123** wishes to bring to the notice of the Court new circumstances which have arisen and which might affect the decision or order of the Court, application must be made without delay by letter to the Registrar for permission to make new submissions. The application should indicate the circumstances and the submissions it is desired to make, and a copy must be sent to the solicitors for the other parties to the appeal.

Opposed procedural applications

8.10.1 See paragraph 7.1 of Practice Direction 7 for applications. **4–124**

Patents

8.11.1 This direction applies to any appeal direct from the High **4–125** Court under sections 12 and 13 of the Administration of Justice Act 1969, from an order for the revocation of a patent made under section 32 or section 61 of the Patents Act 1949 or under section 72 of the Patents Act 1977.

8.11.2 Notice of intention to file an appeal, with a copy of the notice of appeal, must be served on the Comptroller–General of Patents, Designs and Trade Marks, as well as on the respondents.

8.11.3 If at any time before the hearing of the appeal the respondents decide not to file an acknowledgement to oppose the appeal, they must without delay serve notice of their decision on the Comptroller and on the appeal. Any such notice served on the Comptroller must be accompanied by a copy of the petition under section 32 of the 1949 Act or of the statements of case in the claim and the affidavits filed therein.

8.11.4 The Comptroller must, within 14 days of receiving notice of the respondents' decision, serve on the appellant and file a notice stating whether or not he intends to file an acknowledgement.

8.11.5 The Comptroller may appear and be heard in opposition to the appeal:

(a) in any case where he has given notice of his intention to appear, and

(b) in any other case (including in particular a case where the respondents withdraw opposition to the appeal during the hearing) if the Court so directs or allows.

8.11.6 The Court makes such orders for the postponement or adjournment of the hearing of the appeal as may appear necessary for the purpose of giving effect to the provisions of this paragraph.

Public funding and legal aid

4–126 **8.12.1** The Court does not provide public funding or legal aid. Application for public funding must be made in England and Wales to the Legal Services Commission, in Scotland to the Scottish Legal Aid Board, and in Northern Ireland to the Legal Aid Committee.

8.12.2 A party to whom a public funding or legal aid certificate has been issued must as soon as possible thereafter file a copy at the Registry. Any emergency certificate and subsequent amendments and the authority for leading counsel must also be filed.

Effect of application by appellant for public funding/legal aid

8.12.3 Provided the Registrar and the other parties have been notified in writing, an application by an appellant for public funding or legal aid suspends the commencement of proceedings and the time limits in rules 11 and 19 are extended until 28 days after the determination of the application for public funding or legal aid (including any appeals against a refusal of funding).

8.12.4 Notification must be given far enough before the expiry of the original time limits to ensure that the appeal is not dismissed as being out of time. A copy of the order appealed from must be submitted by the applicant with the notification.

Effect of application by respondent for public funding/legal aid

8.12.5 Where a respondent to an appeal has applied for public funding or legal aid, the Registrar should be informed within the original time limit for filing the statement and appendix.

Issuing of public funding/legal aid certificate

8.12.6 Where a public funding or legal aid certificate is granted, the relevant date for the purpose of calculation of time limits under paragraphs 8.12.4 and 8.12.5 is the date of issue of the certificate.

Specialist advisers and advocates to the Court

4–127 **8.13.1** Any party to an appeal may apply in writing to the Registrar for specialist advisers to attend the hearing: rule 35.[1] Such advisers provide assistance to the Court and are strictly independent of the parties to the appeal.

8.13.2 A request for an advocate to the Court to be appointed in an appeal should be made in writing to the Registrar. Any request should indicate whether the other parties to the appeal support the request.

Stay of execution

4–128 **8.14.1** Filing a notice of appeal or an application for permission to appeal does not in itself place a stay of execution on any order appealed from. A party seeking such a stay must apply to the court ap-

---

[1] For Nautical Assessors, see also Supreme Court of Judicature Act 1891 s 3.

pealed from, not to the Supreme Court. The Supreme Court cannot stay an interlocutor of the Court of Session.[1]

Transcription

8.15.1 See paragraph 6.6.6 of Practice Direction 6 for requests for stenographers and transcripts.

4–129

Withdrawal of appeals and applications

8.16.1 Attention is drawn to the provisions of rule 34.

4–130

Applications for permission to appeal

8.16.2 An application for permission to appeal may be withdrawn by writing to the Registrar, stating that the parties have agreed how the costs should be settled. The respondents should notify the Registrar of their agreement.

Appeals

8.16.3 An appeal that has not been listed for hearing may be withdrawn by writing to the Registrar, stating that the parties to the appeal have agreed the costs of the appeal. The nature of the agreement should be indicated. Where appropriate, the letter should also indicate how any security money should be disposed of. Written notification must also be given to the respondents who must notify the Registrar of their agreement to the withdrawal of the appeal and who must confirm that the costs have been agreed.

8.16.4 An appeal that has been listed for hearing may only be withdrawn by order of the Court on application. (See paragraph 7.1 of Practice Direction 7 for applications.) An application for such an order should include submissions on costs and, where appropriate, indicate how any security money should be disposed of. The application must be submitted for their consent to those respondents who have filed an acknowledgement. The application should be filed with the prescribed fee.

Broadcasting

8.17.1 The President and the Justices of the Supreme Court will normally accede to a request to record, film or broadcast proceedings before the Court where the presence of cameras or recording equipment does not affect the administration of justice and the recording and broadcasting is conducted in accordance with the protocol[2] which has been agreed with representatives of the relevant broadcasting authorities. Permission to record, film or broadcast proceedings must be sought from the President or the presiding Justice on each occasion and requires his express approval. Where the President or the presiding Justice grants permission, he may impose such conditions as he considers to be appropriate including the obtaining of consent from all the parties involved in the proceedings.

4–131

---

[1] Court of Session Act 1988 s 41(2).

[2] The protocol ensures that certain types of proceedings and some aspects of proceedings such as private discussions between parties and their advisers are not recorded, televised or filmed. It also regulates the use of extracts of proceedings and prevents their use in certain types of programmes (such as party political broadcasts) and in any form of advertising or publicity.

Enforcement of orders made by the Supreme Court

4–132   **8.18.1** The enforcement of orders made by the Supreme Court in England and Wales is dealt with in paragraph 13 of Practice Direction 40B which supplements Part 40 of the Civil Procedure Rules. This provides for an application to be made in accordance with CPR Part 23 for an order to make an order of the Supreme Court (or the House of Lords) an order of the High Court. The application should be made to the procedural judge of the Division, District Registry or court in which the proceedings are taking place and may be made without notice unless the court directs otherwise.

8.18.2 The Part 23 application must be supported by the following:

(1) details of the order which was the subject of the appeal to the Supreme Court or the House of Lords;

(2) details of the order of the Supreme Court or the House of Lords, with a copy annexed, and

(3) a copy of the certificate of the Registrar of the Supreme Court or of the Clerk of Parliaments of the assessment of the costs of the appeal to the Supreme Court or the House of Lords.

8.18.3 The order to make an order of the Supreme Court or the House of Lords an order of the High Court should be in form no PF68.

8.18.4 An order made by the Supreme Court is a UK judgment and enforcement of such an order in Scotland and Northern Ireland is dealt with in accordance with Schedule 6 to the Civil Jurisdiction and Judgments Act 1982. See Part 74 of the Civil Procedure Rules.

PRACTICE DIRECTION 9—THE HUMAN RIGHTS ACT 1998

Appeals involving declarations of incompatibility

4–133   **9.1.1** Where an appellant or a respondent seeks a declaration of incompatibility under the Human Rights Act 1998, the appropriate section of Form 1 or Form 3 must be completed and the provisions of the relevant Practice Direction must be complied with: see Practice Direction 4 paragraph 4.2.12.

9.1.2 The Crown has the right to be joined as a party in any appeal where the Court is considering whether to declare that a provision of primary or subordinate legislation is incompatible with a Convention right: see rule 40. In any appeal where the Court is considering, or is being asked to consider, whether to make, uphold or reverse such a declaration, the Registrar must notify the appropriate Law Officer(s)[1] if the Crown (through a Minister, governmental body or other person defined in Human Rights Act 1998 s 5(2)) is not already a party to the appeal: rule 40(1).

9.1.3 The person notified under paragraph 9.1.2 must within 21 days of receiving such notice, or such extended period as the Registrar may allow, serve on the parties and file a notice stating whether

---

[1] The Registrar notifies: (i) in appeals from England, the Attorney–General; (ii) in appeals from Scotland, the Advocate General for Scotland and the Lord Advocate; (iii) in appeals from Wales, if appropriate, the Counsel General of the National Assembly for Wales; (iv) in appeals from Northern Ireland, the Attorney General for Northern Ireland.

or not the Crown intends to intervene in the appeal; and the identity of the Minister or other person who is to be joined as a party to the appeal.[1]

9.1.4 If a Minister or other person has already been joined to proceedings in the court below in accordance with the provisions of s 5 of the Human Rights Act 1998, the permission of the Court is not required for the continued intervention of the Crown.

9.1.5 Once joined to the appeal, the case for the Minister or other person must be filed in accordance with Practice Direction 6, paragraph 6.3.

9.1.6 The Court may order the postponement or adjournment of the hearing of the appeal for the purpose of giving effect to the provisions of this direction or the requirements of the Act.

Other Human Rights Act appeals

9.1.7 Where an appellant or a respondent seeks to challenge an act **4–134** of a public authority under the Human Rights Act 1998, the appropriate section of Form 1 or Form 3 must be completed and the provisions of the relevant Practice Direction must be complied with: see Practice Direction 4 paragraph 4.2.12.

9.1.8 Where an issue under the Human Rights Act is raised in respect of a judicial act,[2] the Registrar notifies the Crown through the Treasury Solicitor as agent for the Lord Chancellor.[3]

9.1.9 Except as stated above, no special steps are required for other Human Rights Act appeals.

PRACTICE DIRECTION 10—DEVOLUTION JURISDICTION

General note

10.1.1 The Supreme Court has jurisdiction to hear and determine **4–135** "devolution issues", that is questions relating to the powers and functions of the legislative and executive authorities established in Scotland and Northern Ireland by the Scotland Act 1998 and the Northern Ireland Act 1998 respectively, and questions as to the competence and functions of those established by the Government of Wales Act 2006, whether or not the issue arises in proceedings in England and Wales, Scotland or Northern Ireland.

10.1.2 The Supreme Court can also be asked to scrutinise Bills of the Scottish Parliament (under section 33 of the Scotland Act), Bills of the Northern Ireland Assembly (under section 11 of the Northern Ireland Act) and proposed Orders in Council and proposed Assembly Measures and Bills under sections 96, 99 and 112 the Government of Wales Act 2006.

10.1.3 Such cases can reach the Supreme Court in four ways.

(1) By way of a reference of a question by a relevant officer.

(2) By way of an appeal from certain superior courts of England and Wales, Scotland and Northern Ireland.

---

[1] Human Rights Act 1998 ss 5(2) and 9(5).
[2] Human Rights Act 1998 ss 7, 9(3) and 9(4).
[3] In appeals from Scotland, the Registrar notifies the Solicitor to the Scottish Government; in appeals from Northern Ireland, he notifies the Crown Solicitor and the Departmental Solicitor.

(3) By way of a reference of a devolution issue by certain appellate courts.

(4) By way of a direct reference of a devolution issue by a relevant officer whether or not the issue is the subject of litigation.

10.1.4 Rule 3(2) defines "relevant officer" as meaning

(a) in relation to proceedings in England and Wales, the Attorney General and, in relation to proceedings that particularly affect Wales, the Counsel General to the Welsh Assembly Government,

(b) in relation to proceedings in Scotland, the Advocate General for Scotland and the Lord Advocate, and

(c) in relation to proceedings in Northern Ireland, the Advocate General for Northern Ireland and (when section 22 of the Justice (Northern Ireland) Act 2002 comes into force) the Attorney General for Northern Ireland.

10.1.5 Rule 41 of the Supreme Court Rules provides in general for appeals or references under the Court's devolution jurisdiction (as defined by section 40 of, and Schedule 9 to, the Constitutional Reform Act 2005) to be dealt with in accordance with the Rules, but the Court will give special directions as and when necessary and in particular as to—

(a) any **question** referred under section 33 of the Scotland Act 1998, section 11 of the Northern Ireland Act 1998 or section 96, 99 or 112 of the Government of Wales Act 2006;

(b) any reference of a **devolution issue**;

(c) any **direct reference** under paragraph 33 or 34 of Schedule 6 to the Scotland Act 1998, paragraph 33 or 34 of Schedule 10 to the Northern Ireland Act 1998 or paragraph 29 or 30 of Schedule 9 to the Government of Wales Act 2006.

As to **(a)** above, section 33 of the Scotland Act 1998 provides for the scrutiny of Bills of the Scottish Parliament by the Supreme Court. Section 11 of the Northern Ireland Act 1998 provides for the scrutiny of Bills of the Northern Ireland Assembly by the Supreme Court. Section 96, 99 or 112 of the Government of Wales Act 2006 provide for the scrutiny of proposed Orders in Council, proposed Assembly Measures and Bills of the National Assembly for Wales by the Supreme Court.

As to **(b)** above, a devolution issue is defined by Schedule 6 to the Scotland Act 1998, Schedule 10 to the Northern Ireland Act 1998 or Schedule 9 to the Government of Wales Act 2006. See paragraph 10.1.1 above. Under paragraphs 10, 11, 22 and 30 of Schedule 6 to the Scotland Act 1998, paragraphs 9, 19, 28 and 29 of Schedule 10 to the Northern Ireland Act 1998 or paragraphs 10, 18, 19 and 27 of Schedule 9 to the Government of Wales Act 2006, certain appellate courts may refer a devolution issue arising in proceedings to the Supreme Court.

As to **(c)** above, a relevant officer may make a direct reference of a devolution issue to the Supreme Court under paragraph 33 or 34 of Schedule 6 to the Scotland Act 1998, paragraph 33 or 34 of Schedule 10 to the Northern Ireland Act 1998 or paragraph 29 or 30 of Schedule 9 to the Government of Wales Act 2006 whether or not the issue is the subject of litigation.

References of a question by a relevant officer

10.2.1 A reference of a question by a relevant officer is made by— **4–136**

(a) filing the reference, and

(b) serving a copy on any other relevant officer who is not already a party and who has a potential interest in the proceedings,

within any time limits specified by the relevant statute.

10.2.2 The reference should state—

(a) the question to be determined with respect to the proposed Order in Council, proposed Assembly Measure or Bill to which the reference relates;

(b) whether it applies to the whole Order in Council, Assembly Measure or Bill or to a provision of it,

and the reference shall have annexed to it a copy of the Order in Council, Assembly Measure or Bill to which it relates.

10.2.3 Any relevant officer (other than the one making the reference) who wishes to participate in the proceedings shall within 7 days of service of the reference on him notify the Registrar and the other parties. Any relevant officer who gives notice automatically becomes a respondent to the proceedings.

10.2.4 The relevant officer making the reference shall, within 7 days of filing the reference, file a case with respect to the question referred. The referring relevant officer's case should include a copy of any statement made in relation to the Order in Council, Assembly Measure or Bill in accordance with the relevant statute and any relevant extracts from the Official Report of proceedings in the Parliament or Assembly.

10.2.5 Any other relevant officer who is participating in the proceedings shall file a case with respect to the question referred within 7 days of the notice given under paragraph 10.2.3.

10.2.6 The relevant officer making the reference shall also notify the relevant Assembly or Parliament which passed the Assembly Measure or Bill or approved the draft of the Order in Council, as the case may be, of the making of the reference.

Appeals to the Supreme Court

(a) Permission to appeal

10.3.1 Part 2 of the Supreme Court Rules applies to applications **4–137** for permission to appeal. Permission to appeal to the Supreme Court may be sought only if permission to appeal has been applied for and refused by the court below. The provisions of this section apply, with necessary modifications, to applications for permission to cross–appeal as they apply to applications for permission to appeal. For the procedure in cases where permission to appeal is not required, see paragraph 10.3.3.

10.3.2 An application for permission to appeal shall—

(a) briefly set out the facts and points of law involved in the appeal;

(b) conclude with a summary of the reasons why permission to appeal should be granted; and

(c) not normally be accompanied by supporting documents except

> (i) the order or interlocutor appealed from;
>
> (ii) the judgment appealed from; and
>
> (iii) if separate, the order or interlocutor of the court below refusing permission to appeal to the Supreme Court.

(b) Appeals

10.3.3 Rules 18 and 19 and the following paragraphs apply to a person who has obtained permission to appeal from the Supreme Court and in cases where permission to appeal is not required, for example, where a person desires to appeal to the Supreme Court against a determination of a devolution issue by the Inner House of the Court of Session on a reference under paragraph 7 or 8 of Schedule 6 to the Scotland Act 1998.

10.3.4 A person who desires to appeal to the Supreme Court shall file Form 1 within 42 days of the date on which the order or interlocutor appealed from was made or permission to appeal was granted, as the case may be.

10.3.5 A notice of appeal must be made in Form 1 and signed by the appellants or their counsel or solicitor.

10.3.6 The appellant must also serve a copy of his Form 1 on any relevant officer who is not already a party and who has a potential interest in the proceedings. Any relevant officer who is so served may intervene in the proceedings on the appeal in the Supreme Court if within 14 days of service he notifies the Registrar and all other parties. Any relevant officer who gives notice automatically becomes a respondent to the proceedings.

References by Courts

4–138 **10.4.1** A reference by a court is made by the appropriate officer of the court—

(a) filing the reference,

(b) serving a copy of the reference on the parties, and

(c) serving a copy of the reference on any relevant officer who is not already a party and who has a potential interest in the proceedings.

10.4.2 The reference shall set out—

(a) the question referred;

(b) the addresses of the parties;

(c) the name and address of any person who applied for or required the reference to be made;

(d) a concise statement of the background to the matter including—

> (i) the facts of the case, including any relevant findings of fact by the referring court or lower courts; and
>
> (ii) the main issues in the case and the contentions of the parties with regard to them;

(e) the relevant law, including the relevant provisions of the relevant statute;

(f) the reasons why an answer to the question is considered necessary for the purpose of disposing of the proceedings.

10.4.3 All judgments and orders already given in the proceedings, including copies of any interlocutors and any notes attaching to such interlocutors, shall be annexed to the reference.

10.4.4 Any party to the proceedings in the court making the reference who intends to participate in the proceedings in the Supreme Court shall within 14 days of service of the copy reference on him notify the Registrar and the other parties. Any relevant officer who is already a party to the proceedings automatically becomes a respondent to the proceedings.

10.4.5 Any party who does not intend to participate shall give notice in writing to the Registrar and the other parties accordingly.

10.4.6 Where notice has to be given under this section of this Practice Direction, it shall also be given to any relevant officer who is not already a party and who has a potential interest in the proceedings.

10.4.7 Any relevant officer who is not already a party to the proceedings may intervene in the proceedings on the reference by giving notice to the Registrar, other relevant officers with a potential interest and the court making the reference.

10.4.8 Unless the Supreme Court directs otherwise, once a final judgment has been given on a reference by a court the proceedings shall stand remitted to the court from which the reference came without further order, subject to the disposal of any outstanding issues as to the costs of the reference.

Direct references by a relevant officer

10.5.1 In a case where the devolution issue arises in proceedings **4–139** before a court or tribunal to which the relevant officer is a party, a direct reference by the relevant officer is made by—

(a) filing the reference,

(b) serving a copy of the reference on the parties to those proceedings, and

(c) serving a copy of the reference on any other relevant officer who is not already a party to those proceedings and who has a potential interest.

10.5.2 The reference shall set out—

(a) the question referred;

(b) the addresses of the parties;

(c) the name and address of any other person who applied for or required the reference to be made;

(d) a concise statement of the background to the matter including—

    (i) the facts of the case, including any relevant findings of fact by the court or tribunal; and

    (ii) the main issues in the case and the contentions of the parties with regard to them;

(e) the relevant law, including the relevant provisions of the relevant statute;

(f) the reasons why an answer to the question is considered necessary for the purpose of disposing of the proceedings.

10.5.3 All judgments and orders already given in the proceedings, including copies of any interlocutors and any notes attaching to such interlocutors, shall be annexed to the reference.

10.5.4 Any party to the proceedings in the court or tribunal who intends to participate in the proceedings in the Supreme Court shall within 14 days of service of the copy reference on him notify the Registrar and the other parties. Any relevant officer who gives notice automatically becomes a respondent to the proceedings.

10.5.5 In a case where the devolution issue is not the subject of proceedings before a court or tribunal, a direct reference by the relevant officer is made by—

(a) filing the reference, and

(b) serving a copy of the reference on any other relevant officer who has a potential interest.

10.5.6 Any relevant officer served with a copy of the reference may intervene in the proceedings on the reference by giving notice to the Registrar and the relevant officer making the reference.

10.5.7 Where notice has to be given to any person under the Scotland Act 1998, the Northern Ireland Act 1998 or the Government of Wales Act 2006, as the case may be, the reference shall state the name and address of that person and when he was notified.

10.5.8 A person who has to be notified under paragraph 35 of Schedule 6 to the Scotland Act 1998, paragraph 35 of Schedule 10 to the Northern Ireland Act 1998 or paragraph 30 of Schedule 9 to the Government of Wales Act 2006, as the case may be, but who does not intend to participate in the proceedings in the Supreme Court shall give notice in writing within 14 days to the Registrar and the other parties to the proceedings.

PRACTICE DIRECTION 11—THE EUROPEAN COURT OF JUSTICE

4-140   **11.1.1** Article 234 of the Treaty establishing the European Community provides:

1. The Court of Justice shall have jurisdiction to give preliminary rulings concerning:

   (a) the interpretation of this Treaty;

   (b) the validity and interpretation of acts of the institutions of the Community and of the European Central Bank;

   (c) the interpretation of the statutes of bodies established by an act of the Council, where those statutes so provide.

2. Where such a question is raised before any court or tribunal of a Member State, that court or tribunal may, if it considers that a decision on the question is necessary to enable it to give judgment, request the Court of Justice to give a ruling thereon.

3. Where any such question is raised in a case pending before a court or tribunal of a Member State against whose decisions there is no judicial remedy under national law, that court or tribunal shall bring the matter before the Court of Justice.

11.1.2 When the Court refuses permission to appeal where the application includes a contention that a question of Community law is involved, the Court gives additional reasons for its decision not to grant permission to appeal: rule 42(1). These reasons reflect the decision of the Court of Justice in *CILFIT v. Ministry of Health* (Case C–283/81) which laid down the categories of case where the Court of Justice considered that no reference should be made to it, namely:

(a) where the question raised is irrelevant;
(b) where the Community provision in question has already been interpreted by the Court of Justice;
(c) where the question raised is materially identical with a question which has already been the subject of a preliminary ruling in a similar case; and
(d) where the correct application of Community law is so obvious as to permission no scope for any reasonable doubt.

11.1.3 The Court may order a reference to the Court of Justice before determining whether to grant permission to appeal. In such circumstances proceedings on the application for permission to appeal are stayed until the answer is received. The paragraphs below apply as appropriate.

11.1.4 When the Court intends to make a reference, it will give consequential directions as to the form of the reference and the staying of the appeal (see rule 42(3)) and the parties are invited to submit an agreed draft of the question(s) to be referred. A further statement of facts and issues, for the use of the Court of Justice, may also be appropriate. The Court then makes the reference, with or without judgments. At this stage the appeal may also be disposed of in part.

11.1.5 Within 28 days of the judgment of the Court of Justice, the parties must file written submissions on whether a further hearing before the Supreme Court is necessary or on how the appeal is to be disposed of.

Further proceedings in the Supreme Court

11.1.6 If a further hearing is required before the Supreme Court, **4–141** the parties may file supplemental cases.

11.1.7 If supplemental cases are filed, then:

(a) no later than 5 weeks before the expected date of the further hearing, the appellants must file **the original and 7 copies** of their supplemental case and also serve it on the respondents;
(b) no later than 3 weeks before the expected date of the further hearing, the respondents must file **the original and 7 copies** of their supplemental case and also serve it on the appellants;
(c) no later than 3 weeks before the expected date of the further hearing, any other party filing a case (e.g. an intervener or advocate to the court) must file **the original and 7 copies** of their supplemental case, and also provide copies to the appellants and respondents.

11.1.8 As soon as all the supplemental cases have been exchanged, and no later than 2 weeks before the date of the expected hearing, the appellants must file 10 additional sets of core volumes containing:

(a) appellants' and respondents' cases;
(b) cases of interveners etc, if any;
(c) judgment of the European Court of Justice;
(d) any additional authorities relied on that are not included in the original green authorities' volumes.

11.1.9 The Registry supplies the Court with the original core volumes, appendices and authorities volumes.

Costs

4–142 **11.1.10** The Court of Justice does not make orders for costs. The costs of the reference are included in the order of the Supreme Court disposing of the appeal; and, if necessary, are assessed by the Costs Officers of the Court.

Papers for the Court of Justice

4–143 **11.1.11** Parties should be aware that the Court of Justice will not translate documents which are longer than 20 pages; only summaries are made.

PRACTICE DIRECTION 12—CRIMINAL PROCEEDINGS

Section 1 General Note and the Jurisdiction of the Supreme Court in Criminal Proceedings

1. Introduction

4–144 **12.1.1** The procedure of the Supreme Court is regulated by statute, by the Supreme Court Rules and by the practice directions which supplement the Rules. Copies of these and other documents may be downloaded from *www.supremecourt.gov.uk*.

12.1.2 Practice Directions 1–11 and 13 governing civil proceedings apply to criminal proceedings in the Supreme Court subject to any modifications or additional provisions made by this Practice Direction.

Right of appeal

12.1.3 The right of appeal to the Supreme Court is regulated by statute and subject to statutory restrictions. The principal statutes for criminal appeals (as amended in most cases by section 40 of, and Schedule 9 to, the Act) are:

> the Administration of Justice Act 1960;
> the Criminal Appeal Act 1968;
> the Courts–Martial (Appeals) Act 1968;
> the Administration of Justice Act 1969;
> the Judicature (Northern Ireland) Act 1978;
> the Criminal Appeal (Northern Ireland) Act 1980;
> the Proceeds of Crime Act 2002;
> the Extradition Act 2003;
> the Criminal Justice Act 2003;
> the Serious Organised Crime and Police Act 2005.

Every applicant for permission to appeal must comply with the statutory requirements before the application can be considered by the Court. The Human Rights Act 1998 applies to the Court in its judicial capacity. But that Act does not confer any general right of appeal to the Court, or any right of appeal in addition to or superseding any right of appeal provided for in Acts passed before the coming into force of the Human Rights Act 1998.

England and Wales and Northern Ireland

12.1.4 An appeal to the Supreme Court may only be brought with the permission of the court below or, if refused by that court, with the permission of the Supreme Court. Subject to paragraphs 12.2.2–12.2.4, in criminal matters such permission may not be granted unless the court below has issued the certificate referred to in paragraph 12.2.1.

12.1.5 Subject to paragraphs 12.1.4 and 12.2.1–12.2.6, an application for permission to appeal to the Supreme Court in a criminal matter may be made by either the defendant or the prosecutor, as follows:

(a) from any decision of the Court of Appeal Criminal Division in England and Wales on an appeal to that court[1];

(b) from any decision of the Courts–Martial Appeal Court on an appeal to that court[2];

(c) from any decision of the Court of Appeal in Northern Ireland on an appeal to that court by a person convicted on indictment[3];

(d) from any decision of the Court of Appeal in Northern Ireland in a criminal cause or matter on a case stated by a county court or magistrates' court[4];

(e) from any decision of the High Court of Justice in England and Wales in a criminal cause or matter;[5];

(f) from any decision of the High Court of Justice in Northern Ireland in a criminal cause or matter[6].

Scotland

12.1.6 No appeal lies to the Supreme Court from criminal proceedings in the High Court of Justiciary in Scotland.

Criminal contempt of court cases

12.1.7 In cases involving criminal contempt of court, an appeal lies to the Supreme Court at the instance of the defendant only and, in respect of an application for committal or attachment, at the instance of the applicant from any decision of the Court of Appeal Criminal Division, the Courts–Martial Appeal Court or the High Court[7].

Section 2 Applications for Permission

2. Certificate of Point of Law

12.2.1 Subject to paragraphs 12.2.2–12.2.4, permission to appeal **4–145** to the Supreme Court in a criminal matter may only be granted if it is certified by the court below that a point of law of general public importance is involved in the decision of that court, and it appears to that court or to the Supreme Court that the point is one that ought

---

[1] Criminal Appeal Act 1968 s 33(1) (as amended); Criminal Justice Act 2003, Part 9.

[2] Courts–Martial (Appeals) Act 1968 s 39(1).

[3] Judicature (Northern Ireland) Act 1978 s 40(1)(b); Criminal Appeal (Northern Ireland) Act 1980 s 31(1) (as amended).

[4] Judicature (Northern Ireland) Act 1978 s 41(1)(b).

[5] Administration of Justice Act 1960 s 1(1)(a) (as amended); Extradition Act 2003 ss 32, 114.

[6] Judicature (Northern Ireland) Act 1978 s 41(1)(a); Extradition Act 2003 ss 32, 114.

[7] Administration of Justice Act 1960 s 13; Judicature (Northern Ireland) Act 1978 s 44. For appeals in cases involving civil contempt of court see Practice Direction 1 paragraph 2.1.8.

to be considered by the Supreme Court[1]. An application for permission to appeal without the required certificate may not be filed (paragraph 12.4.3), except as provided by paragraphs 12.2.2–12.2.4.

12.2.2 A certificate is not required for an appeal from a decision of the High Court in England and Wales or of the High Court in Northern Ireland on a criminal application for habeas corpus[2].

12.2.3 A certificate is not required for an appeal by a minister of the Crown or a person nominated by him, a member of the Scottish Executive, a Northern Ireland minister or a Northern Ireland department when they have been joined as a party to any criminal proceedings, other than in Scotland, by a notice given under the Human Rights Act 1998 ss.5(1) and 5(2) and they wish to appeal under section 5(4) of that Act against any declaration of incompatibility made in those proceedings.

12.2.4 A certificate is not required in contempt of court cases where the decision of the court below was not a decision on appeal[3].

12.2.5 In cases where the court below has not certified a point of law of general public importance, the Registrar will at the request of an applicant provide a letter stating that no appeal lies to the Supreme Court. The European Court of Human Rights accepts this letter as setting out the jurisdiction of the Supreme Court in the litigation, for the purpose of determining whether the petitioner has satisfied the requirement, laid down by Article 35 of the European Convention on Human Rights, that all domestic remedies must be exhausted before an appeal can be made to the Strasbourg Court.

Judicial review: criminal matters

12.2.6 There is no appeal to the Court of Appeal from a refusal by a Divisional Court to grant permission to apply for judicial review in a criminal case[4]; and the Supreme Court has no jurisdiction to hear an appeal against a refusal by a Divisional Court of permission to apply for judicial review in a criminal case[5]. So, if a Divisional Court refuses permission to apply to it for judicial review in a criminal matter, there is no further remedy in the domestic courts. The only circumstances in which an application may be made to the Supreme Court for permission to appeal from a Divisional Court in a criminal judicial review matter are when the Divisional Court certifies that a point of law of general public importance arises from its decision.

3. Time Limits

Time within which to apply for permission to appeal

12.3.1 An application for permission to appeal to the Supreme

---

[1] Criminal Appeal Act 1968 s 33(2); Administration of Justice Act 1960 s 1(2); Courts–Martial (Appeals) Act 1968 s 39(2); Judicature (Northern Ireland) Act 1978 s 41(2); Criminal Appeals (Nothern Ireland) Act 1980 s 31(2); Extradition Act 2003 ss 32, 114; Proceeds of Crime Act (Appeals under Part 4) Order 2003, SI 2003/458.

[2] Administration of Justice Act 1960 s 15(3) (as amended); Judicature (Northern Ireland) Act 1978 s 45(3).

[3] Administration of Justice Act 1960 s 13(4); Judicature (Northern Ireland) Act 1978 s 44(4).

[4] Supreme Court Act 1981 s 18(1)(a).

[5] Administration of Justice Act 1960 s1(1) & (2) and the decisions of the House of Lords in Re Poh, Eastaway and Burkett.

Court in a criminal matter must first be made to the court below. If the court below refuses permission to appeal, application may then be made to the Supreme Court.

12.3.2 An application to the Supreme Court for permission to appeal is made in accordance with rule 10 and Practice Direction 3. An application for permission to appeal to the House of Lords

    (a) from a decision of the Court of Appeal under s 33(1) of the Criminal Appeal Act 1968 or

    (b) from a decision of a Divisional Court of the Queen's Bench Division in a criminal cause or matter under s 1(1)(a) of the Administration of Justice Act 1960

must be made within 28 days beginning with the date on which the application for permission was refused by the court below (and not the following day)[1]. This date is not necessarily that on which the point of law was certified. Where the time prescribed expires on a Saturday, Sunday, bank holiday or other day on which the Registry is closed, the application is accepted as being in time if it is received on the next day on which the Registry is open.

12.3.3 An application for permission to appeal must be made within 14 days if made under one of the following provisions: ss 32(5), 114(5) of the Extradition Act 2003; ss 33, 44 and 66 of the Proceeds of Crime Act 2002[2]; and, ss 183, 193 and 214 of the Proceeds of Crime Act 2002[3]. A 14 day time limit also applies to an application to refer a case pursuant to the Attorney General's Reference procedure under s 36(5) of the Criminal Justice Act 1988[4].

Application for extension of time to file application for permission

12.3.4 Subject to paragraph 12.3.5, the Supreme Court or the court below may, on application made at any time by the defendant and in certain limited circumstances the prosecutor[5], extend the time within which application for permission to appeal to the Supreme Court may be made to the Supreme Court or to that court[6]. Such an application to the Supreme Court is incorporated in the application for permission itself, and should set out briefly the reason(s) why the application is being presented outside the statutory period.

12.3.5 No extension may be granted in respect of applications made under ss 32 and 114 of the Extradition Act 2003.

Public funding and legal aid

12.3.6 Paragraph 8.12 of Practice Direction 8 applies to appeals in

---

[1] Criminal Appeal Act 1968 s 34(1) (as amended); Administration of Justice Act 1960 s 2(1) (as amended).

[2] Proceeds of Crime Act 2002 (appeals under Part 2) Order 2003 (SI 2003 No 82), Part 3, Article 12.

[3] Proceeds of Crime Act 2002 (appeals under Part 4) Order 2003 (SI 2003 No 483), Part 3, Article 12.

[4] Criminal Justice Act 1988 Sch 3, para 4.

[5] Criminal Appeal Act 1968, ss 33(1B), 34(2).

[6] Criminal Appeal Act 1968 s 34(2); Administration of Justice Act 1960 s 2(3); Courts–Martial (Appeals) Act 1968 s 40(2); Criminal Appeal (Northern Ireland) Act 1980 s 32(2); Judicature (Northern Ireland) Act 1978 Schedule 1, paragraph 1(2). Section 1A of the Geneva Conventions Act 1957 makes, in relation to protected prisoners, certain extensions to the time limits in the Administration of Justice Act 1960, the Criminal Appeal Act 1968, the Courts–Martial (Appeals) Act 1968 and the Criminal Appeal (Northern Ireland) Act 1968.

criminal proceedings. In criminal proceedings, depending on the route of appeal, application should be made to the court appealed from or, in Northern Ireland, to the Legal Aid Committee.

12.3.7 A copy of the order appealed from must be submitted by the appellant with the notification of the application for funding. The period within which the application for permission to appeal or notice of appeal (as the case may be) must be filed is then extended to 28 days after the final determination of the application for funding, including any appeals. An extension may not be granted to an appellant under the Extradition Act 2003[1].

12.3.8 A representation order will usually provide for junior counsel and solicitors at the permission stage with the addition of leading counsel if permission is granted.

4. Applications for Permission to Appeal

Form of application

4–146   **12.4.1** The provisions of Practice Direction 3 govern the form of applications for permission to appeal.

Case title

12.4.2 In applications where a prosecuting authority is the appellant, the prosecuting authority should be described as follows: "Director of Public Prosecutions (*or other prosecuting authority*) (on behalf of Her Majesty)".

12.4.3 Subject to paragraphs 12.2.2–12.2.4, the Registry cannot issue any application for permission to appeal that is not accompanied by the certificate from the court below required by statute, certifying a point of law of general public importance (see paragraph 12.2.1 above).

Service

12.4.4 In habeas corpus appeals and/or in appeals concerning extradition, the application must be served on the government that is seeking extradition or on the Director of Public Prosecutions if he is acting for that government.

5. Costs

4–147   **12.5.1** Where an application for permission to appeal is determined without an oral hearing, costs may be awarded as follows:

    (a) to a publicly funded or legally aided appellant, reasonable costs incurred in preparing papers for the Appeal Panel;

    (b) to a publicly funded or legally aided respondent, only those costs necessarily incurred in attending the client, attending the appellant's solicitors, considering the application, filing notice of objection and, where applicable, preparing respondent's objections to the application;

    (c) to an unassisted respondent where the appellant is

---

[1] Extradition Act 2003 ss 32, 114

publicly funded or legally aided, payment out of the Community Legal Service Fund (pursuant to s 11 of the Access to Justice Act 1999[1])[2] of costs as specified at (b) above;

(d) to an appellant or respondent, payment out of central funds, pursuant to s 16 or s 17 of the Prosecution of Offences Act 1985, of costs incurred at (a) or (b) above, as the case may be;

(e) to a respondent where neither party is publicly funded or legally aided, costs as specified at (b) above to be paid by the appellant.

Where costs are sought under (c), (d) or (e) above, application may be made by letter addressed to the Registrar or may be included in a bill of costs filed in the Registry conditional upon the application being granted.

12.5.2 Where an application for permission to appeal is referred for an oral hearing and is dismissed, application for costs must be made by the respondent at the end of the hearing. No order for costs will be made unless requested at that time.

12.5.3 Where permission to appeal is granted, the costs of the permission application become costs in the appeal.

12.5.4 Bills of costs for assessment must be filed within three months from the date of the decision of the Appeal Panel or the date on which an application for permission is withdrawn. If an extension of the three months period is desired, application must be made in writing to the Registrar and copies of all such correspondence sent to all interested parties. In deciding whether to grant an application for an extension of time made after the expiry of the three month period the Registrar takes into account the circumstances set out in paragraph 6.2 of Practice Direction 13.

6. Fees

12.6.1 No fee is payable at any stage of an application for permis- **4–148**
sion to appeal in a criminal matter. Fees are payable on the assessment of a bill of costs.

Section 3 Appeals

7. Time Limits

12.7.1 Apart from appeals under the Extradition Act 2003, a notice **4–149**
of appeal must be filed in accordance with rule 19.

12.7.2 Appeals under the Extradition Act 2003 must be filed within 28 days of the grant of permission, starting with the day on which permission is granted. The time for doing so may not be extended[3].

---

[1] Also pursuant to r. 5(2) Community Legal Service (Cost Protection) Regulations 2000 and in accordance with the procedural requirements of rr. 9, 10 Community Legal Service (Costs) Regulations 2000 (as amended).
[2] Or s 18 Legal Aid Act 1988; or, in Scotland, pursuant to s 19 Legal Aid (Scotland) Act 1986 or, in Northern Ireland, pursuant to Article 16 Legal Aid Advice and Assistance (N.I.) Order 1981.
[3] Extradition Act 2003 ss 32, 114.

8. Security for Costs

4–150   **12.8.1** No security for costs is required in criminal appeals.

9. Statement of Facts and Issues

4–151   **12.9.1** The provisions of Practice Direction 5 apply to appeals in criminal proceedings.

12.9.2 In any appeal under the Criminal Appeal Act 1968, the statement of facts and issues must state clearly whether any grounds of appeal have been left undetermined by the Court of Appeal (see also paragraph 12.11.2).

10. Filing of Statement and Appendix

Respondents' consent

4–152   **12.10.1** The provisions of Practice Direction 5 apply to appeals in criminal proceedings but it is not the practice in criminal appeals to require the consent of the respondents to applications for extension of time.

11. Appellants' and respondents' cases

4–153   **12.11.1** The provisions of Practice Direction 6 apply to appeals in criminal proceedings.

12.11.2 In any appeal under the Criminal Appeal Act 1968 in which grounds of appeal have been left undetermined by the Court of Appeal (see paragraph 12.9.2), each party should include in their case submissions on the merits of those grounds and on how they would seek to have them disposed of by the Court.

12. Core Volumes

Form of core volumes

4–154   **12.12.1** The provisions of Practice Direction 6 apply to appeals in criminal proceedings.

12.12.2 It is not necessary for the appellants' solicitors to produce additional volumes for the use of victims attending the hearing. The Registry provides the necessary documents from among the number produced for the use of the Court.

13. Bail

4–155   **12.13.1** The Supreme Court does not grant bail. Applications for bail should be made to the court below. Where bail is granted to a party to an appeal to the Court, the Registrar should be notified.

12.13.2 The attendance of a party to an appeal who is in custody is not normally required or permitted. Where the attendance of a party in custody is required, his solicitors will be informed by the Registrar in writing.

12.13.3 It should be noted that where a party was on bail pending the hearing of the appeal, surrender is usually required on the first day of the hearing.

14. Exhibits

4–156   **12.14.1** Parties who require exhibits to be available for inspection at the hearing must apply to the Registrar for permission for the exhibits to be brought to the Court before the hearing.

15. Victims' Code of Practice

12.15.1 The Victims' Code of Practice governs the services to be **4–157** provided in England and Wales to victims of criminal conduct that has occurred in England and Wales. The Code is issued by the Home Secretary under s 32 of the Domestic Violence, Crime and Victims Act 2004. The Court applies the Code.

12.15.2 Accordingly, all applications for permission to appeal and all appeals are examined to establish whether a victim can be identified and, if so, to determine what services are required to be provided to the victim.

12.15.3 In giving effect to paragraph 12.15.2 the Registrar may consult the Treasury Solicitor, the Court of Appeal Criminal Division and other relevant persons to obtain any necessary information.

12.15.4 The Registry may either directly or through the joint police/CPS Witness Care Units contact victims to inform them that an application for permission to appeal or an appeal has been filed, to explain the appeals procedure, and to report progress on the application and/or appeal, including the date set for the hearing.

12.15.5 Victims may attend the hearing of an appeal or application for permission to appeal or the handing down of judgment. The Registry arranges such attendance and provides the case papers.

12.15.6 If permission to appeal is granted by an Appeal Panel, the Registrar notifies the joint police/CPS Witness Care Units no later than one working day after the day on which permission to appeal has been granted.

12.15.7 The Registry notifies the joint police/CPS Witness Care Units of the result of the appeal no later than one working day after the day of the result.

PRACTICE DIRECTION 13—COSTS

4–158

Note: enquiries about costs should be made to the Costs Clerk (tel: 020–7960 1990). Enquiries about fees should be made to the Registry (tel: 020–7960 1991, 1992).

Drafts and cheques for fees, including assessment fees, should be made payable to '**The Supreme Court of the United Kingdom**'.

Drafts and cheques for security money only should be made payable to 'UK Supreme Court Security Fund Account'.

Section 1

1. Introduction

1.1 Detailed assessments of costs in the Supreme Court are conducted by Costs Officers appointed by the President: see rule 49. One Costs Officer will be the Senior Costs Judge (the Chief Taxing Master of the Senior Courts) or any Costs Judge nominated by him and the second may be the Registrar of the Supreme Court.

1.2 The Costs Clerk is a court officer in the Registry of the Supreme

Court who acts under the direction and supervision of the Costs Officers.

1.3 Detailed assessments are conducted in public.

1.4 The assessment of costs is governed by the relevant provisions of the Supreme Court Rules supplemented by this and the other Practice Directions issued by the President. To the extent that the Supreme Court Rules and Practice Directions do not cover the situation, the Rules and the Practice Directions which supplement Parts 43 to 48 of the Civil Procedure Rules are applied by analogy at the discretion of the Costs Officers, with appropriate modifications for appeals from Scotland and Northern Ireland. The legal principles applied are those also applicable to assessments between parties in the High Court and Court of Appeal in England and Wales[1].

1.5 References in this Practice Direction to:

"the Costs Officer" include the plural;

"costs" and "bills of costs" include expenses and accounts of expenses in appeals from Scotland, and

"solicitor[2]" includes an agent or a costs draftsman.

2. Entitlement to costs

4–159   **2.1** Claims for costs or *"bills of costs"* may be filed in the Registry for assessment in the following circumstances:

    (a) costs payable by appellants, respondents or other persons under an order for costs made by an Appeal Panel or by the Court;

    (b) costs payable by the Legal Services Commission (LSC) or the appropriate Legal Aid Board to appellants, respondents or other persons consequent upon an order for costs made by an Appeal Panel or by the Court to which section 11 of the Access to Justice Act 1999 or the equivalent provisions in the Legal Aid (Scotland) Act 1986 or the Legal Aid, Advice and Assistance (Northern Ireland) Order 1981 apply;

    (c) costs payable by the Legal Services Commission (LSC) or the appropriate Legal Aid Board to solicitors, counsel or other legal representatives acting on behalf of a party whose legal proceedings in the Supreme Court were funded ("a publicly funded party").

3. Orders under paragraph 3.5.1(d) of Practice Direction 3

4–160   **3.1** This paragraph applies to a respondent who is allowed to apply for his costs in accordance with paragraph 3.5(1)(d) of Practice Direction 3 (that is, in circumstances where an application for permission to appeal is refused).

3.2 The application may be made by letter addressed to the Registrar or may be included in a bill of costs filed in the Registry conditional upon the application being granted.

3.3 As a general rule the Registrar does not grant the application in any of the following cases:

---

[1] Kuwait Airways Corporation v Iraqi Airways Company and others: Appeal Committee, 102nd Report (2001–02), paragraph 16, HL Paper 155.
[2] Rule 3 defines "solicitor" as including any person authorised to provide legal services other than as counsel in connection with proceedings before the Court.

(a) where the application for permission was not served on the respondent making the application;

(b) where the respondent making the application did not file notice of objection to the application for permission;

(c) where the application is made by one of two or more respondents and the Registrar is not satisfied that the applicant had an interest in the application for permission that required separate representation.

4. Orders under section 11 of the Access to Justice Act 1999 etc.

4.1 Any costs ordered to be paid by a publicly funded party must **4–161** not exceed the amount which is a reasonable one for them to pay having regard to all the circumstances including

(a) the financial resources of all the parties to the proceedings; and

(b) their conduct in connection with the dispute to which the proceedings relate (Access to Justice Act 1999, section 11).

4.2 Costs which were incurred by one party during a period when another party was publicly funded, and which are not recoverable from the publicly funded party only because of section 11 of the Access to Justice Act 1999, may, in certain circumstances, be payable by the LSC itself.

4.3 The Community Legal Service (Costs) Regulations 2000 and the Community Legal Service (Cost Protection) Regulations 2000[1] are Regulations made under section 11 of the Access to Justice Act 1999 and provide a code governing orders for costs against publicly funded parties and against the LSC.

4.4 A party who seeks costs against the LSC under section 11 of the Access to Justice Act 1999, or who may do so, depending upon the amount of costs payable by the publicly funded party, must file with his bill of costs copies of any documents (including a statement of resources and any notice served by him on the LSC) which he has served upon others in compliance with the Regulations[2].

4.5 Within 21 days of being served with a bill of costs to which section 11 of the Access to Justice Act 1999 applies, a party who is or was publicly funded during any period covered by the bill must respond by filing in the Registry a statement of resources and serving a copy of it on the receiving party and, where relevant, on the LSC.

4.6 The LSC may appear at any hearing relating to an order made against the LSC.

4.7 References in this paragraph to the LSC and to section 11 of the Access to Justice Act 1999 are to be read as references to the appropriate Legal Aid Board and to the equivalent provisions in the Legal Aid (Scotland) Act 1986 and the Legal Aid, Advice and Assistance (Northern Ireland) Order 1981 in cases to which those provisions apply.

---

[1] SI 2000/441; SI 2000/824; SI 2001/822; SI 2001/823; SI 2001/3812; SI 2003/649; SI 2005/2006; and the equivalent provisions in the Legal Aid (Scotland) Act 1986 or the Legal Aid, Advice and Assistance (Northern Ireland) Order 1981.

[2] There is a strict time limit for making an application under section 11 see *R v Secretary of State for the Home Dept ex parte Gunn* [2001] EWCA Civ 891 and the Guidance Notes issued by the Senior Costs Judge.

5. Filing

4–162   **5.1** Bills of costs for assessment must be filed within three months of:

(a) the date on which the final judgment in the appeal is handed down; or

(b) the date on which an application for permission to appeal is dismissed by an Appeal panel; or

(c) the date on which an application for permission or a notice of appeal is withdrawn.

6. Extension of time

4–163   **6.1** If an extension of the three month period for filing a bill is desired, application must be made in writing to the Registrar before the end of that period. Copies of all such correspondence must be sent to all interested parties.

6.2 Applications for extensions of time may be made after the expiry of the three month period. In deciding whether to grant an application the Registrar takes into account all the circumstances, including:

(a) the interests of the administration of justice;

(b) whether the failure to file in time was intentional;

(c) whether there is a good explanation for the failure to file in time;

(d) the effect which the delay has had on each party; and

(e) the effect which the granting of an extension of time would have on each party.

7. Form of bill

4–164   **7.1** The items on a bill should be numbered consecutively as shown in Section 2 below and similarly worded where possible. Parties or their solicitors should adhere to the items shown so far as possible. The standard three column bill paper should be used. See paragraph 16.3 for items relating to counsel's fees.

7.2 Where costs are to be assessed both as between the parties and under the Access to Justice Act 1999 or the Legal Aid (Scotland) Act 1986 or the Second Schedule to the Legal Aid, Advice and Assistance (Northern Ireland) Order 1981, a six column bill should be drawn.

8. Endorsement

4–165   **8.1** The bill must be endorsed before filing with a certificate of service on the parties entitled to be represented at the assessment or their solicitors. Information about the date and time of the assessment is sent to all such parties or solicitors.

9. Documents

4–166   **9.1** The following documents must be filed with the Costs Clerk:

(a) the bill **plus two copies**;

(b) Counsel's fee notes and, where counsel's fees exceed the guideline rates in paragraph 26.5, a detailed note explaining why;

(c) written evidence of any other disbursement which is claimed and which exceeds £500;

   (d) certificates as to
      (i) accuracy,
      (ii) interest and payments,
      (iii) (where appropriate) interest of assisted person or funded client.

9.2 Other papers on which parties intend to rely may be brought to the assessment hearing or filed with the Costs Clerk as he thinks appropriate. At least 4 copies of any such papers must be provided. Where a bill is complex or large, any papers which the Costs Officers will need to pre–read, should be filed at least 7 days before the hearing.

10. Basis of assessment

10.1 Unless otherwise provided for by order or direction, costs in 4–167 the Supreme Court are ordered to be assessed on the standard basis or on the indemnity basis in accordance with rules 50 and 51 of the Supreme Court Rules or the equivalent bases that apply in Scotland and Northern Ireland.

11. Fees for preparing applications for permission to appeal

11.1 The general rule is that a single fee is allowed for one junior 4–168 counsel for preparing applications for permission to appeal. Rarely, if ever, are fees allowed for two counsel, but a fee may be allowed for a Queen's Counsel instead of junior counsel if this is held to be necessary because of the difficulty or complexity of the case or other good reason.[1]

11.2 In a publicly funded application for permission to appeal, a fee for Queen's Counsel is not allowed unless permission has been given by the relevant funding authority.

11.3 For guideline figures for fees on applications for permission to appeal, see paragraph 26.5.

12. Funded parties: applications for permission to appeal

12.1 Where an applicant for permission to appeal is publicly 4–169 funded and the application is dismissed without an oral hearing:

   (a) reasonable costs may be awarded for preparing the applicant's papers for the Appeal panel;
   (b) a publicly funded respondent may be awarded costs incurred in attending the client, filing notice of objection and, where applicable, preparing respondent's objections to the application;
   (c) an unassisted respondent may be awarded costs similar to those at (b) above out of the Community Legal Service Fund pursuant to s ection 11 of the Access to Justice Act 1999 or the equivalent provisions in the Legal Aid (Scotland) Act 1986 and the Legal Aid, Advice and Assistance (Northern Ireland) Order 1981.

12.2 If an application for permission to appeal is dismissed after an oral hearing, the costs of the hearing are allowable in addition to the costs at (a) to (c) above.

---

[1] As to "necessary", see Lord Woolf CJ, *Home Office v Lownds* [2002] EWCA Civ 365.

13. Respondents' Objections

4–170   **13.1** Respondents to an application for permission to appeal who submit objections under rule 13 may apply for costs in accordance with paragraphs 3 and 4 above. For guideline figures for preparing respondents' objections, see paragraph 26.5.

14. Provisional assessment

4–171   **14.1** A provisional assessment procedure exists for the assessment of costs involving public funding and in cases where the parties request a provisional assessment. In such cases a provisional assessment is conducted without the attendance of the parties, and the Registrar informs them in writing of the outcome: rule 49(6). If the result of this procedure proves unsatisfactory to the parties, or if points of disagreement cannot be resolved in correspondence, the Registrar appoints a date for a hearing.

14.2 Large or complex bills, and bills to be assessed as between the parties, are not usually dealt with by provisional assessment procedure but at a hearing before the Costs Officers.

14.3 Any request for a hearing following a provisional assessment must be made within 14 days of the receipt of the letter from the Registrar: rule 49(6). Where an oral hearing is requested, it will take place before a Costs Judge and the Registrar.

14.4 The Scottish Legal Aid Board will be informed of any provisional assessment in an appeal from Scotland in order that it may decide whether or not to intervene.

15. Assessment before Costs Officers

Points of dispute

4–172   **15.1** A paying party may file points of dispute under rule 48 but, if the bill is above **£20,000**, the paying party must file points of dispute. Paying parties who file points of dispute must do so within 21 days of service of the bill upon them, and must at the same time serve a copy of the points of dispute on every other party. The points of dispute must be properly endorsed with a certificate of service. The receiving party may within 21 days from service of the points of dispute respond to the points if they think it appropriate to do so.

15.2 Where the paying party does not file points of dispute and fails to attend an assessment, the Costs Officer may nevertheless assess the bill, but generally allows the bill to the extent that it appears reasonable and (if appropriate) proportionate.

Date of assessment hearing

15.3 The Registrar gives at least 21 days' notice of the day and time appointed for assessment to all those entitled to be heard at the assessment.

Attendance at assessments

15.4 The receiving party or their deputy must attend the assessment. Where additional papers are brought to the assessment, at least 4 copies must be provided. Only the parties or their solicitors who were responsible for the case in the Supreme Court or their deputies have a right to be heard. For the purpose of this paragraph, a deputy may be another member of the solicitor's firm, or the London agent, or the costs draftsman or counsel instructed for the purpose; but those attending must be fully conversant with the matters to be considered.

Counsel

15.5 Where counsel's fees exceed the guideline rates in paragraph 26.5, a detailed note must accompany the bill, explaining why this is justified. Submissions on counsel's fees may be made at the assessment hearing or in writing to the Costs Officer on a provisional assessment.

16. Costs Officers' discretion (civil appeals)

16.1 The Costs Officers have discretion as to the amount to allow. **4–173** In exercising this discretion they bear in mind the terms "unreasonably incurred" and "unreasonable in amount" in CPR 44.4, (or in appeals from Scotland the provisions of Rule 42.10 of the Rules of the Court of Session 1994) and in particular consider to what extent an item assisted the Court in determining the appeal. In the case of applications for permission to appeal, a major consideration is whether the application gave rise to a point of public importance.

16.2 The length of a hearing, the complexity of the issues as indicated by the judgments delivered in the Court, and the general level of fees sought and allowed in the lower courts are taken into account.

16.3 Counsel's fees are assessed in respect of each item of work counsel has undertaken. It is essential therefore in drawing a bill to apportion counsel's work according to the categories set out in paragraphs 26.5 and 26.7. The number of hours spent by counsel in preparation is rarely of assistance to the Costs Officers when assessing the quantum of counsel's fees at any stage of the proceedings.

16.4 The Costs Officers have discretion to allow Queen's Counsel's fees for applications for permission to appeal (subject to paragraph 11).

16.5 The Costs Officers have no discretion to allow fees for more than two counsel unless the Court has, on application at the hearing, made an order that the fees of more than two counsel may be allowed. See paragraph 6.3.7 of Practice Direction 6.

17. Costs Officers' discretion (criminal appeals)

17.1 The Costs Officers do not generally take into account the **4–174** hours spent by counsel in preparation.

17.2 The Costs Officers have discretion to allow Queen's Counsel's fees for applications for permission to appeal (subject to paragraph 11).

17.3 The Costs Officers have no discretion to allow fees for more than two counsel unless the Court has, on application at the hearing, made an order that the fees of more than two counsel may be allowed. See paragraph 6.3.7 of Practice Direction 6.

18. Appeals against assessment in the Supreme Court

Appeals against assessment

18.1 Any party to an assessment who is dissatisfied with all or part **4–175**

of a decision of the Costs Officer may apply in accordance with rule 53 for that decision to be reviewed by a single Justice.

18.2 An application may be made only on a question of principle and not in respect of the quantum allowed on any item. For applications see paragraph 7.1 of Practice Direction7.

18.3 Any application must be made within 14 days after the decision of the Costs Officer or such longer period as may be fixed by him or by the Registrar.

Written grounds of appeal

18.4 An application for a review must be accompanied by written submissions setting out the items or parts of items objected to and stating concisely in each case the nature and grounds of the objections. A copy of the grounds of appeal must be delivered to each party who attended the assessment of those items.

18.5 Any party to whom a copy of the grounds of appeal is delivered may, within 14 days after delivery of the copy to them or such longer period as may be fixed by the Registrar, submit in writing to the Registrar their answers to the grounds of appeal. They should state concisely the reasons why they are opposed to a review of the item(s), and must at the same time deliver a copy of their answers to the party applying for review and to each party to whom a copy of the grounds of appeal has been delivered.

Reference to a Single Justice

18.6 When he has received all the necessary documents, the Registrar refers the matter to a single Justice nominated by the presiding or senior Justice who heard the appeal or application for permission to appeal.

18.7 The nominated single Justice decides whether the matter should be referred to an Appeal Panel and, before he makes a decision, he may consult other Justices who heard the appeal or application. If the single Justice is of the opinion that the matter should not be so referred, the decision of the Costs Officer is affirmed.

Application to the Court

18.8 If the nominated single Justice decides that the matter should be referred to an Appeal panel, the party disputing the decision of the Costs Officer may, within 14 days of the date on which that decision is communicated to the parties, file an application in Form 2.

18.9 The application will be referred to a Panel of Justices, which considers whether it should be referred for hearing.

19. Allocatur (Agreed Costs Figures)

4–176 **19.1** Forms of allocatur are obtained from the Costs Clerk at the assessment hearing and must be returned by the receiving party to the Costs Clerk within one month, signed by all parties who attended the assessment, together with the completed bill and assessment fee. Specimen forms are set out in Section 3 below.

19.2 If a paying party refuses to sign the form of allocatur, the signature of the receiving party will be sufficient, provided the Registrar is satisfied that the paying party has refused to sign without good reason.

20. Certificate of discharge

20.1 A certificate in the following form may be accepted as evidence of payment of any disbursement not exceeding £500 (other than fees to counsel) provided that the paying party does not object, and subject to any direction to the contrary that may be given by the Costs Officer: **4–177**

> We A.B. & Co.,
>
> Hereby certify that all disbursements listed in the assessed bill in the matter of C. v. D. which individually do not exceed £500 (other than those relating to counsel's fees) have been duly discharged.
>
> Signed A. B. & Co.

21. Vouching

21.1 Counsel's fee notes must be receipted except in the case of publicly funded bills. **4–178**

22. Summary

22.1 The completed bill of costs must include a summary (see Section 3 below) showing the respective amounts of profit costs, counsel's fees, other disbursements and VAT allowed. **4–179**

23. Fees

23.1 Information about payment of assessment fees is set out in Section 4 below and the fees are set out in Annex 2 to Practice Direction 7. **4–180**

23.2 The receiving party is responsible for paying the filing fee and the assessment fee.

23.3 The receiving party is responsible for paying the fee on a withdrawn bill.

23.4 Reduced fees are payable when costs are agreed before assessment. Responsibility for informing the Registrar that agreement has been reached lies with the receiving party, but both parties must confirm the agreement in writing.

23.5 Drafts and cheques for fees are payable to "**The Supreme Court of the United Kingdom**".

24. Certificates

Civil

24.1 When the assessment fee has been paid, a certificate of assessment for the costs as allowed will be sent to the receiving party, except in the case of respondents whose costs can be wholly satisfied from money deposited as security for costs (see rules 36 and 54). **4–181**

Criminal

24.2 Where costs have been ordered to be paid out of Central Funds or where costs are paid under Legal Aid Orders issued by the Registrar of the Court of Appeal, Criminal Division, the certificate and counsel's fee notes are sent to the Senior Courts Fees Office to settle the certificated amounts with the parties or their agents and counsel direct.

Courts–Martial

24.3 Where costs are payable to the Secretary of State for Defence in respect of an appeal from the Courts–Martial Appeal Court, the certificate is sent direct to the Ministry of Defence to settle as in 24.2 above.

Criminal (Northern Ireland)

24.4 Where the costs are payable in accordance with section 41 of the Criminal Appeal (Northern Ireland) Act 1980 the certificates are sent to the Northern Ireland Office to settle as in 24.2 above.

25. Interest

4–182　**25.1** Interest is chargeable on orders made in respect of costs assessed as between the parties and orders for costs in favour of successful unassisted parties. The rate of interest is in accordance with the provisions of the Judgments Act 1838, as amended, and interest accrues from the day on which the order of the Court is made or such other date as the Court may specify.

25.2 It is within the discretion of the Costs Officer to vary the period for which interest is allowed in any case where the circumstances make it appropriate to do so.

26. Quantum: guidelines on fees allowed

Solicitors practising in England and Wales[1]

4–183　**26.1** The guideline rates set out below are used. These are consolidated figures that include a mark–up for care and attention. No further mark–up is allowed for care and attention.

26.2 The following table sets out the hourly rates and localities:

Grade of fee earner	A	B	C	D
	£	£	£	£
City of London	402	291	222	136
Central London	312	238	193	124
Outer London	225–263	169–225	162	119
National 1	213	189	158	116
National 2/3	198	174	144	109

An explanation of the grades and details of localities will be found in Section 5 below.

26.3 Claims at the "A" rate must be justified.

26.4 When travel and waiting is claimed, this is allowed at the rate agreed with the client, unless this is more than the hourly rate allowed on the assessment.

Letters and telephone calls are allowed at one tenth (1/10) of the hourly rate.

---

[1] Consolidated rates based on those permitted in the respective jurisdictions are allowed for solicitors practising in Scotland or Northern Ireland.

Counsel

26.5 The following guideline figures are used in assessing payments to counsel:

Applications for permission, civil and criminal

	Junior	**QC** (*subject to paragraph 11*)
Settling application	£1000	£1250
Advice (if any) for Legal Services Commission or Legal Aid Board in Scotland or Northern Ireland	£400	£600
Preparing respondents' objections	£700	£1000
Attending oral hearing by Appeal Panel	£1500	£2000

26.6 If an increase is sought on any of the above items, it must be explained in a detailed note from counsel which accompanies the bill. No other payments are allowed at the permission to appeal stage.

26.7 The general rule is that only one counsel's fees are allowed on assessment for any stage of an application for permission to appeal, unless a public funding or legal aid certificate authorises two counsel (see paragraph 11).

Appeals—civil and criminal

	Junior	**QC**
Settling notice of appeal	£100	£100
Statement of facts and issues	£2000	£4000
Authorities	£800	£1600
Conferences (each, up to a maximum of six)	£500	£1000
Advice	£900	£1800
Brief (based on a 1 day hearing)	£7000	£14000
Brief (based on a 2 day or longer hearing)	£9000	£18000
Refresher (from day two of the hearing)	£1500	£3000

Notes

26.8 Generally counsel for an appellant commands a higher fee than counsel for a respondent.

26.9 The brief fee includes **all work on the brief, the case and the first day of attendance at the Court**.

26.10 The Costs Officers exercise discretion in instances where junior counsel has undertaken most of the work on a particular item.

26.11 For settling a notice of appeal, only one counsel's fee is permitted. The Costs Officers have no discretion to allow fees for more than two counsel unless the Court has, on application at the hearing, made an order that the fees of more than two counsel may be allowed. See paragraph 6.3.7 of Practice Direction 6.

26.12 These fees are intended as a guide. If counsel seek higher fees, they must explain in a detailed note which should accompany the bill.

27. Conditional Fee Agreements

4–184   **27.1** Notification should be given to the opposing parties and to the Registry as soon as practicable after a conditional fee agreement has been entered into[1]. The Costs Officers decide questions of percentage uplift in accordance with the principles set out in *Designers' Guild Limited v Russell Williams (Textiles) Limited (Trading as Washington D.C.)* [2003] 2 Costs LR 20[2].

28. Costs of litigants in person

4–185   **28.1** The amount allowed to a litigant in person may not exceed the loss actually sustained or, where no loss has been sustained, £9.25 for each hour reasonably spent, subject in either case to a maximum for any particular item of two thirds of the sum which in the opinion of the Costs Officer would have been allowed for that item if the litigant had been represented by a solicitor. The two thirds limit does not apply to out–of–pocket expenses which would be disbursements if incurred by a solicitor. (For further information see CPR 48.6 and section 52 of the Costs Practice Direction which supplements it.)

29. Costs of Drafting Bill for Assessment

4–186   **29.1** By way of guidance for smaller bills, the following sums are usually justified:

Amount of bill	Amount allowed
Bills assessed at up to £2000 (excluding VAT)	£300
Bills assessed at £2001–£5000 (excluding VAT)	£500
Bills assessed at £5001–£10000 (excluding VAT)	£700

[1] Notification is not generally needed in Scottish appeals where an agreement has been entered into under Rule 42.17 of the Rules of the Court of Session 1994 but it is helpful to the Costs Officers to be informed of any such agreement when the account of expenses is submitted for assessment.

[2] It is open to the Costs Officers to reduce the percentage uplift recoverable if it is considered to be excessive. A party who seeks a ruling that the percentage uplift should be disallowed on legal grounds should apply to the Court at the hearing for such a ruling.

29.2 For a larger bill the amount allowed is a multiple of the relevant hourly rate for time reasonably spent in drafting the bill.

SECTION 2: FORMS OF BILLS OF COSTS

4–187   *Note: the figures in the following forms are for illustrative purposes only*

Form A: Respondent's bill of costs under paragraph 3.5.1(d) of Practice Direction 3

IN THE SUPREME COURT

ON APPEAL FROM HER MAJESTY'S COURT OF APPEAL (ENGLAND)

BETWEEN

AB	Claimant and Appellant
~ and ~	
CD	Defendant and Respondent

RESPONDENT'S BILL OF COSTS

V.A.T. No. 33 5574 90

Proceedings in the Courts below

The appellant brought a claim in the High Court seeking compensation for personal injuries and other losses suffered in a road accident which occurred on 1st January 1999, as a result of which the respondent (the defendant in those proceedings) was later convicted of various offences including careless driving and driving under the influence of drink or drugs.

At the trial of the claim in July 2001 the appellant was awarded damages totalling £78,256.53 plus interest and costs. The respondent brought an appeal to the Court of Appeal relying upon several infringements of articles 6 and 8 of the Human Rights Act 1998 which had occurred at and before the trial. The appeal was successful. By its order dated 27 June 2002, the Court of Appeal set aside the trial award and awarded to the respondent her costs incurrred in the High Court and Court of Appeal.

Proceedings in the Supreme Court

The appellant sought permission to appeal against the Order of the Court of Appeal dated 27 June 2002. The application for permission was served on the respondent who then filed notice of objection. On 28 July 2003 permission to appeal was refused without a hearing and the respondent was allowed to apply for her costs in accordance with paragraph 3.5.1(d) of Practice Direction 3. The respondent respectfully requests the Registrar to accept this bill as constituting such an application.

Fee earners and hourly rates

The respondent first instructed T U V & Co in this matter in June 2002. The following rates were agreed

Partner - £195 per hour plus VAT
Assistant solicitor - £130 per hour plus VAT
Other fee earners - £95 per hour plus VAT
Routine letters and emails out and telephone calls – one tenth of the relevant hourly rate.

Item No.	Description of work done	V.A.T.	Disbursements	Profit Costs
	Attendances upon the Registry			
	18 July 2002			
1	Filing notice of objection – Trainee solicitor 6 minutes			£ 9.50
2	Travelling and waiting 1.3 hours			£ 123.50
3	Paid fee		£ 115.00	
	Attendances upon the respondent			
4	Routine letters (5: assistant)			£ 65.00
5	Routine telephone calls (7: assistant)			£ 91.00
	Attendances upon the appellant			
6	Routine letters (5: assistant)			£ 65.00
	Communications with Registry			
7	Routine letter (1: assistant)			£ 13.00
	Attendances upon documents			
	12 July 2002 considering the application for permission 24 mins partner			
	28 July 2002 considering the ruling thereon 6 mins partner			
8	Total for partner 0.5 hours			£ 97.50
	Other work done			
	Preparing and checking the bill			
9	Partner 24 mins			£ 78.00
10	Costs draftsman 1.5 hours			£ 142.50
	Assessment of costs			
	Preparing for and attending assessment (including perusal of any Points of Dispute served)			
11	Partner 0.5 hours (estimated)			£ 97.50
12	Costs draftsman 1.5 hours (estimated)			£ 142.50
13	Travel and waiting (costs draftsman) 1.5 hours (estimated)			£ 142.50
14	VAT on total profit costs of £1,067.50			£ 186.81
15	Assessment fee (to be added)			

	Grand totals	
	Profit Costs £	1,067.50
	VAT thereon £	186.81
	Disbursements £	115.00
	VAT thereon £	-
	Total costs claimed £	1,369.31

Form B Appellant's bill for application for permission and appeal

IN THE SUPREME COURT

ON APPEAL FROM HER MAJESTY'S COURT OF APPEAL (ENGLAND)

BETWEEN

AB	Claimant and Appellant
~ and ~	
CD	Defendant and Respondent

APPELLANT'S BILL OF COSTS

V.A.T. No. 22 4462 80

Proceedings in the Courts below

The appellant brought a claim in the High Court seeking compensation for personal injuries and other losses suffered in a road accident which occurred on 1st January 1999, as a result of which the respondent (the defendant in those proceedings) was later convicted of various offences including careless driving and driving under the influence of drink or drugs.

At the trial of the claim in July 2001 the appellant was awarded damages totalling £78,256.53 plus interest and costs. The respondent brought an appeal to the Court of Appeal relying upon several infringements of articles 6 and 8 of the Human Rights Act 1998 which had occurred at and before the trial. The appeal was successful. By its order dated 27 June 2002, the Court of Appeal set aside the trial award and awarded to the respondent her costs incurred in the High Court and Court of Appeal.

Proceedings in the Supreme Court

The appellant applied for permission to appeal against the Order of the Court of Appeal dated 27 June 2002. The application was heard on 28 October 2002 and was successful. The appellant then gave notice that he wishes to proceed with his appeal. It was not possible to agree the Statement of Facts and Issues within the time allowed and therefore, with the consent of the respondent, an application was made for an extension of time. In November 2002 an agreed Statement of Facts and Issues and an Appendix was filed and the Registrar was informed that the appeal was ready to list. The appeal then proceeded to a hearing before the Court on 18 July 2003 and, on 28 July 2003, Orders were made setting aside the Order of the Court of Appeal dated 27 June 2002 and restoring the Order of Mr Justice Alexander dated 26 July 2001. It was further ordered that the respondent should pay or cause to be paid to the appellant the costs incurred by the appellant in the proceedings in the Supreme Court and in the proceedings in the Court of Appeal.

Fee earners and hourly rates

The appellant first instructed E F & Co under a conditional fee agreement dated 8 July 2000 which applied to the claim and to the appeal brought in the Court of Appeal by the respondent. That agreement did not apply to the proceedings in the House of Lords and therefore a further conditional fee agreement dated 28 July 2001 was made which specifies the following base fees and success fees

Partner - £195 per hour plus VAT

Assistant solicitor - £144 per hour plus VAT

Success fee - 100% discounted to 25% if, before or within 2 weeks after the appeal is set down, the parties agree settlement terms which in effect restore the decision herein of Mr Justice Alexander.

Except where the contrary is stated the proceedings were conducted on behalf of the appellant by an assistant solicitor, admitted November 2001.

Counsel's fees

E F & Co instructed Counsel (Miss G H, called 1992) under a conditional fee agreement dated 28 July 2001, which specifies a success fee as defined in the agreement between solicitor and client and base fees, payable in various circumstances, of which the following are relevant

Conferences	£250 plus £50 per half hour or part thereof, plus VAT
Brief for appeal (estimated duration 5 hours)	£2,750 plus VAT
Fee for second and subsequent days	£850 plus VAT
Judgment fee	£200 plus VAT

Item No.	Description of work done	V.A.T.	Disburse-ments	Profit Costs
	APPLICATION FOR PERMISSION			
	Attendances at the Registry			
	8 July 2002			
1	Filing the application 6 mins			£ 14.40
2	Travelling and waiting 1.3 hours			£ 187.20
3	Paid fee		£ 570.00	
	Attending the Appeal Panel			
	28 October 2002			
4	Attending Hearing 1.1 hours			£ 158.40
5	Travel and waiting 1.8 hours			£ 259.20
6	Counsel's base fee for hearing		£ 750.00	
	Attendances upon the appellant			
7	Routine letter (1: partner)			£ 19.50
8	Routine letters (5: assistant)			£ 72.00
9	Routine telephone calls (7: assistant)			£ 100.80
10	Timed telephone calls (Schedule 1: total 1.7 hours)			£ 244.80
	Attendances upon the respondent			
11	Routine letters (5)			£ 72.00
	Communications with Registry			
12	Routine letters (5)			£ 72.00
	Communications with Counsel			
13	Routine letters (2)			£ 28.80
14	Routine telephone calls (6)			£ 86.40
	Attendances upon documents (Schedule 2)			
15	Total for partner 1.1 hours			£ 214.50
16	Total for assistant 36 minutes			£ 86.40
	NOTICE OF APPEAL			
	Attendances upon the Registry and Counsel			
	11 November 2002			
17	Filing the notice 6 mins			£ 14.40
18	Travelling and waiting 1.3 hours			£ 187.20
19	Paid fee		£ 570.00	
	Carried forward -	£ -	£ 1,890.00	£ 1,818.00

	Conference with counsel			
20	Attending with client 1.5 hours			£ 216.00
21	Travelling and waiting 1.2 hours			£ 172.80
22	Counsel's base fee	£ 400.00		
	Application for extension of time (filed by post)			
23	Paid fee	£ 230.00		
	15 January 2003			
24	Filing Agreed Statement of Facts and Issues and Appendix 18 mins			£ 43.20
25	Travelling and waiting 1.7 hours			£ 244.80
26	Paid fee	£ 3,420.00		
	Attending the Appeal			
	18 July 2003			
27	Attending Hearing 4.7 hours			£ 676.80
28	Travel and waiting 1.8 hours			£ 259.20
29	Counsel's base fee for hearing	£ 2,750.00		
	28 July 2003			
30	Attending for Judgment 1.7 hours			£ 244.80
31	Travel and waiting 1.8 hours			£ 259.20
32	Counsel's Judgment fee	£ 850.00		
	Attendances upon the appellant			
33	Routine letter (7: partner)			£ 136.50
34	Routine letters (35: assistant)			£ 504.00
35	Routine telephone calls (27: assistant)			£ 388.80
36	Timed telephone calls (Schedule 3: total 2.7 hours)			£ 388.80
	Attendances upon the respondent			
37	Routine letters (15)			£ 216.00
38	Routine telephone calls (27)			£ 388.80
39	Timed telephone calls (Schedule 4: total 1.6 hours)			£ 230.40
	Communications with Registry			
40	Routine letters (23)			£ 331.20
	Carried forward:	£ -	£ 9,540.00	£ 6,519.30

41	Routine letters (22)			£ 316.80
42	Routine telephone calls (16)			£ 230.40
43	Timed telephone calls (Schedule 5: total 1.6 hours)			£ 230.40
	Attendances upon documents (Schedule 6)			
44	Total for partner 3.1 hours			£ 604.50
45	Total for assistant 18.7 hours			£ 2,692.80
	Other work done			
	Preparing and checking the bill			
46	Partner 24 mins			£ 78.00
47	Assistant 1.4 hours			£ 201.60
48	Costs draftsman's fee		£ 900.00	
	Sub-totals:-	£ -	£ 10,440.00	£ 10,873.80
	VAT and success fees			
49	VAT on solicitors' base fees of £10,873.80	£ 1,902.92		
50	Success fee on solicitors' base fees and VAT thereon	£ 1,902.92		£ 10,873.80
51	VAT on counsel's base fees of £4,750	£ 831.25		
52	Success fee on counsel's base fees and VAT thereon	£ 831.25	£ 4,750.00	
	Assessment of costs			
	Attending assessment including perusal of any points of dispute served			
53	Partner 1.5 hours (estimated)			£ 292.50
54	Travel and waiting (Partner) 1.5 hours (estimated)			£ 292.50
55	Success fee on estimated solicitors' charges (100%)			£ 585.00
56	Costs draftsman's fee for attending the hearing and travel and waiting 3 hours (estimated)	£ 49.88	£ 285.00	
57	VAT on items 53 - 55	£ 204.75		
58	Assessment fees (to be added)			
	Totals:-	£ 5,722.96	£ 15,475.00	£ 22,917.60

Grand totals	£ 44,115.56
Profit Costs £ 22,917.60	
VAT thereon £ 4,010.58	
Disbursements £ 15,475.00	
VAT thereon £ 1,712.38	
Total costs claimed £ 44,115.56	

Page 5

378

Form C: Respondent's bill of costs including separate accounts for Scottish and English agents

IN THE SUPREME COURT

ON APPEAL FROM THE COURT OF SESSION IN SCOTLAND

BETWEEN

AB	Pursuer and Appellant
~ and ~	
CD	Defender and Respondent

RESPONDENT'S BILL OF COSTS

Proceedings in the Courts below

The appellant brought a claim for compensation for personal injuries and other losses suffered in a road accident which occurred on 1st January 1999, as a result of which the respondent (the defender in those proceedings) was later convicted of various offences including careless driving and driving under the influence of drink or drugs.

The claim was heard by the Lord Ordinary (Lady X) in the Court of Session in July 2001 and was successful. The appellant was awarded damages totalling £78,256.53 plus interest and expenses. A reclaiming motion was marked by the respondent in which she relied upon several infringements of articles 6 and 8 of the Human Rights Act 1998 which had occurred at and before the trial. The reclaiming motion was heard by their lordships of the First Division of the Court of Session in June 2002. On 27 June 2002 the First Division allowed the reclaiming motion, set aside the trial award and awarded to the respondent her expenses incurred in the proceedings before them and before the Lord Ordinary.

Proceedings in the Supreme Court

The notice of appeal was served on the respondent who filed an acknowledgement to it. In November 2002 a Statement of Facts and Issues and an Appendix were agreed. The appeal was proceeded to a hearing on 18 July 2003. On 28 July 2003, Orders were made dismissing the appeal and awarding the respondent her costs incurred in the Supreme Court.

Fee earners and hourly rates

EDINBURGH AGENTS' ACCOUNT
V.A.T. No. 43 9876 90
The respondent first instructed W X & Co in this matter in June 2002. The following rates were agreed
Partner - £190 per hour plus VAT
Assistant solicitor - £130 per hour plus VAT
Other fee earners - £95 per hour plus VAT
Routine letters and emails out and telephone calls – one tenth of the relevant hourly rate.

LONDON AGENTS' ACCOUNT

V.A.T. No. 33 5574 90

By her solicitors W X & Co, the respondent instructed Y Z & Co and the following rates were agreed

Partner - £195 per hour plus VAT

Assistant solicitor - £144 per hour plus VAT

Routine letters and emails out and telephone calls – one tenth of the relevant hourly rate.

Except where the contrary is stated the proceedings were conducted on behalf of the appellant by an assistant solicitor, admitted November 2001.

Item No.	Description of work done	V.A.T.	Disburse-ments	Profit Costs
	PART 1 EDINBURGH AGENTS' ACCOUNT			
	NOTICE OF APPEAL			
	Attendances upon Counsel			
	5 December 2002			
	Consultation with counsel			
1	Partner attending with client 1.5 hours			£ 285.00
2	Travelling and waiting 1.2 hours			£ 228.00
3	Counsel's fee	£ 78.75	£ 450.00	
4	Paid fee for certifying Appeal to the Supreme Court		£ 97.00	
	Attending the Appeal			
	18 July 2003			
4	Counsel's fee for hearing	£ 525.00	£ 3,000.00	
	28 July 2003			
5	Counsel's fee for judgment	£ 148.75	£ 850.00	
	Attendances upon the respondent			
	Personal attendances (Schedule 1)			
6	Total for partner 3.2 hours			£ 608.00
7	Total for assistant 1.4 hours			£ 182.00
8	Routine letters (15: Partner)			£ 285.00
9	Routine letters (7: assistant)			£ 91.00
10	Routine telephone calls (27: assistant)			£ 351.00
	Timed telephone calls (Schedule 2)			
11	Total for partner 2.1 hours			£ 380.00
12	Total for assistant 1.6 hours			£ 208.00
	Attendances upon the appellant			
13	Routine letters (2: partner)			£ 38.00
14	Routine letters (4. assistant)			£ 52.00
	Communications with Registry			
15	Routine letters (8: assistant)			£ 104.00
	Communications with Counsel			
16	Routine letters (12: partner)			£ 228.00
17	Routine telephone calls (16: partner)			£ 304.00
18	Timed telephone calls (Schedule 3: total 1.6 hours: partner)			£ 304.00
	Attendances upon documents (Schedule 4)			
19	Total for partner 3.1 hours			£ 589.00
20	Total for assistant 14.7 hours			£ 1,911.00
	Carried forward:-	£ 752.50	£ 4,397.00	£ 6,148.00

Item No.	Description of work done	V.A.T.	Disburse-ments	Profit Costs
	Brought forward	£ 752.50	£ 4,397.00	£ 6,148.00
	Other work done			
	Preparing and checking the bill			
21	Partner 0.7 hours			£ 133.00
22	Assistant 1.4 hours			£ 182.00
23	Costs draftsman's fee	£ 94.50	£ 540.00	
	Assessment of costs			
	Preparing for assessment (including perusal of any Points of Dispute served)			
24	Partner 1.5 hours (estimated)			£ 265.00
	Sub-totals :-	£ 847.00	£ 4,937.00	£ 6,748.00

Totals

Profit Costs	£	6,748.00
VAT thereon	£	1,180.90
Disbursements	£	4,937.00
VAT thereon	£	847.00
Total costs claimed in Part 1	£	13,712.90

Item No.	Description of work done	V.A.T.	Disbursements	Profit Costs
	PART 2 LONDON AGENTS' ACCOUNT			
	NOTICE OF APPEAL			
	Attendances upon the Registry			
	18 July 2002			
25	Presenting the notice of appeal 6 minutes			£ 14.40
26	Travelling and waiting 1.3 hours			£ 187.20
27	Paid fee		£ 1,140.00	
	Attending the Appeal			
	18 July 2003			
28	Attending Hearing 4.7 hours			£ 676.80
29	Travel and waiting 1.8 hours			£ 259.20
	28 July 2003			
30	Attending for Judgment 1.7 hours			£ 244.80
31	Travel and waiting 1.8 hours			£ 259.20
	Attendances upon the respondent and her Edinburgh agents			
32	Routine letters (35)			£ 504.00
33	Routine telephone calls (27)			£ 388.80
34	Timed telephone calls (Schedule 5: total 1.6 hours)			£ 230.40
	Attendances upon the appellant			
35	Routine letters (25)			£ 360.00
36	Routine telephone calls (27)			£ 388.80
	Communications with Registry			
37	Routine letters (23)			£ 331.20
	Communications with Counsel			
38	Routine letters (2)			£ 28.80
39	Routine telephone calls (16)			£ 230.40
	Attendances upon documents (Schedule 6)			
40	Total for partner 3.1 hours			£ 604.50
41	Total for assistant 18.7 hours			£ 2,692.80
	Other work done			
	Preparing and checking the bill			
42	Partner 24 mins			£ 78.00
43	Assistant 1.4 hours			£ 201.60
44	Costs draftsman's fee	£ 94.50	£ 540.00	
	Carried forward:-	£ 94.50	£ 1,680.00	£ 7,680.90

Item No.	Description of work done	V.A.T.	Disbursements	Profit Costs
	Brought forward	£ 94.50	£ 1,680.00	£ 7,680.90
	Assessment of costs			
	Preparing for and attending assessment (including perusal of any Points of Dispute served)			
45	Assistant 2.5 hours (estimated)			£ 360.00
46	Travel and waiting 1.5 hours (estimated)			£ 216.00
47	Costs draftsman's fee for attending the hearing and travel and waiting (estimated)	£ 52.50	£ 300.00	
48	Assessment fees (to be added)			
	Sub total>	£ 147.00	£ 1,980.00	£ 8,256.90

Totals

Profit Costs	£	8,256.90
VAT thereon	£	1,444.96
Disbursements	£	1,980.00
VAT thereon	£	147.00
Total costs claimed in Part 2	£	**11,828.86**

SUMMARY

Part 1	£	13,712.90
Part 2	£	11,828.86
TOTAL	£	**25,541.76**

SECTION 3: SUMMARY AND ALLOCATUR OF BILLS OF COSTS

SECTION 3: SUMMARY AND ALLOCATUR OF BILLS OF COSTS

1   Summary   for Bill

Assessed Off	Value Added Tax[1]	Disbursements	Profit costs

Disbursements	Profit Costs		
	Page 1		
	Page 2		
	Page 3		
	Page 4		

Assessed off ... ...

Add profit costs ... ...

Add VAT on profit costs ... ...

Add counsel's fees ....

Add VAT on counsel's fees...

Other disbursements ... ...

Add VAT on other disbursements...

Total ... ...

Assessment fee 5%

(on total rounded up to next pound)

---

[1] Value Added Tax on disbursements as allowed.

Funded Summary

Profit costs (excluding costs
of assessment) ... ...

VAT on profit costs ... .

Counsel's fees ... ...

VAT on counsel's fees ...

Other disbursements
(excluding assessment fee) ...

VAT on other
disbursements ... ...

Costs of assessment
allowed against Community
legal service fund
(including assessment fee) ... ...

VAT thereon (excluding
assessment fee) ... ...

(or simple form if appropriate)

3.　　**Allocatur**[2]

IN THE SUPREME COURT

BETWEEN

... ...

v.

... ...

APPELLANT'S/RESPONDENT/S* COSTS
(Delete where applicable)

Amount of profit costs and disbursements claimed ... ...

Less assessed off disbursements and profit costs... ... ...　　　　＿＿＿＿＿

Total ... ...

Add VAT[3]　　　＿＿＿＿＿

Total allowed... ... ...

Assessment fee on total allowed[4] ... ...　　　＿＿＿＿＿

Amount to be certified... ... ...　　　＿＿＿＿＿

... ...Solicitor for the appellant

... ... Solicitor for the respondent

REGISTRAR
SUPREME COURT

---

[2] The return of this form together with the bill and the fee within one month of the assessment is the responsibility of the receiving party. The party must indicate their agreement to the castings in the bill by signing the allocatur.
[3] On amounts which attract VAT.
[4] Assessment fee payable to "the Supreme Court Fees Account".

SECTION 4: FEES

For the relevant fees see the order made under section 52 of the **4–189** Constitutional Reform Act 2005 on the website of the Supreme Court or Annex 2 to Practice Direction 7. Drafts and cheques for assessment fees are payable to 'the Supreme Court of the United Kingdom'.

SECTION 5: GUIDELINE FIGURES FOR THE PROVISIONAL ASSESSMENT OF COSTS

4–190   *Solicitors' hourly rates: England and Wales*

1. The guideline rates set out in paragraph 26 for solicitors are broad approximations. Rates include care and attention.

2. The grades of fee earner are those that have been agreed between representatives of the Senior Courts Costs Office, the Association of District Judges and the Law Society. The categories are as follows:

    A. Solicitors with over eight years' post qualification experience including at least eight years litigation experience.

    B. Solicitors, employed barristers and legal executives with over four years' post qualification experience including at least four years litigation experience.

    C. Other solicitors, legal executives and fee earners of equivalent experience.

    D. Trainee solicitors, para legals and fee earners of equivalent experience.

3. "Legal Executive" means a Fellow of the Institute of Legal Executives. Those who are not Fellows of the Institute are not entitled to call themselves legal executives and in principle are therefore not entitled to the same hourly rate as a legal executive.

4. Unqualified clerks who are fee earners of equivalent experience may be entitled to similar rates and in this regard it should be borne in mind that Fellows of the Institute of Legal Executives generally spend two years in a solicitor's office before passing their Section 1 general examinations, spend a further two years before passing the Section 2 specialist examinations and then complete a further two years in practice before being able to become Fellows. Fellows therefore possess considerable practical experience and academic achievement. Clerks without the equivalent experience of legal executives will be treated as being in the bottom grade of fee earner i.e. trainee solicitors and fee earners of equivalent experience. Whether or not a fee earner has equivalent experience is ultimately a matter for the discretion of the court.

The National 1 rates apply to

Aldershot, Farnham, Bournemouth (including Poole)
Birmingham Inner
Bristol
Cambridge City, Harlow
Canterbury, Maidstone, Medway & Tunbridge Wells
Cardiff (Inner)
Chelmsford South, Essex & East Suffolk
Chester
Fareham, Winchester
Hampshire, Dorset, Wiltshire, Isle of Wight
Kingston, Guildford, Reigate, Epsom
Leeds Inner (within 2 kilometers radius of the City Art Gallery)
Lewes
Liverpool, Birkenhead
Manchester Central
Newcastle—City Centre (within a 2 mile radius of St Nicholas Cathedral)
Norwich City
Nottingham City
Oxford, Thames Valley
Southampton, Portsmouth
Swindon, Basingstoke
Watford

The National 2/3 rates apply to

Bath, Cheltenham and Gloucester, Taunton, Yeovil
Bury
Chelmsford North, Cambridge County, Peterborough, Bury St E,
Norfolk, Lowestoft
Cheshire & North Wales
Coventry, Rugby, Nuneaton, Stratford and Warwick
Exeter, Plymouth
Hull (City)
Leeds Outer, Wakefield & Pontefract
Leigh
Lincoln
Luton, Bedford, St Albans, Hitchin, Hertford
Manchester Outer, Oldham, Bolton, Tameside
Newcastle (other than City Centre)
Nottingham & Derbyshire
Sheffield, Doncaster and South Yorkshire
Southport
St Helens
Stockport, Altrincham, Salford
Swansea, Newport, Cardiff (Outer)
Southampton, Portsmouth
Wigan
Wolverhampton, Walsall, Dudley & Stourbridge
York, Harrogate

Birmingham Outer
Bradford (Dewsbury, Halifax, Huddersfield, Keighley & Skipton)
Cumbria
Devon, Cornwall
Grimsby, Skegness
Kidderminster
Northampton & Leicester
Preston, Lancaster, Blackpool, Chorley, Accrington, Burnley,
Blackburn, Rawenstall & Nelson
Scarborough & Ripon
Stafford, Stoke, Tamworth
Teesside
Worcester, Hereford, Evesham and Redditch
Shrewsbury, Telford, Ludlow, Oswestry
South & West Wales

LONDON BANDS

Grade	A	B	C	D
City of London: EC1, EC2, EC3, EC4	£380	£274	£210	£129
Central London: W1, WC1, WC2, SW1	£292	£222	£181	£116
Outer London: (All other London post codes: W, NW, N, E, SE, SW and Bromley, Croydon, Dartford, Gravesend and Uxbridge)	£210–246	£158–210	£152	£111

Scotland and Northern Ireland

The Costs Officers bear in mind the guideline rates for England and Wales when determining appropriate rates in appeals from Scotland and Northern Ireland.

PRACTICE DIRECTION 14—FILING DOCUMENTS IN THE REGISTRY OF THE SUPREME COURT BY ELECTRONIC MEANS

Introduction

14.1 The Supreme Court intends to take full advantage of the opportunities offered by modern information technology and rules 6(1)(d) and 7(1)(d) provide for the service and filing of documents "(with the consent of the party to be served or at the direction of the Registrar) by electronic means in accordance with the relevant practice direction". This Practice Direction makes the necessary provision. **4–191**

Filing of documents

14.2.1 Subject to paragraph 14.4.6, all documents must be filed electronically at the same time as hard copies are sent to the Registry. See rule 7(3) which provides that: **4–192**

> "Except with the consent of the Registrar, the contents of documents
>
> (a) filed in hard copy must also be provided to the Registry by electronic means, and
>
> (b) filed by electronic means must also be provided to the Registry in hard copy."

Other parties should be notified by the filing party that filing has taken place.

14.2.2 Each electronic document must be named in accordance with the file naming convention published by the Registrar.

14.2.3 In the event of a mistake being made, the Registry should be notified immediately.

Submission of electronic documents to the Registry

4–192.1   **14.3.1** Unless otherwise directed or permitted by the Registrar, or where the circumstances in paragraph 14.5.6 apply, the means of submitting electronic documents to the Registry is via e–mail at registry@supremecourt.gsi.gov.uk.

14.3.2 Where the Registrar directs or permits, or in accordance with 14.5.6 below, the party should submit the electronic documents to the Registry on a memory stick, clearly marked or labelled with the title of the case and the identity of the party.

General provisions

4–193   **14.4.1** A document is not filed until the transmission is received and accepted by the Registry, whatever time it is shown to have been sent.

14.4.2 The time of receipt of a transmission will be recorded electronically on the transmission as it is received.

14.4.3 If a transmission is received after 4pm—

(1) the transmission will be treated as received; and

(2) any document attached to the transmission will be treated (if accepted) as filed, on the next day the Registry is open.

14.4.4 A party sending an e–mail is responsible for ensuring that the transmission or any document attached to it is filed within any relevant time limits.

14.4.5 The Registry will normally reply by e–mail where—

(1) the response is to a message transmitted electronically; and

(2) the sender has provided an e–mail address.

14.4.6 Parties are advised not to transmit electronically any correspondence or documents of a confidential or sensitive nature, as security cannot be guaranteed.

14.4.7 If a document transmitted electronically requires urgent attention, the sender should contact the court by telephone.

Format of electronic documents

4–194   **14.5.1** Where an application for permission to appeal is determined without an oral hearing, costs may be awarded as follows:

14.5.2 The electronic version, including pagination, must be identical to the hard copy.

14.5.3 Unless otherwise directed or permitted by the Registrar, core volumes and volumes of authorities must be filed as a single pdf document and bookmarked in accordance with the index so that each individual document can be accessed directly by hypertext link both from the index page and from bookmarks on the left–hand side. Please see the example core volume and accompanying instructions on the Supreme Court website at http://www.supremecourt.gov.uk.

14.5.4 Wherever possible, pdf documents within core volumes *and within volumes of authorities* and otherwise filed with the Court must be converted to pdf from their original electronic versions rather than scanned as images. Where documents are only available in hard copy and have to be scanned, the resultant pdf files should, where the quality of the scan allows, be subjected to a process of optical character recognition (OCR). This is to enable the documents to be text searchable and annotatable by the Court. Please see the example core volume and accompanying instructions on the Supreme Court website at http://www.supremecourt.gov.uk.

14.5.5 Where electronic core volumes or other individual documents exceed 10 megabytes in size they must be submitted on memory stick, clearly marked or labelled with the title of the case and the identity of the party.

14.5.6 The Registrar may permit filing in a different or additional format (e.g. Excel) for good reason.

Hypertext linking within documents

14.6.1 The Supreme Court does not intend at this stage to impose **4–195** detailed requirements as to hypertext linking within documents. However, it wishes to encourage parties to employ hypertext links within documents. In particular, it would be helpful if hypertext links were introduced at the time the core volumes are produced to link:

(a) the statement of facts and issues to documents in the appendix;

(b) written cases to documents in the appendix and to the authorities;

(c) cases to the relevant law reports and to the index of authorities.

14.6.2 The parties should seek to agree on the extent to which hypertext linking is to be used.

Special directions

14.7 The Registrar may give special directions for the filing of **4–196** electronic documents to meet the requirements of particular cases or by way of experiment.

FORMS

Form 1 (Application for permission/notice of appeal)

4–197

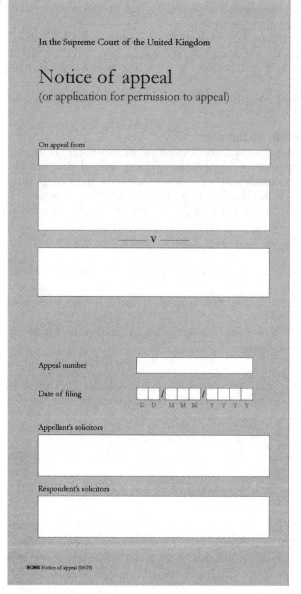

In the Supreme Court of the United Kingdom

Notice of appeal
(or application for permission to appeal)

On appeal from

—— V ——

Appeal number

Date of filing

D D / M M M / Y Y Y Y

Appellant's solicitors

Respondent's solicitors

SC001 Notice of appeal (04.09)

© Crown copyright 2009

1. Appellant

Appellant's full name

Original status

☐ Claimant   ☐ Defendant

☐ Petitioner   ☐ Respondent

☐ Pursuer   ☐ Defender

Solicitor

Name

Address

Telephone no.

Fax no.

DX no.

Postcode

Ref.

Email

How would you prefer us to communicate with you?

☐ DX   ☐ Email

☐ Post   ☐ Other *(please specify)*

Is the appellant in receipt of public funding/legal aid?

☐ Yes   ☐ No

If Yes, please give the certificate number

Counsel

Name

Address

Telephone no.

Fax no.

DX no.

Postcode

Email

Counsel

Name

Address

Telephone no.

Fax no.

DX no.

Postcode

Email

2. Respondent

Respondent's full name

Original status

☐ Claimant   ☐ Defendant

☐ Petitioner   ☐ Respondent

☐ Pursuer   ☐ Defender

Solicitor

Name

Address

Telephone no.

Fax no.

DX no.

Postcode

Ref.

Email

How would you prefer us to communicate with you?

☐ DX   ☐ Email

☐ Post   ☐ Other *(please specify)*

Is the respondent in receipt of public funding/legal aid?

☐ Yes   ☐ No

If Yes, please give the certificate number

Page 3

SC001 Notice of appeal

396

Counsel

Name

Address

Telephone no.

Fax no.

DX no.

Postcode

Email

Counsel

Name

Address

Telephone no.

Fax no.

DX no.

Postcode

Email

3. Decision being appealed

Name of Court

Names of Judges

Date of order/
interlocutor/decision

D D / M M M / Y Y Y Y

4. Permission to appeal

If you have permission to appeal complete **Part A** or complete **Part B** if you require permission to appeal.

PART A

Name of Court granting permission

Date permission granted

| D D | M M M | Y Y Y Y |

Conditions on which permission granted

PART B

☐ The appellant applies to the Supreme Court for permission to appeal.

Page 5

SC001 Notice of appeal

398

5. Information about the decision being appealed

Please set out

- Narrative of the facts
- Statutory framework
- Chronology of proceedings
- Orders made in the Courts below
- Issues before the Court appealed from
- Treatment of issues by the Court appealed from
- Issues in the appeal

399

6. Grounds of appeal

Counsel's name or signature:

400

7. Other information about the appeal

Are you applying for an extension of time?

☐ Yes   ☐ No

If Yes, please explain why

What order are you asking the Supreme Court to make?

Order being appealed   ☐ set aside   ☐ vary

Original order   ☐ set aside   ☐ restore   ☐ vary

Does the appeal raise issues under the:

Human Rights Act 1998?   ☐ Yes   ☐ No

Are you seeking a declaration of incompatibility?
☐ Yes   ☐ No

Are you challenging an act of a public authority?
☐ Yes   ☐ No

If you have answered Yes to any of the questions above please give details below:

Court's devolution jurisdiction?   ☐ Yes   ☐ No

If Yes, please give details below:

SC001 Notice of appeal

401

Are you asking the Supreme Court to:

depart from one of its own decisions or from one made by the House of Lords?

☐ Yes   ☐ No

If Yes, please give details below:

make a reference to the European Court of Justice of the European Communities?

☐ Yes   ☐ No

If Yes, please give details below:

Will you or the respondent request an expedited hearing?

☐ Yes   ☐ No

If Yes, please give details below:

402

8. Certificate of Service

Either complete this section or attach a separate certificate

The date on which this form was served on the

1ˢᵗ Respondent ▢▢ / ▢▢▢ / ▢▢▢▢
D D M M M Y Y Y Y

2ⁿᵈ Respondent ▢▢ / ▢▢▢ / ▢▢▢▢
D D M M M Y Y Y Y

I certify that this document was served on

by

by the following method

Signature

9. Other relevant information

Neutral citation of the judgment appealed against e.g. [2009] EWCA Civ 95

References to Law Report in which any relevant judgment is reported.

Subject matter catchwords for indexing.

Please return your completed form to:

The Supreme Court of the United Kingdom, Parliament Square, London SW1P 3BD

DX 157230 Parliament Square 4

Telephone: 020 7960 1991/1992   Fax: 020 7960 1901

email: registry@supremecourt.gsi.gov.uk

www.supremecourt.gov.uk

Page 11

SC001 Notice of appeal

Page 12

SC001 Notice of appeal

Form 2 (Application form)

4–198

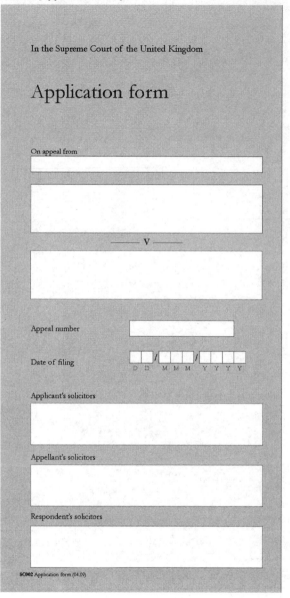

In the Supreme Court of the United Kingdom

Application form

On appeal from

_____

_____

———— v ————

_____

Appeal number _____

Date of filing

DD / MMM / YYYY

Applicant's solicitors

_____

Appellant's solicitors

_____

Respondent's solicitors

_____

SO002 Application form (04.09)

© Crown copyright 2009

1. Details of the applicant

Applicant's full name

Original status

- [ ] Claimant
- [ ] Defendant
- [ ] Intervener
- [ ] Petitioner
- [ ] Respondent
- [ ] Pursuer
- [ ] Defender

Solicitor

Name

Address

Telephone no.

Fax no.

DX no.

Postcode

Ref.

Email

How would you prefer us to communicate with you?

- [ ] DX
- [ ] Email
- [ ] Post
- [ ] Other *(please specify)*

Counsel

Name

Address

Telephone no.

Fax no.

DX no.

Postcode

Email

Counsel

Name

Address

Telephone no.

Fax no.

DX no.

Postcode

Email

2. Nature of the application

The applicant applies for

- [ ] Extension of time
- [ ] Permission to intervene
- [ ] Security
- [ ] Order for substituted service
- [ ] Expedited hearing
- [ ] Review of Registrar's decision
- [ ] Other order *(please specify)*

408

3. Grounds on which application made

On what grounds are you
making this application?

4. Consent to application

The following parties **consent** to this application

See attached letter(s) dated

The following parties **object** to this application

See attached letter(s) dated

5. Other relevant information

410

6. Details of the appellant

Appellant's full name

Original status

☐ Claimant   ☐ Defendant

☐ Petitioner   ☐ Respondent

☐ Pursuer   ☐ Defender

Solicitor

Name

Address   Telephone no.

Fax no.

DX no.

Postcode   Ref.

Email

Counsel

Name

Address   Telephone no.

Fax no.

DX no.

Postcode

Email

411

Counsel

Name

Address

Telephone no.

Fax no.

DX no.

Postcode

Email

7. Details of the respondent

Respondent's full name

Original status

☐ Claimant ☐ Defendant

☐ Petitioner ☐ Respondent

☐ Pursuer ☐ Defender

Solicitor

Name

Address

Telephone no.

Fax no.

DX no.

Postcode

Ref.

Email

Page 7

SC002 Application form

412

Counsel

Name

Address

Telephone no.

Fax no.

DX no.

Postcode

Email

Counsel

Name

Address

Telephone no.

Fax no.

DX no.

Postcode

Email

8. Certificate of Service

Either complete this section or attach a separate certificate

On what date was this form served on the

Appellant

D D / M M M / Y Y Y Y

Respondent

D D / M M M / Y Y Y Y

I certify that this document was served on

by

by the following method

Signature

9. Details of Registrar's order/decision being appealed

Date of order/decision

		/				/				

D D M M M Y Y Y Y

SC002 Application form

414

415

Page 11

SC002 Application Form

Please return your completed form to:

The Supreme Court of the United Kingdom, Parliament Square, London SW1P 3BD
DX 157230 Parliament Square 4

Telephone: 020 7960 1991/1992   Fax: 020 7960 1901
email: registry@supremecourt.gsi.gov.uk
www.supremecourt.gov.uk

Form 3 (Notice of objection/acknowledgment by respondent)

4–199

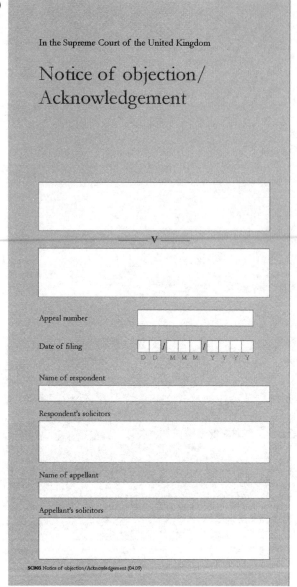

In the Supreme Court of the United Kingdom

Notice of objection/ Acknowledgement

———— V ————

Appeal number

Date of filing
D D / M M / Y Y Y Y

Name of respondent

Respondent's solicitors

Name of appellant

Appellant's solicitors

SC003 Notice of objection/Acknowledgement (04.09)

© Crown copyright 2009

1. Respondent

Respondent's full name

The respondent was served with the
- [ ] application for permission to appeal
- [ ] notice of appeal
- [ ] application

On date

```
[  ] / [   ] / [    ]
 D D   M M M   Y Y Y Y
```

The respondent intends to ask the Court to:
- [ ] refuse to grant permission to appeal
- [ ] order the appellant to give security for costs if permission to appeal is granted
- [ ] dismiss the appeal
- [ ] give the respondent permission to cross-appeal
- [ ] allow the appeal for reasons which are different from, or additional to, those given by the court below
- [ ] Other *(please specify)*

The respondent wishes to receive notice of any hearing date and to be advised of progress. The respondent's details are:

Solicitor

Name

Address

Telephone no.

Fax no.

DX no.

Postcode

Ref.

Email

How would you prefer us to communicate with you?
- [ ] DX
- [ ] Email
- [ ] Post
- [ ] Other *(please specify)*

Page 2

SC005 Notice of objection/Acknowledgement

419

Counsel

Name

Address

Telephone no.

Fax no.

DX no.

Postcode

Email

Counsel

Name

Address

Telephone no.

Fax no.

DX no.

Postcode

Email

2. Certificate of Service

Either complete this section or attach a separate certificate

Appellant

D D / M M M / Y Y Y Y

On what date was this form served on the

Other

D D / M M M / Y Y Y Y

I certify that this document was served on

by

by the following method

Signature

3. Other information about the respondent

☐ The respondent is in receipt of public funding/legal aid

Certificate number

☐ The respondent is applying for public funding/legal aid

Information about the respondent's case

Set out here the respondent's grounds of appeal, reasons why permission to appeal should be refused or why the appeal should be allowed. Include information to explain what the respondent intends to ask the Court to do.

421

Is the respondent seeking a declaration of incompatibility?

☐ Yes ☐ No

☐ The respondent will seek to raise issues under the Human Rights Act 1998
(please give brief details)

☐ The respondent will ask the court to make a reference to the
European Court of Justice *(please give brief details)*

422

Please return your completed form to:

The Supreme Court of the United Kingdom, Parliament Square, London SW1P 3BD

DX 157230 Parliament Square 4

Telephone: 020 7960 1991/1992   Fax: 020 7960 1901

email: registry@supremecourt.gsi.gov.uk

www.supremecourt.gov.uk

SC003 Notice of objection/Acknowledgement

SECTION 6

ADMINISTRATION OF FUNDS, PROPERTY AND AFFAIRS

6A COURT FUNDS

Senior Courts Act 1981

(1981 c.54)

Delete title "Supreme Court Act 1981" and substitute "Senior Courts Act 1981".

6A–1 Accountant General of the Senior Courts

Delete title "Accountant General of the Supreme Court" and substitute: "Accountant General of the Senior Courts".

In section 97(1), for Supreme Court substitute:

Senior Courts

In section 97(2), for the two instances of "Supreme Court" substitute:

Senior Courts

Note

Add at end:

6A–2   and the Constitutional Reform Act 2005 s.59 and Sch.11, para.26 with effect from October 1, 2009 (SI 2009/1604).

Interpretation

6A–22   *In rule 2(2), for the two instances of "Lands Tribunal" substitute "Upper Tribunal".*

Note

At the beginning add:

6A–23   Definitions "Court" and "Order" amended by the Transfer of Tribunal Functions (Lands Tribunal and Miscellaneous Amendments) Order 2009, Sch.2, para.27 (SI 2009/1307, for transitional provisions see Sch.5) with effect from June 1, 2009.

Payment Schedule

In rule 7(3) for "Lands Tribunal" substitute:

6A–31   Upper Tribunal

Note

Add new paragraph at end:

6A–32   Paragraph (3) amended by the Transfer of Tribunal Functions (Lands Tribunal and Miscellaneous Amendments) Order 2009, Sch.2, para.28 (SI 2009/1307, for transitional provisions see Sch.5) with effect from June 1, 2009.

Preparation and amendment of Schedules

In rule 8(1), for "Lands Tribunal" substitute:

6A–33   Upper Tribunal

Note

Delete and substitute:

6A–33.1   Amended by SI 1999/1021 r.2(b) and by the Transfer of Tribunal Functions (Lands Tribunal and Miscellaneous Amendments) Order 2009 Sch.2, para.29 (SI 2009/1307, for transitional provisions see Sch.5) with effect from June 1, 2009.

THE INVESTMENT OF FUNDS IN COURT

Special Investment Account (formerly short term investment account)

In the fifth paragraph for "The rate of interest ... February 1, 2009.": substitute:
The rate of interest changed to 0.5 per cent with effect from July 1, 2009. **6A–162**

Special and Basic rates from October 1, 1965

Add new entries at end of County Court table:

6A–171

1.6.09	1	d/d 2.2.09	1.6.09	1.5	d/d 2.2.09
1.7.09	0.5	d/d 3.6.09	1.6.09	0.3	d/d 3.6.09

6B   COURT OF PROTECTION

GENERAL

The Practice Directions

For "http://www.publicguardian.gov.uk" substitute:
   http://www.hmcs.gov.uk **6B–11**

The forms

In the third paragraph, for "http://www.publicguardian.gov.uk" substitute:
   http://www.hmcs.gov.uk **6B–12**

Court fees

Add after "Court of Protection Fees Order 2007":
   (the Court of Protection Fees Order 2007 (SI 2007/1745) has been amended by the **6B–18**
Court of Protection Fees (Amendment) Order 2009 (SI 2009/513), with effect from
April 1, 2009)

Appeals to the Court of Protection

Delete the third and fourth paragraphs and substitute:
   Where a standard authorisation has been given, the Court of Protection can **6B–21.4**
determine any question relating to:
   1. whether the person meets any of the qualifying requirements/assessments;
   2. the period for which it has been given;
   3. the purpose for which it has been given; or
   4. the conditions subject to which it has been given.
   Once it has determined the question, the court may make an order varying or
terminating the authorisation or ordering the supervisory body to vary or terminate it.
   In the case of an urgent authorisation, the court may determine:
   1. whether the urgent authorisation should have been given;
   2. the period during which the urgent authorisation is to be in force
   3. the purpose for which the urgent authorisation is given.
   The court may make an order varying or terminating the urgent authorisation or
ordering the managing authority of the relevant hospital or care home to vary or
terminate the urgent authorisation.
   There will usually be fee for applications to the court. Legal Aid will be available
both for advice and representation before the court. Details of the fees charged by the
Court and circumstances in which fees can be waived or remitted are available from
the Office of the Public Guardian (*http://www.hmcs.gov.uk* [Accessed January 13, 2009]).

Court of Protection Rules and Practice Directions

Add new paragraph 6B–21.5:

6B–21.5   The Court of Protection Rules 2007 have been amended by the Court of Protection (Amendment) Rules 2009 (SI 2009/582) with effect from April 1, 2009 in order to add supporting rules for the deprivation of liberty jurisdiction. A new part Pt 10A (Deprivation of Liberty matters) is inserted consisting of a new r.82A which provides the procedure for the applications is set out in the practice direction to that part.

6C   NON–CONTENTIOUS PROBATE

Senior Courts Act 1981

6C–1   (1981 c.54)

Delete title "Supreme Court Act 1981" and substitute "Senior Courts Act 1981".

SECTION 7

LEGAL REPRESENTATIVES – COSTS AND LITIGATION FUNDING

7A   GENERAL

Funding Arrangements

CONDITIONAL FEES

Add new paragraph at end:

7A–57   Generally speaking parties are entitled to make, and often do make, an agreement which applies to the period before they made it. Section 59 of the Solicitors Act 1974, which permits a solicitor to make an agreement for remuneration in respect of contentious business "done or to be done by him" contemplates a retrospective agreement. The court went on to express the view that a retrospective success fee is not per se contrary to public policy.

> "There is, in my view, insufficient warrant for effectively precluding solicitor and client from making such an agreement. In some, perhaps many, circumstances a retrospective success fee, or its amount, may be unreasonable, either as between the parties or as between solicitor and client but this will not always be so. The court has, in my opinion, enough weapons in its armoury in the form of the criteria applicable on a detailed assessment and the provisions of the Costs Practice Direction and the Practice Direction on Protocols to disallow or reduce retrospective fees that are unreasonable . . .". *Birmingham City Council v Forde* [2009] EWHC 12 (QB), Christopher Clarke J (at para.[150]).

Success fees

Add new paragraphs to end:

7A–58   In a clinical negligence case, the court was persuaded that the solicitors for the claimant were, at the outset, faced with difficulties and the case had uncertain prospects. The court held that the solicitors knew when the CFA was made that it was one which could easily have been assessed as having chances of success lower than 50 per cent. The solicitor is entitled to enter into a CFA at an early stage. It follows inevitably from that entitlement that the solicitor will be in a position of ignorance compared with that when he has medical records and expert advice. But, given that he is likely to be experienced in the field and to have some knowledge of the claim, his ignorance is relative. A 100 per cent success fee was allowed: *Oliver v Whipps Cross University Hospital NHS Trust and Waltham Forest Primary Care Trust* [2009] EWHC 110 (QB), Jack J.

Where the CFA did not specify how much of the percentage increase, if any, related to the cost to the representative of the postponement of the payment of his fees and expenses, Burton J. held that if the postponement element was nil, there was no need for this to be specified unless doubt existed as to the construction of the agreement. In which event it would be necessary for the court to consider the full construction of the CFA. On the facts of the case the judge was satisfied that the position about postponement had been made sufficiently clear in the documents and the appeal was allowed: *Sidhu v Sandhu & Sandhu* [2009] EWHC 983 (QB), Burton J.

7C SOLICITORS ACT 1974

PART I

RIGHTS AND PRIVILEGES OF SOLICITORS

Rights of practising and rights of audience

In section 19(1)(a), for "Supreme Court" substitute:

Senior Courts   **7C–2**

In section 19(2) delete "section 94 of the Supreme Court Act 1981,".

Note

Add after "County Courts Act 1984 Sch.2":
and the Constitutional Reform Act 2005 s.59 and Sch.11, paras 1, 21(3) with effect **7C–3**
from October 1, 2009 (SI 2009/1604).

Non–British subjects as solicitors

In section 29, for "Supreme Court or of the Supreme Court of Northern Ireland" substitute:

Senior Courts or of the Court of Judicature   **7C–26**

Note

Add new paragraph 7C–26.1:
Amended by the Constitutional Reform Act 2005 s.59 and Sch.11, para 21(4), with **7C–26.1**
effect from October 1, 2009 (SI 2009/1604).

PART II

PROFESSIONAL PRACTICE, CONDUCT AND DISCIPLINE OF SOLICITORS AND CLERKS

PRACTICE RULES

Rules as to professional practice, conduct and discipline

In section 31(1), add after "the professional practice, conduct":

, fitness to practice   **7C–28**

In section 31(1), add after "by the Society are being":
, or have been,

Note

For "Legal Services Act 2007 ... (SI 2008/222)." substitute:
Legal Services Act 2007 s.177 and Sch.16, Pt 1, para.31(2)(a) and (d) (with effect **7C–29**
from March 7, 2008 (SI 2008/222)), and Sch.16, Pt 1, para.31(2)(c) and (e) (with effect
from March 31, 2009 (SI 2009/503)).

ACCOUNTS, ETC.

Accounts rules and trust accounts rules

Delete sections 32(1) and (2) and substitute:

7C–30   **32.**—(1) The Society shall make rules, with the concurrence of the Master of the Rolls—

> (a) as to the opening and keeping by solicitors of accounts at banks or with building societies for money within subsection (1A);
>
> (aa) as to the operation by solicitors of accounts kept by their clients or other persons at banks or with building societies or other financial institutions;
>
> (b) as to the keeping by solicitors of accounts containing information as to money received, held or paid by them for or on account of their clients or other persons (including money received, held or paid under a trust); and
>
> (c) empowering the Society to take such action as may be necessary to enable it to ascertain whether or not the rules are being, or have been, complied with.

(1A) The money referred to in subsection (1) is money (including money held on trust) which is received, held or dealt with for clients or other persons.

(2) [...]

Delete subsections (4) to (6) and substitute:

(4) The Society shall be at liberty to disclose a report on or information about a solicitor's accounts obtained in the exercise of powers conferred by rules made under subsection (1) for use in investigating the possible commission of an offence by the solicitor or any of his employees and for use in connection with any prosecution of the solicitor or any of his employees consequent on the investigation.

(5) Rules under this section may specify circumstances in which solicitors or any class of solicitors are exempt from the rules or a part of the rules.

Note

For "and the Access to Justice Act 1999 Sch.15, Pt II." substitute:

7C–31   , the Access to Justice Act 1999 Sch.15, Pt II and the Legal Services Act 2007 s.177 and Sch.16, Pt 1, para.32(2)(a), (c)–(e), (3)–(7) and Sch.23, with effect from March 31, 2009 (SI 2009/503).

Interest on clients' money

Delete section 33 and substitute:

7C–32   **33.**—(1) Rules under section 32 may require a solicitor to pay interest, or sums in lieu of and equivalent to interest, to a client, any other person or any trust, for whom the solicitor holds money.

(2) The cases in which a solicitor may be required by the rules to act as mentioned in subsection (1) may be defined, among other things, by reference to the amount of any sum received or the period for which it is or is likely to be retained or both.

(3) Except as provided by the rules, a solicitor is not liable to account to any client, other person or trust for interest received by the

solicitor on money held at a bank or building society in an account which is for money received or held for, or on account of—

    (a) the solicitor's clients, other persons or trusts, generally, or

    (b) that client, person or trust, separately.

(4) Rules under section 32 may—

    (a) prescribe the circumstances in which a solicitor may make arrangements to limit or exclude an obligation imposed on the solicitor by rules made by virtue of this section, and

    (b) prescribe the requirements to be met by and in relation to those arrangements.

Note

Add after "Building Societies Act 1986 Sch.18":

  and the Legal Services Act 2007 s.177 and Sch.16, Pt 1, para.33 and Sch.23, with ef- **7C–33**
fect from March 31, 2009 (SI 2009/503).

Accountants' reports

Delete section 34 and substitute:

34.—(1) The Society may make rules requiring solicitors to provide **7C–36** the Society with reports signed by an accountant (in this section referred to as an "accountant's report") at such times or in such circumstances as may be prescribed by the rules.

(2) The rules may specify requirements to be met by, or in relation to, an accountant's report (including requirements relating to the accountant who signs the report).

(3)–(5) [...]

(6) If any solicitor fails to comply with the provisions of any rules made under this section, a complaint in respect of that failure may be made to the Tribunal by or on behalf of the Society.

(7)–(8) [...]

(9) Where an accountant, during the course of preparing an accountant's report—

    (a) discovers evidence of fraud or theft in relation to money held by a solicitor for a client or any other person (including money held on trust) or money held in an account of a client of a solicitor, or an account of another person, which is operated by the solicitor, or

    (b) obtains information which the accountant has reasonable cause to believe is likely to be of material significance in determining whether a solicitor is a fit and proper person to hold money for clients or other persons (including money held on trust) or to operate an account of a client of the solicitor or an account of another person,

      the accountant must immediately give a report of the matter to the Society.

(10) No duty to which an accountant is subject is to be regarded as contravened merely because of any information or opinion contained in a report under subsection (9).

Note

Add after "AJA 1985 Sch.1":

  and the Legal Services Act 2007 s.177 and Sch.16, Pt 1, para.35 and Sch.23, with ef- **7C–37**
fect from March 31, 2009 (SI 2009/503).

Employees of solicitors

Add new paragraphs 7C–37.1 to 7C–37.4:

7C–37.1   **34A.**—(1) Rules made by the Society may provide for any rules made under section 31, 32, 33A or 34 to have effect in relation to employees of solicitors with such additions, omissions or other modifications as appear to the Society to be necessary or expedient.

(2) If any employee of a solicitor fails to comply with rules made under section 31 or 32, as they have effect in relation to the employee by virtue of subsection (1), any person may make a complaint in respect of that failure to the Tribunal.

(3) If any employee of a solicitor fails to comply with rules made under section 34, as they have effect in relation to the employee by virtue of subsection (1), a complaint in respect of that failure may be made to the Tribunal by or on behalf of the Society.

Note

7C–37.2   Inserted by the Legal Services Act 2007 s.177 and Sch.16, Pt 1, para.36 with effect from March 31, 2009 (SI 2009/503).

Employees of solicitors: accounts rules etc.

7C–37.3   **34B.**—(1) Where rules made under section 32(1) have effect in relation to employees of solicitors by virtue of section 34A(1), section 85 applies in relation to an employee to whom the rules have effect who keeps an account with a bank or building society in pursuance of such rules as it applies in relation to a solicitor who keeps such an account in pursuance of rules under section 32.

(2) Subsection (3) applies where rules made under section 32—

    (a) contain any such provision as is referred to in section 33(1), and

    (b) have effect in relation to employees of solicitors by virtue of section 34A(1).

(3) Except as provided by the rules, an employee to whom the rules are applied is not liable to account to any client, other person or trust for interest received by the employee on money held at a bank or building society in an account which is for money received or held for, or on account of—

    (a) clients of the solicitor, other persons or trusts, generally, or

    (b) that client, person or trust, separately.

(4) Subsection (5) applies where rules made under section 33A(1) have effect in relation to employees of solicitors by virtue of section 34A(1).

(5) The Society may disclose a report on or information about the accounts of any employee of a solicitor obtained in pursuance of such rules for use—

    (a) in investigating the possible commission of an offence by the solicitor or any employees of the solicitor, and

    (b) in connection with any prosecution of the solicitor or any employees of the solicitor consequent on the investigation.

(6) Where rules made under section 34 have effect in relation to employees of solicitors by virtue of section 34A(1), section 34(9) and (10) apply in relation to such an employee as they apply in relation to a solicitor.

Note

Inserted by the Legal Services Act 2007 s.177 and Sch.16, Pt 1, para.36 with effect **7C–37.4** from March 31, 2009 (SI 2009/503).

Jurisdiction of Senior Courts over solicitors

Delete title "Jurisdiction of Supreme Court over solicitors" and substitute "Jurisdiction of Senior **7C–42** *Courts over solicitors".*

In section 50(1) for "Supreme Court" substitute:
Senior Courts

In section 50(2) for "Supreme Court was" substitute:
Senior Courts were

Note

Delete and substitute:

Amended by the Constitutional Reform Act 2005 s.59 and Sch.11, para.21(5) with **7C–43** effect from October 1, 2009 (SI 2009/1604).

Part III

Remuneration of Solicitors

Non–contentious business

Orders as to remuneration for non–contentious business

In section 56(1), add new subsection (da):
(da) a member of the Legal Services Board nominated by that **7C–51** Board;

In section 56(5)(d), add after "on the part of the solicitor"
, or any employee of his who is an authorised person,

Note

For "and in part from June 30 ... not yet in force)." substitute:

, in part from June 30, 2008 (SI 2008/1436) and in part from July 1, 2009 (SI 2009/ **7C–52** 1365) (remaining amendments not yet in force).

Effect on contentious business agreement of death, incapability or change of solicitor

In section 63(3), after "on the part of the solicitor" substitute:
, or any of his employees,   **7C–88**

Note

Amended by the Legal Services Act 2007 s.177 and Sch.16, Pt.1, para.59, with effect **7C–88.1** in part (subject to transitory provisions) from March 31, 2009 (SI 2009/503; for transitory provisions see art.4) (remaining amendments not yet in force).

Taxation with respect to contentious business

In section 66(a), add after "retained by, the solicitor":
or an employee of the solicitor   **7C–92**

In section 66(b), add after "business done by him":

or by any employee of his who is an authorised person (within the meaning of section 56(5A))

Note

Add new paragraph 7C–92.1:

7C–92.1   Amended by the Legal Services Act 2007 s.177 and Sch.16, Pt.1, para.62, with effect in part (subject to transitory provisions) from March 31, 2009 (SI 2009/503; for transitory provisions see art.4) (remaining amendments not yet in force).

REMUNERATION—GENERAL

Signature of bill

Add after "(1883) 1 Cab. & El. 118).":

7C–107   In respect of bills delivered after March 7, 2008, s.69 of the Solicitors Act 1974 was amended to state, at s.69(2A):

"A bill is signed in accordance with this subsection, if it is—

(a) signed by the solicitor, or on his behalf by an employee of the solicitor authorised by him to sign..."

Before, a former requirement that the bill had to be signed by a partner was accordingly directory and not mandatory. In the particular case the bills had been signed by a non–practising barrister: *Magantic Services Ltd v Dorsey & Whitney* [2008] EWHC 2662 (QB), Irwin J.

Subsection (2)—Statutory Demand

After the first paragraph, add as a new paragraph:

7C–117   A sum which had not been judicially assessed or determined was not a claim for a liquidated sum that could be the subject of a bankruptcy petition under s.267 of the Insolvency Act 1986, even if the period for challenging the claim under the 1974 Act had expired. The court considered *Re a Debtor (Nos 833 and 834 of 1993)* (above) but held that if public policy required the client to be able to seek assessment of a solicitor's bill, even after having reached an otherwise binding agreement, that was merely a reason why the court ought not to make a bankruptcy order on a petition likely to be the subject of an assessment under the 1974 Act. The availability of assessment did not prevent an otherwise binding agreement converting what had previously been a solicitor's mere estimate of proper costs, into a liquidated sum capable of founding a petition under s.267 of the 1986 Act: *Truex v Toll* [2009] EWHC 396 (Ch), Proudman J.

Charging orders

7C–135   *Delete the last paragraph.*

Add new paragraph at start:

7C–138   Where a district judge of the County Court granted a charging order over land which had been the subject of litigation for costs to be assessed by the court it was held that the detailed assessment had to take place at the Supreme Court Costs Office since the bill fell outside the parameters laid down in s.69(3): *Jones v Twinsectra Ltd* [2002] EWCA Civ 668, April 16, 2002.

PART IV

MISCELLANEOUS AND GENERAL

SUPPLEMENTARY

Rules

Add new paragraphs 7C–143.0 and 7C–143.0.1:

86A.—(1) Rules made by the Society under this Act may— **7C–143.0**
    (a) make provision generally or subject to exceptions or only in relation to specified cases;
    (b) make different provision for different cases or circumstances or for different purposes.

(2) Without prejudice to the generality of subsection (1), any rules prescribing a fee may provide for that fee to be reduced or waived in such circumstances as may be specified in the rules.

Note

Inserted by the Legal Services Act 2007 s.177 and Sch.16, Pt.1, para.74, with effect **7C–143.0.1** from March 31, 2009 (SI 2009/503).

Interpretation

In section 87(1) for "'client account' means an account in the title of which the word 'client' is **7C–143** *required by rules under section 32;" substitute:*
"client account" means an account subject to rules under section 32(1)(a);

Delete "section 128 of the Supreme Court Act 1981" and substitute:
section 128 of the Senior Courts Act 1981

Delete "'controlled trust', in relation to a solicitor, means a trust of which he is a sole trustee or co–trustee only with one or more of his partners or employees;".

Delete "'the roll' means the list of solicitors of the Supreme Court kept by the Society under section 6" and substitute:
"the roll" means the list of solicitors of the Senior Courts kept by the Society under section 6

Delete "'solicitor' means solicitor of the Supreme Court" and substitute:
"solicitor" means solicitor of the Senior Courts

Note

For "Sch.16, Pt 1, para.75(c), with effect from March 7, 2008 (SI 2008/222)." substitute:
Sch.16, Pt 1, para.75 and Sch.23, with effect in part from March 7, 2008 (SI 2008/ **7C–144** 222) and in part from March 31, 2009 (SI 2009/503) (remaining amendments not yet in force) and the Constitutional Reform Act 2005 s.59 and Sch.11, para 21(6) with effect from October 1, 2009 (SI 2009/1604).

SECTION 8

LIMITATION

Note

For "Supreme Court Act 1981" substitute:
Senior Courts Act 1981 **8–103**

SECTION 9

JURISDICTIONAL AND PROCEDURAL LEGISLATION

9A   MAIN STATUTES

Senior Courts Act 1981

9A–0   (1981 c.54)

Delete title "Supreme Court Act 1981" and substitute "Senior Courts Act 1981".

Introductory note

Add new paragraph at end:

By the Constitutional Reform Act 2005 s.59 and Sch.11 Pt I para.1(1) the Supreme Court Act 1981 is re–titled the Senior Courts Act 1981 and throughout the 1981 Act "Senior Courts" is substituted for "Supreme Court". Certain other amendments are also made by the 2005 Act to the 1981 Act, in particular amendments made necessary by the transfer of the judicial functions of the House of Lords to the Supreme Court of the United Kingdom (see s.40 and Sch.9 para.36 of the 2005 Act).

OTHER PROVISIONS

Assistance for transaction of judicial business of Senior Courts

9A–30 *Delete title "Assistance for transaction of judicial business of Supreme Court" and substitute "Assistance for transaction of judicial business of Senior Courts".*

In section 9(6A) for "House of Lords" substitute:

9A–31   Supreme Court

In section 9(8)(a)(i) for "a Lord of Appeal in Ordinary; or" substitute:

a judge of the Supreme Court; or

Note

Delete ". Further amendments to s.9 will be made as other provisions in the 2005 Act are brought into effect (see para.9A–4 above.)" and substitute:

9A–32   and by the 2005 Act, ss 40, 59, Sch.9, para.36(2), Sch.11, para.26, Sch 17, para 22(3), with effect from October 1, 2009 (SI 2009/1604).

Power of judge of Senior Courts to act in cases relating to rates and taxes

9A–46 *Delete title "Power of judge of Supreme or Crown Court to act in cases relating to rates and taxes" and substitute "Power of judge of Senior Courts to act in cases relating to rates and taxes".*

In section 14(1), for "Supreme Court" substitute:

Senior Courts

Note

Add at end:
Amended by the Constitutional Reform Act 2005 s.59 and Sch.11, para.26 with ef- **9A–47** fect from October 1, 2009 (SI 2009/1604).

Judicial bias—"incapable" and "apparent"

At the end of the eleventh paragraph add:
The handling of judicial review claims (especially those involving nationality and **9A–48** asylum issues) in which a judge is required to look at particular documents for interlocutory purposes may pose particular hazards in this respect. In such circumstances, the judge may think it right not to take part in a determination of the merits; all depends upon the circumstances (R. (AHK & FM) v *Secretary of State for the Home Department* [2009] EWCA Civ 287, April 2, 2009, CA, at para.20).

Appeals from High Court

In section 16(1), for "House of Lords" substitute:
Supreme Court **9A–57**

Note

Add new paragraph 9A–57.1:
Amended by the Constitutional Reform Act 2005 s.40 and Sch.9, para.36(3) with ef- **9A–57.1** fect from October 1, 2009 (SI 2009/1604).

Appeals directly from the High Court to the Supreme Court—"leap–frog" petitions

Delete title and substitute: "Appeals directly from the High Court to the Supreme Court—"leap–frog" petitions".
See the AJA 1969 s.13 (para.9B–33 below) **9A–58**

Delete "… and Practice Directions … 4A–13 (above)." and substitute:
and Section 4 paras 4.1.5 and 4.5.9 above.

Jurisdiction to hear appeals from High Court

In the first paragraph, for "appeals to the House of Lords" substitute:
appeals to the Supreme Court of the United Kingdom (formerly to the House of **9A–59** Lords)

Proceedings on case stated by magistrates' court or Crown Court

In section 28A(4) for "House of Lords" substitute:
Supreme Court **9A–93**

Note

Delete and substitute:
Amended by the Access to Justice Act 1999 s.61 and the Constitutional Reform Act **9A–94** 2005 s.40 and Sch.9 para.36(6) with effect from October 1, 2009 (SI 2009/1604).

Power to award interest on debts and damages

Add new paragraph at end:
Under English conflict of laws rules and the Private International Law (Miscel- **9A–124** laneous Provisions) Act 1995 s.11, the assessment of damages in tort is a procedural matter and, therefore, is governed by the law of the forum, but the right to claim interest by way of damages in a claim in tort depends on the proper law and is not in any sense a procedural question for the law of the forum; consequently, where, according to the proper law, a right to claim interest is established, the rate of interest is to be determined by the lex fori (*Maher v Groupama Grand Est* [2009] EWHC 38 (QB); [2009] 1 W.L.R. 1742 (Blair J.), where the judge noted effects on these propositions, as from January 11, 2009, of provisions in Council Regulation (EC) No.864/2007 ("Rome II") concerning the ascertainment of the applicable law as to assessment of damages in non–contractual claims arising out of events occurring after August 20, 2007).

Application for leave by person subject of an order (s.42(3))

Add new paragraph at end:

9A–152.7   In *R. (Ewing) v Secretary of State for Justice* [2008] EWHC 3416 (Admin); December 19, 2008, unrep. (Beatson J.), it was explained that, where a person subject to an order under s.42(1A) wishes to apply, under s.42(3), for leave to apply, under CPR r.54.4, for permission to proceed with a claim for judicial review, it may, depending on the circumstances, be appropriate for the High Court to consider the applications together or in stages; see also Vol.1 para.54.4.1.

C. Section 49(3)

Stay under particular statutes

In the last paragraph, for "In Admiral Taverns ... permission to appeal" substitute:

9A–177   In *Admiral Taverns (Cygnet) Ltd v Daly* [2008] EWCA Civ 1501; November 25, 2008, unrep., CA, the landlord's submission that the court's power to stay under r.3.1(2)(f) and under its inherent jurisdiction are subject to this section was rejected on their appeal to the High Court (see [2008] EWHC 1688 (QB)) and, on a second appeal, to the Court of Appeal. It was held (1) generally, that a court has an inherent jurisdiction (not changed by the CPR) to arrange its appeal business, and when so doing to suspend an order if necessary, and (2) particularly that s.89(1)(a) is to be read as restricting the jurisdiction of the court granting the order, and not as directed to an appellate court considering the exercise of its inherent jurisdiction to stay execution pending an appeal, and (b) does not restrict the exercise of that inherent jurisdiction (though in considering whether to grant a stay, an appeal court will have in mind the purposes of that provision). Consequently, an appellate court that had either granted permission to appeal form an order for possession, or was still considering permission, could stay the order pending determination of the appeal or application for permission to appeal.

Effect of this section

At the end of the third paragraph, add:

9A–198   ; *Watson v Croft Promo–Sport Ltd* [2009] EWCA Civ 15; [2009] 3 All E.R. 249, CA (where the relevant authorities are reviewed)

COMPOSITION OF COURT

Court of civil division

In subsection (5) of section 54 for "House of Lords" substitute:

9A–210   Supreme Court

Note

Add at end:

9A–211   Further amended by the Constitutional Reform Act 2005 s.40 and Sch.9 para.36.

OTHER PROVISIONS

Calling into question of incidental decisions in civil division

In subsection (2) of section 58, for "House of Lords" substitute:

9A–223   Supreme Court

Note

Add at end:

9A–224   Further amended by the Constitutional Reform Act 2005 s.40 and Sch.9 para.36.

Interpretation of this Act, and rules of construction for other Acts and documents

In section 151(1) for "'solicitor' means a solicitor of the Supreme Court" substitute:
"solicitor" means a solicitor of the Senior Courts; **9A–391**

In section 151(3) for "Supreme Court" substitute:
Senior Courts

In section 151(4) for "Supreme Court" substitute:
Senior Courts

Note

For "and the Constitutional Reform Act 2005 s.15(1), Sch.4, para.146 (see para.9A–4 above)." substitute:
the Constitutional Reform Act 2005 s.15(1) and Sch.4, para.146 and the 2005 Act **9A–392**
s.59 and Sch.11, para.1 with effect from October 1, 2009 (SI 2009/1604).

County Courts Act 1984

Transfer to High Court by order of High Court

In section 41(2) for "Supreme Court Act 1981" substitute:
Senior Courts Act 1981 **9A–479**

Note

Add at end:
Amended by the Constitutional Reform Act 2005 s.59 and Sch.11, para.1 with effect **9A–480**
from October 1, 2009 (SI 2009/1604).

Execution of judgments or orders for payment of money

Add new paragraph at end:
Article 8 of the 1991 Order imposes restrictions on the circumstances in which a **9A–583**
judgment or order of a county court for the payment of a sum of money which it is
sought to enforce wholly or partly by execution against goods may be enforced in the
High Court (see para.9B–939 below). Coinciding with the substitution of CPR r.70.5
(Enforcement of decisions of bodies other than the High Court and county courts and
compromises enforceable by enactment) by SI 2008/3327, significant amendments to
art.8 were made by SI 2009/577.

Civil Procedure Act 1997

Rule Committee

In section 2(2)(a), for "Supreme Court" substitute:
Senior Courts **9A–740**

In section 2(2)(d) for "Supreme Court Act 1981" substitute:
Senior Courts Act 1981

In section 2(2)(e) for "Supreme Court" substitute:
Senior Courts

In section 2(2)(f) for "Supreme Court" substitute:
Senior Courts

Note

Add new paragraph 9A–740.1:
Amended by the Constitutional Reform Act 2005 s.59 and Sch.11, paras 1, 4 with ef- **9A–740.1**
fect from October 1, 2009 (SI 2009/1604).

Rule–making process

Add new paragraph at end:
The Lord Chancellor's power under this section is a protected function within the **9A–746**
Constitutional Reform Act 2005 s.19 and Sch.7.

Civil Justice Council

Add at end:

9A–755   The Lord Chancellor's power under this section is a protected function within the Constitutional Reform Act 2005 s.19 and Sch.7.

Disclosure etc. of documents before action begun

In subsection (1) of section 8, for "section 33(2) of the Supreme Court Act 1981" substitute:

9A–759   section 33(2) of the Senior Courts Act 1981

Note

Add new paragraph 9A–759.1:

9A–759.1   Amended by the Constitutional Reform Act 2005 s.59 and Sch.11, para.1 with effect from October 1, 2009 (SI 2009/1604).

Note

For "Supreme Court Act 1981" substitute:

9A–773   Senior Courts Act 1981

Access to Justice Act 1999

Assignment of appeals to Court of Appeal

In subsection (1)(a) of section 57, for "House of Lords" substitute:

9A–848   Supreme Court

JUDGES ETC.

Judges holding office in European or international courts

In section 68(3)(a), for "Supreme Court Act 1981" substitute:

9A–849   Senior Courts Act 1981

In section 68(3)(c), for "Supreme Court Act 1981" substitute:

Senior Courts Act 1981

Note

Delete "(see para.9A–4 above)" and substitute:

9A–850   and s.59 and Sch.11, para.1 with effect from October 1, 2009 (SI 2009/1604)

Vice–president of Queen's Bench Division.

In section 69(2) for "Supreme Court Act 1981" substitute:

9A–851   Senior Courts Act 1981

Note

Add after "Sch.4, para.282":

9A–852   , and subs.(2) amended by the 2005 Act s.59 and Sch.11, para.1 with effect from October 1, 2009 (SI 2009/1604).

Access to Justice Act 2000 (Destination of Appelas) Order 2000

Citation, commencement and interpretation

In section 1(2)(b) for "Supreme Court Act 1981" substitute:

9A–898   Senior Courts Act 1981

In section 1(4)(b)(i) for "Supreme Court Act 1981" substitute:

Senior Courts Act 1981

Note

Add new paragraph 9A–898.1:
  Amended by the Constitutional Reform Act 2005 s.59 and Sch.11, para.1 with effect **9A–898.1**
from October 1, 2009 (SI 2009/1604).

Appeals from the High Court

In section 2(a), for "Supreme Court Act 1981" substitute:
  Senior Courts Act 1981   **9A–899**

Note

Add new paragraph 9A–899.1:
  Amended by the Constitutional Reform Act 2005 s.59 and Sch.11, para.1 with effect **9A–899.1**
from October 1, 2009 (SI 2009/1604).

Consequential amendments

In section 7, for "Supreme Court Act 1981" substitute:
  Senior Courts Act 1981   **9A–904**

Note

Add new paragraph 9A–904.1:
  Amended by the Constitutional Reform Act 2005 s.59 and Sch.11, para.1 with effect **9A–904.1**
from October 1, 2009 (SI 2009/1604).

Tribunals, Courts and Enforcement Act 2007

"JUDICIAL REVIEW"

Upper Tribunal's "judicial review" jurisdiction

In section 15(5)(a) for "Supreme Court Act 1981" substitute:
  Senior Courts Act 1981   **9A–1009**

Note

Add new paragraph at start:
  Amended by the Constitutional Reform Act 2005 s.59 and Sch.11, para.1 with effect **9A–1009.1+**
from October 1, 2009 (SI 2009/1604).

Transfer of judicial review applications from High Court

In section 19(3) for "Supreme Court Act 1981" substitute:
  Senior Courts Act 1981   **9A–1013**

In section 19(4) for "Supreme Court Act 1981" substitute:
  Senior Courts Act 1981

Note

  Amended by the Constitutional Reform Act 2005 s.59 and Sch.11, para.1 with effect **9A–1013.0.1**
from October 1, 2009 (SI 2009/1604).

9B   OTHER STATUTES AND REGULATIONS

Administration of Justice Act 1960

Appeal in cases of contempt of court

In Section 13(2)(c), for "House of Lords" substitute:

9B–18   Supreme Court

In Section 13(4), for "House of Lords" substitute:

Supreme Court

Note

For "and the Access to Justice Act 1999 s.64 and Sch.15, Pt III" substitute:

9B–19   , the Access to Justice Act 1999 s.64 and Sch.15, Pt III and the Constitutional Reform Act 2005, s.40 and Sch.9, para.13, with effect from October 1, 2009 (SI 2009/1604)

Procedure on application for habeas corpus

9B–21   *Delete "and no such application shall in any case be made to the Lord Chancellor."*

Administration of Justice Act 1969

PART II

APPEAL FROM HIGH COURT TO SUPREME COURT

Grant of certificate by trial Judge

Delete Part II title "Appeal from High Court to House of Lords" and substitute "Appeal from High Court to Supreme Court".

9B–30   *In section 12(1)(b), for "House of Lords" substitute:*

Supreme Court

In section 12(3)(b), for the two instances of "House of Lords" substitute:

Supreme Court

Note

Add new paragraph at start:

9B–31   Part II heading amended by the Constitutional Reform Act 2005 s.40 and Sch.9, para.20(2), with effect from October 1, 2009 (SI 2009/1604).

For "and the Courts Act 1971 s.56, Sch.11." substitute:

the Courts Act 1971 s.56 and Sch.11 and the Constitutional Reform Act 2005 s.40 and Sch.9 para.20(3), with effect from October 1, 2009 (SI 2009/1604).

Leave to appeal to Supreme Court

9B–33   *Delete title "Leave to appeal to House of Lords" and substitute "Leave to appeal to Supreme Court".*

In section 13(1) for the two instances of "House of Lords" substitute:

Supreme Court

In section 13(2) for "House of Lords" substitute:

Supreme Court

In section 13(2) for the two instances of "House" substitute:

Supreme Court

In section 13(2)(b) for "House of Lords" substitute:

Supreme Court

Delete section 13(4).

Note

Add new paragraph 9B–33.1:
Amended by the Constitutional Reform Act 2005 s.40 and Sch.9, para.20(4), with ef- **9B–33.1** fect from October 1, 2009 (SI 2009/1604).

No appeal to Court of Appeal

Add new paragraph at end:
As a result of the transfer of the jurisdiction formerly exercised by the House of **9B–34** Lords to the Supreme Court of the United Kingdom, para.4.15 of Practice Directions Applicable to Civil Appeals is replaced by r.16 of the Supreme Court Rules 2009.

Appeal where leave granted

Delete and substitute:
14. *[Repealed by the Constitutional Reform Act 2005 s.40 and Sch.9,* **9B–35** *para.20(5), with effect from October 1, 2009 (SI 2009/1604).]*

Cases excluded from section 12

In section 15(2)(b), for "House of Lords" substitute:
Supreme Court   **9B–36**

Note

Add at end:
Amended by the Constitutional Reform Act 2005 s.40 and Sch.9 para.20(6), with ef- **9B–37** fect from October 1, 2009 (SI 2009/1604).

Courts and Legal Service Act 1990

ALLOCATION AND TRANSFER OF BUSINESS

Allocation of business between High Court and county courts

In section 5(7)(a)(i) for "Supreme Court" substitute:
Senior Courts   **9B–102**

Note

In the first paragraph, add after "Sch.4, para.212":
; and subs.(7) amended by the Constitutional Reform Act 2005 s.59 and Sch.11, **9B–103** para.4, with effect from October 1, 2009 (SI 2009/1604)

Law reports

In section 115 for "Supreme Court" substitute:
Senior Courts   **9B–171**

Note

Add new paragraph 9B–171.1:

9B–171.1   Amended by the Constitutional Reform Act 2005 s.59 and Sch.11, para.4, with effect from October 1, 2009 (SI 2009/1604).

High Court and County Courts Jurisdiction Order 1991

Introductory note

In the last paragraph, add after "... (SI 2008/2934)":

9B–928   ; High Court and County Courts Jurisdiction (Amendment) Order 2009 (SI 2009/577) (making amendments to arts 4A, 5(1) and 9 consequential upon amendments to the CPR relating to fast track claims made by SI 2008/3327 which came into force on April 6, 2009, but haseffect only in relation to proceedings issued before that date, and other amendments)

Delete article 4A and substitute:

9B–935   **4A.** Except for proceedings to which article 5 applies, a claim for money in which the county courts have jurisdiction may only be commenced in the High Court if the value of the claim is more than £25,000.

In article 5(1), for "financial value" substitute:

value

Note

Add after "Article 6B was inserted by SI 2008/2934.":

9B–936   Article 4A was substituted and art.5(1) was amended in relation to proceedings issued on or after April 6, 2009 by the High Court and County Courts Jurisdiction (Amendment) Order 2009 (SI 2009/577).

Enforcement

Delete paragraph (2) of article 8 and substitute:

9B–939   (2) *[amends the County Courts Act 1984, s.85(1)]*

(2) Subject to paragraph (3), where—
    (a) an enactment provides that a sum of money shall be or may be recoverable as if it were payable under a county court order; and
    (b) the recovery of that sum is sought wholly or partially by execution against goods, payment of that sum shall be enforced in accordance with paragraphs (1)(a) to (c).
(3) Paragraph (1)(b) does not apply to the enforcement of—
    (a) a sum of money recoverable under section 15(1) of the Employment Tribunals Act 1996; or
    (b) a compromise sum which is recoverable under section 19A(3) of that Act.

Note

Delete and substitute:

9B–940   Amended by SI 1993/1407; SI 1995/205 art.5, SI 1996/3141 and new paras (2) and (3) inserted in relation to proceedings issued on or after April 6, 2009 by SI 2009/577.

Enforcement of traffic penalties

Add new paragraphs (1)(a)(iii) to (1)(a)(v) to article 8A:

9B–943   (iii) regulation 17 of the Road User Charging (Enforcement and Adjudication) (London) Regulations 2001;
(iv) regulation 21 of the Civil Enforcement of Parking Contraventions (England) General Regulations 2007; and

(v) regulation 13 of the Civil Enforcement of Parking Contraventions (Penalty Charge Notices, Enforcement and Adjudication) (Wales) Regulations 2008;

Delete paragraph (1)(c) and substitute:

(c) amounts payable by a person other than a local authority under an adjudication pursuant to—
  (i) the Road User Charging (Enforcement and Adjudication) (London) Regulations 2001;
  (ii) the Civil Enforcement of Parking Contraventions (England) Representations and Appeals Regulations 2007; and
  (iii) the Civil Enforcement of Parking Contraventions (Representations and Appeals) (Wales) Regulations 2008; and
(d) increased fixed penalties referred to in—
  (i) regulation 17(6) of the Road Traffic (Vehicle Emissions) (Fixed Penalty) (England) Regulations 2002; and
  (ii) regulation 17(6) of the Road Traffic (Vehicle Emissions) (Fixed Penalty) (Wales) Regulations 2003,

In paragraph (2), delete "and expressions which are used in the 1991 Act have the same meaning in this article as they have in that Act".

In paragraph (3)(a), for "a London authority", substitute:

a London borough council, the Common Council of the City of London, Transport for London,

Note

For "and the High Court ... (SI 2001/1387)" substitute:
, the High Court and County Courts Jurisdiction (Amendment) Order 2001 (SI **9B–944** 2001/1387) and (in relation to proceedings issued on or after April 6, 2009) the High Court and County Courts Jurisdiction (Amendment) Order 2009 (SI 2009/577)

Value of claim

Delete title "Financial value of claim" and substitute: "Value of claim"

Delete "value of the financial claim" and substitute: **9B–948**
value of the claim

Note

Add new paragraph 9B–948.1:
Amended in relation to proceedings issued on or after April 6, 2009 by the High **9B–948.1** Court and County Courts Jurisdiction (Amendment) Order 2009 (SI 2009/577).

Charging Orders Act 1979

Note

For "Supreme Court Act 1981 s.153, Sch.5" substitute:
Senior Courts Act 1981 s.153 and Sch.5 **9B–1025**

For "Supreme Court Act 1981" substitute:
Senior Courts Act 1981

Note

For "Supreme Court Act 1981" substitute:

9B–1029   Senior Courts Act 1981

Civil Liability (Contribution) Act 1978

Note

At the end of the second paragraph add:

9B–1090   A party (X) is liable in respect of any damage within the meaning of these provisions if another party (Y) was entitled to recover compensation from X in respect of that damage, whatever the legal basis of X's liability (*BRB (Residuary) Ltd v Connex South Eastern Ltd* [2008] EWHC 1172 (QB); [2008] 1 W.L.R. 2867 (Cranston J.) where X, under the mistaken belief that they were contractually obliged to indemnify a third party (Z) in respect of Y's damage and had suffered judgment on liability to be entered against them, were subsequently allowed, on the basis that they and Z were liable in respect of the same damage, to bring a contribution claim against Z).

Crown Proceedings Act 1947

JUDGMENTS AND EXECUTION

Interest on debts, damages and costs

In section 24(3) for "Supreme Court Act 1981"

9B–1147   Senior Courts Act 1981

Note

For "and the Private International Law (Miscellaneous Provisions) Act 1995 s.4" substitute:

9B–1148   the Private International Law (Miscellaneous Provisions) Act 1995 s.4; and the Constitutional Reform Act 2005 s.59 and Sch.11, para.1 with effect from October 1, 2009 (SI 2009/1604).

Attachment of moneys payable by the Crown

In section 27(3) for "Supreme Court Act 1981" substitute:

9B–1155   Senior Courts Act 1981

Note

Add after "SI 2005/2712":

9B–1156   and the Constitutional Reform Act 2005 s.59 and Sch.11, para.1 with effect from October 1, 2009 (SI 2009/1604)

Litigants in Person (Cost and Expenses) Act 1975

Costs or expenses recoverable

In section 1(1)(a) for "in the Supreme Court or in the House of Lords" substitute:

9B–1210   in the Senior Courts, in the Court of Judicature or in the Supreme Court

In section 1(2)(a) for "House of Lords" substitute:

Supreme Court

In section 1(5), delete "'the Supreme Court'".

Note

Add new paragraph 9B–1210.1:
Amended by the Constitutional Reform Act 2005 s.59 and Sch.11, para.22 with ef- **9B–1210.1**
fect from October 1, 2009 (SI 2009/1604).

Late Payment of Commercial Debts (Interest) Act 1998

(1998 c.20)

9B–1325

Add new paragraphs 9B–1325 to 9B–1364:

ARRANGEMENT OF SECTIONS

PART I

STATUTORY INTEREST ON QUALIFYING DEBTS

Introduction

This Act applies where both contracting parties are acting in the course of business. Its aim is to encourage prompt payment in such cases but in pursuit of this aim uses the "stick" rather than the "carrot" by providing for payment of a fixed sum plus statutory interest at a penal rate in the event of late payment. Anti–avoidance provisions prevent contracting out.

The Act was brought into force gradually by a series of statutory instruments and has been fully in force from August 7, 2002 (SI 2002/1673), and this applies to all commercial contracts (unless exempt—see below).

PART I

STATUTORY INTEREST ON QUALIFYING DEBTS

Statutory interest

1.—(1) It is an implied term in a contract to which this Act applies **9B–1326** that any qualifying debt created by the contract carries simple interest subject to and in accordance with this Part.

(2) Interest carried under that implied term (in this Act referred to as "statutory interest") shall be treated, for the purposes of any

rule of law or enactment (other than this Act) relating to interest on debts, in the same way as interest carried under an express contract term.

(3) This Part has effect subject to Part II (which in certain circumstances permits contract terms to oust or vary the right to statutory interest that would otherwise be conferred by virtue of the term implied by subsection (1)).

"implied term"/"express term"

9B–1327   The principle of the Act is to imply a term into commercial contracts but the implied term is then treated as an express term.

"statutory interest"

9B–1328   When suing for a debt which is covered by the Act the particulars of the claim should include a claim for:

> "statutory interest pursuant to the Late Payment of Commercial Debts (Interest) Act at [appropriate rate—see below] amounting to £x as at the date hereof and continuing at £y per day from today until judgment or sooner payment."

Contracts to which Act applies

9B–1329   **2.**—(1) This Act applies to a contract for the supply of goods or services where the purchaser and the supplier are each acting in the course of a business, other than an excepted contract.

(2) In this Act "contract for the supply of goods or services" means—

   (a) a contract of sale of goods; or
   (b) a contract (other than a contract of sale of goods) by which a person does any, or any combination, of the things mentioned in subsection (3) for a consideration that is (or includes) a money consideration.

(3) Those things are—

   (a) transferring or agreeing to transfer to another the property in goods;
   (b) bailing or agreeing to bail goods to another by way of hire or, in Scotland, hiring or agreeing to hire goods to another; and
   (c) agreeing to carry out a service.

(4) For the avoidance of doubt a contract of service or apprenticeship is not a contract for the supply of goods or services.

(5) The following are excepted contracts—

   (a) a consumer credit agreement;
   (b) a contract intended to operate by way of mortgage, pledge, charge or other security.

(6) [...]

(7) In this section—

   "business" includes a profession and the activities of any government department or local or public authority;

   "consumer credit agreement" has the same meaning as in the Consumer Credit Act 1974;

   "contract of sale of goods" and "goods" have the same meaning as in the Sale of Goods Act 1979;

   "government department" includes any part of the Scottish Administration;

> "property in goods" means the general property in them and not merely a special property.

Note

Amended by the Late Payment of Commercial Debts (Scotland) Regulations 2002 **9B–1330**
(SSI 2002/335), reg.2(2).

"in the course of a business"

Only contracts where both supplier and purchaser are acting in the course of a **9B–1331**
business are covered by this Act. All such contracts are covered unless specifically
exempted.

"excepted contracts"

Excepted contracts include mortgage and contracts governed by the Consumer **9B–1332**
Credit Act 1974.

Note

Section 2A applies to Scotland and is not reproduced here. **9B–1333**

Qualifying debts

3.—(1) A debt created by virtue of an obligation under a contract **9B–1334**
to which this Act applies to pay the whole or any part of the contract
price is a "qualifying debt" for the purposes of this Act, unless (when
created) the whole of the debt is prevented from carrying statutory
interest by this section.

(2) A debt does not carry statutory interest if or to the extent that
it consists of a sum to which a right to interest or to charge interest
applies by virtue of any enactment (other than section 1 of this Act).

This subsection does not prevent a sum from carrying statutory interest by reason of the fact that a court, arbitrator or arbiter would,
apart from this Act, have power to award interest on it.

(3) A debt does not carry (and shall be treated as never having carried) statutory interest if or to the extent that a right to demand
interest on it, which exists by virtue of any rule of law, is exercised.

Note

Amended by the Late Payment of Commercial Debts (Scotland) Regulations, **9B–1335**
reg.2.(4)

"qualifying debt"

The Act applies to a "qualifying debt" as defined. By s.3(1) it applies both to **9B–1336**
contracts providing for a lump sum payment and to those providing for stage
payments. The Act is intended to deal with contracts not already subject to a different
statutory regime: hence s.3(2).

Period for which statutory interest runs

4.—(1) Statutory interest runs in relation to a qualifying debt in ac- **9B–1337**
cordance with this section (unless section 5 applies).

(2) Statutory interest starts to run on the day after the relevant
day for the debt, at the rate prevailing under section 6 at the end of
the relevant day.

(3) Where the supplier and the purchaser agree a date for payment of the debt (that is, the day on which the debt is to be created
by the contract), that is the relevant day unless the debt relates to an
obligation to make an advance payment.

A date so agreed may be fixed one or may depend on the happening of an event or the failure of an event to happen.

(4) Where the debt relates to an obligation to make an advance payment, the relevant day is the day on which the debt is treated by section 11 as having been created.

(5) In any other case, the relevant day is the last day of the period of 30 days beginning with—

(a) the day on which the obligation of the supplier to which the debt relates is performed; or

(b) the day on which the purchaser has notice of the amount of the debt or (where that amount is unascertained) the sum which the supplier claims is the amount of the debt, whichever is the later.

(6) Where the debt is created by virtue of an obligation to pay a sum due in respect of a period of hire of goods, subsection (5)(a) has effect as if it referred to the last day of that period.

(7) Statutory interest ceases to run when the interest would cease to run if it were carried under an express contract term.

(8) In this section "advance payment" has the same meaning as in section 11.

When does the statutory interest start to run?

9B–1338   The question posed in this sub–heading is answered by s.4. Interest runs from the day after the "relevant day" as defined. Where a date has been agreed for payment that is the relevant day (s.4(3)). Where the contract provides for an advance payment see s.11. In other cases the relevant day is 30 days after the date specified in s.4(5).

Remission of statutory interest

9B–1339   **5.**—(1) This section applies where, by reason of any conduct of the supplier, the interests of justice require that statutory interest should be remitted in whole or part in respect of a period for which it would otherwise run in relation to a qualifying debt.

(2) If the interests of justice require that the supplier should receive no statutory interest for a period, statutory interest shall not run for that period.

(3) If the interests of justice require that the supplier should receive statutory interest at a reduced rate for a period, statutory interest shall run at such rate as meets the justice of the case for that period.

(4) Remission of statutory interest under this section may be required—

(a) by reason of conduct at any time (whether before or after the time at which the debt is created); and

(b) for the whole period for which statutory interest would otherwise run or for one or more parts of that period.

(5) In this section "conduct" includes any act or omission.

Discretion

9B–1340   The effect of s.5 is to give the court a discretion to withhold statutory interest where the interests of justice so require. For example, interest may be awarded for a period less than that of the relevant day to the day of the judgment where the claimant has unreasonably delayed in either issuing or prosecuting the claim.

Compensation arising out of late payment

9B–1341   **5A.**—(1) Once statutory interest begins to run in relation to a

448

qualifying debt, the supplier shall be entitled to a fixed sum (in addition to the statutory interest on the debt).

(2) That sum shall be—

(a) for a debt less than £1,000, the sum of £40;

(b) for a debt of £1,000 or more, but less than £10,000, the sum of £70;

(c) for a debt of £10,000 or more, the sum of £100.

(3) The obligation to pay an additional fixed sum under this section in respect of a qualifying debt shall be treated as part of the term implied by section 1(1) in the contract creating the debt.

Note

Amended by the Late Payment of Commercial Debts (Scotland) Regulations (SSI **9B–1342** 2002/335) reg.2(5).

Compensation payment

In addition to statutory interest at a penal rate (see below) the claimant is entitled to **9B–1343** a fixed sum as provided for by s.5A(2).

Rate of statutory interest

6.—(1) The Secretary of State shall by order made with the consent **9B–1344** of the Treasury set the rate of statutory interest by prescribing—

(a) a formula for calculating the rate of statutory interest; or

(b) the rate of statutory interest.

(2) Before making such an order the Secretary of State shall, among other things, consider the extent to which it may be desirable to set the rate so as to—

(a) protect suppliers whose financial position makes them particularly vulnerable if their qualifying debts are paid late; and

(b) deter generally the late payment of qualifying debts.

"rate of statutory interest"

The rate of statutory interest prescribed pursuant to s.6 is currently that set out in **9B–1345** the Late Payment of Commercial Debts (Rate of Interest) (No.3) Order 2002 (SI 2002/ 1675). The rate is eight per cent above the official bank rate. For all relevant rates see Vol.1 para.7.0.17(h). Paragraph 4 of SI 2002/1675 provides that the rate is eight per cent above the official bank rate in force on the June 30 (in respect of interest which starts to run between July 1 and December 31) or on the December 31 (in respect of interest which starts to run between January 1 and June 30) immediately before the day on which statutory interest starts to run.

SI 2002/1675 refers to "the official dealing rate" but this is the rate now known as the official bank rate, as set out at para.7.0.17(h). (Somewhat unhelpfully the statutory instrument's "explanatory note" mentions the "repo" rate which is no longer in use.)

Editorial note

Sections 7 to 10 set out the anti–avoidance provisions of the Act, but see also ss.12 **9B–1346** and 14.

PART II

CONTRACT TERMS RELATING TO LATE PAYMENT OF QUALIFYING DEBTS

Purpose of Part II

7.—(1) This Part deals with the extent to which the parties to a **9B–1347** contract to which this Act applies may by reference to contract terms oust or vary the right to statutory interest that would otherwise apply when a qualifying debt created by the contract (in this Part referred to as "the debt") is not paid.

(2) This Part applies to contract terms agreed before the debt is created; after that time the parties are free to agree terms dealing with the debt.

(3) This Part has effect without prejudice to any other ground which may affect the validity of a contract term.

Forbearance

9B–1348   The anti–avoidance provisions are intended to prevent a commercial contract excluding the provisions of the Act. Thus Pt II applies to contract terms agreed before the debt is created and by s.7(2), does not apply to later terms agreed by the parties dealing with the debt e.g. a term whereby the creditor later agrees to forego interest if payment is made by a new agreed date.

Circumstances where statutory interest may be ousted or varied

9B–1349   **8.**—(1) Any contract terms are void to the extent that they purport to exclude the right to statutory interest in relation to the debt, unless there is a substantial contractual remedy for late payment of the debt.

(2) Where the parties agree a contractual remedy for late payment of the debt that is a substantial remedy, statutory interest is not carried by the debt (unless they agree otherwise).

(3) The parties may not agree to vary the right to statutory interest in relation to the debt unless either the right to statutory interest as varied or the overall remedy for late payment of the debt is a substantial remedy.

(4) Any contract terms are void to the extent that they purport to—

    (a) confer a contractual right to interest that is not a substantial remedy for late payment of the debt, or

    (b) vary the right to statutory interest so as to provide for a right to statutory interest that is not a substantial remedy for late payment of the debt,

        unless the overall remedy for late payment of the debt is a substantial remedy.

(5) Subject to this section, the parties are free to agree contract terms which deal with the consequences of late payment of the debt.

Limited contracting out

9B–1350   Section 8, the key anti–avoidance provision, renders void any contract term which merely purports to exclude the right to statutory interest. Contracting parties are free to agree an alternative to statutory interest provided that it is a "substantial remedy".

Meaning of "substantial remedy"

9B–1351   **9.**—(1) A remedy for the late payment of the debt shall be regarded as a substantial remedy unless—

    (a) the remedy is insufficient either for the purpose of compensating the supplier for late payment or for deterring late payment; and

    (b) it would not be fair or reasonable to allow the remedy to be relied on to oust or (as the case may be) to vary the right to statutory interest that would otherwise apply in relation to the debt.

(2) In determining whether a remedy is not a substantial remedy, regard shall be had to all the relevant circumstances at the time the terms in question are agreed.

(3) In determining whether subsection (1)(b) applies, regard shall be had (without prejudice to the generality of subsection (2)) to the following matters—

(a) the benefits of commercial certainty;

(b) the strength of the bargaining positions of the parties relative to each other;

(c) whether the term was imposed by one party to the detriment of the other (whether by the use of standard terms or otherwise); and

(d) whether the supplier received an inducement to agree to the term.

"substantial remedy"

Any term purporting to exclude the right to statutory interest is void (see s.8 above) **9B–1352** but a "substantial remedy" can be agreed instead. To be "substantial" the remedy must fulfil the Act's primary aim of deterring late payment or, alternatively be sufficient to compensate for late payment. Additionally, it must be fair and reasonable to allow the remedy to be relied on to deny, or vary, the right to statutory interest. In deciding this all the circumstances at the time the contract was agreed are relevant (see s.9(2)) and, without prejudice to this, the factors in s.9(3) will be considered.

Interpretation of Part II

10.—(1) In this Part—   **9B–1353**

"contract term" means a term of the contract creating the debt or any other contract term binding the parties (or either of them);

"contractual remedy" means a contractual right to interest or any contractual remedy other than interest;

"contractual right to interest" includes a reference to a contractual right to charge interest;

"overall remedy", in relation to the late payment of the debt, means any combination of a contractual right to interest, a varied right to statutory interest or a contractual remedy other than interest;

"substantial remedy" shall be construed in accordance with section 9.

(2) In this Part a reference (however worded) to contract terms which vary the right to statutory interest is a reference to terms altering in any way the effect of Part I in relation to the debt (for example by postponing the time at which interest starts to run or by imposing conditions on the right to interest).

(3) In this Part a reference to late payment of the debt is a reference to late payment of the sum due when the debt is created (excluding any part of that sum which is prevented from carrying statutory interest by section 3).

PART III

General and Supplementary

Treatment of advance payments of the contract price

9B–1354   **11.**—(1) A qualifying debt created by virtue of an obligation to make an advance payment shall be treated for the purposes of this Act as if it was created on the day mentioned in subsection (3), (4) or (5) (as the case may be).

(2) In this section "advance payment" means a payment falling due before the obligation of the supplier to which the whole contract price relates ("the supplier's obligation") is performed, other than a payment of a part of the contract price that is due in respect of any part performance of that obligation and payable on or after the day on which that part performance is completed.

(3) Where the advance payment is the whole contract price, the debt shall be treated as created on the day on which the supplier's obligation is performed.

(4) Where the advance payment is a part of the contract price, but the sum is not due in respect of any part performance of the supplier's obligation, the debt shall be treated as created on the day on which the supplier's obligation is performed.

(5) Where the advance payment is a part of the contract price due in respect of any part performance of the supplier's obligation, but is payable before that part performance is completed, the debt shall be treated as created on the day on which the relevant part performance is completed.

(6) Where the debt is created by virtue of an obligation to pay a sum due in respect of a period of hire of goods, this section has effect as if—

    (a) references to the day on which the supplier's obligation is performed were references to the last day of that period; and

    (b) references to part performance of that obligation were references to part of that period.

(7) For the purposes of this section an obligation to pay the whole outstanding balance of the contract price shall be regarded as an obligation to pay the whole contract price and not as an obligation to pay a part of the contract price.

"advance payment"

9B–1355   The Act applies not merely to a conventional contract, e.g. where goods are supplied and payment is then due, but also to contracts where some or all of the payment is to be made in advance. The right to statutory interest arises where the advance payment is not made and s.11 defines the date when the debt is deemed to have been created for the purpose of statutory interest.

Conflict of laws

9B–1356   **12.**—(1) This Act does not have effect in relation to a contract governed by the law of a part of the United Kingdom by choice of the parties if—

    (a) there is no significant connection between the contract and that part of the United Kingdom; and

  (b) but for that choice, the applicable law would be a foreign law.

(2) This Act has effect in relation to a contract governed by a foreign law by choice of the parties if—

  (a) but for that choice, the applicable law would be the law of a part of the United Kingdom; and

  (b) there is no significant connection between the contract and any country other than that part of the United Kingdom.

(3) In this section—

  "contract" means a contract falling within section 2(1); and

  "foreign law" means the law of a country outside the United Kingdom.

"conflict of laws"

Although s.12 has the title "conflict of laws", s.12(2) is in reality an anti–avoidance **9B–1357** provision. It prevents the Act being disapplied by a term stating that the contract is governed by a foreign law when in reality the contract has no connection with the foreign country and would otherwise be governed by the law of a part of the United Kingdom. Section 12(1) operates the other way round to disapply the Act in contracts expressed to be governed by the law of a part of the United Kingdom but which otherwise have no connection with the United Kingdom and the applicable law would be a foreign law.

Assignments, etc.

13.—(1) The operation of this Act in relation to a qualifying debt is **9B–1358** not affected by—

  (a) any change in the identity of the parties to the contract creating the debt; or

  (b) the passing of the right to be paid the debt, or the duty to pay it (in whole or in part) to a person other than the person who is the original creditor or the original debtor when the debt is created.

(2) Any reference in this Act to the supplier or the purchaser is a reference to the person who is for the time being the supplier or the purchaser or, in relation to a time after the debt in question has been created, the person who is for the time being the creditor or the debtor, as the case may be.

(3) Where the right to be paid part of a debt passes to a person other than the person who is the original creditor when the debt is created, any reference in this Act to a debt shall be construed as (or, if the context so requires, as including) a reference to part of a debt.

(4) A reference in this section to the identity of the parties to a contract changing, or to a right or duty passing, is a reference to it changing or passing by assignment or assignation, by operation of law or otherwise.

"change in identity of the parties"

The effect of the Act is not affected by a change in the identity of the parties (e.g. by **9B–1359** assignment under a factoring agreement).

Contract terms relating to the date for payment of the contract price

14.—(1) This section applies to any contract term which purports **9B–1360** to have the effect of postponing the time at which a qualifying debt would otherwise be created by a contract to which this Act applies.

(2) Sections 3(2)(b) and 17(1)(b) of the Unfair Contract Terms Act 1977 (no reliance to be placed on certain contract terms) shall apply in cases where such a contract term is not contained in written standard terms of the purchaser as well as in cases where the term is contained in such standard terms.

(3) In this section "contract term" has the same meaning as in section 10(1).

Postponing payment

9B–1361   Section 14 is in reality another anti–avoidance provision. Any term purporting to have the effect of postponing the time at which a qualifying debt would otherwise have been created is subject to s.3(2)(b) and 17(1)(b) of the Unfair Contract Terms Act 1977 (see para.3H–555).

Orders and regulations

9B–1362   **15.**—(1) Any power to make an order or regulations under this Act is exercisable by statutory instrument.

(2) Any statutory instrument containing an order or regulations under this Act, other than an order under section 17(2), shall be subject to annulment in pursuance of a resolution of either House of Parliament.

Interpretation

9B–1363   **16.**—(1) In this Act—

"contract for the supply of goods or services" has the meaning given in section 2(2);

"contract price" means the price in a contract of sale of goods or the money consideration referred to in section 2(2)(b) in any other contract for the supply of goods or services;

"purchaser" means (subject to section 13(2)) the buyer in a contract of sale or the person who contracts with the supplier in any other contract for the supply of goods or services;

"qualifying debt" means a debt falling within section 3(1);

"statutory interest" means interest carried by virtue of the term implied by section 1(1); and

"supplier" means (subject to section 13(2)) the seller in a contract of sale of goods or the person who does one or more of the things mentioned in section 2(3) in any other contract for the supply of goods or services.

(2) In this Act any reference (however worded) to an agreement or to contract terms includes a reference to both express and implied terms (including terms established by a course of dealing or by such usage as binds the parties).

Short title, commencement and extent

9B–1364   **17.**—(1) This Act may be cited as the Late Payment of Commercial Debts (Interest) Act 1998.

(2) This Act (apart from this section) shall come into force on such day as the Secretary of State may by order appoint; and different days may be appointed for different descriptions of contract or for other different purposes.

An order under this subsection may specify a description of contract by reference to any feature of the contract (including the parties).

(3) The Secretary of State may by regulations make such transitional, supplemental or incidental provision (including provision modifying any provision of this Act) as the Secretary of State may consider necessary or expedient in connection with the operation of this Act while it is not fully in force.

(4) This Act does not affect contracts of any description made before this Act comes into force for contracts of that description.

(5) This Act extends to Northern Ireland.

SECTION 10

10 COURT FEES

In the table, the following entries have been added or amended. Delete entries "— in the Supreme Court" and "— in the county court" following 5.1, 5.3, 5.4 and 5.6.

SCHEDULE 1

FEES TO BE TAKEN

2.7 On an application by consent or without notice where no other fee is specified.	£40
2.10 Register of judgments, orders and fines kept under section 98 of the Courts Act 2003—	

Note: The fee payable under fee 4.1 includes—
  • where the court allows a party to fax to the court for the use of that party a document that has not been requested by the court and is not intended to be placed on the court file.
  • where a party requests that the court fax a copy of a document from the court file.
  • the court provides a subsequent copy of a document which it has previously provided.	

5.1 On the filing of a request for detailed assessment where the party filing the request is legally aided or is funded by the LSC and no other party is ordered to pay the costs of the proceedings.	£140
5.3 On a request for the issue of a default costs certificate.	£60
5.4 On an appeal against a decision made in detailed assessment proceedings.	£200
5.5 On applying for the court's approval of a certificate of costs payable from the Community Legal Service Fund.	£50
5.6 On a request or application to set aside a default costs certificate.	£100
8.1 On an application for or in relation to enforcement of a judgment or order of a county court or through a county court, by the issue of a warrant of execution against goods except a warrant to enforce payment of a fine —	
(a) in cases other than CCBC cases;	£100
(b) in CCBC cases	£70
8.3 On an application for an order requiring a judgment debtor or other person to attend court to provide information in connection with enforcement of a judgment or order.	£50

8.4(a) On an application for a third party debt order or the appointment of a receiver by way of equitable execution.	£100
(b) On an application for a charging order.	£100
8.5 On an application for a judgment summons.	£100
8.7 On an application for an attachment of earnings order (other than a consolidated attachment of earnings order) to secure payment of a judgment debt.	£100
8A.1 On a request for service by a bailiff of an order to attend court for questioning	£100

Note

Add at end:

10–7.1   and SI 2009/1498

SCHEDULE 2

REMISSIONS AND PART REMISSIONS

Interpretation

In Schedule 2, paragraph 1(1)(c) for "section 626 of the Jobseekers Act 1995" substitute:

10–8   section 26 of the Jobseekers Act 1995

In Schedule 2, paragraph 1(1)(h) for "Supreme Court Act 1981" substitute:

Senior Courts Act 1981

Note

Add after "SI 2008/2853":

10–8.1   , SI 2009/1498 and the Constitutional Reform Act 2005, s.59 and Sch.11, para.1 with effect from October 1, 2009 (SI 2009/1604).

Delete the table and substitute:

Full remission of fees—gross annual income

Column 1 *Number of children of party paying fee*	*Column 2* *Single*	*Column 3* *Couple*
no children	£13,000	£18,000
1 child	£15,930	£20,930
2 children	£18,860	£23,860
3 children	£21,790	£26,790
4 children	£24,720	£29,720

10–10

In Schedule 2, paragraph 3(2) for "£2,735" substitute:

£2,930

Note

Add new paragraph 10–10.1:

10–10.1   Amended by SI 2009/1498.

Disposable monthly income

In Schedule 1, paragraph 5(3) delete sub–paras (a), (b) and (c) and substitute:

10–12   £315; plus

(b) £244 for each child of the party; plus

(c) £159, if the party has a partner.

Note

Add after "SI 2008/2853":
and SI 2009/1498

10–15.3.1

SECTION 12

CPR: APPLICATION, AMENDMENTS AND INTERPRETATION

C. STRUCTURE OF CPR

1. RULES AND PRACTICE DIRECTIONS

(b) Process for making or giving practice directions

After the fifth paragraph, add as a new paragraph:

In *Bovale Ltd v Secretary of State for the Communities and Local Government* [2009] **12–17** EWCA Civ 171; March 11, 2009, unrep., CA, in amplification of what is said above, the Court of Appeal explained (at para.23) that, after the amendments to s.5 of the 1997 Act made by the 2005 Act came into effect, it became the custom for new practice directions or amendments to existing practice directions affecting civil proceedings to be issued only after consideration by the Civil Procedure Rule Committee (see para.12–3 above). That Committee is chaired by the Master of the Rolls with persons from the Lord Chancellor's department (the Ministry of Justice) in attendance. After such consideration, practice directions are then issued by the Master of the Rolls (as the nominee of the Lord Chief Justice) and "with the agreement of the Lord Chancellor" (see Sch.2, Pt 1, para.3(1) of the 2005 Act).

After the eighth paragraph, add as a new paragraph:

After the coming into effect of those provisions, in *Bovale Ltd v Secretary of State for the Communities and Local Government*, op cit, the Court of Appeal traced the history of the inherent power of the court to make practice directions and explained the restrictions on that power imposed, first by provisions in the 1997 Act, and secondly by provisions in the 2005 Act. In this appeal the Court held that the lead judge of the Administrative Court, by giving standard directions in a judgment handed down in a particular case ([2008] EWHC 2143 (Admin)), had exceeded his powers. A majority of the judges on the appeal regarded it as significant that, in doing so, the judge did not simply provide guidance as to the interpretation and application of the rules and practice directions applicable to cases of a particular type coming before his court or fill in a gap apparent therein, but attempted to vary them.

(c) Modification or disapplication of rules or practice directions—pilot schemes

Add new paragraph at end:

Practice Direction (Electronic Working Pilot Scheme) supplements CPR r.5.5 and **12–18** came into effect on April 1, 2009. See further Vol.1 para.51.1.6 above.

G. CONSTRUCTION AND INTERPRETATION OF RULES

15. EUROPEAN LAW AND THE CPR

After the first paragraph, add as a new paragraph:

12–59   In *Morgan v Hinton Organics (Wessex) Ltd* [2009] EWCA Civ 107; March 2, 2009, unrep., CA, where it was noted that the presumption that legislation is to be construed so as to avoid conflict with international law may apply where domestic legislation intended to bring a treaty into effect is ambiguous, the Court of Appeal held that the State's treaty obligation under art.9(4) of the Aarhus Convention to provide remedies that are not "prohibitively expensive" (albeit one adopted by the EC for certain purposes) was not a rule of law directly binding on the English court and in the circumstances of that case was, at most, a matter potentially relevant to the judge's exercise of discretion as to costs under CPR r.44.3. In *Football Association Premier League Ltd v QC Leisure* [2008] EWHC 2897 (Ch); November 13, 2008, unrep. (Kitchin J.), the question was whether an application for the joinder of additional parties under CPR r.19.2 should be granted where the application was made after a question raised in the proceedings had been referred to the ECJ for preliminary ruling under r.68.2. In granting the application on terms the judge took into account not only the overriding objective but also the duty of sincere co–operation enshrined in EC Treaty art.10.

SECTION 14

ALTERNATIVE DISPUTE RESOLUTION

A. INTRODUCTION

2. APPELLATE JUDGES' STATEMENTS AND SPEECHES ON ADR

In the second paragraph, for "in 2007 and 2008" substitute:

14–3   between 2007 and 2009

Add at end:

; *http://www.judiciary.gov.uk/docs/speeches/mr–littleton–chambers–080609.pdf* [Accessed July 27, 2009] (Lord Clarke of Stone–Cum–Ebony M.R.).

B. ADR IN THE CONTEXT OF THE CPR

1. CASE MANAGEMENT

(c) Voluntary v compulsory/mandatory ADR and case management

In the first paragraph, for "http://www.lawreform.ie" substitute:

14–6   *http://www.lawreform.ie/publications/consultpapers.htm*

(f) Judicial speeches—ADR case management post Halsey—power to direct ADR

For "during 2007 and 2008" substitute:

14–9   between 2007 and 2009

(h) Case management and cost sanctions

Add at end:

14–11   Further information on costs sanctions is given in para.14–17.

(i) Case management: facilitation of ADR procedures and criteria for referral to ADR

14–12   *Delete title "(i) Case management: facilitation of ADR procedures, criteria for referral to ADR, timing of referral" and substitute: "(i) Case management: facilitation of ADR procedures and criteria for referral to ADR".*

Delete and substitute:

The overriding objective in the CPR requires the court to encourage the use of an ADR procedure, in appropriate cases, and to facilitate the use of such procedure, as one of the elements of active case management (r.1.4(2)(e)). The manner in which the court may facilitate the use of an ADR procedure includes the following:

(i) By ensuring that the opportunity to explore ADR prospects is not prejudiced by the rigours of case management procedures generally.

(ii) By acting as a source of information about professional and commercial bodies providing ADR services (for example, see *http://www.nationalmediationhelpline.com* [Accessed July 27, 2009] and paras 14–24 and 14–27 below).

(iii) By verbally encouraging the parties to consider ADR at a hearing or telephone conference, such as a case management conference or a pre–trial review.

(iv) By ordering a stay of the whole or part of the proceedings, for mediation or some other ADR procedure, pursuant to the application of the parties or one of them (r.3.1(2)(f) and r.3.3(1) and see para.14–13 below).

(v) By ordering such a stay of its own initiative (r.3.1(2)(f) and r.3.3(1)). An appropriate time to make such an order might be upon perusal of the parties' statements about ADR in their Allocation Questionnaires. (See para.14–13 below.)

(vi) By making an order, whether on directions for allocation or a later stage, of the type referred to in the Multi–Track Practice Direction (sometimes referred to as an "Ungley Order"). (29PD4.10(9) and see para.14–13 below.)

(vii) By making an ADR order on the basis of the draft in App.7 to the Admiralty and Commercial Courts Guide (see para.14–22). The draft order includes the following paragraph: "4. The parties shall take such serious steps as they may be advised to resolve their disputes by ADR procedures before the neutral individual or panel so chosen by no later than [*]." See para.14–9 above regarding the issue of the court's power to order parties to take part in a mediation process.

(viii) By making an ADR order on the basis of the draft order in App.E to and Section 7 of the Technology and Construction Court Guide (see para.14–22). Although these Guides refer to their particular courts there appears to be no reason why the type of ADR orders made in these courts could not be made, where appropriate, in other courts. Again, see para.14–9 above regarding the issue of the court's power to order parties to take part in a mediation process. See also paras. 14–22 and 14–23 below regarding ADR in the Commercial Court and the Technology and Construction Court.

(ix) By arranging, in the Admiralty and Commercial Court or the Technology and Construction Court, for the court to provide Early Neutral Evaluation (see the references to the respective Court Guides in sub–paras (vii) and (viii) immediately above). Further, in the Technology and Construction Court the court can provide a judge to act as a mediator; further information about this, and a reference to nine cases having been mediated to date, can be found at *http://www.tecsa.org.uk/mediation__adr–1328.htm* [Accessed July 27, 2009].

(x) By, in a case which is suitable to be resolved by an ADR procedure except for one sticking point, ordering the hearing of that point as a preliminary issue with a view to the case then being referred to ADR (see s.8 of the Technology and Construction Court Guide, para.14–22, although, again, there is no reason why the approach taken by the Technology and Construction Court cannot be taken by other courts, where appropriate).

(xi) By referring a Small Claim to the Small Claims Mediation Service (see para.14–24).

(xii) By making an appropriate costs order (or advising that such an order might be made in the future) in respect of failure to give adequate consideration to ADR prior to the commencement of proceedings (para.14–21) or during proceedings (see para.14–17).

Criteria for referral to mediation is given in Guidance on Judicial Referral to Mediation issued to members of the judiciary in 2007: see para.14–28 below. The Guidance deals with the type of cases suitable for mediation and the indicators and counter indicators for referral.

(j) Case management: the stages at which ADR may be encouraged

Delete title "(j) Case management: the stages at which ADR may be encouraged" and substitute: **14–13**
"(j) Case management: timing and the stages at which ADR may be encouraged".

At the beginning of the first paragraph add:

The issue of timing, as in when is the best stage of a case to use an ADR procedure, is often a complex question. It is dealt with in the *Guidance on Judicial Referral to Mediation* referred to in para.14–2 above (see paras 14–28 and 14–31). In *Nigel Witham Ltd v Smith* [2008] EWHC 12, TCC Judge Peter Coulson Q.C. offered general guidance saying that a premature mediation simply wasted time and could sometimes lead to a hardening of positions on both sides whereas, conversely, a delay in any mediation until after full particulars and documents had been exchanged could mean that the costs that had been incurred to get to that point became themselves the principal obstacle to a successful mediation. He added:

> "The trick in many cases was to identify the happy medium: the point when the detail of the claim and the response were known to both sides, but before the costs that had been incurred in reaching that stage were so great that a settlement was no longer possible."

Delete the final paragraph.

(k) *Case management: where a public authority is a party*

Add new paragraph at end:

14–14   A rather different picture is painted by "Mediation and Judicial Review: An empirical research study" published in 2009 by the Public Law Project (see *http://www.publiclawproject.org.uk/documents/MediationandJudicialReview.pdf* [Accessed July 27, 2009]).This detailed research paper does not contemplate mediation as having a significant role in this area. One of its conclusions is:

> "Any exploration of the role of mediation in judicial review would therefore be likely to focus on the small percentage of unresolved cases that proceed beyond the permission stage and in which both parties have an interest in reaching a settlement but are unable to do so because negotiations have become 'stuck'" (page 35).

3. COSTS WHERE ADR DECLINED

Add new paragraphs at end:

14–17   In *Vale of Glamorgan Council v Roberts* [2008] EWHC 2911 an unsuccessful litigant claimed costs against the successful defendant local authority. His application did not succeed. The court noted that the defendant had not positively suggested mediation and said that it would be going too far to disallow costs incurred by a local authority because that authority did not initiate suggestions for a mediation.

In *S v Chapman* [2008] EWCA Civ 800; [2008] E.L.R. 603; (2008) 152 S.J.L.B. 29 the court found that the defendant was entitled to await the outcome of its application to strike out before deciding whether or not it was either necessary or advantageous to enter into mediation of the substantive issues with the claimant. There was no reason to depart from the normal principle that costs followed the event.

It is often the case, where a party has refused mediation, that the court has a number of factors to consider, in relation to r.44.3(4)(a) and the parties' conduct, rather than (as in *Halsey*) the single issue of whether refusal was unreasonable. The overall nature of the court's discretion on costs can be seen in *Multiplex Construction (UK) Ltd v Cleveland Bridge (UK) Ltd* [2008] EWHC 2280, TCC where Jackson J. made a comprehensive review of costs authorities from which he derived (at para.72) eight principles. These included

> "(v) In many cases the judge can and should reflect the relative success of the parties on different issues by making a proportionate costs order"

and

> "(vi) In considering the circumstances of the case the judge will have regard not only to any part 36 offers made but also to each party's approach to negotiations (insofar as admissible) and general conduct of the litigation."

In two cases, *Whitecap Leisure Ltd v John H. Rundle Ltd* [2008] EWCA Civ 1026 and *Shah v Joshi* [2008] EWHC 1766 the court's overall approach to costs was seen. Features of the parties' conduct included the following. In *Whitecap*, the conduct of each party was described as having been as bad as the other, although one party's obdurate attitude was more striking than the other's conduct, and an offer of mediation was rejected as was a very favourable Pt 36 offer. In *Shah*, mediation was proposed but flatly rejected, as was a Calderbank offer. The parties did undertake mediation shortly before trial, but it was unsuccessful. On the first day of the trial, the judge emphasised to the parties the extreme desirability of a settlement but despite giving an extended adjournment to facilitate a settlement no agreement was reached. In *Whitecap* the court came to deal with costs and ordered that one party should recover only 80 per cent of its costs of the appeal and that the costs of the claim and the costs of the appeal should be set off against each other. In *Shah* an application for indemnity costs in respect of a successful claims and counterclaim was only granted in part; the court took into account all the circumstances, including the losing party's attitude at the time when the other party first proposed mediation. These cases perhaps demonstrate that if a party rejects an offer of mediation, or fails to give ADR adequate consideration when following a pre–action protocol or completing the allocation questionnaire, it will run the risk of an adverse costs order when costs are dealt with and the court considers the overall conduct of the litigation.

4. CONFIDENTIALITY, WITHOUT PREJUDICE AND "MEDIATION PRIVILEGE" IN RELATION TO MEDIATION

(a) Privacy is important, but not without exceptions

Delete paragraphs 14–18 to 14–20 and substitute:

It is very important, for reasons of public policy, that communications between parties to a mediation, and between those parties and the mediator, remain private and confidential. The courts will, generally, be ready to reinforce the cloak of confidentiality under which settlements are reached: **14–18**

> "communications made with a view to an amicable settlement ought to be held very sacred; for if parties were to be afterwards prejudiced by their efforts to compromise, it would be impossible to attempt an amicable arrangement of differences." (per Lord Scott, quoting Romilly M.R. in *Hoghton v Hoghton* (1852) 15 Beav 278, 321 when discussing the "without prejudice" rule in *Ofulue v Bossert* [2009] UKHL 16; [2009] 2 W.L.R. 749).

In the context of ADR, Dyson L.J. said in *Halsey v Milton Keynes General NHS Trust* [2004] EWCA Civ 576; [2004] 1 W.L.R. 3002 (at para.14):

> "…parties are entitled in an ADR to adopt whatever position they wish and if, as a result the dispute is not settled, that is not a matter for the court .   .   . if the integrity and confidentiality of the process is to be respected, the court should not know, and therefore should not investigate, why the process did not result in agreement."

This statement is reinforced by Toulson and Phipps on Confidentiality (at para.15–016):

> "… it would destroy the basis of mediation if, in the case of the mediation failing, either party could publicise matters which had passed between themselves or between either of them and the mediator for the purposes of mediation..."

Finally, in *Cumbria Waste Management Ltd and Lakeland Waste Management Ltd v Baines Wilson* [2008] EWHC 786 (QB), H.H.J. Kirkham said: "… the court should support the mediation process by refusing, in normal circumstances, to order disclosure of documents and communications within a mediation."

There are different ways in which mediation communications are protected and, as the cases mentioned below demonstrate, it can be important to differentiate between the concepts of confidentiality, "without prejudice", legal professional privilege, and (if it exists) "mediation privilege". The cloak of confidentiality is, in fact, multi–layered.

These cases will also demonstrate that, and again this is for reasons of public policy, confidentiality is not absolute and there are exceptions whereby a court may wish to examine mediation matters that usually remain private and confidential. Such exceptions are limited in nature and guarded by the court. Essentially, when considering whether matters in relation to a particular mediation should remain confidential, the court will usually be involved in a careful public policy balancing act, weighing the importance of encouraging parties to settle against, for example, some kind of impropriety.

The final paragraph in this section mentions some less obvious aspects relating to confidentiality.

Issues that relate to confidentiality in its broadest sense are of importance in various ways; they are relevant, for example, to lawyers advising a party before a mediation, to mediation providers when drafting agreements to mediate, to lawyers and mediators in relation to the conduct of a mediation and to lawyers and the courts when there are applications, post mediation, that the court should explore what took place at a mediation.

(b) Farm Assist 2

14–18.1   In *Farm Assist Limited (in liquidation) v The Secretary of State for the Environment, Food and Rural Affairs (No.2)* [2009] EWHC 1102 (TCC) ("Farm Assist 2") the court gave guidance on these matters. It did so in the context of an application by a mediator to set aside a witness summons that was intended to require her to give evidence about what had taken place at a mediation. Having reviewed the authorities Ramsey J. gave the following summary of the different concepts or principles that are applied in the protection of the privacy of mediation:

"(1) Confidentiality: The proceedings (at a mediation) are confidential both as between the parties and as between the parties and the mediator. As a result even if the parties agree that matters can be referred to outside the mediation, the mediator can enforce the confidentiality provision. The court will generally uphold that confidentiality but where it is necessary in the interests of justice for evidence to be given of confidential matters, the Courts will order or permit that evidence to be given or produced.

(2) Without Prejudice Privilege: The proceedings are covered by without prejudice privilege. This is a privilege which exists as between the parties and is not a privilege of the mediator. The parties can waive that privilege.

(3) Other Privileges: If another privilege attaches to documents which are produced by a party and shown to a mediator, that party retains that privilege and it is not waived by disclosure to the mediator or by waiver of the without prejudice privilege."

These three concepts of privilege will be explored in more detail below.

The mediator's application in this case to set aside the witness summons was dismissed for a number of reasons: the parties had, as they were entitled to do, waived the without prejudice privilege and, although the mediator was on the face of it entitled to enforce the confidentiality provision in the Mediation Agreement, it was held that this was "… a case where, as an exception, the interests of justice lie strongly in favour of evidence being given of what was said and done (at the mediation)." These findings, however, had no practical consequences as the mediator did not have any relevant notes or any recall of the issues; further, the case went on to settle in any event. *Farm Assist 2* has attracted the attention of mediators and has resulted in the publication by the Civil Mediation Council of "Civil Mediation Council Guidance Note No.1 Mediation Confidentiality" (see *http://www.civilmediation.org* [Accessed July 27, 2009]).

(c) Confidentiality

14–18.2   As in *Farm Assist 2*, most agreements to mediate include clauses providing that, in addition to the mediation being conducted on a without prejudice basis, the parties and the mediator are required to treat the proceedings as confidential. In *Farm Assist 2* Ramsey J. also found that the confidentiality would have been implied, even if the mediation agreement had not agreed it expressly.

In concluding that the court can override such confidentiality, where it is necessary in the interests of justice, the court in *Farm Assist 2* took into account on the following passage in *Confidentiality* by Toulson and Phipps:

"Generally speaking, confidentiality is not a bar to disclosure of documents or information in the process of litigation, but the court will only compel such disclosure if it considers it necessary for the fair disposal of the case: see. . . *British Steel Corporation v Granada Television Ltd* [1981] A.C. 1096" (para.17–001).

If there is an explicit agreement on confidentiality it will, as with any other type of agreement, fall to be construed by the court. In *Farm Assist 2* the confidentiality provisions were narrowly drawn and not as wide as the mediator might have wished.

Another particular point clarified by this case was the finding that the mediator could enforce the provisions relating to confidentiality, as against the parties. This means that where, as in *Farm Assist 2*, the parties have waived without prejudice privilege the mediator may nevertheless be able to require that confidentiality will be maintained.

Where there is a risk that a party may act in breach of the agreement that proceedings at a mediation be kept confidential he may be restrained by an injunction (*Venture Investment Placement Ltd v Hall* [2005] EWHC 1227 (Ch); [2005] All E.R. (D) 224 and *David Instance v Denny Brothers Printing Ltd* [2000] F.S.R. 869.

(d) Without Prejudice

It is apparent, from the analysis in *Farm Assist 2*, that part of the mediation cloak of **14–18.3** confidentiality is based on without prejudice privilege, and that such privilege can be waived by the parties. For a fuller statement of the without prejudice rule or concept see *Cutts v Head* [1984] Ch. 290; [1984] 1 All E.R. 597, CA; *Unilever plc v The Proctor & Gamble Co* [2000] 1 W.L.R. 2436; [2001] 1 All E.R. 783; *Muller v Linsley & Mortimer* [1996] P.N.L.R. 74 and Vol.1, para.31.3.40 below. There are, however, exceptions to this privilege (helpfully summarised by Robert Walker L.J. in *Unilever* [2000] 1 W.L.R. 2444) which are of importance in the context of mediation and ADR. A number of these exceptions, which are largely based on public policy and the better administration of justice, appear in the following cases.

In *Muller*, the claimant's initial claim had been against his fellow shareholders in a private company following his dismissal as a director of that company. He settled that claim following without prejudice correspondence. Subsequently, he sued the solicitors who had advised him in the initial claim, alleging negligence. It was held that the without prejudice correspondence in the initial claim was disclosable in the subsequent claim. The public policy reasons that would have applied to prevent disclosure in the initial claim did not apply in the context of the subsequent claim: any without prejudice statements or offers made in the initial claim were kept from the court, in that claim, lest they be treated as an admission of liability. Once that claim has been concluded, however, that reason fell away. (See Vol.1, para.35.12.3 and also *Bradford and Bingley v Rashid* [2006] 1 W.L.R. 2066).

The decision in *Muller* seems applicable in circumstances where there is a subsequent claim following an earlier claim and there are relevant mediation communications in the earlier claim that do, on the face of it, appear to be subject to without prejudice privilege. This was the finding in *Cattley v Pollard* [2007] Ch. 353. There the claimants in the initial action were the executors of an estate who sued various defendants, including the solicitors acting in the estate, for misappropriation of estate funds. A settlement was reached at a successful mediation involving some of the defendants. A subsequent action was bought by the claimants against one of the defendants in the initial action who had not been involved in the mediated settlement. The defendant in this subsequent action was concerned about the issue of double recovery by the claimants and sought disclosure of mediation documents. The defendants resisted disclosure, arguing that mediations will not succeed if confidentiality is broken. The court held, following *Muller* and taking account of the overriding objective to deal justly with cases, that there should be disclosure limited to such parts of the mediation bundle as were factually material to the defendant's argument relating to double recovery.

In *Cumbria Waste Management Ltd and Lakeland Waste Management Ltd v Baines Wilson* [2008] EWHC 786 (QB), however, the court found that Muller did not apply and refused to order disclosure of confidential mediation documents for the purposes of a subsequent action. The parties to the mediation did not waive privilege and the court held that the documents should remain privileged, both on the basis that they were subject to without prejudice privilege and were confidential by virtue of the agreement to mediate. H.H.J. Kirkham said that the court should support the mediation process by refusing, in normal circumstances, to order disclosure of documents and communications within a mediation. The court found that the disclosure sought here did not fall within the exception to the without prejudice rule set out in *Muller* and, further, noted that the court in *Muller* gave no consideration to the position of third parties.

Muller and the applicability of the without prejudice rule fell to be considered by the House of Lords in *Ofulue v Bossert* [2009] UKHL 16; [2009] 2 W.L.R. 749. This property case concerned two sets of proceedings between the same parties and, in particular, without prejudice negotiations between the parties during the first set of proceedings. The House of Lords said that the without prejudice rule was based on both the public policy of encouraging the negotiated settlement of actions and the express or implied agreement of the parties that communications in the course of such negotiations should not be admissible in evidence. It was held that the rule did extend to without prejudice negotiations conducted during earlier proceedings involving an issue which was still unresolved. The court further found that, although there were exceptions to the rule where justice required it, as where it was necessary to prevent the rule being used to further impropriety, reasons of legal and practical certainty made it inappropriate to create a further exception to limit the protection to identifiable admissions. Lord Hope referred to Ormrod J.'s words in *Tomlin v Standard Telephones & Cables Ltd* [1969] 1 W.L.R. 1378 when he said that the court should be very slow to lift the without prejudice umbrella unless the case for doing so is absolutely plain. Lord Neuberger explained that if the House of Lords created further exceptions to the without prejudice rule this would severely risk hampering the freedom parties should feel when entering into settlement negotiations.

Another well established exception to the without prejudice rule is that it does not prevent the admission in evidence of what parties said to one another when the issue is whether or not such communications resulted in a concluded settlement agreement (see Vol.1, para.31.3.40 below). At the trial of such issue, the fact that such communications took place between the parties at a mediation does not confer on them a status distinct from any other without prejudice communications sufficient to take them outside the scope of the exception or otherwise to render them inadmissible (*Brown v Rice and Patel* [2007] EWHC 625 (Ch).

As seen in *Farm Assist 2*, parties can waive their entitlement to without prejudice confidentiality and did so in *Chantry Vellacott v Convergence Group* [2007] EWHC 1774 and *Earl of Malmesbury v Strutt & Parker* [2008] EWHC 424 (QB). In the latter case Jack J. made adverse findings in relation to a party's recovery of costs on the basis of that party's conduct during a mediation. He said that "... the claimant's position at the mediation was plainly unrealistic and unreasonable" and found that, had they made an offer which truly reflected their position, the mediation might have succeeded. Subsequently, however, the Master of the Rolls seemed to disapprove of this approach on the basis that it might lead to satellite litigation (see para.19 of the Master of the Rolls' Birmingham Speech referred to in para.14–3 above.)

Note, however, that without prejudice privilege is effectively regarded as a joint privilege and cannot be waived by one party alone (see *Somatra Ltd v Sinclair Roche & Temperley* [2000] 1 W.L.R. 2453; [2000] 2 Lloyd's Rep. 673, referred to in Vol.1 at para.31.3.40).

In *Smiths Group v Weiss* [2002] LTL 22/3/2002, the court followed *Somatra* (see above) when considering whether material, prepared for a mediation that did not result in a settlement, should retain its without prejudice status. It was held that the material should remain without prejudice save in clear and unequivocal circumstances.

The court had to consider whether in all the circumstances it was fair and just to allow a party to rely on the material.

Where the court directs under r.35.12 that there should be a discussion between experts and that they must prepare a statement for the court, any such statement is available for use in the proceedings and is not protected by the without prejudice privilege (see Vol.1, para.35.12.3 below). Consequently, where a mediation takes place after such order, it cannot be argued in subsequent proceedings before the court that the statement cannot be referred to, even though the direction was made by the court with an eye to assisting a contemplated mediation (*Aird v Prime Meridian Ltd* [2006] EWCA Civ 1866; *The Times*, February 14, 2007 CA).

In *Farm Assist Ltd v Secretary of State* [2008] EWHC 3079 (the precursor to *Farm Assist 2*) the issue concerned legal advice privilege rather than the without prejudice concept. Party 1 sought to set aside the agreement resulting from a mediation on account of duress by party 2. Party 2 said that, as the allegations about duress went to party 1's state of mind, it should be able to see the (usually privileged) documents containing the legal advice to party 1. It was held that disclosure be refused, there having been no waiver of legal advice privilege.

(e) Mediation Privilege

14–18.4   In *Farm Assist 2* Ramsey J., having considered "other privileges" (see (3) in 14–18.1 above), noted that in Brown & Marriott *ADR Principles and Practice* the authors discuss the possible existence of and desirability for a distinct privilege attaching to the mediation process:

> "It remains to be resolved definitively by the English Courts (if not by the legislature) whether there is a privilege attaching to the whole mediation process,

including all communications passing within that process, whether the mediation relates to family matters, civil or commercial disputes or any other kind of issue" (para.22–088, 2nd edition).

He went on to canvass the "... the need for a further 'privilege' which arises other than the Mediator's right to confidentiality in relation to the mediation proceedings." In *Brown v Rice* [2007] EWHC 625 the court commented, although did not have to make a finding on the point, that: "It may be in the future that the existence of a distinct mediation privilege will require to be considered by either the legislature or the courts ..."

Mr Justice Briggs has written on "Mediation Privilege?" in an authoritative two part review in the New Law Journal (159 N.L.J. 506 and 159 N.L.J. 550). Having reviewed the various concepts of privilege in relation to mediation he goes on to develop a potential common law solution. This is based on a distinction between the facts that:

"a mediator will act as a conduit for the sharing of such information between the parties as is commonly shared in without prejudice negotiations: (shared information)"

and

"the important part of the mediator's facilitative role (which) is to encourage the parties to share with him or her information, views, hopes and fears about the dispute which the party communicating them does not wish the other party to know, and which the mediator agrees to keep secret from the other party (mediator secrets)."

His thesis likens Mediator Secrets to legal professional privilege, on the basis that parties to disputes should be able to unburden themselves with absolute frankness to a mediator in the same way as with their legal advisers, and to argue that public policy may justify a new privilege strictly limited to Mediator Secrets. He adds that such a privilege would not be likely to interfere with the application to Shared Information in mediation of the recognised exceptions to the without prejudice principle, as occurred in both *Brown* and *Cattley*. Mr Justice Briggs supports the idea of a new privilege by referring to the ability of the common law to recognise a new form of privilege, where, in a new context, the public interest so requires, pointing out that a distinct form of non–status based privilege, in connection with matrimonial conciliation relating to children, has recently been recognised: see *Re D (Minors) (Conciliation: Disclosure of Information)* [1993] Fam 231 at 238. He concludes:

"There is in principle therefore good reason why the courts should now recognise that the undoubted public interest in facilitating the process of mediation as a desirable and often preferable means of dispute resolution, by comparison with the full panoply of a trial, justifies the identification of a narrow form of mediator secret privilege of the type described above. There is no reason why a party to a mediation should not be encouraged to be as frank with the mediator as with his or her legal adviser. The similarity with the underlying justification for legal professional privilege is therefore very close."

Mr Justice Briggs' call for a development in this area is made all the more timely by virtue of the fact that the EU Mediation Directive (Directive 2008/52/EC of the European Parliament and of the Council of 21 May 2008 on certain aspects of mediation in civil and commercial matters) carries the requirement that it be complied with by May 2011. By art.7 of the Directive member states must ensure that, with reference to cross–border mediation, mediators must not be compellable to give evidence in civil proceedings or arbitration regarding information arising out of or in connection with a mediation, except where overriding considerations of public policy otherwise require, or where disclosure of the content of the mediation settlement agreement is necessary in order to implement or enforce it.

(f) Other aspects relating to confidentiality

There are other ways in which mediation confidentiality may be called into question **14–18.5** and a number of these are dealt with in "Mediator Confidentiality—Conduct and Communications" by Burnley and Lascelles (see *http://www.cedr.co.uk/library/articles/ Mediator_confidentiality_SJBerwin.pdf* [Accessed July 27, 2009]). These include, for example, money laundering (Proceeds of Crime Act 2002), breaches of professional conduct, insolvency proceedings in circumstances where the court reserves the power to veto settlement agreements and, arguably, a mediation settlement involving a minor where court approval is required. Other examples might possibly include applications of the Data Protection Act and the Freedom of Information Act.

5. MEDIATION COSTS

14–19   Two important points arise from *National Westminster Bank Plc v Thomas Feeney and Linda Feeney* [2006] EWHC 90066 (Costs) and [2007] (Costs Appeal). First, Eady J. confirmed that: "as a matter of general principle, costs incurred in a mediation would form part of the costs of the action just as any reasonable costs of negotiation would (see Costs Practice Direction para.4.6(8))." Secondly, the successful party did not re-cover the mediator's costs or its costs for preparing for and attending at the mediation because: (a) the mediation agreement entered in to by the parties on the mediation provider's standard terms was on the basis that the mediator's fee would be borne equally by the parties who would bear their own costs; (b) the Tomlin Order agreed when settlement was reached did not deal explicitly with the costs of the mediation; and (c) it was held that the Tomlin Order did not alter the mediation agreement. In *Lobster Group Ltd v Heidelberg Graphic Equipment Ltd* [2008] EWHC 413 (TCC) Coulson J., having confirmed the main point in *Feeney* (that a Tomlin Order will not alter a mediation agreement unless it does so explicitly) went on to make a finding that has significant implications for mediation costs. He introduced some doubt about whether the costs of a mediation would (assuming no contractual agreement of the type in *Feeney*) form part of the costs of the action in cases where a mediation takes place pre proceedings. (This is an important point because, in accordance with the pre–action protocols, mediations are increasingly carried out pre proceedings.) Coulson J. was considering mediation costs as one aspect of an application for security for costs and he was clearly troubled both by the amount of the costs and the fact that they had been incurred some considerable time prior to the issue of proceedings. He put forward a number of reasons for his view that the costs of the pre–action mediation were not recoverable:

> "16. First, unlike the costs incurred in a pre–action protocol, I do not believe that the costs of a separate pre–action mediation can ordinarily be described as 'costs of and incidental to the proceedings' (pursuant to s.51 of the Supreme Court Act 1981). On the contrary, it seems to me clear that they are not. They are the costs incurred in pursuing a valid method of alternative dispute resolution. Those costs were incurred in a form of dispute resolution which had no connection to these proceedings, and which here took place 2.5 years before the proceedings even started."

Clearly, this aspect of the decision, to the extent that it might appear to inhibit pre-action mediation, does not sit comfortably with many recent developments in relation to ADR. This is not least because pre–action mediations are often carried out pursuant to the provisions of the relevant Pre–Action Protocol. It may be that the case will come to be regarded as a decision on its own particular facts. See also *McGlinn v Waltham Contractors Ltd* [2005] EWHC 1419 (TCC); [2005] All E.R. 1126 (Judge Peter Coulson Q.C.) which also considered s.51 of the Supreme Court Act. It was held that (a) the costs incurred in complying with a Pre–Action Protocol may be recoverable as costs "incidental to" any subsequent proceedings and (b) costs in respect of claims dropped by a claimant prior to the commencement of proceedings were not, in unexceptional circumstances, capable of amounting to costs "incidental" to the proceedings.

See also *Earl of Malmesbury v Strutt & Parker* [2008] EWHC 424 (QB) and the com-ments thereon in paras 14–11 and 14–18 above regarding costs sanctions in relation to conduct at a mediation.

6. MISCELLANEOUS MATTERS

14–20   Where the parties freely consent to arbitration there is unlikely to be a denial of ac-cess to a court within the meaning of ECHR, art.6(1): *Deweer v Belgium* (1979–1980) 2 E.H.R.R. 439; *Axelsson v Sweden* No.11960/86, decision of July 13, 1990, unrep., EComHR; *Pastore v Italy* No.46483/99, May 25, 1999, unrep., ECtHR, 2nd chamber. The key is the absence of restraint: *ibid*. Where the court was excessively forceful in its encouragement of the use of ADR, ECHR art.6(1) might be engaged. Any waiver of art.6 rights must be unequivocal: *Zumtobel v Austria* (1994) 17 E.H.R.R. 116; *Rolf Gustafson v Sweden* (1998) 25 E.H.R.R. 623.

For the enforcement of a contractual ADR clause and comparison with an arbitra-tion clause, see *Cable & Wireless Plc v IBM United Kingdom Ltd* [2003] EWHC 316; [2002] All E.R. (D) 277 (Colman J.).

Routinely, the courts will exercise their inherent jurisdiction to stay legal proceed-ings where there is an extant arbitration clause, in effect enforcing the agreement to arbitrate the dispute. It would appear that the English courts may be edging towards the position that they should exercise their jurisdiction to stay legal proceedings where there is an agreement between the parties to negotiate or mediate (albeit an agreement that is lacking in the certainty traditionally regarded as necessary for enforceability and perhaps even non–binding) (ibid.; cf., *Halifax Financial Services Ltd v Intuitive Systems Ltd* [1999] 1 All E.R. (Comm) 303 (McKinnon J.)). See further Vol.2, paras 9A–176 to 9A–177. See also *Ardentia Ltd v British Telecommunications Plc* [2008] EWHC 2111 where one of the parties commenced proceedings before a tiered dispute resolution procedure had been exhausted. The procedure made an exception to the bar on commencing proceedings where, as was the case, interim relief was sought from the court. The court, however, having granted interim relief, then stayed the matter to enable the other issues between the parties to be dealt with under the procedure.

C. ADR IN PRE–ACTION PROTOCOLS AND COURT GUIDES

1. ADR IN PROTOCOLS

Delete the first paragraph and substitute:

14–21 Pre–action conduct is dealt with by Practice Direction—Pre–Action Conduct, as amended in April 2009 (para. C1–001) and the various pre–action protocols listed below. Section II of the Practice Direction is general in its application, whereas Section III deals with the conduct of cases that are not subject to a pre–action protocol (paras 2.3 and 2.4). The Practice Direction reinforces the role of ADR. The aims of the Practice Direction are stated, in para.1, to include enabling the parties to settle without needing to commence proceedings. Parties are to be encouraged to do this by exchanging information and considering using a form of ADR. Paragraph 4 (which falls within Section II and is therefore of general application) deals with parties' compliance with both the Practice Direction and the pre–action protocols and goes on, at para.4.3, to state that one example of non–compliance is a party's unreasonable refusal to consider ADR.

The new para.8 (which falls within Section III and therefore deals with the cases that are not subject to a pre–action protocol) commences with the mantra that starting proceedings should usually be a step of last resort and is one that should not normally be taken when settlement is being actively explored. Parties are warned that the court may require evidence that parties considered some form of ADR (paras 8.1 and 4.4(3)). ADR is defined (para.8.2) so as to include discussion and negotiation, mediation, early neutral evaluation and arbitration. Parties are also reminded that the duty to consider the possibility of reaching a settlement at all times is a continuing one that applies after the commencement of proceedings and up to and during any final hearing (para.8.4).

In the second paragraph, for "(with one exception) … December 18, 2008]" substitute:

(with two exceptions), reference is made to the LSC booklet entitled "Alternatives to Court" available at *http://www.communitylegaladvice.org.uk/media/656/13/leaflet23e.pdf* [Accessed July 27, 2009]

In the third paragraph, for "(again with one exception)" substitute:

(again with two exceptions)

Add new bullet point at end:

- *Pre–Action Protocol for Possession Claims (Mortgage)*, paras 7 and 8.

D. ADR IN PARTICULAR COURTS

1. ADR IN TECHNOLOGY AND CONSTRUCTION COURT

In the fifth paragraph for "(see further "ADR Providers", below)" substitute:

(see further "ADR Providers" at para.14–27 below)

14–23

In the last paragraph, add after "(For further information":

and a reference to nine cases having been mediated

2. MEDIATION IN COUNTY COURTS

In the third paragraph for "http://www.civilmediation.org/provider–organisations.php [Accessed December 18, 2008]" substitute:

14–24   *http://www.civilmediation.org/files/pdf/List%20of%20Organisations.pdf* [Accessed July 27, 2009]

E. ACCESS TO MEDIATION ADVICE AND SERVICES

1. ADVICE ON MEDIATION—WHEN DOES MEDIATION WORK?

In the first bullet point for "http://www.hmcourts–service.gov.uk/CMS/770.htm [Accessed December 18, 2008] (go to "When does Mediation work?");" substitute:

14–26   *http://www.hmcourts–service.gov.uk/cms/7770.htm* [Accessed July 27, 2009];

In the second bullet point for "http://www.adrnow.org.uk/go/subPage__47.html#adv [Accessed December 18, 2008]." substitute:

http://www.adrnow.org.uk [Accessed July 27, 2009].

2. MEDIATION SERVICE PROVIDERS

In the first bullet point add after "'Mediation in county courts",':

14–27   at para.14–24

In the last bullet point add after "'ADR in Technology and Construction Court",':

at para.14–23

SECTION 15

INTERIM REMEDIES

A. INTERIM INJUNCTIONS

9. UNDERTAKING AS TO DAMAGES

(b) Undertakings in interim injunctions generally

After the third paragraph add as a new paragraph:

15–27   In *United States Securities & Exchange Commission v Manterfield* [2009] EWCA Civ 27; January 28, 2009, unrep., CA, where the applicant for a world–wide freezing order was a foreign public agency (C) and the application was made in support of proceedings abroad, the respondent's submission that, because C could offer no cross–undertaking, no freezing order ought to be made, was rejected by the Court of Appeal and it was held that the judge was right to start from the position that a cross–undertaking would not be given and to consider whether this was a case in which it should or should not be dispensed with.

(h) Enforcement and assessment

(ii) *Decision to enforce*

At the end of the second paragraph add:

15–35   The law as to the discharge of freezing orders and the enforcement of undertakings where there has been material non–disclosure (whether innocent or not) was explained in *Dadourian Group International Inc v Simms* [2009] EWCA Civ 169; [2009] 1 Lloyd's Rep. 601, CA; see further Vol.1 para.25.3.5.

After the fifth paragraph add as a new paragraph:

In *North Principal Investments Fund Ltd v Greenoak Renewable Energy Ltd* [2009] EWHC

985 (Ch), May 1, 2009, unrep. (David Richards J.) the judge reviewed the relevant authorities (in particular *Yukong Line Ltd v Rendsburg Investments Corporation* [2001] 2 Lloyd's Rep. 113, CA) and stated (1) that if it is established that the injunction was wrongly granted, albeit without fault on the claimant's part, the court will ordinarily order an inquiry as to damages in any case where it appears that loss may have been caused as a result, (2) that the applicant must adduce some credible evidence that he has suffered loss as the result of the making of the order, and (3) that if the defendant shows that he has suffered loss which was prima facie or arguably caused by the order, then the evidential burden of any contention that the relevant loss would have been suffered regardless of the making of the order in practice passes to the defendants and an inquiry will be ordered.

B. FREEZING INJUNCTIONS

1. INTRODUCTION

At the end of the eighth paragraph, add:

The authorities on dispensing with cross–undertakings in interim injunctions in **15–54** cases where public authorities are seeking to enforce the law were examined by the Court of Appeal in *United States Securities & Exchange Commission v Manterfield* [2009] EWCA Civ 27; January 28, 2009, unrep., CA

5. "DOMESTIC" FREEZING INJUNCTIONS

(b) Assets excepted

(iii) *Legal expenses*

After the second paragraph, add as a new paragraph:

Where the freezing injunction restrains the defendant from dealing with assets to **15–73** which the claimant asserts title, the defendant must establish on proper evidence that there are no funds or assets available to him which can be used by him to pay his legal expenses other than the assets in respect of which the claimant brings his proprietary claim. Once that hurdle is cleared, the court can make an order allowing the defendant to use part of the funds (the equitable ownership of which is claimed by the claimant) for the defendant's legal expenses. That power in the court is a discretionary power. The court, in deciding whether to exercise it, must weigh the potential injustice to the claimant of permitting the funds which may turn out to be the claimant's property to be diminished so that the defendant can be legally represented, against the possible injustice to the defendant of depriving him of the opportunity of having the assistance of professional lawyers in advancing what may, at the end of the day, turn out to be a successful defence (see *The Ostrich Farming Corporation Ltd v Ketchell* December 10, 1997, unrep., CA, and earlier Court of Appeal decisions referred to there; see also *Independent Trustee Services Ltd v G P Noble Trustees Ltd* [2009] EWHC 161 (Ch), January 26, 2009, unrep. (Lewison J.)).

(d) Freezing injunction in aid of proceedings in other jurisdictions

Add new paragraph at end:

In *United States Securities & Exchange Commission v Manterfield* [2009] EWCA Civ 27; **15–79** January 28, 2009, unrep., CA, where the claimants (C) in foreign proceedings (a public agency) in which fraud was alleged applied for a world–wide freezing injunction, the respondent's submission that, on the grounds that C were seeking to enforce a foreign penal law, the English court should decline jurisdiction was rejected. It was held (1) that the substance of what C would seek to enforce (if they prevailed in the action), and in relation to which they sought to preserve assets, was the disgorgement of what they alleged to be the proceeds of fraud, and (2) that in the circumstances, the fact that a civil penalty might be imposed was not of such significance as to form a basis for characterising the proceedings as for the enforcement of a penal law.

D. INTERIM PAYMENTS

4. AMOUNT OF INTERIM PAYMENT (CPR R.25.7(4))

Interim payments and periodical payments of quantum judgment

Add at end:

15–110.1   In *Eeles v Cobham Hire Services Ltd* [2009] EWCA Civ 204; March 13, 2009, unrep., CA, the Court of Appeal explained that, in a case where a periodical payments order (PPO) is made, the amount of the final judgment is the actual capital sum awarded and does not include the notional capitalised value of the PPO, and held that, because he did not consider what capital sum was likely to be awarded at trial, a judge dealing with an interim payment order (IPO) application was not in a position to decide upon a reasonable proportion of that sum, and had therefore erred in that respect. The court reviewed some of the first instance authorities and stated that, for the purposes of an IPO application, (1) a judge should not normally begin to speculate about how the trial judge will allocate the damages, and, as a rule, should stop at the figure which he is satisfied is likely to be awarded as a capital sum, however (2) where the judge is able confidently to predict that the trial judge will capitalise additional elements of the future loss so as to produce a greater lump sum award, for example, where the claimant can clearly demonstrate a need for an immediate capital sum (probably to fund the purchase of accommodation), he may award a reasonable proportion of that greater sum, but (3) before encroaching on the trial judge's freedom to allocate in this way the judge should have a high degree of confidence that the trial judge will endorse the capitalisation undertaken.

APPENDIX 1

COURTS DIRECTORY

County Court Directory

In the table, the following entries have been amended:

AP–9

ABERDARE AA	The Court House Cwmbach Road Aberdare Wales CF44 OJE	Tel: 01685 888575 Fax: 01685 883413 DX: 99600 Aberdare–2
AYLESBURY AY	Walton Street Aylesbury Buckinghamshire HP21 7QZ	Tel: 01296 554326 Fax: 01296 554320 DX: 97820 Aylesbury–3
BARNET BT	Barnet Civil and Family Courts Centre St Mary's Court Regents Park Road Finchley London N3 1BQ	Tel: 020 8343 4272 Fax: 020 8343 1324 DX: 122570 Finchley (Church End)
BODMIN BJ	The Law COurts Launceston Road Bodmin Cornwall PL31 2AL	Tel: 01208 261580 Fax: 01208 77255 DX: 136846 Bodmin 2
Brighton County Court—Family Centre	1 Edward Street Brighton BN2 0JD	Tel: 01273 811333 Fax: 01273 607638 DX: 142600 Brighton–12

BRISTOL BS	Lewins Place Lewins Mead Bristol BS1 2NR	Tel: 0117 910 6700 Fax: (General) 0117 910 6729 (Bailiffs) 0117 910 6762 (Family) 0117 910 6728 (Diary Manager) 0117 910 6760 DX: 95903 Bristol–3
Business List *For Patents County Court* *see under "P"*		Business List Fax: 020 7917 7935/7940 DX: 97325 Regents Park–2
GLOUCESTER GL	Gloucester Family and Civil Courts Kimbrose Way Gloucester GL1 2DE	Tel: 01452 834900 Fax: 01452 834923 DX: 98660 Gloucester–5
HAYWARDS HEATH HH	The Law Courts Bolnore Road Haywards Heath West Sussex RH16 4BA	Tel: 01444 417611 Fax: 01444 472639 DX: 135596 Haywards Heath–6
HITCHIN HI	Park House 1–12 Old Park Road Hitchin Hertfordshire SG5 2JR	Tel: 0844 8920550 Fax: 01462 445444 DX: 97720 Hitchin–2
KIDDERMINSTER KI	Comberton Place Kidderminster Worcestershire DY10 1QT	Tel: 01562 514000 Fax: 01562 514084
KINGSTON–UPON–HULL KH	Kingston–upon–Hull Combined Court Centre Lowgate Humberside HU1 2EZ	Tel: 01482 586161 Fax: 01482 588527 DX: 703010 Hull–5
KINGSTON–UPON–THAMES KT	St James Road Kingston–upon–Thames Surrey KT1 2AD	Tel: 020 8972 8700 Fax: 020 8547 1426 DX: 97890 Kingston–upon–Thames–3
LEIGH LG	Darlington Street Wigan Greater Manchester WN1 1DW	Tel: 01942 405405 Fax: 01942 405459
LINCOLN LN	360 High Street Lincoln LN5 7PS	Tel: 01522 551500 Fax: 01522 551551 DX: 703231 Lincoln–6
NEWARK NK	Newark Court House Beech House 58 Commercial Gate Newark Nottinghamshire NG18 1EU	Tel: 01636 656406 DX: 702180 Mansfield–3
NEWPORT (GWENT) NP	Olympia House 3rd Floor Upper Dock Street Newport Gwent South Wales NP20 1PQ Court House The Magistrates' Court Pentonville Newport Gwent NP20 5HZ	

PENZANCE PZ	Trevear Alverton Terrace Penzance Cornwall TR18 4GH	Tel: 01872 267460 Fax: 01872 222348 DX: 135396 Truro–2
READING RG	160–163 Friar Street Reading Berkshire RG1 1HE	Tel: 0118 987 0500 Fax: 0118 959 9827 DX: 98010 Reading–6
ST ALBANS SI	The Court Building Bricket Road St Albans Hertfordshire AL13 3JW	Tel: 0844 892 0550 Fax: 01727 753234 DX: 97770 St Albans–2
	Walsall Hearing Centre Bridge House Bridge Street Walsall West Midlands WS1 1JQ	General enquiries: Tel: 01922 728855 Fax: 01922 728891 DX: 701943 Walsall–2 Email: enquiries@walsall countycourt.gsi.gov.uk Family enquiries: Email: family@walsall countycourt.gsi.gov.uk Bailiffs enquiries: Email: bailiffs@walsall countycourt.gsi.gov.uk Listing enquiries: Email: hearings@walsall countycourt.gsi.gov.uk
WIGAN WN	Darlington Street Wigan Greater Manchester WN1 1DW	Tel: 01942 405405 Fax: 01942 405499 DX: 724820 Wigan–9
WINCHESTER WC	Winchester Combined Court Centre The Law Courts Winchester Hampshire SO23 9EL	Tel: 01962 814100 Fax: 01962 814260 DX: 98520 Winchester–3
WORKSOP WS	30 Potter Street Worksop Nottinghamshire S80 2AJ	Tel: 01623 656406 Fax: 01623 626561 DX: 743240 Worksop–4

INDEX

LEGAL TAXONOMY
FROM SWEET & MAXWELL

This index has been prepared using Sweet and Maxwell's Legal Taxonomy. Main index entries conform to keywords provided by the Legal Taxonomy except where references to specific documents or non-standard terms (denoted by quotation marks) have been included. These keywords provide a means of identifying similar concepts in other Sweet & Maxwell publications and online services to which keywords from the Legal Taxonomy have been applied. Readers may find some minor differences between terms used in the text and those which appear in the index. Suggestions to *sweetandmaxwell.taxonomy@thomson.com.*

(All references are to paragraph number and all references to material in Volume 2 are enclosed in square parentheses)

481

High Court and County Courts Jurisdiction Order 1991—*cont.*
value of actions, [9B–948] — [9B–948.1]

Homelessness
appeals
allocation, 2BPD.9
assistance
eligibility, [3A–1289] — [3A–1290], [3A–1296]
inquiries, [3A–1281] — [3A–1281.1]
definitions
index of, [3A–1486] — [3A–1487]
dependent children, [3A–1323]
good faith, act or omission in, [3A–1342]
priority need
dependent children, [3A–1323]
priority need and not intentionally homeless
generally, [3A–1361] — [3A–1362], [3A–1375]
review of decisions
generally, [3A–1417] — [3A–1418], [3A–1425], [3A–1432]
threatened homelessness
generally, [3A–1380] — [3A–1381]

Housing and Regeneration Act 2008
general provisions, [3A–1674.1], [3A–1678]

House of Lords (appeals)
allocation, 2BPD.9A

Housing
statutory basis
Local Government Act 1972, [3A–57.4]

Housing Act 1985
jurisdiction of district judges, 2BPD.11

Housing Act 1988
jurisdiction of district judges, 2BPD.11

Housing Act 1996
jurisdiction of district judges, 2BPD.11

Housing associations
meaning
HA 1985, [3A–320]

Human rights
allocation
county courts, 2BPD.15
High Court, 2BPD.7A

Human rights—*cont.*
Convention rights
interpretation, [3D–9]
declarations of incompatibility, [3D–17] — [3D–19]
ECHR judges, [3D–60] — [3D–61]
freedom of expression, [3D–48.1]
judicial remedies, [3D–41]
legislation
declarations of incompatibility, [3D–17] — [3D–19]
interpretation, [3D–16]
public authorities
acts of, [3D–23] — [3D–27.1]
judicial remedies, [3D–41]
proceedings, [3D–34.1]

Human Rights Act 1998 (claims)
disclosure, 31.3.32

Impecuniosity
security for costs, 25.13.12 — 25.13.14

Indemnity costs
generally, 44.4.3

Injunctions
allocation
county courts, 2BPD.8
High Court, 2BPD.2
damages, [9A–198]

Inquests
costs, 44.3.8.4

Insolvency
security for costs, 25.13.12 — 25.13.14

Insolvency proceedings
debt relief orders
conditions, [3E–2860], introduction, cc39.0.6, [3E–2859]
role of court, [3E–2861]

Intellectual property claims
And see Patents Court claims
allocation
generally, [2F–14]
Practice directions, [2F–33]
appeals, [2F–42]
claims under section 19 of the Act, [2F–36]
definitions, [2F–2]
delivery up, [2F–40]
European trade marks, [2F–38]
final orders, [2F–43]
forfeiture, [2F–40]